D1561859

OBSTINATE HEROISM

The Confederate Surrenders after Appomattox

by
Steven J. Ramold

Number 4 in the American Military Studies Series

University of North Texas Press
Denton, Texas

10 9 8 7 6 5 4 3 2 1

Permissions:
University of North Texas Press
1155 Union Circle #311336
Denton, TX 76203-5017

The paper used in this book meets the minimum requirements
of the American National Standard for Permanence of Paper for
Printed Library Materials, z39.48.1984. Binding materials have
been chosen for durability.

  Library of Congress Cataloging-in-Publication Data

Ramold, Steven J., author.
  Obstinate heroism : the Confederate surrenders after Appomattox /
Steven J. Ramold.
      pages cm
  Includes bibliographical references and index.
  ISBN-13 978-1-57441-791-3 (cloth)
  ISBN-13 978-1-57441-802-6 (ebook)
  1. Johnston, Joseph E. (Joseph Eggleston), 1807–1891—Military
leadership. 2. Taylor, Richard, 1826–1879—Military leadership.
3. Kirby-Smith, Edmund, 1824–1893—Military leadership.
4. Confederate States of America. Army—History. 5. United
States—History—Civil War, 1861–1865—Campaigns.
  E545
  973.7/3013–dc23
              2019053461

Obstinate Heroism: The Confederate Surrenders after Appomattox
      is Number 4 in the American Military Studies Series

The electronic edition of this book was made possible by the support
of the Vick Family Foundation. Typeset by vPrompt eServices.

Dedicated to the memory of my Father,
George J. Ramold

and

my brother,
Terry J. Ramold

Contents

List of Illustrations

Preface

The surrender of the Confederate States of America ended the Civil War, the most important milestone event in American history. After four years, massive financial costs, and vast numbers of lives lost, military force had united the nation once again. For such a momentous event, however, the history of the Confederate surrender is not entirely clear. The emphasis of most written accounts is, understandably, on the surrender of General Robert E. Lee to Ulysses S. Grant at Appomattox, Virginia. The events there removed both the Confederacy's most important army and most senior commander from the fight, rendering the South's strategic position immediately hopeless. Monographs usually depict the surrender of the remaining Confederate armies as afterthoughts, the product of inevitable outcomes. This book places these final steps toward peace in a larger context by describing the options available to the other Confederate generals and explaining how the decision to surrender came about only after due consideration of local circumstances. To that end, it is necessary to de-emphasize the role of Lee and the Appomattox surrender, and this study relates the events in Virginia only as needed to explain the actions of Confederate generals in other states. In examining the surrender of the remaining Confederate armies, the role of the respective army commanders is key to understanding their thought processes after learning of Lee's surrender and their own uncertain fate. Two of the senior officers, Generals Joseph Johnston and Richard Taylor, published their memoirs after the conflict ended and also served as the subject of major biographies, thereby providing a substantial amount of information about their part in the decision to surrender.[1] The third general, Edmund Kirby Smith, did not publish a postwar memoir, but his command decisions are widely recounted in two major biographies.[2]

While not its primary purpose, this project addresses the broader question of why the Confederacy lost the Civil War. Such an investigation is necessary as military defeats cannot occur without consideration of the political, economic, and societal events that undermine a nation's will and ability to win. Such was the case with the Confederacy and its sense of identity. Several studies have examined the concept of Confederate nationalism and whether the South's inability to stand together determined its fate. Drew Gilpin Faust, in *The Creation of Confederate Nationalism*, described how cultural elements, such as religion, created a Confederacy that endured great hardships in its pursuit of independence.[3] Conversely, Richard Beringer, Herman Hattaway, Archer Jones, and William Still, Jr., in *Why the South Lost the Civil War*, depict the failure of Confederate nationalism because of the inability of the nation's political and military institutions to adjust to wartime crises.[4] Wartime pressures and the emergence of patriotic identity is also the central theme of Anne Sarah Rubin's *A Shattered Nation*, a study that asserts that Confederate nationalism came about because of wartime pressures rather than antebellum institutions and traditions.[5] The concept that Confederate nationalism failed, however, has been challenged by other historians, most notably Gary Gallagher in his *The Confederate War*.[6]

The adherence to the Confederate cause, whether through a collective sense of nationalism or individual self-interest, certainly existed. No culture, after all, struggles through years of bloody fighting without good reason to do so, especially the considerable number of Confederates still willing to fight when a path to victory no longer existed. As the war progressed, however, increasing numbers of Confederate civilians were unwilling or unable to contribute to the war effort to the extent asked by their government. In instances such as these, nationalism loses its importance as a motivator toward victory; it is difficult to be a nationalist when one is hungry, destitute, or homeless. Rather than abstract ideas such as nationalistic identity, a practical approach to the question of Confederate defeat is found in more prosaic reasons for growing pessimism. A strong sub-current of anti-Confederate resentment existed in several regions of the Confederacy, sapping the nation's resources and diverting it from its broader military objectives. Studies such as Richard Current's *Lincoln's Loyalists* show the lack of monolithic support for the Confederacy, even to the point of many Southerners enlisting under the Union flag.[7] William Freehling, in his *The South vs. the South*, further describes how the internal discord within the Confederacy undermined Southern goals.[8] Even those Southerners who supported the cause of independence were reluctant to risk all to obtain it. Kenneth Noe's *Reluctant Rebels* proves that, after the initial waves of enthusiastic volunteerism, support for the war among army recruits was more tempered as soldiers enlisted in the face of declining chances of victory and growing economic problems at home.[9] Confederate soldiers from areas under Union assault had particular concerns about their domestic situations as described in Stephen Ash's *When the Yankees Came*, a complex account of civilian areas under Northern occupation and the problems such a situation created.[10]

Beyond personal and philosophical reasons for demoralization, some more basic justifications existed. A frequently claimed source of Confederate failure is the discord that existed in the Confederate government, often a byproduct of the debate over states' rights. Herman Hattaway and Richard Beringer's *Jefferson Davis* portrays a litany of political clashes in which the Confederate president engaged, while David Eicher's *Dixie Betrayed* underscores the singular inability of the Confederate Congress to generate effective legislation.[11] The various governors were the biggest proponents of states' rights in their opposition to nationalist legislation, and Joseph Park's *Joseph E. Brown* depicts the efforts of Georgia's strong-willed governor to protect his state's sovereignty.[12] Economic failure, a byproduct of ineffective governance, also damaged the Confederate war effort. Douglas Ball outlines a litany of failed government economic programs in his *Financial Failure and Confederate Defeat*, while Stanley Lebergott shows how Southern merchants failed to overcome a range of wartime problems in his article "Why the South Lost: Commercial Purpose in the Confederacy."[13] The military failures of the Confederacy also demoralized the populace, as defeat emphasized the futility of the people's sacrifices for freedom. Military failure was often the result of flawed strategy, as described in Thomas Connelly and Archer Jones's *The Politics of Command* and Mark Grimsley and Brooks Simpson's edited work *The Collapse of the Confederacy*.[14]

The causes of Confederate defeat were numerous and varied. All played a part in degrading Confederate confidence in the face of Union military might and political commitment to national unification. By 1865, even the most dedicated Confederate citizen could not ignore the obvious problems facing the country, especially as hardships and defeats seemed to occur with greater regularity and severity. More importantly, the implications of Confederate military, political, and economic failure were very much on the minds of all Confederate military leaders when the crucial decision to surrender finally arrived.

Acknowledgments

I would like to thank the many people who have made this project possible. My employer, Eastern Michigan University, granted me a Faculty Research Fellowship that provided the release time to conduct the bulk of the research for the manuscript. In particular, I would like to thank the two outstanding Department Heads, Richard Nation and James Egge, who facilitated my research. The Interlibary Loan staff at Halle Library were also of great assistance. I visited a number of archives around the country, and am always struck by the high level of enthusiasm their staff have for promoting historical research. A particular thanks goes out to Jeffrey Flannery at the Library of Congress' Manuscript Division, who was a great help to my project and who also accommodates my occasional student groups. Dan Wurdinger made a huge contribution to the manuscript by producing the maps, an addition for which I am very grateful. The biggest thanks goes to my wife, Paula. She is, as always, a great source of inspiration, assistance, and insight, and this project would not have happened without her.

Introduction

"Most of the wars memorable in history have terminated with some momentous and splendid crisis of arms. Generally some large decisive battle closes the contest; a grand catastrophe mounts the stage; a great scene illuminates the last act of the tragedy. It was not so with the war of the Confederates."[1]

The Surrender at Appomattox, 1865 by Thomas Lovell (*Image courtesy of the National Geographic Society*).

The scene is a familiar one. General Ulysses S. Grant, surrounded by his staff and senior command officers, sits slouched at a small table. He is clearly fatigued as he watches General Robert E. Lee, sitting at a table across the room, sign the instrument of surrender presented to him by his lone aide. Grant, in his unkempt uniform, appears exhausted; his resolve bolstered only by the support of the officers around him, while Lee, immaculately dressed in his finest uniform, maintains his cool resolve even as he surrenders the cause for which he fought. One might forgive an uninformed observer for surmising that

Grant was in fact surrendering to Lee. Despite the slightly skewed perspective, many Americans know the consequence of the familiar scene. Grant, in
the paper upon which Lee is about affix his signature, magnanimously offered
Lee charitable terms that allowed Lee to surrender with both his and his army's
dignity intact. The Confederate Army, after surrendering their arms and public
property, could go home and begin the process of peace. After all, everyone
knows that the surrender at Appomattox ended the Civil War.

Except, of course, it did not. Lee surrendered his own Army of Northern
Virginia, but, despite his position as senior commander of the Confederate
Army, he lacked the authority to surrender other Confederate armies without
the consent of Confederate President Jefferson Davis. The Confederacy still
had three significant armies in the field, as well as numerous smaller forces
dispersed throughout the South. The three forces, separated from each other
and facing various levels of Union opposition, had the option to continue
fighting, but did not. The last force did not surrender until several weeks after
Lee, but each portion of the Confederate Army made its own decision to lay
down their arms independent of the opinion of the Confederate government.
The other surrenders were, to various degrees, complicated affairs. Perhaps
that is why the events at Appomattox captured the imagination and became the
image framed in the American mind as the end of the Civil War—it is, for lack
of a better term, a tidy surrender. Lee, surrounded by Grant's superior force,
had no opportunity to fight a prolonged battle until forced to capitulate, nor
did he complicate matters by consulting Jefferson Davis for guidance in the
negotiations or permission to sign the surrender document. Isolated from the
Confederate government, Lee consented to a purely military surrender without
the messy complications that a politician might introduce. Lee, of course, was
inclined to accept Grant's terms because they were so charitable, a set of offer-
ings that accomplished the surrender of a key Confederate army while avoiding
the pesky political issues that had caused the war in the first place. There was
even a surrender ceremony to add finality to Lee's capitulation. Three days
after Lee signed the surrender document, his army surrendered their arms,
flags, and equipment before accepting their parole forms and going home.

The surrenders of the other Confederate armies, however, were
nowhere near as tidy and uncomplicated as that at Appomattox. Unlike Lee,

the commanders of the other armies were not surrounded and possessed the ability to continue the fight if they chose to do so. In North Carolina, Gen. Joseph Johnston, commanding both the Department of South Carolina, Georgia, and Florida and the Department of North Carolina and Southern Virginia, grappled with Union Maj. Gen. William T. Sherman's forces near Raleigh. Commanding the Department of Alabama, Mississippi, and East Louisiana, Maj. Gen. Richard Taylor led Confederate efforts to contain two Union incursions into Alabama, a cavalry assault from the north and an infantry assault from the south led, respectively, by Maj. Gen. James Wilson and Maj. Gen. Edward Canby. In Texas, Confederate Gen. Edmund Kirby Smith faced only a distant military threat from a Union army in Missouri led by Maj. Gen. John Pope, but contended with internal turmoil triggered by years of military and economic shortcomings in his Department of the Trans-Mississippi. Each of the Confederate generals had the opportunity to fight on, but each chose to surrender, although the decision came only after the respective commanders assessed their local situations and prospects. Johnston surrendered to Sherman seventeen days after Lee's submission at Appomattox, and Taylor capitulated eight days after that. Kirby Smith held on the longest, not submitting to Union authority until forty-seven days after the events at Appomattox.

But why surrender so soon? The removal of Lee's army clearly meant that the Union could deploy the massive Army of the Potomac against other already outnumbered Confederate forces, but that would take time. The collective memory of the Civil War holds that once Lee surrendered, like the loss of a keystone in an arch, the capitulation of the remaining Confederate forces was inevitable. Such was not the case, however, as all of three remaining Confederate armies had at least minimal options to exercise. The news of Lee's submission to Grant certainly had a negative effect on Confederate morale, both military and civilian, but was not itself the reason that the other Confederate commanders chose to cease fighting. Under only very slightly different circumstances, one or more of the remaining Confederate armies might have surrendered before Lee. Conversely, other shifting conditions, had they occurred, might have allowed Johnston, Taylor, or Kirby Smith to continue the war for at least some time.

None of the generals pondering the question of surrender did so under purely military considerations. Armies do not operate in a vacuum, but instead rely upon the support of their governments and populations, and the Confederacy increasingly lacked the national will to fight. Military defeats, economic disasters, and poor policy-making all combined to create a climate of defeatism that sapped Confederate morale and willingness to sacrifice for the cause of independence. Defeatism in some cases became open defiance of Confederate authority, forcing the government to impose stringent controls that generated few solutions and more resistance. As the national economy collapsed and the number of available soldiers diminished, few civilians, and even a fair portion of the army, could envision a successful outcome of the war. Consequently, the country divided into those who wished to fight on despite the odds and those who demanded peace regardless of the cost.

The divided nature of the Confederacy, in turn, made it impossible for the Confederate leadership to coordinate continued resistance in the waning months of the war. It also created increased urgency to capitulate as Federal armies, after forcing surrenders elsewhere, could concentrate on the remaining Confederate forces. The fragmented nature of the Confederate Army in 1865 also prevented any sort of coordination when it came to surrendering. Were the War Department capable of greater military coordination or the Confederate government more willing to end the war before the final battles occurred, then a single unified surrender might have occurred. The separate commands, however, forced their respective commanders to make the decision to surrender by themselves and determine the mechanism and means by which their surrender would occur. For some, it was a decision taken boldly and done in a timely manner, but for others it was a decision made for them and done in the most chaotic of methods.

Although practical implications promoted the surrender of Confederate armies, abstract ideas made the process more complex. The main problem that the Union faced in obtaining a Confederate surrender was how to accept the capitulation of a government that it did not consider legitimate in the first place. If the Lincoln (and later Johnson) administration did not consider Jefferson Davis the real political leader of the Confederacy, then accepting a surrender from Davis or one of his subordinates was likewise proscribed.

As there was no declaration of war, there could be no peace treaty. Instead, the ending of the war became a "series of unilateral measures," with the Confederacy succumbing by subjugation rather than surrender, the result of military, economic, and cultural disasters that left no enemy for the Union to fight.[2] In addition, if Davis was not a proper leader, then he was not the spokesperson for anyone in the South, especially among those who did not wish to give up. Lincoln recognized this reality when, in his last public speech, he reminded his listeners that "No one man has authority to give up the rebellion for any other man."[3]

Indeed, Davis himself never formally surrendered his government, leaving the end of the war in the even more murky process of individual generals deciding the fate of the nation by their decision to stop fighting. This process has been termed as "conflict termination at the operational level ... not subject to precise delineation," a good description considering the outcome of the Civil War when military authority separate from political authority decided when the war would end. Surrenders arranged among generals were fraught with peril, however, because governments could often not immediately direct the negotiations. Achieving the desired political and military outcomes was a process defined by "requiring the closest communication among civilian leadership and senior military commanders; the former conveying their vision, the latter responsibly rendering clear the effects of the military facts on the ground on that vision, and vice versa," with an exchange of information that required an "ongoing, iterative process."[4]

****

Although all three Confederate generals eventually chose to surrender, the circumstances in which they did so varied widely, based on their individual conditions, prospects, and personalities. Each commander experienced different conditions and limitations that led to his decision to give up after considering all available options. The situations in which Johnston, Taylor, and Kirby Smith found themselves were very different, but have some common themes and circumstances. The surrenders, for instance, represented the varying levels of military leadership exercised by the various commanders in the absence of political leadership by the Confederate government. Johnston, for instance, had some direct political supervision from Jefferson Davis in his talks with Sherman, at least until Davis decided to absent himself, leaving the proceedings in Johnston's hands. Taylor, by comparison, wanted advice from the Confederate government in his dealings with Canby, but Davis had little contact with the rest of the nation following the evacuation of Richmond, leaving Taylor to make the best terms he could. In the Trans-Mississippi Department, Kirby Smith, who also eventually surrendered to Canby in New Orleans rather than Pope in St. Louis, had even less contact with Confederate authority. Since the fall of Vicksburg left his department virtually isolated, Kirby Smith was for all practical purposes the Confederate government in the region, leaving him to make the decision regarding surrender entirely on his own.

The presence or absence of political authority had, by extension, a direct influence on the protocols of how each Confederate commander capitulated. Under the indirect presence of the Confederate president, Johnston engaged in formal negotiations that required three meetings, but unlike at Appomattox, did not have to endure a formal surrender ceremony. In Alabama, however, Taylor engaged in informal negotiations with Canby because general surrender terms, introduced at Appomattox and refined by the talks between Sherman and Johnston, were already established. The informal negotiations, therefore, invariably also led to the absence of a formal surrender process. The surrender of Confederate forces in the Trans-Mississippi was even more informal. Instead of determining the terms under which his army disbanded, Kirby Smith's army largely decided for itself that the war was over and demobilized of their own volition. Without an army to surrender, an official surrender process became moot.

The Confederate government did not play a role in the various surrenders, but the state governments did, although the influence of the executives also varied. North Carolina Governor Zebulon Vance, who had actively defended the rights and interests of his constituents against the policies of the national government, tried to exert some influence on the events occurring in his state but those with greater influence ignored him. As events came to a head in Alabama, the influence of state executives is almost entirely absent, with Taylor advising the governors of events but not deferring to their authority. Kirby Smith, on the other hand, refused to assume the full mantle of control and sought the cooperation of state governors, who unfortunately could not provide him the means to continue the war.

Insufficient support to keep their respective armies fighting was another key element in the decision to surrender, especially in the specific locations where the armies ended their resistance. Joseph Johnston's supply situation in central North Carolina was relatively positive. The problem was that Johnston, in retreating into the area before Sherman's advance, was occupying the region where Lee's army drew its supplies and providing for one army meant the starving of the other. Taylor's supply problems were different. He had a railroad line to provide logistic support, but would soon have nothing to move because of the loss of production and quartermaster facilities to Canby and Wilson's offensives, leaving Taylor to surrender before his army suffered from severe supply shortages. The soldiers of Kirby Smith's army, on the other hand, had suffered from supply shortages for months in spite of an open trade outlet in Mexico. Coupled with the inability of the government to pay them their wages on a reliable schedule, the supply problems sapped morale to the point that self-demobilization became the only option.

Other comparisons and contrasts are evident in the mindset of the surrendering generals. All generals had, despite the decision to cease fighting, an ability to continue the war by maneuvering their armies away from their opposition, an ability denied to Lee's surrounded army. Although near Sherman's forces, Johnston's army had a head start on their foe if Johnston chose to avoid combat and march away, a consideration that led Sherman to negotiate a surrender rather than demand one. Likewise, although Taylor's forces had suffered serious defeats against both Canby and Wilson's forces, neither was in immediate proximity to his concentrated force in southern Mississippi, leaving Taylor two paths on which to take his army, albeit neither of them very appealing. Kirby Smith had the most room to maneuver. With Pope's distant army as the only immediate threat, Kirby Smith had the opportunity to detect Union offensives from a distance and react accordingly, but circumstances nullified that advantage.

The mindset of the Confederate generals was particularly relevant considering their unique responsibilities, how they dealt with their superiors and colleagues, and even the cause for which they fought. Johnston, for instance, negotiated with Sherman while Jefferson Davis, a man he considered his greatest nemesis, looked over his proverbial shoulder. Davis was also unenthusiastic about Johnston holding such an important post, especially as Johnston had become pessimistic regarding the Confederacy's chances of success. The result of these elements was a situation where Johnston was not only prepared to surrender when his options began to dwindle, but also to surrender when Davis gave him instructions to the contrary. Taylor had also become a pessimist by the end of the war, but his personality traits created different outcomes. Taylor often proved a difficult subordinate early in the war, at a time when the Confederates needed cooperation the most. Taylor's other distinguishing characteristic was his lack of formal military training. Although the son of a professional soldier and wartime hero, Taylor earned his high rank due to his social status, name recognition, and battlefield success in the early months of the war. While a capable officer, Taylor's background meant that he often thought more like a civilian than would a professional soldier, something that became evident when Taylor exercised his own discretion and surrendered when the circumstances, not the policy of the government, demanded he do so. Kirby Smith's singular problem was that he had the authority of a military governor, but not the disposition to act like one. The general had the burden of defending the region and commanding the troops within his department, while assuming the role of political leader when normal connections to the national government in Richmond became impossible. Consequently, both the military and civilian populations were unclear of Kirby Smith's role, with many officers viewing him more as a bureaucrat than a commander and many civilians perceiving the general as intruding into civilian political authority.

****

The circumstances in which the Confederate armies found themselves in Spring 1865 were dire to say the least. In terms of numbers, supplies, transport, and resources, all were inferior to the Union formations in their respective departments. The enemy had occupied large portions of the South, and its armies were maneuvering to conquer even more. Just months earlier, Northern voters had reelected Abraham Lincoln as President, signifying their determination to see the war through to the end. Morale among the

Confederate troops was consequently very poor in most units, as the likelihood of victory seemed increasingly distant. Their pay, when it was rarely available, was largely worthless, and their families suffered as a result. Confidence in both political and military leadership was likewise at low ebb. Military defeats put the final touch on the Confederacy's demise in early 1865, but the conditions that denied the Confederate army the ability, and eventually the will, to fight started much earlier, paving the way for the downfall of the nation.

Chapter 1

"What Will the Poor People Do": The Decline of Confederate Confidence and Unity

Wars only end when armies and governments decide to quit fighting. The dates when surrenders occur and the circumstances under which soldiers decide to put down their weapons are relatively easy to define, but armies rarely surrender when they have the means of continuing to fight. Military capitulations are the consequence of much more complicated circumstances, many of which might be months or years in the making. Such was the case with the Confederacy, whose ability to fight decreased over time because of severe political and military shortcomings brought about by many failed government policies and leadership deficiencies. Although the allegorical debate often centers on whether the Confederacy succumbed to a few major wounds or died the death by a thousand cuts, a better analogy is to perceive that the Confederacy died of its untreated wounds. The Confederate government and military faced major problems during the war, but succeeded in resolving virtually none of them. Even worse, attempts to solve the nation's problems tended to make the situation worse. "Every attempt to meet military need, every policy innovation," one historian wrote, "imposed a new toll on the population and set in train a dangerous political dynamic." The Confederates, for instance, solved their lack of soldiers by imposing conscription, a step that deprived the economy of its labor force. Likewise, the government imposed impressment to feed the army on the surplus of the land, but caused only starvation and demoralization.[1] Although easy to critique in hindsight, the political decisions and command shortcomings instituted by the Confederate government derived from the best available information and most noble of intentions. Intelligent people with vast experience created policies with the purest of objectives in mind, but could not foresee the unintended consequences of those actions. Powerful figures and groups, especially those who advocated a philosophy of states' rights, had their own opinions on how the new Confederate nation should operate and challenged the leadership and direction of those in national authority. In addition, the decisions and policies passed with the greatest optimism in Richmond often faced backlash and resistance among citizens who found the legislation to be shortsighted, improperly implemented, or even politically repressive. Many policies, including ones that the Union effectively implemented, generated hostility among the civilian population who had to bear the personal burden of national policy.

The consequence of poorly thought-out, badly executed, and excessively harsh policies from the Davis administration in Richmond was a growing sense of dissent among the civilian population that undermined military efforts in the long-term. Some of this dissent was purely political in nature, especially among Unionists opposed to secession in the first place, but much of it was the product of otherwise loyal Confederate citizens whose ardor for the war cooled as their forced contributions to the war effort increased. In a way, the decline in the civilian willingness to sacrifice for the cause is consistent with other studies that attribute the lack of Confederate success to a weakness of collective nationalism.[2] Looking at civilian support for the war from an "all or nothing" approach, however, prevents a real analysis of how support for the war declined in relative terms, either over time or in response to specific events. Many of those who came to resent and then resist Confederate policies did so only after contributing what they could, or even more than they should, and simply could not or would not give any more. Only military victories, effective government policies, or unified leadership could convince those whose dedication was flagging to maintain their allegiance, but such elements seldom emerged. Making matters worse, the Confederate government and military's response to declining civilian morale was often aggressive and authoritarian, which not only failed to halt the declining civilian morale, but also often prompted others to share their sense of demoralization.

The result was a government that increasingly could not find solutions to the nation's problems and a military that progressively found its ability to fight declining. The latter is of particular concern for this discussion because the ultimate end of the war occurred when Southern soldiers decided to stop fighting. While there were battles in the last days of the war that compelled some Confederate generals to concede defeat, in other cases the inability to fight made surrender inevitable. Armies can only fight if the civilian population can provide them with supplies, support them through political action, and convince them that their sacrifices are worthwhile. As civilian support for the war declined, the Confederacy achieved none of these efforts. When civilians went hungry because the agricultural sector suffered, so did the army. When civilians suffered because their money became increasingly worthless, soldiers became more concerned about the home front than enemy armies. When civilians became convinced that the government was ineffective or even hostile, the dedication to the cause of independence waned in the army camps as well. Such demoralization did not happen overnight, although it did accelerate in the last months of the war, but was instead the product of a long process that convinced many in both the army and at home that victory was impossible.

****

A frequent attribution to Confederate demoralization was the shortcomings of Confederate leadership, with the top leader, President Jefferson Davis, as the most frequent target. Davis initially enjoyed a period of personal popularity, and his decisions gained, with only notable exceptions, widespread acceptance among both the Confederate Congress and state governments in the first months of the war. As the war progressed, however, and difficult choices arose, Davis found himself amassing many opponents driven by both personal animosity and policy disagreements.[3] As the number of critics in the Confederate Congress mounted, Davis became more defensive of his presidential prerogatives and adherence to the principle of strong central nationalism. Consequently, Davis made a common error in that he frequently "delegated responsibility without delegating authority and then refused to exercise the authority he withheld from the responsible commander," thereby creating situations where military or political failure generated criticism of the president's decisions.[4] Instead of finding common ground through compromise, the President and Congress increasingly viewed the other as the problem, creating a deadlock that could not be broken. George Rable summarized the situation well when he wrote how "the military crisis, bitter quarrels between the president and Congress, and even arguments about the future of slavery created a politics of recrimination" instead of a politics of accommodation.[5] Examples of this climate of recrimination exist in the opinions of Davis's critics. Vice President Alexander Stephens offered the postwar view that the President "proved himself deficient in developing and directing the resources of the country, in finance and in diplomacy, as well as in military affairs," and because "he did not understand the purpose of the people, he is certainly not entitled to any high rank as a statesman."[6] Senator Lewis Wigfall began the war as one of Davis's most ardent supporters, but turned into one of his harshest critics when convinced of Davis's incompetence as military leader of the Confederacy. Wigfall also led the Congressional criticism of Davis's Cabinet appointments, especially Judah Benjamin, with whom Davis had a close relationship. Anti-Semitism played a role in the attacks, but Benjamin deserved some of the criticism. According to one assessment, as "attorney general, Benjamin presided over an invisible judicial system; as secretary of war, he had failed to distinguish himself, and as secretary of state he was unable to gain the recognition of a single nation."[7] The lack of respect between the two branches of government reached its low point on March 13, 1865, when Davis urged the Confederate Congress to delay its scheduled recess to settle pressing issues, but undermined his plea by claiming the Congress was not doing its duty. Understandably angered by an accusation "so well calculated to excite discord and dissention," Congress ignored Davis's request and adjourned, for the last time, five days later.[8] Davis's public support also declined as military and economic failures increased. Although Davis did his best to make himself accessible to the public, the nature of his position made him a distant figure to many civilians.

Unaware of the challenges Davis faced, citizens criticized him for various failed policies and campaigns. Critics described Davis as "aloof and abstract, a man who concerned himself more with broad questions of policy than with signals from the electorate … and in the process seemed insensitive to local needs."[9] Thus, as the civilian population suffered, Davis became the target of dissatisfaction. By early 1865, some even demanded the removal of Davis, as a North Carolina resident wrote, "The discontent with the Government increases. Revolution, the deposition of Mr. Davis, is openly talked of!"[10] Because a wide range of policies and decisions seemed to have failed, civilians, unwilling to believe that their nation or cause was faulty on such a scale, often concluded that Davis's primary fault was his inability to judge subordinates or avoid nepotism.[11] Such assessments could only result from the lack of communication and commonality between the government and the people. In his proclamations, Davis seemed only to ask the public for more sacrifice, to trust in divine intervention, and anticipate great victories. When the public could give no more, divine assistance seemed unlikely, and military success became rarer, Davis's statements began to ring hollow. "If brag and brutal abuse could have won success for the Southern Confederacy," a London newspaper decided, "Jefferson Davis would now be the conquering hero of the South."[12]

Davis might have enjoyed a more successful Presidency had he been able to count on support from the state executives. As the war dragged on, however, the state governments became more inclined to press their own agendas rather than cooperate with the Confederate government.[13] In addition, most Confederate governors served only a single term, a sign of the public's preference for candidates perceived as protectors of state interests.[14] As early as 1862, for instance, elections for the Florida legislature unseated many antebellum members who had pushed for secession.[15] In 1863, Alabamans turned out their ardently pro-Confederate governor John Shorter, defeating his bid for reelection by a 3:1 vote margin.[16] Gov. Henry Rector of Arkansas had become so unpopular that he lost his 1862 reelection bid to Col. Harris Flanagin, who was serving in Tennessee and did not actively campaign.[17] The anti-Richmond political trend also manifested itself in Congressional elections. In the transition between the First and Second Confederate

Congresses, for instance, Georgia turned over nearly all of its Congressional delegation (one of two Senators and nine of ten Representatives), in a clear statement of public displeasure with the decision to go to war.[18]

In the face of growing political opposition, Davis often believed himself at odds with the state executives. "The difficulties with which this Government has to contend," Davis complained, "have been materially increased by the persistent interference of some of the State authorities" who, in his opinion were "hindering the action of this Government."[19] Davis often failed to appreciate the conditions with which many governors had to contend, leaving the governors in a range of attitudes relative to their loyalty to Davis and the national government. On the extreme range of opposition was Joseph E. Brown of Georgia, who represented a duality in that he was a staunch supporter of slavery against Federal interference, but that position also made him an ardent states' rights advocate.[20] Brown was an early supporter of secession, but, after the imposition of conscription in 1862, the governor contested most decisions of the Davis administration. In a speech to the state legislature, Brown reminded them of their duty "To guard effectually against usurpation, sustain republican liberty, and prevent the consolidation of the power" lest the government in Richmond commit "encroachment … upon either the rights or the sovereignty of the State."[21]

Gov. Zebulon Vance of North Carolina was another prominent opponent of central authority. Upon his election in 1862, Vance was a staunch opponent of the army's methods of obtaining supplies, and resisted at every turn what he perceived as the excesses of the Commissary and Quartermaster Bureaus.[22] Other executives, fearful of the social revolutionary forces unleashed by the war, supported the Davis Administration despite misgivings about its decisions. Gov. John Milton of Florida, for example, feared the damage to the "social fabric" of the South if the Union should prevail, while Thomas Moore of Louisiana pushed for the continuation of the war to avoid the forced elevation in status accorded to the slaves if the North triumphed.[23] Milton was a defender of states' rights, but recognized that national survival trumped states' rights concerns. "When the independence of the Confederate States shall have been achieved" Milton reasoned, "the rights of the States and the constitutional powers of the Confederate Government will be adjusted by an intelligent, brave, and free people."[24] In Louisiana, Gov. Thomas Moore was another example of a cooperative governor whose tenure was marked by "maintaining a sense of decorum and deference" to Davis instead of "playing the disruptive states' rights card." Moore accommodated Davis because of the military threat to his state, a condition that only Davis could remedy.[25] Despite the lack of military assistance from Richmond, Moore demonstrated his determination to support the Confederate government by implementing stringent, even harsh, local restrictions he believed were in line with national Confederate policy.[26]

****

Even if Davis could have gathered universal political support, he would still have had to address the consequences of many institutional decisions that occurred during his administration. At its founding, the Confederacy lacked both institutional structures and executive experience. Consequently, the government organized many of the departments in a slapdash manner and their leaders, often selected more for regional representation than personal competency, were less than satisfactory. The result was a series of Confederate policies, both economic and military, that Davis created with the best of intentions that often failed in spectacular fashion. Besides not achieving their desired goals, the failed policies also created negative unintended consequences in other facets of the Confederate war effort and undermined confidence in the cause of independence.

The Treasury Department was the source of many Confederate problems, attributed to the policies of its Secretary, Christopher Memminger. Davis selected Memminger, one of the wealthiest people in the antebellum period, because of his standing in South Carolina and his financial acumen despite his lack of previous government service. Memminger brought to the Treasury two deeply flawed perceptions, namely that the war would not be lengthy and that drastic economic measures were not necessary. Consequently, Memminger was slow to create long-term financial institutions and regulations suitable for a nation involved in a full-scale war for its survival. Memminger also failed to diversify the economy, instead favoring the antebellum practice of maintaining the value of hard currency through the sale of cotton to the European powers, but that again presumed a short war and did not foresee Union efforts to isolate the Confederacy.[27] Only later did Memminger recognize the futility of continuing prewar economic policies, leaving him the sole option of issuing large amounts of paper money, which created a ruinous cycle of inflation and eroded faith in Confederate financial measures.[28] The Treasury made some belated attempts to bolster confidence in the currency. In 1863, the Confederate Congress passed the Funding Act, which reduced the amount of currency by requiring anyone holding notes to exchange them for Confederate bonds. The move devastated state treasuries because residents paid their taxes in the unfunded Confederate currency, filling the state coffers with worthless dollars.[29] Another failed attempt at restructuring was the Currency Reform Act, enacted in 1864, whereby the Treasury exchanged the paper notes first issued in 1861 for new issue currency at a 2:3 ratio.[30] By replacing the original notes ("old issue") with fewer replacements notes ("new issue"), Congress hoped to bolster the value of the currency by increasing its relative scarcity, but citizens questioned if they could rely upon the new currency if the Treasury could not maintain the value of the existing notes.[31] The failure of the law led to Memminger's resignation in July 1864, but his successor, George Trenholm, had no better idea of how to improve the nation's financial situation. Ultimately, the Treasury resorted to the basic expedient of accepting donations from the citizens still willing to give "money, jewels, gold and silver plate."[32]

Spiraling inflation was the most notable consequence of Treasury Department policies. In 1863 alone, gold prices in Houston went from four Confederate dollars for one prewar gold dollar coin in May to nineteen by the end of the year. In January 1865, a Confederate sergeant in Louisiana considered himself lucky when he exchanged Confederate currency for gold at only a 3:1 rate. He was fortunate; a Richmond resident reported "Gold is at $65 Confederate dollars per ounce." Specie became the preferred medium of exchange, with a soldier reporting that flour that sold for six dollars per pound in Confederate currency could be had for "15 or 20 cents in silver," while an officer paid a cavalryman to post a letter for him behind Union lines, paying "$2 in Confed. [money] for a 3 cent Yankee stamp." Besides depreciating relative to gold, Confederate currency also suffered in preference to Union "greenbacks," because they retained their value relative to inflation. Newspaper editors in occupied New Bern, North Carolina, reported that "greenbacks are crowding out the Confederate currency down South," while newspapers in Raleigh reported that "Nothing but greenbacks are in circulation." In Louisiana, an officer noted in his diary that he converted eight hundred fifty dollars in Confederate money into "eight dollars in greenbacks, with which I bought a horse." Civilians so coveted greenbacks that officials supervising Union POWs ordered the confiscation of the prisoners' money lest they use them to purchase goods not available to their guards or bribe their way to freedom.[33]

As the inflation rate soared, citizens could only watch with alarm as food prices escalated beyond their means to pay. A clerk in Richmond charted the increase of the local cost of a barrel of flour over the course of the war: forty dollars in August 1863; seventy in October 1863; four hundred in May 1864, before peaking at fifteen hundred in March 1865.[34] As Sherman prepared to commence his March to the Sea in 1864, prices in Georgia spiked upward, with a resident reporting that costs had increased more than 40 percent compared to only the month before.[35] Livestock also sold for high prices. A civilian in Georgia recalled paying eight hundred dollars for a cow that reliably produced two gallons of milk a day, "which I think was doing well," while a soldier noted "I saw an ordinary cow sell here for the enormous price of $1,500."[36] With the currency worthless, bartering became an inevitable consequence. In Jacksonville, Alabama, a woman advertised in the local paper that she wanted to barter "a few pairs of Cotton Cards" for "Flour, dried Fruit, or anything to eat," while across the state in Eutaw another resident announced he had "sugar and salt" available and with which he was willing to "barter for provisions."[37] In addition to food, the prices of general goods also first became expensive and then unaffordable. A South Carolina woman in search of cloth complained, "I was horrified at having to pay $32.45" for a small piece of cloth.[38] Medicine became pricey, with quinine fetching twenty dollars per ounce and castor oil at twenty dollars per gallon.[39] Clothing was very expensive, even in Richmond, where a "genteel suit of clothes cannot be had for less than $700" and "a pair of boots, $200 if good."[40] Footwear was particularly hard to find. An officer in Alabama found it "quite a relief to hear that you can probably get me a pair of shoes for $100" because he could find none for less than two hundred-fifty dollars. Those were reasonable, as a Richmond resident complained that "Shoes wear out fast here, and they are asking from $500 to $1,800 for a pair of boots."[41] The cost of fuel also went up. In 1861, coal in Richmond was six dollars per load, but rose to ninety dollars by November 1864. Early in 1865, the city announced that, due to high fuel costs and a lack of iron allocated from the War Department, the city could no longer maintain the streetlights.[42]

With prices spiraling out of control, many farmers tried to grow more food, but with mixed results. By one estimate, the acreage devoted to wheat, corn, and potatoes tripled between 1861 and 1864 in the states east of the Mississippi River, but acreage did not equate to output if laborers did not tend and properly harvest the crops.[43] In 1862, a plantation woman informed a friend "We only plant 40 acres of cotton" and instead "have planted a larger crop of Irish Potatoes than we ever did before, in view of the need of our Army & the high prices they command."[44] Increased production, however, had unintended consequences. When corn production greatly increased in Mississippi from 1861 to 1863, the result was to drive the price down from $1.50 to $.62 per bushel.[45] There were other problems as well. The loss of labor caused an inevitable and immediate decline in production of even the most fertile land. When conscription went into effect, a Tennessee resident informed his Congressman that "Nine-tenths of the producing labor of East Tennessee … is gone. There are within our borders at this time thousands of families left without any male members capable of labor."[46] The Union occupation of Confederate territory also reduced the amount of land devoted to feeding the Southern population.[47] "However generously the earth might yield of grain, fruits, and vegetables," an Alabama woman wrote in her memoir, "the South was awakening to the painful reality that the produce grown on our narrowing space of Confederate soil was inadequate for the sustenance" of the effort.[48]

The Confederacy might have imported food to feed its populace, but the Union blockade stifled imports as well as exports. The Southern states had annually imported fifty-five million dollars' worth of goods in the antebellum years, but the blockade had reduced trade to a fraction of that amount.[49] A sailor observed that "the whole country is greatly distressed by the blockade" as prices for goods doubled and tripled from their prewar costs and were "extremely difficult to procure at even these prices." The lack of industry forced the Confederates to import large amounts of basic items. Those evading the blockade could reap large profits on common commercial goods, such as "Linseed Oil, Soda, Crushed Sugar, Trace Chains, Horse Shoe Nails … tin cups … frying pans, etc."[50] The blockade also had a psychological effect by creating a sense of economic uncertainty in what had been a stable antebellum economy. A Georgia woman described the psychological pressure of the blockade, writing, "I feel the restraint of the blockade and as port after port becomes blockaded, I feel shut up, pent up."[51] Adding to the blockade-fueled depression was a decline in the number of merchants who, unable to stock their stores, shut their doors. A visitor to Charleston described how "the regular merchants had … sold out their stocks long ago, closed their stores" leaving the city "little more than rows of closed stores" where "a perpetual Sunday or holiday prevailed."[52] As soon as the blockade appeared, blockade-runners took up the challenge of moving cotton out and bringing desired commodities back into Confederate ports. The runners kept imports flowing and raised civilian morale with their daring exploits, but the practice had its critics because the blockade-running depreciated the Confederate currency.[53] Driven by the negative effect on the economy, the Confederate government in 1864 forced privately owned blockade runners to allocate half their capacity for government cargoes, but also to allot shipping space to other wartime bureaus as was necessary. The policy greatly diminished potential profits while the level of risk, represented by a tightening Union blockade, continued to increase.[54] The decreasing likelihood of success played a part in the declining number of successful passages through the blockade (1453 in 1863, 806 in 1864, and 204 in the early months of 1865), but the lack of inducement by profit also played a part. As one successful blockade-runner put it, "the enterprise had lost much of its charm; for, unromantic as it may seem, much of that charm consisted in money-making."[55]

****

Economic issues were not the only policy-related problems that undermined the Confederate government. Many military-related policies, while essential at the time, caused more problems than they solved. The most prominent example was the implementation of conscription to force men to serve in the Confederate armed forces, a decision many perceived as government despotism. Enacted in April 1862, the Conscription Act made all men between the ages of eighteen and thirty-five liable for three years of military service. The legislation also extended the enrollment of one-year volunteers by another two years, as well as providing exemptions based on occupation or slave ownership.[56] Immediately, worries appeared that the law represented a central government bent on violating civilian rights. "It is important … to our country, now bleeding at every pore, that this law should meet a hearty and willing response," a newspaper editor proclaimed, but feared a backlash if recruits "are driven into the ranks at the point of the bayonet—if they go 'like gallery slaves scourged' to their tasks."[57] Once committed to conscription, however, the Confederacy had no choice but to continue the practice despite its growing unpopularity and rejection of other means of attracting volunteers. In March 1865, a conscription agent in rural Virginia had to exempt twenty-six men, virtually all of those collected that month, including two for epilepsy, several for poor vision, and two for insanity. Later in the same month, he examined sixteen men, from age twenty-five to forty-eight (average age thirty-eight), but exempted all of them for reasons ranging from epilepsy to asthma to heart disease to a deformed ankle.[58] Another officer noted that when conscript agents arrived "All must go, … the rosy-cheeked, raven-locked youth of seventeen, side by side with fathers of hoary years & furrowed brows … 'the cradle & the grave' march forth to the common defense."[59] The countryside had been swept so clean of eligible recruits that a clergyman in Charlottesville noted the only people who attended his sermons were old men, veterans discharged due to injury, and grieving widows.[60]

Other criticism centered on the unwise drafting of key employees in important industries. To retain artisans and skilled workers, the government exempted laborers because agrarian economies relied upon a few practiced individuals to service the needs of a region. Farmers, for instance, found it difficult to have the simplest repairs performed, especially on scarce tools. Residents in a North Carolina county, for instance, pleaded with the governor to release the local blacksmith from the army because they had no one "that can shoe a horse or fix our farming tools."[61] The conscription of only a few individuals could economically paralyze whole regions, such as when an agent in western Virginia conscripted three blacksmiths, two shoemakers, two physicians, a miller, and a tanner, removing their services from the local economy.[62]

As its unpopularity grew, the conscription process produced fewer recruits as draft resistance lost its stigma. As the number of draft resisters increased, the level of risk they faced often changed. Early in the war, "outlayers" could exist only by hiding in remote areas and relying upon timely warnings from sympathetic neighbors and family members.[63] By the end of the war, however, many areas held enough resisters and their supporters that those who refused to comply with the draft could live openly.[64] In the face of widespread resistance, the conscription process virtually ceased. Few seemed willing to face the obvious fact that by the end of the war there were simply no more men to conscript, and recovering deserters from the army would provide many more soldiers than drafting the few still at home. In the last quarter of 1864, the entire state of Mississippi could only produce 235 conscripts, leading one draft official to believe that there were more agents looking for draftees than men eligible for conscription.[65] An agent in Virginia jokingly declared the army had become so desperate that the doctors "never discharge a man now until he has been dead for four days," and reported his latest draft roundup found only "the lame, the halt, & the blind."[66] The lack of suitable recruits was evident long before the war ended. In April 1864, Col. John Preston, Superintendent of the Conscription Bureau, could only excuse his bureau's shortcomings on the plain fact that "a large majority of such persons between the ages of seventeen and fifty are already in the service," and there was simply no one left to conscript.[67]

Despite the problems with conscription, the Confederate government had to continue drafting men because they were losing them at an alarming rate. Besides battlefield casualties, desertion became a chronic problem. In June 1863, the War Department reported that there were 136,000 soldiers away from their posts. By the end of the winter of 1864, 40 percent of the Confederate army east of the Mississippi River was absent, while a senior general west of the river believed that there were perhaps 21,000 troops available from a claimed force of 43,054 troops, meaning there nearly were as many AWOL as on duty.[68] As a deterrent, the Army used public executions to punish captured deserters and dissuade those pondering a desertion attempt. "There were six men shot in Alexandria last Friday," a soldier informed his wife, "It seems that we have got too many men. They want to kill some of them off."[69] Even deserters who returned to the army on their own initiative, who usually received only minor punishments, faced the death penalty, such as two men from the Thirty-seventh North Carolina, both leaving widows and children behind.[70] Despite these efforts, the rate of desertions continued to increase as demoralization, defeatism, and realism led many Confederate troops to abandon the war to save themselves or their family members. Particularly distressing was the desertion of veteran soldiers. Confederate authorities could dismiss deserters as the cowardly and weak, but by 1865 even the most steadfast soldiers had had enough. One soldier wrote that "If none deserted but cowards it would be different but some are deserting that has been good soldiers ever since the war commenced."[71]

Finding troops was one problem, but feeding them was another. The Commissary Bureau of the War Department was responsible for provisioning the army, but its leader, Col. Lucius Northrop, faced a plethora of difficulties.[72] With poor organization, limited amounts of increasingly depreciating currency, and unreliable sources of supply, Northrop had to feed large Confederate armies widely dispersed over a vast territory on a weak and vulnerable transportation system by coordinating with the various War Department bureaus, the Treasury Department, and any number of different industries. Transportation was important because the products managed by the Commissary had a limited shelf life, so prompt delivery was essential to prevent spoilage. Such a system, however, never existed, and the interrupted movement of supplies caused hardship to soldiers at the front. By late 1864, troops in Virginia relied upon food sources in the Carolinas and such distances meant many opportunities for the supply chain to break down. While Lee's army starved in Petersburg, depots in Danville, Virginia, only 120 miles away, held half a million rations of bread and 1.5 million rations of meat with no means to deliver it.[73] The Commissary also had no control over the value of Confederate currency, and found themselves obligated to feed large numbers of troops with increasingly worthless money. In 1865, for instance, the Commissary Bureau's obligations and expenses reflected the need to feed a force of 400,000 men at a cost of $2.03 per ration per day. In the end, the Commissary Bureau simply could not overcome the enormous obligation and financial burden.[74]

Because of Northrop's organizational failures, the Commissary Bureau had to resort to impressment, the seizure of private property. Secretary of War Seddon admitted that impressment was "a harsh, unequal, and odious mode of supply," but could not offer any alternative to maintaining the army.[75] As an individual policy, impressment stood out as one of the worst abuses of the Confederate government, but it was only a product of the broader Confederate economic problems. As one historian described the policy, "Impressment was a mistake, but a mistake which the crazy quilt of the Confederate economic structure forced on the government."[76] Impressment might have been more effective if producers believed they were receiving fair market value for their goods, but the price schedule, the fixed price the government paid per unit, was always less than the value of goods on the open market.[77] Farmers complained that the government fixed the price schedule for their goods, but their overhead costs constantly increased.[78] Many regions saw wide discrepancies in pricing: the Commissary offered to buy flour at fourteen dollars per bushel but the market price was sixty; the army offered $675 for a good horse when the market price was as high as $6000.[79] Many farmers defied Confederate attempts to impress their crop by either hiding it or selling it to speculators.[80] Other farmers, instead of incurring the cost of growing foodstuffs for which they would not get fair value, simply produced less, which, in turn, denied supplies to city residents who could not provide for themselves.[81] Farmers held so much food off the market that Union foragers often found plenty of sustenance in areas said to be destitute. A Richmond newspaper editor noticed that "when General Lee calls for provisions to feed his army, we are told that this man and that have given them all, but when the Yankee raiders come along, they find meat-houses and corn cribs or cellars filled with abundance."[82]

The impressment policy employed by the Confederate Army also caused widespread anger because it caused collective hardship and suffering, creating greater dissent against the government due to charges of indifference and incompetence. "It becomes daily more difficult," an observer in Charleston noted, "not to live well, but to live."[83] The impressment of an entire season's crop often left families destitute and desperate, which in turn led directly to desertion by soldiers concerned about their family's welfare.[84] The callous nature of how the army impressed products also generated antipathy among civilians unfortunate enough to be in the army's path. Encamped near Forrest City, Mississippi, in July 1863, Private John Hagan told his wife, "I beleave [*sic*] our troops are doing as much harm in this country as the Yankees … our men steal all the fruit, kill all the Hogs & burn all the fences. … I am disgusted with such conduct & feel that we will never be successful while our troops are so ungrateful."[85] Civilians complained, but the government had no answers or alternatives. "They have ate up nearly all the corn in the country, [and] they press what they get now," Mary Scott wrote of Confederate troops in North Carolina, "What will the poor people do Heaven only knows."[86] In March 1865, far too late to have any real effect, the Congress ended impressment by obligating government agencies to pay market prices for all goods taken by the army.[87]

****

Because of the varied political and economic mistakes committed by the Confederate government, civilians had many reasons to be demoralized. Any discussion of demoralization in the Confederacy, however, must consider the fact that pessimism affected the Confederate ability to wage war, but did not itself end the war. Even as the war ended in defeat, a considerable number of Southern civilians and soldiers wanted to fight on. Hardships inured some to the war, while others had simply lost so much that only some sort of victory could compensate them for their sacrifice. Others continued to fight because the consequences of defeat—freed slaves, Union domination, and loss of their way of life—was simply too frightening to comprehend.[88] Other civilians proved willing to continue shedding blood despite military setbacks. "If we cannot force the invading robbers from our soil," a civilian declared, "we can all die in the effort and thereby emblazon the name of our nation higher upon the escutcheon of fame." He was not the only one to embrace radical action to save the Confederacy. "Why does not the President call out the women if there are [not] enough men?" a North

Carolina woman wondered, "We would go and *fight* too—we would better all die together."[89]

Civilian support buoyed the optimism of soldiers who saw their determination first hand. Soldiers gained new hope from civilians "telling us to fight to the end although compelled to retreat now, never give up & other words of cheer. There was not a man but gripped his sabre the tighter & felt more than ever determined never to give up this struggle till liberty or death be our lot."[90] While many soldiers had become demoralized by 1865, others determined to stay in the ranks although their reasons for doing so differed. On one end of the determination spectrum were soldiers who fatalistically recognized that events were moving beyond their control and the only predictable feature of their lives was the grim determination to hold on. "It appears gloomy enough," wrote a Georgia soldier, "Our only hope is to fight until we conquer a peace."[91] Others found reason to fight on because of the fear of leaving defenseless families and relatives behind. A soldier in Alabama lamented the "woes and misery our people have endured already," but "we owe to them a duty, for strong arms, broad backs, and stern discipline will be needed now."[92] On the opposite end were the soldiers whose determination reached levels of unrealistic optimism, even to the point of finding victories in obvious defeats. In Richmond, Col. Richard Maury found an unseen benefit in recent Confederate setbacks. He approved of the evacuation of Charleston as "It was useless to have a second Vicksburg affair enacted there," and was not upset by the loss of Wilmington because it was "so much the better for General Pierre Beauregard will now be able to concentrate against Sherman and no doubt whip him."[93] Another Confederate agreed, stating "Our armies are now concentrating and soon we will ... have nothing but our country to fight for now."[94]

Growing demoralization, however, began to overcome the determination to continue. The demands of modern warfare fought in an industrial age soon took its toll on the Southern agricultural society, and the population experienced varied, but always increasing, levels of demoralization. The government's shortcomings resulted from the lack of preparation for war and its inability to estimate the actions needed to win against an enemy whose determination matched and exceeded its own. As Armistead Robinson determined, "The Confederacy discovered that Southern society could not sustain a defensive war of attrition while simultaneously maintaining the stability of its domestic institutions."[95] Lee recognized that lack of popular support meant the doom of his army, writing that "Everything, in my opinion, has depended and still depends upon the disposition and feelings of the people."[96] As the war dragged on, however, many civilians allowed themselves to fall into bouts of defeatism, a self-pity in the absence of clear actions to alter the country's predicament. "The people of Miss. and Mobile seem to be sanguine about recognition and peace within the course of sixty days," reported an Alabama resident who held out a futile hope of foreign intervention. "This is our only hope unless the Yankees get tired of fighting."[97] Yet others could simply not conceive how their cause had reached such a dire state, even when the evidence of the country's collapse was staring them in the face. "What a change from 1861, when all were so buoyant and full of fiery patriotism with never a thought of being overcome," an Alabama woman wrote gloomily, "yet day by day the newspapers brought news of defeat after defeat ... our soldiers were ... going into battle ragged and barefoot and half-starved—in vain."[98]

With the loss of hope came despair as white Southerners worried about the future and their place in it, creating a widespread emotional depression. Those traveling around the South on official duties noted the attitude everywhere they went. "There seems to be a great feeling of despondency here as elsewhere about the state of our affairs," an official observed in North Carolina, while a Texas state official reported that "the clouds thicken around us from every quarter, every countenance is filled with despondency."[99] Even worse than the uncertainty of the future to many Southerners was the reality that their relationship with their slaves was about to change forever. "War is a terrible demon," Ella Thomas wrote from Augusta, Georgia. "I lose faith in humanity when I see such efforts to sink ... the white race to elevate the Negro."[100] Others associated defeat itself with slavery, with themselves in bondage. "Conquered, Submission, Subjugation are words that burn into my heart," a Texas civilian lamented, "The war is rushing rapidly to a disastrous close. Another month and our Confederacy will be a Nation no longer, but we will be slaves, yes slaves, of the Yankee Government."[101]

The civilian population became demoralized, and many Confederate soldiers did so as well. The inclination to suffer for comrades or cause remained for many dedicated soldiers, but they expected minimal returns for their suffering. There are many cases when only a relatively slight improvement in their condition—getting paid regularly, having an occasional decent meal, or being informed of what was going on—could have dramatically improved the soldiers' confidence in the outcome of the war. Producing these results, however, proved difficult, and soldiers endured many basic organizational failures that they had every reason to expect to not occur. The Confederacy's financial troubles meant that soldiers often went unpaid for months at a time. In June 1864, Congress increased a private's pay from eleven dollars per month to eighteen, but it made little difference as the currency devalued and inflation increased.[102] Supply problems also sapped morale. An officer found items, like shoes, tents, and overcoats, "an object of curiosity" when he finally obtained them, while a soldier in Virginia complained that during a lengthy march "it rained hard, and the men had not one day's rations in the three."[103] The pervasive hunger convinced many soldiers it was time to desert, with one soldier writing, "Men can't stay here and fight and work and not eat. I tell you they can't and won't."[104] In his postwar memoir, a disgruntled Confederate veteran blamed the failure of logistics for their defeat, claiming, "if we could have gotten a little something to eat, I would be fighting for our beloved South today."[105] Unable to rely upon regular logistic support, soldiers ate what they could forage. Troops near Savannah were reduced to "catching rats and parching acorns," but one soldier could not develop a taste for crabs, saying, "They are just about as much like meat as a maypop is like a vegetable."[106]

Because of the growing pessimism, more and more troops became reluctant to fight in a war they believed to be lost. The growing pessimism morphed into apathy and defeatism, as soldiers who could see no path to victory became blasé about the war or even their own chances of surviving it.[107] A soldier informed his wife that "The Armey [*sic*] hear is very much demoralized. I don't believe that the men will fight much."[108] Others saw no point in minutiae. "I do everything mechanically," a private described, "I shoulder my rifle as usual, walk steady, and perform my duties faithfully and without murmur, but within my heart is sad and weary, and I ask myself what is the use."[109] Such attitudes soon infected troops in the Confederate armies. Driven before the Union advance into the Carolinas, a soldier wrote to his mother, "I can see no hope for our cause. … Our generals are drunkards and the soldiers black with profanity," while a colleague agreed, concluding "there is not any use of fighting any longer. … I would like to hear of some terms of peace before they run clear over us."[110] Likewise, in Lee's army in Virginia, a courier could see proof the army was finished because "Demoralization, panic, abandonment of all hope, appeared on every hand," and an officer observed the "mournful spectacle" of the roadside ditches strewn with the "abandoned muskets of the straggling soldiers. Some were broken, the barrels of others bent and the muzzles choked with mud … unmistakable evidences of a set determination upon the part of hundreds to fight no more."[111] Unable to see any hope of success, some Confederates simply wished for peace regardless of the costs. "If this war was over, could we not enjoy peaceable homes once more?" a soldier wondered, "I hope the day is not far off when we will again be permitted to see loved ones at home."[112] Soldiers recognized more than the politicians and generals that defeat was to occur sooner rather than later. A Louisiana cavalryman was very blunt about the Confederacy's prospects when he wrote "At every point of the Confederacy we have been beaten, and already our armies are fighting mostly in detail. To speak truly, I think we will finally be overpowered and forced to lay down our arms."[113]

****

While the Confederate government, state leaders, and military command-ers recognized that the war would impose hardship and suffering, few could predict the widespread dissent that their actions would generate, and the subsequent resistance that appeared across all social classes, regions, and constituencies of the Confederacy. Because the scope of the dissent proved so great, the Confederate leadership found it difficult to react to the oppo-sition occurring within its own population or conceive means to rectify the situation. The government should have anticipated opposition because wartime burdens fell most heavily on yeoman farmers, the largest portion of the Southern population and those most likely to suffer the greatest losses in terms of property and status while having the least to gain from a war for independence.[114] Those who dissented from the war had the common attributes of residing in regions that were not predominantly cotton-growing areas, opposed Confederate policies and legislation that compelled their compliance in a war that increasingly threatened their economic status, and held strong social networks, usually based on kinship, that permitted group resistance rather than forcing individuals to stand alone.[115] The trend toward centralizing political control in Richmond also had the unintended consequence of creating new reasons for dissent while at the same time reducing the ability of the government to either address or contain dissatisfaction in the populace. Opposition to government decisions, for instance, greatly increased after passage of the Conscription Act in 1862 because it made the decision by citizens not to participate in the war an act of virtual treason.[116] The government might have mitigated the dissent if their policies proved successful, but many new political and military decisions made the circumstances much worse.[117] The revolutionary nature of the Confederate secession also prevented the Confederate elite from perceiving dissenters as less than traitors to their cause. Consequently, nonsupport of Confederate policies by disgruntled or destitute citizens was not an option, as many civilians who philosophically still supported Confederate objectives, but who no longer could sacrifice toward those goals "retreated into a neutrality or noninvolvement that Confederate officials defined as disloyalty."[118] This was particularly true of those who supported the war but whose economic status meant that they either could not or would not sacrifice any more for the nation when their own condition was desperate, generating what Rebecca Christian described as "an attitude of despondency and discontent, even of indifference to the outcome of the war."[119] Rather than find means of alleviating suffering and bolstering patriotism, the Confederate Congress increasingly began to see only enemies within their midst. In the last months of the war, Congress designated anyone leaving the Confederacy, especially those fleeing to Union lines, "as an alien enemy, and his property shall be liable to sequestration." Only days later, Congress passed another law allowing the death penalty for "any person … corresponding with the enemy in any manner."[120] Unable to pacify unhappy citizens, Confederate authorities could only react as a spectrum of opposition began to develop throughout the nation that crossed regional, class, and gender boundaries. Some of the opposition was philosophical, but some anti-government reactions were much more active and even reached the point of violent resistance.[121]

The first hostility to the Confederacy came in the form of Unionists who opposed the secession of their states from the Union. As the war progressed, anyone who opposed the Confederate war effort, regardless of reason or motivation, received the label of "Unionist," much in the same way that any war opponent in the North faced accusations of being a Copperhead. Proper Unionists, however, were those who opposed the creation of the Confederacy on political or philosophical grounds, which separated them from other groups who opposed specific elements of Confederate policy. Several common bonds identified those who clung to their Union loyalties. One was their political identity, as many had identified with the antebellum Whig Party. The nationalistic philosophy promoted by the Whigs served as basis for the initial resistance to secession by most Unionists, who viewed secession as radical and illegitimate. Much of the Unionist opposition in Georgia, for example, originated in anger that secession was forced upon the state by a minority of citizens, a sentiment shared in other places like Arkansas, where less than a third of white residents favored secession when first proposed.[122] Economic interests also defined Unionist allegiance, such as merchants in urban centers with strong commercial ties to the North and yeoman landowners in rural areas outside of the cotton-growing economic mainstream.[123] In regions dominated by small farm economies maintained with few or no slaves, residents had long resisted the political dominance of the large landowners. The war exacerbated the divide created by the secession crisis by further delineating the "us vs. them" nature of Southern life, with many yeoman farmers "who did not own slaves were swearing that they 'would not lift a finger to protect rich men's negroes.'"[124] Geography also played a part, with Unionists generally originating in the "upcountry" regions of several states with long-standing antagonisms with the "low country" political elites. As Unionists fit into categories outside of the social establishment of Southern culture, their political adherence to the Union became a sign of their purported backwardness. Pro-secessionists, according to one Alabama resident, came from the "best people" of the state, while Unionists were "the most miserable, ignorant, poor, ragged devils I ever saw."[125]

Unionists faced various conditions and situations that prevented them from asserting any decisive influence in Confederate affairs. Pro-Confederate portions of the population outnumbered the Unionists, who found themselves forced to remain silent and be at least minimally complicit with national policy. Unionists dared only to openly demonstrate their loyalty to the United States when Federal troops were nearby. The arrival of Union troops in northern Alabama, for example, allowed Unionists to secure their property, exercise their political will, and avoid persecution, but it came with a price. Unionists had to accommodate the demands of the Union occupiers and their constant supply needs, and were often in the crossfire when military clashes took place.[126] Elsewhere, Unionists also disagreed with the Lincoln administration's racial policies, especially the Emancipation Proclamation. Unionists were not abolitionists, and, while the Proclamation did exempt some occupied regions of the South, the loss of property and status alienated many Unionists throughout the Confederacy.[127]

Unionists were ineffective in altering the Confederate bid for independence, but a more assertive portion of the opposition to the Confederate government, broadly identified as "dissenters," had a greater influence. While Unionists resisted the Confederacy from the start and opposed everything that it stood for, dissenters represented those who had at one point supported the cause of independence. As the difficulties of wartime existence increased, however, more and more dissenters from the government's agenda appeared, not necessarily because they disagreed with the nation's goals, but rather because they could no longer contribute as the government demanded. Many became dissenters for the very practical reason that they had already sacrificed a great deal for the cause and either could not nor would not sacrifice any more lest they themselves suffer or starve. Pressed to the point of desperation, dissenters ignored, evaded, or openly defied Confederate laws, especially those related to conscription and impressment. Although often denigrating those less driven toward independence than himself, Jefferson Davis in 1864 had to admit that "it can no longer be doubted that the zeal with which the people sprung to arms at the beginning of the contest has, in some parts of the Confederacy, been impaired by the long continuance and magnitude of the struggle."[128] Contentious policies, such as conscription, led to the decrease in enthusiasm that Davis mentioned, as did the failure of Confederate economic policies, leading to widespread instances of what one author called "economic disloyalty" by placing one's own survival over the needs of the nation.[129]

The state of morale among the civilian population was a major indicator of the extent of dissent in many regions. The decline in morale became very evident relatively early in the war, created by, as one historian wrote, "the growing number of sacrifices, the breakdown of authority, the drain on manpower, and dwindling hope of victory."[130] Many otherwise loyal citizens lost their enthusiasm for the Confederate cause, especially after impressment agents depleted their food stocks with no sympathy for a family's plight.[131] Union depredations often took the rest, but instead of blaming the Union troops who impoverished them, many blamed the government for getting them into the war and then failing to protect them.[132] The division was visible to an Alabama cavalryman who was pleased "to find many family altars where the fire of patriotism still burns," but also found the "majority of the people cold, spineless, apathetic—a set of demoralized extortioners."[133] Because economic problems hit everyone, dissent came from a cross-section of the civilian population, as one Confederate supporter admitted, "Very many of the middle class, a large number of the more intelligent, and nearly all of the lower class of her people are drifting to the Yankees."[134]

The middle class in particular became demoralized because the conflict threatened their individual opportunism. From 1850 to 1860, Mississippi, for instance, went from the third largest cotton producer to the largest, but the average size of farms grew from only 309 acres to 370, indicating that middle-class producers, not large plantation owners, were the generators of the state's wealth now threatened by the war.[135] The appearance of military failure also sapped morale. By 1864, the government measured military success not by occupying enemy soil but by merely preventing the loss of more Confederate territory. Civilians, perceiving that their contributions brought only mere survival questioned if the sacrifice was worthwhile.[136] Even temporary Confederate military successes failed to boost morale, especially when the success had unintended consequences. When Confederate cavalry captured the Union outpost at Athens, Alabama, loyal citizens hoped they intended to stay, but instead the troops withdrew a few days later, leaving the loyalists much poorer than before by commandeering their livestock and destroying the only railroad track.[137]

As dissent became more prevalent, a political element of discord emerged. While no open rebellion occurred against Jefferson Davis's rule, he was very unpopular with many voters. Campaigning in Louisiana in 1864, a Union soldier observed that "the inhabitants exhibit a stony desire for the Union army to hold possession of the town, being tired of being ruled by the power of Jeff D. and Co.," while a Georgia newspaper editor claimed, "We have entirely too many little jackass upstarts filling positions in our government."[138] Without influence in Richmond, political dissenters tried to alter the course of the Confederacy through their state governments, albeit with only limited success. In Alabama, for instance, the state legislature proposed to enter peace negotiations with the Union based upon the Democratic Party's Chicago platform in 1864. Governor Thomas Watts came out in opposition, charging that those who supported the measure would "stamp with infamy alike the names of our gallant dead and living heroes of the war," but more than a third of the state House of Representatives voted for the proposal.[139] Many Georgians, weary of the war, held open pro-peace rallies, creating perhaps the only circumstance where Gov. Joseph Brown and Davis could find common ground. Brown did not like Davis, but he disliked the Union even more. In response to the pro-peace efforts within the state, both Brown and Davis generated emotional statements pleading for national loyalty as the Confederacy's strength waned.[140]

Dissenters defied Confederate law, but resisters were the most dangerous internal group within the Confederacy because they challenged Confederate authority. A deserter, for instance, hiding at home, broke the rules, but many deserters took further action to prevent their arrest and return to service by escalating their resistance to the level of actual violence. Often deserters banded together to fight against efforts to arrest them, and because they could not engage in farming or other practices to support themselves, either had to rely on the support of sympathetic dissenters to feed them or become criminals to support themselves.[141] Joining the deserters were civilians whose actions rose to the level of active resistance for different reasons, be it political Unionism or economic necessity. Because of their unidentified nature, resisters were difficult to assess, with estimations of their numbers and motivations often greatly exaggerated. Confederate authorities in July 1863, for example, estimated that eight to ten thousand deserters and anti-war civilians existed in north Alabama, including many deserters from Mississippi and Texas.[142] While the estimation was greater than the actual numbers, the location of the purported resisters was typical of where such activity tended to occur in that the area was relatively remote, with few railroad connections to the more-populous portions of the state, and dominated by middle- and lower-class farmers.[143] Because of the relatively less development of such regions, pro-government citizens denigrated the resisters as both unpatriotic agents of the Union and uneducated "low" people. An Alabama newspaper editor described resisters as "the Yahoos in North Alabama" who were "little better than the wild beasts with which they herd, and as such, have no more moral influence than a drove of cattle."[144] Denigrating and stigmatizing the resisters made it easier to crack down on them, such as a citizen describing local resisters as both "male & female … unfit to live anywhere. … They are abolitionists, spies, deserters, liars, thieves, murderers, and everything foul & damnable."[145]

In regions where they could concentrate, resisters managed to disrupt local government functions. In Alabama, one resistance group "banded together and committed serious depredations upon good citizens. They pillage, plunder, and steal horses and everything else that is of any use to them." Further described as "a terror to the people," the group was accused of burning the Coffee County courthouse, murdering a number of "the best citizens of that county," and making it "exceedingly dangerous for a loyal man to travel" to the point that the local circuit court judge would not venture there "unless he is protected by the military."[146] An officer complained that deserters "stay at Home all the time, protected and harbored by their friends at Home, defying every attempt to catch them. … Indeed, they are menaces that will burn, rob, or destroy the property of any citizen who would in the least assist in their arrest."[147] Resistance activity took on some common forms, such as theft, intimidation, and clashes with local authorities, but some notable locations showed differences in resistance in various states. In North Carolina, the most visible form of resistance was the "Buffaloes," a group of armed anti-Confederate resisters who reflected class separation in the state by their lower class membership and proclivity to target upper classes' economic assets. A civilian commented that "the country is swarming with deserters" who were "committing depredations on the rich farmers."[148] The Union organized some Buffaloes into formal organizations, but most simply used the cover of the war to engage in banditry. The state was also plagued by bands of "deserters and fugitives who had become outlaws" existing in the boundary zone between Union and Confederate control by "plundering the good and Loyal Citizens." By the last year of the war, bands of up to four hundred resisters roamed the countryside "burning and robbing everything before them" and some judges close to Raleigh did not feel safe holding court sessions.[149]

Louisiana's equivalent to the Buffaloes were their "Jayhawkers," resistance groups that had grown brazen enough to attack Confederate officers in broad daylight. When Jayhawkers operating in central Louisiana captured three officers and turned them over to Union authorities in exchange for reward money, Maj. Gen. Richard Taylor ordered officers not to travel through the area without a substantial escort. He further ordered subordinates to "scour this portion of the country thoroughly, and every man found with arms in his hands, against whom reasonable suspicion exists of a determination to resist the laws, will be shot by you on the spot."[150] The Jayhawkers eventually became such a danger that both sides established a truce so Confederate troops could restore order. Using a Union Navy officer as a go-between, Confederate Capt. William Ratliff proposed to Union Maj. Gen. Francis Herron a truce, under which Ratliff proposed to "capture or drive away the bands of men, commonly known as jayhawkers" if Federal troops "agree to a truce for a limited time," to which Herron concurred.[151]

Arguably, the most widespread resistance took place in Florida. In Taylor County, just southeast of Tallahassee, a band had so intimidated the sheriff that he informed the state treasurer that "I am compelled to stop collecting or assessing taxes for the present" after threats upon his life made him conclude

"I have thought it best to desist."[152] Threatening the sheriff was a group of "over 200 refugees and deserters … in open war with the Confederacy."[153] In the panhandle region, Brig. Gen. John K. Johnson informed the War Department that "Many deserters from the armies of Virginia and Northern Georgia … have organized, with runaway negroes, bands for the purpose of committing depredations upon the plantations and crops of loyal citizens and running off their slaves."[154] The resisters were so brash as to even plot to kidnap Governor Milton and turn him over to the Union blockade, but loyal citizens warned Milton in time.[155] Beyond local criminality, the resisters in Florida evolved into an insurgency, with locals acting as guides for Union raiders, burning transportation and communication lines, and plundering or destroying Confederate logistics. Resistance began with acts of self-defense, but soon escalated into economic warfare that included the seizure of slaves and cattle.[156]

****

Regardless of whether Unionist, dissenter, or resister, the Confederate reaction to the developing opposition was a steady increase in pressure and violence. Initially, state governments relied upon minimal means, such as peer pressure, appeals to state identity, or legislation to contain those viewed as a threat to the collective order.[157] When those measures did not work, state governors used the corrective force at their disposal, such as county sheriffs, to arrest and jail those accused of resistance-related offenses. When local law enforcement proved not up to the task, governors opted to use state forces, such as formal State Troops or short-term militias, to bolster their efforts at suppressing opposition. When the use of militia tended to make the situation worse, governors had no choice but to ask the War Department to use Confederate troops to break up or destroy resistance groups within their borders, a drastic and often unsuccessful tactic.[158] No matter which approach was applied, the efforts to stifle opposition only generated more disagreement as the government action only reinforced the reasons and perceptions that led to opposition in the first place.

Unwilling to admit that open resistance existed, some governors favored a corrective approach to those who might resist Confederate efforts. In Florida, Governor Milton initially applied a policy of reconciliation, believing that many deserters who opposed the Confederacy "left the ranks for the purpose of helping their starving families" and "had little conception of the gravity of their offense in military law," and unnecessarily harsh treatment of those who differed in opinion would only make the situation worse.[159] The most common means of suppressing resistance was through new legislation intended to make specific acts of dissent or resistance illegal and punishable by local authorities. In some states, like Alabama, the legislation was prompted by the first significant numbers of deserters and made aiding deserters a felony.[160] The Arkansas state legislature passed an 1862 law that provided for the death penalty for those who aided the enemy. Not all Arkansans perceived a benefit to the law. One newspaper editor saw the opportunity for vengeance-based violence, as "if anybody has an enemy in north Arkansas, he has only to denounce him as a member of the peace society to insure his death."[161]

When coercion did not work, the Confederate states escalated their use of force by applying all available resources to intimidate the dissenters and resisters, justified by fiery rhetoric to warn those who transgressed and encourage supporters of the cause. Alabama Gov. John Shorter promised that "effective measures shall be adopted for the apprehension of every man—wherever located—who engages in any open act of Rebellion against the authorities of Alabama or of the Confederate States."[162] When local authorities proved unable to contain the resistance problem, governors employed either the existing state troops or ad hoc militias created to deal with the lack of order. As events proved, however, the state forces were singularly ineffective, mostly because their lack of discipline usually led to the unlawful use of force and resulting brutality, which generated further resistance to the Confederate government. In one case, pro-Confederate militia threatened a woman's infant, striking her, and tying her up by her thumbs to reveal the whereabouts of her husband.[163] Instead of remaining passive victims of assaults of state troops, resisters countered with violence of their own. In January 1863, state troops conducted a sweep through northeastern Georgia to round up dissenters and draft resisters, netting about six hundred men. Within months, however, many of the draft dodgers had become deserters, returning to their homes with their rifles and a new determination to avoid recapture. The state attempted another sweep in February 1864, but this time resisters fought back, killing several militia members and forcing them to withdraw without accomplishing their objective.[164]

In places like North Carolina, the campaign against dissenters triggered violent episodes throughout the backcountry, marked by murder, ambushes, assault, arson, torture, and intimidation as pro- and anti-Confederate forces struggled for control. Gov. Henry Clark sent three hundred state troops into Randolph County when the first overt forms of opposition appeared, but failed to root out the resisters. By 1863, a concerned Confederate officer reported resister bands that numbered in the hundreds who operated without fear of reprisal, advising that the only "strong measures of military repression" could hope to contain them.[165] Harsh repression, however, only bred additional confrontation and violence. When a state militia unit hanged eight men in Ashe County, resisters retaliated by ambushing the unit, inflicting a number of fatalities.[166] At the same time, Home Guard troops conducted large-scale operations to root out dissenters, including a sixty-day campaign utilizing eleven battalions of Home Guard troops authorized to suspend habeas corpus at their own discretion, with orders to "arrest all persons suspected of aiding and abetting deserters."[167] The campaign, like others, terrorized the families of dissenters when the dissenters themselves could not be found, including the torture of a young mother to reveal the whereabouts of her husband and the jailing of five pregnant women under conditions that caused some to miscarry.[168] Such large-scale operations by state troops occurred in other states, but likewise failed to achieve anything but short-term results because forces were poorly equipped and comprised of men either too young, too old, or too infirm to face conscription. When sent against resister bands that included veteran troops who had deserted, the militia often found themselves out-fought. In other cases, resisters undermined the militia units by joining these groups and betraying their plans. "Men are enlisted in the State reserves under false names and places," a Mississippian told the government, "who are deserters from the general Confederate service."[169]

When state militias proved incapable of containing resistance, the only resort available to state governors was to request assistance from the Confederate Army. While certainly better equipped than the state troops, the regular soldiers proved to be an unwise choice. Unlike the state troops who might have some sympathy for the resisters, regular soldiers were even more inclined to view resisters as traitors and treat them accordingly. In addition, combat had inured veteran soldiers to extreme violence and made them more willing to inflict harsh treatment. The circumstances, however, that made the state troops ineffective also made Confederate soldiers likewise unable to suppress the growing resistance. A cavalry sweep through rugged terrain in southern Georgia produced few results, with only twenty-two resisters caught in the net. Subsequent patrols also failed to round up many deserters, leaving military commanders to justify their failures by concluding that local authorities had greatly exaggerated the number of resisters.[170] Because they had obligations elsewhere, Regular army operations were invariably of short duration. In April 1864, for instance, the Sixty-fourth Georgia conducted an anti-resister operation through southwest Georgia and the Florida panhandle that temporarily suppressed opposition, but the resisters returned with even more vigor when the Georgians left to join Lee's army.[171] Cavalry action could also be dangerous for the cavalrymen themselves, who searched for desperate men perfectly willing to fight back. In August 1863, for instance, a search by Texas troops through central Louisiana resulted in a counterattack by local resisters that left a number of men on both sides dead.[172]

The level of violence was proportional to the threat posed by armed resisters, and areas with the most active resistance attracted the most violent response by Confederate troops. Such was the case when troops tried to suppress the active bands in central Mississippi in 1864. Upon arriving at his target area, Col. Robert Lowry offered deserters the opportunity to "perform your duties as patriots and freemen" so that when "an unbiased history of this war [is] written, do not have your children to feel disgraced because of the action of their sires."[173] The effort took the usual turn, however, when extralegal violence became common, with accused deserters given the choice of returning to the army or facing summary execution. Using such policies, Lowry reported that after only a few days "I have caught and had to report to me over 350 deserters and absentees" while also admitting "I have executed two men by hanging, and one was shot and killed, having tried to escape." He also had lost one of his own men killed and two others wounded "when a deserter slipped up and fired a shotgun into a group." Lowry reported a successful raid by stating that the local "sheriff has returned to his home and again entered upon his duties" as a sign he controlled the area. However, he also had to confess that there were still plenty of resisters and "Loyalty to the Government is punished by death or banishment from home, and the deserters are … plundering upon good and loyal citizens."[174] By the end of the operation in May 1864, the sweep had rounded up many deserters and executed eleven men without trial, but Lowry's operation only slightly diminished the number of resisters. Barely two months later, the enrolling agent in Jones County informed the governor that resister activity had so increased in violence that "if a man is found dead the civil authorities pays no attention to it—any more than if it was a dog."[175] By comparison, when army units did behave with restraint, their efforts were sometimes more successful. In September 1863, Maj. Gen. Robert Hoke and his division returned to his native North Carolina to both recruit soldiers and to suppress dissent in the western counties.[176] Instead of relying upon brutality and terror, Hoke enticed deserters to return. By offering immediate furloughs for deserters to address any home concerns before returning to the service, Hoke convinced some men to report for duty.[177]

Relative restraint of the type practiced by Hoke, however, was the exception rather than the rule, and Confederate troops usually practiced no more restraint than the state troops in dealing with purported traitors. In Virginia, Brig. Gen. John Echols, concerned about "the large collections of deserters and disloyal men … and of the depredations and outrages committed by them," informed the War Department of his intent to "exterminate them." Seventeen days later, Echols reported "in the guard-house at this place upward of fifty prisoners, deserters, and disloyal citizens." Despite his claims of success, Echols had to admit that citizens were still "being plundered, and that horses and slaves were being driven off and houses plundered," while nearby "A band of robbers had come in and were plundering everybody, driving off horses, negroes." Echols attributed his failed effort to the large number of "haters of our Government and people and institutions," and, convinced that "Loyal people and these people cannot live together," he requested permission to "remove all of these people beyond our lines."

Echols should have credited his lack of success to the tactics he employed. The sweep occurred with the usual torture, abuse, threats, and violence. His soldiers abused women, destroyed or confiscated property, and burned homes. Instead of intimidating the resisters, it merely destroyed what little loyalty to the Confederacy that remained. Furthermore, a follow-on sweep by the State Reserves acted in a similar manner, including taking children into custody until their deserter fathers surrendered themselves, and achieved the same failed results.[178]

As resistance was very active in Florida, it is not surprising that some of the worst examples of brutality occurred there. A Union officer reported to his superiors that "In Walton County 7 citizens were hung last week for entertaining Union sentiments, and a woman … was killed in a shocking manner, and two of her children caught and torn to pieces by bloodhounds."[179] In March 1864, Confederate troops under Lt. Col. Henry Capers tried to remove a band of resisters. Brig. Gen. William Gardner, commander of the District of Middle Florida, warned that Capers's force was prepared to "visit prompt punishment upon deserters," but offered amnesty if deserters returned voluntarily. If not, Gardner promised that "All those who may be found with arms in their hands will be shot without mercy."[180] As Capers and his force advanced, they burned the homes of as many of the resisters as he could identify and arrested their wives and children, shipping them to a fortified camp near Tallahassee. While many locals sympathized with their plight, others justified their imprisonment by reasoning "Desperate cases require desperate remedies," while noting that their husbands and families "made no attempt whatever to come to the rescue. Cowardly and treacherous, as might be expected of the betrayers of their country."[181] Governor Milton, forced into an embarrassing situation by the imprisonment of women and children without trial, demanded that the Confederate army take no such recourse again and allowed the prisoners to transfer to Union blockading ships offshore.[182]

****

Confederate government leaders, even in their most pessimistic estimations, could never have anticipated the general demoralization among the civilian population and even considerable portions of the Confederate Army. From the start, confident in the righteous nature of their cause and the power of their armies, few Confederates believed the war would last very long, and, even if it did, the lure of independence would dampen any internal issues that a lengthy war might create. The reality was quite different. Divided leadership and ineffective policies generated in Richmond created difficulties and resentment throughout the country, consequently diminishing the nation's ability to wage war. As civilian demoralization increased, the troops in the field found themselves facing enemy armies of seemingly inexhaustible reserves of manpower and material, while their own numbers and supplies were glaringly finite. Not surprisingly, by 1865 Confederate armies, facing this climate of defeatism, found it difficult to continue fighting. Even if willing to continue the struggle, Confederate armies operating in the climate of demoralization lacked the tools to do so. Desertion denied the armies needed troops, poor economic policy deprived them of food and supplies, and civilian hardship divided their attentions between the enemy and their families at home. It was a common situation for all the various Confederate commands, and each dealt with the circumstances in their own way, but surrender was the inevitable result.

Chapter 2

"A Raging Leaden Hailstorm": The Battles for the Carolinas

Only days after Lee's submission at Appomattox, Gen. Joseph Johnston surrendered his army to Maj. Gen. William T. Sherman. Like Lee's surrender, Johnston's capitulation was the result of a lengthy military campaign. Despite some daunting manpower, transportation, and logistics problems, Confederate troops resisted the Union advance from its start in Georgia until its end in North Carolina. A defense of the region might have been more viable if enough troops were available, but the only reinforcements were those trickling in from hundreds of miles away, the consequences of disastrous strategic decisions made in other theaters of the war. Southern troops faced a large Union Army that proved able to exploit their numbers and mobility to best advantage. Despite Confederate opposition, difficult terrain, and unfavorable weather, Sherman's army swept northward, causing massive damage. The Confederates, however, did not submit without a fight. A change in command reinvigorated their morale, and, on ground suitable for a fight against a superior foe, the Confederates made one last attempt to deflect Sherman's path and prevent the Union troops from reaching a source of supplies and reinforcements. Although the attack failed, the Confederates reminded Sherman that the war was not yet over, his opponent was still a dangerous one, and further battles were necessary to compel a Southern surrender.

Gen. Joseph Johnston (*Image courtesy of the Library of Congress*).

The central figure in this campaign was Johnston himself. His reappoint-ment to lead the army, after Jefferson Davis removed him from command of the Army of Tennessee during the Atlanta campaign, bolstered flagging Confederate morale, and his decision to strike Sherman when the opportunity presented itself impressed upon Sherman the lingering potency of Confed-erate arms. Johnston himself was a mixed blessing to Confederate fortunes.

His reinstatement to command was only the latest episode in a long history of rivalry with President Jefferson Davis that began at the start of the war and continued after the war as both men exchanged insults and recrimination in their various memoirs and histories of the war. If internal discord was not enough to harm the ability of the Confederate Army, Johnston himself contributed to circumstances that hamstrung the South's military efforts. Because of numerous setbacks earlier, the general had become pessimistic about the Confederacy's ability to continue the war and believed that his reappointment to command was less about his ability to lead and more about Davis's spiteful desire to have him take the blame for an inevitable defeat. There is no evidence that this was Davis's intent, but the move to place Johnston in charge had a fateful consequence for the Confederacy. When circumstances put him in a position to surrender his forces, Johnston, despite the proximity of Davis to provide political oversight, decided to reach terms with Sherman, a move that accelerated the overall surrender of the Confederacy and permanently stained Johnston's reputation in the postwar Lost Cause mythology.

****

Sherman's advance into the Carolinas caught no one by surprise. The general had spent the previous eight months devastating large parts of Georgia, first in his campaign to take Atlanta and then his March to the Sea that culminated with the capture of Savannah. The two campaigns' actions had long-term consequences for the Confederacy. Johnston's failure to contain Sherman in northern Georgia had cost him his command before Atlanta, replaced in favor of Lt. Gen. John Bell Hood. In the end, Hood could not hold Atlanta and withdrew into Alabama, leading to his controversial invasion of Tennessee covered in a later chapter. The culmination of the campaign to Savannah placed Sherman in an inconvenient location. Grant wanted Sherman's army in Virginia to assist in the containment of Lee's army, but was not certain how to relocate such a large force.[1] Sherman wanted to march his army overland through the Carolinas to Virginia to wreck the same economic destruction he had inflicted upon Georgia. Grant preferred to transport Sherman's men by boat, but when Sherman demonstrated that a seaboard passage would not take less time than an overland march, Sherman got his way.

Gen. Ulysses S. Grant (*Image courtesy of the Library of Congress*).

In approving Sherman's plan of advance, Grant's orders to Sherman gave him specific goals but the widest latitude to accomplish them. Grant, despite some initial skepticism, approved Sherman's plan for a march from Georgia to Virginia because the "effect of such a campaign will be to disorganize the South, and prevent the organization of new armies from their broken fragments" as well as "give us a position in the South from which we can threaten the interior." Also, Grant realized the attack would allow Sherman to

Gen. William T. Sherman (*Image Courtesy of the Library of Congress*).

"Break up the railroads in South and North Carolina." Grant also considered how Sherman's move would affect Lee's strategy, judging "It would compel Lee to retain all his present force in the defenses of Richmond, or abandon them entirely." Grant considered the latter option the only risk to the plan because, if Lee could march his army toward Sherman before Grant could intervene, Sherman "would be compelled to beat it, or find the sea-coast. Of course I shall not let Lee's army escape if I can help it, and will not let it go without following to the best of my ability."[2]

Gen. Oliver Howard (*Image courtesy of the Library of Congress*).

Sherman commenced his march on February 1, forming his army into two wings. Maj. Gen. Oliver O. Howard's Army of the Tennessee moved on the right, nearest the coast, and Maj. Gen. Henry W. Slocum's Army of Georgia moved on the left. There were few Confederate troops to hinder his advance, but the terrain proved a more difficult obstacle. "We crossed the Savannah River ... thirty miles from Savannah and when we got across it was nothing but swampy ground in front of us," Private Frederick Marion wrote. "We had to build a road out of poles for twenty miles."[3]

Gen. Henry Slocum (*Image courtesy of the Library of Congress*).

The poles that Marion mentioned were corduroy roads, a means of traversing muddy or swampy ground by placing logs side by side to form a road. Another soldier described the process as "we just cut poles 10 feet long, laid them side by side and piled fine brush on them to keep the horses' feet from going through, and laid long poles on the ends of the brush to hold it down, leaving a way six feet wide in the middle for the horses to pass."[4] While moving forward, Union troops took the opportunity to take a

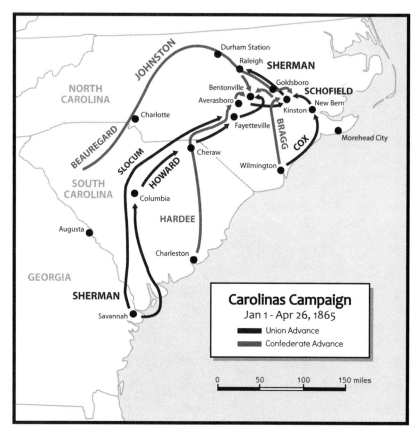

Carolinas Campaign

measure of revenge against the state where the rebellion began. "The boys burned everything that came within their reach. They did not even let a corn crib stand," one Union soldier wrote, leaving a Confederate soldier to observe that Sherman "seems to of have [*sic*] had no opposition. The country in his wake is nothing but a black smoldering ruin."[5]

The Confederates might have taken advantage of Sherman's slow advance through the South Carolina swamps to concentrate against him, but Sherman disguised his objective. Passing between Charleston, South Carolina, and Augusta, Georgia, Sherman directed columns to posture toward both cities, forcing General P. G. T. Beauregard, commander of the Confederate Department of the West, to protect both.[6] While Sherman forced the Confederates to cover potential objectives in South Carolina, he offered no targets of his own. Operating without a base or logistic lines, Sherman offered no point of attack. Even the Confederates had to grudgingly admit Sherman's power, reporting "The enemy … has in reality no lines of communication which can be threatened or cut. His overpowering force enables his move into the interior of the country like an ordinary movable column."[7] The inability to contain Sherman in southern South Carolina was a foregone conclusion because Beauregard could not collect the troops to stop him, confessing to Jefferson Davis that his force was not enough to halt Sherman's advance.[8]

Besides Sherman, Beauregard also had to deal with another Union threat from the west. In January 1865, Grant ordered Maj. Gen. George Stoneman to conduct an expedition that "might penetrate South Carolina well down toward Columbia" in support of Sherman's advance from Savannah with the aim of "destroying the railroad and military resources of the country" and possibly attacking Salisbury, North Carolina. Grant was initially enthusiastic about the plan, but Stoneman needed nearly six weeks to accumulate the horses he required.[9] Stoneman finally got underway on March 20 with six thousand men to support Sherman's operations by cutting the Chattanooga–Lynchburg Railroad to impede Lee's ability to maneuver, followed by attacks on the Danville railroad. Entering North Carolina near the town of Boone, Stoneman scattered the local militia before advancing east, destroying railroad bridges as they went, with the objective of Christiansburg, a town on the Virginia & Tennessee Railroad, from where Stoneman could threaten Lynchburg.[10]

The immediate effect of Beauregard's failure to concentrate Confederate forces occurred when Sherman, only fifteen days after leaving Savannah, reached the state capital at Columbia. Describing Sherman's approach as a "dance of Death," a resident of Columbia could only nervously watch as the Union army approached and wonder "How long before our beautiful little city may be sacked and laid in ashes." Despite promises from local commanders that "Sherman will not come to Columbia," the city's defenders, led by Maj. Gen. Wade Hampton, departed on the night of Feb. 17. The retreat triggered the pillaging of abandoned Confederate stores because "all the shops had been opened and provisions were scattered in all directions." When Union troops entered the city, residents initially reported, "Everything is quiet and orderly. Guards have been placed to protect houses, and Sherman has promised not to disturb private property," although warning that "Some public buildings have to be destroyed."

The calm, however, turned out to be deceptive. That night several fires broke out, which, aided by high winds, soon spread through the heart of the city's commercial district. Residents blamed the fire on Union troops, describing them as "drunken devils … shouting, hurrahing, cursing South Carolina" as "flames broke forth in every direction."[11] Sherman's men were undoubtedly to blame for many of the fires, but Sherman, who later said he had no regrets about the destruction in the city, insisted that the Confederates had to share responsibility.[12] Indeed, Hampton did not follow the advice of local leaders to evacuate civilians from the city or destroy the local liquor supplies. Rather than disperse the cotton stored in the city, Hampton, following established Confederate policy, elected to burn the cotton to deny it to the enemy. Hampton piled the cotton he could not destroy in the streets to use as barricades, which did nothing but hinder the movement of those who sought to leave and provide ready tinder when the fires started. Also, when Hampton learned that civic leaders intended to preemptively surrender the city to avoid fighting, he denied them the option of doing so. Consequently, instead of marching into an uncontested city, Union troops faced sporadic fighting from Hampton's retreating cavalry and perceived the city residents as still combative. Maj. Gen. Joseph Wheeler's men further harmed the city as they withdrew, setting fires to destroy supplies they could not take with them.[13]

Once Sherman's advance toward Columbia became obvious, the Confederate garrison at Charleston became a strategic quandary for the Confederates. The city, with its arsenal and other facilities, was a major contributor to the war effort, and its harbor still received ships despite the tightening Union blockade. Sherman's northward advance, however, isolated Charleston, and holding the city required resources that the Confederacy simply did not have. Maj. Gen. William Hardee reported he needed twenty thousand additional troops to hold Charleston. Gov. Andrew McGrath had promised five thousand state troops, but failed to provide them. Consequently, Hardee informed Jefferson Davis that "I am acting strictly on the defensive, and unless heavily re-enforced must continue to do so."[14] Beauregard and Hardee decided to abandon Charleston and the evacuation occurred the same day that Columbia fell.[15] The loss of Charleston was a huge logistic blow as Hardee could not evacuate a large amount of ordnance in the fortifications. Union officers, upon occupying the city, reported, "we have taken over 450 pieces of ordnance," and "also captured eight locomotives and a number of platform and passenger cars, all in good condition."[16] As the Charleston garrison moved northward to consolidate with Beauregard's forces, many of its troops began to desert, either demoralized by the loss of the city or, upon hearing of the damage inflicted by Sherman's men, left to protect their families. Others, accustomed to garrison life in Charleston, were not up to the rigors of field operations and deserted to avoid the arduous duty.[17]

****

With the situation in the Carolinas reaching a critical stage, Jefferson Davis and the War Department made two drastic decisions. The first was to transfer the Army of Tennessee, encamped in Mississippi, to the Carolinas. Besides leaving a large portion of the Confederacy weakly defended, the transfer threatened to wreck an army already battered by recent disastrous campaigns. After sparring with Sherman's army after it abandoned Atlanta to the Union, the Army of Tennessee's commander, Maj. Gen. John Bell Hood, planned to seize the initiative by advancing into Tennessee and recapturing Nashville, a city in Union hands since 1862. Hood believed the operation would draw Sherman back into Tennessee in pursuit, but Sherman had no such intentions. Instead, he dispatched the Army of the Cumberland under Maj. Gen. George Thomas to monitor Hood's movement while he left on his March to the Sea.[18] Several conditions hindered Hood's operation from the start. The attack suffered from fatal delays, meaning Thomas had more time to prepare and that little food remained in the fields for Hood's troops for forage.[19] Once the operation got underway, encounters with the Union Army were also less than successful. On November 29 at Spring Hill, confusion between Hood and his subordinates allowed Maj. Gen. John Schofield's XXIII Corps to escape encirclement. Hood immediately pursued Schofield to Franklin, where the Union forces were entrenched in a bend in the Harpeth River. In a poorly executed attack, Hood launched thirteen different piecemeal assaults against the

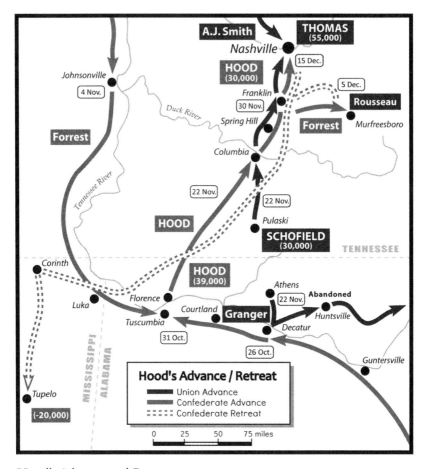

Hood's Advance and Retreat

Union positions, but achieved nothing other than disastrous losses. Among the forty-five hundred casualties were six generals killed, five wounded, and one captured.[20]

After the debacles at Spring Hill and Franklin, Hood lost the initiative but pressed on with his assault on Nashville out of a lack of alternatives. He later justified his actions by claiming "I could not afford to turn southward" because "our army was in that condition which rendered it more judicious the men should face a decisive issue rather than retreat."[21] Hood "besieged" Nashville, although he lacked the troops to surround the city, sever its transportation routes, or halt its flow of supplies. Quite the opposite, Thomas could adequately feed, house, and supply his troops while Hood's poorly fed men slept on the frozen ground. Thomas waited only for the weather to clear before dealing with Hood. When Thomas launched his assault on December 15, the collapse of the Confederate line forced Hood to abandon his campaign. "Hood's retreat revealed the fact that his army had retreated in great haste," a Union cavalry man described, "as the turnpikes were thickly strewn with guns and … he made no effort to carry off his wounded or bury the dead."[22]

As Hood fell back, his rear guard desperately fended off cavalry attacks on the retreating column while Hood's engineers threw a makeshift bridge across the Tennessee River.[23] After crossing the river and arriving in Mississippi, the Army of Tennessee's suffering continued as it sought supplies by encamping along the Mobile & Ohio Railroad. As the soldiers marched to their destinations, the weather deteriorated. A distressed officer wrote to his wife of seeing so many men "barefooted and so nearly naked and the weather so cold." Another veteran recalled that the weather was "the coldest that had been known for many years. The ground was frozen and rough, and our soldiers were poorly clad. … The once proud Army of Tennessee had degenerated to a mob." Discouraged Confederate troops drew comparisons to another winter retreat. "Passed through Moscow, and established a permanent camp … south of town," a demoralized veteran wrote, "This is 'Camp Bonaparte,' which is appropriate—'Bonaparte before Moscow.'"[24]

Only in camp could the Confederates get a clear sense of the disaster that had occurred. Hood began the campaign with nearly forty thousand men. He lost 4,500 men at Franklin and similar losses at Nashville. Thirty-four days later, when the army re-crossed the Tennessee, official returns listed seventeen thousand men available.[25] In addition, more than ten thousand of Hood's troops were in Union POW camps. That number included eight generals, another huge loss of command experience after the earlier command casualties at Franklin. The army felt the losses everywhere. Brig. Gen. Daniel Reynolds found his brigade could muster only one hundred sixty men. He gained some additional troops as stragglers and wounded from the hospitals reported for duty, but noted they were "without guns." Hood's artillerymen had lost half of the approximately one hundred pieces they had at the start of the campaign.[26] Consequently, morale was very low. "Hood's Army is completely cleaned out and demoralized," a soldier admitted. "This campaign has been the most disastrous of the war, and is certainly a very severe blow to us."[27] The losses convinced others the war was lost. "They are utterly despondent and would hail with joy the prospect of peace," a soldier wrote in his diary. "[T]hree-fourths of the Army of Tennessee … are in favor of peace on any terms, no matter how ignominious they may be."[28]

When Beauregard arrived in camp in mid-January, he was shocked to find, instead of a potent army, a demoralized force that was desperately short of food and winter clothing. Beauregard could only describe the troops camped around Tupelo as "in the strict sense of the word a disorganized mob, it was no longer an army."[29] Hood had already forwarded to the War Department a request to be relieved of command, but Beauregard had already seen enough and moved to replace him.[30] His men were glad to see him go. "I like him for his bravery and untiring energy," a veteran soldier recalled, "but he lacked caution and seem to care nothing for the lives of his men."[31] Hood himself took no blame for the Nashville debacle, believing that history would vindicate him because "Time can blot out all things from our memory."[32] After being relieved, he made his way to Richmond and prepared reports on the Nashville campaign that emphasized the shortcomings of the Army of Tennessee to explain his failures.[33]

Hood's replacement was Lt. Gen. Richard Taylor, the commander of the Department of Alabama, Mississippi, and East Louisiana, who had a questionable reputation of his own. The son of Zachary Taylor, the career Army officer, Mexican War hero, and twelfth President of the United States, Taylor eschewed a military career and instead enrolled at Yale, where he graduated in 1845. Taylor moved to Louisiana, eventually becoming one of the wealthiest landowners in the state.[34] Taylor shared his upper-class status with another planter just upriver in Mississippi. In 1835, Taylor's sister, Sarah, married Jefferson Davis, the future President of the Confederacy. The marriage lasted only three months due to Sarah's premature death, but Taylor always considered Davis his brother-in-law.[35] In 1861, Gov. Thomas Moore appointed Taylor colonel of the Ninth Louisiana Infantry, part of the Louisiana Brigade fighting in Virginia. Soon after he arrived, the War Department picked Taylor to command the Louisiana Brigade although the three other regimental colonels had more seniority. Aware that "my known friendship for President Davis … would justify the opinion that my promotion was due to favoritism," Taylor asked Davis to rescind the promotion, but Davis refused.[36] The controversy led to accusations of nepotism that may have had a kernel of truth. Davis's second wife, Varina, later wrote, perhaps jealously, that her husband was "too fond of West Pointers and his first wife's relations."[37] Assigned to Maj. Gen. Thomas "Stonewall" Jackson's corps, Taylor's Louisianans fought well in several battles in the Shenandoah Valley, as well as during the Peninsular Campaign. In May 1862, Union forces captured New Orleans and Davis needed to rally support in the area. To that end, Davis appointed Taylor as the district commander in his home state.[38] Taylor arrived in Louisiana to find the situation desperate, with "no arms or munitions, and no money" and less than seven thousand effective troops.[39]

Despite improving conditions in his district, Taylor developed a mixed reputation. He was prone to personal conflicts resulting from his forceful personality, something that his friends considered his best feature and his enemies his worst. Confident to the point of arrogance, Taylor often had "total irreverence for any man's opinion," and was contemptuous toward those he thought fools.[40] His own father considered Taylor as overly emotional, referring to his son as "perhaps a little hasty as to temper," his personality possibly exacerbated by the rheumatoid arthritis that plagued Taylor his entire adult life.[41] While Taylor had his admirers, he also had detractors from men in all ranks. One described Taylor as "noisy on retreats, with a tendency to cuss mules and wagons which stall in the road," while another wrote that "Dick Taylor has not a single friend that I have met yet, nor does anyone accuse him of being a military man."[42] Taylor also quarreled with subordinates who did not meet his expectations. Taylor, for instance, feuded with Brig. Gen. St. John Liddell to the extent that Liddell asked to be relieved of command rather than continue "this wretchedly mismanaged business under the guidance of a foolish man" who was prone to "exhibiting childishness and absurdities unbecoming an officer."[43] Taylor also may have suffered from an inferiority complex because, unlike his father or many other generals, he was not a West Pointer nor an officer in the antebellum army. If Taylor did not enjoy the confidence of professionally trained officers, he reciprocated the attitude. Taylor's opinion of West Point was that it would accept "a boy of sixteen from his mother's apron-strings, shut him up under constant surveillance for four years" only to produce an officer who was the "most complete illustration of suppressed mental development of which human nature is capable."[44] Consequently, Taylor found it difficult to accept a subordinate role in the military hierarchy, especially if he disagreed with the orders or strategy of his superiors.

This was especially true when Lt. Gen. Edmund Kirby Smith took command of the Trans-Mississippi Department. A Florida native and 1845 West Point graduate, Kirby Smith[45] had fought in several battles of the Mexican War, and, as a brigadier general under Joseph Johnston, suffered a wound at the First Battle of Bull Run. After recuperating at home, Kirby Smith returned to duty as a major general in the Army of East Tennessee. He participated in a joint invasion of Kentucky with Maj. Gen. Braxton Bragg, winning a minor engagement at Richmond, Kentucky, but Bragg's defeat at the Battle of Perryville brought the campaign to a halt short of its objectives. Kirby Smith received a promotion to lieutenant general for his victory at Richmond, and served under Bragg until accepting command in the Trans-Mississippi in January 1863, becoming Taylor's superior officer.[46] Relations between the two senior officers were initially good. When Kirby Smith arrived, Taylor sent his own boat to collect him at Port Hudson and bring him to Alexandria, Louisiana. Kirby Smith originally chose Alexandria as his department headquarters, but Taylor, perhaps concerned about his freedom of command, urged him to relocate to Shreveport.[47]

That was only the first hint of friction between the two men, as Taylor's inability to accept a subordinate position or keep his opinions to himself began almost immediately. Taylor constantly gave unsolicited advice on how to conduct operations in the department, inevitably putting Louisiana in the preferred position for offensive action. Taylor had obvious reasons for favoring the state above others in the department, but his strategic views clashed with that of Kirby Smith. Instead of New Orleans, Kirby Smith viewed Arkansas as the area of greatest strategic effect. Liberating the state,

Gen. Richard Taylor (*Image courtesy of the Library of Congress*).

he believed, removed Union threats to other regions of the Trans-Mississippi Department, nullified Union control of the Mississippi River by putting large portions of its western bank in Confederate hands, and provided a springboard for the occupation of Missouri, thereby making the state's star on the Confederate flag more than just symbolic.[48]

Despite efforts to work together, Kirby Smith and Taylor clashed over efforts to defeat the Union assault on Vicksburg. Incorrectly believing that

Grant's supply line was still on the west bank of the Mississippi, Kirby Smith ordered Taylor to overrun the garrisons there in preparation for crossing the river to reinforce Maj. Gen. John Pemberton's Vicksburg garrison. Taylor wanted to attack and recapture New Orleans, but Kirby Smith thought that, even if Taylor was successful, the subsequent fall of Vicksburg meant the Confederate capture of New Orleans would be short-lived, stating "the hopes of holding it would be placing your command in a cul-de-sac, from which there could be no extrication." Taylor reluctantly obeyed orders, leading to inconclusive fights at Milliken's Bend and Lake Providence, as well as the eventual fall of Vicksburg.[49] Relations between the two generals further soured after newspaper articles critical of Kirby Smith began to appear, most citing sources from within Taylor's headquarters.[50] The feud between Kirby Smith and Taylor came to a head a month later when Union Maj. Gen. Nathanial Banks led an invasion of upper Louisiana by advancing up the Red River, an operation covered in a subsequent chapter. Taylor's leadership led to the defeat of Banks's offensive, but blaming Kirby Smith for snatching an ever greater victory from his grasp, Taylor engaged his superior in a series of insubordinate messages, leading Kirby Smith to relieve him of command in June 1864.[51]

Soon after, Jefferson Davis appointed Taylor, promoted to lieutenant general, to command the Department of Alabama, Mississippi, and East Louisiana.[52] Months later, with no other option after relieving Hood of command of the Army of Tennessee, Beauregard turned control of the army over to Taylor. His time in direct command was brief because the War Department soon ordered the remnants of the Army of Tennessee to contest Sherman's advance into the Carolinas. Both Taylor and Beauregard objected to moving the army by asserting that an "attempt to move Hood's army at this time would complete its destruction," but Jefferson Davis would not relent.[53] Recognizing the inevitable, Taylor retained only Brig. Gen. Francis Cockrell's division and a number of artillerymen who lost their guns during the Nashville campaign to defend Mobile and sent the rest of the Army of Tennessee to the Carolinas. Besides orders from the War Department to do so, Taylor saw the practicality of the move. He recognized the vulnerability of his command if the entire Army of Tennessee left, but he also understood that retaining the army did him no real good, while a few thousand troops might be the difference between victory and defeat against Sherman. "General Taylor reports that a victory over Sherman is essential," Beauregard explained, "and that he can resist a raid without Stewart's corps, [but] cannot fight a battle with it against an army."[54]

Due to the collapsing Confederate infrastructure, the Army of Tennessee's first battle was simply getting to their destination. Leaving its encampments, the Confederate soldiers took various routes across Alabama to Montgomery, thence to Augusta, Georgia, before moving into the Carolinas.[55] Some units managed to move quickly. The Twenty-seventh Alabama covered the distance from Tupelo to Augusta in just eleven days. Others moved slowly: Brig. Gen. Daniel Reynold's brigade of less than two hundred men left Meridian, Mississippi, on February 3, and did not join Johnston's army at Goldsboro, North Carolina, until March 11.[56] The main impediment was the weak railroad system. The railroads at Montgomery could move two thousand men per day to Columbus, Georgia, but only four hundred arrived because of constant repairs. Maj. Gen. Benjamin Cheatham and his staff took three days to cover scarcely one hundred miles because their train repeatedly derailed on the dilapidated line.[57] Troops moving to the Carolinas had to use nine separate railroads of the fragmented Confederate system, requiring transshipment due to different gauges. Consequently, units arrived piecemeal, especially as heavy items such as wagons and artillery pieces traveled separately. Nearly a quarter of the troops transferred to the Carolinas were unarmed after losing their rifles on the retreat from Nashville.[58] Because of the poor transportation and lack of supplies, many veterans suffered during the journey. "The box[car] in which I rode," the soldier remembered, "was old and dilapidated, and as a cold rain was falling we all got wet." With the boxcars already filled to capacity, a soldier recalled that "One or two men froze, riding on top of the cars."[59] Few men received rations before they left, and many engaged in theft and plunder along the length of the transit route. "Our boys had not been paid for ten months," an officer wrote apologetically. "Our brig[ade] behaved shamefully all the way around from Tupelo, Miss. to Raleigh, N.C." Residents of Montgomery described the streets as filled with soldiers "devoted to debauchery and crime." To quell the disruptions, Taylor's staff issued a stern reminder to the regimental and company officers that they "will be held strictly responsible for the conduct of their commands."[60] Desertion also became a problem as demoralized soldiers chose either to stay in the west or to abandon the army on the trip to the Carolinas. One brigade that left Alabama with sixteen hundred men arrived with only nine hundred.[61] Thanks to delays, desertions, and transfers to Mobile, of the sixteen thousand men of the Army of Tennessee present after the Nashville Campaign, less than half arrived to confront Sherman in the Carolinas.[62]

****

The second drastic decision was a change in command in the Carolinas. Clearly unable to halt Sherman, Beauregard lost the confidence of Jefferson Davis, who took the difficult step of appointing Lt. Gen. Joseph Johnston, his greatest personal enemy, as a replacement. Unity in command is vital in any war, but Davis and Johnston maintained a mutual dislike that overshadowed all other considerations. "The two men suffered from a hubris that made it impossible for them to communicate or for either to overlook what he considered to be an insult from the other," one historian observed. "Neither could admit error nor ask forgiveness."[63] The friction between President and general began almost at the start of the war, when Johnston antagonized Davis in an argument over rank. War Department policy established that career officers would retain their relative equivalent rank in the Confederate Army to avoid placing antebellum subordinates over superior officers. In 1860, Johnston had left his field grade of lieutenant colonel to accept the temporary staff position of brigadier general in the Quartermaster Corps. But, citing permanent rank as the criterion, President Davis announced the list of generals, by seniority, as Samuel Cooper, Albert S. Johnston, and Robert Lee, with Joseph Johnson fourth.[64] Johnston took exception, and made his misgivings known to Davis.[65] The feud intensified a few weeks after the First Battle of Bull Run. Sensing that his force was at peak strength relative to Union defenses, Johnston requested immediate reinforcements from Kentucky and western Virginia so that he might move across the Potomac to seek a decisive engagement. Davis demurred, and Johnston took exception to what he perceived as the second-guessing of his strategy by an armchair general, even if he was the President.[66] During the 1862 Peninsular Campaign, Johnston halted Union General George McClellan's advance toward Richmond at the Battle of Seven Pines, but suffered serious wounds that forced him to relinquish command of the Army of Northern Virginia to Davis's military advisor, Robert E. Lee. Lee's subsequent success ensured that Johnston would not regain the post when his health permitted him to return to duty, further antagonizing his relationship with Davis.[67]

After recovering from his wounds, Johnston assumed command of the Department of the West, overseeing Maj. Gen. Braxton Bragg's Army of Tennessee and Maj. Gen. John Pemberton's Army of Mississippi. Johnston was unhappy with the arrangement, as he viewed his position as purely administrative, a situation exacerbated by both Bragg and Pemberton's proclivity to seek directives from the War Department rather than Johnston. Johnston considered it just another snub from Davis, who was trying to micromanage the department from distant Richmond.[68] The command situation demonstrated its flaws in 1863 when Grant began operating against Vicksburg. Concentrated against Pemberton in Mississippi, Grant threatened Confederate control of the state, but Johnston could not conduct a similar concentration without withdrawing Bragg's army from Tennessee. With only a small force at his disposal, Johnston failed to either stop Grant or reinforce Pemberton's garrison at Vicksburg. Johnston attempted a relief effort, but it was too late to save the city, which surrendered on July 4 after a six-week siege. Davis accused Johnston of lacking aggressiveness, while Johnston criticized the President for undermining his authority by directly ordering Pemberton to hold the city when Johnston had ordered him to abandon Vicksburg and join him for joint operations against Grant.[69]

Instead of dying down, the feud between the general and the President continued because of Bragg's inability to contain a Union advance, forcing another leadership debate. After the indecisive battle at Stone's River, Maj. Gen. William Rosecrans led his Union Army of the Cumberland into eastern Tennessee. Johnston lent his support to Bragg, resulting in a Confederate victory at Chickamauga in September. Bragg, however, failed to destroy the Army of the Cumberland (now under the command of Maj. Gen. George Thomas) at Chattanooga, and, when Union reinforcements drove Bragg's

Gen. Braxton Bragg (*Image courtesy of the Library of Congress*).

army back into Georgia, most of his subordinates questioned his poor command decisions. Johnston, still the department commander, had been under pressure to replace Bragg after Stone's River, but had declined. Davis wanted to support Bragg, but when Bragg impetuously offered his resignation, Davis reluctantly accepted. Davis wished to retain Bragg, but no suitable replacement existed other than Johnston.[70] The move made Bragg and

Johnston enemies for the rest of the war, although few were sorry to see Bragg leave. Brig. Gen. William Mackall wrote to Johnston that "I have even heard Bragg's friends say that your presence would be worth 10,000 men to the army."[71]

Davis had criticized Johnston for his purported lack of aggressive action to save Vicksburg, and the charge came up again after Johnston assumed command of the Army of Tennessee. In 1864, Maj. Gen. William T. Sherman led a Union force into Georgia to capture Atlanta. Considerably outnumbered by the opposing force, Johnston relied on delaying tactics to slow Sherman's advance, waiting for Sherman to make a mistake that he could exploit in a counter-attack, but no such event presented itself. Johnston eventually fell back to the defenses of Atlanta, delaying Sherman to the extent that it took him ten weeks to cover scarcely one hundred miles. Davis, however, saw only more lack of forcefulness by Johnston. Davis relieved Johnston of command and replaced him with one of his corps commanders, Maj. Gen. John Bell Hood. Johnston's strategy of exchanging space for time did not sit well with Davis, but his soldiers appreciated his conservation of their lives. "Johnston's removal is not as popular in the army as expected," a worried soldier wrote. "Hood may do something desperate to vindicate & establish his policy." Another soldier agreed, saying, "Johnston was retreating & saving his army … all he has lost is territory. Hood may make the fight & lose his army or get it cut to pieces so … we will be in a bad fix to carry on the war much longer."[72]

Angered by his perceived maltreatment by the President, Johnston became openly associated with Davis's political opponents, especially Texas Senator Louis Wigfall. The Senator was a states' rights advocate who found a firm friend, ally, and confidant in Johnston.[73] Although angered at his demotion, Johnston wanted another suitable command based upon his own merits. Therefore, he was somewhat dismayed when his friends in Congress, led by Wigfall, attached to the bill naming Lee the Commander-in-Chief a formal recommendation that Johnston be put in command of the Army of Tennessee. A professional soldier, Johnston did not believe that Congress should be meddling in the selection of officers; that was the prerogative of the President regardless of Johnston's opinion of Davis.[74] Nevertheless, Johnston had supporters both within and outside of Congress pressing for his reinstatement.

"It is also believed that General Johnston will soon be placed in command of the army of Tenn.," a member of Congress wrote. "I have not much confidence in that army, and think it will have to continue to retreat, or, in military parlance, 'fall back,' and I think Johnston the best man we have for that sort of work."[75] In February 1865, Lt. Gen. James Longstreet urged Lee to use his new CINC authority to reinstate Johnston to command of the Army of Tennessee, an act he believed "will restore that army to organization, morale, and efficiency." Reminding Lee that "I have served under General Johnston," Longstreet considered Johnston as "one of our ablest and best generals."[76]

In February, Lee ordered Johnston to "Assume command of the Army of Tennessee & all troops in department of South Carolina, Georgia, & Florida. Assign General Beauregard to duty under you, as you may. … Concentrate all available forces & drive back Sherman."[77] In his first message after returning to duty, Johnston informed Lee that "It is too late to expect me to concentrate troops capable of driving back Sherman" because "the sentiment of the army of Tennessee is much divided." Johnston was clearly unenthusiastic regarding his new posting and suspicious of Davis's intent. Johnston's wife told a confidant that "He was only put back to be the one to surrender." Johnston also believed he was there merely to be a scapegoat. To a friend who assured him that Davis would support him in any way possible, Johnston replied, "He will not do it. He has never done it … and he has only put me in command to disgrace me." In his postwar memoir, Johnston asserted that, when returned to command, he did not believe that the South could win the war, and accepted the position "with no hope beyond that of contributing to obtain peace on such conditions as, under the circumstances, ought to satisfy the Southern people and their government."[78] Johnston was not optimistic, but his soldiers were enthusiastic about the change in command. An officer in Alabama wrote to Johnston telling him his resumption of command "has filled us with new hope" and requested that his command be "ordered to report to you" on the front lines.[79] Members of the Third Texas Cavalry were pleased to have Johnston, believing that under his command the Confederacy could "recover all that has been lost."[80] The reinstatement of Johnston also received the approval of other officers. In Richmond, Col. Richard Maury was glad Johnston has been "restored to his old army, or rather to what the obstinacy of the Administration and the imbecility of Gen. Hood have left of it." Maury hoped that the Army of Tennessee's new commander would improve its performance. "Johnston believes in the policy of concentration," he opined, "His plan has always been to save his men as much as he could and, knowing our comparative scarcity of soldiers, he never strikes unless all of the chances are in his favor. He, in my opinion, is one of our greatest Generals, second only to Genl. Lee."[81]

Johnston's return bolstered the morale of the Confederate troops, but it could not overcome the reality that Johnston simply did not have enough soldiers. When Johnston took command on February 25, his new command consisted of several different fragments amounting to Hardee's eleven thousand men from the Charleston garrison, Joseph Wheeler's cavalry, and the South Carolina militia. The poorly equipped brigades (three thousand men combined) of the Army of Tennessee were near Fayetteville, but they had just completed a hard march from Mississippi. In addition, there were Wade Hampton's six thousand cavalry and fifty-five hundred men under Braxton Bragg (recently returned to field command) near Wilmington. However, S.D. Lee's brigade from the Army of Tennessee had not yet reached Augusta, with another four thousand troops spread out across Georgia en route to Fayetteville.[82] Johnston had few troops, but certainly did not lack commanders for them. Thanks to depleted commands and the War Department's propensity to distribute generals' stars, Johnston had within his command two full generals, four lieutenant generals, fourteen major generals, and "innumerable brigadiers."[83] The North Carolina Junior Reserves, state troops between the ages of sixteen and eighteen, formed the largest brigade in Johnston's army, forcing him to acknowledge the army was now grinding "the seed corn of the Confederacy."[84]

Meanwhile, another threat appeared along the Atlantic coast. While Sherman prepared to leave Georgia, a Union combined arms operations captured Wilmington, North Carolina, one of the few ports still open and the hub of three railroads.[85] The only significant Confederate force in the area, a division led by Maj. Gen. Robert Hoke, probed the Union lines searching for an opportunity to counter-attack, but found retaking the city an impossible task.[86] Caught between two large Union forces, Johnston initiated discussions with Lee about a possible merger of their two armies. On March 8, Johnston informed Lee that "Sherman has been marching with extended front," and raised the option of combining their armies to deal with Sherman.[87] Lee dithered about what to do. He neither left Petersburg to go to Johnston, which would have necessitated an evacuation of Richmond, nor ordered Johnston to march rapidly to him. Wanting Johnston to fend off Sherman to protect his source of supply in North Carolina, Lee urged Johnston to strike as soon as possible rather than plan on a retreat that would cost Lee his supply base. "Should you be forced back in this direction both armies would certainly starve," Lee reminded Johnston, but "A bold and unexpected attack might relieve us."[88] In response, Johnston provided a more detailed assessment of his situation, relating that his army was finally reaching a reasonable level of consolidation. Johnston still hoped to attack Sherman before he could receive reinforcements from the Carolina coast, otherwise "their march into Virginia cannot be prevented by me." Rather than waiting for either Grant or Sherman to force their two armies to merge, Johnston asked, "Would it be practicable, instead, to hold one of the inner lines of Richmond with one part of your army, and meet Sherman with the other, returning to Richmond after fighting?"[89] In reply, Lee advised Johnston that "a disaster to your army will not improve my condition," and therefore "I would not recommend you to engage in a general battle without a reasonable prospect of success" and to attack only if "an opportunity may occur for you and Bragg to unite upon one of their columns and crush it." Lee explained that he had only a single supply line available to him, which, thanks to the Union's "preponderance in cavalry, and his ability unperceived to mass his troops" made it ill-advised for him to part with even a portion of his force. Instead, Lee continued to press Johnston to "seek a favorable opportunity for battle," but not expect any assistance as "I shall maintain my position as long as it appears advisable, both from the moral and material advantages of holding Richmond."[90]

****

Sherman, however, did not intend to allow the Confederates to dictate his moves. After spending two days destroying military facilities in Columbia, he was ready to resume his march. "Every state seems to have its share of suffering to undergo," a Union officer correctly observed. "All save North

Carolina have been invaded, & its turn is now at hand," as the Union columns headed toward Fayetteville.[91] The city contained extensive industrial works and an arsenal. As Johnston was still organizing the army, he could not hold the city without risking being defeated in detail, so on March 11 he ordered Hampton to cover his retreat, abandoned the arsenal and other manufacturing sites, destroyed the bridges over the Cape Fear River, and retreated north.[92] The loss of Fayetteville was another huge logistical blow, as Johnston could not remove the arsenal machinery. This was particularly devastating because when Sherman's men wrecked the site, they removed the last major facility for making firearms available to either Lee or Johnston's army. The capture of Fayetteville was not surprising as the city was an obvious objective once Columbia fell. Sherman's path, however, was not as obvious, and the Confederates were uncertain if he intended to achieve a junction with a Union force near New Bern or head directly toward the state capital at Raleigh. If Sherman intended to head directly to Raleigh, Johnston had less time to prepare, but if the Union general sought a linkup with the other Union element, then Johnston had the option of defending Raleigh or striking at either Union force if an opportunity presented itself.

Given a choice of defending Raleigh or fighting south of the Neuse River, Johnston preferred the latter for some very good reasons. First, if Sherman managed to merge the two Union forces, then Raleigh was doomed anyway, so if Johnston was going to fight it was better to do so before the Union conjunction occurred. Also, the region above the Neuse was where the Army of Northern Virginia collected most of its supplies, so if Johnston had any hope that Lee might join him in North Carolina that region had to be preserved.[93] Other historians suggest that Johnston decided to seek battle to silence his critics and shed his ignoble reputation of being a "retreater" who would not fight a spirited and decisive battle. Others propose that Johnston, unable to move quickly enough to reinforce Lee, initiated a fight in order to convince Lee to move his army to North Carolina, resulting in "additional meaningless death and destruction on both sides."[94]

The Battle of Averasboro on March 16 determined which direction Sherman was going. As Johnston fell back toward Smithfield, Hardee informed Johnston of his intent to delay the Union advance and to "ascertain whether I was followed by Sherman's whole army, or a part of it, and what was its destination."[95] Hardee formed three defensive lines in a fork in the roads leading to Raleigh flanked by the Cape Fear and Black Rivers, forcing the Union army to make a frontal assault. After a sharp clash, troops of Slocum's Left Wing pushed the Confederates back to their third and final line and threatened to flank them. Hardee withdrew under the cover of darkness, however, and continued his march northeast to Smithfield.[96] Hardee only delayed Sherman's advance for a brief time, but had determined that Sherman's force intended to merge with the other Union force, under Maj. Gen. John Schofield, near Goldsborough (the city changed its name to the current Goldsboro in 1869). Now aware of Sherman's intentions, Johnston sought a battle south of the Neuse before Sherman's junction with Schofield's troops. Aiding Johnston was Sherman's disposition to get to Goldsborough as quickly as possible. Food was plentiful, but many of his troops were barefoot and their uniforms had become threadbare. In addition, Slocum's Wing had suffered more than five hundred wounded men at the clash at Averasboro, and Sherman wanted to move them to proper hospitals to both alleviate their suffering and allow his army to move more freely without the encumbrance of so many ambulances.[97]

As the Confederates withdrew from Averasboro, they continued to harass and limit Slocum's advance, which would very much shape Union tactics in the looming clash. As Hardee led his men toward the town of Elevation to recover from the recent battle, cavalry leader Lt. Gen. Wade Hampton took over the task of hindering Slocum's force as it moved east toward Goldsborough. In course of this action, Hampton described to Johnston a particular piece of ground near the village of Bentonville should the commanding general decide to attack. On the north side of the Averasboro-Goldsborough road, Hampton noted a slight rise capped by trees and covered with dense brush that could both hide an attacking force and limit the ability of the Union forces to maneuver. As both of Slocum's corps were limited to the Averasboro–Goldsborough road, the site provided an excellent opportunity to conduct an ambush attack. Moreover, Union movement toward Goldsborough invited an attack by Johnston. As Howard's army had continued on its way toward Goldsborough, a gap existed between

Gen. John Schofield (*Image courtesy of the Library of Congress*).

his army and Slocum's. Howard had slowed the army's advance when news of the Averasboro fighting began, but was still a day's march away from Slocum. Looking for an engagement, Johnston decided to seize the opportunity, placing Maj. Gen. Robert Hoke's division, recently arrived under Bragg's command from Wilmington, across the Averasboro-Goldsborough road as a blocking force. In addition, Bragg commanded the North Carolina

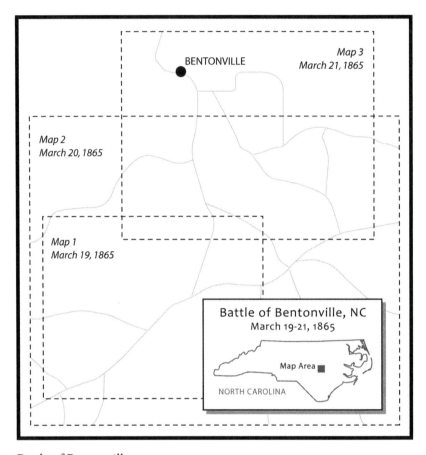

Battle of Bentonville.

Junior Reserves and, just before the battle began, a division under Maj. Gen. Lafayette McLaws from Hardee's command. They would be the only Confederates visible at first to Union troops. The remaining Confederate troops took up hidden positions on the high ground north of the road. To Hoke's right were the soldiers the Army of Tennessee organized into three divisions commanded by Lt. Gen. Alexander Stewart, Lt. Gen. Daniel H. Hill, and Maj. Gen. William Bate. Hardee was also bringing up the rest of his force from Elevation, but, due to faulty maps, he arrived only after an overnight march.[98]

Alexander Stewart (*Image courtesy of the Library of Congress*).

On March 19, Johnston sprang his trap. Seeing the Confederate troops blocking the road, Maj. Gen. Jefferson C. Davis sent two of his three divisions from the XIV Corps forward to assault Hoke's position. North of the road, Brig. Gen. William Carlin looked to repeat Union actions at Averasboro by fixing Hoke's troops in position and then flanking them with one of his brigades. South of the road, Brig. Gen. James Morgan led his division into position to threaten Hoke's lines, but the road on his left and a swamp on his right compressed his line into a narrow front. While pressing their attacks, both Carlin and Morgan sensed the Confederates were attempting more than just a delaying action. The Confederate cavalry, which had always fled after engaging Union skirmishers, were now

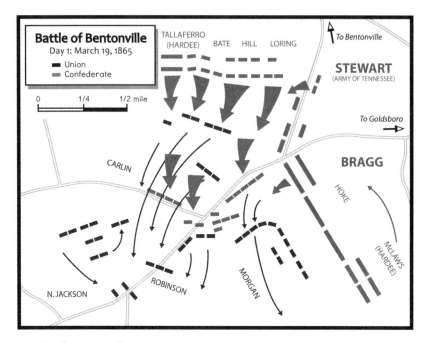

Battle of Bentonville.

fighting more aggressively. Moreover, Union foragers, whose activities to feed the Union Army had become a means of measuring the distance to the enemy, reported that they were meeting resistance almost immediately after leaving camp. One of the foragers recalled, "as we advanced, the firing became more distinct and animated, and seem to be stationary; proof that the cavalry this time was not willing to back out." Further Union probes found "infantry entrench-ments along our whole front," a Union private recalled, "enough of them to give us all the amusement we shall want the rest of the day."[99]

Carlin pressed forward in an attempt to locate and turn the enemy flank, but Morgan ordered his men to prepare defensive positions as quickly as possible. Carlin's probing attack ran into Hoke's main line, but his flank attack failed to cross an open ground dominated by Confederate artillery. Carlin's aggressive assaults, however, unnerved Bragg, who, concerned about Hoke's men holding only lightly entrenched works, requested reinforcements. Unable to dislodge Hoke's men, Carlin's force withdrew, taking a number of Confederate prisoners who revealed that the Confederates were not just staging a delaying action but rather that Johnston was nearby with his entire force. Although originally skeptical of the report, Carlin ordered his men to prepare defensive positions and informed Slocum of the imminent Confederate assault. Slocum, in turn, pressed Maj. Gen. Alpheus Williams to bring his XX Corps forward as quickly as possible and dispatched a rider to inform Sherman and Howard of the situation.

As Carlin's troops returned to their original lines, Johnston delayed his surprise assault to allow Hardee's late-arriving troops to join the attack. Instead of the planned 2:30 pm assault, Johnston did not get moving until after 3:00. Despite the late start, the attack drove Carlin's division back, although with some trepidation. Hardee's troops hesitated to cross an open field swept by Union small-arms fire. "Franklin was fresh in their minds and they hesitated," but Hardee himself exposed himself to enemy fire and urged them forward on what would be their final assault.[100] As "bullets whistled around our ears," a Michigan soldier related to his family, "the rebels came with bayonets and chased us away and we had to run," saved only by reaching a hastily assembled line where the "cannons started to fire and mowed the rebels down." The XIV Corps had at its disposal seventy-two pieces used to great effect "with double shotted canister," which, "with the incessant rattle of musketry caused the very earth to tremble."[101] Driven from their incomplete entrenchments, Carlin's troops fell back to the Averasboro–Goldsborough road, leaving a gap between their lines and Morgan's division on their right. To aid Carlin, Morgan dispatched his reserve brigade to reinforce the left side of the line, but was soon overwhelmed along with the rest of Carlin's division in the Confederate onslaught. Attacking on two sides, Confederate troops nearly surrounded Morgan's division. Only the swamp that had constrained Morgan on his right prevented the Confederates from cutting off the Union position.[102]

Despite the pressure, Morgan's division held its ground, aided by Confederate errors. Bragg, claiming unclear orders, hesitated to allow Hoke to move forward in support of the Army of Tennessee. Johnston's delay in launching his attack had allowed Union reinforcements to arrive, blunting the power of his assault. Although not great in number, the additional Union troops stopped several determined assaults, confronting the attackers with what one Confederate described as a "raging leaden hailstorm."[103] At the critical time when Morgan's division was facing envelopment, the lead brigade of Williams's XX Corps, under Brig. Gen. William Cogswell, arrived, threatening to catch the Confederates between Morgan's breastworks and Cogswell's attack. "The enemy fought bravely," wrote one of Williams's men, "but … when they came up to our line, posted behind slight entrenchments, they received a fire which compelled them to fall back."[104] That, in turn, allowed Morgan to concentrate his fire on Hoke's attackers and drive them back with heavy losses. With their attack spent, the Confederates retreated to their original lines as the rest of the XX Corps arrived to bolster Slocum's position. Direct fighting ceased, but a Confederate soldier recalled that "a heavy musketry fire was kept up till nearly dark on either side."[105]

The next day found the situation little changed. Johnston kept his outnumbered army in its general positions despite the risks of doing so. He wanted to recover his wounded off the battlefield and hoped that Sherman would launch a frustration-driven frontal assault. Neither was a particularly good reason for remaining. Sherman, more concerned about achieving his link with Schofield and proceeding toward Virginia, was not inclined to launch an attack that might divert him from his immediate plans. Collecting his wounded was a humane intent, but Johnston risked the loss of his entire army to save a relatively small portion. By the late afternoon of March 20, both of Howard's two corps, Maj. Gen. John Logan's XV Corps and Maj. Gen. Francis Blair's XVII Corps, had arrived. After the fighting of the previous day, Slocum's men were oriented east/west along the Averasboro-Goldsborough road. As Howard's troops arrived, they moved into position in a north-south orientation on the right of Davis's XIV Corps. To meet the new Union arrivals, Johnston pivoted Hoke's division from its westward-facing lines to a new one facing eastward.[106] To bolster Hoke, Johnston further shifted troops into position on Hoke's left and extended his line north, concentrating his cavalry on his far left. Both sides extensively employed skirmishers to determine the location of the other in the dense underbrush, but a general engagement did not occur. Instead, most of the day was spent engaged in localized probing attacks."[107]

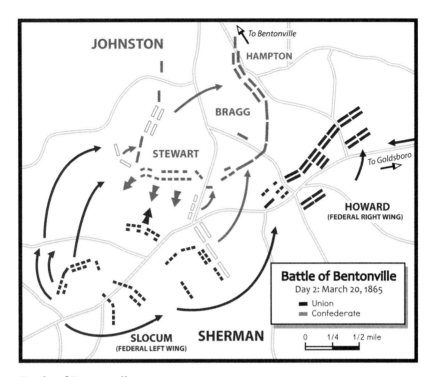

Battle of Bentonville.

The morning of the twenty-first opened with more indecision on both sides. Sherman and Johnston did not want to renew the fighting, but neither could move while in the presence of the enemy. Only late in the morning did the situation change in an unexpected way. Blair ordered one of his division commanders, Maj. Gen. Joseph Mower, to move to extend the army's flank. Mower, an aggressive fighter, took the opportunity to conduct a reconnaissance in force. He pushed his division to the right and forward, easily brushing aside Brig. Gen. Evander Law's cavalry force. Law urgently appealed for assistance from Maj. Gen. Joseph Wheeler's nearby cavalry and informed Johnston of the dire circumstances on his left flank. As Mower pressed forward, he occupied the town of Bentonville itself, deep behind Johnston's headquarters, and unbeknownst to him, was less than a mile from a bridge across Mill Creek that served as Johnston's only route of escape. Johnston immediately ordered all his cavalry to counter-attack. Among them was the

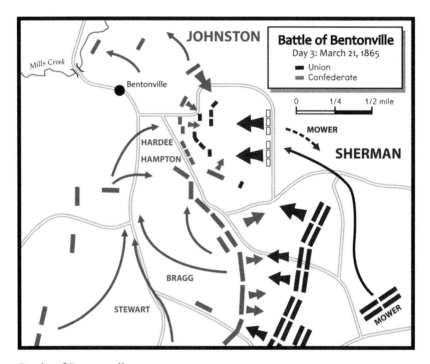

Battle of Bentonville.

Eighth Texas Cavalry, a depleted unit of barely eighty men. Short of troopers, the Texans permitted Hardee's teenaged son, William Jr., to join in their attack despite the assessment of one officer that "it looked like the old regiment was this time surely going to its grave."[108] At the same time, Sherman, now aware of Mower's probing attack, ordered the aggressive Union general to maintain contact with the Union right flank. Mower complied and, under pressure on two sides by Confederate counter-attacks, returned to positions close to his starting point unaware of how close he had come to severing Johnston's line of retreat. The Confederates paid for their desperate attack, no one more than Hardee, whose son suffered a mortal wound in the assault.[109]

While his troops had contained Mower's assault, Johnston concluded that he had tempted fate too long and began preparations to withdraw. Overnight, his troops crossed the Mill Creek Bridge and marched toward Smithfield despite the continuation of the previous nights' skirmishing, during which one Union regiment purportedly fired seventeen thousand rounds.[110] Some Union forces attempted a pursuit, but Sherman, with the path to Goldsborough finally free of Confederate interference, decided that reaching his source of supplies was more immediately important that inflicting any more damage on Johnston.[111] The battle concluded with mixed results. Johnston had put a scare into Sherman, demonstrated that the Confederates were still willing to fight, and temporarily hindered the Union Army's progress to Goldsborough, but at a heavy cost. Johnston suffered approximately twenty-six hundred casualties, a tenth of his force, from an army that could not replace its losses. By comparison, Sherman's force lost about fifteen hundred men, less than 5 percent of his total force.[112] The thin resources left to Johnston were revealed in his last official returns to the War Department submitted a week after the battle when he reported only 14,953 men available for duty; his entire force was smaller than just one of Sherman's corps.[113]

Bentonville had immediate short-term effects on both armies. The clash buoyed Confederate morale after the recent disasters in Wilmington and Nashville, which contributed to the portrayal of the battle in several postwar histories as less than an attempt to delay Sherman and more of a strike to destroy him. Hampton, for instance, later contended "General Johnston's only object in making this fight was to cripple the enemy and impede his advance." That assessment was quite different than the one that Hampton related immediately after the battle, where he described how the army had merely "injured Sherman a good deal, so that he cannot boast of getting through [to Goldsborough] free."[114] The battle may have improved the outlook of some Confederates, but it did little to change the overall pessimism of their commander. Johnston informed Lee that he could not hope to stop Sherman and could only annoy him, and pushed for a consolidation of the two armies as the only hope for further success.[115] Other officers were equally pessimistic of future success. On March 25, Bragg wrote to Jefferson Davis that desertion was commonplace, and the "Officers seem paralyzed, men indifferent to everything but plunder, and the people, as they well may, appear disgusted and dismayed." Bragg saw little hope for the future, telling Davis "I see disasters, disorderly retreats, and utter confusion on our front."[116] To Sherman, the battle reminded him that Johnston was still an adversary who could surprise him. The improvised nature of the battle led to the failure to exploit Mower's advance, something Sherman later regretted. Had he reinforced Mower instead of recalling him, Sherman might have destroyed a large portion of Johnston's command or even forced its surrender. The circumstances of the war would have been much different, and a potential Johnston surrender on March 22 might have hastened Lee's own surrender rather than its eventual occurrence on April 9. Instead, Sherman lost the opportunity to shorten the war, leaving his army to ponder if the bloodshed might continue for the foreseeable future. One Union officer wrote after the battle that "The enemy's forces … will be able to compel one more campaign" because "Johnston is very careful of his men and will make the most of them, and … I hardly expect so long and continuous a campaign as that of last summer, though it is a question of men, and who can endure the draught of blood the longest."[117]

****

Leaving his subordinates to supervise the resupply of his troops in Goldsborough, Sherman traveled to City Point, Virginia, for a conference with Grant and Lincoln. Grant had invited Lincoln to City Point to update him on the progress of the Petersburg campaign, which Lincoln, seeking relief from the political squabbles in Washington, accepted. Sherman's arrival also allowed Lincoln to get a first-hand report of recent operations in the Carolinas and assess the effect upon the Confederate war effort. Sherman was also there to obtain information, specifically if he should continue into Virginia as originally planned or if he should pursue the destruction of Johnston's army. Sherman preferred the former, should Grant wait a short time for Sherman's troops to arrive or if Grant was unable to overcome Lee on his own. The general was disappointed to learn that Grant did not intend to wait, but was already formulating plans to sever the last rail line into Petersburg, turn Lee's flank, and force him out of Petersburg. Although Sherman did not get the answer he wanted, he did have the opportunity to discuss with Grant and Lincoln the means by which to end the war. Although dismayed by Grant and Sherman's contention that the Confederates would likely fight at least one more major battle before considering surrender, Lincoln expressed his

Meeting at City Point, March 1865. ('The Peacemakers' by George Healy (1868)). *Image courtesy of the Library of Congress.*

wish that the Confederates should receive generous terms if they were to ask for peace. The President wanted easy peace terms, something that his Cabinet members did not, which explained why Lincoln put the process of accepting Confederate surrenders in the hands of Grant and Sherman.[118] It is also the likely reason why Lincoln came to City Point without any political advisors. Rear Adm. David Porter, commanding the North Atlantic Blockading Squadron, was also present at the talks, and he recounted that when Vice President Andrew Johnson showed up unexpectedly, Lincoln asked Porter to find a reason to ship him somewhere else. Lincoln likewise refused permission for William Seward to visit when the Secretary of State inquired if the President needed his services.[119]

Because no one took official notes of the discussions, only the recollections of Grant, Sherman, and Porter relate the process and outcome of their meetings with Lincoln, but all point toward a presidential desire for lenient and immediate peace terms. Porter, for instance, recalled that in the discussion that Lincoln had with Grant before Sherman arrived, "he was determined the Confederacy should have the most liberal terms. 'Get them to plowing once,' he said, 'and gathering in their own little crops, eating pop-corn at their own firesides, and you can't get them to shoulder a musket again for half a century.'"[120] When Sherman arrived, he had discussions with Lincoln over two days in which he claimed, "Mr. Lincoln was full and frank in his conversation, assuring me that in his mind he was all ready for the civil reorganization of affairs at the South as soon as the war was over." To ensure the success of the civil reorganization, Lincoln enunciated what later became known as the River Queen Doctrine, which offered lenient terms on the premise that once surrendered Confederate troops "reach their homes, they won't take up arms again." To further the peaceful transition, Lincoln instructed Grant and Sherman to allow "their horses to plow with, and, if you like, their guns to shoot crows with. I want no one punished. Treat them liberally all around."[121] In his postwar memoirs, Sherman recalled Lincoln's instructions as "all he wanted of us was to defeat the opposing armies, and to get the men composing the Confederate armies back to their homes, at work on their farms and in their shops." Specifically, Sherman asserted that Lincoln "authorized me to assure Governor Vance … that to avoid anarchy the State governments then in existence, with their civil functionaries, would be recognized by him as the government de facto till Congress could provide others" as a model for other Confederate states.[122] Porter's recollection of the meeting with Lincoln concurred with Sherman's, stating that "Mr. Lincoln came down to City Point with the most liberal views toward the rebels … and was willing that the enemy should capitulate on the most favorable terms." Porter also remembered how the President emphasized the importance of Grant's and Sherman's roles in obtaining an end of the war because "if Lee and Johnston surrendered, he considered the war ended, and that all the other rebel forces would lay down their arms at once" because all the Confederates had left to fight for was the "hope of being handed down in history as having received honorable terms." Also important, considering future events, was the memory that "Sherman energetically insisted that he could command his own terms, and that Johnston would have to yield to his demands," a position to which Grant "made no objections."[123] When Sherman departed the next day, he did so with an understanding that he could freely engage in possible surrender talks with Johnston rather than follow specific terms dictated by Lincoln, who wanted leniency to achieve a quick resumption of order. Grant, in his memoirs, confirmed that he had the same sense of liberty. Only days later at Appomattox, when writing up the terms, Grant recalled that, instead of issuing specific terms dictated by Lincoln, "I did not know the first word that I should make use of in writing the terms. I only knew what was in my mind, and I wished to express it clearly."[124] A few days later, Grant attended a Cabinet meeting where Lincoln asked "What terms did you make for the common soldiers?" indicating that Lincoln did not know Grant's terms in advance. Lincoln expressed his approval at Grant's reply of "I told them to go back to their homes and families, and they would not be molested, if they did nothing more."[125]

During their talks, Sherman, Grant, and Lincoln did not converse on one item that was to cause Sherman grief in the coming weeks. During a prisoner exchange on February 21, Maj. Gen. Edward Ord, commanding the Union Army of the James, contacted his old friend, Lt. Gen. James Longstreet, whose Confederate I Corps were opposite his lines north of Petersburg. Discussing recent failed attempts at peace talks, Ord suggested that the soldiers themselves might be able to arrange a peace. He suggested a meeting between Lee and Grant (along, oddly enough, with the wives of the ranking officers, who would intermingle and socialize to make the situation less tense) and asked Longstreet to inquire if such a conference could be arranged from the Confederate side. Longstreet contacted Lee, who, in turn, discussed it with Davis. He agreed to a meeting, although Lee was not optimistic about hearing any offer from Grant other than immediate surrender. On the Union side, the government adamantly rejected the proposed meeting. On March 3, the War Department forwarded Lincoln's response in terse language, telling Grant "The President directs me to say to you that he wishes you to have no conference with General Lee unless it be for the capitulation of Gen. Lee's army, or on some minor, and purely, military matter." More precisely, Grant was not to "decide, discuss, or confer upon any political question" with a Confederate counterpart as "Such questions the President holds in his own hands; and will submit them to no military conferences or conventions."

The following day Grant informed Lee that he had no authority to conduct any sort of negotiation, and declined his offer of a meeting. Lincoln had made it perfectly clear to Grant that he forbade generals to discuss political outcomes of the war, but there is no evidence any other officers received the order and the matter did not come up at the City Point meeting two weeks later, leaving Sherman unaware of Lincoln's position on military involvement in political matters.[126]

****

Although Sherman was not aware at the time, he had fought his last military battle. He expected, as he told Lincoln, that at least one more large battle would be necessary to defeat the Confederacy. Sherman returned to his army prepared to fight another battle, and was confident in the successful outcome of the engagement. He had every reason to be buoyant. Sherman had driven his enemy before him for hundreds of miles, devastated much of their countryside, and brushed aside their only major effort to halt his advance. Instead of getting weaker, by merging with Schofield's force Sherman's army had actually become stronger. With his army resupplied and outfitted, Sherman saw only success on the horizon, viewing the recent clash at Bentonville as only a minor delay. Sherman the general was at the peak of his talents. He was a hero to many in the North, feared by many in South, and, he thought, about to play his part in ending the war. Little did Sherman know, however, that everything was about to change. In a matter of days, many Union citizens questioned Sherman's abilities, and even his loyalties, for actions the general took off the battlefield. The change was the result of Sherman's own actions when he thrust himself into a precarious position, because Sherman the general was about to become Sherman the negotiator, a task for which he was woefully unprepared.

Chapter 3

"In the Highest Interest of Humanity": Negotiating Peace in the Carolinas

J ohnston stung Sherman at Bentonville, but knew that he had not stopped him. Preparing his army to defend Raleigh, Johnston soon received the shocking news that Lee had abandoned his defenses around Petersburg, followed by his surrender only days later. The departure from Petersburg also led to the abandonment of Richmond by the Confederate government, making Jefferson Davis first a relocated, then fugitive, President of a country that was rapidly losing its ability and will to fight. The government's flight from Richmond added another dimension to Johnston's struggle with Sherman, as the fleeing President arrived in Johnston's department seeking both protection and assurance that his generals still intended to fight. Davis, however, found neither. Already pessimistic about the Confederacy's fortunes, Johnston, with the concurrence of Pierre Beauregard, the other senior officer in the department, told Davis that his army was incapable of stopping any Union advance. Johnston further suggested to Davis that it was time to surrender his army to save lives and prevent unnecessary suffering by civilians. It would be tempting to consider this as merely the culmination of the rivalry between Davis and Johnston with the two disagreeing about future Confederate prospects as a matter of course, but both men firmly held their respective opinions. Johnston, confronted by an army under Sherman that he already could not stop, would soon face Grant's army as well as it redeployed to assist Sherman. Davis, the political personification of the Confederacy itself, could not bring himself to accept defeat as long as some Southerners were willing to fight. Unable to change Davis's mind, Johnston pressed Davis to allow him to surrender only his own army while Davis continued his flight elsewhere. In one of the most overlooked but momentous events in the Civil War, Davis ceded to Johnston the authority to make the best terms he could with Sherman while at the same time removing himself from the area in search of refuge. Davis's abdication of political authority allowed Johnston to devise with Sherman a wide-ranging surrender document that included most of the Confederate forces that remained east of the Mississippi River, an outcome that Davis certainly did not anticipate.

Under normal circumstances, civilians would have hailed the surrender of an important Confederate army, especially only days after Lee's surrender, as a great Union victory. Johnston's capitulation, however, did not occur in stable circumstances. Johnston's surrender occurred in the shadow of Abraham Lincoln's assassination when suspicion ruled in Union circles. A paranoid Union government, especially Secretary of War Edwin Stanton, deemed the terms that William Sherman offered to Johnston, proffered with the best of intentions and based on the relative position of the two commanders, as unsatisfactory and even treasonous. The government's rejection of the terms not only jeopardized the surrender of Johnston's army, but also threatened to destroy Sherman's otherwise sterling reputation among Northern civilians. Cooler heads prevailed, however, and modified terms allowed Johnston to surrender his army under acceptable circumstances, but the episode demonstrated that deciding how to end wars can sometimes be as difficult as deciding how to fight them.

****

After his discussions at City Point with Grant and Lincoln, Sherman's immediate plans seemed clear as he returned to his army at Goldsborough. Now aware that Grant intended to drive Lee out of his Petersburg defenses, Sherman's new plan was to prepare his army if Lee tried to march to North Carolina to merge forces with Johnston or to seek an engagement with Johnston before Lee arrived. A few days later, Sherman learned that Grant had forced Lee to withdraw on April 2, and he hastened his plans to depart Goldsborough. By then, Sherman's army was ready to move. "By the 8th of April the army looked like itself again," a soldier recalled, "We had received a new outfit of wearing apparel. The wagons were again replenished with rations and ammunition."[1] On April 10, Sherman moved his force toward Johnston's army encamped near Smithfield, guessing that Johnston would try to fight him where he was or retreat toward Raleigh. Sherman's task became easier when, the following day, news arrived that Lee had surrendered to Grant at Appomattox two days earlier. No longer concerned about reinforcements coming from Lee, Sherman pressed his army westward, seeing an opportunity to end the war.[2] The news elated Sherman's men, including one who "smashed his rifle against a cotton tree." When an officer reminded him that he would be billed fourteen dollars to replace the weapon, the soldier replied, "I will gladly pay Uncle Sam for the rifle, for the good news is worth it to me."[3]

The approach of Sherman's troops created a desperate and uncertain situation in Raleigh. Governor Vance tried to negotiate a peace independent of the Confederate government, writing to Sherman on April 12 to request "a personal interview" to achieve not only "a suspension of hostilities" but opening a dialog with the U.S. government "touching the final termination of the existing war."[4] Sherman, in his reply message, expressed "doubt if hostilities can be suspended as between the army of the Confederate Government and the one I command," but agreed to meet Vance "to contribute to the end you aim to reach, the termination of the existing war." Sherman sent a follow up message urging Vance that "you had better send someone out by the train to me as quick as possible" because "as the Confederate army is our only enemy I must take all possible precautions, as you are aware that they do not recognize you as an agent to commit them" to any possible surrender.[5] Vance dispatched two former governors, William Graham and David Swain, to represent him in the discussions with Sherman, but events overtook Vance, as Union troops arrived in Raleigh and he had to flee.[6] Sherman immediately secured the city to prevent any damage, and issued invitations to Vance and other members of the state government to return to the city, a move in line with Lincoln's intentions at City Point.[7] Although no longer a relevant political figure, Vance still pressed military authorities to do their duty to protect the populace. A week after leaving Raleigh, Vance urged Johnston to get his soldiers under control after he witnessed soldiers sacking a train, especially after seeing "soldiers staggering under heavy loads of the plunder" leave the scene "as officers of nearly all grades were standing quietly around" and allowing the pillaging to occur. He also asked Johnston's help to halt the "most complete and outrageous robbery of private citizens now going on to a most distressing extent," which he feared would only get worse by "an army about to be disbanded."[8]

Vance's comment regarding his concerns about the imminent disbanding of Johnston's forces was appropriate, because Johnston himself was considering such a possibility. Johnston elected not to fight for Raleigh, but instead retreat westward toward the railroad line at Greensboro, seventy-five miles away. Sherman had considered that Johnston might move in that direction and hoped to either overtake Johnston or thwart his movement by attacking Greensboro with cavalry from Grant's army before Johnston could arrive. However, Johnston's smaller and less-burdened army could outpace Sherman and Union cavalry was still too far away to assault Greensboro, so nothing stood between Johnston and his immediate objective. The biggest impediment was Johnston himself. Rumors began to arrive that Lee had surrendered, and, although not confirmed, the news was another blow to Johnston's confidence regarding the war effort. He had constantly pushed for a unification of the two Confederate armies as the only hope of success, and that hope now appeared to be gone. Besides his diminished chances of military success once the surrender of Lee was confirmed, Johnston had other more direct reasons to consider an honorable surrender if he could obtain one. The news of Lee's surrender had triggered a steady stream of desertions from both his and Lee's armies that he could not ignore. As he consolidated his forces after the clash at Bentonville, Johnston was aware of numerous reports of deserters from the Army of Northern Virginia making their way home, causing disruption all the way and spreading disillusion in Johnston's force. "Our army is getting demoralized," one officer reported, as "A band of marauding soldiers visited our camp this morning and coolly helped themselves to some … goods that we had just quietly secured from Quartermaster's Department."[9]

To make matters worse, the appearance of so many deserters from Lee's force and the unconfirmed news that Lee had surrendered led to accelerating desertion rates.

Discouraged by defeats, retreating, and lacking essential supplies and support, many Confederate troops found plenty of excuses to end their military service. Desertion had become rampant, especially among the North Carolina troops, whose nearby homes proved to be an irresistible lure. In one brigade, desertion had reduced its number from eighteen hundred to three hundred in just ten days. Desertion diminished the ranks of the North Carolina Junior Reserves, once the largest brigade in Johnston's army, to a sixth of its former size in only a month. Others stayed in the ranks, but simply refused to assume the burden of soldiering any longer. "Whole regiments remained on the ground," Brig. Gen. (and future South Carolina governor) Johnson Hagood wrote in his diary, "refusing to obey" orders to join the westward march. Those that did fall in for the march did so reluctantly, and many threw away their rifles, a clear signal of their intent to fight no longer. A Confederate officer noted in his diary, "Every man had his eye turned homeward … The eagerness of the men to get to their homes now is beyond picture."[10] The result was an almost predisposition by Johnston to accept the inevitable. As a possible indicator of Johnston's mindset, he suspended the execution of four deserters, perhaps unwilling to waste more lives from an army about to disband.[11] Johnston was disinclined to fight, but he had to convince Jefferson Davis that it was time to surrender. Johnston soon had the chance to make his case.

****

The Confederate defeat around Petersburg that led to Lee's surrender just days later also forced the Davis administration to abandon Richmond and become a government in exile within its own country, eventually arriving in North Carolina seeking Johnston's protection. When Grant broke Lee's lines around Petersburg on April 2, Davis informed his Cabinet members at a noon meeting to be prepared to leave Richmond that evening.[12] Leaving unnecessary items behind, the entire administration required only eight trains to move Davis (his wife and children had left Richmond a few days earlier), his Cabinet members, what military stores could be loaded, and the essential possessions of the Confederate government, including its archives and the remaining funds from the Treasury. Although Union leaders estimated the Treasury funds with Davis as somewhere between "$6,000,000 to $13,000,000," the reality was much more modest. When finally caught, Davis's party had "$87,878, in gold, mostly old coinage, $8,822 in silver, 146 pieces of foreign coin (gold and silver) value not yet estimated, and 56 bricks of silver ... the value of the whole being somewhat over $100,000."[13] Their destination was Danville, Virginia, 140 miles southwest of Richmond. Davis selected Danville because of its location between Lee and Johnston's army in case a merger of the two forces became necessary, it was defendable because of the Dan River and supporting railroad lines, and the capital would still be in Virginia, an important psychological consideration. There were also substantial facilities, including two convalescent hospitals, a small arms factory, and supply depot.[14]

The departure of the government generated only depression among the citizens of the soon to be occupied city. "I saw a government on wheels," an officer observed as the trains left Richmond, "It was the marvelous and incongruous debris of the wreck of the Confederate capital."[15] A local woman described how "The people were rushing up and down the streets, vehicles of all kinds were flying along, bearing goods of all sorts and people of all ages and classes who could go beyond the corporation lines." Early the next morning, she was "startled by a loud sound like thunder ... It was soon understood to be the blowing up of a magazine below the city. In a few hours another exploded on the outskirts of the city," and by morning "The lower part of the city was burning." Besides the ammunition stores, other fires broke out after "government employees, having opened up all their supply depots for the public to pillage, put fire to them. There was a strong wind, so the whole commercial sector of the city was reduced to ashes ... I have never seen such a disaster."[16] The next day, Union troops arrived to extinguish the fire and restore order in the city, thereby removing Richmond from an exclusive list. After Davis fled Richmond, only two Confederate state capitals, Tallahassee, Florida, and Austin, Texas, had not fallen into Union hands at least temporarily.

Upon arrival in Danville on April 3, Davis, intending to stay indefinitely pending the merging of Lee and Johnston's armies, insisted on maintaining

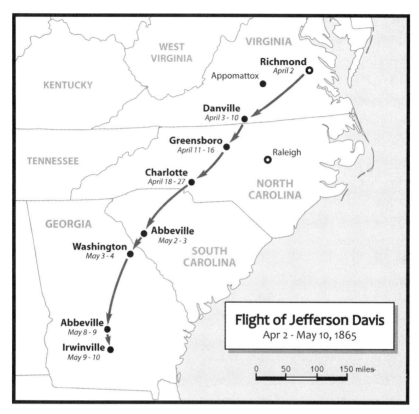

Flight of Jefferson Davis.

the functions of government despite the inability to do so. Union cavalry had cut many of the telegraph lines, so Davis was ignorant of any events beyond his immediate sight and had limited ability to issue orders.[17] Trying to reassure the people that his government was still functioning, on April 4 Davis issued a sweeping public statement in which he expressed confidence in ultimate victory. Richmond, he declared, had been a handicap with which Lee no longer had to contend. Without cities to defend, the Confederate Army would use maneuver and guile to wear down the North's will to fight and secure victory. It was either an exercise in propaganda or a sign of Davis's delusions; the people no longer supported the war and bringing Union armies directly into their home regions would engender less support. Quite the contrary, there was nothing left in the countryside with which to support the army, and mass suffering would have been the only result. Perhaps it was best that Davis's proclamation reached only a limited audience. Because of the destruction of the telegraph lines, very few Confederate civilians ever read it. The proclamation, for instance, did not appear in newspapers in Raleigh, only eighty miles away, until six days later.[18]

Proclamations could not protect Davis and his entourage, however, especially when on April 10 Davis learned of Lee's surrender two days before, news that Secretary of the Navy Stephen Mallory recorded "fell upon ears of all like a fire bell in the night."[19] Danville, with a local garrison of only three thousand defenders to protect the town, was no longer a secure location, so Davis immediately ordered preparations to depart for Greensboro, North Carolina, where Johnston's army could protect him.[20] It was a prudent move because Grant was already deploying forces southward, ordering Maj. Gen. Philip Sheridan to take most of the cavalry and the VI Corps toward Greensboro. The move was to reinforce Sherman, but its unintended consequence was to put Union troops on the road toward Davis's location.[21]

Unlike the prepared evacuation of Richmond, the departure from Danville was not well organized, with an officer writing that the "streets are choked with government wagons trying to force their way out of town. Soldiers and officers of every degree and description throng the town, mingled in one promiscuous mass." Commissary officers were distributing stores in hopes of avoiding rioting, but "crowds of savage and blood thirsty looking stragglers … appear awaiting an opportunity to do some ugly deed."[22] The disorder continued even after Davis's party departed when hungry civilians pillaged the remaining stores, resulting in an ammunition explosion and "in an instant the building and its contents, including over fifty persons, were blown to atoms."[23] Davis made his escape from Danville, but it was close one. Union cavalry just missed Davis on his transit to Greensboro, burning a railroad trestle just moments after Davis's train had passed over it.[24] Upon his arrival, Davis found his reception in Greensboro much less enthusiastic than the one in Danville, with the city either unprepared or unwilling to welcome him. Greensboro had recently hosted pro-peace rallies, and even those loyal to the Confederacy feared reprisal if Union cavalry discovered them aiding the fugitives.[25]

Davis had little time to complain about the reception he received because he was here to talk with his senior officers, and requested Johnston and Beauregard to come as soon as possible. Both generals arrived on April 12 and held the first of several meetings with Davis and his Cabinet members. Johnston later recalled that, instead of receiving briefs on the military situation, "the President's object seemed to be to give, not to obtain information." The President's bellicosity stunned both generals, as did his belief that deserters and draft-dodgers would return to the army in this time of emergency and that Lee's troops would escape to join Johnston's army. Wishing to bring Davis back to reality, Johnston called the determination to fight "the greatest of human crimes" in the face of overwhelming Union advantages. He considered continuing the war as pointless, as the Confederacy had "neither money nor credit, nor arms but those in the hands of our soldiers, nor ammunition but that in their cartridge boxes, nor shops for repairing arms or fixing ammunition, the effect of our keeping the field would be, not to harm the enemy, but to complete the devastation of our country and the ruin of its people." Davis rejected Johnston's opinion, stating "neither soldiers nor civilians have shown a disposition to surrender," and he would continue to fight if he had to "rally our forces west of the Mississippi."[26] Davis may have been determined, but others besides Johnston considered continued resistance a futile effort. Although certainly not a person inclined to surrender, Maj. Gen. Joseph Wheeler, in his postwar memoirs, recognized that defeat had come. Besides having no arsenals in their possession, Wheeler pointed out "All arms in General Lee's department have been surrendered. Thirteen hundred returned soldiers from the wrecked Army of Tennessee had no arms. The powder-mill in Augusta was in the hands of the enemy."[27] The meeting concluded without reaching any consensus.

That evening, Secretary of War (and former general) John C. Breckinridge arrived with news confirming that Lee had indeed surrendered. At a late meeting with Johnston and Beauregard, Breckinridge agreed with the generals that the war was over, but they together needed to convince Davis. Johnston emphasized to Breckinridge "that the only power of government left in the President's hands was that of terminating the war, and that this power should be exercised without delay."[28] Meeting again the next morning,

Davis resisted the idea of surrender broached by Breckinridge, insisting that the remaining armies would fight and that the Confederacy's attrition strategy could still prevail, despite the loss of Virginia. He emphasized the powerlessness of the South's position if its surrender was unconditional.[29] Davis asked Johnston for his opinion, and Johnston quickly asserted that the President's rosy outlook was flawed. "My views are, sir, that our people are tired of the war," Johnston replied, "feel themselves whipped, and will not fight." He reminded Davis that desertion was causing his own army to disappear, "melting away like snow before the sun," and he could not contain Union forces. Johnston concluded that the best that the country could hope for were suitable surrender terms, which he believed Sherman willing to grant. When queried, Beauregard fully agreed with Johnston, as did most of the Cabinet members; Judah Benjamin was the only one who stood with Davis. Davis remained unconvinced of the need to surrender, and when he expressed doubt that he had the authority to surrender, Johnston reminded Davis that plenty of instances in history existed where "military commanders had found it convenient to initiate negotiations for peace."[30]

After considering this statement, Davis made the momentous decision to allow Johnston to approach Sherman about surrender terms. One revisionist history of the events in Greensboro believed that "it was useless for Davis, as head of the civil government, to attempt to treat for peace, but that Johnston should make the preliminary overtures to Sherman," a move that conveniently removed Davis from the process and placed any subsequent surrender squarely on Johnston's shoulders. Johnston, in turn, would not take the responsibility of establishing talks without Presidential authority. He insisted that Davis give him written instructions on what terms the Confederate government would accept, which Davis provided: disbanding of Confederate army and recognition of Union authority, but only if state governments were preserved, political rights preserved, property (presumably including slaves) protected, and amnesty for any actions during the war. The terms, demanding a return to prewar status quo, were clearly irrational, but Davis was either still recklessly optimistic of the Confederacy's chances or was purposely trying to undermine the talks with Sherman by asking for impossible concessions. To legitimize the proposed talks, Johnston asked Davis to write directly to Sherman requesting talks via Johnston. Per Johnston's request, Davis admitted to Sherman that, "the recent campaign in Virginia have changed the relative military condition of the belligerents." He inquired if Sherman would engage in talks to "stop the further effusion of blood" by allowing a "temporary suspension of active operations … to permit the civil authorities to enter into the needful arrangements to terminate the existing war." Sherman, per his understanding of the River Queen doctrine, replied that he was "fully empowered to arrange with you any terms for the suspension of further hostilities … and will be willing to confer with you to that end" on the basis of the "terms and conditions as were made by Generals Grant and Lee at Appomattox Court-House."[31] As the meeting ended, Davis asked Johnston what path his army intended to take if the talks with Sherman proved fruitless. When informed by Johnston that he intended to fall back into South Carolina, Davis instead urged him to attempt a defense of North Carolina by making a stand around Charlotte. If that proved unsuccessful, Davis instructed him to make plans for a retreat to Texas, a goal that Johnston found preposterous.[32] Despite his public optimism and determination to fight when consulting with his advisors, Davis was much more pessimistic in private. That evening, he wrote to Varina, "Everything is dark … I have lingered on the road and labored to little purpose."[33]

After giving permission to negotiate with Sherman, Davis departed Greensboro for Charlotte, ninety miles to the southwest. Davis's decision to leave remains a curious one. While he had no faith in the outcome of the negotiations between Sherman and Johnston, Davis had always been quick to exercise his presidential prerogatives and the choice to distance himself from the proceedings ensured he would have less influence on subsequent events. At the same time, Davis's departure signaled to Johnston that he was to act at his own discretion, a suggestion that Johnston exercised in the coming days. The departure from Greensboro also marked the end of Davis's government in a practical sense. While the President and a few Cabinet members carried on their exodus, they were never again in a location that had reliable communications. Cut off from the rest of the world and with residents in the remaining parts of the Confederacy unaware of where he was, Davis had become for all practical purposes a political nonentity. Perhaps the uncertainly of how close he should remain to the Sherman/Johnston discussions explained Davis's desultory progress toward Charlotte. Upon leaving Greensboro, Davis moved slowly, averaging less than twenty miles per day.[34]

On the other hand, if the negotiations were as pointless as Davis believed, his proximity to Sherman's army put him and his remaining government at personal risk, and distance would provide some protection. Besides Sherman's troops, Stoneman's cavalry were still roving through North Carolina when local newspapers informed him of the evacuation of Richmond. Stoneman ordered his troops to begin moving southeast in a bid to intercept Davis. Unknown to him, his troops burned the bridge over the Dan River just a short time after Jefferson Davis's fleeing government had passed over it, nearly capturing the Confederate leader. Reuniting his command at Danbury, North Carolina, Stoneman led his force toward Salisbury, a major transportation and logistics center. Pushing aside a small Confederate garrison, Stoneman's troopers needed two days to destroy the city's industrial and military facilities. The damage amounted to four textile factories, seven thousand bales of cotton, ten thousand small arms and thirty-five tons of powder, and forty tons of food-stuff, although Stoneman reserved some items for distribution to the city's poor. "We meet many country people bearing off the remnants of half-ruined articles, such as pieces of machinery, half burnt cotton, wool, etc.," a Confederate officer later observed. "Stoneman appears to have destroyed immensely in the town, and the ruins are still smoking." Stoneman completed his work and moved on, unaware that if he had stayed just a few hours longer he might have captured Davis's party, who arrived to discover cavalry had burned the "depots, arsenal & all public property."[35]

****

On April 15, six days after Lee's surrender at Appomattox and one day after the shooting of the President, Sherman forwarded to Grant and Stanton copies of his correspondence with Johnston in preparation for their meeting that Sherman confidently predicted "will be followed by terms of capitulation." Sherman also provided some foreshadowing of the problems soon to damage his reputation. While promising both Grant and Stanton that "I will accept the same terms as General Grant gave General Lee, and be careful not to compli-cate any points of civil policy," Sherman also reported that "I have invited

Governor Vance to return to Raleigh with the civil officers of his State." He also noted other conversations with North Carolina state officials "all of whom agree that the war is over, and that the States of the South must resume their allegiance, subject to the Constitution and laws of Congress, and that the military power of the South must submit to the national arms. This great fact once admitted, all the details are easy of arrangement."[36] Sherman, believing the nation could achieve that peace most readily by utilizing the existing political systems in the South, naively negotiated with a predisposition to retain certain Confederate leaders in power, an opinion that got him in deep trouble.

Johnston met Sherman on April 17 near Durham Station, North Carolina. After some initial small talk, Sherman asked where Johnston would like to hold their conference. Johnston replied that he had passed a small farmhouse a short distance away, and Sherman agreed to hold the meeting there. Sherman opened the meeting with a bombshell by showing Johnston a telegram confirming an assassin had killed President Lincoln. Shaken by the news, Johnston considered the act "the greatest possible calamity," and hoped that Sherman did not believe it was the outcome of a Confederate plot. Sherman replied that he believed Confederate Army were not involved, but did not rule out the death was ordered by the Confederate government.[37] Sherman then laid out his offer to Johnston by explaining the terms that Grant had given Lee. Johnston, in his reply, changed the entire nature of the discussion by asking Sherman if the two could not "arrange the terms of a permanent peace." Sherman, likely taken aback by such an unexpected offer, stated that, even if he did seek such an outcome, he was not convinced that Johnston had authority to make such a deal, but, after Johnston "intimated that he could procure authority from Mr. Davis," Sherman was intrigued by the idea. Further pushing the boundaries of the discussion, Johnston also inquired about possible terms of amnesty. Sherman replied that the Grant/Lee terms applied to all soldiers, but could not approve amnesty for Davis or other civilian government officials, thereby, at least at that point, remaining within the limits of a purely military discussion.[38]

The generals decided to continue their talks the following day. Johnston had not achieved his goal of obtaining a ceasefire, but he could afford to be patient. Johnston had decided to negotiate, but he was not entering his talks with Sherman empty handed because, unlike Lee, he had options. Because Grant's army surrounded the Army of Northern Virginia, Lee had no choice but to accept Grant's very generous terms. Moreover, Lee did not have the opportunity to confer with Jefferson Davis, but instead had to accept the terms as a purely military agreement without any political implications or approval. Sherman's army, however, did not surround that of Johnston. The Confederate army was a two-day marching distance away from Sherman's, so he was not only not surrounded but also could detect any attempt by Sherman to place him in such a position. His smaller and more mobile army, one of the few benefits from the lack of wagons, could also move at a more rapid rate than Sherman's force. If the contest became a marching challenge, Johnston also had the advantage that as his army could deplete the resources of an area, forcing the following Union army to scrape up only what remained. In short, Johnston, unlike Lee, had the ability to prolong the war, perhaps not indefinitely but certainly longer than Lincoln, Grant, or Sherman would have preferred. The proximity of Jefferson Davis, who could compel Johnston to continue fighting even if the general preferred not to do so, also tempered any proclivity that Johnston might have had to surrender. Although intended as a critique, Maj. Gen. Joseph Wheeler summarized Johnston's options: "Lee could not retreat to supplies; Johnston might. Lee had no hope of reinforcement. If Johnston had fallen back, southward, Richard Taylor had some troops in Alabama; [Nathan] Forrest had troops in Alabama; there were troops beyond the Mississippi."[39]

Johnston was fully aware of his bargaining chip of being able to move away. At the first meeting between the two generals, when Sherman offered the Grant/Lee terms, Johnston "replied that our relative positions were too different from those in the armies of Virginia to justify me in such a capitulation."[40] Also, when queried by Davis of his intentions if negotiations with Sherman failed, Johnston replied that he intended to fall back to South Carolina, indicating not only his awareness of his options but forethought in how they might be implemented.[41] More importantly, Sherman was aware that Johnston could slip away, recalling in his later memoirs that "I knew well that Johnston's army could not be caught; the country was too open; and, without wagons, the men could escape us, disperse, and assemble again at some place agreed upon, and thus the war might be prolonged indefinitely."[42] Sherman, therefore was aware that Johnston not only might not accept the same terms that Grant offered to Lee, but was likely not to accept them under their differing circumstances, leaving Sherman to offer more generous terms. Thus, Johnston's option to move away meant he, as Jacqueline Campbell wrote, "retained some negotiating power and avoided creating a culture of terror in the South" by ending the war in a respectable manner.[43]

If Johnston did opt to break off negotiations if they proved fruitless, his next question would be in which direction to go. One source incorrectly claims "Johnston's only avenue of movement remaining was toward Richmond, a city already destitute, which would have been brought fully to famine had the rebel army gone there."[44] He could have attempted to move west into the Appalachians, but the lack of supplies and transport would likely make such a move a disastrous one when Johnston could not feed his troops. His mobility would also have been impaired if Stoneman's cavalry managed to destroy key bridges and other transportation bottlenecks. Rather, Johnston had only one realistic option, a southward march toward Georgia. Such a movement was not only obvious but also had at least some chance of success. It was the obvious route because Sherman, whose columns had mainly passed through the coastal regions of the Carolinas, had inflicted relatively little damage to the Piedmont region between the coastal strip and the front range of the Appalachians. The roads were intact and, since Sherman's troops were concentrated southeast of Raleigh at Smithfield, no Union troops barred their way. From a supply standpoint, whether Johnston could have used the route depended upon how quickly they could move from one supply source to another. At least until the peace brought about general plundering, North Carolina depots in regions beyond Union control were well-stocked.[45] Johnston would have had to rely upon the depots because of the scarcity of food elsewhere. Major General Stoneman, commanding Union cavalry in southwest North Carolina, reported to the War Department that "Cavalry cannot live up there now, as there is neither hay, grain, nor grass as yet."[46] Johnston might have received access to some railroad links as well. The Confederates placed great emphasis on repairing tracks in the aftermath of Sherman's operations, and Johnston was attentive to the re-establishment of railroad links. Resources and labor were in low supply, but it was a priority and the Confederates had pulled off impressive feats of railroad repairs in the past.[47] Moreover, the railroads around Augusta, Georgia, were still relatively undamaged. Despite the arsenal, depots, and warehouses in the city, Sherman had bypassed it on both his March to the Sea and advance into the Carolinas, so the city provided not only supplies, but also a rallying point for any troops that Johnston might have hoped to accumulate. Besides his own force, Johnston might have added the militias from the Carolinas and Georgia, the small garrison at Augusta itself, and the troops still trickling in from the Army of Tennessee. The additions would not have been great in number, a few thousand soldiers at most, but would have been welcome nevertheless.[48]

Johnston had an escape path that he could possibly use, but the qualifying issue was whether it was worth using. The troops that Johnston might have gained by marching to Augusta would likely have been more than offset by the losses incurred on the march, especially to desertion from North and South Carolina troops as they passed through their home states. An officer in Johnston's command recognized the futility of trying to lead the army elsewhere when he wrote, "If we pass through the States of South Carolina, Georgia, Alabama, and Mississippi, we will have no army."[49] Johnston would have ended up with not only a smaller force, but, due to the probable desertion of veteran troops, a less battle-worthy one. Even if Johnston could have reached Augusta with his entire army, he had nowhere else to go as every Union soldier pursued him. One historian described Johnston's plight as "Kirkpatrick was on his front with as large a cavalry force as his; Stoneman was on his rear with a cavalry force as large as his; Wilson, with at least five times his cavalry, was in Georgia; nearer the depots of supplies in South Carolina, than was Johnston in North Carolina. Moreover, Sheridan was within a few day's march in Virginia with ten thousand cavalry, capable of overtaking him as soon as his departure became known."[50] Columbia and Atlanta were in ruins, and Savannah and Charleston were in Union hands. Grant and Sherman's combined armies were behind him, while Canby and Wilson's forces were in front of him. Even if Johnston could have eluded the ring of Union troops around him, the next closest supply depot was in Louisiana, more than seven hundred miles away and on the other side of the Mississippi River.

Secretary of War John Breckinridge (*Image courtesy of the Library of Congress*).

Any attempt by Johnston to escape by marching away from Sherman, therefore, would only have delayed the inevitable; the Union Army would corner Johnston in Georgia a few weeks later instead of North Carolina immediately. Sherman certainly bargained with Johnston's ability to maneuver in mind, but at the same time Johnston also must have negotiated while heedful of his own limited strategic options.

When the negotiations resumed on April 18, Johnston again steered the discussion toward a broader surrender of Confederate forces. As part of this effort, Johnston offered to bring Secretary of war John Breckinridge into the conversation. Johnston had two reasons for doing so. First, Breckinridge could confirm to Sherman that Davis had conferred on Johnston permission to negotiate, settling the doubts that Sherman expressed the previous day. Second, in case Davis was reluctant to accept any terms subsequently negotiated, Breckinridge could reinforce Johnston's arguments in favor because he himself had been a participant. Sherman, however demurred because he was concerned about discussing civil issues with a representative of the Confederate government. Sherman only consented to speaking with Breckinridge in his capacity as a major general in the Confederate Army.[51] With Breckinridge present, the discussion, led by Breckinridge, diverted into "rule and maxim of international and constitutional law, and of the laws of war,—international wars, civil wars, and wars of rebellion."[52] Sherman found Breckinridge's tirade on legal and constitutional justifications for the rebellion both pointless and amusing, joking that he was not sure who was surrendering to whom. Johnston introduced a set of surrender terms proposed by Postmaster John Reagan. Now completed, he handed them to Sherman, who found them "too general and wordy" and proceeded to revise them to his own liking. In his rewritten terms, Sherman offered the conditions of the Grant/Lee agreement, but also an armistice while their respective governments considered the terms that were to hold until given forty-eight-hour notice. In addition, all Confederate armies would disband and deposit their weapons in the care of their respective states, the state governments, upon taking an oath of loyalty, would remain in power, and civilians would, "so far as the Executive can" retain their political and property rights.

By any definition, Sherman was very generous in his terms to Johnston, leading to the inevitable question of why. There were, for instance, some practical reasons to come to terms in an expedited manner. The armies had ceased to move when the prospect of negotiations arose, and despite the arrival of supplies from their coastal supply bases, Sherman's men still needed to forage to feed themselves and their animals. After only two days, the shortage of supplies meant that Sherman's troops had to go on half-rations.[53] The relative position and capabilities of both armies also complicated the supply situation. If Johnston moved his army in an attempt to escape, he could not only move quickly because of his sparse logistic lines, but also deplete any region of resources through which Sherman would have to pursue him, leaving Sherman's army even more bereft of support as they moved away from their coastal bases. Another theory is that Sherman, because of his fondly remembered relationship with the South in the antebellum period, was more willing to grant his enemy concessions than perhaps other Union generals were inclined to offer. Sherman often commented on how much he respected and almost identified with the Southerners with whom he made acquaintance during his prewar Army career, which led him to have more faith in their ability to become loyal citizens again than perhaps any other Northern figure, especially if the South had come to learn the folly of disloyalty.[54] Sherman enunciated his beliefs regarding the future loyalty of the South and made suggestions on how the Union should treat the region in a May 1865 letter when he wrote "I have had abundant opportunities to know these people both before the war, during its existence, and since their public acknowledgment of submission. I have no fear of them armed or disarmed, and believe that by one single stroke of the pen nine-tenths of them can be restored to full relations to our Government so as to pay taxes, live in peace, and in war I would not hesitate to mingle with them and lead them to battle against a national foe." In addition, Sherman believed the Southern states capable of the self-Reconstruction envisioned by Lincoln, warning that "we must deal with them with frankness and candor, and not with doubt, hesitancy, and prevarication. The nine-tenths would, from motives of self-interest, restrain the other mischievous tenth," expressing confidence that "We have a vast political majority which cannot be lost, unless by seeming acts of oppression a reaction is created in their support. Their resources are all gone and their confidence in their leaders is turned to hate. ... Jeff. Davis, Toombs, Cobb, Benjamin, Slidell, and other political leaders will receive less mercy at the hands of their countrymen than ours." Sherman believed that a harsh Reconstruction would only produce resentment, and that if the administration wanted a model for comparison of government by "military occupation and military governors, I invite your attention to the occupation of Spain by Napoleon's best armies from about 1806 to the close of his career," referencing the French Emperor's disastrous occupation of Spain.[55]

There were also practical military matters. Sherman, among many other Union generals, was concerned that the Confederate Army might resort to guerilla warfare and if the Southern army dispersed into small bands it might take a great deal of time, effort, expense, and lives to hunt them down. Sherman stressed his desire to prevent this outcome in a letter to his wife, indicating that "There is a great danger of the Confederate armies breaking up into guerrillas, and that is what I most fear."[56] Sherman was also concerned about how the news of Lincoln's assassination would affect the mood and behavior of his troops, with Sherman forced to act to end the war quickly lest his army seek retaliation that would further enflame the conflict on both sides. The violent reaction of Union troops to the news of Lincoln's assassination, albeit short-lived, confirmed his fears.[57] Sherman, informing his troops of the assassination, warned, "We have met every phase which this war has assumed, and must now be prepared for it in its last and worst shape, that of assassins and guerrillas." Johnston also considered the effect of the Lincoln assassination, believing that a widespread surrender of Confederate forces would protect them from Northern retribution and retaliation.[58]

Other suggestions regarding Sherman's attitude at the negotiations suggest that he was both out of his element and in over his head when dealing with diplomacy. Some sources describe Johnston and Breckinridge as "wily" in their efforts to outwit Sherman, who was overcome by the enormity of the situation and the skill of his Confederate opponents.[59] While undoubtedly a novice at diplomacy, Sherman, who had been a practicing lawyer, had the legal skills to ensure that Johnston and Breckinridge did not receive conditions to which the Confederates were not entitled. Quite the opposite, Sherman seems to have grasped the broader implications of with whom he was negotiating but also the implications of the possible outcome. Whereas Sherman was not in direct communication with the White House and War Department and was, as he himself admitted, acting on his own initiative, Johnston had clearly indicated to Sherman that he was not only in contact with Jefferson Davis but authorized by him to enter into negotiations. Consequently, while it was Johnston sitting across the table from Sherman, it was, in a greater sense, Jefferson Davis's representative. Once Johnston broached the idea of surrendering forces in a wide area of the South, Sherman had to have realized that successfully to attain the prize that Johnston offered he needed to do more than just offer military terms that Johnston would accept but also political terms that Davis would accept.

This possible viewpoint by Sherman also explains why Sherman would wade into the murky diplomatic waters in the first place. Whereas a seasoned veteran of the political scene in Washington might view the proposed negotiations between Sherman and Johnston as an exercise that required preparation, tact, and adequate assessment of the possible outcomes, Sherman was not a political animal. Instead, Sherman was professional soldier who, as a byproduct of his West Point training and military experience, had learned to seize opportunities when he saw them because such moments tended to be both uncommon and fleeting. Moreover, generals who failed to seize opportunities when they appeared tended to be defeated, relieved of command, or both. With this view in mind, not only would Sherman have seized this chance to end the war, but other generals would likely have done so as well. As a military leader, Sherman also may have had the recent clash at Bentonville in mind. Johnston was able to attack because the wings of Sherman's army were widely separated due to the nature of the road network and the need to forage for supplies. If the campaign became a pursuit, the possibility would exist again for Johnston to launch limited attacks on isolated parts of Sherman's army because of the transport/supply requirements. In addition, when Sherman opted not to exploit Brigadier General Mower's advance that threatened to cut off Johnston's retreat, Sherman had not seized an opportunity when it presented itself, something that perhaps he was determined not to repeat again.

When informed of the agreement, Sherman's subordinates were supportive of his terms, although some later tried to distance themselves from it. In a later biography of Maj. Gen. Henry Slocum, the author claimed that Slocum "expressed his doubts of the agreement being approved … on account of Sherman having permitted civil questions to be embodied in the military."[60] The rest, however, stated their approval. Slocum later recalled that he had "conversed with nearly all these officers, among them [Maj. Gen. John] Logan, [Maj. Gen. Oliver] Howard, and [Maj. Gen. Francis] Blair, and heard no word of dissent from any of them."[61] That Logan and Blair both endorsed the agreement was significant because they were political generals who saw no issue with Sherman issuing such an agreement.[62] One Union officer considered the meeting as not only proper, but enlightened. "The fratricidal struggle of four long and weary years virtually ended on the day when two great men came together in the heart of the State of North Carolina," Maj. George Nichols wrote later in the year, "intent, with true nobility of soul and in the highest interest of humanity, upon putting a stop to the needless sacrifice of life."[63]

Johnston, having achieved the broad surrender he had sought, immediately signed the agreement and immediately sent it to Greensboro to Davis for his approval. Davis, however, had already left town, bound for Charlotte, forcing Johnston to send the documents by courier in pursuit.[64] Sherman also informed his superiors. On April 18, Sherman dispatched Maj. Henry Hitchcock by steamer to DC to deliver messages to Grant and Halleck in person rather than use the unreliable telegraph line. The letters informed Grant and Henry Halleck of his negotiations, which he believed "will produce peace from the Potomac and the Rio Grande." After clarifying that Breckinridge participated in the discussions only "in his capacity as major-general," Sherman summarized the terms he extended to Johnston, allowances that he believed represented "an absolute submission of the enemy to the lawful authority of the United States" and that "they will in the future be perfectly subordinate to the laws of the United States." In justifying his terms, Sherman emphasized that he pressed utmost that the "dispersion and disbandment of these armies is done in such a manner as to prevent their breaking up into guerrilla bands." To that end, he also allowed the Confederates to stockpile their weapons in state arsenals to give local authorities "the means of repressing guerrillas, which we could not expect them to do if we stripped them of all arms." Sherman felt so secure about the military situation that he proposed leaving only Schofield and the X Corps to supervise the surrender proceedings while he led his other five corps to a point in Maryland where they could be demobilized. "The question of finance is now the chief one, and every soldier and officer not needed should be got home at work," Sherman opined, while also reminding Grant "it is important to get the Confederate armies to their homes as well as our own."[65]

Because he did not leave until late in the evening, Hitchcock did not arrive in DC until the afternoon of April 21. Grant, upon reading Sherman's terms, was so concerned about their implications that he urged Stanton to call a Cabinet meeting as soon as possible. Convening that evening at the hotel where President Johnson was staying (he had agreed to allow the Lincolns to remain at the White House during the mourning period and funeral for the dead President), the Cabinet listened while Grant read the terms that Sherman had negotiated. The reaction in the room varied from incredulous silence to blustering outrage. Attorney General James Speed plunged into wild conspiracies, fearing that Sherman intended to use the terms to make himself a military dictator, with the Potomac his proverbial Rubicon.[66] While the other department heads sat, stunned by what they had heard, Stanton took control of the meeting. Grant had shown Stanton the terms earlier in the day, and Stanton had already prepared a list of reasons to reject the agreement. After listening to Stanton's reasoning, which he himself described as a product of his indignation at Sherman's actions, the Cabinet voted to reject the agreement in "the bitterest terms" and instructed Grant to inform Sherman of their decision. In addition, Stanton ordered Grant to "proceed immediately to the headquarters of General Sherman and direct operations against the enemy."[67] The implications of Stanton's order were clear: in directing operations against the enemy, Grant was not there to renegotiate the terms, but rather to direct military efforts that would result in a complete Confederate surrender. Moreover, by sending Grant to direct the efforts, Stanton was effectively sidelining Sherman, essentially relieving him of command without a formal process. What Stanton hoped to gain by this is unclear, unless he believed that Sherman might refuse orders to reject the agreement, but Stanton had no reason to presume that was the case.

Wasting no time, Grant departed that same evening to confer with Sherman accompanied by only a small retinue. By the following afternoon, the group had reached Fort Monroe, where Grant briefly conferred with Maj. Gen. Henry Halleck, who had recently assumed field command of the Department of the James. Grant informed the former Chief of Staff of his mission before continuing on to Raleigh, arriving early in the morning of April 24. While Grant was making his way south, Sherman and Johnston continued to correspond. Sherman was still confident that the Johnson administration would approve his suggested terms, but was concerned about Northern public opinion in the aftermath of the Lincoln assassination. "The feeling North on this subject is more intense than anything that ever occurred before," Sherman admitted, "and I fear much the assassination of the President will give such a bias to the popular mind which, in connection with the desire of our politicians, may thwart our purpose of recognizing 'existing local governments.'" Sherman reassured Johnston that "I doubt if the Confederate military authorities had any more complicity with it than I had," but had to believe that "this assassination of Mr. Lincoln will do the cause of the South more harm than any event of the war, both at home and abroad." Sherman closed by stating his belief that Major Hitchcock was expected the next day and they would have a sense of the "feeling about Washington arising from this new and unforeseen complication."[68]

Grant's arrival was a surprise to Sherman, as he had not informed Sherman of his mission when he left DC or even when his steamer docked in Morehead City the evening before. Hitchcock had telegraphed Sherman of his arrival at Morehead City, but Grant instructed him not to inform Sherman of his presence. Ignoring his orders to direct operations against the enemy, Grant hid his arrival in a bid to allow Sherman to redress his negotiating errors and defuse any controversy before it became public. Despite his efforts at secrecy, Grant's appearance did attract notice. "The quiet of this morning was somewhat broken by the announcement that Genl. Grant had just passed through Morehead city enroute to Raleigh," a Union private noted in his diary, "It was supposed to receive the surrender of the miserable remnant of the Southern Confederacy."[69] In a private session, Grant informed Sherman that the Cabinet had rejected his terms and showed him the orders to assume operations against the enemy. Grant recalled that Sherman, while irritated by the orders to cede control of operations to Grant, was not surprised that the President rejected his terms. Grant also showed Sherman a copy of the March 3 dispatch from Lincoln rejecting his surrender discussions with Longstreet and ordering him to avoid non-military discussions. Sherman stated that he was not aware of the correspondence, and later wrote that if the War Department had made him aware of the command it "would have saved a world of trouble."[70] Nevertheless, Sherman agreed to do as Grant ordered.

In a telegram sent early the next morning, Sherman informed Johnston that he was invoking the forty-eight-hour provision and ending their cease-fire. In a separate note, Sherman explained to Johnston that "I am instructed to limit my operations to your immediate command and not to attempt civil negotiations. I therefore demand the surrender of your army on the same terms as were given General Lee at Appomattox, of April 9, instant, purely and simply." Grant sent his own message to Stanton that "Word was immediately sent to Johnston terminating the truce, and information that civil matters could not be entertained in any convention between army commanders." Besides informing the government that negotiations upon terms of their own liking were underway, Grant, after having a chance to talk to Sherman, tried to rationalize Sherman's motivation for his original agreement with Johnston, but his explanation seemed contradictory. "General Sherman," Grant claimed, "has been guided in his negotiations with Johnston entirely by what he thought was precedent authorized by the President" based upon the discussions at City Point the previous month. Grant also asserted that Sherman "was not surprised" that the government overturned his original agreement, "but rather expected their rejection," a strange statement considering the seriousness with which Sherman took the negotiations, which leaves an observer wondering why Sherman would agree to terms that he knew to be futile.[71]

At that point unaware of the controversy he had unleashed in Washington, Sherman also wrote to Stanton to explain himself, a move that only made the situation worse. Sherman opened the letter by describing his first agreement as "terms on which General Johnston proposed to disarm and disperse the insurgents on condition of amnesty," seeming to put the onus of the negotiations on Johnston rather than himself. To a certain degree this was true; the broad terms drafted by Reagan and presented by Johnston shaped Sherman's surrender statement. Sherman's name was on the document and Johnston was offering to surrender to him, so Sherman could not disguise his part in the process, something Stanton surely recognized. Sherman next was quick to "admit my folly in embracing in a military convention any civil matters," which was not much of an apology as he just as quickly wrote that "such is the nature of our situation that they seem inextricably united … and would warrant a little bending to policy." This statement undermined his apology because it posited that he in reality had done nothing wrong because events dictated that a general in the field had to decide when to cross the boundary between civil and military matters rather than duly appointed politicians, an opinion sure to enrage Stanton even further.

Sherman, while intending to mend his relationship with Stanton, ended the letter in the worst possible way. Asserting that "I still believe the Government of the United States has made a mistake" in rejecting his terms, Sherman then wrote, "but that is none of my business," forgetting that in trying to enact a wide-ranging surrender document, he had made it his business. Closing with a reminder of the "four years' patient, unremitting, and successful labor" that he had given to the nation, Sherman promised that "You may assure the President I will heed his suggestion."[72] Sherman could not possibly have written a letter more likely to outrage Stanton. Looking for contrition from Sherman, Stanton instead perceived Sherman as simply trying to avoid responsibility or even suggest that the government's position was wrong. If Stanton had any qualms about leaking his reaction to the terms to the press, he must have felt fully justified after reading Sherman's note.[73]

On the same day that Sherman wrote to Stanton, he also wrote to Grant, whose opinion meant more to him. Wishing to "record the fact that I made my terms with General Johnston under the influence of the liberal terms you extended to the army of General Lee," Sherman offered more a justification of his actions rather than an apology. "I have not the least desire to interfere in the civil policy of our Government," Sherman emphasized, but admitted that "occasions do arise when a prompt seizure of results is forced on military commanders not in immediate communication with the proper authority." Sherman further admitted that the "terms signed by General Johnston and myself were not clear enough," but nevertheless believed that any misunderstandings "would have been easily remedied" if only the government had asked him to explain his motivations, which he then provided to Grant. Repeating his assertion that he followed Grant's lead when he "stipulated that the officers and men of Lee's army should not be molested at their homes so long as they obeyed the laws at the place of their residence," Sherman explained his other surrender conditions in terms of military practicality rather than political or legal nuance. Sherman, for instance, insisted that no "action on our part in no manner recognizes for a moment the so-called Confederate Government, or makes us liable for its debts or acts," nor could any Southern state legislature act with legitimacy because the "laws and acts done by the several States during the period of rebellion are void because done without the oath prescribed by the Constitution of the United States." In the meantime, before the state government could be made legitimate, Sherman claimed the government had "a right to use any sort of machinery to produce military results, and it is the commonest thing for military commanders to use the civil Government in actual existence … as the very best possible means to produce … entire and complete submission to the lawful authority of the United States." Sherman further rejected the idea that he had absolved all Confederate leaders of responsibility for their wartime actions, instead affirming "that is for the judiciary, and … I will use my influence that rebels shall suffer all the personal punishment prescribed by law, as also the civil liabilities arising from their past acts." He closed his explanation with the primary rationalization that his actions had created a situation where "the rebel armies will disperse, and instead of dealing with six or seven States" the army would now only have to deal with dispersed cavalry bands.[74]

On April 24, Johnston received word from Davis that the Confederate President had approved Sherman's terms, but scarcely an hour later the message from Sherman announcing the Federal government's rejection of the terms and the suspension of the ceasefire arrived at his headquarters. Based upon Davis's continued desire to continue the war that he expressed in their last meeting, Johnston tried to preempt Davis by suggesting "We had better disband this small force to prevent devastation of the country." Davis rejected the idea, and, through orders issued by Secretary of War Breckinridge, instructed Johnston to maintain his army by withdrawing to a more secure location. Breckinridge, not as pessimistic as Johnston but not as optimistic as Davis, tried to suggest some means of salvaging the situation. Instead of surrendering his entire army, Breckinridge suggested that Johnston retreat with as much of his army as he thought possible. "Can you not bring off the cavalry and all of the men you can mount from transportation and other animals, with some light field pieces?" Breckinridge inquired. "Such a force could march away from Sherman and be strong enough to encounter anything between us and the Southwest. If this course be possible, carry it out and telegraph your intended route." The remaining Confederate troops could accept Sherman's terms or "they might still save their small-arms and find their way to some appointed rendezvous."[75] Johnston, after conferring with Beauregard and his senior commanders, offered the opinion that "We have to save the people, spare the blood of the army, and save the high civil functionaries. Your plan, I think, can only do the last." Instead, Johnston suggested that Breckinridge assign some troops to escort President Davis to a place of safety while he negotiated with Sherman "to prevent invasion" and needless bloodshed. Johnston, unwilling to disobey a direct order from the President but equally disinclined to fight any more battles, adopted a middle-ground to seek new options. He ordered his commanders to be prepared to move the army toward Salisbury the following morning while at the same time he replied to Sherman requesting another meeting that might lead to revised terms that both governments could accept, if Sherman was inclined to "agree to other conditions." Sherman quickly replied that he would meet with Johnston at the same site as their earlier meetings the following day. Rather than consult Breckinridge any further, Johnston simply informed the Secretary of War that "I have proposed to General Sherman military negotiations in regard to this army." In his postwar memoir, Johnston justified his unilateral decision to negotiate on the plain fact "that it would be a great crime to prolong the war."[76]

Sherman again met with Johnston at Durham Station. Grant, despite deciding to remain in Raleigh for the time being, did not attend. The Union troops were by that time aware of his presence, but the Confederates remained uninformed. Johnston came alone, as Breckinridge had rejoined Davis's entourage, but Sherman arrived with some of his corps commanders, including Maj. Gen. John Schofield, who joined Sherman and Johnston in their discussion while the other generals waited outside. Why Schofield was accorded this privilege is uncertain, but, as someone whom Grant seemed to favor, he was possibly there as Grant's proxy. When Johnston arrived, Sherman, perhaps sensing from Grant the hostility that his rejected terms had created in Washington, offered only the terms extended to Lee. Johnston, aware that he could yet move his army away, replied that those terms were not acceptable and requested further guarantees and concessions, especially regarding the safety of his men after they returned home. Sherman agreed that Johnston's requests were not excessive, but, considering the attitude in Washington, doubted that the administration would approve such provisions if included in the revised terms. Schofield offered a solution. The two generals, Schofield suggested, should draft a formal surrender document using the terms given to Lee, but also issue a further document that addressed Johnston's concerns. The formal surrender document would placate the Johnson administration while the secondary document served merely as the instrument to carry out the formal surrender. Both generals agreed to the proposed solution, and, after Schofield prepared a draft, sent the revised terms to Raleigh for Grant's approval. He did so immediately, somewhat to the surprise of Johnston who had no idea Grant was so close.[77]

The main draft of the surrender terms was not significantly different from that accepted by Lee, but the terms did have some additional items that reflected the consequences of Lee's surrender and the reality facing Johnston's troops, especially those from distant states. Johnston had broached the subject of additional terms the previous day when, in a note to Sherman, he wrote how the "disbanding of General Lee's army has afflicted this country with numerous bands having no means of subsistence but robbery, a knowledge of which would, I am sure, induce you to agree to other conditions."[78] The other conditions, which Sherman consented to and Grant approved, not only addressed the need to get Johnston's troops to their homes as quickly as possible to avoid the pillaging that Lee's troops had committed but also allowed them to maintain civil order as well. Unlike the terms granted to Lee, the agreement between Sherman and Johnston allowed the Confederates to "retain their transportation" and use their wagons to transport the soldiers home instead of surrendering them as military property, with artillery horses pressed into service to pull the wagons if necessary rather than surrender them as a military asset. An element from Sherman's original proposal was also included in that "Each brigade or separate body to retain a number of arms equal to one-fifth of its effective total, which, when the troops reach their homes, will be received by the local authorities for public purposes." Suitably armed, the Confederate troops could suppress criminal activity while they marched home and, once accumulated in the state arsenals, the state governments could also use the arms to enforce law and order, an admission that not only was disorder the norm in many parts of the South but that the Union Army could not be everywhere to impose control. To promote the acceptance of the terms, Johnston himself accepted the first parole form.[79] On the same day, Secretary of War Breckinridge inadvertently contributed to Johnston's surrender when he ordered that surplus officers with no troops to command go home, as well as soldiers from Maryland now that their home state was deep within enemy territory. Whether Breckinridge was simply performing some administrative tidying, trying to allow some of Johnston's officers to escape the terms of the surrender, or simply accepting the inevitable is unknown, but the order added to the impression that the Confederate Army was soon to be no more.[80] Sherman did his best to promote the idea. He assigned Schofield the task of overseeing the paroling of Johnston's men, who issued a public statement that "for us the war is ended, and it is hoped that peace will soon be restored throughout our country." To further the peace, Schofield promised that "All good and peaceable citizens will be protected and treated with kindness" and "All who are peaceably disposed are invited to return to their homes and resume their industrial pursuits." Schofield further offered to temporarily loan from the quartermaster's department animals and wagons to those who needed them, as well as food for the needy from the commissary department. Lastly, Schofield promised restraint by his troops, but warned "those who disturb the peace or violate the laws will be punished with the severity of martial law." He closed with the declaration that "Between the Government of the United States and the people of North Carolina there is peace."[81]

****

Believing that he had successfully resolved the situation caused by Sherman's initial terms, Grant telegraphed Stanton that Johnston, in negotiation with Sherman and not himself, had signed a surrender document "on the basis agreed upon between Lee and myself for the Army of Northern Virginia."[82] Grant's mission was, from his estimation, a success. He had revoked the excessive terms initially offered by Sherman and retained the peace that Sherman and Johnston had reached, all without embarrassing his chief subordinate.

Despite Grant's best efforts to put the situation right, Stanton seemed determined to cast Sherman in the worst possible light and provoke further tensions. "Your dispatched received," Stanton replied to Grant's note, further agitating the situation by reporting that the "arrangement between Sherman and Johnston meets with universal disapprobation. No one of any class or shade of opinion approves it. I have not known as much surprise and discontent at anything that has happened during the war. ... The hope of the country is that you may repair the misfortune occasioned by Sherman's negotiations."[83] If Grant thought he had defused a potentially embarrassing situation, he was quite wrong. The national media had become aware of Sherman's controversial original terms to Johnston and inflamed public opinion against Sherman. To make matters worse, an enterprising journalist did not break the story, but rather the leak came from the Secretary of War himself.

Chapter 4

"The Tinkering of Politicians": The Consequences of Peace in the Carolinas

I t goes without saying that the assassination of Abraham Lincoln had a profound effect on national events as the Civil War ended. Besides the regret that Lincoln died just as the nation had achieved victory in its long crisis, citizens mourned the loss of a political figure who had become a symbol of everything the Union sought to preserve. With the surrender of the Confederate armies still incomplete, many Northerners wondered how the assassination might affect the outcome of other possible surrenders, as a war that seemed won only days ago now appeared less certain. From a political perspective, the President's death placed his administration's policies in jeopardy. Postwar Reconstruction plans were now in the hands of his Vice President, Andrew Johnson, a Tennessee Unionist and former slave owner, who did not share Lincoln's enlightened view regarding African Americans. Members of Congress who disagreed with Lincoln's objectives, especially his expansion of executive authority, saw the opportunity to redress political imbalances.

The most immediate effect, however, were efforts by the Secretary of War, Edwin Stanton, to undermine Sherman's role in achieving peace with Johnston. Already an influential member of Lincoln's Cabinet since his appointment to the post in 1862 (replacing the ineffectual Simon Cameron),

Stanton had also served in the previous administration of James Buchanan as Attorney General. Capably directing the Union war effort under Lincoln's direction, Stanton found himself, upon Lincoln's death, as the most powerful man in Washington. With Andrew Johnson concentrated upon learning the obligations of his new position and Secretary of State William Seward incapacitated by injuries inflicted by a would-be assassin, Stanton seized the opportunity to influence Johnson's decision-making by becoming his primary advisor, directing the prosecution of Lincoln's murderers, and formulating policies relative to postwar Reconstruction policy. In this capacity, Stanton objected to the peace terms agreed upon by Sherman and Johnston in North Carolina. Unaware of Lincoln's directives at City Point, Stanton objected to Sherman's negotiations without direct political oversight, and furthermore resented the possibility that a successful outcome might enhance Sherman's standing with the public. The combination of events—the paranoia in Washington after Lincoln's assassination, Stanton's political standing, and the uncertainty about who directed postwar policy—all combined to lead Stanton to the conclusion that General Sherman needed to be reminded who was in charge.

****

While Grant was still making his way to North Carolina, Stanton, seeking to undermine the popular Sherman by controlling the discourse on the surrender controversy, arranged to have the list of objections to Sherman's terms that he had presented at the Cabinet meeting leaked to the Northern newspapers. By all evidence, Stanton took this action without consulting President Johnson first, as Johnson, when he met with Sherman in person for the first time, assured him that he was not aware of Stanton's actions until reading the newspapers himself. Johnson was likely trying to separate himself from any controversy over the Secretary's actions, but such a unilateral move by Stanton was not out of character. Grant later described the Secretary as someone who "felt no hesitation in assuming the functions of the executive, or in acting without advising with him," while at the same time constantly looking over Grant's shoulder because of his "natural disposition to assume all power and control in all matters that he had anything whatever to do with."[1]

In this targeted piece of justification, Stanton listed nine specific reasons why he rejected the original terms arranged between Sherman and Johnston. The note generated an effusion of journalistic outrage at what Sherman had done. The *New York Herald* characterized Sherman's agreement as a "virtual surrender," and claimed that the general negotiated as if he was "the chief officer of the United States government." The editor pressed Sherman to obtain the "capture or satisfactory surrender of Johnston's army" as the only means to "repair the single but stupendous mistake" that threatened to "overshadow his glorious reputation."[2] The *Philadelphia Inquirer* openly accused Sherman of being "willing to give up all for which the country has been fighting for four years" and "when the soldiers understand the favor which was to have been extended to the Rebels, they will be more indignant than civilians." The editor closed with the claim that "Sherman has sealed his fate," and then questioned, who would "be willing to trust him now?"[3] Other newspapers, while opposed to Sherman's terms, at least gave him the benefit of the doubt. A Detroit newspaper believed that Sherman, acting in the "spirit of magnanimity [that] was the prevailed feeling in the North" after the surrender of Lee, "thought that his course was justifiable." Unfortunately for Sherman, the newspaper admitted that "He is evidently more of a soldier than statesman," and "his far abler political adversaries" fooled him into offering "extremely lenient" terms. Rather than castigate Sherman, however, the editors asserted "The error of Gen. Sherman was on the right side, and reveals his character as a generous and humane soldier, anxious to stop the slaughter."[4]

The public debate over Sherman's actions was intense, even in his native Ohio. In Cincinnati, the *Enquirer* believed that Sherman acted under the lure of political office, claiming "he has the White House on the brain." The editor further predicted that "General Sherman will be relieved by General Grant, and be required to answer for his assumed offense before a Military Court."[5] The editor of the *Cincinnati Gazette* believed Sherman's actions to be more treasonous than ambitious, calling the agreement "a double disgrace" and an "act of insubordination." The editor further demanded that the government remove Sherman from command, asserting that "His extreme vanity has ruined him; and he must now go where so many have gone before—to the shelf. He has proven himself a … dangerous man, and one in whose hands power cannot safely be trusted. … He can do no good in the army. He can do no harm out of it."[6] The editor of the *Cincinnati Daily Commercial*, however, took umbrage with this interpretation. "We do not think it becomes any friend of the country to assume hastily that he is a ruined man, and to exult in his fall," he wrote, reminding his readers that Sherman "has a military man's contempt for all the details of politics and the tinkering of politicians." Reiterating that "a man may be one the best generals in the army without having been 'educated up' in politics," the editor failed to see any malevolence in Sherman's original terms, pointing out that "all the rebel armies would have been disbanded, but ours would not." He further discounted the threat posed by Confederate weapons stored in state arsenals because "the State capitals of North Carolina, Virginia, Kentucky, Tennessee, Missouri, Arkansas, and Louisiana are in our possession and that arms deposited therein would have been in our hands." Although perhaps not the ideal means of achieving peace, the editor observed that "Sherman's treaty would have closed the war entirely in our favor."[7]

Within days, however, the tone of accusations against Sherman became more muted and reasonable as the general's supporters rallied to his defense and the search for Lincoln's killers crowded Sherman from the headlines. Many editors became more judicious when it became evident that Sherman's negotiations were not the grave political crime they had first charged. Instead of Sherman trying to "play the part of Cromwell, and carve his way to power by the sword," the editor of the *Brooklyn Daily Eagle* wrote in his defense, "if he had made up his mind to depose the President and overthrow the government, why did he send his plan to Washington for concurrence? It is a queer sort of treason that expects a voluntary accomplice in the very administration which it seeks to oust." In addition, "If Sherman thought of joining the rebels, he selected an odd time for it. … At this state of the war he could not be a traitor without being also an idiot."[8] Even the *New York Herald* became more sensible in its comments regarding Sherman, reporting that while "Sherman has undoubtedly failed in his attempt to assume the role of a diplomat, his reputation as a great, gifted, and patriotic general is as untarnished as ever." Its editors even engaged in a bit of self-reflection, commenting that "It is not a little singular that, after four years of a tremendous civil war ... the partisan press has not risen to the dignity of the crisis and still goes maundering along in the old, squabbling, impertinent, reckless, blundering way?"[9] Some editors even speculated that a backlash might cost Stanton his job, leaving one editor to report "Secretary Stanton's friends indignantly deny that he will leave the Cabinet."[10]

The one group who remained fiercely loyal to Sherman throughout the tumult were Sherman's troops, who almost universally supported their commander. "We know that most of the editors is composed of a pack of blowpipes and cowards," Private Frederick Marion strongly asserted. "Sherman is pure in the eyes of his army and it will not do for any citizen to run him down before us."[11] Maj. Gen. Henry Slocum observed a group of soldiers torching a wagon, and, upon dispatching an officer to investigate, learned that it contained "New York papers for sale to the soldiers ... filled with the vilest abuse of General Sherman."[12] Some soldiers hinted at even more dire consequences. "They had better look a little out or they will have General Sherman's Army to reckon," an Indiana private wrote regarding the press. "We don't propose to have our General called such names, 'Sherman a Traitor!' The idea!"[13] The press coverage also incensed the soldiers because, in smearing Sherman's achievements, newspapers redefined his campaigns as little more than pillaging expeditions, which made his troops equally culpable in any illegal or improper behavior. "The indignation of the army rose to such a pitch that it would have taken but a word and the army had marched to Washington and cleaned out the contemptible, cowardly brood," one outraged soldier wrote. "The army felt the insult more keenly than General Sherman himself because the Copperhead papers were again loud in denouncing Sherman's army as a horde of robbers and cutthroats, commanded and led by a heartless brute."[14]

The news of the controversy unleashed by Stanton's leak took several days to reach North Carolina. When the newspapers revealed Stanton's attack on his actions, Sherman flew into a towering rage. One of his generals observed Sherman pacing "like a caged lion" as he described Stanton as a "mean, scheming, vindictive politician" seemingly intent to "rob military men of credit earned by exposing their lives in the service of their country" while aided by his oldest nemesis, the press, whom he labeled the "engine of vilification." The officers stood mostly quiet as Sherman "unbosomed himself with an eloquence of furious invective" that might have convinced a "foreigner unacquainted with the American character … that here was the beginning of a mutiny of a victorious general against his government."[15] Sherman calmed down enough to write a letter to Grant, a note that laid out Sherman's position with clear evidence but also conveyed the simmering rage of its writer. Sherman reiterated that it was Stanton, not himself, who had acted in a rash and uninformed manner by rejecting his initial surrender terms without asking for the reasoning behind them. Claiming that "my rank, if not past services, entitled me at least to the respect of keeping secret what was known to none but the cabinet," Sherman accused Stanton of impugning his character. Sherman repeated that he "never saw or had furnished me a copy of President Lincoln's dispatch to you of the 3rd of March" that ordered Grant to avoid discussion with the Confederates of anything other than military matters. Nor, Sherman reminded, had he received an "official hint of a plan of reconstruction" that would have defined what terms the government allowed him to offer. Quite the opposite, Sherman pointed out that when President Johnson had disapproved the terms, he immediately moved to "compel the surrender of General Johnston's whole army on the same terms you prescribed to General Lee's army."

Sherman further defended his military decisions. Reminding Grant that, whereas he had Lee's army "surrounded and in your absolute power," Sherman had no full control of Johnston's force. Instead, he disposed his force so that Johnston's "escape was only possible in a disorganized shape," but did not press his advantage because he "did not wish to break General Johnston's army into bands of armed men." Sherman found it particularly disturbing that critics questioned his abilities after he had in the "last year, worked day and night, summer, and winter, for the cause and the Administration, and who have brought an army of 70,000 men in magnificent condition across a country deemed impassable." Sherman could not resist in indulging in a bit of righteous self-pity, closing the letter with a diatribe about how "non-combatants, men who sleep in comfort and security whilst we watch on the distant lines, are better able to judge than we poor soldiers, who rarely see a newspaper, hardly can hear from our families, or stop long enough to get our pay," but invited them to "follow my path, for they may see some things and hear some things that may disturb their philosophy." Sherman further requested that, "As Mr. Stanton's singular paper has been published I demand that this also be made public," and the letter appeared in the Northern newspapers soon thereafter.[16]

While his disgust for Stanton increased, Sherman discovered another perceived enemy. Aware of the controversy brewing in Washington, Major General Halleck informed Stanton that he had impulsively issued orders to his subordinates to "pay no regard to any truce or orders of General Sherman suspending hostilities." He further suggested that Stanton forward similar orders to other commanders so they could "take measures to intercept the rebel chiefs and their plunder" which Halleck, per rumors he had heard in Richmond, estimated at "six to thirteen millions."[17] Sherman was in Hilton Head, South Carolina, conferring with Rear Admiral John Dahlgren when newspapers informed him of Halleck's inopportune orders. Dahlgren noted that Sherman "let loose" on Halleck, impugning his bravery by claiming he "had not been under fire once." Dahlgren sympathized with Sherman, reminding him that it was not in his interest to add more enemies because "Halleck's cold blood would be more than a match for Sherman's fiery humor" in political circles. Dahlgren himself had received criticism when an earlier naval assault on Charleston failed under his direction, so he recognized the uninformed howling of the press. "All the little dogs are loose on Sherman," Dahlgren recalled. "How they bark! He is a great sinner against the mass of respectable mediocrities."[18] Grant immediately countermanded Halleck's orders, but Sherman suffered another public insult. The best Grant could do was to try to pacify Sherman, suggesting he should wait before blasting Halleck as the entire situation was "a difference of opinion which time alone will decide who was right."[19] Regardless of Grant's advice, the act of repeating the rumors of a vast horde of gold in Davis's hands only moved to delegitimize Halleck's abilities in Sherman's eyes. In a note to a member of Grant's staff, Sherman declared the "idea of Jeff. Davis running about the country with tons of gold is ridiculous," considering the number of wagons required.[20]

Halleck, meanwhile, tried to repair his relationship with Sherman. "You have not had during this war … a warmer friend and admirer than myself,"

Halleck asserted, claiming he was merely "carrying out what I knew to be the wishes of the War Department" when he sent his inflammatory orders. Unable to "reconcile the friendly expressions" that Halleck had shown him earlier in the war with the "deadly malignity" of his recent orders, Sherman informed Halleck that he "cannot consent to the renewal of a friendship" against anyone who would support the "diabolical plot" against him. Sherman escalated the rivalry by advising Halleck that "I will march my army through Richmond quietly and in good order," but advised him to avoid drawing attention to himself because Sherman would not be responsible if "some of my old command" lashed out at him for the "public insult to a brother officer."[21] Halleck wisely remained out of sight as Sherman's troops passed through the city. "Halleck & others have hurled the anathemas against" Sherman, one of his men wrote to his wife "but he still towers above all … The soldiers under Sherman are jealous of his honor."[22]

****

While the generals, politicians, and journalists clashed over the propriety of Sherman's actions, troops in the field were acutely aware that their war was ending. Unlike the negotiations to surrender Lee's army, which unfolded quickly, Johnston's surrender took much longer, leaving Johnston's men several days to ponder and react to the surrender process. Confederate troops viewed the negotiations between Sherman and Johnston in a negative light. "There appears to be no doubt of the existence of an armistice between Johnston and Sherman," Captain John Dooley recorded. "They are trying to mollify our bitter discomfiture and crushing humiliation." An officer reported that, due to the negotiations, "Desertion every night is frightful."[23] Johnston knew of the reaction to his negotiations, noting how his discussion with Sherman "produced great uneasiness in the army" as soldiers did not want to become POWs, leading to, according to Johnston "not less than four thousand in the infantry and artillery, and almost as many from the cavalry" to desert.[24] Other officers, however, were ready to submit. Upon hearing that Sherman and Johnston were discussing peace terms, Brig. Gen. Laurence Baker, commanding North Carolina's Second Military District, offered to surrender his command before the final terms were even set. This elicited scorn from locals, who accused Baker of "running about the country in search of someone to surrender to."[25]

Once Confederate troops learned the final surrender terms, the reaction was a mix of relief and frustration. "The submission is entirely upon our part," an officer wrote disapprovingly, "but it is on much better terms than were expected."[26] Another officer reported that the enlisted men took the surrender much more personally. "Many expressed disgust and indignation when the surrender of the army was announced," he recorded. "An epidemic of drunkenness, gambling, and fighting prevailed while we were waiting for our final orders."[27] One of the unhappy soldiers, on the day Johnston signed the final surrender terms, recalled, "If crying would have done any good, we could have cried all night." Within days, however, Johnston's men had largely accepted their fate. "After turning in our guns, and getting our paroles, we feel relieved," the soldier wrote. "No more picket duty, no more guard duty, no more fighting, no more war. It is all over, and we are going home."[28] Union troops had an understandably different reaction to the surrender. Private George Childress noted, "tomorrow we are to go to the station to see Gen. Joe E. Johnston's Rebel Army surrender to Gen. Sherman."[29] When the news of Johnston's surrender became official, the Union men rejoiced. "Johnston's Army has surrendered to us," Private Charles Tanner wrote to his family. "You never saw men act like they did in your life when they heard of it. They was up all night last night," although Tanner was concerned about the soldiers' proclivity to fire their rifles into the air, creating a situation where Tanner believed "I had rather been on the skirmish line than in camp. I would not have been in half the danger."[30]

After the initial enthusiasm ebbed, Union soldiers, like those in the Confederate camps, recognized their fortune at surviving the war and recognized the common ground that enlisted men on both sides shared. Union Captain George Pepper observed how the respective reactions to the surrender changed when enlisted men began to mingle. "They came in the sense of enemies; they came, if need be, to kill and destroy," Pepper noted of the contact between the two forces, "Now they are friends—friends to protect both life and property—friends and brothers. ... Yesterday a demon; today an angel."[31]

Despite the agreement between Sherman and Johnston, not all soldiers felt bound by it and many tried to avoid becoming subject to the surrender terms. The issue first popped up at Appomattox, where several small cavalry units opted to leave before the surrender went into effect to avoid any surrender terms limiting their actions. Most notable was Fitzhugh Lee's cavalry brigade, who fled before Lee signed the surrender. His escape, however, was short lived. Although the cavalryman had "fond, though forlorn, hope that future operations were still in store" for his command, he soon understood the "impracticality of longer entertaining such hopes" and disbanded his command after receiving their paroles. Brig. Gen. Martin W. Gary, with two hundred cavalrymen, also passed through the lines and returned to his native South Carolina. Other officers, separated from Lee's command, who would otherwise have been covered in the surrender terms, chose to remain away rather than return for their paroles.[32] These instances were clearly attempts to avoid surrender, but the question became murkier regarding Col. John Mosby's command. Known as the "Gray Ghost" for his ability to strike at Union formations and disappear into the countryside, Mosby and his cavalry command had plagued the Union in northwest Virginia and the Shenandoah Valley. Although in proximity to Lee's Army of Northern Virginia, whether its surrender applied to Mosby was uncertain. Mosby led a partisan unit rather than formal army formation that, independent of Lee, answered to the War Department instead. In addition, Union forces did not surround Mosby's command and he had freedom of maneuver. Mosby requested a series of ceasefires to consult with his men and receive instructions from Jefferson Davis. Grant, tired of the delays, sent instructions that Mosby must surrender immediately or he would dispatch an entire corps of Union infantry to the area. Unwilling to see the widespread devastation of the region as Union troops hunted for him, Mosby instead chose to disband his troops rather than surrender, but it was a moot point. To avoid postwar persecution, the members of his band had to sign parole forms in the presence of a Union officer. Instead of surrendering together, Mosby's Rangers surrendered individually, including Mosby himself.[33]

Once it became clear that Johnston might surrender, some of his troops also took the opportunity to escape. Whereas Lee's negotiations were brief and his surrender sudden, Johnston and Sherman negotiated over several days, providing opportunity for evasion because, as Johnston later wrote,

"It was very commonly believed among the soldiers that there was to be a surrender, by which they would be prisoners of war, to which they were very averse."[34] Other soldiers, however, only used the threat of becoming a POW as a justification to desert. "Thousands under pretense of not being willing to remain to be surrendered," a Confederate officer reported, "stole mules … deserted their colors, endeavoring to get home." Officers, especially those who had resigned commissions in the antebellum army, were also concerned they might face accusations of violating their prewar military oaths.[35] Between April 19 and 24, Johnston estimated that nearly eight thousand Confederates deserted, taking with them "artillery horses and mules belonging to the baggage train" because, according to one officer, "The eagerness of the men to get to their homes now is beyond picture."[36] One such soldier was Private Henderson Deans of the Sixty-sixth North Carolina, who recalled that he escaped because "I had sworn that the Yankees would not ever take me prisoner, that I would die first." Deans's company commander, Capt. Jesse Williams, asked if any of his men wished to follow him up "the old Plank Road from Greensborough to Fayetteville" because he believed "we can get around Sherman's army and not one of us will be taken prisoner." Deans remembered that "I was on my feet so quick I did not know whether I was standing or sitting," and, after burying his "old Springfield rifle that I toted so many hundreds of miles," Deans and his friends "got to the Plank Road a little before sunset, turned down it to Fayetteville … all 7 got home safe."[37]

Once aware of the terms of surrender, senior cavalry officers Wade Hampton and Joseph Wheeler also tried to escape the surrender terms.[38] Johnston concluded that both generals were personally not subject to the surrender since they were not present at the time, but their troops were in the proximity of Bennet Place and therefore the surrender applied to them. Wheeler issued a farewell to his troops on April 29, and headed southeast through South Carolina and into Georgia. He could not elude the net of cavalry searching for Jefferson Davis, however, and Union troops arrested him east of Atlanta.[39] Hampton separately tried to reach Davis, but, in poor health, instead returned to his home in Yorkville, South Carolina.[40] His sudden disappearance led to rumors of his whereabouts, including a Northern reporter who claimed "Wade Hampton refused to be surrendered, and is reported to have been shot by Johnston in an altercation."[41]

With the negotiating done, all that remained was implementing the terms of the surrender. Unlike many commanders who kept their troops in the locale of the surrender on occupation duty, Sherman immediately withdrew the bulk of his troops. He had good reasons for doing so. As he indicated in his earlier letter to Grant, Sherman wanted to alleviate the government of the expense of surplus troops, as well as demonstrating his belief that the defeated Southerners would be loyal citizens that did not need a harsh occupation. Sherman, therefore, left in North Carolina only the X Corps under Schofield's command, a force "who were thought necessary to maintain law and order."[42] Schofield and a few supporting forces covered a large area. "Major General Schofield now commanding the center of Sherman's army, will be left in command of the whole middle district, from Virginia to the Savannah River, with his headquarters at Raleigh," a newspaper reporter informed his reader. "Brevet Major General [Judson] Kilpatrick, now commanding General Sherman's cavalry, will also remain to assist, holding his headquarters at Greensboro. These two Generals will together suppress banditti and promote order … and thus restore confidence in currency and enterprise."[43]

Before his departure, Sherman continued to work closely with Johnston to ensure a smooth demobilization of Confederate forces. "I have further instructed Gen. Schofield to facilitate, what you and I and all good men desire," Sherman informed Johnston, "the return to their homes of the officers and men composing your army." Sherman made further arrangements to release all the Confederate prisoners within his command and permit the resumption of commerce. There were, however, limits to Sherman's largess. Although stating his willingness "to risk my person and reputation … to heal the wounds made by the past war," an attitude that Sherman believed was shared by many in both armies, "there are some unthinking young men, who have no sense or experience, that, unless controlled, may embroil their neighbors" and cause local unrest. "If we are forced to deal with them," Sherman warned, "it must be with severity; but I hope they will be managed by the people of the South."[44] Sherman also issued orders to his subordinates that, wherever they may be, granted them the authority to accept Confederate paroles under the established surrender terms up to May 25 "on pain of being considered outlaws and treated accordingly."[45]

For his part, Johnston also worked to implement the surrender terms and urge others to comply as well. Besides spreading word about the ceasefire and subsequent cessation of hostilities, Johnston also informed state leaders of his decision to stop fighting. In a letter to Georgia Governor Joseph Brown, for instance, Johnston explained that the "disaster in Virginia, the capture by the enemy of all our workshops for the preparation of ammunition and repairing arms, the impossibility of recruiting our little army … or of supplying it except by robbing our own citizens," had led him to enter into "a military convention with General Sherman to terminate hostilities in North and South Carolina, Georgia, and Florida. I made this convention to spare the blood of the gallant little army committed to me, to prevent further sufferings of our people by the devastation and ruin inevitable from the marches of invading armies, and to avoid the crime of waging hopeless war."[46]

Under Schofield's supervision, the paroling of Johnston's men went smoothly. Per Sherman's orders, Schofield had the troops from the most distant states prepared for movement first, and Confederate troops from Arkansas, Louisiana, and Texas began to depart on May 3.[47] The rest began their journey home the following day. "Came to Salisbury today," Captain Samuel Foster wrote in his journal. "The Confederate Army will go to pieces here. The South Carolina and Georgia, Alabama and Mississippi troops will march on foot directly home. The Tennessee, Arkansas, and Texas troops will turn west from here and cross the Blue Ridge into East Tennessee, and there take the R.R. for Chattanooga and to Nashville, where we will take a steamboat for New Orleans." Texas troops continued by steamer to Galveston before making their way home by whatever means was available.[48] Although the organized return generally worked well and kept lawlessness to a minimum, some soldiers took their own path. "The papers were all arranged for our capitulation and we were to march home in regular order," Private John Curry of the Fortieth Alabama recalled. "[B]ut after the first day or two every man was his own commander and went his own way."[49] On May 4, Schofield reported to Sherman that the "paroling of Johnston's army and delivery of arms have been completed and his troops started south yesterday. The most of the North Carolina troops went home without waiting for their paroles. My paroling officers think the number paroled will amount to 30,000 [the actual number was 20,640]. I will make full reports as soon as practicable."[50] Among the senior officers who surrendered under the Sherman/Johnston agreement were two full generals (Johnston and Beauregard), one lieutenant general (D.H. Hill), eighteen major generals, and twenty-three brigadier generals.[51] Not included in this list was Brig. Gen. John Pemberton, the loser of Vicksburg and one of the superfluous generals in Johnston's command. He tried to join Davis's party, but failed to link up with him at Charlotte, North Carolina. Instead, he rejoined his family and awaited his chance to surrender.[52]

In sharp contrast to the lack of foresight at Appomattox, Johnston's demobilization was much more orderly. At Appomattox, Grant had achieved his goal of procuring Lee's surrender, but his terms contained little anticipation of future events or provided for controlling Lee's troops once they received their paroles. Even before Lee's formal surrender, his army was already starting to disintegrate. A Confederate officer in southern Virginia recorded "Stragglers from Lee's army are flowing by us in crowds. The army is completely disorganized and every one for himself is the sole idea," while in another portion "infantry skulking from their regiments, invalids, trumpeters, etc. The country is full of deserters."[53] When Davis was in Danville, an officer observed, "The first news we received of his [Lee's] surrender, came to us from the stream of fugitives which now came pressing into our lines at Danville. … It was, indeed, a rabble rout."[54] The situation did not improve after the surrender because the terms did not provide transportation for the Confederate troops to their homes, forcing them to make their own way the best they could. As Confederates troops walked home, they became, at best, a disciplinary problem, or, at worst, a criminal problem. Unregulated and unruly, the troops, some parolees but others deserters, took what they needed to survive without regard for civilian suffering or the niceties of military law. "Paroled rebel prisoners throughout the country are becoming very troublesome," a Tennessee correspondent informed his readers, and even ardent Confederate supporters wanted the Union to control the troublesome parolees. "We all think the presence of Federal troops would benefit this place, as all Southern rule is gone," a frightened woman wrote. "Scarcely a day passes without hearing of some outrage being committed by men calling themselves returned Confederates."[55]

Demobbed soldiers generally targeted military warehouses to feed themselves, but helped themselves to civilian property when no other source was available. A Georgia resident noted that troops heading home "are playing havoc with stock all through the country. The Texans are especially noted in this respect." Citing the long distance they had to travel to their home state, the Texans took horses from private stables and even "the buggies of quiet citizens on the square," leaving the woman to note that "everybody I know has had horses stolen or violently taken from him."[56] In a postwar memoir, a soldier whitewashed the mass theft by demobilized soldiers by admitting the pillaging of public property, but asserting that there "was little pillage of private property," and justifying the robbery because "A foot-sore and weary soldier might occasionally help himself to a stray horse or mule … but this was rare."[57] Civilians went to great lengths to protect themselves. A traveler passing through Louisiana had to take a circuitous route to cross the Ouachita River as "all the ferry boats … had been hidden or sunk to prevent the marauding soldiers with which the country was infested from crossing."[58] Besides causing problems for civilians on their route home, parolees from Lee's army also collected in places that Union authorities did not want them. Grant ordered Maj. Gen. Edward Ord, commanding the occupation of Richmond, to cease providing aid to paroled men from Lee's army, and inform them they must leave the city and "must get to their homes in their own way."[59]

Besides denying transportation, the surrender terms did not provide Lee's men with provisions, so soldiers had to beg, borrow, or steal to survive. Civilians still loyal to the cause were willing to help, but many were unable, as they had nothing for themselves.[60] "A great many soldiers are passing & calling," a resident of Patrick County, Virginia, wrote of parolees from Lee's army. "If you were here you would think they would eat me out of house & home but I had paid my gov. taxes in corn, so I told them they were eating their own provisions."[61] As parolees reached North Carolina, they requested supplies from Johnston's quartermasters, but, when refused, took what they wanted, especially horses and mules for transport. "Stragglers made an effort to get our mules last night, but failed," an officer wrote of rustlers from Lee's army, "after a few shots from our Irish guards who are sleeping on this campaign with one eye open."[62] Everywhere that Lee's disbanded army went, disruption and disillusionment appeared. A Confederate officer trying to return to Richmond found "the disbanded army are running wild over the country, stealing, plundering, murdering, and seizing trains of car wherever they can find them."[63] As Lee's men reached their home states, the thievery and pillaging continued. In Washington, Georgia, soldiers from Lee's army stole food and confiscated horses and mules for transport.[64] When Jefferson Davis, fleeing from Union pursuit, asked a group of demobilized soldiers near Abbeville, South Carolina, to assist him in restoring order, he was rudely rebuffed by a Confederate private who informed him that "Our lives are just as precious to us as yours is to you. The war is over and we are going home."[65]

Instead of leaving the demobilization to his subordinates, Johnston personally stayed until all his men left their encampments, distributed $54,000 in silver coins (less than two dollars per man), and provided supplies, such as cloth and yarn, that they could use to barter.[66] Sherman instructed his commissary offices to provide the Confederates with ten-days' rations for twenty-five thousand Confederate troops.[67] It was not just a kind gesture. Johnston had counted on the supplies in the remaining Confederate depots to feed his troops on their way home, but mixed mobs had pillaged the commissary stores along the intended routes home.[68] To move the rations and provide for supplies in future days, Johnston distributed the remaining army wagons and ambulances to each brigade.[69] To avoid clogging the roads and overwhelming the local resources, Johnston's men assembled at Salisbury, North Carolina before moving home by way of Morgantown, North Carolina, and Abbeville and Newberry, South Carolina.[70] To facilitate their transit, Johnston's staff officers "concluded to get ahead of the disbanded army on the way home, so we could find forage for man and beast."[71] In many places, however, the shattered infrastructure of the country made progress difficult. Confederate engineers tried to maintain pontoon bridges across the demobilization routes, but an officer reported, "a large number of mules of pontoon train have been stolen," delaying the crossing of several rivers.[72]

Despite his efforts, however, the demobilization in North Carolina was not without its difficulties. Officers could barely contain their soldiers as men wandered out of camp, foraged for alcohol, and recklessly gambled away their now-useless Confederate notes.[73] Other troops opted not to wait. "A large number of them did not wait for their paroles," a correspondent noticed, "but started off as soon as they learned of the capitulation, and are now engaged in pillaging and robbing the destitute people."[74] Nearby cities, like Beaufort, attracted former Confederate troops, where a Union soldier observed, "The town is utterly full of rebel soldiers today, paroled prisoners from the rebel armies" and "some are tight, of course, and boisterous."[75] Other troops were more than just rowdy. "We hear that our soldiers are doing badly as they go through South Carolina and Georgia," an officer lamented. "The report is that they are robbing everything as they go, and the people cannot help themselves."[76] Other issues also prevented the timely return of many soldiers. While the Union provided basic transport, most Confederate soldiers had to walk at least some distance because of the shattered railroad system. The continuing war west of the Mississippi delayed other returning soldiers. Attempting to return home, a Texan heard rumors that paroled soldiers were to be "put in the Penitentiary until the troops west of the Miss[issippi River] are all surrendered." The rumors were unfounded, but it prompted the man to suggest that instead of merely returning home, "every man here would take his rifle and march across there and assist the Yanks in putting them down," seeing little use in resistance "after the armies on this side have surrendered."[77]

Union efforts, whether intentional or not, aided the relative success of the demobilization, including efforts to avoid humiliating their defeated foe. Officers set the example when, as the demobilized armies prepared to depart, former friends took the chance to reacquaint themselves and adversaries met on more friendly terms. During the surrender negotiations, William Hardee and John Schofield struck up a conversation about life in the antebellum army, seeking a common ground of discussion.[78] Nearby, when Union troops apprehended Brig. Gen. James G. Martin and his aide for a violation of the general truce, Union Brig. Gen. William Palmer apologized to Martin, "Regretting that your brother officer and yourself should be placed in this delicate situation," before releasing him.[79] Once peace arrived, a South Carolina soldier wrote with relief that "The terms of surrender were very liberal and as yet we have had none of the Yankee's bravado of triumph," while another soldier noted in his diary that the Union troops did not celebrate their victory and reported he had been "treated very kindly."[80] However, not all Confederates were ready to embrace the peace. A reporter talking to soldiers recently paroled from Johnston's army observed, "As the rebel troops moved off, the prevailing sentiment among them was 'We are overpowered, but not subdued.' Remarks such as these were quite common, in doleful chorus: 'I hate the sight of a Yankee … Before I'd let a Yankee marry a sister of mine, I'd kill her.'"[81]

****

The process to arrange a surrender for Johnston's army was finally over, but the debate over the correctness of Sherman's attitudes continued for a long time. Historians have generally shared Stanton's view that Sherman intruded into the political sphere where he did not belong, reiterating the position that Grant took in his later memoirs when he criticized Sherman because he took the "question of Reconstruction out of the hands of president and Congress."[82] In a later biography of Stanton, supporters of the Secretary of War claimed that the initial "agreement, far from being a mere military convention terminating hostilities, was a virtual treaty of peace. It recognized the legality of the insurrectionary state governments, promised immunity to all persons who had taken part in the rebellion, and permitted the Confederate troops to deposit their arms in their respective state arsenals, thus providing Southern state governments with a supply of war material."[83] Others assert that Sherman was out of his element, too much an amateur in the way of diplomacy to see that he had exceeded his authority and "too pleased with his military success to imagine any opposition to his agreement."[84]

Critics, however, ignore many elements that shaped not only the original surrender terms but also Sherman's belief in what he could accomplish in his meetings with Johnston. First, no evidence exists that Sherman was aware of the May 3 note from Lincoln to Grant forbidding generals from any discussions with the Confederates other than that of a military nature. That left Sherman to base his actions upon the City Point discussions and Lincoln's broad instructions regarding a Confederate surrender. Also, the relative military positions of Sherman and Johnston were quite different from those of Grant and Lee, meaning there was no guarantee that Johnston would accept the Lee/Grant terms because he could still maneuver away. Unlike Lee, Johnston was in consultation with Davis, meaning Sherman had to construct surrender terms that satisfied not only Johnston but Davis as well. Next, Stanton castigated Sherman for involving himself in political affairs, but ignored the common intermeshing of military and political matters, a situation that Stanton himself often created, including with Sherman. Lastly, while Stanton railed about the possible effect of Sherman's initial terms, what Sherman offered was much in line with Lincoln's already-stated Reconstruction policy and the eventual Union process to demobilize its own army.

In their negative assessments, critics of Sherman generally take Stanton's critique of the original terms at face value, but Stanton's charges against Sherman are not necessarily valid. On the credible side of Stanton's leaked statement to the press, he rejected the terms because "It was an exercise of authority not vested in Gen. Sherman, and … he had no authority to enter into any such arrangement." The justification, however, was not entirely accurate, because the government had not provided clear instructions if surrender negotiation occurred beyond Lincoln's City Point instructions. Nor did the government provide approved negotiators, such as James Polk did during the Mexican War. If Polk could send a negotiator more than 2,000 miles to represent his interests, Lincoln could certainly send one three hundred miles to Sherman.[85] Other justifications that Stanton listed reflected the state of over-reaction present in Washington. Stanton accused Sherman of drafting an agreement that would "reestablish the rebel State governments," which might recreate their armies to "conquer and subdue the loyal States." Stanton claimed the terms provided a "ground of responsibility by the Federal Government to pay the rebel debt," while at the same time putting into "dispute the existence of loyal State Governments." Most damningly, Stanton accused Sherman of offering terms that could not create a "true and lasting peace, but relieved rebels from the pressure of our victories and left them in condition to renew their effort to overthrow the United States Government."[86]

Stanton's reasoning, however, was badly flawed. First, Stanton was fully aware that Sherman's agreement to retain the state governments was necessary to prevent civil anarchy throughout the South, an event more likely to rekindle violent conflict than the state arsenals warehousing former Confederate weapons. The possible redemption of Confederate debts was purely speculation on Stanton's part, as the Sherman/Johnston agreement makes no mention of it. Stanton also falsely believed that the surrender could usurp federal and Constitutional legislation, such as the admission of West Virginia, the Emancipation Proclamation, and the XIII Amendment. Sherman did not press the slavery issue with Johnston because he later claimed that the Confederate general agreed with him that slavery, as an institution, was dead. Lastly, the claim that the terms would not have provided a lasting peace was purely conjecture on Stanton's part, whereas Sherman was fully aware of the weaknesses of the Confederate military and their inability to renew the war against the Union at any time in the foreseeable future.

Based on his claim that Sherman usurped the authority of the government, Stanton had legitimate right to challenge the general's decisions. At the same time, however, Stanton attacked the credibility, patriotism, and even loyalty of one of the Union's most prominent generals. Had Stanton allowed Grant to defuse the situation in a discreet manner, the whole affair would likely not have gained much public attention. By dragging the matter into the press, however, Stanton created a public firestorm that damaged the reputations of both Sherman and himself.

Stanton's reaction to Sherman's negotiations is surprising because, as a political process, warfare required commanders to engage in activities far beyond purely military considerations. The most notable was example Maj. Gen. Nathanial Banks's dual role as commander of the Department of the Gulf and military governor of Louisiana. A prominent antebellum politician, Banks promoted Unionist candidates for political office and conducted local elections with the aim of restoring a loyal Louisiana to the Union.[87] Banks was the most prominent political general engaged in civic activities in occupied regions, but not the only one. In occupied Tennessee, Maj. Gen. George Thomas assumed significant powers over local political and economic policy.[88] In Missouri and Arkansas, Maj. Gen. John Pope allowed Gov. Thomas Fletcher of Missouri to withdraw provost marshals from contested areas of the state in favor of local law enforcement, relax restrictions on commerce, and reward those who demonstrated their support for the Union cause.[89] In the case of Sherman, Stanton's shock that the general would engage in political activity was at odds with the fact that Stanton himself dragged Sherman into political situations because he perceived in Sherman someone not in alignment with administration goals. Sherman, for instance, was the only senior commander who did not appoint provost marshals to duties other than those of a military nature, an inaction that challenged Stanton's plan to use the occupying army and its provost marshals to regulate the occupied Confederacy.[90] After Sherman captured Savannah, Stanton took the opportunity to visit Sherman and measure his adherence to government policy, including abolitionism. During the visit, Sherman and Stanton discussed issues ranging from the relocation of freed slaves to the readmission of states under Lincoln's Reconstruction plan.[91] Both men believed they understood each other better after the meetings, but both were also still wary. Sherman resented being involved in discussions that implied he should make military plans relative to their effect on the former slaves. "If it be insisted that I shall so conduct my operations that the negro alone is consulted," Sherman complained, "I will be defeated."[92]

Stanton's charge that Sherman acted beyond the will of the government is also false because Sherman's actions coincided with past actions by the Lincoln administration and future actions by the Union Army. Although he did not mention it in the defense of his actions, Sherman might have had Lincoln's plan for Reconstruction in mind when negotiating with Johnston. Sherman was aware of Lincoln's plan for the reintegration of the South as described in the President's Proclamation of Amnesty and Reconstruction issued in December 1863. Lincoln planned to Reconstruct the country by reestablishing the prewar political system as quickly as possible, and pushed for the rapid readmission of the Southern states to the Union with the corresponding reallocation of full political rights and protection of property, minus slavery. Sherman's original terms with Johnston followed the goals of Lincoln's Proclamation of Amnesty very closely in providing a means for states to quickly rejoin the Union while protecting the property and political rights of those willing to pledge their loyalty.[93]

Sherman's terms also matched actions that the government would soon apply to the Union Army. One of the most criticized parts of Sherman's plan was the process by which the Confederate troops demobilized themselves by marching home and depositing their weapons in their respective state arsenals. Sherman realized the Southern state governments might need the weapons to suppress guerillas and impose order. His critics, however, believed that Sherman had allowed the Confederates to retain the potential for future aggression. The assessments of Sherman's actions, however, are unfounded on two points. First, the paroled Confederates were not prisoners of war and Sherman could not legally hold them. Second, the Union Army itself eventually followed a demobilization pattern like the one Sherman proposed for Johnston's troops. After assembling in central locations in the field, Union regiments moved via transport provided by the Quartermaster Corps to the location in their respective states where the Army first accepted them into service. Once there, the soldiers turned in their weapons for storage in the state arsenal, received their final pay and discharges, and went home.[94]

Besides these unsubstantiated charges, other more personal reasons existed for Stanton's actions. Several historians have accused Stanton of viewing Sherman as a potential political rival that the Democrats might forward as a presidential candidate who agreed with their goal of limited postwar Reconstruction. Moreover, if Sherman's negotiations led to a final Confederate surrender, then his prominence in the public mind would be even greater than it already was. Considering Sherman's well-known antipathy to anything resembling politics, such a concern was far-fetched. Another politically oriented theory is that Stanton's reaction was a manifestation of his political outlook and opportunities. William Marvel suggests that Stanton, whose political beliefs had evolved to become more in line with the Radicals in Congress, was worried that Sherman's lenient inclination toward the South clashed with the harsher retribution proposed by the Radicals with whom he shared a common stance.[95]

Another very real possibility was that Stanton simply overreacted to the Lincoln assassination, which made him inclined to see conspiracies everywhere. Stanton's critics commented on his temperament. Maj. Gen. Lew Wallace described Stanton as "cold, sharp, blunt" and in a "state of incessant irritability" that prevented him from listening to "argument or appeal, or to be amiable and courteous."[96] Others were also unflattering in their description of Stanton's personality and abilities, writing that in the "harrowing crisis" after Lincoln's death "the reins of government dropped into the hands of the Secretary of War; and a pilot more unfit to ride the whirlwind and direct the storm than Edwin M. Stanton could not have been found." Critics acknowledged that Stanton "never wanted for energy," but recalled that "in moments of storm and stress he was apt to lose his head" and instead of waiting for "real facts of a case; he would boil over with rage whenever the course of affairs did not run to his liking."[97] Subsequent historians have not altered their assessment of Stanton's persona, with one describing Stanton as "an excitable man given to panicking under stress, and events of the last week had pushed him to the breaking point."[98] The sense of over-reaction in Washington was clearly evident. When Sherman arrived in Washington on May 12 to consult with Grant he found "strong military guards around his house, as well as all the houses occupied by the cabinet and by the principal officers of Government; and a sense of insecurity pervaded Washington, for which no reason existed." Weeks after the assassination, Maj. Gen. August Kautz, one of the officers appointed to try the conspirators accused of killing Lincoln, told a friend that "Stanton had directed that each member of the Court be accompanied by an escort to and from the Court indicating that the Court might be assassinated."[99]

Given that Stanton was an excitable man, the crisis of the Lincoln assassination was the exact situation where he would be likely to overreact. He certainly had reason to be under stress. Lincoln was dead, Secretary of State William Seward was fortunate to escape his assassin, and Stanton believed one of the conspirators intended to target him as well. Such a high-strung personality as Stanton's could easily create the illusion of vast conspiracies at every turn. Stanton's volatile reaction to the assassination, however, isolated him from outside influences that might have allowed a more reasoned and rational view of developing events. Many of the critics of Sherman's original terms, both contemporary and subsequent, assert that Sherman did not recognize, or should have recognized, the climate that permeated Washington, DC, after the assassination and dealt with Johnston in a more accommodating manner. That presumes, however, that Sherman was aware of the charged atmosphere in Washington. Rather than concluding that the bubble of paranoia that surrounded Washington was the norm and that Sherman did not understand the situation there, a more reasonable interpretation might be that Stanton was the one out of touch with the military and political reality and that Sherman was the one acting, at least from his own perception, in a normal and constructive fashion. Had Stanton acted more rationally and responsibly, the resulting clash between himself and Sherman need not have occurred. Fortunately, the end of the war overshadowed the entire matter, as the simmering feud between Sherman and Stanton might have damaged the Union war effort. At the subsequent Grand Review of the Armies in Washington, Sherman made a public display of his contempt for Stanton. After leading his troops up Pennsylvania Avenue, Sherman entered the Presidential box. He warmly greeted Grant and President Johnson, but rebuffed Stanton's extended hand.[100] One of Sherman's soldiers witnessed the event, observing how "Secretary of War Stanton … advanced and offered his hand. But Sherman feigned not to see him." The soldier admitted that "At first sight this may seem a small, spitefull [sic] revenge," but pointed out that one had to consider "the mean, contemptible tricks Stanton had played on Sherman."[101]

****

While the nation debated the propriety of Sherman's actions, a key element of finally ending the Civil War occurred with almost an afterthought when Jefferson Davis's attempt to escape ended in Georgia. After isolating himself from events by leaving the surrender arrangements to Johnston, Davis continued southward, arriving in Charlotte on April 18. Upon hearing the news of Lincoln's assassination when he reached the city, Davis was emboldened to continue the nation's struggle.[102] The arrival of cavalry reinforcements also improved Davis's mood. Buoyed by the new troops, Davis reiterated his stubbornly held belief that "the struggle will attract all the scattered soldiers and daily, and rapidly, gather strength" to continue the war.[103] With his enthusiasm revived, Davis had mixed feelings when news arrived of the terms to which Sherman and Johnston had agreed. The terms, though very generous, did not address the demand for Confederate independence, so Davis asked each of his Cabinet members to submit written opinions on whether to accept the terms or not. The Cabinet members unanimously agreed that the best course was to accept the terms. Davis questioned if he had the authority to authorize a surrender, but his advisors reasoned "the President is the … commander-in-chief of its armies," and could "ratify the military convention under consideration, and execute its provisions relative to the disbandment of the army."[104] Davis accepted their advice and informed Johnston to accept Sherman's terms. Almost immediately, however, Davis received word that the Johnson Administration had rejected the first agreement.[105] On April 24, Davis was further shocked to learn that Johnston had surrendered to Sherman without consulting the government. "Johnston has surrendered … something unparalleled [and] without good reason or authority," one of the President's party recalled, "So we are falling to pieces."[106] Just as he had to abandon Danville after Lee's surrender, Davis now had to hasten his departure from Charlotte thanks to Johnston's surrender.[107]

After another slow journey, Davis and his group arrived in Abbeville, South Carolina, where the President convened another planning meeting. Hoping for more aggressive proposals than he received from Johnston and Beauregard, Davis instead received only more advice to end the war.[108] As Davis's journey continued into Georgia, he announced the temporary disbanding of the government with the intent of reforming it in the Trans-Mississippi Department.[109] To facilitate faster travel, Davis discharged most of his military escort and headed south with his small party and a ten-man escort.[110] Davis reunited with Varina soon thereafter, but the net was closing around them. Union cavalry seemed to be everywhere, with each soldier eager to collect the "seventy-five thousand dollar ransom on his head."[111] Cavalry finally cornered Davis near Irwinville, Georgia. The Fourth Michigan Cavalry, searching for "the fugitive rebel, Jefferson Davis," followed a tip and came upon Davis's encampment at dawn. Davis surrendered at gunpoint, and soon found himself incarcerated at Fort Monroe, Virginia.[112]

****

As the initial hysteria caused by Lincoln's assassination died down, so did the personality clash between General Sherman and Secretary Stanton, and their disagreement over the peace negotiations with Joseph Johnston caused no long-term damage to the reputation of either man. Both men had bigger obligations to attend to, and, with Grant acting as a buffer between them, managed to perform their duties without any significant difficulties.

Stanton was soon at odds with President Johnson over Reconstruction policy, and, when Johnson tried to fire him, found protection from the new Tenure of Office Act passed by Congress. Johnson defied the law and fired Stanton anyway, precipitating the first impeachment of an American president. Grant, when President, later nominated Stanton to the Supreme Court, but, stricken with asthma made worse by long work hours at the War Department, Stanton died in 1869 before he could take the bench.[113] Sherman garnered promotion thanks to Grant. Promoted to Lieutenant General in 1866, Sherman became the General of the Army, its ranking officer, when Grant became President in 1869. His relationship with Grant, however, never fully recovered from the difficulties generated during the controversy with Johnston, exemplified when Sherman moved his headquarters from Washington, DC, to St. Louis because Sherman resented the interference of the Secretaries of War appointed over him by Grant.[114] Sherman stayed at his post even after Grant left the Presidency, retiring from the Army in 1884, seven years before his death.

From the discord surrounding the Sherman/Johnston surrender controversy, some positive elements did emerge. There were still Confederate armies yet to surrender, and the troubled negotiations between Sherman and Johnston clarified what terms Union generals could extend to their Confederate counterparts. Senior officers limited their subsequent discussions to whether Confederate leaders were amenable to accepting the general terms extended to Lee by Grant, but with the additional allowances that Schofield suggested at Sherman and Johnston's last meeting. Besides clarifying the division between military and political authority when dealing with enemy political leaders, the controversy, as it turned out, made other surrenders easier to negotiate because the limitation on what Union generals could offer removed the need to discuss other issues that might have complicated the negotiations. By extending a single option, the clarified Union policy placed the decision of continuing the war on Confederate shoulders, a burden that other Confederate generals proved unwilling to bear.

Chapter 5

"Make the Enemy Pay Dearly in Blood": The Mobile Campaign

oseph Johnston was not the only Confederate general struggling to contain Union offensives in early 1865. In Alabama, two Union forces attacked Confederate Lt. Gen. Richard Taylor's Department of Alabama, Mississippi, and East Louisiana, each with enough troops to deal with Taylor's depleted army by themselves if the circumstances required. One advanced toward the city of Mobile, while the other, discussed in later chapters, was a cavalry force moving through the northern part of the state. Forced to fight two different types of battles in separate parts of Alabama, Taylor did his best, but circumstances were against him. As previously revealed, Taylor did not have the services of the Army of Tennessee and instead had only a relatively small but well-fortified contingent to defend Mobile and an outnumbered cavalry force to contend with the other Union incursion. The War Department expected Taylor to defend his entire department with these small assets, a task that Taylor privately believed was impossible. Taylor's pessimism was reinforced when, after asking for reinforcements, he received notice from Lee informing him that the "Army of Tennessee is now in North Carolina confronted by Sherman and I see no prospect of its return to Alabama within any given period." Moreover, considering the "difficulty of communication," Lee told Taylor that the "defense of your Department must be left entirely to your judgement," meaning Taylor was to bear the responsibility for subsequent actions.[1]

Alone against two large Union armies, Taylor could only divide his forces and hope that fortifications and skill could overcome the preponderance of enemy numbers. While supervising the defense of the department from afar, Taylor had to rely upon his subordinate commanders to deal with the Union invaders at the local level. In Mobile, that was Maj. Gen. Dabney Maury, an officer who elicited only lukewarm confidence from the garrison and citizenry because of his indecision and inability to predict Union intentions. Given months to prepare for an anticipated Union attack, Maury, despite a lack of funds and labor, made Mobile as impregnable as possible by constructing several daunting defensive positions on the most likely approach to the city. Maury could not complete his ambitions defensive plans, however, and, when Union forces arrived in overwhelming numbers, his fortifications proved imperfect, his men too few, and his chance for victory too thin.

****

By 1864, Mobile was the most important blockade-running port on the Gulf of Mexico, and the city was a major transport and industrial center, growing with the pace of the Industrial Revolution. From a small community of only fifteen hundred residents in the early nineteenth century, Mobile's population swelled to thirty thousand in 1860. Although many residents left to join the Confederate Army, the city's population increased during the war as refugees arrived from other locations, peaking at forty thousand by 1865. The city had significant railroad, lumber, shipbuilding, and transportation facilities, most notably the southern terminus of the Mobile & Ohio Railroad, and was establishing a diversified economy when the war began.[2] Grant had wanted to attack Mobile earlier in the war. In December 1863, at a planning conference in Nashville, Grant proposed a multi-part attack throughout the Western Theater for the following spring. Grant, supported by Sherman marching overland from Mississippi, proposed to attack Mobile while a separate force raided the valley of the Tombigbee River north of the city. With Mobile secured, Grant intended to use the city as a base to attack Atlanta. The plan came to naught, however, due to shifting events and Lincoln's lack of enthusiasm for the offensive.[3]

Gen. Dabney Maury (*Image courtesy of the Library of Congress*).

The job of defending Mobile fell to Maj. Gen. Dabney Maury. A West Point graduate, Maury had served during the Mexican War, where he lost an army after a severe wound. Assigned desk jobs, Maury was a staff officer in the New Mexico Territory when the war began, but resigned his commission in loyalty to his native Virginia. He served under Maj. Gen. Earl Van Dorn at the Battle of Pea Ridge and during the siege of Corinth before assuming command of the

District of the Gulf at Mobile in May 1863. His immediate task was to prepare the fortifications of his new command. Like most major Confederate cities at the start of the war, Mobile's residents demanded protection whether they were under immediate Union threat or not. The task of fortifying the city initially fell to Danville Leadbetter. An 1836 graduate of the U.S. Military Academy, Leadbetter had served in the Army on various projects around Mobile, and, when he left the army in 1857, remained to pursue various business opportunities. When the Civil War broke out, Leadbetter received a commission as a major in the Confederate Engineering Corps and orders to improve the Mobile defenses. The main issue with defending the city was where to place the primary defenses. The city itself was thirty miles north of the narrow inlet into the bay, forcing a debate over which area would receive priority. In the end, the need to defend the inlet to allow blockade-running determined that the main defense would be at the south end of the bay.[4]

The main defensive position at the inlet was Fort Morgan, on the tip of the peninsula that formed the entrance's eastern side. During the War of 1812, it was the site of Fort Bowyer, which twice came under British attack.[5] The assaults emphasized the importance of Mobile, and Congress authorized the construction of a masonry fortification which became operational in 1834. Fort Gaines, a smaller masonry fort, covered the western side of the inlet on Dauphin Island.[6] Despite his efforts to improve the defenses at Forts Morgan and Gaines, Leadbetter was pessimistic of their ability to stop a determined Union naval assault. The gap between the two forts was too wide for the guns to dominate, so Leadbetter concentrated on the field fortifications around the forts on the premise that the positions could hold out against a Union landward assault long enough for a counter-attack by the Confederate Army. To forestall a direct assault, Leadbetter relied on a field of pilings to reduce the available width of the channel and "torpedoes," later called naval mines, to funnel any attackers toward the forts.[7]

The efforts, however, came to naught when, in August 1864, a Union naval force under the command of Admiral David Farragut assaulted the entrance to Mobile Bay. Leading a mixed flotilla of ironclads and wooden warships, Farragut forced his way past Fort Morgan and into the bay. He lost the ironclad USS *Tecumseh* to a torpedo and several of his ships were damaged by gunfire from the forts and in close combat with the Confederate ironclad CSS *Tennessee*, but after several hours of fierce fighting, Farragut's forces had captured the *Tennessee* and gained control of the bay.[8] Only three days later, Colonel Charles Anderson surrendered Fort Gaines to Union troops under Maj. Gen. Gordon Granger. Although defended by six hundred men and supplied for a six-month siege, the fort's walls were easily penetrated by Union shells fired by ships offshore and army batteries established ashore. After a two-week siege, Fort Morgan likewise surrendered. While a great success, the Union could not capitalize on its victories. While the capture of the forts closed Mobile as a blockade-running port, the army committed only three small brigades to the attack, enough to take and hold Forts Morgan and Gaines but not enough to take Mobile, giving the Confederates another opportunity to construct a defensive line.[9]

The loss of Forts Morgan and Gaines forced authorities in Mobile to plan for a close defense of the city. To that end, Maury turned to Lt. Col. Victor von Sheliha, who assumed the responsibility of protecting Mobile when Leadbetter transferred to the Army of Tennessee.[10] The Prussian-born von Sheliha utilized many contemporary European innovations in his fortifications, especially the use of naval torpedoes, but the scale of the operation was too much for even his expertise. Accepting blame for the capture of the outer defenses, von Sheliha submitted his resignation in August 1864 but agreed to stay on until a replacement arrived.[11] With the lower bay in enemy hands, Confederate defensive plans evolved until engineers planned no fewer than fifty-eight forts and batteries to defend the region, all interconnected with trenches and breastworks. The daunting geography of the area required such an extensive defensive system. The Mobile and Tensaw Rivers, which split into numerous short channels where they emptied into the bay, separated the city from the east bay. One such channel of the Tensaw, the Blakely River, itself split just before it emptied into the bay, creating an additional channel, the Appalachee River, with an island in between. To control access to both rivers, engineers constructed Battery Huger on the island at the point where the river forked, with Battery Tracey three hundred yards north, on the west bank of the Blakely River. But the heights on the east side of the bay about a mile away overlooked these

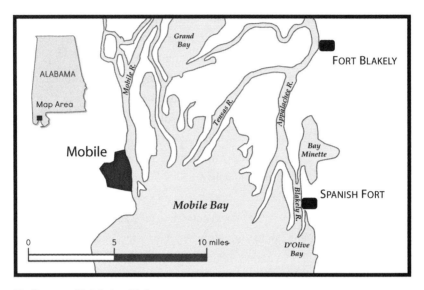

Defenses of Mobile, Alabama.

batteries, so, to cover both positions, engineers began to reconstruct and improve an older earthen fort, known as Spanish Fort, erected when Spain controlled the area decades earlier. High ground five miles to the north threatened Spanish Fort, requiring the construction of Fort Blakely.[12] Altogether, the positions and their twenty-six hundred yards of field fortifications required a minimum of sixteen batteries of artillery and five thousand men just to occupy the forts. In upper bay, von Sheliha relied most heavily on mines, both in the channels and in the bay. Although never available in sufficient numbers, the mines denied important areas of the bay to Union shipping and inflicted significant losses.[13]

Confederate engineers, however, faced many problems that proved difficult to overcome. The same geography that hampered any Union advance proved a burden to the defenders as well. Many positions lay in the low watery geography of the area, leading to many water-borne ailments among their garrisons. "The quarters are not very good and are very much crowded," one lieutenant reported. "The water is very bad and very unhealthy. Most of the garrison is suffering from diorrhoea [sic]." Tools to construct the defenses were also in short supply. An inventory of engineering equipment in the Department of the Gulf included a mere 674 shovels, 122 spades, 179 picks, 141 axes, and 346 wheelbarrows in workable condition, with nearly the same number of each item broken and awaiting repair. Cooperation between the Confederate Army and Navy at Mobile was also lacking, with each service resisting placing its resources under the control of the other. The Navy had only a handful of ships left after the defeat in the bay and preferred to husband their use, but Maury wanted the surviving ships in the bay to support his land operations and operate in conjunction with makeshift Army gunboats. The most important task was to protect the obstructions that von Sheliha had erected in the main channel leading to the city, but the Navy was hesitant to risk its ships to protect some wooden poles.[14]

Weak logistics and support for the garrison also stymied construction of the fortifications. The loss of Vicksburg was a ghost that haunted all Confederate commanders facing a potential siege, and Mobile was no different. Maury was under orders to keep at least a four-month supply of food on hand for ten thousand men, and he contracted for the use of five large warehouses to house what he could collect. Ammunition supplies were also a concern, so Maury accumulated as many weapons and as much ammunition as he could, although lead was in short supply. To rectify that shortcoming, Maury convinced the city leadership to dig up the lead pipes feeding water to the city. Stockpiled for a future attack, many troops did not receive ammunition until almost the last moment.[15] Transportation was also in short supply. Just before the Union assault, when Maury needed all the logistical support he could get, he lost one of his supply steamers, "laden with Q.M. [quartermaster] and commissary stores," which sank after colliding with another boat, the "result of sheer carelessness." Maury also had only limited use of the railroad network to supply the garrison. The Mobile & Ohio line on the west side of the city was still intact, but Union cavalry raids from Pensacola thoroughly disrupted the eastside Mobile & Great Northern, a sixty-two-mile track connecting Mobile and Pollard, Alabama, and the fifty-six-mile Alabama & Florida line that formerly connected Pollard and Pensacola.[16] Defending Mobile also came at a massive cost. For just April and May 1864, von Sheliha spent $607,748 on laborers, both free whites and impressed slaves, to build Mobile's defenses.[17]

Despite the efforts at fortifying the city, Confederate defeats created a sense of foreboding, as residents knew that a Union assault was only a matter of time. Hood's disastrous defeat at Nashville and the departure of the Army of Tennessee cast a pall over Mobile, as the city now seemed a likely target. Maury had been continuing the improvement of the city's defenses, but the new threat added to the pressures upon him. He notified the War Department that he considered his food supplies to be inadequate and asked for additional troops to stiffen his defenses. Maury had made such requests before. In November 1864, well before Hood's defeat at Nashville, Maury requested that "4,000 or 5,000 veteran infantry should be sent here at the earliest practicable moment." Astonishingly, Maury announced that "troops from distant localities are to be preferred over those from this region of country. A few Virginia regiments would be peculiarly well suited for a tour of service here." Maury asked specifically for Virginia troops because "it would be peculiarly gratifying to me to command some troops from my own State." The War Department quickly replied that "Re-enforcements cannot under more pressing exigencies elsewhere be spared for the doubtful contingency of an unreported attack." Maury had requested out-of-state troops because he believed them less likely to desert.[18] For the same reason Maury was hesitant to use state militia as reinforcements as those who did serve shifts in the city defenses tended to be sickly, underequipped, and of not much use.[19] Maury became so desperate for manpower he accepted a group of 450 "galvanized" Confederates—Union deserters and prisoners of war who agreed to switch sides rather than sit in a POW camp. Their reliability was questionable, but Maury was willing to take whatever troops he could find.[20] The result was a mixed bag of troops, with varying levels of experience and capability. Maury had five infantry brigades from the Army of Tennessee and fifteen hundred former artillerymen who had lost their guns during the Nashville Campaign. The hope was to find cannon for them, but to use them as infantry in the meantime. Maury also had three regiments of state militia and six regiments of cavalry.[21] While Maury maintained his headquarters in Mobile, Brig. Gen. St. John R. Liddell commanded the outer defenses. A West Point dropout, Liddell had acquitted himself well in various campaigns, but had developed personality clashes with Gen. Richard Taylor, causing Liddell's reassignment to Mobile. Much to his chagrin, Taylor was soon his superior again when Davis appointed Taylor to the command of the Department of Alabama, Mississippi, and East Louisiana.[22]

****

In the summer of 1864, Grant was still intent on attacking Mobile. Sherman was moving toward Atlanta and Grant was looking to support his attack. While Mobile itself was of no advantage to the Union, using the rivers that passed through it to attack the industrial and logistic centers in the interior of the state became an attractive proposition. The first problem to overcome, however, was to find a suitable general to lead an attack. Maj. Gen. Nathaniel Banks, a Massachusetts political general, had commanded the Department of the Gulf since December 1862, but failed military operations had tarnished his reputation. Grant was determined to remove Banks, but replacing the powerful political general was fraught with potential pitfalls, especially if it caused a negative backlash amongst Banks's friends in Congress. "I do not see that anything can be done this spring with troops west of the Mississippi," Grant wrote to Halleck, pondering the future. "I think, therefore, it will be better to put the whole of that territory into one military division, under some good officer." Grant further suggested that Halleck himself, bearing the credibility as Lincoln's military advisor, should "go in person and take charge of the Trans-Mississippi division."[23] Halleck seemed willing to go, telling Grant "Wherever you and the Secretary of War think I can be of most service I am ready to go. I am willing to serve anywhere and everywhere," but Halleck had little faith in the administrative ability of Secretary of War Edwin Stanton and suggested the best case would be for him to stay in Washington. "There must be some military head here to keep things from getting into a snarl," Halleck explained. "There must be some common head to make the different bureaus act in concert and with promptness. It is impossible for the Secretary of War or his assistants to attend personally to these matters."[24]

Unwilling to push Halleck to accept the position, Grant's second choice was Maj. Gen. Edward Canby. In March 1862, Canby, commanding the Department of New Mexico, had halted a Confederate offensive at the Battle of Glorieta Pass. Winner of one of the few Union victories early in the war, Canby received a promotion to brigadier general, but the advancement

Gen. Edward Canby (*Image courtesy of the Library of Congress*).

moved him behind a desk, first at the War Department, then as "commanding general of the city and harbor of New York" in 1863, before returning to the War Department as assistant to the Secretary of War. In May 1864, Canby assumed command of the new Military Department of the West, overseeing both the Departments of the Gulf and of Arkansas, but his presence caused some confusion and uncomfortable command relationships. The War Department, instead of reassigning him elsewhere to clear the situation, retained

Banks as commander of the Department of the Gulf. Although he led his department, Banks had to clear all orders and actions through Canby, and their relationship was especially awkward as both men had their headquarters in New Orleans. "General Canby has charge of everything," a Treasury Department employee noted in a report, "and Banks seems to be ignored. ... The sooner Gen. Banks goes home, the better it will be." Banks did not go home, staying in New Orleans until mustered out at the end of the war.[25]

While he could not rid himself of Banks, Canby did improve the situation within his department. He issued orders to maximize the troops available and improve their mobility and morale. He reduced the number of camp followers who were, in Canby's opinion, "amassing wealth by their connection with the Army," and reduced the number of surplus animals and supply personnel, proclaiming "Every superfluous man or animal that has to be fed and transported or protected is an embarrassment." That included the large number of artillery pieces that, again in Canby's opinion, overburdened and slowed the army. "It has been one of our misfortunes since the commencement of the rebellion to rely too much upon artillery," Canby complained, as the excessive number of guns required too many horses to pull them, supplies to maintain them, and soldiers to guard them. Instead, Canby established a quota of one gun per thousand men, plus a number in reserve. In addition to providing more troops, the reduction in artillery alleviated the shortage of transport. "There is great abuse in the quantity of transportation that is carried into the field" in Canby's opinion, and he intended to put a stop to it.[26] Canby also improved the security behind the lines of the department, gaining troops in the process. He organized units of Invalid Corps troops, new recruits, and local militias to perform garrison and provost duties in secure areas. Canby ordered "neutral foreigners" not subject to the draft to register as a separate category "to be employed whenever necessary as a local police or constabulary force" in place of troops on occupation duty. This allowed him to consolidate effective troops, especially after he reduced the number of posts along the Mississippi River, and recalled troops from extraneous details and duties. Because he did not want to spare the troops to keep an eye on them, Canby ordered all "registered enemies of the United States" to report to New Orleans for deportation beyond Union lines.[27] Clarity of command aided Union efforts to prepare for military action, but other problems continued to occur beyond Canby's control. Canby's biggest problem was not accumulating troops, but holding on to them once he had them. In May 1864, Grant had decided that the troops west of the Mississippi that had fought with Banks on the Red River would remain inactive for the time being, as they required resupply and new transport. A month later, however, Grant decided they should reinforce his own advance and ordered Canby to detach the XIX Corps for service in Virginia.[28] Canby complied, but the loss of one of his few organized units ended any hope of immediate offensive action in 1864. The absence of the XIX Corps meant that Canby would not have enough troops to capitalize on the naval victory at Mobile Bay in August 1864. A month later, Canby also had to dispatch troops to Missouri to contain a Confederate cavalry raid, further delaying any other offensive action.

Compounding the unpredictable number of soldiers was the scope of Canby's command. He was obligated to not only hold onto the areas occupied by the Union when he arrived, a zone that began in the Indian Territory in the West, stretched down the Mississippi River Valley, and then turned eastward along the Gulf of Mexico to Pensacola, but also to undertake offensive action to expand the conquered area. The region where the War Department expected Canby to take offensive action was vast, including Texas, southern Arkansas, western Louisiana, Mississippi, Alabama, and parts of Florida. Canby's plans also suffered a setback when he almost died. In November 1864, a Confederate sniper wounded Canby in the groin. Canby did not relinquish command, but instead allowed greater discretion by his field commanders for the next two months while he recovered. Despite these problems, Canby created a noticeable increase in the efficiency and capability of the troops under his command. When ordered in February 1865 to commence operations against Mobile, most observers expected a quick operation. A government official in New Orleans predicted only weak Confederate opposition and that Canby would soon be "rattling among the dry bones at Mobile and throughout Alabama."[29]

Canby had the best of intentions to act immediately upon Grant's January 1865 orders to attack Mobile, but the weather foiled any attempt at movement. Canby informed Halleck, "The rainy season ends here ordinarily ... next month, and a few days of dry weather will make the roads from the Gulf to the interior practicable," but the rains continued. In March 1865, a month after he planned to move, Canby was still in New Orleans because, "For the last forty days we have had but seven of favorable weather" and the city had been subject to "heavy easterly and southeasterly gales" that had made it impossible for his transports "to cross the bar" into the Gulf of Mexico. All Canby could promise was imminent action as "About half of the Sixteenth Corps is now here, and the remainder will arrive within the next two days … The navy will not be ready for several days, but our movements for getting into position for co-operation will go on at once."[30] Grant was unsympathetic, replying in a blistering message that "I wrote to you long ago urging you to push forward promptly and to live upon the country. … Take Mobile and hold it, and push your forces to the interior to Montgomery and Selma. Destroy railroads, rolling-stock, and everything useful for carrying on war, and when you have done this take such positions as can be supplied by water."[31] Grant could issue demands, but he could not control the weather, and nearly three weeks passed before Canby could begin his operations against Mobile, in late March 1865. In the meantime, Stanton had to suppress Grant's urge to replace Canby with Philip Sheridan as soon as the latter commander was available for the duty.[32]

Meanwhile, Canby's preparations for the assault did not go unnoticed, although no one was sure which region the Union intended to attack. Confederate intelligence sources noted "the enemy are concentrating forces from Arkansas and Nashville at New Orleans. From the strength of this force it is evident they intend immediate operations against either Mobile, Galveston, or Red River."[33] Commanders in the Trans-Mississippi Department repositioned troops for the presumed thrust up the Red River or the less likely attack on Galveston, but could do little to prevent a movement against Mobile if Canby chose that objective. The Union buildup at New Orleans put all Confederate commanders on edge, fearful that they would be the ones to fall under the Union blow. Across the Mississippi River, Lt. Gen. Edmund Kirby Smith considered a repeat of the Red River Campaign as the most likely Union objective, telling a subordinate "An attempt in force is about being made against either Mobile or the Texas coast, while a formidable naval expedition ascends [the] Red River."[34]

The residents and garrison at Mobile were concerned about a possible
Union assault while contending with the difficulties of daily life. The influx
of Confederate troops, coupled with economic and military failures, led to
hardship for Mobile's civilian population, manifested in several minor food
riots. Civilians jostled to buy limited amounts of goods in competition with
army quartermasters, while attempts to grow food often failed due to marauding soldiers and eager impressment agents.[35] Despite the bread riots, life in
Mobile proved pleasant for the troops sent from the Army of Tennessee.
Garrison duty was not particularly arduous, and the city itself provided various forms of entertainment, ranging from drink to theater to pleasant scen-
ery along the bay. Soldiers were unhappy, however, when on the eve of the
Union attack Maury ordered the closing of the city taverns. Deprived of their
main source of entertainment, some Confederate troops suddenly had a less
positive view of Mobile. "Now I am in Mobile and thus far since I came
time drags heavily," a soldier cut off from recreation objected. "The place
has no attractions for me."[36] Discipline was also still harsh, especially under
the pressure of an anticipated Union attack. Only days before the Union
assault began, a Mobile newspaper noted "Privates Elam and Winn of the 21st
Alabama Regiment were shot to death by musketry at Blakely" for desertion
to the enemy more than a year earlier.[37]

Despite the leisurely existence in Mobile, there existed more a hope that
Mobile could hold out rather than a certainty. After the Union Navy seized
control of the bay, there was always an undercurrent of disbelief that the
army could not defend the city. "I trust you will be able to hold Mobile," Gov.
Thomas Watts told Gen. Maury, but if they could not he preferred Mobile
"remain a heap of ashes before the Yankees pollute it with their footsteps,"
not exactly a ringing endorsement of the Army's ability to defend the place.[38]
The *Richmond Dispatch* was also tepid in its confidence, reporting in March
1865 that "The preparations for the defense of Mobile are very complete.
Provisions for a six-months' siege have been accumulated. General Taylor
has done everything for the successful defense of the city."[39] Maury himself
gave mixed signals about the hope of success in various public statements.
On one hand, he assured the population that the "fortifications are strong …
our troops are veterans" and he had every reason to be "confident of victory."

On the other hand, he also requested that noncombatants evacuate the city and to withdraw as many slaves and as much property as possible.[40] There was also a lack of confidence in Maury's leadership. An officer wrote from Spanish Fort in March 1865 that "the Maj Gen Commanding, who has by some been irreverently dubbed the Lord of Panic, issued his battle order." Soldiers also referred to Maury as "Puss in Boots," because "half of his diminutive person seemed lost in the huge cavalry boots he wore and which were in vogue."[41] The long wait for the Union to act had caused many enlisted men to question Maury's nerve. The constant threat of a Union attack created both tension and lethargy, as Confederate soldiers prepared themselves for battle based upon "reliable" rumors, only to find out an assault was not imminent. Just days before the Union campaign began, a Confederate officer described his men as being of mixed readiness with "half my men working in the trenches and nearly all the other half playing marbles before their quarters," uncertain as to exactly what was their fate.[42]

****

As the weather finally began to clear and river levels fell, Canby was finally able to begin repositioning his men for the assault in February, as transports began moving troops from their Louisiana garrisons to staging areas on Dauphin Island, a process that took some weeks. "I have seen enough of New Orleans to do me," Sergeant Charles Treadway wrote to his family. "One has to be very careful whare [sic] he puts his foot or he will mire or get snake bit."[43] Typical of other Union units, an Indiana regiment began its movement toward Mobile on February 17 by packing its essential equipment and storing unnecessary items, a process that took two weeks before the unit finally arrived at Dauphin Island on March 3.[44] Rear Admiral Henry K. Thatcher undertook the transfer of troops with a force of twenty ships comprised of transports, ironclads, and gunboats. Such a large naval force was necessary because, to the initial force Canby had gathered at New Orleans, Grant had allocated an additional eighteen thousand infantry in the form of the XIII Corps assembled from its scattered duties along the length of the Mississippi River Valley, plus a cavalry division of five thousand men from Thomas's Army of the Cumberland.[45] The Confederates could not help but notice such a movement of ships and men. "Quite an increase in the Yankee fleet during the morning," a Confederate officer noted on March 11, "transports and gunboats numbering nineteen."[46] Canby's plan for the offensive was to effect "the reduction of the enemy's works on the east side of Mobile Bay, the opening of the Tensas and Alabama Rivers, turning the strong works erected for the defense of Mobile, and forcing the surrender or evacuation of the city."[47] The directive that Grant gave to Canby identified the Confederate river defenses as the target for the Union offensive, with the aim of giving the Union access via the rivers into the interior of Alabama. If he could take the city with minimal effort, then Canby could occupy Mobile, but the overall strategy did not have the city as the prime objective. Canby's assault would be supported by Maj. Gen. Frederick Steele's force from Pensacola. Steele's part of the operation was to lead his force from Pensacola toward Pollard, Alabama, to cut the Mobile & Great Northern railroad and distract the city's defenders. If possible, Steele was to head north toward Montgomery, but, if that proved impossible, he was to support the attack on Mobile instead.[48]

The key defensive position near Mobile was Spanish Fort, which stood about ten miles east of Mobile on a point of land jutting into Mobile Bay that was the previous site of a Spanish stone fortification. The location allowed Confederate engineers to make "the most earnest endeavors at securing that important position permanently" by building fortifications that featured the ability to "countersink our guns commanding the river, and to protect the battery by a bastion line in rear." Considered the more important position because of its ability to cover both the landward and seaward approaches to Mobile, Spanish Fort received the most attention and labor to the extent that engineers suspended construction on Fort Blakely for much of late 1864 to concentrate on the more southerly position.[49] Maury described the defenses as "The works of Spanish Fort consisted of a heavy battery of six guns on a bluff of the left bank of the Apalachie River, three thousand yards below Battery Huger. This was strongly enclosed in the rear. On commanding eminences five hundred to six hundred yards to its rear were erected three other redoubts, which were connected by light rifle-pits with each other. The whole crest of the line of defence was about two thousand five hundred yards, and swept around old Spanish Fort as a centre, with the right flank resting on Apalachie River, the left flank resting on Bayou Minette."[50]

Gen. Frederick Steele (*Image courtesy of the Library of Congress*).

Around the primary battery of six heavy guns, Maury ordered the construction of "a line of three redoubts connected by rifle pits, which crowned the higher ground to the rear.[51] A Union officer later described Spanish Fort as "a bastioned work, nearly enclosed, and built on a bluff whose shape projects abruptly to the water."[52] The anchors of the position were five redoubts that reinforced a two-mile long arc of fortifications that stretched from Bay Minette in the north to D'Olive's Bay in the south. The old Spanish

Fort itself, armed with four heavy guns to protect the rear of the position and cover the water approaches, was redoubt #1. Redoubt #2, also known as Fort McDermott, mounted nine guns and six mortars, covered the Confederate right flank at D'Olive's Bay, with redoubt #3, also known as Fort Blair, with four guns and four mortars eight hundred yards to the north. Redoubt #4, also

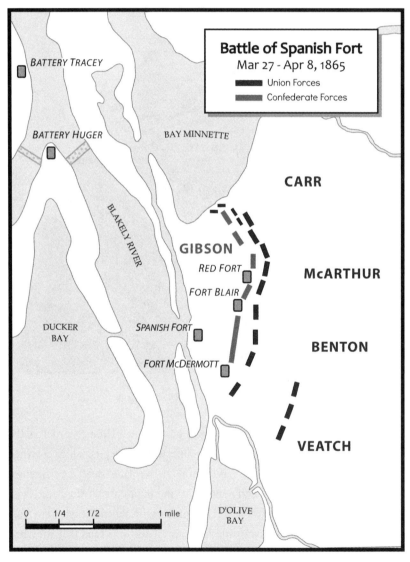

Spanish Fort.

sometimes referred to as "the Red Fort," supported the center of the line and the point at which the defensive line angled to the northwest toward Bay Minette. At the extreme end of the line was redoubt #5.

The redoubts had additional protection in the form of iron mantlets, sheets of metal that covered the gun embrasures when the barrel was not protruding to fire. The mantlets shielded the gunners and defending troops from Union sharpshooters and artillery fragments that might otherwise come through the gun ports. The mantlets were so effective a soldier decided that being near the guns was "the safest place as there is more protection there than anywhere else."[53] Confederate sharpshooters fired from positions protected by "Beauregard screens," which General Beauregard had first used in the Charleston defenses. The screens were wooden boards placed into cuts and notches on the top of a parapet and covered with dirt to disguise the shooter's position. Defenders numbered about twenty-six hundred men at the time of the Union attack.[54] Maury ordered Brig. Gen. St. John Liddell to local command on the eastern shore of the bay. He took direct command of Fort Blakely and placed the senior brigade commander, Brig. Gen. Randall Gibson, in charge at Spanish Fort. Gibson had his own brigade of Louisiana troops, Ector's Brigade of Texas and North Carolina troops, Holtzclaw's Brigade of Alabama troops, a brigade of Alabama Reserves, and artillerymen to man the forty-seven guns allocated to the fort.[55]

As formidable as these fortifications appeared, the defenses at Spanish Fort were not complete. Maury and his chief engineer, Lt. Col. von Sheliha, had dug entrenchments to connect redoubts #2, #3, and #4, had cleared a field of fire in front of the position out to as a much as a third of a mile, and planted obstacles including abatis, telegraph wire, and torpedoes. Both Maury and von Sheliha considered this area the main defensive line because both believed Bay Minette prevented any movement against the left flank. Consequently, redoubt #5 was merely a small dirt-mound fort and no trenches connected it to redoubt #4, some six-hundred yards to its right.[56] The Confederates knew the defenses on their left were weak, but "we had not time to complete them."[57] The fortifications also did not extend forward enough to cover a line of small hills in their front. Gibson reported the shortcoming, noting his lines "were placed so far back on the retreating slope that the infantry could only command its crest, but not the ravine beyond." These hills

Gen. St. John Liddell (*Image courtesy of the Library of Congress*).

provided cover for the Union advance, with a Union soldier describing the terrain as "Our part of the line was behind the brow of the hill where they could not rake us with their shot," although indirect fire from the Confederate mortars was still a concern.[58]

The Confederates knew the position needed improvement, but seemed unconcerned about remedying the situation even as the Union assault seemed imminent. One Confederate soldier described how officers assigned his regiment to work on the "extension of the rifle pits on the western defenses,"

Gen. Randall Gibson (*Image courtesy of the Library of Congress*).

but mentioned the men were "not pushed … but allowed to be leisurely."[59] The failure to improve the fortifications on the Confederate left was more than an unfortunate situation caused by lack of resources; it was a major blunder on Maury's part. The entire Confederate defensive position practically invited a Union attack at that location, and even a cursory look at the Confederate defenses and geography of the area revealed the advantages of controlling the terrain along Bay Minette. If the Union could gain a foothold there, it could in short order place guns to enfilade the defenders inside Spanish Fort, cut connections to Fort Blakely, impede Confederate supply steamers

in the bay, and fire upon Batteries Tracey and Huger. The vulnerability of
the position was not lost on some enlisted men. While there was no shortage of confidence on the Confederate side, some soldiers were pessimistic
of the outcome, with one remembering, "We felt ourselves to be in a trap as
soon we took in the situation."[60]

Immediately before the Union assault began, Maury arrived at Spanish
Fort to assess the circumstances for himself. The defensive works were still
incomplete, and Gibson requested reinforcements, provisions for his men
(including whiskey and tobacco), and entrenching tools so his men could dig
additional rifle pits. Gibson got little of what he requested, but the switch-
ing of two regiments improved his force. Amongst Gibson's men were a
brigade of the Alabama Reserves, state militia made up mostly of boys thirteen to eighteen years of age. These "boy reserves" were poorly trained and
were not the equal of veteran troops, as their behavior demonstrated later
when the battle commenced. An officer remembered telling the boy-soldiers
"when going to the skirmish line to shelter themselves as much as possible.
They thought it was 'not soldierly,' and they stood up and were shot down
like sheep" by Union sharpshooters.[61] Referring to the young militia troops,
a Union artilleryman later noted, "They pressed schoolboys and gray haired
men into service ... but they died like sheep, so they sent them home."[62]
Maury ordered the withdrawal of some of the boy reserves to Blakely, replacing them with a regiment of Alabama troops of Gen. James Holtzclaw's
brigade from Fort Blakely. Gibson was replacing quantity with quality, but
the change did not improve his situation. Two days later, as the Union assault
began in earnest, Maury ordered the rest of Holtzclaw's brigade shifted to
Spanish Fort, an improvement for Gibson but still not enough men to cover
entrenchments of such a scale.[63]

****

Canby's force took two routes toward Spanish Fort, as he did not have
sufficient transports to carry his entire force and he did not want to clog
the few roads. The XIII Corps, which began moving out from Fort Morgan
on March 17, faced varied weather and terrain conditions on the sixty-mile
march toward Spanish Fort. A soldier from the Seventy-seventh Illinois,
noting the warm weather, observed the troops "started in heavy marching

order," but "they soon began to lighten up by throwing away their extra blankets, shirts, etc., and the road sides were lined with them for miles." Within two days, however, rain slowed the progress toward Spanish Fort, forcing the men to extract wagons and guns from the resulting mud. Confiscating fence rails from a local plantation, a soldier recorded the troops "carried our rails for about a mile to a very swampy place in the road where we each one laid our rail down, cordaroying [corduroying] the road as we went so that our trains and artilery [sic] could pass over." It was back-breaking work that the troops did not enjoy, observing that an enlisted man "didn't out rank a mule very much." Even Brig. Gen. William Benton dismounted to help extract a stuck wagon, leading an overworked soldier to conclude "he was a good as a mule."[64] An Iowa soldier observed that the XIII Corps moved fourteen miles on March 18, but only five the next day. That minimal progress came only after arduous labor to extract wagons and teams from the morass, construct corduroy roads, and otherwise manage the swampy terrain that "seemed to have no bottom in places." Corduroy-ing the roads took time, but there were trees available. A Missouri officer observed that "nothing but pine trees grow. This has been a great country for the manufacture of Resin and Turpentine. In some places the trees for miles are scraped and ready for gathering the pitchy stuff off the pines." It was hard work for the enlisted men, but officers found it much less ardu-ous, as one noted "Twas truly a funny sight. Men, Negro women, horses, mules, and teams all mixed up splashing through the water."[65] The terrain also hindered the movement of supplies, leading to reduced rations, with soldiers receiving "only one cracker to a man … 11 such crackers are the usual ration."[66] Besides the muddy roads, supplies were short because the stormy weather caused two Union transports to run aground and damaged another, causing havoc on the Union logistics support.[67]

Other impediments also delayed the Union progress. One was the unex-pected and deadly discovery that the Confederates had planted "torpedoes" in the roads leading to Mobile. "The march over to here was a very exciting one in consequence of the torpedoes that were placed in roads and timber by hundreds," a soldier recalled, "I saw 18 in one pile that had been taken out of the road." Union soldiers learned to treat the deadly devices with respect.

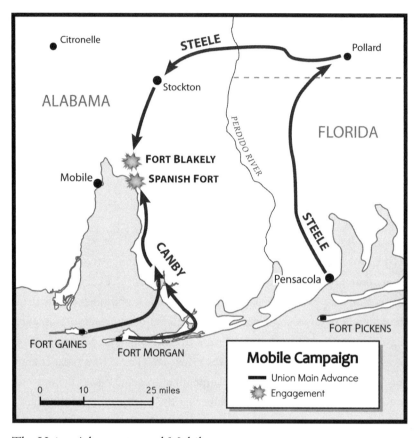

The Union Advance toward Mobile.

"The rebels have planted torpedoes all over creation," Sergeant William Clayton wrote to his family, "The first day 4 or 5 horses were killed by them and two or three men wounded," but soldiers soon learned how to avoid them. Clayton described the mines as "a common shell fixed with a cap so that a man's weight upon it will cause it to explode."[68] Captured rebels often pointed out the buried torpedoes, as they "did not approve this kind of warfare and denounced it as cowardly ... but they seem to be reduced to such a state that they have lost all honor & self-respect."[69] Canby's decision to fortify his camp every night also slowed his march. Canby had no cavalry screen as his two cavalry divisions were supporting Steele's column, and had only advance pickets to warn of Confederate action. Consequently, after laboring through the muddy countryside all day, soldiers had to dig breastworks for protection against a possible surprise Confederate attack.[70]

While the XIII Corps slogged its way toward Spanish Fort, the XVI Corps had a much more leisurely journey. Four days after the XIII Corps began its march, the Navy began shuttling the XVI Corps to the mouth of the Fish River, twenty-two miles south of Spanish Fort, and then upriver several miles where they would wait for the XIII Corps to arrive.[71] Private Abner Dunham of the Twelfth Iowa described the approach to Spanish Fort, glad to leave Dauphin Island but apprehensive about the coming battle. "Followed several boats carrying the 2nd Division proceeded up the bay to the mouth of the Fish River," Dunham wrote to his parents. "It is reported that we are to capture a fort opposite Mobile which the boats cannot get at. If so, we will probably see fun soon." Dunham and his fellow soldiers knew fighting was imminent as "we have no teams along and but few of the officers have their horses," further noting "The boys are all anxious to get the work done for suspense is worse than fighting." They would not be alone, as Dunham recorded "the 13th Corps has arrived on the opposite side of the Fish River now pontoons are being laid for it to cross upon." The last portions of the XIII Corps, after more than a week of marching and road-building, arrived at the rendezvous point on the Fish River on March 23 and Canby immediately issued orders to move toward Spanish Fort.[72] The only delay was the presence of a Confederate force in the vicinity. Liddell, initially believing he was facing only Steele's force from Pensacola, sought an engagement on open ground and ordered Brigadier General Gibson to position a brigade to confront the enemy above the Fish River, but immediately recalled Gibson as the size of the Union force became evident.[73]

After more than a week, Union troops arrived at Spanish Fort on March 26 and began establishing their line of defense. Federal troops settled in "a mile or two back from the forts and threw up some breastworks by cutting up some logs and piling them up and throwing dirt over them … then our band got up on top of our works and serenaded the rebels."[74] An Iowa soldier informed his family of the army's arrival "about two miles from the fort." The regiment advanced forward until they "reached the top of a hill and found ourselves in full view of the fort on the bay, and only 1200 yards distant.

We stacked arms and commenced throwing up a breastwork." The work was dangerous, however, as Confederate shells began to fall nearby, but "Men were posted to give warning when they fired and every man dropped to the ground until the shell passed over and then up and at it we went again." Working under these conditions, the Union troops moved their lines forward another five hundred yards by nightfall.

As the Union troops began to dig, it became evident, to the relief of many of them, that Canby did not intend to storm the defenses, an act that would result in many casualties. "I do not think that we will assault the rebel works," a Union private wrote favorably. "It would be a needless loss of life as every one of us is of the opinion that they cannot be taken in that way." The decision bolstered the soldier's opinion of Canby, characterized by one soldier as "he seems in no hurry and moves cautious. I believe he will not sacrifice men unnecessarily."[75] He was not the only soldier to approve of the use of siege-craft to take Spanish Fort. "Since our ill-fated charge on the fortifications at Vicksburg hardly a man in the Regt can think of charging again without shuddering," a Wisconsin soldier related to his parents. But "They have just made a detail for Sappers & Miners & that is another indication that the head ones intend to take the place by regular siege."[76] Not all Union soldiers took the attack seriously, however, as some took the opportunity for a pickup baseball game, at least until "a shell burst directly over our heads and the pieces of shell and splinters from trees come falling around us but did not hit anyone. We stopped our play & sought shelter behind the works."[77]

As Union troops began to encircle Spanish Fort, Gibson decided to launch a spoiling attack to disrupt their plans, gauge their strength, and buy more time to dig. Early the next morning, Col. Francis Campbell led his brigade of Louisianans toward the Union lines under the cover of darkness. They surprised Union skirmishers from the Forty-seventh Indiana, but soon ran into determined opposition and returned to their own lines before sunup. The sortie only halted the Union advance for a few hours and gained very little. Gibson reported to Liddell that he "Drove in the enemy's skirmishers this morning at daylight, capturing guns, knapsacks, and blankets."[78] On the other side, Union troops were dismissive of the Confederate assault. "The rebs came out and tried to drive our skirmishers back, but they made a complete failure," an Iowa soldier remembered. "Our boys would not drive worth a cent."[79]

Undeterred by the spoiling attack, Union troops moved forward from their original defensive line a mile from the fort "without much resistance and formed a line within about half a mile of Spanish Fort" and began to build observation posts on the hilltops and emplace heavy siege guns.[80] "The toil of the besiegers was incessant and severe," a Vermont officer later recalled. "[I]n some places the ground was rocky, in others it was filled with stumps and roots and covered with large logs. The details had become so wearing on the men that the officers sometimes took the muskets and went on duty themselves as sharpshooters, while the men rested and slept."[81] The Confederates were also digging. Motivated by the "blue waves" of Union infantrymen that surrounded their position, the defenders of Spanish Fort did all they could to improve their incomplete defenses, despite the weariness of constant labor.[82] As the soldiers dug, the artillerymen set about their deadly task. "The rebs replied with energy and as our works were not overly strong, they had the best end of the bargain," a Union soldier wrote with grudging respect. "They do some of the best artillery firing I ever saw. They plant a shell exactly where they want it."[83]

By March 28, the second Union defensive line was nearly complete. "The line of battle advanced by degrees until a position was secured within about 800 yards of the fort," Colonel Lucius Hubbard informed Canby, "the enemy the while delivering from his works a spirited fire of musketry and artillery."[84] As Union troops continued to dig, their advance was covered by a large number of sharpshooters; one brigade alone had 250 such riflemen to provide protection by sniping at Confederate artillery positions.[85] As the two armies closed, many Confederate gunners owed their lives to the iron mantlets that protected their positions. "Artillery duels became a daily occurrence," a Confederate artilleryman later wrote. "Our embrasures, when we were not in action, were always closed with square sheet of iron an inch or so thick and about 3 feet square. These screens were sufficient to resist the sharpshooters' bullets. They were specked all over with the white splotches of the enemy's bullets."[86] Confederate sharpshooters were also active and a constant threat to the Union advance. An Illinois soldier noted his brigade employed "to construct a line of rifle pits about half way between our line and the rebel works" had to "remain there until the next night as we could not go out or back in daylight without encountering the rebel fire."[87] Private Abner Dunham's regiment faced the same perils. "After dark our Regt. moved out on the front line," he told his parents. "Our skirmishers are within 50 yards of them. … In the day time we will have to lay low for the sharpshooters will pick us off."[88]

Despite the violence with which they attempted to halt the Union advance, the Confederates could only watch while the Union troops crept closer. When the siege began, the Union lines were typically six hundred yards from the Confederate outposts. Within five days, they were an average of one hundred yards away. "We fired so lively that they dare not show their heads over the works," Union Private James Newton described in a letter to his mother. "We were so close that they could not depress their cannon enough to touch us."[89] Seeking to ease the Union pressure on his lines, on March 30 Gibson ordered another spoiling attack to drive back Union sappers near Fort Blair. A small assault force numbering only thirty men from Co. E of the Fourth Louisiana moved forward under the cover of an intense artillery barrage. The cannon fire had ignited trees and underbrush in front of their positions, hiding their approach. They surprised and captured twenty-one Union soldiers on forward picket duty, along with their commanding officer, Captain Riley Sterns, of the Seventh Vermont. Sterns described the attack later: "The charge was so sudden and vigorous that we could offer but little resistance. I gave the command to fire, which was obeyed by the majority of my men, but the next instant every man had at least one musket at his head, with a summons to surrender. I found two muskets and a revolver pointing at me." An observer of the attack wrote scornfully that the "7th Vermont run again for the 2nd or 3rd time & left the left of our line exposed," but his troops stood their ground, "holding the line."[90]

As the Union vice tightened, Gibson ensured that the defenders of Spanish Fort did not just sit and take punishment. He directed, often at great personal risk to himself, artillery bombardments against specific Union threats of advancement and exhorted his men to persevere. On March 30, Gibson issued a circular to his men, writing of his "admiration of their valor and endurance, and his entire confidence in their ability to defend this position. Thousands of anxious hearts turn toward you. Let every officer and man resolve to do his whole duty, to stand firm at his post, and to make the enemy pay dearly in blood for every inch he may advance."[91] Perhaps resigned to the fact that he could not drive Canby's force away from his position, Gibson urged his men to entrench all the harder and deeper. Gibson also issued a General Order urging "energy at this hour. You must dig, dig, dig. Nothing can save us here but the spade."[92] Gibson's fears were well-placed. By March 31, the First Indiana Heavy Artillery, with its eight 30-pounder guns, had moved into position on a slight rise on the south shore of Bay Minette that both enfiladed the Confederate positions at Spanish Fort and put Batteries Tracey and Huger under its fire. Consequently, supply steamers from Mobile operated only at great hazard during daylight hours and supporting fire from the river batteries was less effective at halting the inexorable Union advance. Confederate gunners from Fort Blakely, on the other side of Bay Minette, moved a battery to engage the Indianans, but had to retire back into their lanes as General Steele's column began to invest Fort Blakely.[93]

Despite the arrival of the first heavy Union guns, the situation at Spanish Fort was still a stalemate. An officer described the Confederate position as "an exceedingly strong works. Cannot be assaulted successfully and don't propose to attempt it … this is the sixth day of the siege of this work and our casualties up to noon yesterday only amounted to 500, mostly wounded."[94] The Union troops were taking casualties and the siege was difficult, but the Confederate situation at Spanish Fort was becoming desperate. Gibson begged Liddell for reinforcements, reporting "have a great deal to do here, and have only 1,700 infantry, with two corps d'armee in my front pressing up night and day." Liddell sent a disappointing reply; not only had he been ordered by Maury to send no more troops to Spanish Fort, Gibson was to turn over Ector's Brigade to reinforce Fort Blakely. As a poor replacement, Maury had positioned one of his steamers to evacuate Spanish Fort if it became necessary. For his part, Liddell made sure to note that "The order to withdraw [Ector's] troops emanates from General Maury, not myself. I have no desire to withdraw the troops," removing himself from the decision. In the end, the Texans and North Carolinians remained, more from the difficulty in moving them than a decision to let them stay.[95]

Seeking to break the stalemate in the first days of April, Canby began shifting more of his heavy guns to support the emplacement along Bay Minette. The First Indiana Heavy Artillery soon had company, joined by the Sixth Michigan Heavy Artillery, with eight 10-inch mortars, and the Eighteenth New York Independent Battery, with six 20-pounder Parrott rifles.[96] The newly arrived guns attracted notice. "When we first besieged the fort the Rebs had the advantage of us in heavy ordnance," a Wisconsin private told his parents, "but now there is no less than 16 30-pounders—Parrots—in the front occupied by the 16th Corps besides nearly a dozen 10-inch mortars."[97] Confederate troops in their trenches certainly noticed the increase in Union firepower. "About sundown a terrific cannonading commenced along the entire extent of the lines on the 'Eastern Shore' and continued for about three hours," a Confederate soldier later recalled. "It was decidedly the heaviest firing since the siege began. One ammunition chest was blown up at Battery McDermott."[98] Among the weapons firing at Spanish Fort were several improvised "tree mortars," tree trunks hollowed out to fashion a makeshift artillery piece. "Our Division has a lot of men at work making wooden mortars," a soldier informed his parents, "which throw a six inch shell to be taken out by the skirmishers … two men can carry and work them."[99]

The increased Union bombardment put even more pressure on the Confederate defenders. To an inquiry on his situation, Gibson replied on April 1 "Enemy firing 8-inch mortars on all the batteries and using heavier guns and increasing their number. He is now erecting a heavy battery upon my extreme right, which will give me great trouble" while the Union infantry "presses forward his zigzags and parallels closer and closer every day." Gibson was correct to be concerned about the Union ability to move earth. "I never saw such digging as the enemy does," he reported to Maury on April 3, "He is fast converting his advanced skirmish line into his main line." To counter the Union sapping, Gibson asked, "Can I get 100 negroes with 50 axes and 50 picks?"[100] Unlike the Confederate troops, who were short of equipment to prepare fortifications, the Union troops had the proper tools. Canby had issued orders before leaving Dauphin Island that "Each division commander will see that his command is provided with 300 spades or shovels, 300 axes, and 90 picks for entrenching purposes. One wagon to each brigade will be allowed for the transportation of these tools." Properly equipped, Union troops were capable of massive, if inelegant, feats of engineering. One brigade commander reported, "During the siege of Spanish Fort the brigade excavated seven thousand cubic yards of earth, and expended one hundred sixty-nine thousand rounds of musket ammunition."[101]

All that Gibson could do was to order his men to dig deeper. Canby had started the siege with the field guns attached to XIII Corps and three batteries of heavy guns manned by the Indiana, Michigan, and New York troops, but additional heavy guns began to arrive. By April 8 he had ninety guns (thirty-seven field guns, thirty-seven siege guns, and sixteen mortars) pounding Spanish Fort. The Union bombardment was tremendous; a Confederate soldier later wrote "The shells from one end of their line could reach the other end of ours, and 'raked us fore and aft.'"[102] The only restraint on the bombardment was ammunition, which was initially slow in arriving due to the swampy terrain between the gun positions and the logistics hub on the Fish River. By April 8, however, the construction of additional corduroy roads and the transfer of the main supply depot to Starke's Landing, just five miles from the front lines, alleviated the ammunition supply problem. With improved roads and a shorter supply line, the Union bombardment increased in tempo. Throughout the siege, Canby's gunners fired 8,673 artillery rounds at Spanish Fort while the infantry expended just under half a million rounds.[103] The augmented Union artillery fire proved a great boost to Union morale. An exuberant office described how "we opened on them with mortars, Parrotts, Napoleons, siege howitzers, etc. Fun! How we did warm the Johnnies!"[104] The firing was so intense that Confederate troops found "the only leisure time we have is when the enemy are firing on us. As I write shells are bursting and passing over me every few minutes."[105]

At the same time, the Confederate situation from both a supply and morale perspective was becoming more uncertain.[106] By April 4, ammunition of all types was running low, and Gibson sought to remedy the situation by offering a thirty-six-hour leave of absence to any soldier who "turns into the ordnance department twenty-five pounds of lead" from expended enemy shells. Gibson's furlough offer had a noticeable effect. "The soldiers did not hesitate to risk their lives while not in action roaming around in the exposed open ground behind us gathering bullets," a Missouri soldier recalled, explaining the risky action as "A furlough was a furlough."[107] Although a statement of Gibson's determination to hold his ground, the rest of his message gave signs of diminished morale by his troops. Gibson had to note "All missiles must bear undoubted signs of having been thrown by the enemy," indicating that he did not trust his men not to turn in their own limited amount of ammunition. He also issued a warning that "Any men … destroying serviceable cartridges, either our own or such as the enemy's that fall into our hands, will be severely punished," implying that troops were perhaps destroying ammunition to force an end to the fighting. Lastly, Gibson addressed the risk of desertion by the Alabama Reserves by reminding the command that it was "forbidden that a single one of the recruits … be allowed, on any pretext or at any time, night or day, to go beyond the main line of works." Gibson permitted his troops to "fire on and arrest any one of these men attempting to pass beyond the main works … to desert to the enemy, to ruin ourselves and our country by giving information to those who seek to destroy our lives and homes." As a remedy to desertion, Gibson ordered a "secret police should be organized in each company to watch them, detect, and kill them at once."

That Gibson detected a decline in morale should not have been surprising. The Union troops maintained their relentless attack, the arrival of additional siege guns threatened the Confederates in even their most secure positions, and casualties began to mount. On the right side of Gibson's line, the commander of the Louisiana Brigade reported on April 6 "I have lost in my brigade, out of 500 guns, 22 killed and 64 wounded since operations began here." Gibson, describing his troops' plight, reported to Maury "Not an officer or man had taken any unbroken rest. … Two weeks of constant work, night and day, with the musket and spade."[108] Gibson also had difficulty evacuating his casualties. Torpedoes kept the Union gunboats at a distance, but they still controlled the open bay. Consequently, "Steamboats could not come to the fort without great risk" to remove wounded troops, and a soldier wrote "our wounded were carried at night in canoes and yawls" to steamboats bound for city hospitals.[109]

The intensified Union bombardment made it almost impossible for the Confederate gunners to respond. "The very air was hot," a Confederate observer noted, "The din was so awful it distracted our senses. We could hardly hear each other speak. The cracking of musketry, the unbroken roaring of artillery, the yelling, shrieking, and exploding of the shells, the bellowing boom of the mortars, the dense shroud of sulphurous smoke thickening around us. … Men hopped about, raving, blood bursting from ears and nostrils, driven stark crazy by concussion."[110] As the barrage continued, the defenders came to hate the Union mortars. A Confederate veteran described the mortar barrage as "both day and night, those fearful things came down upon our heads. There was no shelter from these bombs. … They would go six feet in the solid earth and exploding tear up a space fifteen or twenty feet square. They went through that tremendous bomb-proof roof … as if was paper … They practiced on us to get the range, and then we 'got it.'"[111]

Despite their determination to hold, the Confederate position at Spanish Fort was becoming intolerable by April 7. Gibson informed Maury of the minimum amount of support he needed to hold the position. Because Union troops "made great progress yesterday and last night in his approaches," Gibson stated he needed "subterra shell [land mines], hand-grenades, more negroes, a company of sappers and miners, a cutter or launch from the navy, [and] two howitzers." Gibson must have known that such items were not available, possibly indicating that he was already planning to abandon the fort but needed an excuse to do so.[112] Maury was aware of Gibson's dire circumstances at Spanish Fort, but the citizens of Mobile were not. Even as Gibson made his emergency demands, the *Mobile Advertiser* reassured its readers that "At the rate of progress the Yanks are making over the bay … it will take them just five years and three months to take Mobile."[113] At the same time that Gibson was pessimistically measuring his options and the newspaper editors were bolstering the confidence of their readers, at least some Union troops could see progress and the promise of a breakthrough. An Illinois officer wrote his wife on April 7: "We are beginning to look upon the capture of Mobile as a thing in the future & think when that event is consummated that we will not have long to serve & this will probably be our last campaign. I hope it may be so."[114]

Gibson did not get the workers, weapons, and tools that he requested, and by April 8 considered whether the continued defense of the fort made any strategic sense. Holding out a few more days would delay Canby's advance, but at the cost of losing soldiers which could not be replaced. After the battle, in calculating his situation, Gibson reported "all my artillery was about silenced; that the enemy had greatly increased his; that his working parties were greatly re-enforced at every point and carefully protected against sorties, were pushing forward at a rate that would bring up to our main works." His only conclusion was that he "could no longer hold the position without imminent risk of losing the garrison."[115] Union movements confirmed Gibson's decision that it was time to abandon the fort and save what soldiers he could evacuate. General Canby, upon gaining an advantageous position late in the afternoon, ordered the direct bombardment of Spanish Fort with "fifty-three siege guns and thirty-seven field pieces. Of these, ten siege rifles and five siege howitzers on our left center enfiladed the enemy's left and center, and five siege howitzers close in on our extreme right enfiladed his center."[116] The ferocity of the bombardment stunned the defenders. One Confederate described the pounding as "if a dozen earthquakes were turned loose," while another recalled, "we thought the mouth of the pit had yawned and the uproar of the damned was about us."[117] Gibson tried to reply, but reported "My artillery was soon disabled and silenced, and the fire from his advanced lines showed them to be well filled."[118]

Under the cover of the bombardment, the XVI Corps probed the left flank of Gibson's position on the south bank of Bay Minette and found only the thin defenses held by Holtzclaw's Alabamians. At 5:30 in the afternoon, the Eighth Iowa, commanded by Lt. Col. William Bell, with two companies deployed as skirmishers in front of the rest of regiment, tested the Confederate defenses by assaulting a small hill. When the skirmishers ran into only limited resistance, Bell ordered the rest of the regiment forward, and informed his brigade commander, Col. James Geddes, of his progress and urged him to move reinforcements into the gap created by the Iowans. Geddes immediately ordered the other regiments in the brigade to move forward. In the meantime, the Iowans, at the eventual cost of six dead and forty-four wounded, overran five hundred yards of fortifications and captured more than four hundred

Confederate troops. Some Confederates fought hard before becoming prisoners, while others "refused to surrender and were shot in their ditches."[119] Confederate troops of the Fourteenth Texas, dismounted cavalry serving as infantry in Gibson's provost guard, counter-attacked, but to no avail.[120] A veteran of the Fourteenth described the attack as "the enemy massed their forces on our left and drove our boys from their works … Our line was driven back in great confusion." An officer rallied thirty men around the regimental flag and ordered a charge, but the assault had no effect. Instead, "Someone gathered up the colors and we retreated … in great confusion, every man pretty much his own commander."[121]

In his subsequent report, Lieutenant Colonel Bell described the flank attack as "executed with as much regularity as could be expected considering the nature of the ground. As soon as the regiment gained the crest of the hill where our skirmishers were … the regiment moved by the right flank in rear of the enemy's rifle-pits, and carried them for a distance of 500 yards, either killing, wounding, or capturing the entire force of the enemy occupying the same." Bell described the thin Confederate defenses as "a series of small pits without direct connection with each other. This enabled us to attack them in detail, and we had carried a considerable portion of their works before their main force was aware that we had turned their left." Bell recalled that the counter-attacking Texans "advanced until within thirty or forty yards of us, calling out 'we surrender,' and then fired on us." In reply, Bell wrote that "I ordered my command to fire and fix bayonets, which was done with a will. The enemy broke and ran … and we saw them no more." With great pride, Bell reported that his men captured "3 stand of colors, 5 pieces of artillery, and 450 prisoners, 7 of them commissioned officers. … My regiment might have had a greater number of flags had they been less anxious to engage the enemy."[122]

Just as Union troops were poised to overrun more of Gibson's position, however, the advance stalled. The attack, which had succeeded to a degree much greater than had been expected by a simple probing of the Confederate lines, caught Canby by surprise and he was not prepared to order a general assault. Even if an attack on all points was possible, the attack by Geddes's brigade occurred so late in the afternoon that Canby was not willing to risk a night engagement. A general assault was not possible, but Geddes himself halted his brigade's advance before they could fully exploit their advantage. The counter-attack by the Fourteenth Texas, although repulsed, probably led Geddes to expect a more vigorous Confederate reaction, so he halted his men and ordered them to dig in. Geddes was also concerned about possible fratricide. The attack had succeeded so well that the rest of the Union force was unaware of their gains. The advancing Iowans had to wave their flags to signal the Union gunners to cease fire to avoid hitting their own troops.[123] The attackers, however, believed they could have achieved more. "Last evening a charge made by the 3rd Brig. on our right that was entirely successful," a Wisconsin private later recalled. "It resulted in forcing back their left flank until we gained position from which we could rake the enemy's breastworks. If they had only been driven a little further we would have captured the whole garrison, but the Gen'l seemed to think he had done well enough for one day."[124] Some Confederates also expressed surprise by the sudden halt in the Union progress. "The main attack was on our left … and pushing back the feeble picket line we had there, got to the bay between us and Blakely, thus cutting us off," a Confederate soldier later wrote. "From that point they came on down our line driving our slender force before them. … Why they did not come right on and take us, too, we could never understand."[125] Most likely, the Union advance stopped because their officers believed that Gibson would redeploy his remaining troops, shore up his defenses, and continue to resist. Gibson had fought this long; surely he would continue to do so.

Gibson, however, had no intention to keep fighting. His first obligation was to preserve his limited number of troops to fight another day, and the loss of his left flank fortifications was enough to convince him that it was time to go. In the aftermath of the war, many officers were critical of Gibson's decision, especially as he did not consult Liddell, who would have been obligated to get confirmation of any evacuation from Maury. Gibson, however, always claimed that Maury authorized him to withdraw without permission if he believed Spanish Fort was lost. However, in deploying all his troops and resources into the defense of Spanish Fort, Maury appeared to have committed himself to stopping the Union advance at that point rather than seeing Spanish Fort as only a hindrance to the Union advance, and would not have allowed Gibson the discretion to abandon the fort.[126] Whether an evacuation was at his option or not, Gibson made the decision to leave Spanish Fort immediately under the cover of darkness. He ordered Col. Francis Campbell and his Louisiana brigade to maintain a brisk fire against all points of the Union lines to allow the remnants of Ector and Holtzclaw's battered brigades to exit the fort first, with the Louisianans to conduct a fighting retreat. Gibson wasted no time; by 10 p.m. the Confederate gunners had spiked their last cannon and had moved toward the evacuation point on the beach at the north-west corner of the fort.[127] The Confederate activity went largely unnoticed, although one perceptive Union officer noted in his diary "Reb pickets fired a good deal. Suspicious; things looked like preparations to leave."[128]

Most of the fort's defenders managed to escape thanks to a prepared line of retreat. Many soldiers, shoeless to remain silent, crossed over to Battery Huger on treadway that was twelve hundred yards long, less than two feet wide, and "concealed by the high grass and covered with moss" before reaching transports that took them to Mobile.[129] The escape up the treadway to Battery Huger was not the end of the danger. Upon reaching Huger, a Confederate veteran recalled "We had to cross a marsh about one and a half miles … to where we could get on a steamboat." Describing the marsh as "covered with reeds … making a matting over the soft mud, beneath which it was bottomless," Private Douglas Cater remembered, "Only two or three men could step in one place before the matting would be broken, and … woe to the man who placed the weight of his body on it. I have feared that some of our reported missing men were victims of that marsh." Another memoir, however, remembered the terrain differently. General Maury recalled the "marsh was quite practicable for infantry at that time. The flood had subsided and the ground had dried" to the point that his primary concern was discovery by Union forces that might "cut off the escape of the garrison."[130] The Confederates considered their escape path to be a great success and hidden secret, but only poor timing prevented Canby from cutting off their escape, as Union forces were aware of the treadway. Canby had requested landing boats from the Navy to monitor the shoreline, "but the launches were at Ship Island and Pensacola, and, although sent for, could not be got up in season."[131] The treadway saved many Confederate troops, but the escape path itself became part of the postwar debate over Confederate conduct at

Spanish Fort. Because an escape route was included in the defenses of Spanish Fort, Maury, in a postwar memoir, claimed "it was never intended that [the] garrison should be lost," suggesting that he intended Spanish Fort to serve only as a delaying position. Considering his extensive preparations, even to the extent of delaying construction and supply at other positions, this seems dubious and self-serving. Maury further praised General Gibson for including a means of escape, although, according to General Liddell, Maury had opposed the construction of such structures in the weeks leading up to the siege. Liddell claimed in his own postwar memoir that his efforts to establish "infantry connections" between the two forts were restricted because they were "considered by General Maury to be superfluous," but Liddell was pleased to take the credit for the treadway as "It eventually saved the garrison of Spanish Fort."[132]

About the same time that the Confederates were moving down the treadway, Union troops became aware of what was happening and moved forward. "The agony is over," Union Captain Thomas Stevens noted in his diary on April 9. "Spanish Fort was evacuated by the enemy between 11 & 12 o'clock last night, and soon after midnight I had the honor of leading 'C' Co. up the declivity & over the parapet into it … the first organization to enter the works."[133] Other accounts also mention the relative ease with which the Confederate works fell. "About midnight we found out they were leaving as fast as possible," a Union private wrote to his parents, "so we pushed on & occupied the fort, capturing several hundred prisoners. The largest share of them got away on transports."[134] Units vied for the honor of being the first to take portions of the fort. A soldier from the Twelfth Iowa proudly told his parents "Company K of our regiment and a Company of the 47th Illinois went on double quick and occupied Spanish Fort before the 13th Corps had any idea of what was going on and it lay immediately in front. As soon as our boys got in they set up a cheer and we fell in line. … Our boys feel glorious."[135] While Gibson did an admirable job of evacuating most of his garrison, he did leave some men behind. Of the 2,888 men that Gibson reported under his command, 556 officers and enlisted men, more than half of them wounded, became Union prisoners.[136] Private Milo Scott, an artilleryman, noted in his diary that he and his comrades received orders to withdraw after "one section of our Battery [was] taken … [and] some men captured. Evacuated the fort at night." Falling back to the waterline, Scott could not locate the assembly point so "myself and others were captured at 12 midnight."[137] After talking with several of the prisoners, a Union interrogator noted the troops, "mostly Alabama & Mississippi men … do not seem to feel very bad at falling into our hands."[138] After talking to some of the prisoners, another soldier mentioned "They all seem heartily sick of the war. Some of them go so far as to say that the … inhabitants of Mobile are praying for our success."[139]

While successful in pulling his troops out of an impossible situation, the Spanish Fort garrison played no additional part in the defense of Mobile. In his subsequent report to General Taylor, Gibson described his casualties. "I have not been able to get the exact number of casualties on the evening of the evacuation," Gibson admitted, but "I estimate our loss to have been about 20 killed and 45 wounded, and 250 captured, making a total loss of 93 killed, 395 wounded, and 250 missing, out of a force of less than 2,000 men." By comparison, on the Union side Canby suffered fifty-two men killed, five hundred seventy-five wounded, and thirty missing.[140] Nearly a thousand troops waded through the swamps of Minette Bay to Fort Blakely, but Maury sent the escaped troops to Mobile instead of reinforcing Fort Blakely. A biographer of Liddell described the refugees from Spanish Fort that arrived at Fort Blakely as "tired bodies," so perhaps Maury thought them too exhausted to be of any use to Liddell, or he was more concerned about maintaining unit cohesion by keeping units together.[141] Although the troops survived, no Confederate considered it any sort of success. "Spanish Fort was evacuated last night about midnight. Nearly all the garrison were saved," a Confederate survivor recorded, but "All the guns, munitions, commissary, and quartermaster's stores were lost."[142]

****

After the war, Dabney Maury distracted any discussion of his shortcomings at Spanish Fort by engaging in a revisionist campaign. Maury claimed the Union commander had committed an "indefensible blunder" in attacking up the east side of the bay, acted timidly in the face of an overwhelmed Confederate force, and executed a poorly planned overall strategy for the campaign. If Canby had landed on the west shore, Maury declared, "he would have found his work shorter and easier, and might have captured my whole army" as Maury was not prepared to hazard the "near 40,000 non-combatants within its line of defense, whose sufferings under a siege would soon have paralyzed the defense by a garrison so small as ours." Maury further made oblique accusations of timidity by Canby's army by pointing out they had "entrenched itself every night," an act "absurd to us, who knew that there was no force in Canby's front." In comparison to Canby's allegorical lumbering Goliath, Maury depicted his own David of a force as a "little army" who had "withstood his great armament and armada for three weeks, and had then bravely made good its retreat."[143]

Maury's defense of his actions was self-serving because his claims of weak Confederate defenses on the western side of the city were simply not truthful. Danville Leadbetter, the engineer in charge of protecting the city, advocated for an integrated defensive system for the entire area. After touring the western defenses, a Union soldier wrote, "They are very heavy and if there had been sufficient force here to man them, and the outer line, many would have fallen to rise no more, this side of eternity."[144] Attacking on the western side of the bay also presented no advantages. The plan for the operation, as dictated by Grant, was for Canby to occupy Selma, necessitating an advance up the Alabama River. Even if Canby did advance up the west side of the bay, he would still have had to attack Fort Blakely, Spanish Fort, and Batteries Tracey and Huger to gain access to the river.[145] The charge of timidity was also misplaced. The Union objective was the occupation of the interior of Alabama, and Canby could not fulfill that goal if he lost too many men in attacking Mobile. There was no reason to rush an attack, and painful lessons had taught commanders to be prudent. A Vicksburg veteran noted that at that battle "it was charge! charge! charge!," but at Mobile "a little more good sense is shown, and a regard had for human life."[146] Under different circumstances, Canby might have acted more aggressively, but he determined that a measured approach to minimize casualties was the appropriate method to deal with Maury's defenses. Instead of blundering, Canby's campaign is best summed up as a "sound, intelligent operation at a time when there was no need for impetuosity," and would likely have received more notice for his victories had they not been overshadowed by events in Virginia.[147]

Chapter 6

"Crushed but Not Yet Conquered in Spirit": Peace in Alabama

Like all ceremonies, surrenders possess symbolism, although the imagery is sometimes unintentional. In a small town in southern Alabama five weeks after the campaign to take Mobile began the symbolism was about as plain as it could possibly be. The senior Union commander, Maj. Gen. Edward Canby, arrived at the agreed-upon spot twelve miles north of Mobile on April 29, 1865, with a suitable cavalry escort, provisions for a post-discussion lunch, and a set of generous terms that he hoped would end the war in this part of the country. His Confederate counterpart, Lt. Gen. Richard Taylor, had a less auspicious arrival. The train that was to take him to the negotiations broke down, forcing Taylor to find alternative transportation. His subsequent arrival to meet Canby spoke volumes about the condition of the Confederacy. Taylor arrived only after overcoming transportation problems, a common Confederate weakness. The lack of fighting men was evident when Taylor, instead of a large escort, appeared accompanied only by his aide, Col. William Levy. Rather than a proper train, Taylor reached the surrender site in an almost undignified manner, with both men sitting on the front of a dusty handcar. Rather than an impressive steam engine, two slaves, whose services to the Confederacy were, like the soldiers in Taylor's army, about to end, propelled his humble transport.

The symbolism was not lost on Taylor, who in his memoir recalled that the circumstances of his and Canby's separate situations revealed the "fortunes of our respective causes."[1]

The events that led to Taylor's surrender began when Canby seized Spanish Fort. In capturing the position, Canby had greatly reduced the odds that the Confederates could hold Mobile. General Maury had staked the future of the city on his key defensive position in the east bay, but his gamble had failed. With the capture of Spanish Fort, Maury's future became murkier at the same rate that Canby's became clearer. The battles for Mobile, however, were still not over. The occupation of Spanish Fort improved Canby's military position, but his ultimate objective of moving into the interior of Alabama still required the capture of Fort Blakely, itself no easy task. The capture of Spanish Fort had required a significant amount of time and blood, and Canby was not eager to spend more of either commodity. Fortunately for Canby, and unfortunately for Maury, the battles around Fort Blakely resulted in satisfactory outcomes for the Union much sooner than he had anticipated, and Mobile fell into Union hands without the need for a pitched battle. Although dismayed by the Union occupation of their city, Mobile residents soon became accustomed, if not accepting, of the changes brought about by military defeat.

The loss of Fort Blakely and Mobile also presented a quandary for Richard Taylor. Without a base of operation and supply in Mobile and facing another large Union force in central Alabama, Taylor found himself with few military options. He could not defend his department with the small force at his disposal, and the nearest Confederate armies were far away from his isolated command. With limited options after the surrender of Lee's and Johnston's armies, Taylor was increasingly inclined to accept Union overtures of peace. Aiding in the likelihood of peace was Taylor's own personality. Unlike the West Point-trained generals in the Confederate Army, Taylor was a wealthy civilian who rose to high military rank, inculcated not in the ethos of professional soldiers but rather in the business considerations of debit and gain, and consideration of when to cut one's losses. By the time that Union troops took Mobile and Taylor found himself with limited options, Taylor, more than any professional soldier in his position, proved willing to make decisions regarding his department on his own counsel.

****

While Canby directed the operations against Spanish Fort, Steele's force conducted its operation northeast of Mobile. Steele's contingent consisted of Brig. Gen. John Hawkins's division of USCT troops and two cavalry divisions under Brig. Gen. Thomas Lucas reinforced by two brigades from Brig. Gen. Christopher Andrews's division of the XIII Corps, a total of eighteen thousand men.[2] Commencing the movement, however, proved difficult as the delays that upset Canby's timetable also affected Steele's. In late February, Private Isaac Jackson wrote to his brother that his regiment had "packed all our surplus baggage" and had "nothing but what they will carry on their backs" in preparation for leaving Pensacola.[3] Corporal Henry Hart anticipated "a long march before us" because the "men are allowed only one shift of underclothing, one pair of pants, one jacket and blouse, and a blanket or overcoat, but not both. What is left is packed in boxes and stored in Fort Pickens."[4]

On March 19, two days after Canby set his force in motion toward the Fish River, Steele's force left Pensacola, moving in two components. As his infantry moved forward, Steele dispatched an advance cavalry detachment under Lt. Col. Andrew Spurling toward the towns of Evergreen and Sparta, Alabama. Arriving five days later, Spurling's command destroyed a significant portion of railroad stock before rejoining Steele's column on March 26. Spurling later received the Medal of Honor for actions at Evergreen when he personally captured three Confederate soldiers.[5] While the cavalry could move with reasonable rapidity, the process for the infantry was slow going. After covering twelve miles the first day, Steele's force encountered swampy and rain-soaked terrain, bringing the advance to a crawl. Soldiers had the backbreaking work of extracting wagons from the morass, meaning the army was moving only short distances per day. The slow pace also caused a shortage of food. Private Isaac Jackson related that "rations are getting very short. This thing of carrying 6 days rations is not so pleasant as one might think. The last of the 6 days meat was eaten for supper last night and 3 days to go on." A week later, the situation had not improved, as Jackson wrote,

"Feel very hungry. Issue only half rations since 27th. Get one small hard tack (1/2 lb.) for a meal." The next day, however, Steele's force reached the main road connecting Mobile and Montgomery, and Jackson reported the army marched "18 or 19" miles in a single day as they emerged from "the pine forest with an occasional cabin, very seldom with anyone living in them."[6]

The terrain delayed their progress, but Steele's column initially met little resistance after leaving Pensacola other than a skirmish with a small Confederate cavalry force led by Brig. Gen. James Clanton. After the rendezvous with Spurling's detachment, Steele continued to march northward, continuing the posture toward Montgomery. On March 26, he directed General Andrews to occupy Pollard in the hopes of finding supplies for his hungry men, but the Confederates had already withdrawn the stores he sought. At the same time, Steele learned that steamers from which he intended to resupply his men could not pass sandbars in the Escambia River. While Steele managed to cut the railroad and disperse the cavalry in front of him, the inability to feed his men meant that he had to forego his planned advance toward Selma and Montgomery and instead turned toward Mobile to support Canby. Steele relayed his dire situation to Canby, who pulled Brig. Gen. James Veach's Division of the XIII Corps off the line to escort a wagon train to Steele's position.[7] Steele's column routed the last Confederate opposition near Holyoke on April 1 before linking up with the supply column from Canby and investing Fort Blakely on April 2, seven days after the siege of Spanish Fort had begun.[8] Steele's approach to Fort Blakely occurred largely undetected because of the superiority of his cavalry. Without cavalry of his own, Liddell posted pickets as far out as he dared, but Union horsemen outpaced and outmaneuvered the pickets, forcing them to surrender or retreat to their lines.[9] The Union soldiers were glad their long expedition was over, one recalling "being 13 days on the march, and going 120 miles. … We had some hard times." [10]

Upon his arrival at Fort Blakely, Steele found a daunting defensive position manned by around twenty-one hundred men. Although delayed by the construction emphasis on Spanish Fort, Fort Blakely was ready when the Union assault commenced. The works at Blakely consisted of a three-mile long arc, with its left flank covered by the Tensaw River and its right covered by Bay Minette, defended by nine redoubts equipped with forty-one guns.

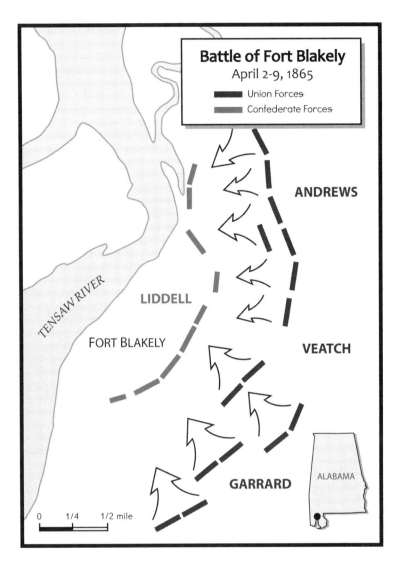

Fort Blakely.

The redoubts supported two lines of trenches, the inner line fifty yards behind the other. In addition to the earthen defenses, "a strong abatis of fallen trees ... and also three or four lines of chevaux-de-frise" also protected the fort.[11] Hidden within the abatis were poles strung with wire a few inches off the ground to trip unwary attackers, and several hundred "torpedoes,"

consisting of artillery rounds fitted with pressure fuses.[12] A Union observer
noted, "They have the vicinity of their works filled with torpedoes. ... They
are planted in the ground with the cap part up with a thin covering of dirt
over it. Some are in clusters of 12, some are in long connected together with
a wire. A line of men passing over them if one man hits the wire all will
explode. I counted 15 in a space about 50 feet in diameter."[13] The Confederate
troops were particularly well equipped with mortars. The mortars consisted
of about forty short-range Coehorn mortars manufactured in Mobile, as well
as several "wooden mortars made of gum [tree] stumps, hollowed out to eight
and ten-inch caliber ... they were only available at short range and with very
small charges." Three understrength brigades of Missouri, Mississippi, and
Alabama troops held the supporting trenches.[14] Overall, Fort Blakely was
a much better defensive position than was Spanish Fort. "It is the key to
Mobile," a Union soldier described, "hence the rebs made their defense of
the city here. They had a very strong position, as strong as art and nature
could make it."[15]

To deal with Fort Blakely, Steele received reinforcements from Canby.
Veach's division, which had escorted the resupply column, remained under
Steele's command, and he received Brig. Gen. Kenner Garrard's Second
Division from XVI Corps.[16] Steele initially tried to take Blakely by storm,
but the Confederates repulsed his first assault, and he was content to press
a siege and await assistance from Canby's larger force.[17] Their approach
was similar to that at Spanish Fort, as soldiers established their initial camps
"about ½ mile from the Reb's works" and began moving forward to the
point of contact with Confederate resistance. From there they began moving
their lines forward to within six hundred yards of enemy positions despite
Rebel artillery fire. A soldier described, "We are kept digging day and night
which is very hard duty."[18] The Confederates were also doing more digging.
Concerned that a Union siege might erode the prepared defensive works,
Maury ordered additional engineers to Fort Blakely to maintain the ramparts
and outer works.[19] Despite the additional excavation and repulse of the initial
Union assault, confidence was in short supply at Fort Blakely. A Confederate
veteran who had survived the siege of Vicksburg noted the troops "began to
feel sort of squally" as a similar process seemed to unfold around them.[20]

The pessimism seemed well founded, as the siege of Fort Blakely proceeded along similar lines to those at Spanish Fort. Artillery fire from the fort made sapping a dangerous and difficult experience. The Confederate gunboats *Morgan*, *Nashville*, and *Huntsville*, which mounted guns heavy enough to smash earthen fortifications, supplemented the fire from the forts. By April 8, however, troops had cleared sufficient trees for a clear line of shot, and Union artillerymen soon drove the boats away.[21] The Union gunners could deal with the vulnerable gunboats, but had more trouble with the guns in the fort. The Union attackers had no heavy artillery with them, only the field guns that had accompanied Steele's column. "We fired 165 shots at the rebs yesterday from our gun," one artilleryman wrote. "We have been under a severe fire several times since we have been here. We had 5 guns firing on us for about an hour at one time."[22] Union troops, however, were most concerned with the mines strewn in front of Blakely. "The rebels have filled the ground with torpedoes, and not scarcely a day passes but what some poor scout gets blowed up," Private Jerry Flint recalled. "The most of them are eight or ten-inch shell, with a percuss[ion] cap, buried in the road or along a stream where the army will be apt to go for water. A man was killed close to our camp by one of those machines yesterday." The terror of sudden death from an unexpected explosion created the desire to retaliate, and Flint recorded that his companions "swear that if they ever get into the fort they will bayonet twenty rebels for every one of our men killed by a torpedo. And they are the men to keep their word."[23]

Liddell, like Gibson at Spanish Fort, did what he could to fend off the Union assault, maintaining a constant artillery barrage against the advancing Union excavations while expanding his works where possible. As at Spanish Fort, the Confederates attempted to push back the Union sappers with probing attacks, but accomplished nothing except taking casualties they could not afford.[24] The forays inflicted casualties on the Union attackers, but did not dampen their confidence. "There has been nothing more than heavy skirmishing yet although our men have rifle pits within 50 yards of the rebel works," a Union soldier wrote. "We have lost about one thousand in killed and wounded. Everybody is confident of success."[25] Life in the Confederate lines was no safer, as the defenses at Blakely provided little cover. Liddell's own headquarters was within range of both Union artillery and sharpshooters. Graphic proof of this occurred when an officer speaking to Liddell observed a Union shell land in front of his tent but fail to explode.[26]

Despite the dangers, Liddell still held all his redoubts and was fully prepared to defend his position, but the sudden news of the fall of Spanish Fort on April 8 doomed Fort Blakely. Now free to move against other objectives, Canby's approach to Fort Blakely changed. Fearful that the Confederate troops who successfully evacuated Spanish Fort would reinforce Blakely, Canby wanted immediate action against the position. The other concern was that the Confederates might abandon Fort Blakely. Having failed to snare the entire Spanish Fort garrison, Canby wanted to ensure the same did not happen at Blakely. The Confederate defenders themselves seem to give no hint of their intentions. "Learned this morning that Spanish Fort had been taken by assault about midnight of the 8th," an Illinois private wrote in his diary. "From the unusual quietness of the rebels in Fort Blakely, it was supposed that they was either evacuating or strengthening their lines."[27] To prevent the escape of the Blakely garrison, Canby allocated two divisions from the XVI Corps to Steele. Canby also quickly shifted guns to the new objective, which had immediate effect. The Indiana gunners who had proven so accurate at Spanish Fort were among the first to arrive and made their presence felt. In the afternoon, the artillerymen engaged the steamboats supplying the fort, severely damaging one and driving off the remainder. Without adequate supply, Fort Blakely's days were numbered, but Canby had a shorter timeframe in mind.[28]

To ensure the capture of the Blakely garrison, Canby ordered Steele to conduct a general assault as soon as possible, and Steele sent orders for the attack to begin as soon as the reinforcements from the XVI Corps arrived. The plan was for an advanced line of "heavy skirmishers" comprised of half of the Union attack force to engage the Confederates to cover the second assault wave coming up behind them. The first Union force to engage the Confederates was the Seventy-third USCT, under the command of Lt. Col. Henry Merriam, who manned the north end of the Union line. As the Seventy-third pushed forward in a probing attack to test the left flank of the Confederate defenses, their skirmish line came under fire from Blakely's defenders, which forced them to take cover. Merriam ordered the rest of his regiment, backed by additional troops from his brigade, to move forward to protect his exposed skirmishers. Seeing the USCT troops advancing, other Union troops took their actions as a sign to begin the assault, and by 6 p.m. Union troops attacked on all points of the line.[29]

Unlike at Spanish Fort, where the capture of the position was almost anti-climactic after the Confederates abandoned their lines, the forced entry into Fort Blakely provided many vivid descriptions and recollections. A Union soldier at Spanish Fort, Private Henry Bert, observed the attack on Fort Blakely from afar. "There was a tremendous artillery firing commenced," Bert wrote to his sister. "A charge was then going on and in about five or ten minutes more the firing ceased and another more strong and louder yell was uttered and was continually kept up for more than half an hour" until the attack came to a successful end.[30] A correspondent for the *Cincinnati Gazette* witnessed the assault much closer, describing the advance with great flourish and detail. "Each man must climb and clamber for himself, and that over a distance of nearly seven hundred yards, through masses of matted timber, which really seemed insurmountable," he wrote. "Wreaths of thin, blue smoke were curling around the rebel ramparts, lit up continually by spurts and flashes of vindictive fire." After crossing the space between the two lines, the correspondent watched as "A short, sharp struggle takes place at the foot of the rebel rampart. Our men have flung themselves across the ditch, and are clambering up the outer slope of the works. Another moment, and something flashes like a meteor through the smoke and fire. Thank God, it is the sacred banner of the stars! It floats as ever amid the storm of battle, the emblem of liberty and light … placed there also by the stout hands which bore them and the stern bayonets that guarded them."[31]

Writing with less flowery language, Private Isaac Jackson wrote to his brother relating how "The rebel works were about 600 or 700 yds. from us. With fallen timber all the way across and other obstructions that we knew nothing of. … We ran about 1/3 of the way and stopped for breath and then up again and for the fort. … crossed a ravine and took breath on top of a hill for another run." The pauses were useful, as Jackson and his comrades still had to reach the main line protected by "an abattis [*sic*] of brush. On top of the hill was another (but more dense than the first) and a short distance from that was the third one—more formidable than the other two, being composed of short stubby pine limbs & long sharpened stakes in with it. Between the 2nd & 3rd was a wire stretched so as to throw a man on those sharp stakes. But it was a little too far off for the purpose intended. The wire tripped nearly every man."[32] Small arms fire from the Confederate defenders took its toll on the advancing Union troops, but accounts by the attackers most frequently mention the numerous torpedoes in front of Blakely's ramparts as the deadliest devices. In his memoirs, Lt. William Eddington described how "I had not gone far when a man next to me on my left stepped on a torpedo with his left foot. It blew his leg off below the knee and his right leg off above the knee."[33] Once Union troops cleared the torpedoes and gained the peak of the parapet, however, the overwhelmed Confederate troops were more likely to surrender than fight to the death. One overpowered Mississippi soldier related the futility of resistance by stating "There were so many that they overpowered us and took all our army prisoner," confirmed by a Union soldier who recalled that, once inside the fort, "The fight was rather short but hot while it lasted."[34]

After the brief clash to take Fort Blakely, claims soon arose that USCT troops killed a large number of Confederate prisoners, perhaps in retribution for the massacre of USCT troops at Fort Pillow, Mississippi, almost exactly a year earlier. There had been other instances of racially motivated battlefield violence in the past months, so both sides reasonably concluded that any clash between USCT and Confederate troops might lead to another incident. The Confederates were certainly wary of such a possibility. As Steele's troops began to surround Fort Blakely, Liddell sent a message to his brigade commanders "to inform you that the force of the enemy now in our front is composed principally of negroes, and will not spare any of our men should they gain possession of our works."[35] There is also evidence that the potential for revenge was on the mind of Hawkins's men. Private William R. Murphy of the First Mississippi Light Artillery, was captured with several other Confederate soldiers east of Fort Blakely when "ordered to plant torpedoes" to impede Steele's advance. While transferred to Ship Island, Murphy and his co-prisoners were "guarded by a 'nigger' company, who told us that if they had captured us they would have killed us."[36]

Although the potential for retaliation was present, it is unclear if the subsequent fatalities were premeditated or an unintended byproduct of the emotion of the charge. Determining the extent of any suspected massacre is difficult because some Confederates continued to fight even as their comrades were surrendering, leading to violence directed against those who had stopped fighting and accusations of unnecessary deaths inflicted by Union troops upon the prisoners. During the charge toward the fort, for instance, a Confederate picket raised his hands in surrender, but when the main charge passed by him the soldier retrieved his weapon and fired, but Union troops killed him with a return volley.[37] When the Eleventh Wisconsin entered the fort, most Confederates immediately surrendered, but a small group did not. The Confederate officer in charge yelled, "No quarter to the damned Yankees," indicating that he would neither surrender nor take prisoners, and the resisting Confederates were killed only after a violent hand-to-hand struggle.[38] The officer that ordered for no quarter to the enemy paid for his resistance with his life, shot in the head at point-blank range.[39] In the chaos and emotion of the fight, surrendered Confederates were still at risk of injury or death due to the confusion of the moment or adrenaline-fueled aggression. As Brig. Gen. Cockrell surrendered to a Union officer, a Union private prepared to shoot Cockrell, but the officer saved Cockrell at the last moment.[40] Similar situations where Confederates continued to fight even as others tried to surrender occurred in the portion of the line charged by Hawkins's USCT troops. In the most notable incident, as a Mississippi regiment surrendered to the advancing Union men, a nearby battery fired a blast at the USCT troops and then tried to surrender. Angered by what they perceived as treachery, the Union troops killed two of the artillerymen.[41]

Further undermining accusations of massacre is the absence of prolonged violence, further suggesting that any killing that did occur happened in the heat of combat. Unlike in other "black flag" incidents during the Civil War, especially those when USCT troops were the victims, there was no prolonged violence after combat had ended nor were there murders of the helpless or unarmed. Even those accounts that claim a massacre took place are devoid of evidence of killings beyond the approximately twenty minutes it took for the Union to overwhelm Fort Blakely, unlike at Fort Pillow when Confederate troops killed USCT troops long after the battle ended.[42] Further complicating any claims of a massacre is the difficulty of determining exactly how many Confederates, if any, USCT troops killed after surrendering. Fearful of surrendering to black troops that might seek revenge for past massacres, many of the defenders fled their positions or tried to surrender to white Union troops on their right, so the number of Confederates who remained in dangerous positions is unclear.[43] Capt. Henry Crydenwise of the Seventy-third USCT, described how during the attack "The rebs in their rifle pits to my rear & left became frightened" and as Crydenwise organized his men to consolidate his position, "the rebs … continued to fire upon us."[44] Moreover, in the aftermath of the battle, official reports credited Hawkins's division with the capture of 123 Confederates, belying the claim that the USCT troops took no prisoners.[45] An Arkansas soldier later wrote in his memoirs that "Blakely was the Yankee Fort Pillow. The place was stormed, the garrison shot down or bayonetted at their posts," but made no specific distinction of who was doing the killing.[46] The claim, however, does not hold up to scrutiny. One source estimated that USCT troops killed perhaps fifty Confederates in the forts until officers could get the men under control.[47] However, the confusion of combat, the growing darkness, and the separated redoubts make it impossible to determine which Confederates died during the charge, as a result of the hand-to-hand combat to take Fort Blakely, or after they were in Union custody.

With the forts in Union hands, chaos reigned as Union attackers celebrated, Confederate defenders surrendered or attempted to flee, and commanders on both sides tried to determine what was going on. Some Confederates fled down to the banks of the Tensaw River, but with no escape path comparable to the treadway at Spanish Fort, their only option was to give up or swim. By not surrendering, however, they made themselves vulnerable, and, as a Union officer described, "Numbers of them jumped into the river and were drowned in attempting to cross, or were shot while swimming."[48] CSS *Nashville*, anchored in the Tensas River, and other Confederate steamers evacuated about two hundred men who swam out to her. General Liddell either could not swim or thought it beneath his dignity to do so. Lt. John Bennett, commanding the *Nashville*, sent a boat to retrieve him, but approaching Union troops prevented the rescue and Liddell became a prisoner.[49] With the capture of their commanding officer, the last gasp of Confederate resistance ceased and the fighting stopped. In addition to Liddell, Brig. Generals Cockrell and Thomas were also captured, along with most of the garrison. Some Confederate troops reached Mobile after their rescue by the river steamers, swimming across the Tensaw River, or making their way through the swamps, but casualties on both sides were remarkably low. The most reliable estimate is that about seventy-five Confederates died during the entire siege and assault, while Union losses were about 150 killed and 650 wounded over the course of the campaign. The loss of Fort Blakely was crippling to Maury's force. Union officers reporting to Canby listed the "prisoners captured at Fort Blakely as 232 commissioned officers and 3,386 enlisted men" and captured materiel as "32 pieces siege and field artillery, 6,000 rounds artillery ammunition, 100,000 rounds ammunition for small-arms, 36,000 pounds corn, 13 serviceable mules, 7 bales sand-bags, 5 army wagons, and 3 wall-tents."[50]

As at Spanish Fort, critics soon questioned the choices that led to the loss of Fort Blakely. Liddell was critical of Maury for not allowing him to keep the survivors from Spanish Fort that arrived in his lines, claiming "if General Maury had permitted me to keep the Spanish Fort garrison, I could have repelled the assault … As It was, my line was nothing more than a good skirmish line, whose fire was entirely too weak." Liddell also asserted his position was "in a very incomplete state," and more time and labor would have improved his odds. Maury, in turn, shifted some of the blame to Liddell, claiming he intended to evacuate Fort Blakely, but stated that Liddell gave him every indication he could hold the position longer than he did.[51] Maury also disapproved of Liddell's failure, if he could not hold the fort, to deny its resources to the enemy. Maury had some legitimate complaint in this regard, as at least one Union officer was not impressed with the Confederate efforts to deny them the fruits of their victory. Although complimentary of the Confederate design of the forts, Captain Thomas Stevens noted that the captured guns "were all spiked, but most of the spikes can be withdrawn without much trouble," and he wondered "Why they did not destroy the ammunition," which seemed plentiful. He could only conclude the Confederates "evidently had not men enough to man their works, or they would never have abandoned such strong ones."[52] A Confederate officer confirmed

Stevens's opinion, explaining the loss of Fort Blakely as "Our lines were very weak, the men being about two yards apart."[53]

Although the fighting was over at Fort Blakely, the position continued to claim lives. The torpedoes planted by the Confederates remained in place, and, common to the use of land mines still today, were still a menace for a long time after. "There were torpedoes planted in front of their works," a soldier recalled, "as the Brigade came back after the fight several men were killed and wounded. They were exploding all night long."[54] One Union officer described how, after his men captured a supply of "commissary whiskey" from Fort Blakely, they "imbibed a little too freely of the latter, thereby losing their heads and running over the torpedoes. They lost their lives after the war was over."[55] Many Confederate prisoners feared that the Union troops would kill them in retaliation. During the assault, a soldier watched as some Confederate troops "threw down their guns and begged for mercy, for they thought they would be killed because they had planted the ground full of 'torpedoes' over which we had to pass. … They knew they had done wrong by fighting with torpedoes."[56] There was no retaliation for the deaths caused by the hidden weapons, but the Union high command compelled the Confederate prisoners to undertake the hazardous task of removing them. An officer noted that "Gen. Steele took some of the rebels out and made them take up the torpedoes."[57] The devices proved as deadly to the Confederates clearing them as to the Union troops who had to attack over them, as a Union soldier wrote approvingly: "General Steele is making the prisoners take them up. Two of them have been killed—Amen."[58] Other sources state the order to clear the mines came from higher up, recalling that General "Canby ordered the prisoners under guard to dig up all the torpedoes. I saw 'Rebs' digging them up, but I didn't want to be in their way or hinder them at their work, so I stayed pretty well back." Rather than disturb the torpedoes by digging them up, Confederate prisoners learned to detonate them in place, with a Union soldier observing "They would put a burning pine knot on them and that would explode them."[59]

With Fort Blakely now under Union control, the only barrier between Canby and Mobile were the two gun batteries barring the entrance into the rivers. Battery Huger contained eleven heavy guns while Battery Tracey contained five 7-inch pieces. Supplementing the two batteries were several warships of the Confederate Navy that altogether mounted twenty-six guns.[60] The waters around both batteries also hid naval torpedoes to keep the Union fleet at a distance.[61] Although well-sited to control the rivers and upper portions of Mobile Bay, Battery Tracey and Battery Huger together stood little chance to stop Canby's advance. Both aided in the defense of Spanish Fort and Fort Blakely, but a shortage of ammunition meant their fire was sporadic and ineffective. Union fire from batteries established on the south side of Bay Minette, on the other hand, was very accurate, disabling several Confederate guns.[62] Canby ordered "some heavy guns to bear on a small sand fort the rebels still held out on a small island or sand bar out in the water," and soon Union shells were hitting the batteries.[63] The Union guns on the eastern bluffs dominated the batteries below, and General Maury recognized the inevitable. "Batteries Huger and Tracey are the only barriers left to prevent the enemy from reaching the city," a Confederate hastily wrote in his diary. "They may last a few days longer but must eventually fall."[64] Maury ordered the battery defenders to maintain fire on any Union advance, consume as much of their ammunition as possible, and then withdraw when forced to do so.[65] The defenders were more than ready to leave, with one gunner telling his wife, "the disgraceful fall of Blakely will no doubt precipitate that of Mobile." After two days, the troops manning the batteries evacuated under the cover of darkness on April 10. The next day, deserters informed the Union Navy of their departure and nearby troops took possession of the batteries.[66] With no positions left to defend, the Confederates scuttled the floating batteries in the Spanish River to block the channel, while the surviving warships and steamers sailed up the Tombigbee River to Demopolis, Alabama, to escape capture.[67]

The loss of the eastern forts made the defense of Mobile impossible. Not only had Maury lost half of his command, the defense of the forts expended most of his available ammunition. Continued defense of the city would also place thousands of noncombatants at risk, leaving Maury the only choice but to withdraw the remaining troops. On April 10, while Canby dealt with Batteries Huger and Tracey, bells rang throughout the city indicating that the evacuation of the city was to commence. The evacuation, although unexpected by the residents, occurred with minimal disruption. To prevent general panic, Maury quickly moved as many troops as possible out of the city, to avoid both panicking the populace by having them witnessing the retreat and possible pillaging by his own men as they passed through town. Instead, he kept only a minimal rear guard to maintain order, spike the heavy guns they could not take with them, and supervise the removal of stores and equipment by civilian workers and impressed slaves. For the rest of the day and all of April 11, the Confederates dismantled what items they could move and did their best to destroy what could not. "Rolled all the shot and shell into the bay, destroyed all the powder by emptying all the cartridge bags in the bay," a member of the rear guard recorded. "On account of the nearness of the enemy, the evacuation had to be conducted as quietly as possible," and "None of the batteries were blown up" to avoid civilian casualties.[68]

Maury's staff also supervised the loading of supplies and the sick and wounded troops onto a handful of railroad cars and several ships. The laden ships, comprised of impressed steamers, former blockade-runners, and CSA Navy vessels, steamed up the Tombigbee River, with the Navy stringing a line of torpedoes behind them to deter pursuit. The Confederates destroyed the Navy Yard, leaving only "some lumber and a quantity of soft coal" to be captured by their Union counterparts.[69] Maury himself did not depart until the morning of the twelfth, leaving with forty-five hundred troops and twenty-seven field pieces.[70] The Confederate evacuation was not flawless, however. Maury left behind a large amount of ordnance amounting to eighteen field guns, thirty-four heavy guns, ninety-eight coastal guns, and five hundred stands of small arms.[71] Overall, the assessment of one officer was that "The evacuation was badly conducted. Many more valuable stores could have been saved with proper management. ... Mobile was left with great reluctance by both officers and men. The men, though low-spirited, behaved well." Many, however, left with great sorrow, including one officer who left behind "a dear wife, child, sister, and two little nieces in great grief."[72]

The nearby battles had ended, but the city of Mobile itself was still in peril. One of the tasks assigned to the rear guard was to burn the thirty thousand bales of cotton accumulated in the city center, which they did before hastily leaving. A nearby cotton press also caught fire, threatening to spread the flames to other buildings. Maury also left behind some supplies, which nearly caused a riot. A local woman reported "a commotion has sprung up, down the street, and the people threatened with a mob. A quantity of commissary stores having been left by our military authorities, and being turned over to the poor, each one of that class, helping himself freely, and endeavoring to carry off as much as possible each one tries to be first, and consequently much scuffling and rioting" occurred. Before either the fire or the riot could spread, however, the citizens of Mobile took matters into their own hands. The rioters were forced off the streets by "citizens, who appear with loaded guns & various weapons," while others, including the fire company of free African Americans, extinguished the cotton fire, saving about half of the bales.[73] Control of the city was also maintained by "Several companies, known as home-guards, made up chiefly of non-combatants and foreigners—generally Germans" that kept looters in check as the army withdrew.[74]

For Mobile, the transition period from Confederate to Union control was brief. Union troops under the command of Maj. Gen. Gordon Granger entered the city on the heels of Maury's departure, and demanded its immediate surrender. Mayor Robert Slough had no alternative but to accede to Granger's request, announcing, "Your demand has been granted, and I trust, for the sake of humanity, all the safeguards which we can throw around our people will be secured to them."[75] Slough may have had Columbia, South Carolina, in mind when he made that statement, but Canby's men were not inclined to burn the city for which they had fought so hard and so long.[76] Union troops entered the city and hoisted the national flag over the Customs House, signifying their conquest. "I saw some soldiers dressed in blue coming along Royal Street," a resident later wrote. "[T]hey went to the top of the Battle House [Hotel] and hoisted it [the Union flag]. They took off their caps and gave three cheers 'for the capture of Mobile.'"[77] For many residents, the reality of their situation did not impose upon them until the actual appearance of Union troops marching down their streets. "I believe I was never so gloomy," Mobile resident Mary Waring wrote in her memoirs of the day of occupation. "I began to realize what had and was taking place." Apart from now-freed slaves, citizens stayed off the streets and "the city had the quietness of the grave," a female resident wrote. "Every blind was closed, and the streets completely deserted by all … If the plague had entered the city, it could not have had a gloomier appearance."[78]

Slowly, most Confederates came to accept the occupation as conditions returned to normal. On April 13, Gen. Granger, placed in command of the occupied city, issued a general order stating "All stores, shops, and other places of business will be opened, and the legitimate business of the city resumed without delay, under such restrictions as the military authorities may, from time to time, find it necessary to impose." Within a few weeks of the occupation, a Union soldier observed, "The stores are being opened with good stocks of goods and everything begins to wear a business aspect."[79] The resumption of a passable normality contributed to improved relations, with one Union occupier commenting that "The people of Mobile submit to Yankee rule quite cheerfully. They treat our soldiers with respect, in fact, I think they like the change."[80] The deportment of the Union troops, who behaved reasonably well and helped those civilians in need, promoted the general calm of the city. "Soldiers of the Union army, who were expected to burn and destroy, have been seen … distributing their coffee and bread to starving women and children," a newspaper reporter wrote. "Every soldier … gave his ration, and with such wonderful satisfaction, that spectators wept at the sight." Much more jarring to the civilians than the occupying Union troops was the sudden change in their relationship with their former slaves. Only three weeks after Mobile fell under his authority, Thomas W. Conway, General Superintendent of the Freedmen's Bureau for the Department of the Gulf, issued a statement that "All person formerly held as slaves will be treated in every respect as entitled to the rights of freedmen, and such as desire their services will be required to pay them." Conway issued the order after, upon his arrival in Mobile, he "found the freedmen locked up in yards, and forced by their former owners into submission of their will. As soon as the following order was issued, he unlocked the gates and set thousands at liberty. The former owners had to recognize the rights of the freedmen, pay them for their work, or let them go."[81]

The fighting may have moved beyond the city, but Mobile still had one more tragic day before the Civil War ended. On May 25, a catastrophic explosion destroyed much of the city's waterfront properties and facilities.

Laborers hired by the Union Army had transferred captured ammunition to an ordnance depot established in a two-story brick warehouse on Beauregard Street. For reasons never determined, the powder and shells stored inside, said by one source to be around two hundred tons, detonated with frightening results. Capt. Thomas Stevens wrote to his wife, "The Ordnance Depot in the city blew up killing hundreds of soldiers & citizens, & wounding hundreds more. Whole squares of brick buildings were blown down & destroyed. … A number of buildings were burned, as well as several steamboats, & trains of cars standing on the rail-road track. It seemed to lift the whole city from its foundations." A local resident described how during the explosion "the very earth shook and houses trembled on their foundations … the air was filled with flying timbers, bales of cotton, barrels of rosin, mules and horses, and hundreds of human beings … Every building within the radius of a mile was more or less shattered." An Iowa private reported that three days after the explosion one "can hear an occasional shell burst in the fire of the ruins in town yet."[82] An Illinois soldier encamped several miles away noted "the concussion nearly took the tops of our heads off. It was sometime before we got over the effect of the jar." Nearing the explosion site, he observed "a fearful sight to behold. The dead bodies of men had been gathered up but the dead horses and mules … and arms and legs and pieces of men and animals were laying everywhere among the ruins and shreds of flesh was sticking to the walls and buildings all around."[83] An Iowa soldier attributed the blast to general carelessness. "I have wondered that such explosions were not more frequent," he wrote. "While at Spanish Fort, ammunition of all kinds was piled up on the wharf, having been taken from the magazines for shipment. Some of the packages would break open and powder was laying around loose everywhere."[84] In the aftermath of the explosion, Gen. Granger tightened security in the city by requiring all paroled Confederates to obtain a pass to enter the city, impressing civilians to clear the debris, and issuing rations and tents to those injured and made homeless by the blast.[85]

****

After the loss of Mobile, Taylor's primary efforts were to consolidate his remaining troops. Maury's surviving forces from Mobile retreated along two routes. Those on the railroad cars of the Mobile & Ohio headed north toward Taylor's headquarters at Meridian. The steamers laden with troops and supplies headed up the Tombigbee River to Demopolis at the confluence of the Tombigbee and Black Warrior Rivers before rendezvousing with the rest of Taylor's army at Meridian.[86] Because Canby did not press Maury's retreating force, the thirty-seven-mile march to Citronelle was leisurely, as the men "sauntered on from day to day in the balmy spring air."[87] Once all available troops had reached Meridian, Taylor set about putting them in some sort of order, including reorganizing the troops who had fled the city with Maury into a new three-brigade division.[88] The main question facing Taylor was what to do next, a decision he had to make quickly to preserve his remaining forces. After the defeat at Mobile many troops were demoralized, a condition made worse by the news of Lee's surrender. "Arrived in Demopolis," one of Maury's soldiers wrote on April 14. "A most miserable camping ground, very low and swampy. No rations issued yet, the command greatly in need of something to eat." Besides a lack of food, the soldiers had no information, news, or instructions, with the soldier noting the camp was in a "Great confusion … What will be our next move, puzzles all."[89] Even with all his available troops at Meridian, Taylor's reduced force had few options regarding their movement. The north/south axis of the Mobile & Ohio Railroad only led to places the army could not or did not want to go, and Taylor found himself controlling only a ribbon of territory between the Union occupation of the Mississippi River Valley and the devastated industrial centers in central Alabama, essentially cut off from the eastern portion of the Confederacy.[90]

With less than ten thousand troops available, Taylor's options were limited to attempting a defense of the Mobile & Ohio Railroad or uniting with another Confederate force. He soon found that defending the rail line was an unlikely option. Taylor received notice from Milton Brown, President of the Mobile & Ohio, informing him that "The services rendered during the evacuation of Mobile were large & our expenses heavy" so he demanded "payment of six hundred thousand dollars. We cannot continue to run for less." Taylor did not have that much cash, and lacked the ability to raise it.[91] With the railroad no longer at his disposal, Taylor pondered either a long trip eastward toward Joseph Johnston's army in the Carolinas or a short trip westward to Edwin Kirby Smith's army in the Trans-Mississippi Department. On April 14, Taylor telegraphed Jefferson Davis, then in North Carolina, for instructions because "Ignorant of the policy of the Government, I cannot decide," but Davis never received the message.[92] Forced to act on his own initiative, Taylor decided to abandon Mississippi and Alabama and move his forces eastward in a bid to reinforce Johnston. Although a much longer and more uncertain route, Taylor's decision was, if not the most logical, the most practical. First, many of the Mobile defenders were troops detached from the Army of Tennessee, so his troops would likely approve of a reunion. In addition, despite the shorter distance, a movement toward the Trans-Mississippi Department was not necessarily easier. Reaching the Mississippi River was easy enough, but crossing the river itself posed an impossible task. Any assemblage of troops along the river would attract Union gunboats and invite attack by the Federal garrisons scattered along the river from Memphis to New Orleans. Even if Union forces chose not to attack, finding the boats to move the troops across was a far from certain task.

Lastly, and perhaps most obviously, Taylor would not take his men to the Trans-Mississippi Department because that would mean placing himself again under the command of Kirby Smith. Neither man had forgotten nor forgiven their earlier personality clashes, nor would Taylor ever have given Kirby Smith the satisfaction of seeming to give Taylor refuge after his military failures.

Taylor began to deploy his men away from Meridian and into camps scattered along the railway toward Demopolis in preparation for the eastward march, but demoralization became worse and desertion was an inevitable result. "I know nothing of our destination," Sgt. William Chambers wrote as the army marched eastward in the rain. "It is said we will go to Cuba Station, Ala. [twenty miles east of Meridian] but I suppose we will go further than that … I think our destination is the army of Gen. Johnston in North Carolina." Although Chambers correctly guessed his objective, he was not optimistic. "It seems like following a 'forlorn hope,' and it is with extreme reluctance that the men will go." Chambers was correct, as two days later he noted in his diary "Several more of the command have deserted. About fifteen of our brigade are missing. I really doubt whether one thousand men of this force will cross the Alabama River. It seems to be a settled fact that the days of the Confederacy are numbered."[93] A Louisiana officer reported that "A few men desert every night … Many are deserting from all the regiments," including his own, relating his own command had left Mobile "with seventy men for duty, and turned out this morning only eleven."[94] Recognizing their fate, Confederate troops at Cuba Station referred to the place as "Camp Farewell," acknowledging that their time as soldiers was likely near an end.[95]

While Taylor weighed his options, Thomas requested that Canby occupy Selma and Montgomery, rather than Wilson, so Wilson's cavalry could participate in the hunt for Jefferson Davis. Canby complied, informing the War Department that "The Sixteenth Corps was put in march for Montgomery" accompanied by four thousand cavalry to "break up all communications between Johnston's and Taylor's armies." At the same time, "Steele with his original infantry force and some artillery was sent by water to Montgomery" and the cavalry force organized into a brigade under "[Brig. Gen. Joseph R.] West for operations west of the Tombigbee."[96] When Union troops reached Selma barely two weeks after a Union cavalry raid discussed in the next chapter had reached Montgomery their reception was decidedly cool. "Before the 2nd of April, the people did not know what war is. They had not suffered," Private Henry Hart believed. "[B]ut Wilson's men had "burned and completely destroyed all shops and stores and workhouses. … There is not a store opened yet." Consequently, "The people are very social and treat us with respect. … They feel crushed but not conquered in spirit." A week later, Hart found the populace even more rebellious than when he first arrived, describing how residents "hate the word Union; they despise the Stars and Stripes. The ladies of this place avoid walking under it where it hangs over the walk by going into the street. … They are as opposed to us as ever. It will be years before they take up arms again from the fact they are crushed and exhausted complete in men and resources for war. I think the states will come back into the Union, not for love of the Union, but preferring being in the Union as before than rigid military rule."[97] The only warm reception in Selma came from freed slaves. "Where ever the boat landed the negroes would do anything for us," a Union soldier recalled. "Give us anything they had, show us where the good meat was to be had. We lived on the fat of the land.

We have been living on Ham, Chicken, Butter, Egg, Molasses, Sugar, Coffee, Cornmeal (and plenty of it)."[98]

At the same time, the XVI Corps reached Montgomery, where Maj. Gen. Andrew Smith determined to impose a peaceful occupation. To that end, Smith's "guerillas," renowned for their pillaging ability, found themselves forbidden to forage.[99] Rather than pillage, Smith gave strict orders that "foraging parties must always be under the immediate command of a commissioned officer, who will be specially instructed to remain with his men and to prevent them, by any means necessary, from taking anything else."[100] Smith's efforts to prevent pillaging were largely successful, but the citizens of Montgomery, as in Selma, still harbored resentment at their recent defeat and occupation. "Four years ago I stopped here soon after the formation of our government," a demobilized Confederate officer wrote disgustedly in his diary. "How different the scene now. Yankee officers riding & driving everywhere."[101] Sensing the public mood, one Union soldier was opposed to granting the Southerners an easy Reconstruction. "For my part I believe in making these head men among the secessionists suffer a little," he opined. "Make them feel, if it is possible for such men to feel, that the United States is able to punish traitors as well as put down treason."[102]

****

The Union occupation of Selma and Montgomery greatly complicated Taylor's plans for an eastward march, as did the arrival of news that Lee had surrendered at Appomattox. On April 19, Canby offered a ceasefire to allow peace talks to occur if Taylor would accept the same terms offered to Lee.[103] Aware of the difficulties facing him and increasing desertion among his men, Taylor proved receptive. Taylor's willingness to consider surrendering to Canby reflected not defeatism, but rather Taylor's sense of practicality, as he was not an officer prone to martial statements or over-exuberant expectations. Instead, he was a practical man who looked at situations as they were instead of how he would have liked them to be, an example of which occurred the previous autumn. To bolster sagging civilian morale, Jefferson Davis visited Georgia and Alabama in September 1864, and the President, after visiting Hood's army after its battering at Atlanta, held a conference with Taylor, who had recently assumed command of the Department of Alabama,

Mississippi, and East Louisiana. Upon hearing from Davis that General Hood believed his army to be in fine shape and morale, Taylor dispelled the President of that notion, advising him to be wary of "listening to narrators who were more disposed to tell what was agreeable than what was true." Taylor told Davis what he believed to be true, specifically that Hood's army was in poor condition, civilian morale was plummeting, and the Trans-Mississippi Department would be of no further assistance to the Confederate effort. In Taylor's opinion, the most optimistic assessment was that the Confederacy could handle limited Union attacks during the upcoming winter lull, but could not contain major offensives once spring arrived, a view that proved highly accurate.[104] Taylor further pressed Davis to ignore "certain senators and representatives, who ... talked much wild nonsense" and instead take a more objective look at how the bid for independence was to be achieved.[105] The following year, Taylor was even less than confident of success. On March 7, Taylor informed Beauregard of Wilson's presence in northern Alabama and confided that if it was more than just a raid he had no means of impeding its progress. Beauregard characterized Taylor's position as unable to "resist anything more than a mere cavalry raid" and, believing that Wilson intended to reach Selma and Montgomery, inquired, "shall the valuable machinery and stores be sent farther east?"[106] Taylor's biggest concerns had come true, and he had to consider whether continued resistance to Union military might would produce any positive gains, especially when news confirming Lee's surrender arrived. On April 20, Taylor made one more attempt to contact Davis, transmitting his earlier telegram again through Maj. Gen. Howell Cobb's headquarters in Georgia, but with equal lack of success.[107] With no political guidance, Taylor pondered his options for two more days before agreeing to meet with Canby.[108]

Taylor's decision to parlay with Canby after the failure to contact Davis was an unconventional one, but also consistent with the personality of Taylor, especially as Maj. Gen. Nathan Forrest, his principle subordinate, did not object. Forrest was an unlikely commander. Born into relative poverty, the self-educated Forrest had made himself one of the wealthiest men in Tennessee through shrewd trading in cotton, slaves, and other commodities. Forty years old when the war began, Forrest enlisted as private in the Seventh Tennessee Cavalry, purchasing weapons and horses for the regiment when none were forthcoming. Quickly promoted to lieutenant colonel, Forrest participated in various campaigns in the Western Theater, as well as conducted many independent raiding operations, gaining promotions and praise for his efforts. Wherever he served, all the senior officers held Forrest in high regard; one stated "His natural qualifications as a soldier were phenomenal" and he had "great ability as a military leader."[109] However, the massacre of USCT at Fort Pillow in April 1864 and his impulse to accept any challenge to his authority or integrity tainted his reputation. He was quick to offer a challenge to duel, even with other senior officers. One private described Forrest as "a great officer and a fine cavalry leader, but he was tyrannical and hot-headed."[110]

In North Carolina, Johnston made the crucial decision to surrender without Davis's approval, but only after Davis allowed him to initiate discussions within the latitude the President permitted. Taylor, however, began discussions with Forrest's support without any consent or advice from Davis, an act that most professional officers would never consider unless under threat of annihilation by the enemy. Importantly, neither Taylor nor Forrest were professional soldiers, a vital consideration in the circumstances in which they found themselves. Professional soldiers, especially West Pointers, viewed their craft within the framework of the civil-military relationship, with submission to the President as Commander in Chief, as well as other forms of civilian leadership, as a primary duty and obligation of any officer. Opening negotiations to surrender not only an army, but an entire department, would be the antithesis of that training. Taylor and Forrest, however, were not professional soldiers. Forrest was an intuitive, even natural-born, leader and Taylor had grown up in the army world of his famous father, but neither had any sort of formal military training. Instead, both were self-made men who had risen in wealth and social standing by their own ability and decision-making instead of asking for opportunities or subordinating their own interests, tools they would rely upon when it came to surrender as well. Taylor and Forrest were practical men, and the situation in which they found themselves in April 1865 meant they had to made practical decisions for what was best for their commands.

Gen. Nathan Forrest (*Image courtesy of the Library of Congress*).

The only mitigating factor that might have prevented Taylor from opening discussions with Canby was the arrival of Davis in the department, the
topic of many local rumors. Taylor discounted any stories of Davis's imminent arrival or postulation on the President's intentions.[111] Instead, Taylor
believed the Union capture of Davis to be inevitable, especially when he
received word that Sherman and Johnston were negotiating, and was inclined
to act on his own best judgment when it came to the future of his department.

Although hesitant to assume the responsibility of surrendering, Taylor took the first step toward that end. The two commanders had already exchanged notes regarding the exchange of prisoners, and Taylor used the correspondence to broach the subject of surrender in very tactful terms without using the word. "The tenor and tone of your communications … induce me to believe that a personal interview between us, although informal in its inception and character," Taylor proposed, "may be attended with results consonant with the views, I think we both entertain." He further hoped, "if such should be the case can be reduced to writing and become the basis of final action within the sphere of authority confided to us." Taylor suggested, and Canby agreed, to a meeting on April 29.[112] Immediately rumors began to spread through both armies about a possible surrender. "It is now rumored that Dick Taylor has given his men 'Indefinite Furlough,'" a Union soldier wrote home. "It is said that some of his men have arrived at this place and that their furloughs have no date [for them to return to duty]. If this is so, it is a new wrinkle in military affairs."[113] Forrest, to stem the rumors, told his troops not to satisfy the "morbid appetite for news and sensation rumors," but instead spread his own rumors that "General Lee has not surrendered" and "Grant has lost in battle and by desertion 100,000 men," tales he hoped would entice "every man to stand firm at his post and true to this colors."[114]

Taylor chose to meet with Canby under circumstances similar to those of Johnston. Canby's forces were in proximity to Taylor's but did not surround him, and Taylor had at least a two-days' march on Canby plus access to the Mobile & Ohio Railroad. In addition, like Johnston, Taylor's paths of retreat were limited in both scope and distance. The distasteful option of moving to the Trans-Mississippi was still available, although Taylor believed that recent rains had made the river impassable.[115] He could have retreated up the rail line into northern Mississippi, only to find himself pressed between Canby's pursuing troops, Thomas's IV Corps in Chattanooga, and the Union garrisons along the Mississippi. That area, already depleted by years of foraging and raiding, could not long support an army. Nor could the farmland of central Alabama if Taylor tried to move eastward, which would have invited Wilson's cavalry to reverse its course to contain him. Taylor could only conclude that his best option was to meet with Canby to see what his Union counterpart had to offer.

On April 29, Canby traveled twelve miles north of Mobile to a place known as Magee's Farm, the site his staff officers suggested for their meeting. Unlike the humble house where Sherman and Johnston met, Magee's Farm was the residence of a well-to-do former state legislator and county sheriff.[116] Canby arrived at the site first, at the appointed place and time. Perhaps wishing to impress his rival without appearing overbearing, Canby's escort was a single brigade of cavalry, as well as a military band and a large contingent of officers in formal military dress. Taylor's arrival on his humble handcar was less imposing.[117] If Taylor expected a gloating victory, he was disappointed. Taylor later remembered that "General Canby met me with much urbanity," and conferred with Taylor less as a defeated enemy than as a respected counterpart. Talks began immediately, and both men, broadly aware of the language in the original Sherman/Johnston terms, agreed to a ceasefire during the length of negotiations subject to a forty-eight-hour notice of suspension. With the initial discussions completed, Canby invited Taylor to join him in a sumptuously prepared luncheon, which, Taylor fondly recalled, offered the opportunity to reacquaint with several prewar friends and the "joyous popping of champagne corks." It is not a great stretch of the imagination that the setting, and bountiful alcohol, was part of Canby's efforts at promoting reconciliation and furthering the talks. This suspicion seems confirmed when, after the military band struck up "Hail, Columbia," a Union military anthem, Canby excused himself from the table to instruct the band to play "Dixie," in honor of their guests. Not to be outdone, Taylor thanked Canby for the gesture, but requested the band take up again "Hail, Columbia" as emblematic of a reunified America that "would soon be a happy land once more."[118] Canby and Taylor adjourned their meeting with plans to reconvene in a few days.

In the meantime, both generals sent orders to maintain the armistice. Canby reined in his troops, ordering the garrisons at Selma and Montgomery "In consequence of new arrangements which are now progressing, you are instructed to desist from further hostilities or destruction of property."[119] Small clashes continued, however, despite the best efforts of commanders on both sides. After sniping by Confederate troops near Selma, General Steele ordered the burning of a train depot at Harrell's Crossroads. In response,

Lt. Col. Samuel Jones informed Steele "I beg to assure you, general, that if any firing was done by any portion of our troops on the Alabama River or elsewhere, it was without the consent and against the orders of Lieutenant-General Taylor."[120] For their part, most Union officers also avoided unnecessary confrontations and did their best to accommodate civilians who wished for the end of the war. "The citizens appear quite friendly and express much satisfaction at the conduct of the troops," Union Brig. Gen. Christopher Andrews noted. "The rebels seem to think the war is really at an end."[121]

The magnanimous tone of the meeting ended two days later, however, when Canby informed Taylor that he was obligated to invoke the forty-eight-hour notice and end the ceasefire. President Johnson had disapproved of the ceasefire as part of the broader rejection of the original Sherman/Johnston negotiations and ordered Canby to demand Taylor's immediate surrender or renew his offensive. In his notification to Taylor, Canby was almost apologetic in his tone, and, in offering terms like what Grant offered Lee, admitted "I say to you frankly what I would not say if I did not believe that the circumstances of both armies were such that you may accept them for your army without reproach from any quarter." The only alternative, Canby mentioned, was a resumption of military action following the previously agreed upon notice.[122] Taylor received additional bad news when telegrams confirmed that Johnston had surrendered in North Carolina. No longer able to march toward Johnston, Canby's only options were to fight it out against Canby's vastly superior forces or accept his terms. Deciding that "folly and madness combined would not have justified an attempt to prolong a hopeless contest," Taylor asked Canby for a meeting to accept his terms.[123] Taylor, in a letter advising his generals of his thoughts, concluded that it was "not improbable the surrender of General Lee's army and other recent disasters ... will make it my duty to surrender the troops under my command." He promised "I shall make every effort to secure an honorable and speedy cessation of hostilities" that would include "such terms as will insure them transportation and subsistence to their homes and a right to remain thereat unmolested by Federal authorities, protection of the horses belonging to enlisted men, and private arms, baggage, and horses of officers." The alternative, Taylor warned, was futile resistance that would leave his command "hunted down like beasts of prey, their families will be persecuted, and ruin thus entailed not only upon the soldiers themselves, but also upon thousands of defenseless Southern women and children."[124]

Although Taylor agreed to surrender on May 2, the distance between his headquarters and Canby's, as well as the need to inform all portions of his dispersed command, meant the actual surrender did not occur until May 4, the date of Lincoln's funeral in Springfield, Illinois. Canby and Taylor met at Citronelle, Alabama, forty miles north of Mobile. Considering Taylor's somewhat undignified arrival at Magee's Farm, Canby likely selected the site to facilitate the Confederate general's limited travel options.[125] If that was the reason, the logic was ironic because a destroyed bridge forced Canby's party to abandon their train only a few miles outside Mobile and continue by hand car. Taylor spared Canby the same inauspicious arrival by arranging for a train to meet Canby's party south of Citronelle.[126] Despite the presence of a large contingent of officers, no one kept official record of the negotiations, and, like the Sherman/Johnston talks, only the memoirs of the participants relate what occurred. After a lengthy discussion regarding the disposition of various cotton supplies, transportation routes, and steam ships, Taylor signed a formal surrender agreement. The terms were nearly identical to the second agreement between Sherman and Johnston. The only difference was specific wording allowing Confederate soldiers to keep their horses, which the other agreement had only implied.[127]

The average soldier, of course, had no direct information on what was transpiring and had to rely upon rumor for any information. One Confederate soldier initially heard both armies had arranged a sixty-day truce, followed by "news" that hostilities would resume immediately, to, finally, hearing that all Confederate troops would be imprisoned as POWs. Confirmation of their paroles came only on May 9, five days after the formal surrender. Taylor softened the news by assuring his command that his surrender was "not the consequence of any defeat," but merely "yielding upon the best terms" that permitted a "preservation of our military honor."[128] Although others complained of the surrender and wished to fight on, most endorsed Taylor's decision to stop fighting. "The armies of both Lee and Johnston having both been surrendered to overwhelming numbers, there was no other course for Gen. Taylor to pursue," one relieved soldier wrote. "To have continued the struggle would have been madness—nay, it would have been murder. … No other army was surrendered on better terms than we are."[129] Other soldiers agreed with that assessment. "Our fate is at last decided," a soldier wrote in resignation. "Humiliating as it is, it is much better than we could expect from our vindictive foe."[130] A cavalry-man noted in his diary that the news of the surrender left the "boys all gloomy and restless," and to take their minds off their predicament resorted to "all kinds of sport for amusement. The camp rings with yelling and discharging of musketry from morning until night."[131] Union troops, as expected, were jubi-lant. "A national salute was fired on account of the surrender of the department of the Gulf by the rebels," a private wrote. "All hostilities was ordered to cease and we felt our work was done."[132]

Taylor spared no time fulfilling his surrender obligations. He dispatched most of Holtzclaw's Brigade to Demopolis to spread the news of the surrender and guard public stores, and sent two regiments of Gibson's Brigade to Meridian on the same mission.[133] Taylor also arranged for the surrender of Confederate naval forces. An Illinois soldier reported, "All the Confeder-ate property [is] being surrendered to the government. The rebel fleet which had been run up the Tombigbee River to Demopolis consisting of 17 trans-ports, one gunboat, and two rams was brought down to McIntosh Landing and turned over to us."[134] Like Johnston, Taylor assisted in the dismantling of Confederate control in his former department. Canby facilitated Taylor's inclination to maintain order by deferring to Taylor and respecting his rank and position. Canby, for instance, instructed his subordinates to follow Taylor's suggestions on how to deploy their occupation troops. Taylor also suggested courses of action to Canby. He asked Canby to protect public property and maintain law and order, and further requested Canby secure the assets of the State Bank of Tennessee lest it depart with deposed Governor Isham Harris. On other issues, however, Canby rejected Taylor's advice. Taylor objected to the use of USCT units to police civilian areas, and Canby quashed Taylor's advice to the governors of Alabama and Mississippi to assemble the state legislatures to repeal their respective ordinances of secession.[135]

The final task related to the surrender was to provide the paperwork that would allow his men to go home, so Taylor appointed Gen. Randall Gibson, who had defended Spanish Fort, to supervise the issuing of paroles in Meridian, a location conveniently located for most soldiers. Resigned to their fate, Confederate troops, either by marching or by railroad, arrived to accept their paroles. One soldier recalled that since they were surrendered, "they would carry their guns no longer, so they filled the ordnance wagon with guns, piled them around it, and leaned them by trees on the road side." The only organizational problem was that the process of paroling so many men took time, and the same soldier mentioned that "Some [men] had grown impatient and left without them."[136] Slowing the process was the arrival of troops from other commands who wished to surrender along with Taylor's men. Some Texas troops from Johnston's army, having failed to get home on their own, instead "flagged a wood train and informed the Federals in charge that we desired to … surrender. We were taken on board and … we surrendered to General Canby."[137]

The only disruption in the paroling process was instigated by the Confederate troops themselves. An officer noted "Deserters are coming in by the thousands to be paroled."[138] As deserters flooded in to claim their paroles, they faced derision by the Confederate troops who had remained steadfast to the end. Observing the reaction of troops to one such deserter, a Louisiana private witnessed his compatriots seize and place "a big fellow astride a rail held high up by a number of hands, yells of derision and contempt all around him."[139] Another Confederate noted "Many men who had never seen any service and some who had quit … were also at Meridian to receive paroles. Some of them were handled roughly by our soldiers, much to the amusement of the Federals who were guarding us."[140] The number of absent men angered the veterans who had fought to the last. "I am ashamed of many of the people in the south," one private expressed. "Gen. Taylor surrendered seven thousand men and when I left Meridian about thirty thousand had been paroled. … A few brave men were left in the field to meet the enemy while at least two thirds of the men who could fight had become tired and quit. Such men do not deserve freedom."[141] By the time the parole process had ended, Canby's staff had issued releases to just over forty-two thousand Confederate officers and men. As in North Carolina, there was no official surrender ceremony.

The demobilization of Taylor's army was much simpler than the complex arrangement that General Schofield created in North Carolina. Schofield had to transport men from all parts of the Confederacy back to their homes. Most of Taylor's men, however, were from either Alabama or adjacent states. Instead of arranged transport, most just signed their paroles, collected rations from Union quartermasters, and walked home, although some, especially those from Texas, accepted transport at least part of the way.[142] Two groups, however, received extensive organized transport. The Union had transferred all Confederate troops captured during the Mobile Campaign, mainly those who could not escape from Spanish Fort, to Ship Island in the Gulf of Mexico. These men received transport to New Orleans and thence to their homes. The other group were North Carolina troops formerly attached to Brigadier General Cockrell's division. The only troops from the eastern part of the Confederacy, they received transport to Vicksburg before obtaining railroad passes to go home.[143]

As Taylor's men surrendered, so too did Forrest's. Even though Forrest was present at Taylor's surrender, his future remained uncertain, including rumors that he intended to fight his way to Mexico. Brig. Gen. Edward Hatch, commanding the Union garrison at Eastport, Mississippi, reported to General Thomas that "Forrest, with the Mississippi State militia, and what militia he can draw from Alabama, intends attacking this place and then moving upon Memphis, Tenn. As the Secesh citizens inside my lines are very anxious to leave, there may be some truth in the rumor." Due to the rumors, Thomas took a hard approach with Forrest. "Send, under flag of truce, a summons to Forrest to surrender upon the terms given by General Grant to Generals Lee and Johnston," Thomas instructed his district commanders. "Inform him, at the same time, of the rumors which have reached you, and that you are prepared for him, and if he attempts such a reckless and bloodthirsty adventure he will be treated thereafter as an outlaw, and the States of Mississippi and Alabama will be so destroyed that they will not recover for fifty years." Rather than leave his men to their fate, Forrest had already decided to surrender instead of joining the exodus to Mexico. Isham Harris, the governor of Tennessee, urged Forrest to continue fighting despite Taylor's surrender, an idea that Forrest found unreasoned. Replying to Harris, Forrest

considered continued combat against an enemy that might outnumber his ten
to one "nothing but murder," and considered, "Any man who is in favor of
a further prosecution of this war a fit subject for a lunatic asylum." To make
his position clear, he told his men, "you may all do as you damn please, but
I'm a-going home."[144] Forrest signaled his intent to abide by Taylor's surrender,
and by May 9 Maj. Gen. Elias S. Dennis, the commander of the District
of Northeast Louisiana, arrived in Gainesville, Alabama, to parole Forrest's
troopers, many of whom were "very restless, and were anxious to get home."
To keep the troops occupied, their brigade commanders relaxed camp discipline and organized athletic competitions until Dennis's staff could process
their paperwork.[145]

Once procured, parole forms allowed Confederate soldiers to go home.
As with Johnston's capitulation, under the terms of the surrender, "Transportation and subsistence to be furnished at public cost for the officers and men
after surrender to the nearest practicable point to their homes."[146] Fortunately
for many Confederate soldiers, their home states were relatively close, so
their treks home were generally uneventful. In their progress home, Confederate veterans became powerful symbols of the Confederacy's fate. "We met
several men returning from the army in Mobile ... they appeared weary and
ill, one having been wounded in the foot," a civilian remembered. "At all
times could be seen hundreds of Confederate soldiers wending their way
home, many of them in rags and bare-footed."[147] While some had only a short
distance to travel, some Confederates had to take a roundabout way to get
home. Milo Scott was a Georgian, but he was serving with a Louisiana artillery battery when captured near Mobile. Union authorities shipped him from
Mobile to Vicksburg, where he began his long walk home. It took him nearly
two weeks, but Scott reached his destination and "found my folks all well."[148]
Other Confederates faced unplanned and unnecessary delays. The Union
shipped surrendered Confederates from the Trans-Mississippi Department
from Taylor's army to Mobile to await trains home, but an official of the
Mobile & Ohio Railroad ordered his station managers to deny free passes to
Confederate soldiers. With Canby's blessing, Taylor had the official arrested
and forced him to relent after threatening to turn him over "to those soldiers
whom you have attempted to wrong, and they would hang you." Trains then

took the demobbed troops westward to places like New Orleans, where Union officers counter-signed their parole forms to permit further transit.[149]

The disinclination to humiliate the Confederates in North Carolina likewise occurred after Taylor's surrender, where again a surrender ceremony was not insisted upon. One Confederate noted that the Union troops did not celebrate their victory and reported he had been "treated very kindly."[150] The entire proceedings were void of any exulting Union troops. A surrendering Louisianan noticed the process was "perfectly businesslike and humdrum" with "no excitement, no disorder. The Federal troops were kept well in hand, were not allowed to insult us, and they showed no disposition to do so."[151] Preparing to demobilize, a Confederate officer reported, "Our guns have all been turned in to our own Ordnance officers" without Union supervision, as "we suppose to save us from further humiliation there has not been a Yank in sight of us yet."[152] In Selma, an Iowa artilleryman observed, "The Rebel soldiers were coming in from the different armies … but we all got along fine together at all times."[153] An Indiana soldier recalled in his diary that the Confederates were glad the war was over, and freely mixed with the Union troops as if they were "warm friends." Another described how after "these dejected, battle-worn veterans halted in our camps, rested peacefully in our tents, shared our coffee and hardtack, and, seated around our camp-fires, they spoke freely of their blasted hopes and broken fortunes."[154] The willingness by Union troops to share their food stemmed from their sympathy toward their former foes. "The South is almost destitute of anything, their homes have been destroyed by fire," a Union sergeant recognized. "[T]he Armies have taken all the stock and provisions, their Negroes have all run off and left them, and now they have been defeated in the war."[155] Consequently, the Union tried to aid their counterparts. "The Federals were very liberal," a paroled soldier remembered. "They furnished rations and transport to every man. They held this open for several months, for we Missourians did not return to our own homes until June."[156] Canby further provided rations to destitute civilians and allocated captured horses and mules to local farmers to work their land.[157] As elsewhere, however, not all soldiers shared the sense of harmony. "Gen. Kirby Smith has not surrendered and the war may continue in the Trans Miss Dept. for several months," a Confederate informed his family. "I am anxious to get on soil not occupied by the enemy. I think I can then breathe easier. There is no love in my soul for Yankees, neither can there ever be."[158]

****

Taylor had estimated that, with the departure of the Army of Tennessee months earlier, he could fend off only a Union raid, and his prediction came true. Confronted by a large and well-equipped Union army, even the strong defenses around Mobile crumbled after a suitable amount of pressure, despite efforts to deflect criticism by the defeated Confederates. With limited options, no hope of support from other Confederate armies, and nothing left to defend in his own department, Taylor followed Johnston's lead and surrendered his army without first obtaining political permission from Jefferson Davis, who was in no position to make such a decision anyway. In the end, Edward Canby's army was sufficient to defeat Taylor's force and bring the war in his department to an end. However, Canby's operations were only part of a much wider Union offensive in Alabama. In the northern part of the state, the Union Army prepared to unleash another large force that would redefine the use of cavalry, destroy the last Confederate industrial centers east of the Mississippi, and force the surrender of Confederate troops across three states.

Chapter 7

"Attacked and Harassed beyond Endurance": Wilson's Raid in Northern Alabama

U nion military operations in Alabama in the last weeks of the war were a clear demonstration of not only the power of the Northern armies, but also the decline of Confederate military capability. Across the Confederacy, from Grant's prolonged siege of Petersburg to Sherman's advance across the Carolinas, large Union armies conducted operations with varied levels of Confederate resistance. The best effort by Richard Taylor to defend Mobile was for naught as Edward Canby surrounded and then reduced the extensive fortifications around the city. Even if Taylor managed to hold off Canby, disaster loomed from another direction. A massive cavalry force under Maj. Gen. James Wilson advanced from northern Alabama toward vital Confederate industrial facilities in the central part of the state. The Confederates had counted on the relative isolation of these sites to protect them from attack, and generally the locations would have been safe from a long overland infantry assault. Wilson's mass of cavalry, however, managed to overcome both distance and Confederate defenses to not only destroy the last Confederate industrial sites east of the Mississippi, but also force the surrender of many remaining pockets of Confederate resistance.

The most important element of Wilson's assault, however, was that it was a surprise, both to the Confederates and the Union. The Confederates

Gen. James Wilson (*Image courtesy of the Library of Congress*).

certainly believed that a Union cavalry assault from northern Alabama was possible. After the debacle around Nashville, the remnants of the Army of Tennessee reformed their shattered ranks in camps in northern Mississippi under the observation of Wilson's cavalry, which spent the winter in its encampments in northern Alabama. When the Army of Tennessee departed on its trek to the Carolinas, Wilson's men remained in Alabama, confronted only by inferior numbers of Confederate cavalry from Taylor's diminished command. Maj. Gen. Nathan Forrest, arguably the Confederacy's most effective cavalry leader, defended the area, and Taylor was confident that Forrest could deal with any Union force, especially after Ulysses Grant transferred a large portion of the infantry from Union Maj. Gen. George Thomas's Department of the Cumberland to the Carolinas. Left with only Wilson's horsemen to conduct offensive operations, Thomas allowed Wilson to assemble the largest cavalry force of the Civil War, in numbers of which even Grant was unaware, and unleashed them in a massive assault that lasted nearly a month and covered more than five hundred miles. Starting in northern Alabama, Wilson's troopers ended their campaign in Georgia and Florida, and bagged a very important prisoner in the process.

****

Wilson was the primary offensive force in the middle South because of a lingering antipathy Grant held for George Thomas. A common criticism of Grant, especially regarding his postwar memoirs, is that once Grant formulated an opinion of someone, even if incorrect, he seldom changed it. Unfortunately for Thomas, Grant believed him too deliberate and prone to defensive warfare for his liking. Grant especially formed this view when he had to relieve Thomas when the Army of the Cumberland was besieged by the Army of Tennessee at Chattanooga, concluding that Thomas should have crushed Bragg without additional assistance. Thomas's quiet demeanor, sometimes assessed as cold, also contributed to the image of someone more prone to thinking than doing.[1] Evidence of Grant's opinion of Thomas occurred when Grant promoted Sherman, although Thomas outranked him, to lead the Middle Military District when Lincoln promoted Grant to Lieutenant General. Sherman also shared Grant's assessment of Thomas. Although Thomas proved he was an aggressive fighter when the Army of the Cumberland engaged in the heaviest fighting around Atlanta, Sherman chose Thomas's force to remain behind in Chattanooga when Sherman prepared to leave Atlanta. Sherman's subsequent March to the Sea is rightfully celebrated, but Sherman took much of his army to Savannah against minimal opposition, while Thomas, with a smaller portion had to deal with the only real Confederate opposition available in the western theater. One officer in support of Thomas called Sherman's March a "holiday excursion" because he was "marching unopposed through the South" while Hood's main Confederate force was "confronting us at Nashville."[2]

Matters came to a head when Hood arrived outside of Nashville. Thomas delayed in counter-attacking Hood for three very good reasons. First, Thomas waited to remount Wilson's cavalry not only to contain Confederate movements, but also to be in a position to conduct a vigorous pursuit, as it was the best means of inflicting damage on a retreating enemy.[3] Second, the weather prevented a counter-stroke, especially after several ice storms rendered the roads impassable; Maj. Gen. Jacob Cox described the area as covered by a "glare of ice."[4] Lastly, there was no need to rush an attack as Hood was no immediate threat to take the city. Grant, viewing the operation from a distance, saw things quite differently and overreacted to the situation. In a series of almost catty telegrams between himself and Secretary of War Stanton and Maj. Gen. Henry Halleck, Grant expressed his lack of faith in Thomas and worried incessantly about a situation that Thomas had well in hand. Grant, envisioning unlikely scenarios such as Hood marching to the Ohio River, offered ludicrous solutions like arming the civilian employees of the Quartermaster Corps.[5]

The situation reached a point where Grant was prepared to relieve Thomas of command. Critics charged that Grant became paranoid about the situation in Nashville to divert attention from his own prolonged and costly siege at Petersburg and deflect blame from himself for approving Sherman's March to the Sea before eliminating Hood's army.[6] Maj. Gen. James Wilson, who owed his rank to Grant's mentorship, supported Thomas in his clash with Grant. "Under these conditions it must be conceded that the possibility of Hood's marching around Nashville or getting away from Thomas," Wilson later wrote, "was about the wildest and the most desperate and hopeless military undertaking possible to imagine." Wilson concluded that "Grant lost his head and failed to act with his usual sound sense" by "assuming to understand the situation better than the level-headed Thomas."[7] When, on December 15 and 16, Thomas dealt Hood the hammer blows that broke his army and sent it reeling back into Mississippi, Grant sent only tepid congratulations.[8]

Thomas's victory did nothing to change Grant's opinion of him. On December 28, 1864, Thomas informed Grant of his plan to encamp his army for sixty days to rearm/resupply before he intended to either march toward Selma and Mobile or advance east into western Virginia.[9] Grant, however, believed Thomas incapable of a swift march to Selma, describing him as "too ponderous in his preparations and equipments to move through a country rapidly enough to live off of it" and thought sixty days was too much time to prepare. Instead, Grant gave Thomas the option of preparing a campaign on short notice or losing most of his troops to other operations.[10] Thomas responded that he intended to strike at Selma, waiting only until the roads, described as in "an impassable condition for wagons and artillery," dried out and the weather improved.[11] Grant was still not satisfied, and consequently removed Maj. Gen. John Schofield's XXIII Corps from Thomas's command and transferred it to the recently captured Wilmington, North Carolina, as well as the two divisions of Maj. Gen. Andrew Smith's XVI Corps sent to bolster Maj. Gen. Edward Canby's army in New Orleans. The reductions left Thomas with only the IV Corps and Wilson's cavalry to defend an area that stretched from the Ohio River on the north to the Gulf of Mexico on the south, and from the Mississippi River on the west to the Appalachians in the east.[12]

An 1860 West Point graduate, Wilson was the assistant topographical engineer for the Department of Oregon when the war began. He participated in the recapture of Fort Pulaski, served as aide-de-camp to Maj. Gen. George McClellan during the Antietam campaign, as assistant engineer to Grant at Vicksburg, and as inspector general of the Army of the Tennessee. In October 1863, when chief engineer under Sherman's command, Wilson received a promotion to Brigadier General, and a few months later was Chief of the Cavalry Bureau in Washington. The following summer, Wilson received his first combat experience while leading a cavalry division during Grant's Overland Campaign and Philip Sheridan's campaign in the Shenandoah Valley.[13] In October 1864, Wilson received a promotion to Brevet Major General and assumed command of the Cavalry Corps of the Military Division of the Mississippi, placing him once again under Sherman's leadership. Grant gave Wilson high praise, telling Sherman "I believe Wilson will add

50 per cent to the effectiveness of your cavalry."[14] Wilson immediately provided results. While, on paper, he had fifty thousand cavalrymen, upon arrival in Nashville there were only six thousand immediately available, with the remainder scattered on countless details. Wilson superseded the commanders in the various departments and took control of the cavalry himself, which allowed him to mass their numbers just as Hood was about to undertake his Tennessee Campaign.

His preparations, however, were not complete and subsequent uneven performances demonstrated the difficulties of his command. At Franklin, Wilson's cavalrymen prevented Forrest's troops from flanking Schofield, thus ensuring the Union victory, but had a difficult time covering the Union withdrawal to Nashville. Schofield was displeased with the young cavalry general, claiming his "immediate flank and rear were insecure, while my communication with Nashville was entirely without protection."[15] When Thomas broke Hood's siege of Nashville, Wilson's cavalry was a key element in the move to flank the Confederates and drive them back, and further improved his standing when his cavalry harassed Hood's retreat back into Mississippi despite bad weather, little food or forage, and desperate localized counter-attacks.[16]

In the aftermath of the Nashville campaign, Wilson requested mounts, weapons, and equipment to put his force into peak condition for upcoming battles. Writing to General Thomas in late December 1864, Wilson requested permission to erect a winter camp where he could prepare his forces for the spring campaigns. "A camp on the north bank of Tennessee … would seem to possess all the requisites," Wilson wanted, specifically a location where he could menace Confederate troops in northern Mississippi, be supplied by steamboats, and remote enough that "the men could be kept together, and away from the demoralizing influence of large towns." To take full advantage of the opportunity "to prepare the Cavalry Corps for efficient field service," Wilson believed "from seventy to ninety days in camp will be necessary." To accomplish his task, Wilson wanted all cavalrymen on detached duty returned to their regiments so they could gain the benefit of full preparation and training. Wilson also wanted at "least 10,000 Spencer carbines—15,000, if they can be obtained," because the rapid-firing rifles not only gave the cavalry decisive firepower but "troops armed with the Spencer carbine, or rifle, consume less ammunition than any other, and are more effective." What Wilson needed most of all were horses, and lots of them. "I shall require also about 10,000 horses," Wilson informed Thomas, as only two of his six divisions were anywhere near full strength. To obtain the needed animals, Wilson not only made the usual requests through the Quartermaster Corps, but also instituted reforms to improve the horses he already had. Instead of the usual practice of discarding cavalry horses that were "reduced in flesh, sick, or sore backed," Wilson established facilities to recuperate the horses for future use, as he reasoned "that similar measures [should] be taken, to restore the jaded and broken-down horses, to those adopted for sick and wounded men." Wilson promised that if his plan was implemented "the Cavalry Corps can take the field in the spring with 25,000 men," and he promised "the rebels can be thrown entirely on the defensive; their cavalry can be broken up, or driven behind their infantry for shelter; their railroads and other lines of communication can be cut; and, finally, their infantry can be attacked and harassed beyond endurance."[17]

Troops began to assemble along the Tennessee in mid-January, although some had to move a considerable distance. The Second Division left Louisville for northern Alabama, but progress was slow as many of their horses, former plow or carriage animals, were not broken for saddle riding and the mules issued to carry their spare equipment proved recalcitrant.[18] On the march to Alabama, the Seventy-second Indiana cavalry lost "eight or ten men by bushwhackers" who managed to approach unsuspecting Union troops because they were "dressed in our uniform."[19] Once in the Tennessee Valley, Wilson's men found themselves at hard labor constructing cabins for themselves and stables for their horses.[20] Charles Goodrich, a Wisconsin cavalryman, informed his wife from his newly established camp, "We marched here yesterday and are camped on a narrow valley surrounded by high wooded hills. A brook runs through the valley and we are completely sheltered from the cold winds, making this the best of winter camps." Within a week, Goodrich informed her "The appearance of the valley where we are camped has changed. The thick brush and timber have disappeared, replaced by snug little cabins, ranged in straight rows and separated by broad and neatly swept streets. We are now hauling lumber about twelve miles and building stables for our horses. It looks as if we will stay here for some time."[21]

Wilson initially had some problems with obtaining supplies. Poor weather prevented the establishment of regular logistics, and food became scarce. An Illinois soldier complained, "we have no rations. Hardly nothing but hardtack and a little coffee and but very little of that."[22] An officer also mentioned that "Boats with rations cannot get up the river on account of ice. The men getting some meal ground at the mills, but living mainly on parched corn."[23] Hungry soldiers from the Fourth Ohio Cavalry mocked General Wilson as he passed their camp by chanting "Hard tack! Hard tack!" at him. Angered at their insolence, Wilson had the men fall under arms and kept them standing in formation all day.[24] Their impertinence was justifiable, with a disgruntled soldier remembering that "When all the provisions were gone, corn that was intended for the horses was issued to the men. For three days all of us had nothing to eat but corn."[25] Finally, boats made it up the Tennessee River in late January, and the supply problems ended. "We have been short of rations for two or three days, having to resort to parched corn and hominy" an Indiana officer reported, "but the boats came up yesterday and we are now all right in the eating line."[26]

Once established in their camps, Wilson drilled his men incessantly to achieve a unified and disciplined force. Wilson would later write, "The final victory over Forrest and the rebel cavalry was won by patient industry and instruction," which corrected the common faults of the "absence of instruction, organization, and uniformity of equipment."[27] To achieve this result, Wilson had to do more than instruct his men in cavalry tactics; he had to make them better soldiers. An officer under Wilson's command recalled that during the time in winter camp, "The government of the corps was made step by step more careful and rigid. Infractions of discipline were promptly and sometimes conspicuously, punished" to reinforce the necessity of order. Over the objection of soldiers who claimed the right to elect their own officers, "Vacancies in offices were filled by appointment of those seen to be the most meritorious, though often to the great dissatisfaction of the men of particular companies." In particular, Wilson emphasized that the troopers had to take great "care of the camps, horses and equipments, although it was exceedingly difficult to keep them in good condition when the rain poured upon them nearly every day. It was hard work." If companies received good evaluations, Wilson employed them away from camp on scouting and foraging operations. During one such ride, "half from the Fourth and half from the Third Iowa, was absent several days, marched as far as Florence, Ala, and brought back fifty-six prisoners and many captured animals."[28]

While Wilson trained his men for their upcoming operations, he was still short of horses, a problem that was not unique to his command. The entire region south of the Ohio River had been subject to the impressment of animals by both sides for months, leaving few horses available. Even before Wilson began assembling his men on the Tennessee River, Union commanders were taking harsh action to find mounts. In December 1864, as Hood threatened Nashville, the Union took the drastic step of impressing animals in Louisville, something common in enemy territory but seldom done in loyal states. Secretary of War Stanton authorized Thomas "to seize and impress horses and every other species of property needed for the military service … at Nashville and Louisville, and wherever property can be had."[29] The army was quick to act. "One morning the citizens of Louisville awakened from their slumbers to find every street and pike leading out of the city picketed by mounted cavalrymen" with orders to seize serviceable horses and mules. An officer later recalled that "every effort was made to secrete their valuable horses. Some were found in cellars and in kitchens, and some in parlors."[30] The fight to drive Hood back from Nashville and subsequent pursuit, however, took a toll on the horseflesh in Wilson's command, forcing him to replace the animals he lost and rest those that he retained.[31] To accomplish this, Wilson went to extraordinary measures, including attempts to acquire ten thousand broken-down animals in recuperative camps near Louisville, Kentucky, reasoning that his troops could tend to the horses in their winter encampments in northern Alabama.[32] Wilson's efforts and appeals proved very successful, a situation that generated both resentment from other commands and questions of whether Wilson's troops, expected to be inactive over the winter months, should continue to receive preferred status. As Wilson established his camps, Halleck sent Grant a message suggesting that perhaps it was time for Wilson to start sharing his resources. "You will remember that since about the 1st of

October all cavalry horses purchased in the West and Northwest have been sent to General Thomas, to the entire exclusion of Missouri, Arkansas, Mississippi, and Louisiana," Halleck reminded Grant. "Consequently, these departments must now have a large number of dismounted cavalry" at a time when Grant was pressing for a movement toward Mobile to support Sherman's upcoming advance into the Carolinas. "The question now arises whether we shall continue to send all cavalry horses to General Thomas," Halleck posed to Grant, or if he should distribute the limited number of horses to other commands in "due proportion." For the time being, Grant decided to continue funneling horses to Thomas, but was also prepared to detach parts of Wilson's command if Thomas was not going to employ them in a timely manner. The decision to concentrate resources in Wilson's hands, however, put other troops at a disadvantage. Col. Simeon Brown, commanding the Eleventh Michigan Cavalry in northern Kentucky, informed Brig. Gen. Edward Hobson that he had problems with guerillas close to his encampments but "We are in a bad fix now, seven rounds of cartridges to a man; not horses enough to mount ten men besides the pickets."[33]

****

Despite its hardships, Wilson's force was in excellent shape compared to his adversary. After the departure of the Army of Tennessee left him with almost no infantry to command, Richard Taylor relied heavily upon his cavalry to cover the vast areas of his department and repel Union incursions that he hoped would be limited to short-term raids. Such an arrangement required Taylor to grant wide latitude to his cavalry command, and Taylor was fortunate to have a capable leader. As one of his first acts upon taking command, Taylor nominated Nathan Forrest for promotion to lieutenant-general and placed him in command of all the cavalry in the department with his headquarters at Verona, Mississippi. Taylor had an excellent working relationship with Forrest, although he initially had some concerns about his cavalry commander's tendency to consider all variable and potential difficulties before undertaking an action. In his first meeting with Taylor, Forrest made a negative impression when he seemed intent to point out every obstacle, leaving Taylor with a sense that Forrest "had no stomach for this work." Taylor soon realized the value of his subordinate's methods when, once the best option was determined, he carried out any plan with vigor.[34] Forrest immediately issued orders to tighten up discipline and end the depredation on civilian property. He warned that the "rights and property of citizens must be respected and protected," and the "illegal organizations of cavalry prowling through the country," which Forrest considered nothing more than "roving bands of deserters, absentees, stragglers, horse-thieves, and robbers," were ordered to report for service under legitimate command or face punishment "even to extermination" under his belief "that kindness to bad men is cruelty to the good."[35] Allowing Forrest to suppress the criminal bands as a means of finding additional cavalrymen was a positive step, but what Taylor needed most of all was additional infantry to replace the losses from the Nashville campaign. It soon became clear that he was not going to get them. In March 1865, Lt. Gen. Pierre Beauregard, the theater commander west of the Appalachians, informed Taylor not to expect the return of any troops from the Army of Tennessee for the foreseeable future, and to expect increasing desertion rates as the government could not provide money to pay long overdue wages. Taylor's only option was to press the state governors to send more militia and state troops.[36]

The problems facing the Confederates, however, seemed insurmountable. In January, while Wilson was assembling in his winter camps in northern Alabama, Forrest reported to Taylor "My command is greatly reduced in numbers and efficiency by losses in battle and in the worn-down and unserviceable condition of animals" because "during the retreat from Nashville I was compelled almost to sacrifice my command." Forrest needed additional horses for his artillery and to induce disillusioned men who were "scattered through the country or have gone to their homes" to return to their units. Desertion plagued Forrest's command after the decision to consolidate several decimated regiments. Forrest furloughed other regiments to return to their native counties to find recruits and round up deserters, but the economic plight of their families caused many of those men to remain at home.[37] Even common soldiers in the Union Army were aware of the Confederate desertion problem. "Deserters are coming in every day from Forrest's army," a Union soldier wrote to his brother. "They report him to have only 4,000 strong and that he is about ready to leave. He thinks the

Yankees are getting too thick for him here."[38] Consequently, Forrest would
be at a disadvantage when the spring campaign began. After the reorganization, Forrest had two divisions of cavalry to deploy against Wilson. Brig.
Gen. James Chalmers commanded one division and Brig. Gen. William
Jackson led the other. On paper, Forrest also had a third division led by Brig.
General Abraham Buford, but its brigades were scattered across Mississippi
and Alabama on detached duty or committed to the defense of Mobile.[39]
While Wilson estimated that Forrest had approximately twelve thousand
troops available, an inspection of Forrest's command by the War Department in February believed that he had only about six thousand effective
troops. Moreover, Wilson's men were concentrated and Forrest's, widely
dispersed on a variety of duties as well as separated to avoid overtaxing
the logistic support in any one area, were not. When the spring campaigns
began, Forrest would have only a single cavalry brigade in central Alabama
to impede Wilson's advance.[40]

Although concentrated in Mississippi along the Mobile & Ohio Railroad, the Confederates were aware of the vulnerability of central Alabama.
Taylor made plans to defend the key cities and sites in the region, but planning was all he could do, as troops, equipment, horses, and cash were all in
short supply. Taylor's department was in such poor financial condition that a
few days before Wilson began his raid Beauregard informed Secretary of War
John Breckinridge "Lieutenant-General Taylor calls most urgently for funds"
because "any attempt to proceed here on credit will inevitably prove a signal
failure before the expiration of sixty days from this time." Despite these
shortcomings, Taylor ordered preparations for the defense of Demopolis,
Selma, Opelika, and Montgomery in the hope that state militia might supplement local defense forces if Union troops did arrive. Taylor also requested
permission to explore the possibility of relocating war industries away from
threatened areas, balanced against the interruption of badly needed products
from those factories.[41]

****

As Wilson trained and prepared his troops, there was no shortage of suggestions on how he could employ them. Wilson fully intended to use his troops
to best effect once the weather allowed him to do so, but, as he was several

links down the command chain, it was not up to him to decide the objectives. What complicated the decision-making process were the various commanders who set the goals for future operations. Grant, as ranking general, had the last word on broad strategic objectives, and his priorities in early 1865 were the conduct of operations that would hasten the end of the war. To that end, Grant envisioned Wilson leading a diversionary force of about five thousand cavalry to support Sherman's attack into the Carolinas by threatening Mobile and the Confederate industrial centers in central Alabama. Wilson objected to the plan, arguing the raid would not achieve the desired results and would be at risk versus Forrest's much larger force.[42] Grant did not press the issue with Wilson, but did detach one of Wilson's divisions, the Sixth under Brig. Gen. Joseph Knipe, to support Canby's advance on Mobile. To outfit Knipe's division, Wilson had to take horses from Brig. Gen. Edward Hatch's Fifth Division, further disrupting the efforts to get all the cavalrymen mounted.[43] Sherman, as commander of the Military Division of the Mississippi, was Thomas and Wilson's immediate superior. He favored a raid into Alabama, but in January 1865 was in Savannah, Georgia, after his March to the Sea, more than five hundred miles away from Wilson's camps along the Tennessee River and almost six hundred from Thomas's headquarters in Nashville. Moreover, Sherman, preparing to move into the Carolinas, faced more pressing matters than what was going on in Alabama. Therefore, Sherman gave Thomas generalized instructions regarding operations west of the Appalachians and left the matter in his hands. "Before I again dive into the interior and disappear from view," Sherman wrote, "I must give you, in general terms, such instructions as fall within my province as commander of the division." Sherman suggested that Thomas take his main infantry force and Wilson's cavalry to Columbus, Mississippi, to sever the Mobile & Ohio Railroad before marching east toward Tuscaloosa and "burning up Selma, that is the navy-yard, the railroad back toward the Tombigbee, and all iron foundries, mills, and factories" before returning to Chattanooga via northern Georgia. Sherman did not see the operation as an invasion, but rather an emulation of his March to the Sea. "I believe such a raid … will have an excellent effect," Sherman rationalized, as he believed that Southern civilians perceived such raids as leading to "the sure and inevitable destruction of all their property. They realize that the Confederate armies cannot protect them, and they see in the repetition of such raids the inevitable result of starvation and misery."[44]

From his instructions, it appears that Sherman was unaware of the size of Wilson's cavalry force or what Wilson and Thomas intended to do with it. Thomas was Sherman's senior commander in the Military Division of the Mississippi and the ranking officer on the scene, and therefore in the best position to plan and execute operations in the region, but his unpopularity with Grant restricted his options. Grant pressed Thomas to threaten central Alabama in support of Canby's assault on Mobile, but at the same time denied him the troops to conduct such an operation when he authorized Schofield to transfer the XXIII Corps to North Carolina. Wilson was operating under Thomas's immediate command, so Thomas used Sherman's instruction and ignored Grant's to give Wilson the greatest flexibility. No evidence exists, in fact, that Thomas informed Grant of the scope of Wilson's planned operations. In turn, when the time came to move, Thomas allowed Wilson to make his own decisions in terms of route and unit deployments.[45] Just before he embarked on his assault, however, Wilson, in a wise political move, made sure to credit Sherman for inspiring his subsequent campaign. "I am just about starting to carry out your ideas in Central Alabama," Wilson wrote to Sherman in March, although he had to admit "I shall not be able to follow the route you indicate." Nevertheless, Wilson assured Sherman that the goal of his attack was to support his operations in the Carolinas and "to have your column made invincible against the whole force the rebels can combine."[46]

****

By March, as the temperatures rose and the roads dried, Wilson finalized plans to break camp and renew combat against Taylor and Forrest. Deciding that a few strong units were better than several half-strength ones, Wilson ordered his division commanders to consolidate their horses in those divisions deemed the most combat-ready, leaving the remaining regiments dismounted until horses could be obtained for them.[47] To improve the firepower of the units participating in the raid, the troopers without horses gave up their Spencer carbines to those who did.[48] Wilson had two reasons for seeking as many Spencers as he could get. First, it would simplify his logistics if he could standardize his weaponry as much as possible. Second, the Spencer was simply the best firearm a cavalryman could possess because the Spencer was reliable, accurate, and, with its seven-shot magazine, could fire up to twenty rounds per minute. The Spencers were so desirable that in 1864 the Army offered to reequip regiments with the weapon if they volunteered to reenlist. Wilson also coveted the Spencers because, having learned the hard lessons of cavalry operations in battle, he intended to use his troops more as dragoons rather than traditional cavalry and the Spencers offered the greatest volume of fire against fortified positions.[49]

As Wilson looked forward to testing his rebuilt force, he and Thomas finalized their plans for the upcoming campaign. Operating in conjunction with the Union attack toward Mobile, Wilson would lead his cavalry south, destroying economic resources on the way, on a path toward the industrial center at Selma. Once securing Selma, Wilson would either continue south to aid in the attack on Mobile or go east toward Montgomery.[50] While he had broad freedom of movement, what Wilson did not have at his disposal was his full command. Despite his best efforts, he could not obtain sufficient horses for all his men, nor could he prevent other operations from dispersing his force. Wilson had lost the services of his Third Division, under Brig. Gen. Judson Kilpatrick, six months earlier when Sherman needed cavalry for his March to the Sea. In February, Wilson received orders to transfer Knipe's Seventh Division to Canby for the attack on Mobile, taking the horses of Brig. Gen. Edward Hatch's Fifth Division. Consequently, Hatch and his command stayed behind at Eastport, Alabama, in the hopes of acquiring horses in a timely manner, which never came. Wilson also did not have the services of his Sixth Division. Thomas instructed Wilson to leave this unit, under Brig. Gen. Richard W. Johnson, behind to contain partisan activities in central Tennessee and northern Alabama over Wilson's objections. The reductions meant that only three divisions, each divided into two brigades, would partic- ipate in Wilson's planned attack. The First Division, under Brig. Gen. Edward McCook, comprised 4,096 men, a force slightly larger than Brig. Gen. Emory Upton's Fourth Division of 3,923 men. The largest division was Brig. Gen. Eli Long's Second Division, made up of 5,127 troopers. With the addition of the Fourth Cavalry regiment from the Regular Army, attached surgeons and medical personnel, and several personnel from the Quartermaster and Engineer Corps, a total of 13,480 men embarked on the campaign.[51]

Wilson could not take all his troops, but he did have his best divisions with the most capable commanders. McCook, a prewar lawyer from Ohio, had risen from the regimental command of the Second Indiana Cavalry to division command in various armies in the West and had participated in numerous raids before joining Wilson's command. Eli Long, a Kentucky native, had served in the antebellum army after graduating from the Kentucky Military Institute in 1855. Earlier in the war, Long had served as a captain in the Fourth Cavalry of the Regular Army, the unit now serving as Wilson's escort, before promotions placed him in brigade commands in other units. He had participated in numerous operations in the Western Theater, suffering five separate wounds in the process. Emory Upton was a late edition to Wilson's senior leadership. Before December 1864, the Fourth Division was under the command of Brig. Gen. Benjamin Grierson, who had conducted the successful raid in support of Grant's Vicksburg operation the year before. The Fourth Division went to Missouri as part of the force assembled to deal with a Confederate incursion from Arkansas, but in October, Wilson ordered Grierson to assemble his forces in Nashville to oppose Hood's advance toward the city. A month later, however, Grierson had not complied with Wilson's orders and was reportedly at his home in Jacksonville, Illinois, where, according to an officer staff sent to investigate, "he had been absent several weeks."[52] Wilson relieved Grierson of his command and transferred leadership of the division to Upton, who many viewed as a rising star in the Army. A New York native, Upton had graduated from West Point in May 1861, and received a posting in the artillery, where he fought in the early battles of the Western Theater. By 1864, Upton had risen to command an infantry brigade in the VI Corps, where he was engaged in the heavy fighting of Grant's Overland Campaign and the Valley Campaign, receiving wounds in both operations. After recovering from his injuries, he transferred to the Western Theater to assume his divisional command under Wilson, one of the few officers during the Civil War to command troops in all service branches.[53] Wilson was understandably satisfied with the leaders of his divisions, telling a friend "the three

Gen. Emory Upton (*Image courtesy of the Library of Congress*).

divisions with me are the model cavalry of the world … and I'm willing to prove it in any test the Lieut. General [Grant] may choose to apply."[54]

Wilson had a potent force and capable subordinates, but what he did not have was favorable weather. Wilson had hoped to launch his attack in the first week of April to coincide with the Union advance toward Mobile, but heavy spring rains turned the Tennessee Rivers and its tributaries into untraversable torrents. "The prospect of moving does not seem very good as the Rain is making bad roads," a Wisconsin soldier noted on March 2, "and the river is so very high."[55] Three days later, the conditions had not improved. "We still lie here, but under orders to be ready to march at an hour's notice," an Indiana officer wrote to his wife on March 5, but the "Tennessee River … is now so high that large steamboats come paddling over corn fields more than half a mile from the river banks." The rain also proved damaging. "We lost, through the negligence of somebody, a vast amount of forage which our horses greatly needed," a soldier reported regarding the flooding of a supply depot near the Eastport encampment.[56] "I never was as much annoyed before in my life," Wilson wrote to a friend in a frustrated tone. "I don't remember ever to have witnessed such heavy rain storms." Wilson was not exaggerating about the rain. A woman in central Alabama recorded the rivers were "higher than it had been in years. At Cahaba, which was on a high bluff, the water was so high that the people were sailing about in boats."[57] The rains also hindered Confederate mobility as Forrest was also unable to move. "It has rained almost every other day and the country is flooded with water," Forrest informed Taylor. "Tombigbee River is a mile wide. … To move with troops, wagons, or artillery until the streams run down is utterly impossible."[58] By March 10, however, the rains had stopped and Wilson hoped the Tennessee would soon become fordable. "We crossed the Tennessee River and turned over all our baggage" one soldier wrote, pleased to be leaving the remote encampments, writing, "Finally we have started—after so long a time to equip."[59] It still took several days to get the entire Union force across the Tennessee, and it was not until March 22, five days after Canby began his advance toward Mobile, that Wilson commenced an operation that he believed would last sixty days. Most of Wilson's troopers were glad to be on the move after months in their dreary camps and hardships of the recent floods. "Never can I forget the brilliant scene as regiment after regiment filed gayly [*sic*] out of camp," an exuberant officer wrote, "decked in all the paraphernalia of war, with gleaming arms, and guidons given to the wanton breeze." Another officer, impressed by the massed ranks of horsemen, believed that the operation would be an absolute success. "The war had now become one of conquest!" Captain Joseph Vale claimed, "Not of territory or peacefully disposed citizens … but a complete conquest and subjugation of the insurgent power in arms in the field."[60]

Once beyond the Tennessee River Valley, however, the soldiers found themselves in a region devastated to a degree that it affected the decision-making

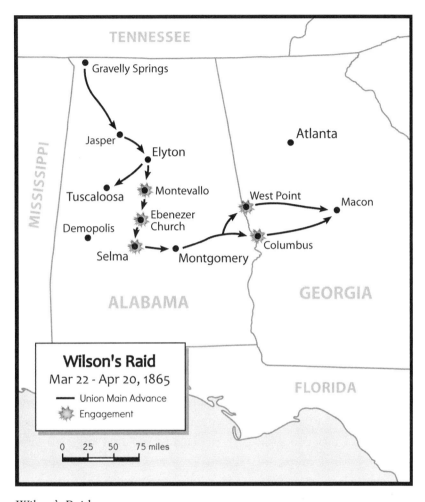

Wilson's Raid.

of both armies. Northern Alabama had suffered greatly from the effects of inflation, economic failures, impressment, and draft resistance in addition to repeated foraging and economic warfare by Union armies. The result was a wide swath of desolation that led both sides to consider the area unable to support a traditional force of any size engaged in combat operations. Wilson had established his winter encampments in the Tennessee Valley as far south as he could construct them and still keep them supplied. Further, it forced Wilson to move through the region quickly lest Confederate resistance force them to remain on ground that could not support them. Wilson directed his subsequent deployments and movements upon the need to rapidly cover the required distance. In doing so, Wilson gained the vital element of surprise by disguising his objectives to Taylor. Wilson's divisions rode on separate roads to prevent competition for scarce resources and to mislead any guess to his intentions. McCook's division initially rode toward Tuscaloosa and Upton's toward Columbus, with only Long's division moving on the direct route toward Selma. To improve mobility and maintain forward progress, Wilson eschewed a large wagon train and prepared to live off the land once he moved through the devastated portion of the state. "Once through the sterile region of North Alabama," Wilson wrote to Sherman just before departing, "I think I can get along pretty well." [61] Each cavalryman "carried five days' light rations, one hundred cartridges, two extra horse-shoes and eight nails, with two days' grain for horses." Each company had several mules that carried "five days' hard bread and ten days' sugar, coffee, and salt." Trailing behind the three divisions "was a small [250] wagon-train carrying eighty rounds more of cartridges, twenty days' sugar and salt, and forty-five days' coffee. … Fifty of the wagons carried a light pontoon equipment of thirty canvas boats." Protecting the wagon train were fifteen hundred dismounted men, under the command of Captain William E. Brown, who would impress horses along the way to improve their mobility. Wilson believed that such a minimal amount of logistic support would be sufficient to get his force "through the northern part of Alabama, a region very poor at the best, and now wasted by two years of war within its borders."[62]

The desolation in northern Alabama also affected Confederate strategy and planning. After the disastrous retreat from Nashville, Hood had led his troops back to northern Mississippi to seek supplies from the Mobile & Ohio Railroad, the only reliable transportation route in the department. After the Army of Tennessee departed for the Carolinas, Forrest's cavalry remained in Mississippi from necessity and strategic limitations. Forrest was obliged to protect the vital railroad line, and the lack of forage and food in northern Alabama forced him to leave the region almost unprotected. Selma and Montgomery were obvious targets, but only a small contingent policed the area because it could not support many troops. Forrest and Taylor were not overly concerned, as they considered the shattered region a barrier against Union incursions. Consequently, Taylor's forces were out of position when Wilson's large cavalry force, organized to pass through the area as quickly as possible, began its assault. According to one source, there were no Confederate troops within 120 miles of Wilson when his attack began. The only Confederate forces in the region were a detachment of Forrest's cavalry and state troops who, without the formal logistics support, had to fend for themselves to the continued detriment of farmers in the region.[63]

Success for Wilson could only occur, however, if his plan to move rapidly and without hindrance came to fruition. As the army moved south, many soldiers, from top rank to privates, commented on the desolation and difficult terrain. "The entire valley of the Tennessee, having been devastated by two years of warfare," Wilson later wrote in his after-action report, "was quite as destitute of army supplies. … In all directions for 120 miles there was almost absolute destitution."[64] Gen. Upton reported on March 24 "The road was exceedingly mountainous and forage scarce," but his division still "made sixteen miles." The next day was more of the same, covering thirty miles although the "Country almost destitute of forage."[65] Besides finding little food for their animals, the Union troops encountered relatively few civilians in this ravaged part of the state. "Not a sign of civilization …," a Missouri cavalryman wrote in his diary, "except towards night we met a man in rags, who drove a miserable herd of cattle, in a homemade cart."[66] An Indiana soldier described his brigade's movement "over a low, sandy ridge of table-land, for 12 miles … this ridge was uninhabited, and we did not pass a house."[67] While soldiers saw few people, there was occasional opposition, as a Wisconsin cavalryman recalled: "There was two bush-whackers taken today & it was said that they were shot this morning."[68] Despite the two bushwhackers, Union troops found a considerable amount of pro-Union (or perhaps anti-Confederate) sentiment as they moved south, with locals willing to readily provide information and what products they could afford to sell.[69] The absence of Confederate resistance in the opening days of the offensive was another byproduct of the war's effect on civilians in the area. As Confederate forces consolidated in northern Mississippi along the Mobile & Ohio in the months before the raid, Wilson's force and other Union units in the Tennessee River Valley were engaged in an unintentional counter-insurgency campaign. Union troops had provided a form of pacification of pro-Confederate civilians by supplying food to those in need, especially among the poor. At the same time, Union forces had dealt with irregular Confederate units operating in the area by reprisal raids and employing Unionist informants, resulting in the location and elimination of several partisan bands in the region.[70]

The relatively friendly welcome and absence of hostile partisans encouraged Wilson to forge ahead even as his wagon train fell behind. By March 25, only three days into the raid, the wagon train was already falling behind. Cavalrymen could maintain a pace on muddy roads, but the wagons bogged down, with "every wagon stuck in the mud, and it looked as though they might stay there till next August."[71] Major James M. Hubbard, commanding the troops assigned to the pontoon bridge sections, later reported his men had to deal with rain that required them "to lift a great many of the wagons out of the mud," double-team their mules to get wagons over hilly terrain, and struggle over bad roads that slowed their progress to such an extent "the mules were not unharnessed and that men had no sleep."[72] Besides the endless labor, there were other hardships. "A detail of 10 men from each company, 400 in all, was made to bridge the swamp," Sergeant Benjamin McGee of the Seventy-second Indiana later recounted. "As the swamp was nearly a mile wide, this was no small job." Besides constructing the bridge in the dark, soldiers had to deal with "a vast sea of mud growing full of trees, vines, and thick underbrush … a paradise for miasma, bullfrogs, serpents, and alligators."[73] Compounding the problems was the lack of forage to feed the horses and mules, which weakened without sufficient food, and find replacements for exhausted and lame animals. As Wilson's troopers sped forward, the men with the wagon train also had to eliminate enemy resources. "Each day … the Regiment went out for forage and brought in all the horses that could be found in the country," a weary soldier wrote. "Orders were given to burn all cotton, cotton presses, and cotton gins, bridges, and everything that would be useful to [the] rebels."[74]

After five days of difficult riding, Wilson's troopers cleared the barren region as they converged from their separate paths on the small town of Jasper. Wilson also expected to meet Confederate resistance at any time from this point forward. He had a good grasp of Confederate dispositions, writing to Sherman just before he left: "From all I can learn Forrest has his forces mostly about West Point, on the Mobile & Ohio Railroad; two regiments at Verona, and one at Baldwyn, with his artillery at Columbus. They have been expecting our movement all winter, and … may annoy us somewhat," but had no updated intelligence information after he left.[75] Wilson succeeded in stealing a march on Taylor, but the Confederate commander was preparing for the inevitable Union advance. Informing his subordinates on March 2, nearly three weeks before Wilson left the Tennessee River, to expect Union cavalry action, Taylor anticipated that Union troops "Intend to make raid through Alabama," but had no idea of the scope of the operation. A week before Wilson's departure, Forrest ordered Chalmers's division, minus a brigade left behind to protect the Mobile & Ohio Railroad, to move as soon as they were ready from Columbus, Mississippi, to Selma, while Jackson's was ordered to Montevallo, Alabama.[76] Neither division was in position by the time that Wilson emerged from the rain-soaked hills of northern Alabama, a result more from Confederate confidence that Union forces could not operate in the country north of the Black Warrior River and less that Wilson's move caught them by surprise. Although Wilson did not take the Confederates by surprise, his rapid movement through northern Alabama did give him the advantage by forcing Taylor and Forrest to react to Union movements instead of initiating the action.

Forrest immediately sent orders for his scattered command to assemble for duty, but widely dispersed units and unreliable communications prevented all his available troops from getting the message. Nearly six hundred men charged with patrolling the area around Vicksburg received the order to rendezvous with Forrest too late to participate, while others were disinclined to obey.[77] Such events did not immediately concern Taylor. Paying more attention to the Union threat around Mobile, Taylor originally believed Forrest needed only a few days to drive back the expected small Union raiding force before joining in the defense of Mobile. On March 25, Taylor, in response to a letter from Alabama Governor Watts offering what state troops he could muster, thanked Watts and reassured him that he was taking action to protect the state, stating the "Enemy's main force evidently intend attacking Mobile from eastern side … troops enough are on the march to whip it, as well as any force coming from the north."[78] Taylor, continuously underestimating Wilson's strength and objectives, believed far too late that Wilson's force was relatively small and his objectives only regional in scope, considering it to be a "mere demonstration" in support of Canby. To that end, he anticipated that only a portion of Forrest's command was needed to "meet, whip, and get rid of that column" before turning its attention elsewhere. Telegrams between Taylor and Forrest during the first week of the offensive continually referred to Wilson's columns as a "scouting" force or a "large raid" that would presumably return to the Tennessee Valley if confronted rather than a large army intent on taking Selma.[79] Nor was Taylor the only one without a firm grasp of Wilson's intent. General Beauregard received reports that incorrectly claimed that Wilson's main objective seemed to be Demopolis, Alabama, a move to support Canby, rather than Selma.[80]

Taylor and Forrest did not gain a realistic grasp of Wilson's intentions until the Union troops entered Jasper, ninety miles south of his starting point, on March 26. The armies reunited in Jasper to mass for the assault on Elyton and nearby Selma in a much more fertile and productive part of the state, described as "a fine country" with "plenty of forage."[81] As the first real town to fall into Union hands, Jasper was something of a disappointment. A cavalryman later wrote he "expected to find a smart little village, at least, but were never so disappointed in our lives, as it was the poorest excuse for a town we ever did see."[82] Jasper also saw the first damage wrought by Wilson's force, as his troops "began our work of distruction [*sic*] of their Iron Factories. We could see fires in every direction for three days."[83] Learning from interrogated prisoners that Forrest had only two cavalry brigades, those of Buford and General Philip Roddey, near Selma with Chalmers and Jackson's divisions still west of Tuscaloosa, Wilson decided to pick up the pace of the advance to strike Selma before Confederate reinforcements could arrive. To exploit this intelligence, however, Wilson had to get his force across the two branches of the Black Warrior River (the northern Mulberry Fork and the southern Locust Fork), a process made extremely difficult by the recent rains. Confident that the Confederates would be more intent in defending Selma than attacking his wagon train, Wilson ordered his trailing column to head toward Selma at their best possible speed and moved forward with his cavalry.[84]

On March 30, Wilson's men entered the town of Elyton (modern Birmingham) forty miles southeast of Jasper and ninety miles north of Selma. Once the town was safely in possession, Wilson paused to inform Thomas of his progress. "We have destroyed several very extensive iron-works," Wilson reported, "and will to-day burn those at Columbiana," thirty miles southeast of Elyton. He noted, "The enemy seems not to have expected us in this quarter. … Chalmers' and Buford's divisions, the latter made up of Lyon's and Roddey's commands, are all I can hear of in this part of the State," an accurate assessment of Confederate strength in the region and reflecting Wilson's excellent intelligence-gathering ability. Wilson closed by stating confidently, "I am pushing everything for Selma with all possible speed, and shall reach there in three days, unless the enemy can do more than present appearances seem to indicate."[85] Wilson had good reason to believe that the Confederates were not yet prepared to face them. Around Elyton his troops found evidence that there were Confederate troops in the area in the form of "the first evacuated fortifications which Rowdy [Roddey] had built two weeks ago" before the Confederates realized the size of Wilson's force and abandoned efforts to defend the town.[86]

As at Jasper, Union troops set about eliminating the facilities in Elyton. A detachment of Upton's men, assigned the task of destroying all facilities of military value, wrecked the industrial works in town, consisting of five coal mines, a rolling mill, and the Red Mountain, Central, and Bibb and Columbiana Iron Works.[87] The demolition was thorough, but made some allowance for civilian needs. "The men are set at work breaking up the Looms in [the] Factory," an observer noted, but "we found a large supply of meat in one of the buildings and we told the poor factory hands to come and take it."[88] Other civilians, however, suffered from the pillaging of private property despite Wilson's strict orders against such behavior. Robert Merrill, a Wisconsin soldier serving as a company clerk, described Elyton as "a small town of about 30 houses & a dozen stores & shops" that fell victim to wide-spread plunder, as the "Destruction of stores & goods was very general." Searching for ink and stationary, Merrill noted "I found some useful and valuable articles here from offices & stores where they had hid them with ammunition, etc. We thought we were entitled to them."[89]

At Elyton, an excursion secondary to the main attack began. Wilson detached Brig. Gen. John Croxton's brigade to attack Tuscaloosa, sixty miles southwest of Wilson's location. Croxton had orders to destroy any military targets he encountered, but the main purpose was to distract Forrest's troops and disguise Wilson's future intentions.[90] The move forced Forrest to dispatch Brig. Gen. William "Red" Jackson in pursuit of Croxton.[91] Departing on April 1, Croxton headed toward Tuscaloosa with the assistance of a Unionist resident of the area who offered to guide them by way of back roads to avoid Confederate pickets. Once near Tuscaloosa, Croxton received advice from local slaves that directed him past Confederate pickets to a bridge across the Black Warrior River north of town. Arriving at sundown, Croxton initially planned to wait until morning to take the bridge, but the sound of Confederates removing the planking forced him to act immediately.[92] As the Union troops entered the town, there was a brief exchange of gunfire with local militia and cadets from the local university. Realizing the futility of armed resistance, the Confederate defenders surrendered, but Croxton paroled by them when he left down two days later. Croxton's troops destroyed a hat factory, a nitre works of the Ordnance Bureau, a cotton mill and warehouses, a tannery, and most of the buildings of the state university. Under normal circumstances, Croxton would have spared the university, but Governor Watts had insisted that its students, who received military training, were state employees, which in turn made its facilities a legitimate military target. The only public building spared was the State Insane Asylum. After finishing the task of destroying anything of military value, Croxton ordered that food stores captured by his men be distributed to the poor.[93] After leaving Tuscaloosa on April 5, Croxton had no idea that his adventure was just beginning. His brigade, separated from Wilson's main force, was the target of all Confederate forces in the area while also constrained in its movements by high water and bridges either destroyed or heavily defended. For the next three weeks, Croxton led his men through the western and central parts of the state to rejoin Wilson's column while avoiding Jackson's pursuing cavalry. He had several brushes with enemy forces but avoided a general engagement while destroying anything of military value as he went. Eventually back-tracking to Elyton, Croxton led his men eastward through Talladega before crossing into Georgia near Carrolton. Croxton's brigade finally rejoined Wilson's command in Macon, Georgia, on April 29 after covering 653 miles. In exchange for 172 casualties, he had destroyed many military and industrial sites and distracted a considerable number of Confederate troops.[94]

After completing their destruction in Elyton, Wilson's main force prepared to leave on March 31. South of Elyton, the land beyond the Black Warrior River was untouched and provided plenty of forage. "We reached Montevallo and entered here into a fertile country," a Union trooper wrote. "We lived entirely off the country, found forage and provisions in plenty here, contrary to our experience before we reached this place."[95] The land south of Elyton provided more supplies, but it also contained more Confederates. Brig. Gen. Emory Upton's brigade, probing through the countryside near Montevallo, forty miles south of Elyton, ran into the first organized Confed-erate opposition to Wilson's Raid. Upton's men had "floored over" a damaged railroad bridge over the Cahaba River in order to destroy the "Red Mountain, Central, Bibb, and Columbiana iron works, Cahaba rolling mill, five collier-ies, and much valuable property" when they engaged a scratch force of Confederate cavalry under the command of Brig. Gen. Philip Roddey and some Alabama state troops under Brig. Gen. Daniel Adams.[96] The Confed-erate troops could not prevent the destruction of the facilities in Montevallo, but they did alert Wilson to the presence of real opposition, especially when Forrest and his escort force, in the van of his divisions, arrived late in the day to assess the situation.

Wilson knew that Forrest was in the area when, in a stroke of luck, on April 1 Union troops near Randolph, Alabama, captured a courier bearing messages for Forrest from one of his subordinates.[97] The inter-cepted communique revealed that Forrest's forces were not only widely spaced, but separated by the Cahaba River as well. It emboldened Wilson to strike at the small force that Forrest had assembled before he could consolidate his command. The only way that Confederate reinforcements could quickly join Forrest was via a bridge over the Cahaba River south of Centreville; without the bridge, the arriving Confederate cavalry would have to find a place to ford the rain-swollen river.[98] Wilson detached Col. Oscar LaGrange's second brigade to capture the bridge in hopes of linking up with Croxton's first brigade returning from the raid on Tuscaloosa. LaGrange captured the bridge and learned from Confederate prisoners that Croxton had succeeded in destroying facilities in Tuscaloosa, but had been driven north by Jackson's division. Unable to rendezvous with Croxton and outnumbered by Confederate troops heading for Selma, LaGrange destroyed the Centreville bridge after a sharp skirmish and fell back to Centreville on April 2.[99] Instead of bolstering his command, Forrest's reinforcements had to find a ford because they did not have a pontoon bridge, the result of an unintended consequence. In December 1864, Union Col. William J. Palmer, leading a small force of cavalry, encountered a Confederate wagon train in northern Alabama. Besides taking one-hundred-fifty prisoners "including 2 colonels, 2 captains, and 6 lieutenants" and destroying "between 750 and 1,000 stand of arms," Palmer reported the destruction of many wagons in a "train, which extended for five miles, and consisted of seventy-eight pontoon-boats and about 200 wagons." Palmer was promoted to brigadier general for his success, and, unwittingly, prevented the consolidation of Forrest's command months later.[100]

The destruction of the bridge at Centreville disrupted Forrest's immediate plans. He had intended to engage Wilson as far north of Selma as possible with as many troops as he could promptly assemble, while another group of reinforcements crossed the Centreville bridge to attack Wilson from the rear. Some of the arriving Confederates joined Forrest as planned, but most did not make it in time.[101] Forrest, instead of falling back to Selma, opted to make a stand at a spot where he could merge his small force, consisting of his personal escort, the cavalry brigades of Brig. Gen. Philip Roddey and Col. Edward Crossman, and a small number of local State Troops, with Brig. Gen. James Chalmers's lead brigade moving up from the south. In addition, Forrest ordered Brig. Gen. William Jackson's troops to cross the Cahaba River as quickly as a ford could be located and attack Wilson's column from the rear. The site Forrest chose was near the Ebenezer Church, close to modern-day Stanton, Alabama, where high ground fronted by a deep creek provided the best defensive terrain in the area. The Confederate consolidation, however, was not to be. Chalmers arrived too late to assist and Jackson could not locate a ford in time, leaving Forrest's small command to confront the troopers of Brig. Gen. Eli Long's division leading Wilson's advance.

Although initially caught by surprise by the appearance of Confederate veterans, Union troops reacted quickly. Two Indiana regiments collided with Confederate troops in a close-range fight where Forrest suffered a serious wound before killing his attacker. As other Union troops arrived, they began to flank the Confederate portion of the line held by the inexperienced State Troops, who crumbled before the rapidly maneuvering Union horsemen. Forrest withdrew before he could be encircled, and fell back toward the field fortifications at Selma, twenty-five miles to the south. The sharp clash had left a dozen Union troops dead and forty wounded. Forrest did not make a report about his casualties, but he had lost three artillery pieces and, even worse considering the dire need for troops, three hundred men taken prisoner.[102] One question to come out of the clash at Ebenezer Church is why Forrest chose to fight there at all. He knew he would not be able to halt Wilson's advance, and, while he wanted time to prepare the defenses of Selma, the losses he suffered did not offset the small amount of time gained by fighting. Perhaps the best answer is that Forrest preferred to fight in open country, where he could improvise and use the element of surprise as he had done so many times in the past, rather than from fixed fortifications like those at Selma that made his efforts predictable. Regardless of his reasons, Forrest had to fall back to Selma, a city the Confederacy could not afford to lose.

****

Wilson's plan for a lightning campaign into central Alabama seemed to be a success. Despite the problems faced in creating his rebuilt force, he appeared on the cusp of great victories. Wilson had overcome rain-swollen rivers, desolate landscapes, and long distances to carry his army deep into enemy territory. Along the way, he had inflicted considerable materiel damage on the Confederate industries his men had encountered. Even more importantly, he, by brushing aside Forrest's defensive stand at Ebenezer Church, had bested the Confederacy's best cavalry general in combat, an accomplishment that very few Union officers could claim. For all his effort, however, Wilson knew the most difficult part of his mission still remained. He had not come just to raid the Alabama countryside, but to destroy his enemy's sources of military support found in nearby industrial centers. If Wilson wanted to reach his goal, he had to attack prepared and defended cities, and the first, Selma, was next on Wilson's agenda.

Chapter 8

"Don't Butcher Us All": Wilson's Raid from Selma to Macon

James Wilson, although a youthful general of only twenty-seven years, had demonstrated his mastery of cavalry warfare. John Schofield had criticized his efforts to contain Hood's advance into Tennessee the previous winter, but Wilson proved his worth during the pursuit of Hood's army and the subsequent improvement of his cavalry arm during the winter encampments along the Tennessee. From a disorganized and largely dismounted force in 1864, Wilson created a force with potent firepower and increased mobility, despite the lack of horses for all his troopers. His improved force, too large for even the Confederacy's most capable cavalry general to halt, had moved through northern Alabama and devastated all military-related targets in its path. Such cavalry operations had occurred throughout the war, and Wilson's men demonstrated they were proficient in the standard use of cavalry as a raiding force suitable for economic warfare against civilian targets.

Wilson's task, however, was about to take a very different turn. Instead of merely raiding sparsely or undefended targets by utilizing the speed of cavalry to catch the enemy by surprise, Wilson's intent was to use cavalry in a strategic fashion by destroying enemy sources of supply. To do so, Wilson had to assault positions where the enemy knew of his presence and had troops in prepared positions to greet him. Previously, cavalry commanders had eschewed such attacks, but Wilson embraced the idea of proving what massed cavalry with modern repeating rifles could accomplish. In the remaining weeks of the campaign, Wilson's men repeatedly assaulted fortified positions, proving that aggressively handled cavalry were the equal of veteran infantry, or even superior considering their speed and mobility. The first test of Wilson's theories on cavalry operations came at the vital industrial city of Selma, Alabama.

****

Selma was an ideal location for an iron industry thanks to its proximity to resources, but also because of its relatively secure location and access to Mobile via the Alabama River as the railroad system declined. The government invested in the antebellum iron facilities, which consisted of four furnaces and two rolling mills, making it a major industrial center featuring sixteen furnaces and six rolling mills by 1864. In addition, the city contained an arsenal and powder works of the Ordnance Bureau, an iron foundry operated by the Confederate Navy, and five civilian-operated iron works.[1] Forrest, still blood-smeared from the fight at Ebenezer Church, arrived in Selma on April 1 to prepare the city for the coming Union assault, but he was not optimistic.[2] Unlike at Ebenezer Church, he would be facing Wilson's entire force from a fixed position that limited his ability to maneuver. He was also, after the clash at Ebenezer Church, in even greater need of troops than before. To provide the soldiers he needed, Forrest began rounding up every able-bodied male resident he could find, declaring that men capable of fighting "must go into the works or into the river." The works now occupied by Forrest's troopers and makeshift soldiers arched over the city with both flanks resting on the Alabama River. Brig. Gen. Frank Armstrong's brigade held the western side of the work while Roddey's held the eastern side, leaving the State Troops and local "volunteers" in the middle where the veteran troops could support them.[3]

At first glance, the Union attackers considered the defenses quite formidable. Private William Crouse described Selma as "protected by two lines of entrenchments, the outer or main line consisting of a high parapet of earth faced by a deep ditch, and at the inner edge of this ditch was a row of pine stakes sharpened." The Confederates were certainly confident in the strength

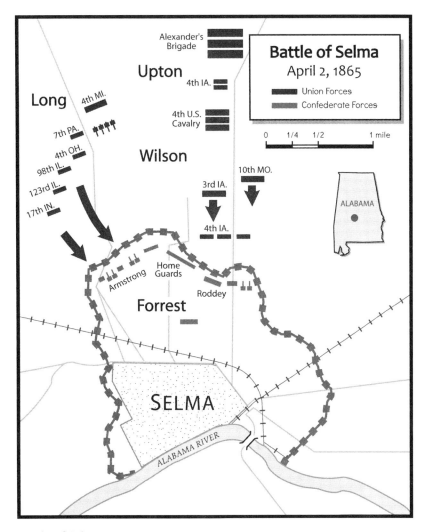

Battle of Selma.

of their defenses. A Union attacker described how "as our troops were forming they held up [a] white handkerchief and beckoned our troops to come
on," presuming the Union troops would prefer to surrender rather than attack
such staunch fortifications.[4] Another soldier was incredulous that Wilson
would even consider attacking such a site. "To charge the enemy at this point,
it was necessary to pass over an open field enfiladed by artillery and swept

by musketry," a Pennsylvania trooper described. "It was scarcely presumed by officers or men that General Wilson would order dismounted dragoons to make an assault upon such formidable earthworks."[5]

As Wilson positioned his men to storm Forrest's position, timely intelligence information once again gave him an advantage. Soldiers from Upton's division had captured a British engineer who designed the Selma defenses and who had provided a detailed description of the breastworks. Wilson had not yet deployed all his troops until mid-afternoon, but was determined to assault the city before darkness fell. Wilson did not want to give Forrest time to improve his defenses, and scouts also reported that Brigadier General Chalmers's division, arriving too late to participate at the Ebenezer Church fight, was approaching the city from the northwest, threatening to disrupt the entire assault. General Long's division, dismounted and fighting on foot as Wilson had planned, led the assault against Armstrong's troops on the Confederate left flank. Wilson selected Long's division to lead the assault because they were "most accustomed to fighting on foot."[6] While Long deployed his troops and awaited the signal to attack, he became concerned about the pressure from Chalmers's rebel troops behind him. To fend off Chalmers, Long dispatched two regiments to block the Confederate advance and cover the rear of the assault. The evolving situation convinced Long he had to attack before Upton's division could get into position, and he ordered his troops to advance in, an observer noted, "a single line without support." After sending the Indiana and Michigan troops to cover his rear, Long attacked the dug-in Confederates with only 1,258 soldiers.[7]

Upton's men, most of whom were also dismounted, upon seeing Long commence the attack ahead of schedule, also moved forward to cover Long's left flank and concentrate their attack at the seam between Armstrong's veterans and the militia in the center of the line. Leading the way was a wave of escaped slaves with axes to clear the abatis and palisades.[8] "None of us thought the enemy would assault the works, exposed as they would be in an open field for some hundreds of yards," a Confederate officer later remarked. "I ... could plainly see the deadly effects of our fire, though it did not check the enemy, who by this time had gotten so near that they were in equal danger in advancing or retreating."[9] The Confederate fire was at first deadly accurate and resulted in many Union casualties. An Illinois soldier wrote afterward, "Our command suffered considerable, owing to having a wide open field to cross, and a strong picket fence with a deep ditch inside and a high embankment."[10] Nevertheless, the Union troops attacked "with a will that surprised the egotistical rebels."[11] The Confederates had the advantage of a well-prepared position, but the firepower from the Union Spencer carbines proved an equalizer. "As soon as our boys got the range of the works they poured such an accurate and continuous sheet of lead from their 'seven shooters' over the parapet of the works," Private Edward Straub described, "and soon struck down so large a number that the few remaining rebels crouched down, appalled and paralyzed with terror."[12]

As the Union assault pressed forward, the militia in the center broke and ran before Forrest could redeploy Roddey's troops to stem the collapse. "The militia began to falter and gradually quit their places behind the breastworks," a Confederate officer later wrote. "Roddy was, therefore, directed to move over and fill the breach; but before it could be effected the enemy had reached the exposed, deserted section of the lines and surmounted it. … In the meantime, the militia had thrown away their arms, and were swiftly seeking their horses, and divesting themselves, as they fled, of all that would betray their late connection with the defense of Selma."[13] As the Union troops crested the breastwork to engage the remaining Confederate veterans, "the uninjured, with the slightly wounded, first by scores, then by hundreds, and in a few moments, by regiments, threw down their arms, and amid loud cries of 'We surrender!' 'Don't fire any more!' 'We are conscripts!' 'For God's sake, Yanks, don't butcher us all,' etc., they surrendered where they lay." As the Confederate position buckled, "A wild panic now spread from right to left along the enemies' whole line, and all not killed or captured, except those occupying the forts, throwing down their arms, rushed in a disordered mob of frightened fugitives, into the city."[14] Forrest tried to rally the defenders at a second improvised defensive line inside the city, but it was to no avail as Wilson himself led the Fourth U.S. Cavalry Regiment in a follow-up assault that moved to flank the Confederate position. Armstrong's men skirmished with Union troops as they retreated through the city, giving Forrest an opportunity to organize a breakout of as many troops as he could muster.

Forrest collected most of Chalmers's troops, a fair number of survivors of Roddey's command, and his own escort and retreated, but Armstrong's entire brigade was either killed or captured. They left a city in chaos, as "the streets were choked with horses, with soldiers, and citizens hurrying wildly to and fro."[15] The entire assault had lasted only twenty-five minutes.

By 7:00 pm, Wilson was in control of Selma, having suffered forty-six killed and three hundred wounded for the effort. The attack was especially costly among senior officers, who suffered 40 percent of the casualties.[16] Brigadier General Long, leading the assault himself, received a serious head wound, requiring Wilson to appoint Colonel Robert Minty commander of the Second Division. General Long remained with the division until the end of the campaign before leaving to seek long-term medical care. Although he lived to practice law for another thirty-eight years, Long suffered paralysis of the left side of his body and diminished speaking ability for the rest of his life.[17] On the Confederate side, Forrest suffered similar casualties, as well as twenty-seven-hundred men made prisoner, and the loss of "twenty-nine guns in position … many colors, and large quantities of stores were taken."[18] Union troops placed their prisoners in a stockade previously used to house Union POWs. Confederate officers objected to what they considered a snub to their standing and "were highly indignant, but cooled considerably when General Wilson ordered all such to be ironed."[19] In the aftermath of the attack, many of Wilson's men were understandably proud of their achievement. Frontal assaults rarely succeeded during the Civil War, nor did conventional wisdom hold that cavalry could defeat entrenched infantry in a stand-up fight. "A fortifyed [sic] city … is captured and sacked by Cavalry," one of the troopers bragged, "without using one spade or throwing up a single breastwork [but] by only one grand rush on their works."[20] Most soldiers attributed the low Union casualties to Wilson's style of leadership. "The Confederate generals have all been fooled, from Forrest down," Private Ebenezer Gilpin wrote. "General Wilson, who looks the dare-devil as he gallops past, is as cautious as an old maid. He waits until 'the sign is right,' then goes in with a dash. It is done so quickly, it is over before you know you are hurt. … We struck them like lightning."[21] A correspondent for the *Cincinnati Commercial* further glorified the victory. "I met an ex-rebel officer yesterday who told me that there were twenty-one batteries concentrating their fire upon the Federal troopers," the reporter informed his readers. "He said it was the grandest sight of the whole war to see that Yankee cavalry come up the road under such a fire. … The charge of the six hundred at Balaklava wasn't equal to that."[22]

After his all-out push to Selma, Wilson now had to pause. His needed to destroy the war-related facilities in Selma, a process that took several days. Wilson also allowed time for his subordinates to get their commands back into order, assess the health of their mounts, and resupply themselves with whatever articles they needed before the march continued. Wilson assigned Brig. Gen. Edward Winslow, one of Upton's brigade commanders, to supervise the destruction of all military facilities. Before the process began in earnest, soldiers took the opportunity to tour the target of their efforts. Ebenezer Gilpin and a friend examined the iron foundry with its "immense machinery, hundreds of guns of all sizes, some very fine naval guns, and thousands of shot and shell," as well. The ladies of Selma also attracted attention. Gilpin noted, "The fair ladies of Selma are busying themselves feeding and caring for the captured Confederates. Our boys sympathize with the Johnnies, and as a consequence, walk home with the girls."[23] The supervised destruction of the foundry commenced at sundown on April 4. A witness related that "shells are exploding one after another, then in platoons and squadrons … never stopping, a bright light flashing and wavering, throwing shadows over the housetops" and described the sound of the burning foundry as "war music."[24] Another observed the destruction as "Large conflagrations everywhere. Shells exploding and gunpowder blowing up. The beautiful city is in ruins."[25] Two days later, Winslow turned his attention to the arsenal. "The Arsenal was burned this Evening," a Wisconsin cavalryman wrote, "The explosions were many & resembled a battle."[26] To another soldier, "The bursting of shells, blowing up of foundries, workshops, and the arsenal, was enough to confound and bewilder the most well-balanced mind."[27] Overall, the Union troops were very thorough, and destroyed anything that could be of benefit to the Confederate war effort. "It was a great manufactoring [sic] place, almost every other house was an Arsonal [sic] or something of the kind. We lay there for a week and when we left the town looked as though it was on fire."[28]

Wilson also put to the torch as many as twenty-five thousand bales of cotton found in the city, per one soldier, "at the time, many of us considered a useless destruction."[29] Among the destroyed facilities in Selma was the printing equipment of the *Chattanooga Rebel*. The owners of the newspaper fled Chattanooga to Atlanta when the Union occupied its home city, but had to move when Sherman occupied its new location in August 1864. The editors printed in three Georgia communities before settling in Selma, but the paper finally met its end. Enterprising Union troops used the equipment to print a single edition of a new newspaper, *The Yankee Cavalier*, but destroyed the equipment a few days later when Wilson abandoned the city.[30]

As Winslow's men continued their task in Selma, Wilson organized a meeting with Forrest to discuss a prisoner exchange. Wilson did not want the prisoners to slow his march, but the conference had other purposes. Croxton had not yet rejoined Wilson's force and he hoped surreptitiously to learn of his whereabouts through discussions with the Confederates without divulging his lack of information. Wilson also wanted to gauge Forrest's strength and determine if the Confederate general still posed a threat to his future operations. The generals met on April 8 at Cahaba, about fifteen miles west of Selma. Wilson, in his postwar memoirs, recounted the meeting began formally enough, but quickly became more open, with each side "treating each other like old acquaintants." Ever the realist, Forrest had to admit to Wilson "you have beaten me badly, and for the first time I am compelled to make such an acknowledgment." Wilson diplomatically complimented Forrest on his stout defense of the city, placing the credit for the victory more on his larger force than on any tactical brilliance on his own part. Getting down to business, Wilson pressed the issue of a prisoner exchange, but Forrest declined because he lacked the authority to make such a deal, but promised to forward the idea to his superiors able to do so. As part of these discussions, Wilson learned that Forrest held but a few of Croxton's men amongst his prisoners and that Croxton was near Elyton. While this meant that Croxton's command would not be rejoining the rest of the Union force anytime soon, it also indicated that the detached Union force was in no imminent danger and could continue to operate on its own.[31] Viewing Forrest as unable to resist his advance, Wilson made plans to leave Selma immediately and continue his march. As Wilson made plans to depart, Confederates elsewhere came to realize the extent of their loss. "News this morning that Selma, Ala. has been captured by a raid," a Confederate officer wrote. "The loss of Selma is a great one, as our only remaining iron works were there."[32] The loss of Selma, occurring so close to the loss of Richmond, became events impossible to disassociate. "The fall of Richmond soon followed the fall of Selma," an officer wrote in his postwar memoirs, "and the Confederate flag went down to rise no more forever."[33]

Wilson intended to maintain his rapid pace as he moved forward. He had acquired enough animals to mount the troops that had escorted the wagon train and decided that he no longer needed the encumbrance of so many vehicles. He intended to impress enough material to build a bridge across the Alabama River and presumed he could do the same in the future, so he opted to thin out his wagon train by ridding himself of most of his pontoons.[34] More difficult to shed was the large number of escaped slaves that had followed Wilson to Selma or who had congregated there seeking their freedom in the week that Wilson occupied the city. Wilson did not consider their welfare to be his responsibility, and he subsequently "directed the column to be cleared of all contraband negroes, and such of the able-bodied ones as were able to enlist to be organized into regiments, one to each division." Wilson assigned officers to each of these makeshift regiments and issued the new troops captured Confederate uniforms until he could provide proper clothing. When the march ended, the Army designated the regiments as the One hundred thirty-seventh, One hundred thirty-eighth, and One hundred thirty-ninth USCT.[35] The one thing that Wilson wanted to bring with him but could not was his wounded troops. Wilson took as many as he could in his wagon train, but had to leave in Selma those who could not travel. Medical officers provided supplies before the army departed, and they received very good care. When Union troops arrived on April 27 to occupy the city, a Union soldier reported "Wilson left his wounded here and no men were ever treated better than they are by the ladies of this town. They just flock in to the Hospital to do what they can for them."[36]

The army was ready to leave, but the weather again interfered as rains swelled the Alabama River. Wilson had planned for this contingency,

however, and ordered his troops to gather "tools, rope, materials, etc., sufficient to construct a pontoon bridge … Send parties to the neighborhood of
the shops and press all the carpenters that can be found … to build pontoons"
before their destruction of the city began.[37] The high water made constructing
the bridge both difficult and dangerous as it often broke and several men
nearly drowned. On April 8, the bridge was finally completed. Instead of a
leisurely daylight crossing, Wilson ordered his command across as quickly
as possible in case the bridge failed again. The last to move, McCook's First
Division commenced its crossing at 10:00 pm, with a trooper describing the
weather as "raining and intensely dark." The crossing was treacherous, and
to provide illumination the soldiers "set fire to the business buildings on the
wharf to light up the river and to guard against driftwood."[38] The fire got out
of control, a soldier noted, and "the Main Street was destroyed."[39] The officers
in charge of bridge construction did not sanction the burning, and expressed
disapproval of the arson. "Several buildings were fired on the evening of
the 2nd instant," an officer wrote to Wilson, "and quite a number of private
dwellings were thereby consumed. This burning being done without authority destroyed supplies which would have been useful to the army, and did no
particular damage to the enemy."[40] Once across the Alabama, the weather
and terrain hindered Wilson's progress more than Confederate opposition.
Because of the rain, "The roads were swampy and full of holes," one soldier
recalled, and they "were compelled to build corduroy road for half a mile
across a swamp."[41] Although slowed by the terrain, Wilson acted decisively
regarding his next objective. He had obtained enough information from local
sources to conclude that the Union advance against Mobile was proceeding
well enough that he could reinterpret his orders. Rather than ride south to
support the investment of Mobile, Wilson opted to head east toward the state
capital, and first Confederate national capital, at Montgomery, fifty miles
away. Besides its symbolic value as the cradle of the Confederacy, Montgomery was an important transportation hub, with two railroads serving the
city, as well as steamboats operating on the Alabama River. There were also
factories that produced shoes and uniforms, nitre and lead works operated by
the Ordnance Bureau, and an arsenal that produced canteens, haversacks, and
horse tack.[42]

Despite its significance, Confederate authorities were uncertain if they were going to defend Montgomery. Brig. Gen. William "Wirt" Adams, commanding the Confederate troops around Montgomery, pledged to the city residents that he intended to defend the city and made perfunctory preparations to do so. Adams worked in conjunction with Governor Watts, who was obviously not in favor of abandoning his capital until all options had failed. Watts, however, had no practical sense of what it would take to stop Wilson. He appealed to President Davis for help, whose only option was to pass the request on to Maj. Gen. Howell Cobb, commanding troops in southern Georgia. Davis instructed Cobb to coordinate whatever action he intended to take with Watts and promptly disowned the matter. Although intimating that he intended to protect the city, Adams had at his disposal only about eighteen hundred soldiers, almost all cavalry. It was too late to issue calls for militia volunteers and he had no weapons for them if he did attempt such a call. Adams's troops placated the public by occupying fortifications near Montgomery, but Adams had no intention, ability, or orders to defend the city. Quite the opposite, on April 14, Taylor instructed Adams to "attempt no defense at Montgomery if the enemy moved against him in force."[43] Complying with Taylor's orders, Adams led his men out of Montgomery. Whether Watts was part of the ploy is uncertain. On one hand, he issued statements declaring that the army would defend the city "as long as there is a reasonable hope" of protecting Montgomery. On the other hand, a newspaper claimed that Watts "determined several days before the enemy reached the city to give it up."[44] Public posturing aside, the city leadership recognized the urgency of the situation and began to prepare for the worst, including the expansion of the city's fire brigades (adding fifty free African Americans) and an ordinance requiring the destruction of all liquor before the enemy arrived.[45]

The arrival was not far off. On April 11, three days after leaving Selma, Union troops ran into Confederates guarding a bridge near Hayneville, Alabama, just six miles from Montgomery. The defenders had demolished part of the bridge to build a barricade on the far shore. General McCook, leading Wilson's column, did not have sufficient troops to force a crossing and awaited reinforcements before assaulting the position the following morning. The next morning, however, a soldier reported "the Rebs were gone and soon our Brigade were in hot pursuit."[46] With nothing to stop the Union entry into the city, Governor Watts evacuated the state government to Union Springs, forty-five miles to the southeast. As Union troops approached the city, "The panic in Montgomery was most shameful," an observer wrote scornfully. "The speculators were busy putting afloat all kinds of extravagant rumors and buying up supplies at greatly reduced prices, whilst the city officials were at time just awaiting the appearance of anything … in blue clothes to which they may surrender the city."[47] When the first contingent of blue uniforms reached the outskirts of town, "the city authority came with a white flag, surrendering Montgomery" as "Genl. Adams … had skedaddled the night before."[48] The advance pickets "Met the mayor with a deputation of citizens 2 miles from the city, who surrendered the city to General McCook, asking clemency for the citizens and protection for their public works. They feared a repetition of the scenes at Selma." McCook, as soon as he accepted the city's surrender, gave a brief speech to the civilians who assembled to witness his arrival. Promising security in exchange for a pledge of non-interference, McCook assured the populace that he would protect their personal property and maintain order.

To back up his words, "General McCook permitted no straggling or pillaging." The residents welcomed the arrival of Union troops to restore order, as General Adams, in his haste to retreat from Montgomery had "given it up to pillage. The rebel troops had broken open the stores and carried away everything of value, burned all the corn, cotton, and commissary stores in the city."[49] The fires set by Adams's men created a significant risk that Montgomery might have burned to the ground, as the Confederates had torched both cotton held in warehouses and bales dragged into the streets as makeshift barricades. The city survived, but Wilson estimated that ninety thousand bales of cotton had gone up in flames. The destruction did not sit well with the residents left to deal with the conflagration; a Union surgeon observed, "The rebel troops before our entrance had burned 85,000 bales of cotton, valued at $40,000,000 in gold. The citizens expressed a great deal of anger at the occurrence."[50]

Union troops were favorably impressed with the beauty of the city during their brief stay, as well as the respect paid by its residents. "The inhabitants received the troops, if without manifestations of joy, at least without any evidences of dislike," a soldier reported, noting that "Montgomery, the capital of Alabama, is a beautiful city, and contains a large number of elegant residences."[51] Unlike Selma, Montgomery had no significant industrial facilities and Wilson moved on after staying only three days, and the city escaped major damage. Soldiers barely had time to sightsee, although one private did make note of the city's fortifications as being "strongly fortified and could have been defended had a proper force of rebels assembled in time."[52] Although the Union forces destroyed war-related industries in the area, civilians recognized that Union troops acted with restraint and damaged no civilian homes. "The good order preserved during our stay was a subject of remark and congratulation by the citizens," Colonel Wickliffe Cooper of the Fourth Kentucky Cavalry reported, but that did not prevent him from following orders from General McCook. Cooper reported he "destroyed the following property: Three steam-boats; Montgomery Arsenal, containing 20,000 stand of small-arms; 1 foundry and molding shop with contents; 1 locomotive; 20 pontoons; nitre-works and contents; cartwheel foundry and contents; Pensacola and West Point Railroad depots and contents, and 20 cars and machine-shop containing 4 unfinished cars."[53]

After finishing with the industrial and military sites in Montgomery, Wilson selected Columbus, Georgia, eighty miles away, as his next target. Because Columbus was such an obvious place to attack, Wilson worried about his ability to cross the Chattahoochee River if its defenders burned the bridges before he arrived. Wilson could improvise a bridge across the Chattahoochee as he did at Selma, but that would take time and deny him the element of surprise. To both improve his chances of catching the defenders at Columbus unaware of his intent and provide an alternate route if his plans did not go as expected, Wilson ordered McCook to assault West Point, Georgia, forty miles north of Columbus, to divert Confederate attention and to seize the bridges across the Chattahoochee. McCook acted immediately, sending a brigade commanded by Col. Oscar LaGrange toward West Point with the rest of the division to follow behind him. "On the morning of the 17th, Colonel LaGrange, taking the 2nd and 4th Indiana, and one section of our battery, marched rapidly at 1:00 am and by daylight reached West

Point," a Union soldier later wrote. "[W]e left the main Columbus Road and took a road over the hills, travelling north-east ... to prevent the rebels from destroying the bridges."[54]

The anchor of the West Point defenses was Fort Tyler, described as "a remarkably strong earth-work, thirty-five yards square, surrounded by a ditch twelve feet wide and ten deep, situated on a commanding eminence and protected by an imperfect abatis." The position, although outwardly daunting, was defended by a garrison of only 265 men made up of local militia, armed civilians (the youngest of whom was twelve years old), and other scraped-together personnel, along with two field guns and a large 32-pounder siege gun.[55] While the Union troops, both before and after the battle, believed the fortifications to be daunting, the Confederates were less impressed. The physician at Fort Tyler told the commanding office, Brig. Gen. Robert C. Tyler, that the fort "is a slaughter pen." Tyler responded, "I know it, but we must man and try to hold it." Tyler had pledged to hold the fort and save the city. When citizens named the fort in his honor and presented him with a flag for the position, Tyler pledged to fight until the end if needed, telling the citizens should "that flag be lowered to the enemy you will find my dead body at the foot of its staff."[56]

Although dominating the high ground, the fort was isolated from the town itself with no supporting fieldworks, allowing LaGrange to contain it with the Second and Fourth Indiana cavalry while "pieces of artillery amused the fort by a steady, well-directed fire" until the rest of the brigade could arrive. While dismounted troopers from First Wisconsin, Second Indiana, and Seventh Kentucky engaged the defenders from behind cover with their Spencer rifles, the Fourth Indiana slipped past the fort, seized the bridges across the Chattahoochee, and scattered a small group of Confederate cavalry.[57] Trying to catch the defenders unaware, LaGrange sent his dismounted troopers forward, supported by his small artillery detachment, which "began a brisk cannonade, dismounting one 12-pounder, driving the cannoniers [sic] from the heavy guns that stood exposed."[58] The initial assault stalled as Union troops took the forward ditch, but could not scale the inner wall. Conversely, Confederate troops could not lean over to fire at the Union troops without exposing themselves. "The enemy got so close that we could not see them," a Confederate soldier recalled, "so we held our guns above our heads at full length of arms and pointing the muzzle downward fired, thinking the shot might be effective perhaps." The Confederates had to raise their rifles because it was too hazardous to stand up, as "the sharpshooters made it too hot and dangerous for our men to put their heads up, as it is almost certain death." Because "there being no headlogs for the infantry nor embrasures for the cannon. Every man killed or wounded was struck in the shoulders, neck, or head." One of the attacking cavalryman recalled the effectiveness of their Spencer carbines, telling a friend, "they dared not raise up and shoot at any of our boys. If they did, 'Mr. Spencer' said 'Lay down, Johnny!'"[59]

Desperate, both sides tried to break the stalemate. The Confederate defenders began "throwing hand grenades, or bombs, into the ditch," a Union soldier remembered, but "being defective, I do not think any of them exploded." Union troops fashioned makeshift bridges with lumber scavenged from nearby houses and charged the inner works, with a Wisconsin regiment being the first to enter the fort itself and force the garrison to surrender.[60] Col. James H. Fannin ordered a ceasefire after a Union sharpshooter killed Tyler and the artillerymen could not service the fort's guns.[61] The victory came at a cost. "General Tyler, the rebel commander, and 60 others were killed, and many wounded," one of the victorious troops wrote. "We lost 5 officers and 20 men killed. Captain Hill, commanding the 2nd Indiana, a brave and dashing officer, was severely wounded, with 40 others."[62] The day after the battle, LeGrange destroyed what was valuable in the town and prepared to move out. A Confederate soldier observed, "the Federals burned the two commodious depots filled with government supplies and hundreds of freight cars loaded with machinery, merchandise, etc., together with about sixteen locomotives."[63] LaGrange also ordered the bridges, the hard-won objective of his mission, destroyed because "We learned that General Wilson had taken Columbus the evening before, with 2000 prisoners, a great amount of artillery and stores." The destruction of the bridges left a sense of pointlessness to the entire clash, a good example of the futility of a war already long lost. In his postwar history, Edward A. Pollard described the battle at West Point as "an episode of desperate Confederate valour in the dreary story of a country overrun almost without resistance" and an honorable example of "obstinate heroism."[64]

Before leaving, LaGrange arranged for the care of both Union and Confederate troops left behind. A local doctor reported, "he supplied us with everything we required for the comfort and sustenance of his and our wounded" consisting of "Seven hogsheads of sugar, 2,000 sacks of corn, 10,000 pounds of bacon and other stores … left in charge of the mayor to provide a hospital fund for both parties, with instructions to distribute the excess among the poor."[65] LaGrange rounded up the prisoners and began marching them toward Macon. "The Negroes were dismounted & prisoners mounted," a soldier remembered, showing the racial value placed by Union troops on their slave laborers. Union officers allowed some of the Confederate prisoners to return home while on the march to Macon, while holding those who arrived at the city in "a place about an acre square … I was told that the Confederate government built this pen to keep Yank prisoners in, but it seems that we were caught in a trap of our own making. We were kept in this pen about a week and then paroled."[66]

As LaGrange overwhelmed the defenses at West Point, Wilson took the main column toward Columbus, a shipping point and industrial hub situated on the fall line of the Chattahoochee River. A dozen steamboats plied the river starting in the 1840s, and the city was a stop on the rail line from Montgomery to Savannah. The city's major industrial product before the war was textiles, with four mills operating by 1860, along with a paper mill and an iron foundry. When the war began, these facilities shifted to war production augmented by other factories constructed under the direction of the Confederate government. Besides uniforms for the Confederate Army, the city's mills produced tents and "India rubber cloth," waterproof fabric with a rubber lining. The demands of the Confederate Army were so great that in late 1861 the Quartermaster Bureau set up a large depot to supplement the local production, but eventually superseded the smaller mills.[67] Local factories produced some weapons. Greenwood & Gray produced "Mississippi" rifles and carbines for the army, while Haiman Brothers were a major producer of swords and bayonets.[68] The most important industrial site at Columbus was the naval works and construction yard operated by the Confederate Navy. Established in 1848 as the Columbus Iron Works, the yard produced cannon, mortars, armor plate, and marine machinery in a complex that included a foundry and rolling mill, eight warehouses, a small dockyard, and a separate building for assembling marine engines. The products of the company were so valuable that, instead of competing for its output, the Confederate Government leased the entire complex outright for its own use in September 1862.[69]

The relative isolation that made Columbus an attractive industrial site also made it unprepared for a major assault. Engineers had constructed some basic fortifications to ward off cavalry raids, but as Wilson's column approached, the vulnerability of the place became evident. Its defense fell on the shoulders of Maj. Gen. Howell Cobb, commanding troops in southern Georgia. Col. Leon von Zinken, a Prussian immigrant who had formerly commanded the Twentieth Louisiana, led the city garrison. In addition to a detachment of cavalry from Forrest's command, the city's defenders included local militia units, Alabama militia from the counties west of Columbus, and some hastily armed and drilled companies from the local works, altogether about three thousand men with two batteries of artillery.[70] Needing additional troops, von Zinken issued a call for help on April 15, asking "all able-bodied men of this city to report to headquarters with whatever arms they have to assist the commanding officer in making a resolute defense of their homes." The message apparently did not convey the proper sense of urgency, as on the same day the *Columbus Daily Sun* featured an opinion that "We are satisfied that the enemy will not move in any considerable force from Montgomery for several days."[71]

Cobb endorsed von Zinken's appeal for additional soldiers, but believed that defending Columbus was futile. Recognizing the nature of raiding warfare, Cobb realized that, even if he managed to hold the city, Wilson would simply flank around him and devastate the countryside. Without supplies, the Confederates defenders would inevitably have to surrender, giving the city to Wilson anyway.[72] Cobb kept his misgivings to himself, as the defenders already had too many problems. There were prepared defenses on the Alabama side of the river, but not enough troops to man them, so von Zinken ordered a line of rifle pits to cover the bridge approaches to the city. Three bridges crossed the Chattahoochee River at Columbus: a railroad bridge along with two covered footbridges that connected Columbus to the

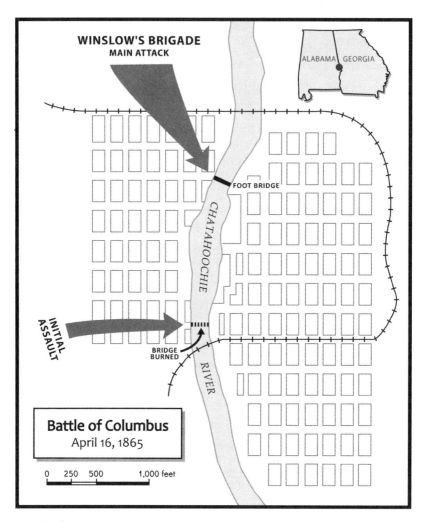

Battle of Columbus.

small Alabama towns of Girard to the south and Phenix City to the north on the opposite bank of the Chattahoochee, forcing von Zinken to spread his force out to guard all of them.[73]

On April 16, the main Union column was close enough to strike. Following the example at Selma, Wilson approached Columbus swiftly to gain as much surprise as possible. Also like Selma, he had his troops fight on foot, but kept the Fourth Cavalry as a mounted reserve to exploit any breach in the

Confederate lines. His optimistic plan, however, came to nothing.[74] Wilson's force first encountered the city's defenders when Upton's Fourth Division drove off a Confederate picket force thirteen miles west of Columbus. Worried that he had alerted the enemy to his presence, Upton drove forward as quickly as possible, and his Second Brigade drove through Girard toward the southern bridge. Running into a small force of militia, Upton brushed them aside as they presented little resistance. Largely untrained, the militia realized their perilous situation and began a hasty withdrawal, one soldier moving so quickly that he ran into his commanding officer, "knocking off his hat. I never stopped to pick it up for him, for every fellow was for himself now."[75] The attack failed, however, as the Confederates had removed the planks across the span. Union troops could not replace the planks as artillery covered the bridge, and the Confederates set it afire.[76]

Stymied at the lower bridge, Upton ordered his Second Brigade to distract the Confederates while he organized his First Brigade, commanded by Brig. Gen. Edward Winslow, to attack the other footbridge. Winslow's troops, hidden by a line of hills, were still unseen by the Confederates. Upton ordered Winslow to lead his men north to the Opelika Road and prepare for another assault. It took time for Winslow to get into position and, having hurried up the road to Columbus, had to pause to allow his men to rest and feed their horses. By the time that was done, Wilson had arrived and learned of Upton's intention to force the second footbridge by a night assault. The alternative was to await reinforcements and daylight, while hoping the Confederates did not reinforce their positions or burn that bridge as well. Upton's confidence won Wilson over, promising his commander, "I'll sweep everything before me."[77]

Well after sundown, the Third Iowa Cavalry, fighting on foot, led the assault on the second bridge using the lighter colored soil of the road as a guide in the dim moonlight. Behind them, mounted to exploit a breakthrough, were the Tenth Missouri (commanded by Lt. Col. Frederick Benteen who was later at Custer's defeat at the Little Big Horn) and Fourth Iowa Cavalry regiments. The darkness both aided and hampered the attack. The limited visibility allowed the Fourth Iowa to close with and engage the Confederate outer works without being detected, causing a breach. However, darkness, along with unfamiliarity with the Confederate defenses, caused confusion when the Tenth Missouri moved forward. Passing through the gap created by the Third Iowa, the Missourians found themselves behind the outer Confederate works but in front of the inner works. Uncertain of their location and caught between Confederate gunfire from two directions, the Tenth withdrew and received orders to dismount to assist the Third Iowa in clearing the outer works. Sensing an opportunity, Upton committed the now-dismounted Fourth Iowa to the assault, and Confederate resistance collapsed. Surging over the Confederate works, Union troops, ordered not to stop to take prisoners, pressed toward their goal. Overcoming a final redoubt on the western side of the river, Union troops rushed the bridge. Confederate defenders had saturated the span with turpentine and cotton wicks to burn it if their defenses collapsed, and had situated two cannons loaded with canister as a final defense. The artillerymen tasked with igniting the bridge could not distinguish between advancing Union troops and retreating Confederate troops because the two were so intermingled, and wound up neither torching the structure nor opening fire. Union troops from the Fourth Iowa were the first across the bridge, seizing the two guns and driving off the last defenders.[78]

Suppressing the fading Confederate resistance as it went, the Iowans almost captured General Cobb, but he managed to escape in the darkness and confusion.[79] Behind him, all was chaos. Fires, lit to illuminate the darkened streets, pierced the darkness as Confederate troops tried to flee while local militia fled for their homes. Union soldiers, weary and hungry after their long march and hard fight, intruded into yards and gardens as they made camp, often forcing the residents to make them something to eat. The Medical Corps established field hospitals and began the difficult process of collecting the wounded hidden in the darkness and battlefield obstacles. They found surprisingly few. Upton's division suffered five dead and twenty-eight wounded in the attack on the upper bridge, a small number considering the confusion and violence of the clash. Wilson attributed the low casualties to the inability of either side to shoot accurately, believing the "Darkness had protected the fighting men of both forces." Wilson also reported the capture of fifty-seven guns and twelve hundred prisoners. Wilson and his subordinates immediately established their headquarters in the city and set about posting a provost guard and reestablishing order. The next morning, Mayor Francis F. Wilkins issued a statement calling for calm and reassuring citizens that, upon a promise from Wilson, "private property will be protected. It is ordered that all citizens remain on their premises." Wilkins also announced that Wilson "further requires of the citizens 30,000 rations, which must be furnished by 12 o'clock noon." Wilson certainly needed the rations, but, as the citizenry could not possibly raise the needed goods in time, Wilson presumably used the demand as a justification for any foraging conducted by his troops.[80] In defeat, civilians tried to put the loss of Columbus in the best light. "Columbus is now in the hands of the enemy," a woman wrote in her diary. "[T]he militia fought manfully in its defense, but having ten to one with which to contend, they were forced to succumb."[81]

The day after taking Columbus, the destruction began of "everything within reach that could be made useful for the continuation of the Rebellion."[82] General Winslow, who had so efficiently wrecked the industries in Selma, received the same the task in Columbus. He quickly accumulated a list of targets for destruction in Columbus and Girard that included three warehouses, three arsenals and nitre works, four newspaper offices, six foundries and blacksmith shops, six factories and mills, the naval armory and yard, and the railroad depot. Winslow's destruction included the sixty-eight heavy guns at the arsenal. Unable to destroy the heavy iron barrels, Winslow noted, "Nearly all were thrown into the river." Among the destruction was 125,000 bales of cotton, valued at more than $60 million, "an immense amount," Wilson notified the War Department, "all of which were burned." At the naval yard, the biggest prize was the nearly complete CSS *Jackson*, an ironclad armed with six 7-inch guns and covered in four inches of armor plate. Nearly 220-feet long and displacing 2,000 tons, the ship, according to Winslow, "would, if fully completed, have been a formidable antagonist for our river gun-boats or rams. ... I am informed she would have been ready for active service in two weeks."[83]

Winslow followed his orders to demolish anything of military value in Columbus, but also made Wilson aware of the burden his efforts were placing on the local populace as civilian pillaging added to the formal destruction of the city's industries and the informal destruction of pillaging by Union soldiers. Winslow reported to Wilson that "No private buildings in Columbus were destroyed, and no buildings fired except by order and with proper authority," but there was still hardship. "More than 5,000 employees [from the workshops] are thrown upon the community for other support," Winslow informed his commander, and "There are thousands of almost pauper citizens and negroes" who "formed one vast mob, which seized upon and carried off almost everything movable, whether useful or not."[84] The pillaging mob consisted of representatives of any demographic in the city at the time. "The stores and shops are open, and the contents, without cost, are at the mercy of fancy or desire," a Union officer wrote. "There is evident demoralization among the females. They frantically jam and jostle in the chaos, and seem crazy for plunder. There are well-dressed ladies in the throng."[85] Although there was little Wilson could do to alleviate the economic hardship in the city, he ordered Winslow to spare from destruction grist mills and other facilities needed to feed the population, as well as distribute from captured Confederate quartermaster stores supplies of clothing and tools.[86]

As the demolition of Columbus's facilities continued, Wilson dispatched Minty's division eastward toward Macon, ninety-five miles away, with the other divisions to follow soon after. Minty ran into little opposition other than a contested crossing of the Flint River that ended when "40 prisoners were captured and 2 cotton factories destroyed."[87] The Union advance from Columbus caused concern in Macon because Cobb, hoping that the Columbus defenses held Wilson, began preparations to defend Macon far too late. When Wilson began his march toward the city, General Cobb gave his engineers the authority to impress slave labor to improve the city's fortifications, but they, in turn, reported that they could do little because they lacked axes and shovels. Cobb also ordered all soldiers on furloughs and details to report themselves to the nearest military unit for immediate service, as well as the requisitioning of all horses and mules along Wilson's expected route of advance. Cobb's efforts were undermined, however, by his decision the following day to evacuate industrial equipment and military stores from the city, giving the impression that he was disinclined to mount a serious defense. Civilians began to panic, with those with the means to flee the city doing so in chaotic fashion.[88]

Meanwhile, Minty's Division, with the Seventeenth Indiana in the lead, pressed toward Macon. On the twentieth, the Indianans, led by Lt. Col. Frank White, pushed back some Confederates attempting to burn the bridge over the Ocmulgee River south of Macon, using blankets and water carried in their kepis to douse the flames.[89] Pressing onward, the regiment encountered a Confederate delegation led by Brig. Gen. Felix Robertson with a request for a truce from General Cobb. Robertson informed White that Sherman and Johnston had signed an armistice in North Carolina that encompassed all of Georgia, and Cobb intended to abide by the terms that required both sides to cease offensive operations. Cobb, on his part, had already withdrawn the state troops from Macon's fortifications to avoid unnecessary conflict. White relayed the message to Minty with a request for instructions. Minty, in turn, instructed White to tell Robertson to return to Macon while Minty passed the request for a ceasefire up to Wilson. Robertson refused to do so without a written response from the Union forces, and Minty, believing that Robertson was there to simply deceive and delay him, provided his request in writing but gave Robertson only five minutes to withdraw. The Confederates did not retreat within the allotted time, so Minty ordered his riders forward, scattering Robertson's escort force. White then pressed forward to Macon, where General Cobb surrendered the city unconditionally. Wilson later congratulated White for his aggressive action. Among the prizes at Macon were four generals (including Cobb and Robertson), three hundred other officers, more than three thousand enlisted men, three thousand stands of arms, five regimental colors, a herd of horses and mules, and sixty artillery pieces.[90]

Cobb immediately protested that Wilson was in violation of the truce. Cobb, in his message, apparently thought that the ceasefire would prevent Wilson from occupying Macon, but Wilson had no intention of stopping short of occupying the place. When Cobb demanded that Wilson withdraw outside of city limits, Wilson informed him that he was not about to take his word regarding the peace talks and would act on the purported ceasefire only when it was confirmed by Union authorities and not before. Wilson only became convinced that the armistice was in place when he asked Maj. Gen. Gustavus Smith, commander of the Georgia State Troops and someone whom Wilson

knew from before the war, if Lee had surrendered. When Smith confirmed
the rumor was true, Wilson accepted the truce and thereafter acted accordingly. In a conciliatory tone, however, Wilson informed Cobb that he and
staff should consider themselves under parole and that he further concluded
the war was over. Committed to peace and an end to the bloodshed, Wilson
informed Cobb that from that point onward "any man killed on either side is
a man murdered." On the twenty-first, Wilson received a formal notification
from Sherman, over the enemy's telegraph wires and through the headquarters of General Joseph E. Johnston, that the reported armistice was a
reality and that he was to cease further operations.[91] Wilson established his
headquarters in Macon, leaving a resident sorrowfully to report "The army
of General Wilson reached Macon in the afternoon and poor old Georgia
was done for."[92]

Upon receiving confirmation of the armistice, Wilson immediately took
steps to implement it and prevent unnecessary burdens on local civilians. He
posted his men to maintain order and worked with General Cobb to provide
sustenance for his troops, prisoners, and animals, as "to have been compelled
to forage for them would have resulted in the devastation of the entire country in the vicinity of the city."[93] Wilson also had to provide support for a
large number of escaped slaves that had followed his army across Georgia.
Describing the mass following in their wake to Macon, an Illinois soldier
observed, "the column was at least two miles long, some mounted and other
afoot, all in the best humor and ready to fight or do anything we say. Here
I see ten mounted, well-armed, as black as midnight, and headed by a white
sergeant."[94] Macon residents had heard of the "hundreds of negroes, who had
been gathering behind him since he had occupied Columbus. The citizens
expected the worst and that squad[s] of citizens were asking for protection
from loot, rapine, and the torch."[95] To calm the fears of residents and send
a clear signal he did not tolerate plundering, Wilson instructed his officers
to recover any pillaged items from their men. "Marched out about three
miles when the command was halted," an Ohio cavalryman recorded, "and
searched for private property, gold, silver, watches, and jewelry, which it
was supposed the men had appropriated during the campaign. Officers found
some pilfered goods in the first company searched. The others, being warned

in time, succeeded in secreting what they had in the sand under their feet until the search was over."[96]

Wilson also set about obtaining the surrender of Confederate forces near his location and granting them paroles. On May 4, Wilson ordered Brig. Gen. Edward McCook southward to Tallahassee to seek the surrender of Confederate forces in Florida. McCook did not arrive in Tallahassee until May 10 because he stopped to suppress disorder in Thomasville. Reporting that "an organized and partially armed band of about 300 citizens and paroled soldiers seized a train," McCook pursued the offenders and placed them in town jail. To impress upon the citizenry the seriousness of the crime, McCook requested to retain one of the thieves and "have him shot by military law, if possible," but Wilson rejected the idea. McCook then continued to Tallahassee with only a few staff officers and five hundred cavalrymen from the Second Indiana and Seventh Kentucky cavalry regiments. McCook wanted to avoid the impression of a confrontation, so he employed a smaller force, sufficient to ward off any "scouts" in the region, but not large enough to appear overtly intimidating. As he approached Tallahassee, McCook left his troopers four miles outside of town and entered with only five staff members to confer with city leaders.[97] Once McCook secured the city, he accepted the surrender of nearby Fort Ward and organized foraging parties to feed his command. Food was scarce, but McCook solved the problem by agreeing to swap surplus Army animals for food from the locals. One thing McCook did not anticipate was the large number of freedmen who arrived in Tallahassee. Many local planters resisted freeing their slaves and instead requested that McCook use his authority to force them back onto the plantations. Instead, McCook ordered a public reading of the Emancipation Proclamation for the "benefit of those who seem to be ignorant of the fact," that the slaves were free, and announced that he intended to enforce all government policies pertaining to emancipation.[98]

His prime task, however, was to parole the Confederate troops and get them back to their homes. Private Robert Merrill, a clerk on McCook's staff, described the process, noting in his diary that he "went up to the office this morning & found that there was a crowd." On the seventeenth, he moved to Madison, about sixty miles east of Tallahassee with "a lot of blank Paroles &

to see some more of Florida."[99] Due to the distances involved and scarcity of transport, the Union Army organized trains to bring parolees to central locations. One train, "more than thirty-two cars long," transported Confederate troops from Lake City, one hundred miles east, to sign their paroles. After they obtained their releases, the same train returned them to Lake City. Upon arrival, a soldier eager to see his awaiting family tragically "jumped off, fell under the train, and was crushed in their sight."[100] Despite this needless death, McCook completed his task by May 21, reporting to Wilson that the "number paroled and already reported is 7,200 and, will doubtless reach 8,000 when the returns are completed." In addition, he provided an inventory of the military property he had gathered, which included 150 horses and mules, 44 wagons and ambulances, 40 artillery pieces, 2,500 rifles, 10,000 rounds of artillery ammunition, 122,000 rounds of small arms ammunition, and, oddly, 325 pikes and lances. McCook was pleased with the outcome of his mission, and mentioned that "In my intercourse with the citizens and surrendered soldiers of this Florida command I found only the most entire spirit of submission to my authority, and in the majority of instances an apparent cheerful acquiescence to the present order of things." His only "collision with any of the authorities" was a pastor of the Episcopal Church who "omitted the customary prayer for the President of the United States," but McCook convinced him of the "error of his ways … He prayed for the President that afternoon."[101]

Despite his success in Tallahassee, McCook became the center of an embarrassing clash over turf and wartime glory. The Confederate troops in Florida were officially the responsibility of Union Maj. Gen. Quincy Gillmore, commanding the Department of the South, through his subordinate in the District of Florida, Brig. Gen. Israel Vogdes. About the time that Wilson dispatched McCook to Tallahassee, Maj. Gen. Samuel Jones, commanding Confederate troops in Florida, contacted Vogdes to meet "With the purpose of disbanding the C. S. troops now in Florida." Jones's offer took Vogdes by surprise, so he requested instructions from Gillmore. Four days later, Gillmore granted Vogdes permission to accept Jones's surrender and issue paroles to all Confederate troops at a site to be determined. With the recent fallout from the Sherman/Johnston negotiations fresh in mind, Gillmore reminded Vogdes to "confine your official correspondence with rebel officers to matters pertinent to the execution of the convention of surrender," and directed Vogdes that "while we are to be humane toward surrendered enemies, these men are still rebels to whom any forgiveness is an act of grace and not of justice." Gillmore desired a stern tone toward the Confederates, but Vogdes took a different tack. In his May 12 response to Jones, Vogdes agreed to accept from Jones "all arms and public property," instructed Jones that he would receive "forms furnished from these headquarters" to issue paroles to his men, after which duplicate copies would be forwarded to him. In short, Vogdes proposed that Jones not only surrender his own army with no supervision, but also do the paperwork himself.[102]

Before Jones could reply to Vogdes's message, McCook arrived in Tallahassee, accepted the Confederate surrender, and began issuing paroles with Jones's approval. Angry that McCook had snatched his glory from him, Vogdes tried to drive off his rival. Vogdes provided McCook with a copy of his orders from Gillmore, "directing me to receive the surrender of General Jones and all the forces under his command," and reminded him that "As Tallahassee is recognized as being within the limits of the Department of the South, I have the honor to request you to desist from further proceedings in the matter of surrender of troops within the limits of this command," because he could not "recognize your right to receive the surrender of troops within this district."[103] McCook declined to recognize Vogdes's authority and continued his work with Wilson's blessing. In a note to George Thomas, Wilson noted "Generals Gillmore and Vogdes complain of what they called General McCook's encroachment upon their commands in going to Florida; but as General McCook … had received the surrender of the troops and stores before the arrival of the protest, I was not disposed to pay any attention to it." [104] Unable to dislodge McCook, Vogdes had to concede. He informed McCook that Gillmore had "applied to Washington to have the limits of his department strictly defined" and asked that McCook consider himself "as being within the limits of his department … and therefore … will carry out the instructions that may from time to time be sent to you from these headquarters." McCook, upon completing his mission, withdrew his force to Macon and turned the responsibility for Tallahassee over to Vogdes, who occupied the city on May 27.[105] In remote areas of the state, officers prompted their men to report to Union authorities in an orderly manner, completing the surrender process without undue difficulty until the last Confederates received their paroles at Port Bay on June 5.[106]

While Wilson was securing the surrender of Confederate troops in Florida, General Thomas was doing the same in northern Georgia. Thomas had ordered Brig. Gen. Henry Judah to contact Brig. Gen. William T. Wofford, commanding Confederate forces in northern Georgia, to gauge whether Wofford was willing to surrender. If Judah found "they desire to have peace," Thomas instructed his subordinate to inform Wofford that "I will accept his surrender upon the same terms as Lee surrendered to General Grant."[107] Wofford, in reply, declined to surrender because he was concerned about the lack of law and order in the state if his limited authority disappeared. Thomas was sympathetic to Wofford's position, but, with Jefferson Davis still at large, Thomas had to assume that Wofford was acting to facilitate Davis's movements.[108] Thomas, therefore, pressed the issue with Wofford by implying that he would apply more stringent surrender terms if the Confederates did not immediately surrender, while promising a quick occupation to restore order if he capitulated. Compelled by Thomas, Wofford surrendered on May 2, and Union troops promptly moved into Georgia with the "duty of protecting the defenseless, oppressed, and impoverished citizens of Northern Georgia" and, strictly prohibited from committing any "act of oppression, wanton destruction of or depredation upon private property."[109]

Federal authorities selected Kingston, Georgia, as the site for formal surrenders and issuing of parole slips, and more than four thousand soldiers and deserters arrived over the next two weeks to receive their paroles.[110] Throughout the surrender proceedings, Wofford was tireless in his efforts to help the citizens of Georgia. General Judah related to Thomas his "high appreciation of the personal character of General Wofford," and attributed to Wofford's leadership and example the "the earnest desire of the people and the Confederate soldiers to return quietly to their homes, and give all aid they can to the Federal authorities in restoring the supremacy of the Federal civil authority." Judah cited as an example Wofford's willingness to allow a Union courier to pass through his lines "without even an inquiry as to the object of his mission." Wofford worked closely with Judah to facilitate the military occupation of the countryside to suppress the remaining bands of scouts and arrange Union aid for the destitute. He obtained permission for local authorities "to adopt some general plan to feed the destitute" by distributing "a great number of beef-cattle in this county purchased for the Confederate armies and now running at large in the woods" and to take possession of "a lot of wool, some 7,000 or 8,000 pounds" to provide the poor with "warm clothing in this coming winter, and without which they will suffer greatly. These things can be well spared by the Government without loss to it, and confer great humanity and generosity upon a poor, destitute people."[111] That was not the only location that needed help. Wofford sent an urgent appeal to General Wilson in Macon for assistance because around Atlanta "reside about 15,000 poor and penniless men, women, and children, who must, of necessity, starve unless the public shall supply their wants." Wilson, following Thomas's lead, informed Brig. Gen. Edward Winslow that he was "authorized to make such issues of rations to the poor people of North Georgia," to "Seize any railroad iron or supplies you can find to advance your work" of completing the railroad to bring in further supplies, and allow indigent farmers to round up "the straggling government stock" of horses and mules "scattered over the country to help them farm."[112]

For his assistance in the transition period and concern for the plight of common citizens, Wofford earned the respect of the Union Army and the people of Georgia alike. Thomas, impressed by Wofford's willingness to bring peace, used his influence to hasten his amnesty process. "Being convinced of his sincerity and honorable conduct," Thomas wrote to General Judah, "I have asked to be permitted to administer the President's amnesty oath" to him because his compliance with Union authority did "show that he is worthy of such an act of clemency on the part of the Executive."[113] In late 1865, thankful citizens elected Wofford to represent them in the House of Representatives, but Congress refused to seat him and other Southern congressmen elected without federal sanction. Unwilling to leave Washington empty-handed, Wofford urged prominent politicians to provide economic assistance to poor civilians through the Freedmen's Bureau.[114]

****

With the dissolution of the Confederate Army, Union commanders turned to the problems of postwar occupation. Wilson's presence in Macon stabilized the region after the Confederates surrendered, but it was also a burden. His army could no longer forage, so Wilson required regular supplies of food and forage for 13,000 troops and 21,000 animals, and informed Thomas and Sherman he needed a reliable supply line from Savannah, preferably by railroad. Sherman's first impulse was to order Wilson to Decatur, Alabama, close to his start point on the Tennessee River, rather than repair the local railroads. Wilson, however, believed such a movement was impossible because of the lack of supplies in Decatur and railroads made impassable by his earlier raids.[115] Grant, however, wanted to redeploy troops in case the Confederates in the Trans-Mississippi Department continued to hold out, as well as demobilize any surplus soldiers to reduce military expenditures. To that end, he arranged for the opening of a short-term railroad supply line to Macon, while confirming Sherman's order to move his surplus troops to Decatur as soon as possible. Wilson himself was to remain in Macon to oversee the occupation, retaining only Croxton's brigade to control the area.[116] Wilson wanted another combat command if the war was to continue in the Trans-Mississippi, so, with few troops to command and nothing to do in Macon, in June he requested the dissolution of his own command to free himself up for reassignment. On June 26, Wilson announced that "The organization known as the Cavalry Corps, Military Division of the Mississippi, is hereby discontinued," but the war was already over. Wilson stayed in Georgia as the commander of the District of Columbus, part of the Department of Georgia, until he went home on leave in December 1865.[117]

Wilson's campaign through Alabama and Georgia was an impressive achievement. In the twenty-eight days since he left his camps on the Tennessee until the arrival in Macon, Wilson's main column moved 528 miles, an average of nineteen miles per day. It took Wilson only seven days to cover the 215 miles from Montgomery to Macon, an average of more than thirty-one miles per day.[118] Aiming to destroy Confederate war-making capability, Wilson certainly succeeded, destroying or capturing according to one source "2 gunboats; 90,000 small arms and much artillery; 10 iron works; 7 foundries; 8 machine shops; 5 rolling mills; the University buildings; many county courthouses and public buildings; 3 arsenals; a naval foundry and navy yard; 5 steamboats; a powder magazine and mill; 35 locomotives and 565 cars; 3 large railroad bridges and many smaller ones; 275,000 bales of cotton; much private property along the line of march; many magazines of stores; and had subsisted his army on the country."[119] The material captured by Wilson's First Division alone was substantial, amounting to more than twenty thousand small arms, eight artillery pieces, more than twenty industrial sites, and more than three hundred railroad cars at the cost of ninety casualties.[120] For the entire expedition, Wilson suffered ninety-nine men killed in action (thirteen officers and eighty-six enlisted men), 598 wounded (thirty-nine officers and 559 enlisted), and twenty-eight missing (seven officers and twenty-one enlisted men). The 725 casualties from a force of 13,480 equals a 5 percent casualty rate, a low number considering the length of the operation and the sharp engagements at Ebenezer Church and Selma.[121]

Although a remarkable military achievement, Wilson's expedition has earned relatively little historical acclaim because it came so late in the war. In his memoirs, Ulysses Grant considered Wilson's campaign, along with Canby's operations around Mobile, as "eminently successful, but without any good result" because "The war was practically over before their victories were gained."[122] Grant based his opinion on hindsight, and no one could have known at the time that when Wilson, or Canby for that matter, launched his campaign that the war was in its last days, so the outcome of the operation should be evaluated on its own merits. Grant also did not consider the effect that Wilson's troops had on other events. By wrecking Confederate facilities, scattering Taylor's forces, and positioning his force in Macon, Wilson had denied Joseph Johnston the capability of moving his army past Augusta if he had tried to move away from Sherman instead of negotiating in North Carolina. Johnston never mentioned Wilson's presence as a reason for his decision to sit down with Sherman, but the existence of a blocking force in Georgia and ruined facilities in Alabama and Georgia would have limited Johnston's options if he had tried to continue the war.

****

Although a spectacular success, momentous events soon overshadowed the accomplishments of Wilson and his troopers. The surrender of great armies and the assassination of Abraham Lincoln dominated the nation's attention, denying Wilson and his troopers a greater fame that they rightfully deserve. Wilson's campaign through Alabama and Georgia was the apex of cavalry operations, as the coming decades saw the introduction of new weapons and methods that soon rendered the mounted soldier a relic of the past. Under different circumstances, however, Wilson might have had another chance to demonstrate what his troopers could do. The sole remaining Confederate army, in the Trans-Mississippi Department, still held out. Its commander, Gen. Edmund Kirby Smith, refused to surrender because no Union army immediately threatened his command, appearing to leave him the option of continuing the war until a Union force could compel him to give up. Kirby Smith commanded a region noted for its vast distances, undeveloped transportation, and industrial base concentrated in isolated interior regions, a situation very like the one that Wilson had just overcome. Wilson certainly wanted the opportunity to bring his style of cavalry warfare to the Trans-Mississippi, but the war took a very different course and Kirby Smith confronted problems more daunting than Union cavalry.

Chapter 9

"The Absolute Dictator": Leadership in the Trans-Mississippi Department

As Confederate forces in the Trans-Mississippi Department surrendered, a reporter for a Cincinnati newspaper summed up the efforts of the Confederate leadership to sustain the war effort. Referring to the top military officers in the department, the correspondent observed that "It is very evident that Magruder and Kirby Smith wanted to rekindle the Southern heart, but the surrender shows that the people refused to give them even a shadow of support." Resistance was not favored because "The fair land of Texas has never been laid waste by war, and the inhabitants were so averse to inviting it, that they convinced the brood of mercenary generals ... the time to emulate the 'magnanimous' example of Lee [had] arrived." Although an important local event, the reporter, in a flourish of insight, recognized that the surrender of the last major Confederate army would receive relatively little notice or bear any great historical significance. "It is ... scrupulously true to say that the great American rebellion is a thing of the past. The insurgent armies are scattered and their material given up, even to the last battle flag," the reporter concluded, but the surrender in Texas, "though the literal end of the war, will excite little interest compared with that attached to every bulletin when Grant and Lee were clinched in the death struggle. The war ended, in fact, when Lee capitulated, and all subsequent surrenders have declined in importance by a regular diminuendo."[1]

The reporter's prediction proved very accurate. Lee's surrender was the precursor to a cascade of other surrenders that culminated with the last Confederate capitulations west of the Mississippi River, and the meeting between Grant and Lee did become the image in American historical memory regarding the end of the Civil War. The allegory used by the reporter was also appropriate. A musical term to describe a decrease in the volume of sound, *diminuendo* was an apt description of Confederate efforts in the Trans-Mississippi Department. From a great sound and fury at the onset of the war, the contributions and capabilities of the department declined until, at the time of its surrender, only a murmur of effort existed. The outcome could have been different. The Trans-Mississippi Department held many strategic, political, and economic opportunities that could have provided an alternate outcome to the Civil War if utilized in a different manner. The region, however, faced a multitude of other problems—underdeveloped infrastructure, geographic isolation, and lack of strategic vision, to name but some—that left the area underutilized and increasingly difficult to hold. Instead of playing a prominent role in the Civil War, the Trans-Mississippi became a relative backwater to the larger conflict, leading to its inevitable collapse when the surrender of other Confederate armies left it alone to face Union forces. The inability to influence the outcome of the war was also the byproduct of poor military and political leadership, both in the region and from Richmond, which squandered the Trans-Mississippi's advantages and made its eventual surrender a predictable outcome.

****

For such a large portion of the Confederacy, the Trans-Mississippi region always suffered from a lack of strategic relevance when viewed from Richmond. At the start of the war, the War Department divided the Trans-Mississippi region into several small departments with commanders who lacked the concentrated resources and geographical reach to coordinate the area. The region then became a sub-district of a much larger Western Department, but that organizational structure created an area too large for a single commander to manage. To rectify that situation and to address the growing

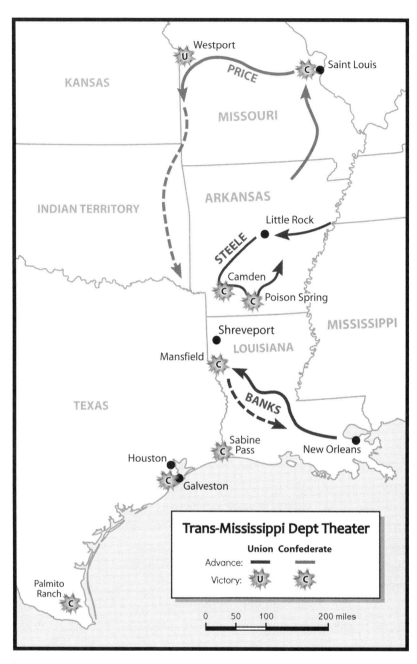

Trans-Mississippi Department.

Union interest in the area, the War Department established the Trans-Mississippi Department in May 1862, with its own internal districts in west Louisiana, Arkansas (including the Indian Territory), and Texas (including the New Mexico Territory). As a proper department, however, the Trans-Mississippi Department had built-in problems. The best characterization of the Trans-Mississippi Department was a region that was a "vast territory, thinly populated, undeveloped, practically without railroads, cut off from its principal source of military supplies, having but precarious and infrequent communication with the … government." In all, the Trans-Mississippi Department encompassed an area of 735,000 square miles with a population (excluding Native Americans) of 2.7 million.[2]

General Edmund Kirby Smith shouldered the burden of leading the department for most of its existence, a tenure marked by great victories and significant lost opportunities. Kirby Smith, however, was not Jefferson Davis's first choice to lead the department. Originally, in September 1861, Jefferson Davis placed the defense of the entire western region in the hands of General Albert S. Johnston, whose command area stretched from the Gulf of Mexico to Kentucky and from the Appalachians to the Ozarks. Johnston concentrated more on defending Kentucky and Tennessee than the huge area west of the river, so, in December 1861, Davis offered command of the region west of the Mississippi River to Maj. Gen. Braxton Bragg, then commanding the Department of West Florida. Bragg, however, declined the offer, stating he found a posting to the Trans-Mississippi "not enticing" because of the limited hope for success there.[3] Davis next considered Maj. Gen. Earl Van Dorn, but decided against offering him the post because critics accused the general of constant "negligence, whoring, and drunkenness."[4] Consequently, Van Dorn led only the Confederate forces in Arkansas, but as a sub-district of Johnston's Western command. Brig. Gen. Paul Hébert held a similar position under Johnston in Texas.[5]

The defeat of Van Dorn's army at Pea Ridge in March 1862 forced Davis to find a suitable department commander. Van Dorn's withdrawal to the valley of the Arkansas River and, two months later, transfer of his remaining troops eastward to reinforce the besieged Confederate garrison of Corinth, Mississippi, left only a token force behind to protect the southern half of

Gen. Edmund Kirby Smith (*Image courtesy of the Library of Congress*).

Arkansas. The proximity of Union forces led Gov. Henry Rector to demand protection of the region. He suggested that Texas, Arkansas, and Louisiana "should form a department" and appoint their own general if the War Department did not provide one.[6] The Union capture of Island No. 10 in April 1862 and New Orleans in May created an even greater sense of urgency, and in May 1862 the War Department established a separate Trans-Mississippi Military Department.[7]

Again, Davis's plan for the new post did not go as he wished. The President wanted Maj. Gen. James Magruder to take command, but Magruder, despite some success around Yorktown, under-performed during the Peninsular Campaign. Magruder took one of the district positions in the Trans-Mississippi Department, but never received overall command.[8] Davis instead appointed Maj. Gen. Thomas Hindman, a prewar Arkansas resident, to the post. Hindman, however, soon triggered dissent within his own command over his attempts to impose martial law and impress private property.[9] After only a short tenure, Hindman found himself demoted to district commander in Arkansas and replaced by Maj. Gen. Theophilus Holmes. Although close in age to Jefferson (and Robert Lee and Joseph Johnston, for that matter), the frail, sickly, and nearly deaf Holmes was physically not up to the task of department command.[10] Unable to effect real improvement in the area, Holmes did not object when Davis relieved him of command in February 1863.

Davis turned to Lt. Gen. Edmund Kirby Smith to replace Holmes.[11] Kirby Smith's problems with his subordinates, particularly those with Richard Taylor discussed earlier, were the least of his worries when he took charge. As he prepared to depart for his new command, Kirby Smith received instructions from Secretary of War James Seddon, who mentioned "deplorable accounts … of the disorder, confusion, and demoralization everywhere prevalent." Seddon warned Kirby Smith to expect an army "dwindled, by desertion, sickness, and death … who are disaffected and hopeless" and a population "in a state of consternation, multitudes suffering for means of subsistence."[12] Kirby Smith, upon his arrival, found that Seddon had not exaggerated the condition of the department, a situation made worse when Union troops isolated Kirby's Smith command by capturing Vicksburg. Just days later, Jefferson Davis sent a lengthy letter to Kirby Smith underscoring the difficult position in which the general found himself. Acknowledging that "your difficulties must be materially enhanced" by the fall of Vicksburg, Davis stressed to Kirby Smith, "You now have not merely a military, but also a political problem involved in your command." Quelling the anxiety of the state governors who believed themselves ignored in Richmond, Davis explained, would require Kirby Smith to understand that supply from the Cis-Mississippi would be, at best, difficult, and his "department must need be ... self-sustaining."[13]

In appointing Kirby Smith, Davis, as critics often accused him of doing, imposed upon the general the responsibility to achieve results but not the authority to accomplish them, as there was no clear directive giving him power over civil affairs.[14] The absence of authority led Kirby Smith to doubt the real parameters of his power for the duration of his leadership. An 1864 law, for instance, gave Kirby Smith the option to suspend habeas corpus in the department if necessary, but he never utilized this power because he doubted that the War Department would support him in the face of a public backlash.[15] Too late did Kirby Smith try to claim the authority he believed he needed. Just weeks before he surrendered, Kirby Smith wrote to Senator Robert Johnson that, since "Communication with Richmond is growing more difficult daily," he pushed the "necessity of granting more powers to the Dept. Commander," especially over economic matters, because "they are necessities created by the circumstances" of his isolated command.[16]

Kirby Smith never received such powers, a critical weakness in the governing of the Trans-Mississippi when the general had to make non-military decisions. Besides commanding the armies in his department, Kirby Smith became, by default, a political leader as well because there was no other suitable option. The governors of Texas, Arkansas, and Louisiana might have produced a single leader or governed collectively, but Jefferson Davis, already at loggerheads with pro-states' rights governors over policy decisions, was not willing to cede any power to state executives. Davis also had the option of sending a political leader to the department to aid Kirby Smith. An obvious choice, since the President himself could not leave Richmond, was to create a political position, appointed by Davis and having the equivalent rank of a Cabinet position, who would act as Davis directed. Such a position, however, had no constitutional validity and, as the official was appointed and not elected, would face opposition from the state governors. Any civilian official, regardless of who selected him, also faced Davis's reluctance to give real authority to anyone. Granting pseudo-political power to a senior military officer like Kirby Smith made the most sense to Davis. Davis was realistic enough to know that whomever he selected had to make important decisions, implement political policies, and control considerable economic assets, but, as Commander in Chief, Davis could always override any choice he deemed improper or remove such leaders as he saw fit.

Kirby Smith had to act like a political leader, but to do that he had to establish his position relative to the elected officials of his department. Soon after his arrival, Kirby Smith invited the state governors to meet on August 15 at Marshall, Texas, to set department priorities and establish a program to make the region "self-sustaining and self-reliant in every respect" with the "support and advice of the representative men of the States composing my department."[17] At this first meeting, Kirby Smith accepted reports on the status of each state; inquired how to improve morale, restore confidence, and suppress dissent; asked how to fund the department and bolster the currency; appointed commissioners to make diplomatic contact with Mexico; and established the boundary between military and civil authority. The response of the governors reflected a mix of cautiousness about their political position and the realities of the military situation. The leaders unanimously recommended that only Kirby Smith should, at his discretion, exercise the powers entrusted to him by the Davis administration, but also insisted on the maintenance of existing laws, thereby giving them the means to assert civil power over the military in state affairs. The executives admitted that procuring and selling cotton was the only reliable means of funding the department, but were wary of turning control of the commodity over to Kirby Smith.

For his part, Kirby Smith did not push an agenda on the governors. Either wary of engaging in political debates with elected leaders or more concerned with military affairs, Kirby Smith's approach to the conference was one of deference to civil authority. An observer of the conference asserted that the general was aware that his authority did not include "any higher or greater powers than … delegated to him, were limited to those which the President might confer upon another, and did not extend to those vested by the Constitution in the President," which did not include the power to tax, regulate commerce, or any other power reserved by the Confederate Congress.[18] Not everyone was as confident. Fearful that "General Kirby Smith has extraordinary powers … equal to those of the President," one civilian worried that he might secede from the Confederacy and "establish a new federation over here."[19]

****

Without an elected or appointed government official to run the Trans-Mississippi Department, Kirby Smith had to perform both military and political duties and that meant he had to create institutions that paralleled the bureaus and departments operating in the Cis-Mississippi. In this regard, he was largely successful. In July 1863, the War Department authorized Kirby Smith to establish a separate Conscription Bureau, removing any confusion over who was empowered to conscript troops. By September, Kirby Smith had appointed a chief Quartermaster, Paymaster, and Ordnance officer for the department.[20] The government established other offices as time passed. In January 1864, Congress authorized Davis to appoint a Treasury agent for the Trans-Mississippi Department, and a month later permitted the hiring of a postmaster agent to manage the mail.[21] Kirby Smith also created several local sub-agencies like a "clothing bureau" and "transportation bureau" to tackle specific problems related to industrial development instigated by Kirby Smith or already in progress before he arrived.[22]

Once the perception that the war would be a short one disappeared, Confederate officials planned to expand the small industrial base in the region.[23] At the same time, Union encroachment made industrial planning difficult, as the cities that could most likely provide the workers for new works were also the obvious targets for Union incursions. Consequently, most new facilities opened only after Kirby Smith took command and the course of the war had identified what areas were most secure. One of those areas was eastern Texas. Marshall, Texas, just forty miles west of Kirby Smith's headquarters in Shreveport and connected by one of the few railroads in the department, became the most important logistics and production center. By mid-war, the city was producing uniforms and hats for the army, tanning hides for the leather industry, and contained a variety of support facilities for the Quartermaster Corps. Other industrial works sprang up to support the facilities in Marshall. The Quartermaster Depot established a huge facility at Mound Prairie, Texas, that included facilities for grinding grain, sawing lumber, making shoes, spinning cotton, shoeing and outfitting horses, and producing iron. The Field Transportation Bureau, responsible for moving goods and obtaining horses and teams, established several branch offices throughout the state. The region was largely self-sufficient when it came to cloth. Utilizing the labor of more than two hundred inmates at the state penitentiary at Huntsville, the Quartermaster Corps manufactured more than two million yards of cotton and woolen cloth for conversion into clothing in quartermaster shops in Tyler.[24]

Tyler, Texas, one hundred miles west of Shreveport, became the center of ordnance production. In 1862, the Texas state government issued a contract for five thousand rifles, at thirty-five dollars apiece, to a newly established gun foundry established near Tyler. The new plant proved a failure, however, and the Confederate government purchased the plant outright in 1863. Although never a major firearms producer, the plant repaired imported rifles and produced other accoutrements such as ammunition boxes and canteens. The facility's greatest contribution was as the main source of ammunition for the Trans-Mississippi Department. In a single order delivered in December 1864, the factory provided "69,000 Enfield cartridges, 18,000 Buck & Ball ditto, [and] 3,000 Miss. Rifle B & B cartridges." Other smaller and privately owned works scattered around the state supplemented the Tyler works by producing secondary articles such as percussion caps, pistols, and swords.[25] Despite the success of the Tyler works and supporting plants, however, firearms were never in sufficient supply, After the fall of Vicksburg cut off outside supplies of rifles, Kirby Smith approved steep fines for any soldier who lost or damaged his weapon and approved twenty-day furloughs for any soldier who could obtain weapons from home.[26]

Despite these successes, Kirby Smith failed to solve other problems. As in other parts of the Confederacy, currency was the cause of, and solution to, many economic complications in Kirby Smith's jurisdiction. When General

Holmes assumed command, the department was already $13 million in debt to suppliers and other creditors, but cash to pay them was simply not available.[27] In the first two years of the war, the Confederate government appropriated nearly $79 million for the Trans-Mississippi Department, but managed to deliver only twenty million. The late portion of the war was no better. Between July 1863 and April 1864, the Treasury only managed to deliver $27 million in notes and $18 million in bonds to the Trans-Mississippi Department. By December 1864, another $47 million in currency and bonds had arrived against debt obligations of $313 million.[28] In addition to its creditors, the Army could not pay its soldiers, an endemic problem in the Trans-Mississippi Department, with the absence of pay contributing to widespread desertion and absenteeism. Officers told conscripts and volunteers who entered the army after August 1863 not to expect any pay at all for the foreseeable future, until all veteran troops received their back pay.[29] By the end of the war, all of the Trans-Mississippi Department troops were months in arrears when it came to their pay.[30] In one of his numerous appeals to the War Department for assistance, Kirby Smith pled for his men, many of whom "have not been paid a dollar in sixteen months; some not a dollar in nearly two years."[31] In March 1865, Kirby Smith wrote a pleading letter to Senator Robert W. Johnson hoping that "The enclosed letters clearly demonstrate the importance of sending funds in large amounts immediately, to the relief of the Department" because unless given money "I cannot be held responsible for the consequences."[32]

Kirby Smith's financial problems were particularly burdensome because he had a potential source of economic support by selling cotton through Mexican ports free from Union blockaders. The benefits of trade with Mexico were not lost on the Confederate Congress, who explicitly exempted Mexico from its international cotton embargo imposed as an early-war foreign policy.[33] Selling cotton across the Mexican border was an obvious solution to many Confederate problems, but the business attracted unwanted participants. Speculators, lured by the quick wealth that crises often provide, were the first to see the benefit of selling cotton across the border, where their cotton fetched as much as nine times what they paid for it.[34] The speculators, however, soon had rivals for control of the cotton crop. The shortcomings of the supply bureaus meant that many purchasers, including War Department agents (operating under the authority of Maj. Simeon Hart of the Quartermaster Corps), Confederate government purchasers (from other civil and military bureaus) sent out from Richmond, military authorities from the Trans-Mississippi Department, and Texas state officials all vied for the same cotton.[35]

Further problems emerged when the Confederate military and government tried to impose controls, thereby restricting individual property rights. In December 1862, for instance, Lt. Gen. Theophilus Holmes, the new commander of Trans-Mississippi Department, announced that "the exportation of cotton from the District of Texas is prohibited, except by authorized agents of the Government" to weed out speculators. Subordinates reported to Holmes that the new regulations "had already a good effect, bringing down the price of cotton 5 cents a pound."[36] The War Department, however, ordered Holmes to rescind the order immediately because of objections from the Treasury Department, upon whose jurisdiction Holmes was treading, and assertions that "Congress alone can pass an act of embargo," making Holmes policy "not in accordance with the laws of the land."[37] Without any source of supply for his army, Holmes had no alternative but to impress cotton, his quartermaster stating, "It is a question of supply or no supply."[38]

Despite the efforts by military leaders to control the sale of cotton, speculators and private citizens organized a system of routes and sales points that became a funnel for cotton to the Mexican border. Those selling cotton preferred the route to Brownsville and thence the Mexican town of Matamoros, 250 miles from San Antonio and 450 miles from Houston. Brownsville and Matamoros were far enough up the Rio Grande that only a significant Union military effort could threaten either city, while sandbars at the entrance to Matamoros's port at Baghdad, twenty-five miles east at the mouth of the Rio Grande, deterred the Union Navy.[39] Flush with cotton profits, Matamoros became a bustling trade center whose prewar population of eight thousand soon swelled to more than fifty thousand. An observer noted, "There were millions of dollars' worth of merchandise in the place … Never was a place of the same size crowded with more people, and made a display of more goods."[40] Like all boomtowns, however, Matamoros's prosperity lasted only as long as the war.[41]

The problem was getting cotton to Brownsville. The lack of railroads meant a lengthy journey by ox- or mule-teams from Brownsville to the closest railhead at Alleyton, west of Houston, a journey that could take six to eight weeks.[42] The wagon trains also consumed a large amount of both man and animal power. A typical wagon train of ten to fifteen wagons needed twenty men or more, along with approximately one hundred oxen and horses. One source estimated that over the course of the war "To transport this immense amount, nine thousand wagons were requisite, drawn by fifty thousand head of cattle, and sixteen thousand head of horses and mules. The employees are estimated at ten thousand."[43] The route had other risks as well. Because of a lack of funds, the state could not maintain the roads and bridges, and there were few amenities for travelers along the way. Bandits pounced on undefended wagon trains, causing the editor of the *Weekly State Gazette* to warn, "It is no longer safe to travel. Assassination and attempts to assassinate on that road are of daily occurrence."[44] When asked if it was safe for a woman to travel through southern Texas to Matamoros, an agent in Mexico replied that such a trip "would be worse than going through purgatory and more than I would inflict upon any respectable Lady."[45]

Besides the problems of conducting the cotton trade on their side of the river, Kirby Smith also had to contend with the political and economic situation south of the border. After Benito Juarez became the President of Mexico in 1861, the U.S. government recognized Juarez as the legitimate leader, especially when Juarez did not recognize the new Confederate government.[46] Support from the U.S. was vital to Juarez after France, under the rule of Napoleon III, used Mexico's default of its European loans as a pretext to occupy Mexico with the aim of reestablishing a French empire in North America. After taking Mexico City in June 1863, the Imperial Army pursued Juarez into northern Mexico, where Juarez continued his war against the French occupation and its figurehead leader, Emperor Maximilian.[47] Kirby Smith and the Confederate government hoped that the French presence on its border might bring long-sought European recognition and assistance. In consolidating their hold, however, the French complicated the Confederacy's efforts to supply itself via Matamoros for several months by confiscating cargoes of military goods because they could not establish if the products were for use by the Confederates or by Juarez's forces.[48]

The necessity to sell cotton to fund the department finally forced Kirby Smith to impose some sort of central authority, something he pledged to the state governors he would not do at their meeting in Marshall in 1863. To provide a fair and uniform process for obtaining cotton, in August 1863 Kirby Smith established the Cotton Bureau, a centralized cotton-purchasing organization under his direct control.[49] The Bureau's task was to collect cotton, transport it to Mexico, oversee its sale, use the proceeds to procure war materiel, and deliver those supplies to the army in the field. Kirby Smith authorized the Bureau to purchase, in Confederate currency or promissory notes, up to half of a cotton-grower's crop every year. Planters received a permit to export their remaining crop, but only if they did business with the Bureau. Kirby Smith justified his Cotton Bureau by explaining that the only alternative was general impressment of cotton supplies, whereas his system was more fair, orderly, and least likely to generate abuse.[50]

Despite Kirby Smith's optimism about the success of the venture, the Cotton Bureau faced difficulties over the course of its existence. The organization lacked transport to move cotton to the border, had limited operating funds to buy cotton, and its small staff often could not locate cotton before speculators got to it first.[51] Not surprisingly, cotton speculating, the type of business the Cotton Bureau was intended to prevent, grew even more profitable as producers searched for economic survival. Speculators were more than willing to not only pay top dollar for cotton, but pay for it cash, as well as arrange to move the cotton to the border at their own expense.[52] Not functioning as efficiently as hoped or promised, the Cotton Bureau was in crisis by the summer of 1864, as the Bureau had not obtained sufficient cotton to meet the outstanding debt.[53] The criticism of Kirby Smith's handling of the cotton trade escalated into claims of mismanagement and embezzlement.[54] Kirby Smith ignored the rumors for a time, but eventually tried to separate himself from the baseless accusations in January 1865 by placing his chief of staff, Maj. Gen. Simon Buckner, in charge of the cotton trade.[55]

The biggest challenge to the Cotton Bureau came from a local competitor in the form of the state of Texas. In 1864, a Military Board appointed by the new governor, Pendleton Murrah, approved his plans for a new Texas Loan Agency to fund the state government.[56] Under the scheme, cotton-growers could sell cotton on the foreign market only after selling half of their crop to the state. The state purchased the cotton with state bonds, which planters considered a more reliable investment than the uncertain Confederate currency. Most importantly, the state ensured the security of the transaction by transporting the cotton to the border at its own expense.[57] Murrah believed his plan superior to Kirby Smith's Cotton Bureau because "There is no illegal force, no illegal and oppressive exactions made of the producer," and the cotton grower received what is "due him for the property of his hard earnings."[58] The competing systems, however, only created more chaos, especially when both organizations claimed ownership of the same cotton.[59] Despite offering a better deal to the growers, the state had no more success in obtaining and moving cotton than other organizations. The Texas state government obtained more than 13,000 bales over the course of the war, and, even if every bale reached a buyer in Matamoros, that represented only 12 percent of the cotton that passed through Matamoros.[60] After several months of competition between the Loan Agency and the Cotton Bureau, in July 1864 Kirby Smith persuaded Murrah to rescind his state plan.[61]

Kirby Smith had fended off an internal rival, but, as criticism mounted, the Cotton Bureau's days were numbered. Nine months after the Cotton Bureau began operation, Jefferson Davis declared that the general had acted improperly and "there is no authority in law for the impressment of cotton for the purposes designed by you."[62] In reply, Kirby Smith suggested placing the Bureau's financial arrangements in the hands of Peter W. Gray, the newly appointed Assistant Secretary of the Treasury for the Trans-Mississippi Department, to avoid any appearance of impropriety.[63] Despite this new oversight, Congress decided to investigate the Cotton Bureau's activities and recommend changes. In December 1864, anticipating the closure of the Bureau, Kirby Smith ordered its officers to halt operations, release all their civilian employees, and return troops assigned to them to their regiments.[64] In the end, the Cotton Bureau was a great failure and a squandered asset that, if properly managed, could have been a great benefit to the Confederacy. The inefficiency of the Cotton Bureau can be seen in that, while the Bureau purchased approximately 72,000 bales of cotton, it took delivery of only 47,000 bales due to wastage and inefficiency, broken contracts, poor transportation, and the closing of the Bureau prior to delivery. Because of this shortcoming, the Bureau ended its existence in a financial deficit.[65] Instead of becoming a source of economic power, the cotton trade to Mexico was one of the great squandered opportunities of the Confederacy.[66]

****

Managing the economic health of his department was only one of Kirby Smith's problems, as he had to contend with internal discord that paralleled that occurring throughout the Confederacy. As in other regions, the spectrum of opposition to the Confederate government existed west of the Mississippi River. While present in other parts of the Confederacy, Unionism was particularly strong in Texas. The state had long campaigned to join the United States in the aftermath of its independence from Mexico, and many citizens found it difficult to change their loyalties so easily.[67] That did not stop Confederate authorities from reacting to Unionist activity, whether real or imagined. German immigrants, motivated by their general anti-slavery sentiments and resentment at Southern efforts to assimilate them into the mainstream culture, were the most notable Unionists, even forming local militias to deter conscription officers. In response, in 1862 army officers imposed martial law to crack down on the local German immigrant population, filling the jails with anyone suspected of Unionist sympathy.[68] The retaliation prompted Confederate loyalists to act on their own accord against suspected enemies. In August 1862, for example, a band of vigilantes attacked a group of immigrants bound for Mexico, killing many of them and capturing the rest in a clash known as the "Battle of the Nueces."[69] The most notorious act of vigilantism occurred in Gainesville, Texas, in that same year. Pro-Confederate civilians claimed to possess evidence that Northern sympathizers planned to attack military and civilian targets.[70] By October 1862, Texas authorities had rounded up nearly 150 residents in and around Gainesville and prosecuted them in front of a "citizens' court" under the supervision of an army provost marshal, culminating with the issuing of twenty-one death sentences. In a following round of trials, authorities in Gainesville rounded up a further sixty prisoners and hanged nineteen of them.[71] One postwar memoir simply wrote off the hangings, and other violent outrages against anti-Confederate behavior, as "deplorable affairs; ones which may be regretted, and yet be accounted for as a result of the passions engendered by an unfortunate Civil War."[72]

The lengthy conflict also generated many dissenters among the landed lower class. As a frontier state with cheap land, Texas contained many yeomanry who had nothing to gain and everything to lose from the war, and were hesitant to sacrifice for the success of the upper class that dominated the state. Confederate authorities also included among the dissenters those who inhibited the economic functioning of the department, such as those who refused to accept Confederate money, speculated in goods after the imposition of the blockade, and placed the pursuit of profits through the Mexico trade over the Southern cause.[73] Dissent also manifested itself in the determination of many to avoid the draft. A Confederate officer in central Texas reported that "500 to 700 men met … in Austin County, and that they determined to resist the draft and conscription to the last extremity."[74]

Unlike in other parts of the Confederacy, open resistance to authority coalesced early in the war, promoted by economic depression, a heightened sense of vulnerability on the frontier, and heavy-handed responses by Confederate officials. The widespread resistance generated a sense that much of the department was not safe for loyal citizens, causing an exasperated enrolling officer to declare that "we are on the very eve of an insurrection, and that the secession portion of our population are daily in great danger."[75] The main risk to loyal civilians were, as in other regions, the bands of armed deserters that occupied remote areas in large numbers; by the summer of 1862 an estimated 3,000 resisters/deserters lurked in the northern counties of Texas alone.[76] A Confederate officer requested the protection of "armed men to assist in the enforcement of the conscript law" because in counties north of Dallas "bodies of men are assembling, armed and equipped, to resist the enrolling officers. These squads are increasing daily in strength by deserters, both from the army and from conscription … and, if unnoticed, will eventually become formidable."[77] Just months later, a Texas official reported to the state government that "twenty men had perished by violence. Some had been waylaid and shot; others taken from their homes … and hung, and their houses robbed; and some had been mobbed and murdered in jail and irons. No man felt secure, even at home."[78]

The violence might have been an aberration if localized in the north Texas counties, but resister violence occurred in every corner of the department. In Brownsville, Brig. Gen. James Slaughter reported that hundreds of eligible men lived in the city, making no effort to hide from conscription agents too intimidated to do their duty.[79] In the "Big Thicket" country north of Houston, authorities arrested a group of resisters, but one of their number had a "small pearl-handled pen knife that he had hidden in his boot" that he used to pry up the floorboards of the jail and permit their escape. A punitive expedition into the region launched from Houston tried to burn the resisters out of their camps and into the open, but only managed to start a range fire that scorched more than 3,000 acres of countryside.[80]

As in other states, authorities turned to repressive measures to restore order. When Kirby Smith took command in the department, he pushed for aggressive action against armed bands, instructing his subordinates that "deserters must be arrested and brought back to their commands or exterminated."[81] Pursuant to Kirby Smith's orders, the army conducted a series of cavalry sweeps through regions plagued by deserter bands, but with the same lack of long-term success. In one such raid, an officer in October 1863 instructed his troops to "Extend pardon to all that you believe come in voluntarily, arrest all others alive wherever found, and let them all understand that they must go to the army and stay obedient to Country or be killed." The move had the blessing of Kirby Smith, who urged all officers to move immediately and with force as "the camp of deserters must be broken up at all hazards," directing them to "use every exertion to effect their extermination as soon as possible."[82] In most instances, however, anti-deserter sweeps usually came up empty because resisters hid, fled, or fought back. During an August 1863 operation in Louisiana, for instance, a sweep resulted in a counter-attack by local resisters that left many men on both sides dead.[83] The failure of counter-desertion operations often led to brutality, especially when state troops tried to deal with deserter bands and failed. In one operation in southern Texas in November 1863, state troops employed harsh measures, including impressing the families' food supplies, horses, and firearms, because to do nothing proved, in the words of their commander, that "our laws are powerless" to arrest deserters who supported themselves by becoming "robbers and bushwhackers."[84]

****

The inability to stabilize the economy and maintain law and order created a lack of confidence in the leadership of the department. The brunt of the doubt fell on Kirby Smith, who, in turn, himself generated uncertainty about his abilities. He had reoccurring health issues throughout his military career, for instance, ranging from wounds received in battle (against the Comanche in 1859 and at First Bull Run) to various fevers, dysentery, and eye issues during his tenure in the Trans-Mississippi that took him away from his duties.[85] Others doubted that Kirby Smith himself believed the Confederacy could win the war. A few months after taking command, Kirby Smith wrote to Richard Taylor that "The difficulties of my position are well known to you—a vast extent of country to defend; a force utterly inadequate for the purpose; a lukewarm people … who appear more intent upon the means of evading the enemy and saving their property then of defending their firesides."[86] Kirby Smith's most prominent critics, however, were his political superiors, who often found him wanting.[87] The Confederate Congress, upon receiving complaints from their constituents, often questioned Kirby Smith's competence. In October 1864, Missouri Congressman Thomas Snead wrote to General Price, "I am sorry that I cannot share the admiration which you all bestow on General Smith. I do not think that he is competent to command the Department of the Trans-Mississippi, and I hope that he will for that reason be superseded."[88] Nor did Texas Senator William Oldham endorse Kirby Smith's leadership, accusing the general of abusing the legitimate civilian leadership of the region. "No Roman pro-consul was ever more absolute than the military commanders of the Trans-Mississippi Department," Oldham declared, believing that Kirby Smith "considered himself not only the commander of the armies and soldiers in his district, but the absolute dictator, the proconsul, of Texas."[89]

Such accusations had little merit, as Kirby Smith's record clearly showed that he tread very carefully when dealing with the governors of his department, never seizing dictatorial powers when circumstances suggested such a move was prudent. Rather, Kirby Smith's greatest shortcoming was one that he could not avoid because it was the very nature of his command. Due to his unique responsibilities in the isolated department, Kirby Smith was both a military and political leader, but was also neither. Kirby Smith was in a conundrum because he was expected to assume some of the Richmond government's authority. Kirby Smith did so, but only in the context of how it affected the state governments, a position established at the 1863 conference in Marshall. While Kirby Smith had considerable political authority, he was hardly a dictator. Jefferson Davis had imposed great bureaucratic burdens upon him, so Kirby Smith dealt with issues the best he could, giving him the public perception of a failed politician.[90] At the same time, Kirby Smith was also the military leader of the department, albeit in a removed capacity. Officially, Kirby Smith led all troops within his jurisdiction, but he did not personally direct battles except for leading the operations against Steele's column during the Red River Campaign, a fight that ended badly for him. Therefore, any military victories, such as Taylor's successes against Banks, were his at a command level but not at a battlefield level since Taylor directed the fight. By claiming part of the credit as department commander, however, Kirby Smith exacerbated the jealousy between himself and Taylor, especially as Kirby Smith never accepted similar amounts of blame for military defeats. The troops in Kirby Smith's department had both victories and defeats, but Kirby Smith's credit or responsibility for either was never clear, making his role as military leader very indistinct despite his rank. Given the burden of his political duties, such unclear roles were inevitable. "Had General Smith been at the head of the army, with no other duties but to operate against the enemy, the results of his department might have been very different," one observer considered, but "his duties were not those of a General at the head of an army, but assimilated to those of a civil governor and legislator."[91]

The best assessment of Kirby Smith is that, while he administered his department, he did not lead it. He did reasonably well at managing the affairs of the Trans-Mississippi Department, but did little to aid the overall Confederate war effort. Kirby Smith could organize institutions and improve efficiency, but he lacked the charisma and record of accomplishments necessary for a successful leader. He could issue orders to subordinates, but he could not inspire them. At the same time, he managed the limited resources of his department as best he could, but could not provide enough economic security to get civilians to consolidate their support for his ideas. Governor Allen of Louisiana believed Kirby Smith "a man of personal courage and high probity," but found him "almost too gentle and retiring for his position—too facile and yielding to the impudent and importunate demands of often unworthy subordinates." Perhaps more charitably, a major biographer of Kirby Smith minimized his leadership failures by determining that he was in an unwinnable situation from the start, undermined by flawed Confederate strategy, economic limitations impossible to overcome, and civilian morale fractured long before Kirby Smith took command.[92] Even Senator Oldham, a frequent critic, had to admit that Kirby Smith was one of only a "few men competent to the discharge of the manifold and responsible duties of the position," further assessing that "little less than the genius of a Napoleon could have mastered and controlled the elements and produced efficient and practical results."[93]

****

In the end, the Trans-Mississippi Department played a role in the Civil War much less than its resources and geography might have indicated. Plagued by its low priority status in Richmond and led by commanders of doubtful quality, the department managed to establish a credible level of domestic production considering the dearth of industrial bases before the war. Kirby Smith's inability to harness the region's cotton wealth to fund the army and maintain the domestic economy, however, undermined the impressive achievements in Marshall, Tyler, and other new industrial centers. Many of the problems, such as the government's financial shortcomings and the political chaos south of the border, were beyond Kirby Smith's control, but others were not. The general could have done more to curb the speculators that sapped the region's wealth for their own gain or to establish clearer policies regarding the impressment and use of cotton to fund the armies, but he was hesitant to challenge the authority of the state executives at a time when he needed their local political support. Kirby Smith was both a political leader and a military leader, but was unable to accomplish each task at the same time. To be both meant that he would have to assume the powers of a dictator, and he was simply unwilling to do that. He also demonstrated leadership shortcomings through his inability to deploy troops across the Mississippi River, a failure that portended other military shortcomings when Union assaults forced Kirby Smith to defend his department.

Chapter 10

"A Rabble of Dead-Heads": The Defense of the Trans-Mississippi Department

E dmund Kirby Smith faced a constant stream of criticism throughout his tenure as department commander. Detractors especially targeted his lack of action, as he seemed to go months between any armed clashes when major battles took place in the Cis-Mississippi with a lethal regularity. The lack of offensive action stemmed from several causes. The isolation of Texas was both a blessing and a curse. There was little prospect of invasion, but there was also no imminent threat to motivate the army and populace. A Texas soldier wrote to this wife from Galveston, "No prospect for a fight here & I don't think anywhere else on this side of the river."[1] In addition, since Kirby Smith lacked the offensive power to conduct anything other than a large raid, he ceded the operational initiative to the Union. The Red River campaign was the best example of this limitation, as Kirby Smith managed to defeat Union incursions after they began but could not take preemptive action to disrupt Union plans. The lack of offensive power also came from the shortage of weapons. Assessments of Kirby Smith's strength were always misleading because, thanks to the chronic need for rifles, the number of troops available for operations was less than the number of troops listed as available for duty.[2]

The final problem was Kirby Smith's own lack of strategic vision. Kirby Smith, unable to deploy his army across the Mississippi River and not strong enough to recapture key territories, often grasped at the ideas of others. In March 1865, Maj. Gen. James F. Fagan proposed a cavalry invasion of Arkansas with the unrealistic goal of recapturing Little Rock as the first step toward retaking the state. Kirby Smith gave his consent and deployed an infantry division in case Fagan was successful, but the improbable attack never took place.[3] Unable to find a direction or strategy, Kirby Smith seemed to his critics far too willing to do nothing. "The troops of that Department were never organized into an army," Senator William Oldham charged, "but were divided, and subdivided, into more than a dozen bodies ... each under its own commander and dispersed throughout the Department." Oldham further described an army that "made no bold aggressive movement during the war, although several were made by small fractions of it, which usually failed from weakness and want of support. The main body of the troops remained quietly in camp in summer as well as winter."[4] The lack of military initiative cost Kirby Smith dearly in the end. While Johnston and Taylor fought last-ditch battles to fend off the inevitable, Kirby Smith never had the opportunity to mount a last-minute face-saving clash that enabled him to surrender under more honorable terms.

****

In October 1862, the Union made its first determined effort to seize and hold a coastal enclave by attacking Galveston, Texas. Confederate Brig. Gen. Paul O. Hébert failed to protect the city, leading to his dismissal. His replacement was Maj. Gen. John Magruder, who, reinforced by troops from New Mexico, retook Galveston. On New Year's Eve 1862, Magruder's assault, led by four makeshift gunboats, caught Union forces by surprise. After losing two ships, the Union garrison surrendered, and, although the blockade remained in place for the rest of the war, the Federals made no further attempts to take the city.[5] The next Union assault did not occur until September 1863, when Union forces tried to seize the Sabine Pass, on the Texas-Louisiana border. The War Department charged Maj. Gen. Nathanial Banks, the most prominent Union "political general," with establishing a Federal presence in Texas.[6] He chose to target Houston, but rather than a direct assault through Galveston, Banks opted for an approach up the Sabine River to encircle Houston from the rear.[7] In September 1863, a flotilla carried five thousand troops of Maj. Gen. William B. Franklin's XIX Corps to seize Sabine Pass. Confederate artillery, however, disabled two Union gunboats, and, without support from the Navy, Franklin abandoned the operation and took his troops back to New Orleans.[8] Repulsed from Sabine Pass, Banks again invaded Texas a few months later. In November 1863, two divisions of the XIII Corps under the command of Maj. Gen. Napoleon Dana landed at Brazos Santiago at the mouth of the Rio Grande. The goal of the operation was to seize Brownsville and cut the Confederate cotton trade to Mexico. Dana took Brownsville, but he could do little more with his small force. Eventually, Banks wearied of the failed campaign, and withdrew the bulk of Dana's force and ceded Brownsville back to the Confederates, leaving only a garrison at Brazos Santiago.[9]

Banks did not give up his goal of attacking the Trans-Mississippi Department. Instead of the Texas seaboard, Banks intended to advance up the Red River toward the Confederate administrative and logistic center at Shreveport, Louisiana. Banks embarked on his Red River Campaign in March 1864 with the highest of hopes, but it proved to be one of the most disappointing Union efforts of the Civil War. The plan had ill-defined goals, with one officer later writing "No one knew who started the expedition … or what its object was. No one cared to father it after it was over, for it was one of the most disastrous affairs that occurred during the war."[10] Banks believed there was vast amounts of cotton available for confiscation, and the Confederates certainly believed the purpose of the raid was to seize cotton. Once the invasion began, the Confederate army appropriated all cotton near the Red River, burning what they could not remove. Admiral Porter reported to his superiors, "The rebels are retreating before the army, and, as usual are destroying everything that can fall into our hands, treating public and private property alike."[11] The Union also undertook the expedition to confront French adventurism in Mexico by "re-establishing the national authority in Western Texas as soon as possible."[12] Banks launched his assault with more than 30,000 troops accompanied by a large naval contingent. Rear Admiral David Porter, leading the naval force, was not enthusiastic about the operation, considering the Red River the "most treacherous of all rivers." At the same time, Maj. Gen. Frederick Steele,

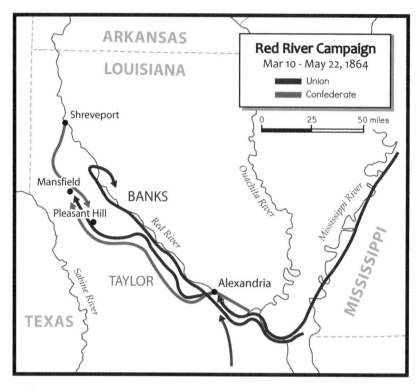

Red River Campaign.

then commanding the Department of Arkansas before later participating in Canby's campaign against Mobile, led seven thousand men south from Little Rock to assault Shreveport in support of Banks's advance, although Steele was also not optimistic regarding the outcome of the operations.[13]

As Banks's army neared Mansfield, his army was strung out along the river with a gap of several miles between his two corps and the naval flotilla twenty miles further back. The separated nature of Banks's army gave Taylor, who had fallen back toward Shreveport, an opportunity to turn and fight. Reinforced by an infantry division recently arrived from Texas, Taylor assaulted the forward Union division and nearly turned its flank. The following day, as Union troops consolidated near Pleasant Hill, Taylor, given a choice of withdrawing after his victory pushing his luck, decided to attack. Driving his men the twenty miles to Pleasant Hill, Taylor launched a frontal assault

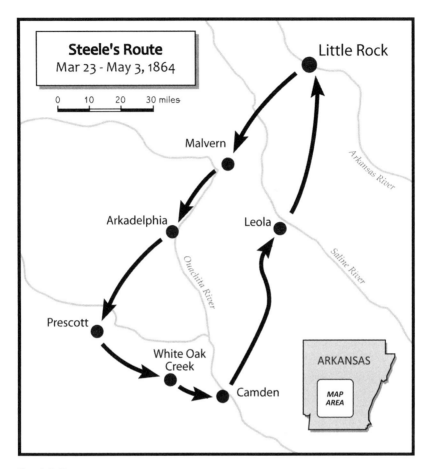

Steele's Route.

so bold that Union defenders thought the Confederates "full of whiskey," an attack that failed in the face of "thirty pieces of artillery playing upon the rebels." Unnerved by Taylor's sudden assault, Banks ordered a withdrawal to Natchitoches to replenish his forces from his supply ships. With water levels falling, however, Banks chose to fall back even further, another fifty miles to Alexandria.[14]

As Banks retreated, Taylor met with Kirby Smith to draft plans for further pursuit, but found Kirby Smith had other goals. Kirby Smith wished to deal with Steele's column, ninety miles from Shreveport, before turning on

Banks. Unbeknownst to Kirby Smith, Steele had already decided to retreat when he learned of Banks's misfortunes.[15] Seeing a greater threat to the north, Kirby Smith took the Arkansas and Texas troops from Taylor's command and sent them to pursue Steele.[16] Although stripped of most of his infantry, Taylor continued to press Banks as he retreated first to Alexandria and then to his start point at the mouth of the Red River.[17] Meanwhile, Kirby Smith's efforts to destroy Steele's force came to nothing, as Union troops repelled efforts to halt their retreat to Little Rock. Kirby Smith redirected troops south to support Banks, but the Union force was gone before they could arrive.[18] By the end of the campaign, the Confederates had suffered about 4,300 casualties compared to the Union's approximately 5,000.[19]

The campaign generated recrimination on both sides. In the aftermath of the failed expedition, the Committee on the Conduct of the War, a joint Congressional investigative body charged with examining decisions made by the Lincoln administration, conducted hearings on the Red River debacle. Testifying before the committee, Banks blamed everyone but himself for the failure, citing such adverse conditions as low river levels, poor communications, and inadequate logistic support.[20] Others, however, but the blame squarely on Banks. When questioned about the goals and purpose of the campaign, Major General Franklin testified that they were unaware in specific terms of exactly what was the purpose of the expedition other than to use Shreveport as a future base for offensives into Texas.[21] The Confederates experienced even greater internal discord. Fixated on defending his department, Kirby Smith committed a major strategic blunder. He successfully repelled both Union forces, but, while inflicting serious losses, did not destroy either column. Moreover, by concentrating on Steele's smaller force, he allowed Banks's larger force to escape.[22] Expecting that Jefferson Davis would want an explanation of what had occurred, Kirby Smith submitted an official report that defended his actions during the Red River Campaign, emphasizing his inadequate forces and the "wide distances which separated my commands" and "made it impossible to effect rapid concentration."[23]

Kirby Smith could spin tales for Jefferson Davis in Richmond, but his subordinates had a different view. In a public statement, only days after Banks decided to withdraw, the department commander announced it was "an appropriate occasion to pay a well-merited tribute to the endurance and valor of the troops engaged in these battles." Kirby Smith gave all the credit to the soldiers, but he did not specifically praise any of his senior subordinates. Taylor felt slighted in Kirby Smith's congratulatory message, but promised Kirby Smith that "no unkindness, even from a quarter whence I had some reason to expect the reverse, will turn me from the great work before me."[24] While engaging in his "great work," Taylor found time to erode his relationship with Kirby Smith even further. On April 28, while still dealing with Banks, Taylor wrote Kirby Smith to question his command decisions, asking why he chose to "chase after a force of 10,000 in full retreat" instead of achieving the "certain destruction of an army of 30,000 men." If allowed to act as he wished, Taylor claimed he could have easily defeated Banks's entire expedition by exerting "no more than ordinary energy for its accomplishment." Kirby Smith returned the letter by responding, "This communication is not only improper but unjust. I cannot believe but that it was written in a moment of irritation or sickness." Instead of letting the matter drop, Taylor continued to criticize Kirby Smith's leadership. On May 24, in response to Kirby Smith's orders to prepare for a possible invasion of Missouri to capitalize on the recent Union setbacks, Taylor declined to participate and instead again asked "that I may speedily be relieved from duty in this department."

In reply, Kirby Smith pointed out that when he issued his plans for the campaign, "You then distinctly expressed your approval of the movement," but his attempt at a calm discourse failed when Taylor responded with another insubordinate letter that alternated between passive-aggressive accusations and self-martyrdom. "The campaign as a whole has been a hideous failure," Taylor accused. "The fruits of Mansfield have been turned to dust and ashes. Louisiana, from Natchitoches to the Gulf, is a howling wilderness and her people are starving."[25] Fed up with Taylor's insubordination, on June 10 Kirby Smith issued orders relieving Taylor of command and ordered him to "proceed to Natchitoches, La., and there await the pleasure of the President of the Confederate States." The following day, Kirby Smith wrote to Jefferson Davis to explain his reason for sacking Taylor. He included copies of Taylor's impolitic letters as evidence of his insubordinate behavior, emphasizing that, unlike Taylor's "improper and disrespectful" statements, he was acting from a "self-control that has been sustained only by love of country and a desire of promoting her best interests."[26] While he awaited Davis's response to his letter, Kirby Smith replaced Taylor as commander of the District of Louisiana with Maj. Gen. Simon Buckner.[27]

The nasty exchanges between Kirby Smith and Taylor split opinion in both the army and among civilians. Lt. Edward Cunningham defended Kirby Smith's decisions because "Some persons say the campaign was successful, but it might have been so much better had this or that been done differently. Very true, but it might have been so much worse."[28] Kirby Smith, already unpopular because of his policies before the campaign, recognized that his command was in jeopardy. In a letter to his mother, Kirby Smith pessimistically believed "My administration may cease at any moment," as the "difficulty with Taylor has made me bitter enemies" in both the army and administration.[29] Kirby Smith survived the spat with Taylor, but neither general distinguished himself in the matter.

****

Union attacks in the Trans-Mississippi were a great concern to the various generals who commanded the department, but opportunities for offensive action did exist. Although major expeditions to the Cis-Mississippi were not possible, there were objectives in Union-held territory on the west side of the river open to assault, mainly in Missouri. The limited numbers of troops and weapons, however, along with the need to defend key locations, prevented any large-scale infantry assault into Missouri after the failed 1861 offensive that ended at Wilson's Creek.[30] In place of conventional offensives, the commanders of the Trans-Mississippi Department conducted a series of cavalry raids to disrupt Union military plans, obtain supplies and recruits, and bolster Confederate support in the state. Three such raids, each of roughly a month's duration, occurred between December 1862 and October 1863, sustaining the war effort west of the river and placating War Department demands for the armies in the department to contribute more to the overall war effort.

Pressure from the War Department was the impetus for Kirby Smith to approve another, even larger, operation in September 1864. The repulse of the Red River Campaign suggested that Union morale and strength were at low ebb, to the point where a major effort might achieve substantial gains. In the

Cis-Mississippi, the War Department pressured Kirby Smith to take offensive action to redirect Union efforts away from Sherman's advance toward Atlanta and Grant's Overland Campaign toward Richmond.[31] The proposal for another strike into Missouri came from Brig. Gen. Joseph "Jo" Shelby, a native Missourian. Shelby believed that the Union offensives had depleted their garrisons in Missouri, leaving the state vulnerable to a Confederate offensive with little risk or cost while acquiring many recruits and gathering badly needed supplies.[32] While the plan was Shelby's idea, a more senior

Sterling Price (*Image courtesy of the Library of Congress*).

officer had to lead the operation, and Kirby Smith placed Maj. Gen. Sterling Price in command. Price was an odd choice, as he had not led a cavalry force since the Mexican War, and certainly not one of this size. Kirby Smith himself, by that point in the war, had assessed Price's military abilities as "good for nothing." However, Kirby Smith had already reassigned Richard Taylor due to his clashes with himself and General Buckner declined to lead the operation, leaving Price as the only command option.[33]

In August 1864, Kirby Smith issued orders for Price to lead the assault into Missouri, instructing him to acquire as many "mules, horses, cattle, and military supplies" as he could. Kirby Smith also needed soldiers. "Rally the loyal men of Missouri," he directed Price, "and remember that our great want is men." Price was to strike toward St. Louis, and if that objective was not obtainable, he was to cross the state and make his retreat "through Kansas and the Indian Territory." In short, it was an all-or-nothing gamble. If Price could not reach St. Louis, then he was to convert the invasion into a raid by doing as much damage as he could as he withdrew. Being practical, Kirby Smith realized that the capture of St. Louis "will do more toward rallying Missouri to your standard than the possession of any other point," but unless he could capture "its supplies, and military stores" his force could not stay in the state.[34]

Crossing the Arkansas River between the two main Union garrisons at Little Rock and Fort Smith, Price moved toward Missouri with 12,000 cavalry in three divisions, commanded by Maj. Gens. James Fagan and John Marmaduke, and Brig. Gen. Jo Shelby. As the operation began, signs began to surface that the raid was not going as expected. The cavalry officers, especially Shelby, became exasperated at the slow pace of the column. Price seemed to consider his force as a traditional army, and instead of slashing movements by lightly equipped forces, the cavalry moved at the pace of marching infantry. An immense wagon train, a traditional feature of infantry operations but of no use to the cavalry accustomed to living off the land, slowed the column. Consequently, any element of surprise, if it had even existed, was gone. The slow pace also made the capture of St. Louis, the goal of the attack, impossible, as Union reinforcements and improved defenses made the city impervious to Price's smaller force.[35]

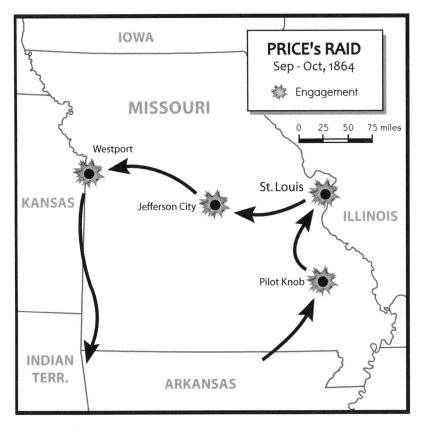

Price's Raid.

Deterred by the large force he believed was in his path, Price turned away from St. Louis and instead directed his attention against Jefferson City, the state capital, 120 miles to the west. Marching along the south bank of the Missouri River, Price again moved at a pace that frustrated his cavalry officers. Price skirmished with Union forces outside the city, but opted not to mount an assault after determining its defenses were too daunting. Instead, Price announced he would follow his instructions from Kirby Smith and withdraw from Missouri via Kansas and the Indian Territory. In doing so, Price moved away from the growing Union strength in St. Louis, but moved toward the Union Army of the Border, commanded by Maj. Gen. Samuel Curtis.[36] Seeking an engagement with Price, Curtis ordered a division under

Maj. Gen. James Blunt to impede Price's advance while Curtis assembled the main force further west. In the meantime, Price allowed his men to forage and loot at their leisure, damaging their reputation and credibility with the local population. The accumulation of food and loot caused the wagon train to swell to more than five hundred vehicles, stretching "eight or ten miles in length." General Shelby's aide, Maj. John Anderson, described the force as becoming "a rabble of dead-heads, stragglers, and stolen negroes on stolen horses" that gave the force the "appearance of a Calmuck horde."[37]

Price's westward advancement came to a halt at Westport, Missouri, where Price found himself greatly outnumbered and between two Union forces. In a confused and violent fight along Brush Creek, Union troops threatened to envelop Price's entire command. Price ordered a withdrawal to the south, and for the next five days Price fell back toward the Arkansas line with Union forces in pursuit. After several running battles, the last at Newtonia, Missouri, on October 29, Curtis ordered his troops to break off the pursuit and Price's battered column struggled toward Arkansas unimpeded. Upon crossing the border, Price furloughed his Arkansas brigades to go home and recruit replacements while he took the remaining troops to encampments in southwestern Arkansas, arriving two months after he began his campaign.[38]

In the aftermath of the failed operation, all participants tried their best to depict the raid as a success. In his report to Kirby Smith, Price proudly claimed he inflicted damage amounting to $10 million, tore up Missouri's railroad system, and raised 5,000 new recruits. However, he also admitted "a number of desertions took place among the Arkansas troops," so his gain was negligible.[39] If Price's report did not reflect reality, Gen. Jo Shelby's report was pure fantasy. Shelby had been one of the biggest critics of Price during the operation, characterizing the operation as the "stupidest, wildest, wantonest, wickedest march ever made by a general [Price] who had a voice like a lion and a spring like a guinea pig." Shelby had to put the raid in the best possible light because, as a Missourian himself, he needed the raid to be deemed a success. "Although the expedition was full of hardships and suffering in some respects," Shelby wrote, diminishing the negative effects of the raid, "General Price ... stamped his expedition as one of the most brilliant of the war." Shelby's report promoted the number of Union troops diverted from other operations, the amount of enemy supplies destroyed, and the "electric hope, pride, strength, and resistance sent coursing through every vein and artery of the South."[40] As the commander who had authorized the operation, Kirby Smith tried the hardest to find some sort of victory, or at least avoid most of the blame. In November 1864, Kirby Smith informed President Davis of the raid in a letter worded in such a manner as to deflect any possible criticism. According to Kirby Smith, Price's Raid had accomplished a long list of ancillary and unprovable benefits, including the diversion of reinforcements away from Sherman in Georgia. "I consider General Price as having effected the objects for which he was ordered into Missouri," Kirby Smith concluded, "and the expedition a success."[41] Kirby Smith also tried to spin the raid in a positive light by explaining that the "cavalry expedition into Missouri was directed by me … as a diversion in favor of our army in Georgia."[42]

Although the participants tried to sell the idea of the raid as great success, subsequent analysis ranged from a middling claim that the raid was ineffective to a damning criticism that the movement "marked a general Confederate collapse along the border of Arkansas and Missouri."[43] Price had disrupted military supply and railroad systems, but the Union was not planning any major military operations from Missouri, so the strategic consequences of the raid were minimal. Price obtained five thousand recruits, but most were unarmed and Kirby Smith had little ability to equip them. The recruits were a fraction of what Price promised to attract, especially compared to the personnel losses he had suffered to get them. Lastly, Price's available force in December was a third of what it had been in August, reduced by combat, desertion, furloughs, and disease, leaving it described as "terribly disorganized, and not in a fit condition to fight any body of men."[44] General Holmes viewed the remaining Confederate forces as an "army of prisoners, and self-supporting at that."[45] Unit rosters after the raid showed that Kirby Smith commanded twenty-nine brigades, organized into eleven divisions in a four-corps formation, but three of the corps were barely larger than a standard division.[46]

The failure of the raid particularly diminished the morale of Kirby Smith's cavalry units, who found their regiments about to change to solve other problems. Kirby Smith found himself in late 1864 with two related problems when it came to cavalry and horses. First, his army was unbalanced compared to other armies of the era. In Civil War armies, cavalry generally comprised about a tenth of the army, with the rest of the force consisting of a smaller percentage of artillery and the vast remainder made up of infantry formations. In Kirby Smith's army, however, the cavalry represented more than half of his available combat force. Had Price's Raid accomplished any sort of positive result, Kirby Smith might have justified retaining that many horsemen, but growing Union power in Missouri demonstrated that the chances of success from future raids were slim.[47] The other related problem was that Price needed horses to haul supplies to keep his army fed, as well as to move cotton to Brownsville to fund the department. Kirby Smith's artillery batteries were also short of horses, and the lack of mules to move supplies often forced army garrisons to forage near their positions, depleting the food supply and causing anger and demoralization among the local civilians.[48]

Forced to think defensively after Price's failure, Kirby Smith concluded that he could solve both problems by dismounting some of his cavalry regiments, converting them into infantry, and transferring their horses where needed. He was not naïve enough to believe that the decision would go over well among the cavalry, because he had not accumulated so many cavalry units by accident. Besides the vast distances of the department and lack of other modes of transportation that made cavalry units so useful compared to slow-marching infantry, the horse-based culture of the frontier made cavalry service more attractive. Mounted units were more readily recruited than infantry because, as an English observer noted, "At the outbreak of war, it was found very difficult to raise infantry in Texas, as no Texan walks a yard if he can help it."[49] Even locals admitted the preference of riding to walking. "The chief objection to enlistment was the repugnance to infantry service," Texas Governor Francis Lubbock wrote in his memoirs. "The predilections of Texas for cavalry service, founded as it is upon their peerless horsemanship, is so powerful that they are unwilling in many instances to engage in service of any other description."[50] In addition, earlier instances that necessitated the dismounting of cavalry for even short emergencies faced stiff resistance. "To lessen the consumption of corn," after his losses at the Battle of

Pea Ridge in 1862, General Hindman "found it necessary to dismount four regiments of Texans and three of Arkansians. This produced much dissatisfaction, and there were many desertions in consequence."[51] In September 1863, General Magruder ordered the troopers of the Thirty-seventh Texas cavalry to dismount and join the defenses of nearby Galveston to repulse a rumored Union invasion of the port. The soldiers resisted the order despite reassurances the assignment was only temporary, and about one hundred men deserted rather than submit.[52]

Despite the negative consequences, Kirby Smith informed Jefferson Davis that he intended to dismount six thousand of his cavalry and redistribute their horses as part of a general reorganization and consolidation of decimated formations.[53] Perhaps as a punishment for his failures in Missouri, Price's command was the first to lose their horses, although Kirby Smith exempted Shelby's division. Price himself agreed with Kirby Smith's decision, although he advised his commander, "I would respectfully recommend the postponement of any action" until after the transfer of horses occurred to allow the "division commanders to get their men in hand."[54] Despite efforts to persuade the cavalrymen to accept their new assignments, the loss of their horses caused many to desert. A Louisiana soldier noted the effect of dismounting by writing, "They dismounted three regiments … and about one half of them ran off. One regiment all left but about eighty men. There were several captains and five or six lieutenants that left the crowd."[55] Because desertion was the typical reaction, officers took additional precautions, actions that insulted the soon-to-be dismounted cavalry. "The 3rd Louisiana Brigade of Cavalry, under Col. [Isaac] Harrison, were marched to Natchitoches under plea of recruiting their horses," a soldier told his family, but the next morning "a Division of Infantry was placed around them & they [were] ordered to deliver up their horses to the Quartermaster." The soldier further noted that "On the day after tomorrow, we will march to Natchitoches … it may be that we will be dismounted. God grant it may not be, for the Army will lose many a man if such a thing is undertaken."[56] Rather than desert, some soldiers took matters into their own hands. Private Joe Scott of the Thirty-first Texas Cavalry did not take kindly to being dismounted, considering his unit "had seen some of hardest service that Confederate soldiers were ever subject to" during Price's Raid. Resentful of the "feeling we had been treated very badly," Scott determined "to recover my horse." He illegally obtained a requisition form, gathered his horse from the assembly pen, and demanded the right to enlist in another cavalry unit.[57] Like many of Kirby Smith's efforts, he had extended the department's ability to resist the Union as much as he could, but it was not enough and he damaged his own army's morale in the process.

****

Kirby Smith and Price had achieved little with the raid into Missouri, an operation that turned out to be the Trans-Mississippi army's last offensive action. Although no Union forces immediately threatened the Trans-Mississippi Department, Maj. Gen. John Pope planned to change that. Pope had achieved success early in the war, but suffered a crushing defeat at the Second Battle of Bull Run, which led to his assignment to the relatively remote Department of the Northwest. In this capacity, Pope suppressed an uprising by the Dakota tribe, and spent the subsequent months dealing with other Native American threats to white settlers. The task repaired much of the damage to his reputation, and in November 1864 Grant added the Departments of Missouri and Kansas to Pope's command.[58] In addition, Grant offered to send additional troops if Pope could properly utilize them. With these reinforcements, Grant suggested "If you can break up Price where he is you may find it practicable to make a campaign in Northeast Texas, subsisting entirely off the Country."[59] Pope confirmed an offensive was feasible if Grant could provide him five thousand cavalry mounts, because the "cavalry is nearly all dismounted, the horses having been taken south by General Canby and not yet replaced."

Pope envisioned an offensive very different from the earlier attempts to attack Texas. Rejecting a "movement up [the] Red River" because such a move would "drive the enemy before us into Texas" toward their own reinforcements, Pope envisioned a direct assault on the center of Confederate positions. Pope planned to "to move in three columns from the Arkansas River toward the Red River … the main column to move from Little Rock, the other two from Dardanelle and Fort Smith. The junction of the two first-named columns will be made on Red River." Pope then

Gen. John Pope (*Image courtesy of the Library of Congress*).

proposed to "march rapidly upon Marshall, Tex.," to capture the industrial and military facilities there. As the Confederates could not allow the loss of such an important site, Pope concluded it was "almost certain that if they deliver battle at all they will do so near Marshall." Presuming that he could defeat Kirby Smith's attempt to hold Marshall, Pope then planned to bypass Shreveport and head south in a movement that "threatens Galveston, Houston, and Austin."

If he could complete his plan, Pope believed the Union would "completely possess Texas" as any remaining Confederate troops would be scattered, isolated, and unsupplied. Pope, however, could not attack immediately, informing Grant he could not expect an offensive until at least June 1 because "depending as we shall do on the country for supplies, it would be desirable to wait until the corn and wheat crops in Eastern Texas were sufficiently advanced."[60] Grant was impressed with Pope's plan and gave it his blessing, despite Pope's assertion that he could not advance for at least two more months. Just weeks before, when George Thomas told Grant that he could not conduct operations for sixty days after defeating Hood at Nashville and conducting a winter campaign, Grant took it as a sign of defensive thinking and removed most of his troops. Even as Grant approved Pope's planned offensive, events took a different turn when Lee surrendered barely two weeks later. Convinced the fight was going out of the Confederate Army, Grant began to hedge his bets about a thrust into Texas.[61] Pope himself was also hopeful that Kirby Smith would see reason and surrender, telling the War Department "I incline strongly to believe that no campaign west of Mississippi will be necessary," and instead, "I would think it well to wait a couple of weeks to see what Kirby Smith may do." Grant concurred, replying to Pope that he could "suspend preparations for campaign west of the Mississippi for the present," but "If Kirby Smith attempts to hold out, a force will be sent to overrun the whole country west of the Mississippi."[62]

****

Pope's plan had every likelihood of success, as morale in the Confederate Army declined because of late pay, poor supplies, and concern for suffering families at home. The deterioration of the army's spirit should have surprised no one, as by the last months of the war the Confederate leadership often could not provide the basics of life, such as uniforms and monthly pay. In March 1865, the commander of an ordnance works in Texas, after receiving sixty troops to act as a guard force, requested new uniforms for them as "They are almost naked … They claim that they have not changed their clothing since they left their homes in Missouri."[63] Desertion rates soared and the soldiers that did stay became increasingly unruly and mutinous. By early 1865, a Union officer reported from Galveston that among the Confederate garrison "Much discontent exists among the troops, who have not been paid for eighteen months. Rations are scant and soldiers are obliged to furnish their own clothing."[64]

Desertions also occurred among troops who had lost faith in the long-term success of the Confederacy. In February 1865, a cavalryman noted that "Missouri and Ark[ansas] troops are deserting daily and going home to fight no more." Other officers informed their superiors of "Arkansas soldiers reported deserting by the hundreds" and, from a Missouri regiment "Last night 30 of Perkins' men deserted, about 20 deserted 10 days ago."[65] Unable to pay his men, Kirby Smith offered a more liberal furlough policy. Emulating a policy enacted by the Union Army, soldiers could get furloughs of twenty days or longer, depending upon the distance to their homes. Only 10 percent of a company received a furlough, and the remaining members could only go on furlough when other soldiers returned, using peer pressure to prevent desertions.[66] The furloughs were long overdue because of a general agitation among the troops for the welfare of their families. Many soldiers, however, did not bother to ask for furloughs and deserted anyway, utilizing, as one claimed, "the doctrine of secession, they threw themselves upon their individual rights, and … seceded from their colors and their commanders."[67]

Everywhere he looked, Kirby Smith could see signs that the army and populace were growing weary of the war. Despite its isolation, the population of the Trans-Mississippi were aware of the Confederacy's declining fortunes from the fall of 1864 into early 1865. Although outwardly confident, Kirby Smith himself dealt with bouts of pessimism, confessing in a letter to his mother, "The bad news from the Cis-Mississippi has cast a gloom over all."[68] The situation in the Trans-Mississippi became even worse when devastating news arrived from Virginia. Because of delays in communications, the news of Lee's surrender did not reach Shreveport until April 20, eleven days after the event.[69] The surrender in Virginia had a particularly hard effect in the Trans-Mississippi Department because it came as other defeats became evident, creating a seeming cascade of calamity. "What are our prospects?"

a Texas private despaired. "The dark cloud is settling upon our bleeding country; today our cause is at the lowest depths of despair."[70] Concerned lest poor morale further impair his already fragile situation, Kirby Smith issued an address admitting that "The crisis of our revolution is at hand. Great disasters have overtaken us," but appealed to the soldiers to "Stand by Your colors." He reminded the soldiers of the "great resources of this department, its vast extent, the numbers, the discipline, and the efficiency of the army," but also asked them to fight to "secure to our country terms that a proud people can with honor accept," suggesting that he might negotiate a peace with the enemy.[71]

Even as the army was teetering on internal collapse, there were still signs of determination. Because many demoralized soldiers had already deserted and Union military forces were not nearby, a significant portion of the enlisted men in the Trans-Mississippi remained steadfast to their units. When Kirby Smith announced his determination to fight on, a Missouri soldier responded "let come what will—we'll fight the Yankees alone," a defiant attitude shared by a soldier in Louisiana who announced, "Everybody but me is whipped, but I don't think all is lost by any means yet."[72] Besides personal bravado, appeals to nationalism and common heritage also defined the will of the soldiers to resist. One cavalryman believed that all loyal soldiers and civilians should make "a strong pull and a pull together. Now is the time to immortalize this Army, and if we ever have been any account, now is the time to prove it."[73] A prominent example of the remaining Confederate determination in the Trans-Mississippi Department was the last mission of the gunboat CSS *Webb*. On April 23, 1865, the *Webb*, under the command of Lt. Commander Charles Read, made a final attempt to escape down the Mississippi River. Read managed to sneak past some Union patrols, but ran out of luck a few miles south of New Orleans. Caught by craft with superior firepower, Read beached his ship and fled with his surviving crew. Read's audacious efforts earned him great respect. "Poor Charley Reed [*sic*] couldn't run the 'Webb' through [to the Gulf of Mexico] though he tried hard," an observer noted, "but it 'Twas a gallant act and gallantly carried through."[74]

****

Efforts such as Read's aside, the determination to continue the war in the Trans-Mississippi constantly diminished. While successful in fending off Union attacks throughout the department, remaining on the defense sapped the morale of the region's defenders. Instead of undertaking offensive action to win the war on their own terms, the Trans-Mississippi soldiers could only defend their own ground and try to outlast Union efforts to defeat them. Had Confederate supply organizations provided sufficient sustenance and weapons, the army might have sustained such a defense for a long time. The absence of such materiel support, however, created a perception that Confederate troops were not winning the war, but merely surviving, and the lack of an obvious path to victory exaggerated mundane shortcomings in the department's administration. Kirby Smith deserves much of the credit for protecting his jurisdiction, and, if some logistic efforts and command relationships had worked better, his outcome might have ended differently. Instead, he found himself winning battles, but losing the war. As public morale declined, the willingness of the army also suffered. The clarity of this reality became painfully evident when Kirby Smith had to make the ultimate decision to continue the war or accept Union requests for his surrender.

Chapter 11

"The Exercise of One Manly Virtue": The Surrender of the Trans-Mississippi Department

Although constantly questioned in his decision-making, Edmund Kirby Smith had, by April 1865, protected his department from threats at all points. He had arrived in a department that lacked basic organization, administration, and logistics, but had improved all such situations. Although a man of military training, he had plunged into domestic economic policy and had dealt with the vagaries of diplomacy. Insubordinate district commanders had challenged his authority, but Kirby Smith had survived their efforts to undermine his leadership. Isolated on the west side of the Mississippi River, he had launched what practical offensive operations were within his grasp. By any measure, Kirby Smith was a tested, if imperfect, leader who had seen the Trans-Mississippi Department through some dark days. The area's economic conditions were bad, supply and currency problems were mounting, and the state governments provided more problems than solutions. Nevertheless, the public and the army had stood by Kirby Smith despite their misgivings about him. Their loyalty, however, soon faced a serious test when a Union peace offer arrived.

Of all the challenges that Kirby Smith and the people of the Trans-Mississippi Department faced, surrendering was both the easiest and most difficult to accept. Considering the dire economic circumstances faced by the department and the prospect of fighting the Union armies by themselves, accepting the end of the war certainly made sense. After surviving for so long, to continue fighting would only destroy what little the people had left. Without a country left to serve, soldiers could only see their families and homes as entities worth defending. Submitting to Union demands, however, was a difficult prospect to accept because such a surrender would occur under unusual circumstances. No Union army menaced the centers of Confederate power, or was even engaged in an active offensive against the department. Quite the opposite, the best Union estimates were that an offensive would not occur for at least two months. Generals Grant, Sherman, and Canby's massive armies were free to attack the remaining Confederate region, but would need weeks to arrive. Even if they did, the vastness of the Trans-Mississippi offered a chance to prolong the war. All these elements combined to place Kirby Smith in the difficult position of determining how he could best fulfill his obligations to defend the department during a war that gave every indication of coming to an end.

****

On April 18, Union Gen. John Pope dispatched his chief of staff, Col. John Sprague, to deliver an offer to Kirby Smith to surrender. Pope informed Grant of Sprague's mission, taking care to emphasize that was only "offering the terms accorded by you to General R. E. Lee." Furthermore, because Pope himself did not intend to meet Kirby Smith or engage in any sort of negotiations, he gave Sprague instructions in case Kirby Smith should enquire about specific issues. Sprague was to remember that the terms in the letter were "purely military and in no manner relates to civilians or civil affairs," but if any Confederates wished to leave the country rather than sign a parole he was to "not oppose any considerable objection." Sprague was also not to object should Confederate troops return to their homes without their paroles if they left their weapons and public property behind. Pope further instructed Sprague to inform Kirby Smith that, should he surrender, the occupation of his department would be limited, with "only sufficient force … to garrison important points."[1]

Sprague's eight-hundred-mile journey to deliver Pope's letter took two weeks. Because an overland journey was too dangerous, Sprague took a steamship from St. Louis to the mouth of the Red River. Once there, he contacted the closest Confederate forces to relay to Shreveport his request to meet with Kirby Smith. Two of Kirby Smith's staff officers offered to take any written message to their commander, but Sprague declined, explaining that he "had much to say beyond the contents of my dispatches." Escorted to Shreveport, on May 8 Sprague presented Pope's letter to Kirby Smith that explained the terms he offered and the conditions under which he offered them. Prefacing his letter with official reports of the victories by Grant, Sherman, and Canby, Pope offered Kirby Smith the same surrender terms "accorded to and accepted by General R. E. Lee." If Pope had simply extended the offer, there was a possibility that Kirby Smith would have at least considered it or even accepted it, but Pope overplayed his hand. In addition to offering his surrender terms, Pope wrote that he thought it suitable to point out to Kirby Smith that "the great armies of the United States are now available for operations in the Trans-Mississippi Department; that they are sufficiently strong to render effective resistance impossible." If Kirby Smith refused his terms, "you will be made responsible for unnecessary bloodshed and for the devastation and suffering which must follow the movement of large armies into Texas and extensive military operations in that State," but Pope hoped that he would surrender under the same terms "accepted by your General-in-Chief" to "spare the necessity of further hostile operations."[2]

Instead of accepting the offer, Kirby Smith rejected the terms in a terse note, because he believed Pope's "propositions for the surrender of the troops under my command are not such that my sense of duty and honor will permit me to accept."[3] Unwilling to sever this line of communication, however, Kirby Smith retained the note and asked Sprague if he could linger at Shreveport for a few days until the general had an opportunity to confer with the state governors, which Sprague agreed to do. One factor that both complicated Kirby Smith's efforts to arrange a surrender and made a sit-down with the state governors so necessary was the status of Jefferson Davis. Like Richard Taylor in his situation after the loss of Mobile, Kirby Smith was uncertain how to proceed in the absence of any information regarding the Confederate President. Kirby Smith had not received any communications from Davis and did not know his whereabouts, but neither had he heard any news that Davis was in Federal custody.

Consequently, Kirby Smith was unsure how to proceed. While perhaps convinced that his department could not continue the war on its own, the arrival of Jefferson Davis might instill renewed morale and optimism that Kirby Smith was incapable of generating. Acting on this possibility, Kirby Smith perhaps stalled Colonel Sprague to either allow Davis time to arrive, and therefore assume the burden of command, or see if the French in Mexico might offer some alternatives to outright surrender, which was a manifestation of wishful thinking.[4] The rumors of Davis trying to make his way to the Trans-Mississippi through Cuba were compelling enough that, a few days after hearing about Lee's surrender, Kirby Smith planned to send an envoy to Havana to locate Davis and bring him to the department via Matamoros.[5] While many soldiers and civilians would have welcomed Davis's arrival in the department, a significant portion of the army saw little reason to celebrate the President's possible arrival. "There is but little doubt that the Confederacy is fast collapsing," Lt. Col. David Pierson wrote to his father from Shreveport. "This Dept. might hold out for a year longer by falling back into Texas, but neither the people nor the army will sustain such an undertaking." Pierson further related the rumors of the President trying to reach the Department "with all the specie he could get," but "if Mr. Davis gets into this Dept., he will make a last effort to sustain himself, but his efforts will all be in vain. The soldiers are disheartened & disgusted and determined not to sacrifice their lives to gratify anybody's ambition."[6]

Colonel Pierson's comment about Davis was astute, as the question whether Davis was still in charge or not limited Kirby Smith's ability to act. If Union forces had captured Davis or if Davis was so disconnected from the mechanisms of command that he was no longer in charge in any practical sense, then Kirby Smith could pursue whatever course of action he wanted in concert with the governors of the Trans-Mississippi. But if he did so, and Davis suddenly appeared, then Kirby Smith looked at best as a panicky usurper and at worst as an outright traitor. After leaving Danville, however, Davis was increasingly out of touch with the rest of the Confederacy and, more importantly, no one outside of Davis's party knew his destination. The presumption among both Union and Confederate commanders was that Davis would attempt to reach the Trans-Mississippi Department and continue the war from there. Earlier, Davis had attributed to the region an ability to maintain the war that did not mesh with reality. He made a virtue of the region's under-developed nature, stating the region was safer from Union attack because it "would not be flanked by rivers or railroads."[7] Some believed Davis might receive European assistance to reach his destination. "It was mentioned, in the gossip of recent European letters," a Cincinnati newspaper reported, "that the rebel iron-clad Stonewall Jackson had left for the coast of Florida, with the presumed purpose of conveying Davis and his family to Europe." The CSS *Stonewall*, constructed in France for the Confederate Navy, did get as far as Cuba, but Spanish authorities impounded the ship on May 24.[8]

Despite not knowing where Davis was, authorities in the Trans-Mississippi pinned all their future hopes on his arrival. In his postwar memoirs, Gov. Henry Allen of Louisiana asserted that "It was believed by many … that Mr. Davis would cross the Mississippi River and come to Texas. If he had done so, there would have been a stand made." Allen's statements, however, were unrealistic memories, as he also incorrectly believed there was "still an army of nearly one hundred thousand men under arms here, and this would have been joined by probably as many more from the East. Most of the men who deserted at the last moment before surrender would have tried to have gotten over. All the 'exchanged prisoners' would have come." Allen was either delusional or misinformed, because there were no massive armies in the department, no way for Cis-Mississippi soldiers to cross the Mississippi, and "exchanged prisoners" would be violating their paroles if they tried to fight again.[9] Brig. Gen. Alexander Terrell was more pragmatic, believing that Davis might make it to Texas but to no purpose since "he could not cross the Mississippi with an army, and, if he came without one to continue the struggle, it could only end in disaster and ruin."[10]

Kirby Smith convened with the state governors at Marshall on May 9. At the first conference in August 1863, Kirby Smith had done his best to assure the local governors that he was not assuming dictatorial powers. At the second conference, when the governors looked for him to take charge and give clear guidance, Kirby Smith also refused to assume dictatorial powers and instead left the future of his department in the governors' hands.[11] For Kirby Smith, at least, the purpose of the conference was clear. It was not to discuss how to continue the war, but rather how the general and the governors could bring the fighting to an end without having to formally surrender to save their own sense of honor and political legitimacy.[12] This was first evident in Kirby Smith's invitation to meet. While recognizing that the "surrender of General Lee and the perilous situation of the armies in North Carolina & Alabama seem to preclude the probability of successful resistance in the States east of the Mississippi," Kirby Smith claimed that the "army under my command yet remains strong, fresh, and well-equipped" and could continue the war under the "perfect concord of the civil and military authorities, the application of all our energies, and the united & devoted support of the people." The main problem, according to Kirby Smith, was the lack of communication with Jefferson Davis. Based on the premise that "the seat of Government of the Confederate States ... may be transferred to the Western side of the Mississippi" when Davis arrived, Kirby Smith was in the position of having to "meet the exigencies of the times, and questions of grave political importance" yet aware that he "should carefully avoid any appearance of usurping functions not entrusted to my discretion." He therefore requested a conference with the governors to "indicate such a policy as you may deem necessary to maintain with honor and success the sacred cause in which we are engaged."[13] These were hardly the words of a commander willing to take charge in time of an obvious emergency.

If Kirby Smith was looking to the state executives for answers, however, he was to be disappointed because the local governments had long-since ceased to be relevant to the ongoing struggle. The governors in the region lacked forceful authority because they lacked support from weak legislatures, the long political dominance by the military in local affairs, the deference of authority to Kirby Smith upon his arrival, and the reliance upon emergency powers to circumvent traditional political controls. The result, when the wartime crisis reached its peak, was a lack of alternative political power, with the legislatures either unable or unwilling to act because they had been ignored for so long and governors who did not govern. The Missouri and

Arkansas legislatures holding sessions in exile in Texas, representing regions occupied by the Union, had become irrelevant by late 1864. The Texas state legislature met for the last time in November 1864, adjourning after debating little and accomplishing even less. Likewise, the Louisiana legislature met for only a brief session in January 1865 before it disbanded under internal pressure. Like their legislatures, the governors were more symbols of authority than exercisers of it. Govs. Thomas Reynolds of Missouri and Harris Flanagin of Arkansas held no more real authority over their occupied states than did their legislatures, and Texas Gov. Pendleton Murrah was hardly a voice of the people after he won the gubernatorial race in August 1863, an election marked by low voter turnout with only 15,000 Texans casting ballots. Only Gov. Henry Allen of Louisiana exercised any real authority, but solely through the force of his own considerable will.[14]

Consequently, when the governors met with Kirby Smith, the participants found it difficult to reach a consensus. Governor Allen of Louisiana offered to go to Washington to discuss surrender terms directly with Lincoln, but both Kirby Smith and Colonel Sprague refused the offer. Governor Reynolds of Missouri sent a mixed message, claiming that the "people & authorities of the territory held by the Confederacy should decide" whether to continue the war or not, but "Should the war be discontinued, we desire time & facilities and supplies to leave the Country with our personal possessions."[15] Governor Murrah of Texas was concerned lest Kirby Smith, who Murrah believed had accumulated too much authority, ignore or overrule his state's interests. He told the legislature just before that conference that "Texas is the only civil power left intact west of the Mississippi River" and "as General E. Kirby Smith is vested with so much power … the executive should have a more reliable means of correspondence" between Murrah and Kirby Smith so that the general's "mind should not be left to impressions obtained through indirect ways as to the interest, the policy, and the condition of the State."[16]

Finally coming to the realization that victory was not possible and Jefferson Davis was not likely to reach the Trans-Mississippi (those meeting did not know Davis had been captured three days earlier), on May 13, the governors issued an unrealistic and naïve set of proposals that, considering the recent controversy of the Sherman/Johnston negotiations, were doomed to fail. The governors demanded that the Union allow all officers and soldiers of the Confederate army to disband without paroles and with their citizenship intact, permit the states to maintain troops to keep order, tolerate the continued operation of the existing state governments until state conventions established new leadership, grant any Confederates who wished the right to leave the country, and agree to a specific date for the withdrawal of all occupation forces before the Confederate Army would officially disband. The notable thing about the demands formulated by the governors is that they protected their own rights and authority above all else. If accepted, the governors would retain a large measure of authority and would be subject to no punitive measures, especially imprisonment or prosecution, for being active leaders of the rebellion.[17]

Upon returning from his conference with the governors, Kirby Smith informed Colonel Sprague of the governors' decision on May 15. His reply included two lengthy documents. The first was the note rejecting Pope's terms that he had written several days before. In his reply to Pope, Kirby Smith asserted "I regret that your communication should have been accompanied with a threat, or that you should have supposed that personal considerations would have influenced me in the discharge of my duties." He further emphasized directly to Sprague that since there was no Union army immediately threatening his department, "the prevailing opinion was that more liberal terms should be granted to the Army of the Trans-Mississippi Department than those accepted by General Lee."[18] The second document listed the terms of surrender generated at the Marshall Conference. He prefaced his introduction to the terms requested by the governors with the premise that the requests were "necessary to the public order, and the proper security of their people," which, if suitable to Pope, "would authorize me to relinquish further resistance."

While Pope considered the matter, Kirby Smith presumed a truce would go into effect and that "aggressive movements against this department should be suspended." In the formal memorandum presented to Sprague, Kirby Smith relied on posture and semantics to bolster his otherwise weak bargaining position. Claiming that his army was "menaced only from a distance," which was true, and that "it is large and well supplied and in an extensive country full of resources," which was false, Kirby Smith asserted it would be dishonorable for him to surrender under Pope's terms because "An army which is well appointed and supplied, not immediately threatened, and with its communications open, cannot afford to surrender." Instead, Kirby Smith reminded Sprague that "Many examples of history teach that the more generous the terms proposed by a victorious enemy the greater is the certainty of a speedy and lasting pacification, and that the imposition of harsh terms leads invariably to subsequent disturbances." If Pope would accept the governors' terms, it would avoid the "impression that there is a wish on the part of the victorious Government not to pacify the country ... but to humiliate a people who have contended gallantly in behalf of principles which they believe to be right."

In presenting the governors' suggested terms, Kirby Smith, with perhaps false confidence, suggested that the "propositions are of a character so reasonable under the circumstances that it is difficult to conceive of any objection" by Union authorities, and tried to control the discourse by asserting "The propositions ... contain terms, which the Trans-Mississippi Department can rightly claim and the United States Government can justly concede." In addition to supplying the terms, Kirby Smith also informed Sprague that Governor Allen had requested permission to accompany Sprague to Pope's headquarters to discuss their terms with the "proper authorities." Sprague, acutely aware of the political storm caused by Sherman's mistake of dealing with Confederate officials, informed Pope that the "application of Governor Allen to accompany me to Washington I did not see fit to comply with."[19] With that, Sprague's mission ended. He began the long journey back to St. Louis, but by the time that he arrived, the Confederates had surrendered to other Union authorities.[20]

****

Although Sprague could not procure a surrender from Kirby Smith, his visit still had a positive outcome from the Union's perspective in that Kirby Smith's negotiations with the colonel created confusion and declining morale among the Confederate Army. When news of Lee's surrender first arrived, Kirby Smith had pledged to his soldiers that he would fight it out. By negotiating with Sprague and not rejecting Pope's peace overture outright, however, many rebel soldiers concluded that Kirby Smith was not being forthright and honest. This was particularly the case in Louisiana, where both Kirby Smith and Governor Allen told the soldiers that they would continue the struggle, but were confounded by rumors that not only Kirby Smith but also Governor Allen were trying arrange some sort of surrender. Fueling the rumors, Allen had begun to sell off state-owned property, both to alleviate the suffering of those in need of state aid and to prevent state property from falling into Union hands.[21] Weak from hunger, penniless due to lack of pay, and bored due to inactivity, troops in Louisiana began to leave almost immediately and in large numbers, with regiments deciding to "disband by the hundreds in open daylight."[22]

The desertion by Louisiana troops was only a small part of the overall process of self-demobilization that was occurring throughout the department, as a once formidable army became only a hollow force in a matter of weeks. On paper at least, Kirby Smith appeared to have a considerable force when Colonel Sprague arrived with his message. Besides the small garrisons in the Rio Grande valley and larger formations in east Texas, Kirby Smith's army occupied a line that stretched from Alexandria, Louisiana, on the Red River through Shreveport to his industrial/logistical center at Marshall, Texas. According to information the Union obtained from a deserter in late April, "Kirby Smith was at Shreveport with a force of 10,000 cavalry and an infantry force of 20,000" although another deserter claimed the number of infantry was closer to 30,000. Overall, Kirby Smith believed his defensive position was more than adequate, claiming in early 1865 that his army was "larger, in finer order, and better supplied than ever" because recent "Crops have been bountiful," meaning the army could "successfully defend their territory for an indefinite period."[23]

If Kirby Smith perhaps overstated his logistical strength, his defenses were in good shape. The Mexican border secured his southern flank, while vast open plains and deserts on the western side of his command did not lend themselves to an overland assault. There were also long approaches to his department via the Arkansas/Indian Territory, regions that had defied numerous Union attacks during the war. The Union Navy could seize coastal towns along the Gulf of Mexico, but would find themselves in isolated pockets surrounded by hostile territory. A Union Army advancing up the only obvious invasion route, another invasion attempt up the Red River, would encounter stiffer opposition in the form of additional forts at Alexandria and the iron-clad CSS *Missouri*.[24]

However, as the Louisiana desertions proved, appearances were deceiving and the army was falling into disarray. In a postwar memoir, Col. John Edwards recalled that by April the army's "Organization, discipline, pride, honor, manhood, dropped speedily away, and the country was filled with innumerable bodies of armed men without leaders and without restraint." Edwards was confounded how "sixty thousand well-armed, well-appointed, well-fed, healthy and well-officered men, with not an enemy nearer than two hundred miles, spontaneously ... and disgracefully surrendered everything, without the exhibition of a single heroic impulse or the exercise of one manly virtue."[25] Other observers were more pragmatic. "There were none in favor of the continuation of the war," Senator William Oldham wrote dejectedly. "They believed that a continuation of the contest would be madness ... and it would be worse than folly, with the small force in the Trans-Mississippi department to maintain a war against the whole military power of the United States."[26]

The collapse of discipline among the troops in Shreveport units and at Alexandria, a vital defensive position blocking Union access to the Red River, exemplified the dissolution of Kirby Smith's military power. Even before the news of Lee's surrender reached the region, the situation in Shreveport was deteriorating, becoming noticeable when "depredations and robberies began to be so prevalent ... that a special patrol ... guarded the city" and "It became dangerous for even General Smith or any staff officers to be caught in the streets at night." By early May, the disillusioning state of the war, the news of Lee's surrender, and rumors that the Union was offering surrender terms "caused a culmination in the excitement" when soldiers bitter at the "hopeless surrender of the cause for which they had fought ... began to leave for home, openly and unmolested." Rumors began to surface that angry soldiers intended to burn and pillage the city, leading officers to collect ammunition and ship it to other locations. By May 19, desertion had decimated most of the Confederate regiments in and around Shreveport, with departing soldiers helping themselves to not only wagons and their teams, but also the contents of the Quartermaster depots. To prevent further widespread disruptions, the next day Major General Buckner issued widespread furloughs, sending the troops home in the hopes of perhaps recalling them at some point in the future, but many soldiers declared they were going home without "furlough, discharge nor parole," rejecting any further obligation to the Army. By the twenty-first, the city was in a state "terrible beyond portrayal," with the streets strewn with ruined supplies and discarded government documents, compounded by the decision to open all the government stores, which caused a riot among the remaining civilians in the city.[27]

The situation in Alexandria was even more dire. The only troops remaining on duty at Alexandria did so under the greatest of reservations because, aware of the lawlessness around them, many feared for the safety of their homes and families.[28] "I regret to be compelled to report that the demoralization of the garrisons of the forts is still progressing," Brig. Gen. Joseph Brent informed Kirby Smith on May 4. "Last night there were nearly fifty desertions." Even worse, the soldiers "took arms and ammunition with them." Brent could only conclude "I think the demoralization has reached such a point as to be beyond the control of the officers," citing as evidence that he had recently received a group of exchanged prisoners, but "twenty-five Missouri soldiers … declined to be exchanged" and remained in Union custody after taking "the oath of allegiance to the Federal Government."[29] Only the officers remained willing to fight. Lt. Col. William Purves of the Third Louisiana Cavalry announced that he would fight because "The gallant Forrest and Wade Hampton have refused to surrender as long as they can get a rebel to follow them," but had to confess that "My men are deserting me daily."[30]

By May 17, the situation had not improved, and Brent instructed the commander of one of his cavalry regiments to "use your own discretion in granting leaves of absence to your men for such time and purpose as you think best consistent with preserving your regimental organization" rather than run the risk of the entire regiment deserting altogether. Brent, facing the reality of the situation, stated to his subordinate that "The fact can no longer be concealed that the whole army and people, with scarce an individual exception, are resolved to fight no more, and to break up the army at all hazards. All is confusion and demoralization here, nothing like order or discipline remains." Breaking up his formations was not an attractive option because "the whole country [is] filled with deserters with arms in their hands." Realizing that "the men are thoroughly demoralized, and all may leave at any moment" to "go home to defend their families," Brent concluded that "violent measures to restrain desertions" would produce "no good results, and would only tend to exasperate the soldiery and cause them to commit many depredations on citizens."

Consequently, Brent could only determine that the "army is destroyed and we must look the matter square in the face and shape our actions (personally and officially) accordingly," and instructed the colonel to consider himself "free to act as you think best." The only thing keeping any of the Confederate troops in position were the rumors of a possible Union advance. On the same day that Brent advised his officers to be generous with their furloughs, Col. William G. Vincent of the Second Louisiana Cavalry, forwarded to Kirby Smith word that "the Sixteenth Army Corps, U.S. Army, is under marching orders at New Orleans for [the] Red River," and postulated that if Sprague's mission was unsuccessful, "they will enter."[31] The Union Army was not preparing such a movement as Vincent feared, but he could do nothing if Grant did decide to send the XVI Corps into the area. On May 19, Vincent informed his superiors that "Everything here … is disorder and confusion" because the "orders and compulsory measures to make the few remaining men do their duty on this front are now at end," he lacked rations for his men, and deserters had stolen his remaining means of transport.[32]

Events in the Trans-Mississippi Department took an even more serious turn when news arrived in mid-May that a significant portion of Kirby Smith's command had unilaterally surrendered to Union troops. At the time that Maj. Gen. M. Jeff Thompson took command of the northern sub-district of Arkansas in March 1865, he was perhaps the poorest Confederate general. Only recently released from a POW camp, his sole possessions were "a pair of borrowed pantaloons … my portfolio and two shirts in a pair of saddlebags."[33] When he reached his new headquarters, he found his estimated ten thousand troops unruly, scattered, and averse to leaving their

families north of the Arkansas River. There were also several bands of guerillas and "independent companies" operating beyond Confederate control, but
Thompson soon eliminated them "for they were irritating the whole people."
He was pleased to report that, when a group of irregulars passed near his
headquarters, "Capt. [Harvey] Richardson and posse turned out and killed
them much to my gratification."[34]

Thompson had barely assumed command when rumors of Lee's surrender
began to circulate among his troops. On April 18, the rumors were confirmed
when Thompson received a letter from Maj. Gen. Joseph Reynolds,
commander of Union troops in Arkansas, offering surrender terms like those
offered to Lee. "If these terms are accepted at once," Reynolds urged, "the
men of your command will yet have time to raise crops this season and
provide for their families during the coming winter."[35] Thompson, although
"women begged me to surrender, old men begged me, some implored with
tears," declined to surrender.[36] After Thompson rebuffed Reynolds, Maj. Gen.
Grenville Dodge, commanding the Department of the Missouri, dispatched
Lt. Col. Charles W. Davis to confer with Thompson. Upon arriving in
Thompson's headquarters, Davis updated the Confederate commander on
the recent Union victories at Mobile, Selma, Columbus, Montgomery, and
Macon.[37] Over the next two days, Thompson obtained clarification from
Davis on a few issues, such as where a possible surrender would take place,
if soldiers could retain their personal property and horses, and if those who
did not wish to live under Union control were free to leave. Satisfied with
Davis's answers, Thompson agreed to surrender.[38]

Having conceded, Thompson took pains to emphasize that he was
compelled to do so to protect civilian property. In a message to Dodge,
Thompson disagreed with the contention that the Confederacy was through,
stating "though dark clouds now obscure our prospects, yet I have every
faith in our ultimate success, and am only induced to surrender now to spare
the people of this already desolated country the horrors of an invasion in
their present condition."[39] Thompson felt the need to justify himself, but the
common soldiers were simply ready to go home and resented that they did
not go sooner. "The thing is going to pieces so fast that one cannot count the
fragments," an officer observed regarding Thompson's troops, finding them

"very much incensed against their officers" for not accepting his earlier offer to accept their surrender "which would have put these men all at home in time to raise a crop this year."[40] As in other regions, deserters and stragglers came out in large numbers for their paroles. Thompson noted "men started to tell others that it was all safe, and soon the hills were filled with squads."[41] The issuing of paroles went smoothly, and a month later Lieutenant Colonel Davis informed General Pope he had paroled 7,454 men (636 officers and 6,818 enlisted men). Davis reported, however, that he had collected very little public property from the Confederates. Emphasizing the weakness of Thompson's force, Davis mentioned that "General Thompson had no transportation, except 300 or 400 dugout canoes, and no public animals or property of any other description," and his only resources was $5,000 in Confederate money. He closed with the observation that the Confederate soldiers "seemed highly pleased at the surrender, and said that all they wanted now was to be allowed to live at home."[42]

Thompson's surrender stunned Kirby Smith, and, with the situation around Shreveport collapsing, he determined the best hope for continued resistance was a concentration of Confederate forces in Texas. To that end, on May 18 Kirby Smith left Shreveport to relocate his headquarters to Houston, leaving General Buckner, his chief of staff, in charge with orders to organize what troops he could and march to Houston when possible. The decision to relocate to Houston, while understandable considering the situation in Shreveport, was disastrous. Because there was no railroad line, Kirby Smith and his staff had to go overland, meaning he was out of touch with events for a full week. Moreover, many soldiers viewed the move as a sign of weakness instead of strength of the military situation, generating rumors that "the General is going to run away" to Mexico.[43] Instead of following Kirby Smith to Texas, for instance, many Arkansas and Missouri troops saw the redeployment as an abandonment of their states to the Union, and consequently began to desert.[44] Two days after Kirby Smith departed, Maj. Gen. James Churchill, commander of Arkansas troops in the department, issued orders to prevent the full dissolution of his command by announcing that liberal "furloughs will be granted all men who desire to go home to cut their wheat" in the hopes that at least some of them might return at a later date rather than lose all of them by desertion.[45]

The news of Kirby Smith's decision also had a negative effect elsewhere in Louisiana. When Kirby Smith and Buckner communicated the relocation plan to Maj. Gen. Henry Hays at Natchitoches and Brig. Gen. Joseph Brent at Alexandria, they were instructed to hold their positions in case the Union assaulted up the Red River again, but only temporarily to preserve their commands and then fall back into Texas. Hays, however, had no faith that his command would stand and fight, and, communicating directly with Brent, advised his subordinate, if Union formations arrived in Alexandria in force, to make his own terms of surrender rather than risk a fighting retreat. Hays's opinion of his own troops was that they were little more than a "lawless mass" who would soon desert whether he ordered them to stay or not.[46] Many other Louisiana troops also fit that description. Some, especially those encamped at Mansfield some miles south of Shreveport, began to desert soon after the news of Lee's surrender arrived. One soldier returned to camp from a detail to find it deserted. Inquiring to the whereabouts of his regiment, the soldier learned that the men had deserted, leaving their weapons behind and "swearing they are going back home regardless of the consequences." A similar determination was reached in the Twenty-sixth Louisiana as most of regiment deserted as it moved from Natchitoches to Mansfield despite the vigilance of its officers. Other Louisianans left when they felt aggrieved. The men of the Third Louisiana, which had maintained its discipline, were incensed when Kirby Smith ordered Arkansas troops to prevent them from deserting. The indignant Louisianans left virtually en masse, taking with them their weapons and many wagons and teams.[47]

If Kirby Smith believed Shreveport to be too disorderly, he found the rest of his department to be no less so. On his journey to Houston, he encountered "mobs of disorderly soldiery, thronging the roads, interrupting travel and making life and property exceedingly insecure." By the time he reached Hempstead, northwest of Houston, Kirby Smith learned that most of the soldiers in East Texas had disbanded and went home on their own initiative. At almost the same time, Magruder reported that his troops along the Rio Grande were doing the same, leaving the state virtually undefended.[48] The disorder in the countryside was so great that it was unsafe for Kirby Smith to travel and he was, as he wrote, "compelled to remain 36 hours in

Huntsville" until it was safe to resume his trip. Upon his arrival in Houston, Kirby Smith found he had no army, and therefore had to request "Governor Murrah to employ State troops still under his control to collect and protect public property."[49]

Kirby Smith soon found that the situation in Houston was, if possible, even worse than that in Shreveport. In Louisiana, soldiers were deserting, but at least they were a not public threat. In the area around Houston, the army only narrowly averted the threat of mutiny. On May 14, the day after Kirby Smith abandoned Shreveport, the garrison at Galveston, about four hundred men, attempted to desert en masse, but their commander, Col. Ashbel Smith, persuaded them to stay. Other troops in the area, as Magruder informed Kirby Smith, "will fight no longer" and endangered the region by refuting any effort by Magruder to "instill a spirit of resistance into the men." Quite the opposite, Magruder reported his efforts to bolster their spirits only resulted in him becoming "antagonistic to the army and an object of their displeasure." The soldiers were determined to divide the military supplies stored in the city amongst themselves and go home, and Magruder could only allow them to go to "induce them to preserve their organization, and to send them in regiments to their homes, with as little damage to the community as possible." Maj. Gen. John Walker added his own concurrence, stating that "my observation convinces me that the troops of this district cannot be relied upon. They consider the contest a hopeless one, and will lay down their arms at the first appearance of the enemy," while his cavalry remained but only because they were "waiting for what they consider the inevitable result, viz, surrender." Rather than risk another possible mutiny, Magruder allowed many of the Confederate troops around Galveston to go home and consolidated those who remained. To Col. Ashbel Smith, Magruder sent instructions to immediately release his "most unmanageable regiment of men," while telling the troops who remained that those "who behave properly shall have honorable discharges … as they have been true to their trusts," implying that the unruly soldiers would receive dishonorable discharges. Magruder also ordered Colonel Smith to reduce the size of his outlying garrisons and transport as much of his supplies as possible to a central location. Smith was to also "spike all guns that cannot be brought away" and was specifically reminded to "not forget the telescope from the observatory."[50] Magruder's efforts were only partially successful at reestablishing order as on May 24 the steamer *Lark*, the last blockade-runner to make it into Galveston, was pillaged by a mob as soon as it tied up to the dock.[51]

Further south, the situation in Brownsville was no better. The day after Kirby Smith abandoned Shreveport for Houston, Brig. Gen. James Slaughter informed Magruder that "great dissatisfaction exists among the troops on this frontier; at least one-half have already or will desert their colors. They say, 'We are whipped. It is useless for the Trans-Mississippi Department to undertake to accomplish what the Cis-Mississippi Department has failed to do.' War meetings have been held, speeches made, but all without the desired effect. Force could not be used, as the rest of the troops could not as a body be depended upon."[52] Concerned that his command might soon become a disruptive mob, Slaughter soon grasped an opportunity to surrender. On May 20, Brig. Gen. Egbert Brown, newly appointed to command of the Union troops in the area, arrived at the mouth of the Rio Grande and sent a party under a flag of truce to sound out Confederate intentions and to assess their strength at Brownsville. The party reported the Confederate troops ready to lay down their arms as they were "anxious for peace and earnestly opposed to any further resistance," especially the cavalry under Col. John Ford, but Brigadier General Slaughter was prepared to continue the war.[53] His men, however, were not. On May 20, Lane's Rangers, the most important unit under Slaughter's command, opted to disband.[54] The disintegration of discipline continued, and, finally realizing the gravity of the situation, on May 25 Slaughter prepared to abandon his command and flee to Mexico, paying his way by selling his cannons to the Imperial commander across the river in Matamoros. Colonel Ford, however, learned of the scheme and forced Slaughter to pay off his troops, who had not seen their wages in months, before allowing him to head south.[55]

As Kirby Smith transited from Shreveport to Houston, state leaders and military subordinates took it upon themselves to negotiate the peace that he had seemed unwilling to undertake. On May 19, Confederate officers at Alexandria reported that Brigadier General Brent had passed the post bound "for the mouth of Red River, to put himself in communication with the Federal authorities, but was rebuffed."[56] On May 22, Arkansas Governor Flanagin sought terms for the state of Arkansas by way of two peace commissioners dispatched to make contact with Union forces, but Union officers declined the offer to talk.[57] On the same day, Texas Governor Murrah and Major General Magruder also unilaterally decided to seek surrender terms for the state of Texas. Instead of rejecting the commissioners, U.S. Navy officers on blockade duty off Galveston granted the peace delegates, Col. Ashbel Smith and William Ballinger, passage to New Orleans. Ignoring the state's recent history, Magruder instructed Smith and Ballinger to seek the "pacification of the State of Texas on the basis of the treaty of 1845, by which she was annexed to the United States."[58] Before Smith and Ballinger reached New Orleans, however, officers with much more authority had already arranged the surrender of the entire department. Leaving Maj. Gen. James Fagan in charge in Shreveport, on May 20 Major General Buckner, Kirby Smith's chief of staff, and Maj. Gen. Sterling Price made their way down the Red River. Collecting Brigadier General Brent on his way back from his failed mission to discuss terms with Canby, Buckner arrived in New Orleans on May 24, ready to talk peace whether Kirby Smith wanted it or not.[59]

Although Buckner claimed Kirby Smith authorized him to discuss terms, there are no orders anywhere telling him to negotiate, and Kirby Smith's instructions when he left Shreveport indicate that he expected Buckner eventually to join him in Houston. Moreover, when Kirby Smith reached Houston he telegraphed Buckner inquiring, "When shall I expect you? Will any troops accompany you?" Considering Kirby Smith sent the telegraph to Shreveport and not New Orleans, it represents the best evidence that Kirby Smith was unaware that his subordinate was discussing terms with Canby. Indeed, Kirby Smith was very surprised when he heard the news that his department had capitulated without his knowledge or permission.[60] Moreover, if Kirby Smith believed that it was time to surrender, he could have accepted the terms offered by Colonel Sprague in Shreveport instead of traveling all the way to Houston to accept the same terms. If Kirby Smith did not give explicit permission for Buckner to negotiate, there seemed to be a presumption of permission in Shreveport. Senator Oldham, traveling through the region after the fall of Richmond, learned that "Gens. Price and Buckner had a few days before

Gen. Simon Buckner (*Image courtesy of the Library of Congress*).

gone down the Red River with authority from Gen. Smith to negotiate with Gen. Canby the terms of surrendering the Trans-Mississippi Department." Senator Oldham did not condemn Buckner for initiating surrender talks, as he summarized the mood of the populace as "the people were prepared to give up the cause. Neither the people nor the soldiers were more inclined to keep up the contest west than east of the river. The war is at an end."[61]

Buckner's decision to surrender the department without conferring with Kirby Smith was only part of the unique nature of this surrender compared to earlier capitulations. The other surrenders occurred in a climate of magnanimity, as a meeting of equals among officers. In Buckner's case, he did not expect such consideration as it was clear that he was the one surrendering. The earlier discussions had at least the tone of negotiations, as exemplified by the meetings on neutral ground between the two armies. Buckner, however, made his way to the enemy's headquarters to ask for terms, a clear sign of a defeated adversary. More importantly, Buckner had no basis of negotiations. Unlike Johnston and Breckinridge, who had prepared proposals to give to Sherman, Buckner came seeking the best terms he could obtain. He did not bring up the suggested surrender terms drafted by the governors in Marshall, nor did he introduce any ideas of his own. Instead, he had only his desire to see the war end as soon as possible.

Upon his arrival, Buckner first conferred with Maj. Gen. Peter Osterhaus, Canby's Prussian-born chief of staff, as Canby was en route from Alabama. Osterhaus must have been somewhat surprised to see Buckner, as just a few days before the Union general related to Canby intelligence that claimed that Buckner intended to "cut himself a way through Texas into Mexico with the more exasperated portion of his army."[62] Osterhaus was not initially convinced that Buckner had the authority to surrender, but, when Buckner convinced him of the sincerity of his mission, found rooms for them at the St. Charles Hotel pending Canby's arrival that afternoon.[63] The meeting between Buckner and Canby, described as "agreeable as possible under the circumstances," was a short one, as there was little to negotiate. Mindful of the controversy from the Sherman/Johnston talks, Canby offered only the terms Grant extended to Lee. With Sherman's recent experience in mind, Canby informed Grant that "I have had a conference to-day with Buckner,

Price, and Brent," but was clear that "I have explained to them that no other terms could be given" other than those given to Lee.[64]

With no leverage of his own, Buckner had no choice but to accept. The meeting was very brief, although Canby requested a meeting later in the evening where Buckner would sign formal documents prepared in the meantime. Like Johnston's surrender, the terms embraced all Confederate military personnel within the jurisdiction of the surrendering force, as well as providing for transportation of all paroled soldiers to their homes. In his discussions with Buckner, Canby had an unexpected ally in Richard Taylor, his former foe in Alabama. When the surrender discussions ended, Canby graciously offered Taylor the opportunity to travel with him to New Orleans so he could reunite with his family. Canby asked Taylor to attend the meetings, both to lend a voice of reason if Buckner should attempt a difficult negotiation and to vouch for Canby's sincerity regarding any terms he might offer. Buckner left no indication of what extent Taylor's presence played in his decision to submit, but it is likely to have convinced him to at least a small degree.[65]

After the meeting ended, Canby immediately informed Grant that the "arrangements for the surrender of the Confederate forces in the Trans-Mississippi Department have been concluded." In addition to dissolving the Confederate forces, the surrender talks also included elements designed to prevent a potential guerilla campaign by reluctant soldiers. Canby informed Grant that Buckner agreed that "Confederate military authorities will use their influence and authority to see that public property in the hands of the agents of the late rebel Government are duly surrendered to the U.S. authorities."[66] When news of the agreement reached the press, editors recalled that Buckner had been the first Confederate general to surrender a substantial force, at Fort Donelson in 1862, making him "the Alpha and the Omega of the downfall of the Confederacy."[67] Public reaction to the surrender in New Orleans was subdued, with no newspaper reports of either celebration or dejection. Canby issued no public statement or orders celebrating the event. General Osterhaus seemed the only Union official elated at the outcome, stating in his memoirs that his participation in the negotiations "will always be a highly valued recollection, that it was my good fortune to see my name under these final agreements."[68]

While some historians have been critical of Buckner, claiming that he surrendered when intact portions of the Confederate Army remained under Kirby Smith's command, the most likely scenario is that Buckner, like Joseph Johnston, was more inclined to spare lives and property than continue a hopeless war. In a letter to his wife, Bucker explained he had to act because the "troops were deserting by divisions, and were plundering the people as well as the government property." Although Buckner stated in the letter "I could not communicate with my commander," he also asserted the "military convention which I negotiated was … a relief to all the parties concerned." He closed the letter by taking a swipe at Kirby Smith by stating that he surrendered with as much dignity as he could muster instead of taking the option to leave "the country at any time in a clandestine manner, it is not suited to what I regard as the true dignity of my character, to sneak out." To Buckner, pragmatism won out over senseless destruction, a decision that was entirely within his character. As his biographer described, "Buckner was, however, never given to chasing moonbeams."[69]

The surrender in the Trans-Mississippi had an odd duality in that while it was largely irrelevant considering the small number of troops left to surrender, it also could not have happened at a better time, because the mass desertions were causing even more chaos. "So far as I know there is not a Confederate soldier in arms in the State," Arkansas Gov. Flanagin wrote a few days later. "The command at Marshall is furloughed. I felt no hesitation in acting as I would act if no such thing as a Confederate force existed. I do not believe that there are 3,000 men under arms in the department."[70] Even after news of the surrender became widely known, the disorder continued for several days until Union troops could establish control. General Brent, upon his return to Alexandria after the surrender, ordered all "Confederate troops on the front lines of the District of West Louisiana … to abstain from all hostilities against the United States," but that did nothing to prevent the troops from disruptive behavior. In Shreveport, the officers of the Eighth Missouri, one of the few intact Confederate units, reported "Disorder reigns supreme. All discipline at an end. Men go when they please, come when they please. Fire their guns as often as, and where they please, and burn as much funds as they wish."[71] In Texas,

Kirby Smith, yet unaware that Buckner had surrendered, informed his chief of staff that the "Texas troops all disbanded. Public property all seized" and that he was to inform "General [Samuel] Cooper commanding Indian Territory of conditions of things and tell him to have the Indians take care of themselves." Many tribes in the Indian Territory had aligned themselves with the Confederacy, most notably the Cherokees under the command of Brig. Gen. Stand Watie, but had suffered badly for their choice. The Confederacy had often failed to supply and support them, and now Kirby Smith was abandoning them to their fate.[72]

The first notice that Kirby Smith most likely received regarding his now-surrendered condition was a note from Canby dated May 27 informing him that he was sending an officer for the purpose of "conferring with you in relation to the details of the terms of the military convention held in this city."[73] Kirby Smith, a general without a command, found he could do nothing but accept the inevitable. In a note dripping with self-pity, Kirby Smith described to Colonel Sprague how in only two weeks his "army of over 50,000 men and a department rich in resources" had evaporated, and he had to admit that "I am now without either. The army in Texas disbanded before my arrival here" after his men "dissolved all military organization, seized the public property, and scattered to their homes." Thus, he could only inform Sprague that his former "department is now open to occupation by your Government. The citizen and soldier alike, weary of war, are ready to accept the authority and yield obedience to the laws of the United States," leaving him powerless to do anything other than request "patient moderation" by the Union Army to "insure peace and secure quiet."[74] The same day, Kirby Smith also issued a self-serving farewell address to his troops that puts the blame for the surrender on their shoulders. He opened the statement by claiming he relocated his headquarters to Houston to concentrate his forces toward achieving an honorable surrender, but their lack of discipline prevented such an outcome. Instead, Kirby Smith complained, "I am left a commander without an army—a General without troops. You have made your choice. It was unwise and unpatriotic, but it is final. I pray you may not live to regret it. The enemy will now possess your country, and dictate his own laws. You have volunteerly [sic] destroyed your organizations, and thrown away all means of resistance." He closed by instructing his men to return to their families and civilian lives and to hope for the best.[75]

However, Kirby Smith still had a task to perform. When Buckner signed the terms of surrender in New Orleans, he insisted that the document was not official until signed by Kirby Smith. The reason is open to debate. Buckner may have simply wanted to follow the chain of command or not want to take the long-term blame for the surrender by having his name affixed to it. His reluctance to assume final responsibility might also be an indicator that he did not have Kirby Smith's permission to negotiate in the first place.[76] The reason Buckner wanted Kirby Smith to agree to the terms was moot because Canby also insisted that an indirect surrender was not enough and the Confederate commander had to sign. Canby directed his staff to send formal surrender documents through the Confederate delegation "to General E.K. Smith for his signature." The USS *Fort Jackson* arrived in Galveston on June 2 with Brig. Gen. Edmund Davis, a Texas Unionist and future governor of the state, to meet with Kirby Smith and obtain his signature, making the surrender official, on June 2.

As with Johnston's eventual surrender terms with Sherman, the signees arranged some last-minute supplemental terms. Union authorities agreed to accept the surrender of all Confederate forces, including the Confederate Navy, within Kirby Smith's jurisdiction, and Kirby Smith agreed, in the interests of public safety, to keep some of his own troops on duty at posts in the interior until Union troops could replace them. Although not written up in the formal agreement, the Confederates also agreed to surrender all forts in the Indian Territory, dispatch commissioners to effect the surrender in remote parts of west Texas and the New Mexico Territory, and designate points where the few Confederate troops still on duty could collect their paroles. On behalf of General Canby, Davis informed Kirby Smith that the Union would immediately release all prisoners of war from Texas, and provide transportation for them to Galveston "with a view of saving them from a long and tiresome march through the country."[77] After signing the document, both Kirby Smith and Magruder expressed concerns about what would happen to them next, but Davis assured them that their paroles protected them from Union retribution and even offered to take them to

New Orleans if they wished. Kirby Smith and Magruder declined, but some members of their staffs accepted the offer.[78]

Like the other surrenders, the dismantling of the Confederate formations was reasonably trouble-free and the reaction of Confederate troops was generally calm. A swirl of rumors surrounded the Johnston and Taylor surrenders, but the average soldier in the Trans-Mississippi knew nothing about the surrender talks until Buckner had already decided their fate. When General Price returned to Shreveport and announced the surrender to his soldiers, he received a mixed response. "Some of the men jump for joy," one of his officer related, "while others curse and gnash their teeth … others are cast down, silent, and dejected."[79] Reaction to the surrender was muted because only well-disciplined troops remained to hear the news. Any soldier inclined to desert had already done so, leaving only those with the personal resolve to stay. As one soldier put it, "I cast my lot with the Confederacy and would go down with her." He was one of the minority that waited for his parole before he could resume his civilian life, albeit "with worse than nothing to begin life with."[80] Railroads were either unavailable or not functioning, so, unlike other surrenders, the Union could not provide much transportation to surrendered Confederates. Paroles in hand, soldiers made their way home the best they could. In the days after the surrender, soldiers "hurried silently, and sadly homeward," an observer noted, "not to receive the triumphant greeting … but to be greeted with sadness and tears."[81]

As most of the army had already returned home, the number of paroles issued in the Trans-Mississippi was relatively low. Union officers at Shreveport issued the most paroles, 15,000, with only about 2,500 paroles issued elsewhere. General Buckner, like Joseph Johnston, stayed to assist with the paroling, which considerably aided the process. Under the direction of Maj. Gen. Francis Herron, the Union commissioners began issuing paroles on June 8 and receiving all surrendered military property, including "Twenty-one pieces of artillery and 500 stand of small-arms." Because of the pillaging of military warehouses in Shreveport, Herron believed that "There will be but little public property turned over aside from artillery and ordnance stores," although he praised the efforts of Buckner and other senior officers to comply with the surrender terms. In addition to paroling the Confederate troops,

Herron was also busy getting essential infrastructure working, informing his superiors that "The stage routes are mostly operating, and in a few days the telegraph will be at work to Galveston, Camden, and other points."[82]

The only major issue was the transfer of Union troops to remote locations, but the Confederates complied with their obligations in this matter. In the Rio Grande valley, Confederate officers, including Col. John Ford in Brownsville, supervised the paroles of their men and maintained order.[83] At the same time, Brig. Gen. Henry McCulloch, commanding the North Sub-district of Texas, instructed the frontier defense regiments to maintain their positions until relieved by Union cavalry, but told all other troops to go home stating that their ad hoc furloughs "will be regarded as a permanent discharge."[84] For individual Confederate soldiers, the surrender meant only uncertainty. "It is rather a discouraging thing to have arrived at my age, and to find myself turning grey, getting toothless, and wrinkled, and not to have done anything or made anything in the world," a disheartened Confederate officer wrote, aspiring for himself only "a home, a wife, and five or ten million dollars."[85] Other soldiers would have been content with much less. "I am without money or clothing," a demoralized soldier told his family. "The money that I was to get … was to be paid in Confederate money, so it is no use."[86]

****

Kirby Smith's surrender opened the door for Federal troops to occupy Texas without having to resort to invasion, but the supervision of Texas was a reluctant duty for many Northern soldiers. Union troops began to hear rumors that they might deploy to the Trans-Mississippi Department only days after the other Confederate armies surrendered. "We have had several rumors in camp about being discharged," a Massachusetts artilleryman wrote to his family, "but there is a rumor about going to Texas."[87] At least some troops favored the move as a demonstration against French interests in the New World. "Woe be to Mexico when he opposes American soldiers," an Indiana soldier wrote in his diary. "We will teach the frog eaters what fighting is."[88] Most Union troops, however, were not enthusiastic about going westward instead of home. When soldiers of the Seventy-seventh Illinois were "ordered to draw … clothing sufficient for a two month campaign," a member of the regiment observed "we were not pleased with this order as we had thought our campaigning was done."[89] A cavalryman voiced the opinion of many when he complained, "I enlisted for the war, and now that it is over I am desirous of leaving the service" rather than "make triumphal marches over a played out Confederacy."[90] Other Union troops believed they were included in the expedition only because ambitious officers sought promotions. "We soon learned that some of our officers are anxious to go to Texas, and were trying to hold the regiment for such service," a Michigan soldier related. "I tell you we protested, and gave them to understand that we would make them rue the day they ever took us off down there."[91] Understandably, troops that headed home instead of Texas were happy at the news. "About noon we heard that we were not going to Texas," an artilleryman wrote. "This caused a great deal of rejoicing in the Battery."[92]

Although prepared for a fight, the Union troops that arrived in the Trans-Mississippi under the command of Maj. Gen. Philip Sheridan were an army of peacetime occupation. Sheridan ordered Maj. Gen. Gordon Granger, upon his arrival at Galveston, to "carry out the conditions of the surrender of General Kirby Smith to Major-General Canby." He was also to "notify the people of Texas that … all slaves are free" and "all acts of the Governor and Legislature of Texas since the ordinance of secession are illegitimate."[93] The first Union troops, from Maj. Gen. Andrew Smith's XIII Corps, arrived on June 19. The locals responded with little attention, other than to remark "their conduct is orderly and credible to themselves as well as their officers, and we trust our citizens will have no occasion to regret their presence."[94]

As Federal troops spread out to occupy the rest of the region, they encountered sullen but passive expressions from civilians, and soon settled into the tedium of occupation duty. Bored U.S. troops at Brownsville sought entertainment in Matamoros, but "got drunk, in fact, abusing the Mexican Guards & police," causing Mexican authorities to bar U.S. troops from the town. One of their officers was pleased with the order as he thought the locals were "the very scum of the earth—criminals, renegades from all nations, and the worst of them are the run-away 'Yankees' … a mean set of cut-throats." The search for leisurely activity was not surprising. The same officer was extremely bored, telling his wife "We have nothing going on to relieve the monotony."[95] In addition, Union troops in Texas faced numerous issues: harsh weather conditions and associated health problems, shoddy accommodations, unreliable mail service, and poor water and rations. Union troops, especially USCT regiments in the XXV Corps, were also the targets of civilian violence.[96] A Galveston newspaper noted one such instance, stating "the sentence of Edward Cantwell, a paroled prisoner, has been commuted from hanging to imprisonment for ten years. Cantwell, some time since, got into a difficulty with some negroes, and in the course of the altercation he stabbed one of the negroes, a United States soldier … from the effect of the wound the negro died."[97] A former Confederate residing in Logansport, Texas, on the Sabine River, acknowledge that the locals had to "adjust ourselves to the new order of things" when a company of USCT troops arrived on occupation duty.[98]

Some Union soldiers, unhappy at their prolonged duty, despaired that they might ever get home. In August, a bored Private Washington Carson of the Forty-second Illinois wrote his fiancé, Kate, that "Texas can't boast of anything but cattle." By October, Carson regretfully told Kate that "There is no sign of our getting out of the army. Sometimes I almost think that we won't be mustered out this winter," blaming the situation on officers who "want to stay in the service, for they are making more money now than they could if they were at home" and spend their time "drinking whiskey and enjoying themselves." Carson did not finally return home until the Forty-second mustered out in November and the unit disbanded January 10, 1866.[99]

As Union troops occupied the Trans-Mississippi Department, some Confederates were leaving it. Johnston, Taylor, and other Confederate generals had surrendered only after military clashes convinced them it was time to submit. When they did surrender, the generals stayed to share the fate of their troops. In the Trans-Mississippi, with no final climactic battles or even any Union troops prepared for immediate offensive action, the Confederate surrender triggered an exodus of senior leaders into Mexico. Because the Confederacy surrendered more to internal collapse rather than Union military pressure, leaders could salve their pride by asserting that they themselves had not given up, but could not make such a claim as Union troops occupied the region. The only solution was to leave, thus allowing the preservation of honor without a form of personal submission. Among the exiles into Mexico were senior leaders of the state governments and military. By June 1865, Generals Edmund Kirby Smith, John Magruder, James Slaughter, Jo Shelby, John Walker, Alexander Terrell, Thomas Hindman, and Commodore Matthew Maury, along with Governors Isham Harris, Thomas Reynolds, and Pendleton Murrah, had fled to Mexico, some after harrowing journeys.[100] The largest contingent that went to Mexico were the troops under the command of Brig. Gen. Jo Shelby. The number of enlisted men who accompanied Shelby is uncertain, as sources range from several hundred to as few as 150. Shelby's route to Mexico took him through San Antonio, which became an assembly point for those heading south. "Fugitive generals had gathered there," a Confederate officer wrote, "and fugitive senators and fugitive governors and fugitive desperadoes, we all, men sententious of speech and quick of pistol practice."[101]

After a harrowing journey though Texas, the party crossed into Mexico and marched to Monterrey, the largest city in northern Mexico. From there, most of the fugitives continued to Mexico City, but Kirby Smith headed to Vera Cruz and took a steamer to Cuba. He was relieved to be a private citizen again, writing to his wife "The weight of cares & responsibilities taken from my shoulders makes me almost a new man." Although safe in Cuba, Kirby Smith made inquiries if it was safe for him to return. He wrote to Ulysses Grant seeking special consideration regarding his desire to return to the United States, and Grant, after consulting President Johnson, offered the same parole terms given to his troops. Accepting the parole, Kirby Smith returned home in November 1865.[102] The rest of the group arrived in Mexico City at the behest of Emperor Maximilian, who wished to determine the intentions of the former Confederates. Many sought appointments in the Mexican Army, but the Emperor, who believed Juarez was nearly defeated, declined their offer of service.[103] Although unwilling to employ them in his army, Maximilian was uncertain what to do with the Confederates in his empire. They could prove a useful counterweight to both the U.S. and Juarez's rebels, but harboring the Confederates reduced the chance that the U.S. would recognize Maximilian's legitimacy in Mexico.[104] Therefore, Maximilian took an approach that did not force the exiles to leave, but did not provoke the United States. The Emperor offered the Confederates land at favorable terms in a region east of Mexico City where they could engage in plantation farming. Most of the exiles took the offer, establishing a colony named Carlotta, after the Emperor's wife. The enterprise was not a success, however, largely due to Maximilian's declining fortunes. The French were withdrawing their troops from Mexico, allowing Juarez to regain the upper hand in the struggle for power. Within months, the Mexican government fell and Maximilian was a prisoner. Denied their protector, most of the exiled Confederates returned to the United States, accepted their paroles, and tried to resume their lives.[105]

****

All the Confederate generals endured criticism for their actions, both by historians later assessing the war and fellow Southerners as the Lost Cause mythology sought to explain away Confederate defeats. In the assessment of who or what led to Confederate defeat, however, Edmund Kirby Smith's name is strangely absent. Considering his unique position of department military commander and practical military leader over such a large portion of Confederate territory, few of the significant studies on why the Union won the war or the Confederacy lost it make any significant mention of Kirby Smith. If histories do mention Kirby Smith, it is in reference to his early Cis-Mississippi campaigns or authorization of raids such as those conducted by Sterling Price in 1864.[106] Only specific biographies of the general provide the lengthy analysis of Kirby Smith's decisions and leadership that the general histories view as largely irrelevant to the demise of the Confederacy. The aforementioned Cincinnati newspaper reporter who proclaimed in 1865 that the clash between Grant and Lee would hold the public's imagination was more accurate than he believed. Edmund Kirby Smith, the general who not only commanded but virtually ruled over a vast portion of the Confederacy, is little known and his faults and virtues largely forgotten. His decisions, for good or ill, determined the fate of thousands of square miles of Confederate territory, and, leading the last Confederate army to surrender, faded into history, obscured by the familiar image from Appomattox.

Conclusion

"The Confederacy only exists in the history of the past. I would have stood by her flag, but we, our courage and patriotism to the contrary not withstanding, are beaten, whipped, and have no alternative but to surrender."[1]

With the surrender of Kirby Smith's army, the Union government began the process of tidying up the remaining extraneous issues from the war. The paroling of isolated pockets of Confederate troops continued until mid-June, when Secretary of War Stanton informed President Johnson that the last Confederate troops in the field had received their papers to go home.[2] The Union also set about releasing and transporting the thousands of Confederate POWs held in northern camps. Brig. Gen. William Hoffman, the Union Commissary-General of Prisoners, initially proposed that each camp release fifty men per day to avoid the disorder like that caused by the unsupervised parole of Lee's troops. If approved, Hoffman informed Grant that he could empty the seventeen POW camps under his jurisdiction of their 50,000 inhabitants in less than sixty days.[3] Grant approved the plan, and instructed Hoffman to release first "those who have been longest in prison and from the most remote points of the country," and all would receive transportation "to the nearest accessible point to their homes, by rail or by steamboat."[4] By July, however, a considerable number of POWs remained, so the War Department instructed Hoffman he was to "proceed immediately to discharge all the prisoners of war of the rebel Army and Navy."[5]

Enlisted men returned to their homes relatively quickly, but Johnson complicated the process when he issued an order exempting from parole high-ranking Southern military officers and civilians that fell under fourteen different categories, including antebellum graduates from the nation's military academies, prewar military officers and elected officials who left their positions to join the rebellion, and those whose property exceeded $20,000 in value. These prominent Southerners had to apply to Johnson for a presidential pardon, explaining why Johnson should grant them one.

If approved, the pardon included a requirement that the applicant make an oath of allegiance.[6] Some senior officers balked at the terms, but in the end accepted the reality of the situation. Maj. Gen. Dabney Maury initially refused to swear an oath because he did not regret his wartime service, but decided that Confederate officers should set an example to their men in peace as they had in war. Like his men, Maury decided to "take the oath and go to work."[7] Lt. Gen. Nathan Bedford Forrest shared Maury's attitude, and as soon as President Johnson appointed William L. Sharkey governor in Mississippi, Forrest applied for parole.[8] Receiving paroles, however, did not mean the former Confederate leaders were free from Union control, especially when they tried to assert influence as civilians. When state officials, for instance, nominated former Adm. Raphael Semmes to serve as a probate judge in Mobile, Gen. George Thomas, supervising Reconstruction in the district, refused to permit his appointment. Although subsequently criticized for imposing the parole terms, Johnson did limit the potential ramifications by defining some wartime actions considered treasonous in other circumstances to go unpunished.[9]

The hesitancy to allow former Confederate officers to wield any sort of influence was a byproduct of Union reactions to late-war state policies. As the Confederacy collapsed, many state governors attempted to maintain their legitimacy by reconvening the state legislatures and continuing to administer their states even as Union military units arrived as wartime invaders or postwar occupiers. Universally, the War Department issued orders to Union commanders to prevent such political action to the point of arresting anyone who tried to govern without military approval. In Georgia, for example, Gen. James Wilson, when occupying Macon, had to suppress Gov. Joseph Brown when he tried to call the legislature into session, bypassing Wilson by asking the Johnson administration for instructions regarding postwar policy, and browbeating the general. In instructions to Wilson, Stanton, declaring that "restoration of peace and order cannot be intrusted [*sic*] to rebels and traitors who destroyed the peace," told Wilson to take "prompt measures to prevent any assemblage of rebels as a Legislature," including arresting anyone he deemed necessary. On May 9, Wilson obeyed the orders and arrested Governor Brown, a fate shared by all the sitting Confederate governors who had not fled the country.[10] Johnson clarified the situation relative to the Confederate state executives on May 9, when he issued an executive order declaring all laws of the Confederate government, including the certification of state elections, to be invalid.[11] Johnson justified the removal of elected officials and imposition of government-approved governors based upon a legal opinion from James Speed, his Attorney General. Speed concluded that the "rebellion and treason" of the Confederate states left the Federal government with the obligation to "declare their late State organization a nullity."[12]

In other areas, Johnson also moved quickly to normalize the nation, particularly efforts to restore property rights and reestablish the national economy. In May, the Treasury Department ceased seizing property of Confederates who had not paid taxes since the war began, and in June lifted restrictions on trade between the regions except for items still considered contraband. The Union seizure of abandoned property also ended by federal fiat in the same month.[13] Also in May, Johnson appointed to the occupied states the federal bureaucrats, such as tax collectors, customs officials, postal workers, and federal judges, needed to restore antebellum governance.[14] In June, the President formally lifted the blockade and allowed unrestricted trade in all American ports.[15] It was not until more than a year later, however, that Johnson formally declared the end of all hostilities, on August 20, 1866.[16]

Another topic that Johnson had to address was the French occupation of Mexico, and, even more pressing, Ulysses Grant's determination to remove the French by force. Grant viewed the foreign occupation of Mexico as a violation of the Monroe Doctrine and believed that the French-imposed regime had not remained neutral during the Civil War and had engaged in actions hostile to U.S. interests.[17] With the Confederacy defeated, Grant was free to act on his beliefs. He immediately dispatched to the Mexican border a large force under the command of Maj. Gen. Philip Sheridan, ostensibly to occupy the Trans-Mississippi Department but also prepared to engage Imperial forces if necessary. Sheridan shared Grant's views on the French presence in Mexico, stating, "I have always believed that the occupation of Mexico was a part of the rebellion; and I believing that the contest in our own country was for the vindication of republicanism, I did not think that that vindication would be complete until Maximilian was compelled to leave."[18]

Sheridan was also familiar with the Rio Grande Valley. After he graduated from West Point, his first service post was with the First Infantry Regiment at Fort Duncan, near Eagle Pass, Texas.[19] To demonstrate his resolve, Grant allocated to Sheridan a force of up to 80,000 troops. In addition to the XIII and XVI Corps from Canby's command, Grant allocated to Sheridan XIX Corps from Pope's command, the IV Corps from George Thomas's Army of the Cumberland, the XXV Corps from Maj. Gen. George Meade's Army of the Potomac, and two cavalry brigades.[20]

Sheridan wasted no time in making his presence felt. After visiting Brownsville to see the situation on the border firsthand, Sheridan dispatched scouts into Mexico to provide additional intelligence information and ordered the local commander, Gen. Frederick Steele, to "make demonstrations all along the lower Rio Grande" to show the Imperialists the military strength he had at his disposal.[21] Sheridan also encouraged rumors that he was there to invade Mexico, prompting wild claims that he was merely "awaiting the arrival of the troops … at San Antonio, to cross the Rio Grande on behalf of the Liberal cause." Sheridan reinforced the stories with less than subtle inquiries into the "quantity of forage we could depend upon getting in Mexico" and the repositioning of a "pontoon train to Brownsville." At Grant's suggestion, Sheridan ordered his ordnance officers to "condemn" thousands of rifles and "abandon" them along the banks of the Rio Grande where Juarez's troops could easily claim them.[22]

By mid-June, Grant could report to the President that, among other provocations, French troops had fired on Sheridan's men, and asserted that the false Mexican government was engaged in "hostility against the Government of the United States." Raising the concern that veteran Confederate troops might bolster Maximilian's armies, Grant urged Johnson to sanction military action that would "protect against the establishment of a monarchical government in Mexico by the aid of foreign bayonets."[23] Grant initially seemed to sway the Johnson to his way of thinking, but Grant did not anticipate the influence of Secretary of State William Seward. Throughout the war, Seward had feared a formal alliance between France and the Confederacy and believed an overly aggressive posture toward the French presence in Mexico might trigger such an alliance. He therefore took a cautious approach, making the French aware that the U.S. did not condone their presence but not pushing the issue to the point of insulting the French. While this cautious approach clashed with the more direct personas of Grant and Sheridan, Seward successfully stymied any French/Confederate alliance by skillfully dangling the one prize that the French wanted most of all—the recognition of Maximilian's rule by the U.S. government.[24] With the war over, Seward believed a cautious approach was the best method to deal with the situation in Mexico. Informed by sources in Europe, Seward was convinced that France was determined to cut its losses in Mexico, and military action was unnecessary to remove them or maintain the Monroe Doctrine. Unlike Grant, he had no philosophical opposition to Maximilian. If the Mexican people did not want him as a leader, Seward reasoned, then they should remove him themselves. Moreover, Seward believed that American interference in Mexico was just as undesirable as European interference in the Civil War. The best course, Seward believed, was continued delegitimization of Maximilian's reign, believing that "Grant's proposals would … wound French pride and produce a war with France."[25]

Seward soon found a way to forestall Grant's military plans. The general had developed a close relationship with Matías Romero, Juarez's ambassador to the U.S., and the two men had discussed the nature of any American military incursion against Maximilian. Grant initially envisioned William Sherman leading the army, but he declined. Sheridan was Grant's second choice, but he was already committed to the occupation of Texas. Grant and Romero next approached John Schofield, but Schofield drove a hard bargain. Concerned about both his position in the U.S. Army and his reputation should the expedition fail, Schofield made demands. He would act only if assured of a leave of absence from the U.S. Army; he would not resign his commission in case he was out of work a few months later. Schofield accepted Romero's officer of a salary of $100,000 to lead the American volunteers in Mexico, but Schofield wanted it all up front, not just for himself but for all senior officers whom he might appoint. Romero resisted Schofield's demand for command of all Mexican military forces by reaching a compromise where Schofield would lead any forces that the Mexican government chose to put under his command.[26]

By August 1865, Schofield was ready to go to Texas to assume command of the troops that Grant believed would soon liberate Mexico, but Seward acted first by poaching Schofield. Playing on Schofield's vanity, Seward convinced him to undertake a mission to Paris to confer with Napoleon III about the situation in Mexico, knowing that Napoleon would not discuss the issue with him in person, as formal diplomatic discussions had to go through the American ambassador. Before heading to Europe, however, Seward recommended that Schofield conduct a fact-finding mission to Texas to assess the situation so that he might have first-hand knowledge of what was going on there, a task that would itself take at least several weeks before his European mission would even start. Romero, in addition to seeing his plans derailed, was disappointed that "Schofield does not recognize Seward's real purpose" of defeating Grant's objectives in Mexico.[27] Schofield, filled with Seward's flattery, conducted his tour of the Mexican frontier before taking passage to France, where Napoleon III paid him but scant notice. Eventually he returned home, but the chance to lead a victorious army into Mexico had passed.[28] By the following spring, Seward's patient approach had proved successful. In May 1866, Napoleon III announced that he would withdraw all of his troops from Mexico to reinforce metropolitan France in the face of growing Prussian influence, and the last French soldiers departed on November 13.[29] Left without his European patron, Maximilian's government collapsed months later, and the captured Emperor died before a firing squad in June 1867.[30]

****

The tragic war that cost more than 600,000 lives, and damaged the health of tens of thousands more, was finally over. Two and half million slaves, now described as freedmen, found themselves residents of a different country than the one they had always known, one where their place was uncertain but their futures seemed, at least for the moment, full of opportunity. The once prosperous economy was in ruins and would need years to recover. The South was now occupied territory, with victorious Union troops, many of them African American, policing every major city and transportation route. The Confederacy had failed as a political, military, and cultural experiment. Reality, however, proved to be malleable. In the years after the war, the Lost

Cause mythology put a very different veneer on Confederate failures. Interpersonal clashes, poor strategic plans, and bad leadership disappeared from the memory of the Confederate Army, just as the deficiencies of Jefferson Davis's leadership evolved into tales of sage executive decisions. The internal divide and sagging morale of the demoralized populace gave way to fables of the diehard Confederate home front who stoically sacrificed to keep the cause of independence alive. These mistruths find their way into that familiar image from Appomattox. Nowhere in the picture are the hungry civilians fearful of raids by foraging soldiers of both sides, the masses of demoralized soldiers who deserted, or the dead from battles fought after the outcome of the war was long decided. Instead, the historical memory of Confederate capitulation is the clean and tidy image, represented by Lee's dignified visage, which hides the messy and complicated reality of Confederate defeat.

Endnotes

Notes for Preface

1. Joseph E. Johnston, *Narrative of Military Operations during the Civil War* (New York: Appleton, 1874). Craig L. Symonds, *Joseph Johnston: A Civil War Biography* (New York: Norton, 1992). Richard Taylor, *Destruction and Reconstruction: Personal Experiences of the Late War* (New York: Appleton, 1879). T. Michael Parrish, *Richard Taylor: Soldier Prince of Dixie* (Chapel Hill: University of North Carolina Press, 1992).
2. Robert L. Kerby, *Kirby Smith's Confederacy: The Trans-Mississippi South, 1863–1865* (New York: Columbia University Press, 1972). Joseph H. Parks, *General Edmund Kirby Smith, C.S.A.* (Baton Rouge: Louisiana State University Press, 1954).
3. Drew Gilpin Faust, *The Creation of Confederate Nationalism: Ideology and Identity in the Civil War South* (Baton Rouge: Louisiana State University Press, 1988).
4. Richard E. Beringer, Herman Hattaway, Archer Jones, and William N. Still, Jr., *Why the South Lost the Civil War* (Athens: University of Georgia Press, 1986).
5. Sarah Anne Rubin, *A Shattered Nation: The Rise and Fall of the Confederacy, 1861–1868* (Chapel Hill: University of North Carolina Press, 2005).
6. Gary W. Gallagher, *The Confederate War: How Popular Will, Nationalism, and Military Strategy Could Not Stave Off Defeat* (Cambridge, Massachusetts: Harvard University Press, 1997).
7. Richard N. Current, *Lincoln's Loyalists: Union Soldiers from the Confederacy* (Boston: Northeastern University Press, 1992).
8. William W. Freehling, *The South vs. the South: How Anti-Confederates Southerners Shaped the Course of the Civil War* (New York: Oxford University Press, 2001).
9. Kenneth W. Noe, *Reluctant Rebels: The Confederates Who Joined the Army after 1861* (Chapel Hill: University of North Carolina Press, 2010).
10. Stephen V. Ash, *When the Yankees Came: Conflict and Chaos in the Occupied South, 1861–1865* (Chapel Hill: University of North Carolina, 1995).
11. Herman Hattaway and Richard E. Beringer, *Jefferson Davis, Confederate President* (Lawrence: University Press of Kansas, 2002). David J. Eicher, *Dixie Betrayed: How the South Really Lost the Civil War* (New York: Little & Brown, 2006).

12. Joseph H. Parks, *Joseph E. Brown of Georgia* (Baton Rouge: Louisiana State University Press, 1977).

13. Douglas B. Ball, *Financial Failure and Confederate Defeat* (Urbana: University of Illinois Press, 1991). Stanley Legergott, "Why the South Lost: Commercial Purpose in the Confederacy, 1861–1865," *Journal of American History* 70, no. 1 (June 1983): 58–74.

14. Thomas L. Connelly and Archer Jones, *The Politics of Command: Factions and Ideas in Confederate Strategy* (Baton Rouge: Louisiana State University Press, 1973). Mark Grimsley and Brooks D. Simpson, eds., *The Collapse of the Confederacy* (Lincoln: University of Nebraska Press, 2001).

Notes for Introduction

1. Edward A. Pollard, *The Lost Cause: A New Southern History of the War of the Confederates* (New York: E.B. Treat, 1867), 726.

2. Robin Wagner-Pacifici, *The Art of Surrender: Decomposing Sovereignty at Conflict's End* (Chicago, IL: University of Chicago Press, 2005), 66. Neff, 203 and 207. *New York Times*, April 12, 1865.

3. Jeremi Suri, *Liberty's Surest Guardian: Rebuilding Nations after War from the Founders to Obama* (New York: Simon & Schuster, 2012), 47.

4. John D. Waghelstein and Donald Chisholm, "The Road Not Taken: Conflict Termination and Guerrillaism in the American Civil War," *Journal of Strategic Studies* 29, no. 5 (October 2006): 900.

Notes for Chapter 1

1. Stephanie McCurry, *Confederate Reckoning: Power and Politics in the Civil War South* (Cambridge, MA: Harvard University Press, 2010), 359.

2. See Richard E. Beringer, Herman Hattaway, Archer Jones, and William N. Still, Jr., *Why the Confederacy Lost* (Athens: University of Georgia Press, 1986) or Anne Sarah Rubin, *A Shattered Nation: The Rise and Fall of the Confederacy, 1861–1865* (Chapel Hill: University of North Carolina Press, 2005).

3. Paul D. Escott, "The Failure of Confederate Nationalism: The Old South's Class System in the Crucible of War," in Harry P. Owens and James J. Cooke, *The Old South in the Crucible of War* (Jackson: University of Mississippi Press, 1983), 20.

4. Richard M. McMurry, "The Enemy at Richmond: Joseph E. Johnston and the Confederate Government," *Civil War History* 27, no. 1 (March 1981): 11.

5. George C. Rable, *The Confederate Republic: A Revolution Against Politics* (Chapel Hill: University of North Carolina Press, 1994), 278.
6. Alexander H. Stephens, *Recollections of Alexander H. Stephens* (New York: Doubleday, 1910), 327–328.
7. Edward S. Cooper, *Louis Trezevant Wigfall: The Disintegration of the Union and Collapse of the Confederacy* (Madison, NJ: Fairleigh-Dickinson University Press, 2012), 124–125. James C. Clark, *Last Train South: The Flight of the Confederate Government from Richmond* (Jefferson, NC: McFarland, 1984), 30–31.
8. John H. Moore, "The Rives Peace Resolution—March, 1865," *West Virginia History* 26, no. 2 (April 1865): 159–160.
9. Paul D. Escott, "Joseph E. Brown, Jefferson Davis, and the Problem of Poverty in the Confederacy," *Georgia Historical Quarterly* 61, no. 1 (Spring 1977): 60.
10. Beth G. Crabtree and James W. Patton, *Journal of a Secesh Land: The Diary of Catherine Ann Devereaux Edmonston, 1860–1866* (Raleigh, NC: Department of Cultural Resources, 1979), 658. Carl Sandburg, *Abraham Lincoln: The Prairie Years and the War Years* (New York: Houghton, Mifflin & Harcourt, 2002), 622.
11. Timothy B. Smith, *Mississippi in the Civil War: The Home Front* (Jackson: University Press of Mississippi, 2010), 187.
12. *London Morning Star*, June 4, 1867.
13. Harry N. Scheiber, "The Pay of Troops and Confederate Morale in the Trans-Mississippi West," *Arkansas Historical Quarterly* 18, no. 4 (Winter 1959): 355.
14. Malcolm C. McMillan, *The Disintegration of a Confederate States: Three Governors and Alabama's Wartime Home Front, 1861–1865* (Macon, GA: Mercer University Press, 1986), 125–126.
15. John E. Johns, *Florida during the Civil War* (Gainesville: University of Florida Press, 1963), 96.
16. Joseph W. Danielson, *War's Desolating Scourge: The Union's Occupation of North Alabama* (Lawrence: University Press of Kansas, 2012), 127 and 139. McMillan, 114–115.
17. Leo E. Huff, "The Martial Law Controversy in Arkansas, 1861–1865: A Case Study of Internal Confederate Conflict, *Arkansas Historical Quarterly* 37, no. 2 (Summer 1978): 160.
18. Kenneth C. Martis, *Historical Atlas of the Congresses of the Confederate States* (New York: Simon & Schuster, 1994), 85 and 87.
19. *The War of the Rebellion: A Compilation of the Official Records of the Union and Confederate Armies*, 130 vols. (hereafter as ORA) (Washington, DC: Government Printing Office, 1880–1901), Series 1, Volume 42, Part 3, 1275.

20. Isaac W. Avery, *The History of the State of Georgia from 1850 to 1881: Embracing the Three Important Epochs: The Decade Before the War of 1861–5; the War; the Period of Reconstruction* (New York: Brown and Derby, 1881), 47.

21. Allan D. Candler, *Confederate Records of Georgia* (Atlanta, GA: Byrd, 1909), 3: 89 and 738–739. Thomas R. Hay, "Joseph Emerson Brown, Governor of Georgia, 1857–1865," *Georgia Historical Quarterly* 13, No. 2 (June 1929): 93–94.

22. Paul D. Escott, *Many Excellent People: Power and Privilege in North Carolina, 1850–1900* (Chapel Hill: University of North Carolina Press, 1985), 39. ORA, Series 4, Volume 3, Part 1, 690–692. David D. Scarboro, "North Carolina and the Confederacy: The Weakness of States' Rights during the Civil War," *North Carolina Historical Review* 56, no. 2 (April 1979): 133.

23. Rable, 279–280.

24. ORA, Series 1, Volume 6, Part 1, 342 and Volume 53, Part 1, 212–213. *Journal of the Proceedings of the Senate of the General Assembly of the State of Florida at the Thirteenth Session* (Tallahassee, FL: Florida Sentinel, 1864), 32. Daisy Parker, "John Milton, Governor of Florida: A Loyal Confederate," *Florida Historical Quarterly* 20, no. 2 (April 1942): 356–360. McMillan, 113–114. William M. Robinson, Jr., *Justice in Gray: A History of the Judicial System of the Confederate States of America* (Cambridge, MA: Harvard University Press, 1941), 191. Johns, 122, 205, and 212.

25. John M. Sacher, "Our Interests and Destiny are the Same: Gov. Thomas Overton Moore and Confederate Loyalty," *Louisiana History* 49, no. 3 (Summer 2008): 265–266 and 271–272. ORA, Series 1, Volume 6, Part 1, 869.

26. Lynda L. Crist, *The Papers of Jefferson Davis, Volume 7* (1861) (Baton Rouge: Louisiana State University Press, 1992), 331–332. Edward S. Cooper, *Traitors: The Secession Period, November 1860-July 1861* (Madison, NJ: Fairleigh Dickinson University Press, 2008), 50–61. *New York Times*, March 4, 1861. John D. Winters, *The Civil War in Louisiana* (Baton Rouge: Louisiana State University Press, 1991), 64. Ezra J. Warner, *Confederates in Gray: Lives of the Confederate Commanders* (Baton Rouge: Louisiana State University Press, 1987), 194–195. ORA, Series 1, Volume 15, Part 1, 504–510.

27. Douglas B. Ball, *Financial Failure and Confederate Defeat* (Urbana: University of Illinois Press, 1991), 162–163. E. Merton Coulter, *The Confederate States of America, 1861–1865* (Baton Rouge: Louisiana State University Press, 1950), 62–63.

28. Gary M. Pecquet, "State Finances in Arkansas, 1860–1865," *Arkansas Historical Quarterly* 48, no. 1 (Spring 1989): 68. Ball, 119.

29. Richard L. Zuber, *Jonathan Worth: A Biography of a Southern Unionist* (Chapel Hill: University of North Carolina Press, 2011), 151–152 and 155.

30. Raphael P. Thian, *Correspondence of the Treasury Department* (Washington, DC: Government Printing Office, 1879), 589–592.

31. Ernest A. Smith, *The History of the Confederate Treasury* (Harrisburg, PA: Harrisburg Publishing, 1901), 59–61. Richard C.K. Burdekin and Marc D. Weidenmier, "Inflation Is Always and Everywhere a Monetary Phenomenon: Richmond and Houston in 1864," *American Economic Review* 91, no. 5 (December 2001): 1621–1622. John M. Godrey, *Monetary Expansion in the Confederacy* (New York: Arno Press, 1978), 119. Gary M. Pecquet, "Public Finance in Confederate Louisiana," *Louisiana History* 29, no. 3 (Summer 1988): 286–288.

32. Jaime A Martinez, "The Question of Bread Is a Very Serious One: Virginia's Wartime Economy" in William C. Davis and James I. Robertson, eds., *Virginia at War: 1865* (Lexington: University of Kentucky Press, 2012), 46. Craig A. Bauer, "The Last Effort: The Secret Mission of the Confederate Diplomat, Duncan F. Kenner," *Louisiana History* 22, no. 1 (Winter 1981): 78–79. Charles W. Ramsdell, *Laws and Joint Resolutions of the Last Session of the Confederate Congress* (Durham, NC: Duke University Press, 1941), 129–130 and 147–149. Henry D. Capers, *The Life and Times of C.G. Memminger* (Richmond, VA: Everett Waddey Co., 1893), 368.

33. *New Bern* [North Carolina] *Times*, March 12, 1864. *Raleigh Weekly Standard*, Januay 11, 1865. Arthur W. Bergeron, *The Civil War Reminiscences of Major Silas T. Grisamore, C.S.A.* (Baton Rouge: Louisiana State University Press, 1993), 180. Bromfield L. Ridley, *Battles and Sketches of the Army of Tennessee* (Mexico, MO: Missouri Printing, 1906), 458–459. Arch F. Blakey, *General John H. Winder, C.S.A.* (Gainesville: University of Florida Press, 1990), 169. James M. Day, *Senate and House Journals of the Tenth Legislature, First Called Session of the State of Texas* (Austin: Texas State Library, 1965), 6–7.

34. John B. Jones, *A Rebel War Clerk's Diary at the Confederate States Capital* (New York: Lippincott, 1866), 2:5, 78, 217, and 240. Gordon Wright, "Conditions in the Confederacy as Seen by the French Consuls," *Journal of Southern History* 7, no. 2 (May 1941): 195–214.213.

35. Rebeca L. Felton, *Country Life in Georgia in the Days of My Youth* (New York: Arno Press, 1980), 273.

36. T.H. Galloway, *Dear Old Roswell: Civil War Letters of the King Family of Roswell, Georgia* (Macon, GA: Mercer University Press, 2003), 106. Thomas W. Cutrer and T. Michael Parrish, *Brothers in Gray: The Civil War Letters of the Pierson Family* (Baton Rouge: Louisiana State University Press, 1997), 257.

37. *Jacksonville [Alabama] Republican*, December 29, 1864. *Eutaw* [Alabama] *Whig and Observer*, June 9, 1864.

38. John F. Marszalek, *The Diary of Miss Emma Holmes, 1861–1866* (Baton Rouge: Louisiana State University Press, 1994), 166.

39. John F. Reiger, "Deprivation, Disaffection, and Desertion in Confederate Florida," *Florida Historical Quarterly* 48, no. 3 (January 1970): 280.

40. Jones, *Rebel War Clerk*, 2:328.

41. John K. Volmer, *From That Terrible Field: Civil War Letters of James M. Williams, Twenty-First Alabama Infantry Volunteers* (Tuscaloosa: University of Alabama Press, 1981), 147. William T. Mumford, diary entry for January 19, 1864. William T. Mumford Diary. History Museum of Mobile (Jack Friend Research Library); Mobile, Alabama. Michael B. Chesson and Leslie J. Roberts, *Exile in Richmond: The Confederate Journal of Henri Garidel* (Charlottesville: University of Virginia Press, 2001), 309 and 338.

42. Michael J. Varhola, *Everyday Life during the Civil War* (Cincinnati: Writer's Digest Books, 1999), 59. Mike Wright, *City under Siege: Richmond in the Civil War* (New York: Madison Books, 1995), 99 and 222.

43. Wright, "French Consuls," 204.

44. Crabtree and Patton, 140 and 368.

45. James D. Clayton, "Mississippi Agriculture, 1861–1865," *Journal of Mississippi History* 24, no. 3 (July 1962): 133–134.

46. William A. Strasser, "Our Women Played Well Their Parts: East Tennessee Women in the Civil War Era, 1860–1870," (M.A. thesis, University of Tennessee, 1999), 14. Martinez, in Davis and Robertson, 43. Diane Lindstrom, "Southern Dependence upon Interregional Grain Supplies: A Review of the Trade Flows, 1840–1860," *Agricultural History* 44, no. 1 (January 1970): 102–104.

47. Richard D. Goff, *Confederate Supply* (Durham, NC: Duke University Press, 1969), 43–53.

48. Parthenia A. Hague, *A Blockaded Family: Life in Southern Alabama during the Civil War* (New York: Houghton, Mifflin, and Co., 1888), 129.

49. David G. Surdam, *Northern Naval Superiority and the Economics of the American Civil War* (Columbia: University of South Carolina Press, 2001), 92–95.

50. ORA, Volume 17, Part 1, 67 and Series 4, Volume 1, Part 1, 557 and 955–958. Richard Maury, diary entry for February 9, 1865. Richard Maury Papers. Virginia Historical Society; Richmond, Virginia. Steven Strom, "Cotton and Profits Across the Border: William Marsh Rice in Mexico, 1863–1865," *Houston Review* 8, no. 2 (Summer 1986): 94–95.

William Diamond, "Imports of the Confederate Government from Europe and Mexico," *Journal of Southern History* 6, no. 4 (November 1940), 496–497. Paul B. Barringer, *The Natural Bent: The Memoirs of Dr. Paul B. Barringer* (Chapel Hill: University of North Carolina Press, 1949), 47.

51. Virginia I. Burr, *The Secret Eye: The Journal of Ella Gertrude Clanton Thomas, 1848–1889* (Chapel Hill: University of North Carolina Press, 1990), 257.

52. David Williams, *Rich Man's War: Class, Caste, and Confederate Defeat in the Lower Chattahoochee Valley* (Athens: University of Georgia Press, 1999), 94. W.C. Corsan, *Two Months in the Confederate States: An Englishman's Travels through the South* (Baton Rouge: Louisiana State University Press, 1998), 65. Diffie W. Standard, *Columbus, Georgia, in the Confederacy: The Social and Industrial Life of the Chattahoochee River Port* (New York: William-Frederick, 1954), 47. Stephen C. Neff, *Justice in Blue and Gray: A Legal History of the Civil War* (Cambridge, MA: Harvard University Press, 2010), 205.

53. Johns, 106. Surdam, 95–96.

54. Frank E. Vandiver, *Rebel Brass: The Confederate Command System* (New York: Greenwood Press, 1956), 118–119. Coulter, 292–292. Parker, "John Milton," 358. Surdam, 96.

55. Willard E. Wight, "Some Letters of Lucius Bellinger Northrop, 1860–1865," *Virginia Magazine of History and Biography* 68, no. 4 (October 1960): 473. Robert B. Ekelund, John D. Jackson, and Mark Thornton, "The 'Unintended Consequences' of Confederate Trade Legislation," *Eastern Economic Journal* 30, no. 2 (Spring 2004): 200. C. Augustus Hobart-Hampden, *Never Caught: Personal Adventures Connected with Twelve Successful Trips in Blockade-Running during the American Civil War* (Carolina Beach, NC: Blockade Runner Museum, 1967), 196.

56. Albert B. Moore, *Conscription and Conflict in the Confederacy* (New York: Macmillan, 1924), 14–15. Later legislation increased the upper age range to forty-five and then fifty years of age, while also lowering the minimum age to seventeen.

57. *Washington* [Arkansas] *Telegraph*, October 8, 1862.

58. Scott County, Virginia Enrollment Office Records. Virginia Historical Society; Richmond, Virginia.

59. William C. Davis and Meredith L. Swentor, *Bluegrass Confederate: The Headquarters Diary of Edward O. Guerrant* (Baton Rouge: Louisiana State University Press, 2005), 650.

60. William Blair, *Virginia's Private War: Feeding Body and Soul in the Confederacy, 1861–1865* (New York: Oxford, 1998), 109.

61. Margaret M. Storey, *Loyalty and Loss: Alabama's Unionists in the Civil War and Reconstruction* (Baton Rouge: Louisiana State University Press, 2004), 70. Paul D. Escott, "Poverty and Government Aid for the Poor in Confederate North Carolina," *North Carolina Historical Review* 66, no. 4 (October 1984): 464. Escott, "Joseph Brown," 61. Martin Crawford, *Ashe County's Civil War: Community and Society in the Appalachian South* (Charlottesville: University of Virginia Press, 2001), 144.

62. "Returns from Scott County." Virginia Enrollment Office Records.

63. William T. Auman, "Neighbor against Neighbor: The Inner Civil War in the Randolph County Area of Confederate North Carolina," *North Carolina Historical Review* 90, no. 1 (January 1984): 86–87.

64. Williams, Williams, and Carlson, 182–183.

65. Georgia Lee Tatum, *Disloyalty in the Confederacy* (Chapel Hill: University of North Carolina Press, 1934), 104.

66. Davis and Swentor, 654, 655, 658, and 661.

67. ORA, Series 3, Volume 5 Part 1, 695–699.

68. *New York Times*, October 8, 1864. Arndt M. Stickles, *Simon Bolivar Buckner: Borderland Knight* (Chapel Hill: University of North Carolina Press, 1940), 261. Beringer, Hattaway, Jones, and Still, 435. Brian H. Reid and John White, "A Mob of Stragglers and Cowards: Desertion from the Union and Confederate Armies, 1861–1865," *Journal of Strategic Studies* 8, no. 1 (January 1985): 64–77. ORA, Series 1, Volume 24, Part 3, 407; Volume 41, Part 4, 1140–1141; and Volume 46, Part 2, 337.

69. John Cawthon, "Letters of a North Louisiana Private to his Wife, 1862–1865," *Mississippi Valley Historical Review* 30, no. 4 (March 1944): 546.

70. Michael C. Hardy, *The Thirty-seventh North Carolina Troops: Tar Heels in the Army of Northern Virginia* (Jefferson City, NC: McFarland, 2003), 168–169. John K. Folmar, *From that Terrible Field: Civil War Letters of James M. Williams, Twenty-first Alabama Infantry Volunteers* (Tuscaloosa: University of Alabama Press, 1981) 157.

71. Hairston Watkins, letter to sister dated January 30, 1865. Elizabeth Seawell Hairston Papers. University of North Carolina (Southern History Collection); Chapel Hill, North Carolina.

72. Thomas R. Hay, "Lucius B. Northrop: Commissary General of the Confederacy," *Civil War History* 9, no. 1 (March 1963): 5–7.

73. Carol Taylor, "Feed the Troops or Fight the Drought: The Dilemma Texas Beef Contractors Faced in 1861–1865" in Kenneth W. Howell, *The Seventh Star of the Confederacy: Texas during the Civil War* (Denton: University of North Texas Press, 2009), 290. John H. Brubaker, *The Last Capital:*

Danville, Virginia and the Final Days of the Confederacy (Danville, VA: Womack Press, 1979), 34. Hay, "Lucius B. Northrop," 15.

74. "History of the Commissary Department of the Confederate States of America," 50. Fontaine W. Mahood Papers. Virginia Historical Society; Richmond, Virginia. Daily, every 100 men were, at least on paper, to receive 75 pounds meal @$5 per bushel, 45 pounds flour @ 50 cents per pound, 2 quarts salt @ $5 per bushel, 4 quarts beans @ $6 per bushel, 5 pounds rice @ 30 cents per pound, 6 pounds coffee @ $5 per pound, 12 pounds sugar @ $3 per pound, 4 quarts vinegar @ $2.50 per gallon, 1 ½ pounds candles @ $3 per pound, 4 pounds soap @ $1 per pound, 20 pounds bacon @ $3 per pound, 25 pounds beef @ 75 cents per pound, 45 gills molasses @ $10 per gallon for a total cost of $202.38.

75. ORA, Series 4, Volume 2, 1009 and Series 1, Volume 48, Part, 1422 and Volume 53, 981–982.

76. Vandiver, *Rebel Brass*, 93. Rebecca Christian, "Georgia and the Confederate Policy of Impressing Supplies," *Georgia Historical Quarterly* 29, no. 1 (March 1944): 8–9. Robert A. Taylor, *Rebel Storehouse: Florida in the Confederate Economy* (Tuscaloosa: University of Alabama Press, 1995), 114 and 124. Frank E. Vandiver, "Makeshifts of Confederate Ordnance," *Journal of Southern History* 17, no. 2 (May 1951): 189.

77. *Washington (AK) Telegraph*, October 21, 1863.

78. Christian, 7–8. Reiger, 284. Blair, *Virginia's Private War*, 117.

79. Henry Cleveland, *Alexander H. Stephens* (Philadelphia, PA: National Publishing, 1866), 789. Christian, 13. James W. Daddysman, *The Matamoros Trade: Confederate Commerce, Diplomacy, and Intrigue* (Newark: University of Delaware Press, 1984), 142.

80. Winters, 114 and 124.

81. Christian, 9–10. Florence F. Corley, *Confederate City: Augusta, Georgia, 1860–1865* (Columbia: University of South Carolina Press, 1960), 89. David Williams, "Bitterly Divided: Georgia's Internal Civil War," in John D. Fowler and David B. Parker, *Breaking the Heartland: The Civil War in Georgia* (Macon, GA: Mercer University Press, 2011), 23.

82. *Richmond Examiner*, March 26, 1865.

83. Wright, "French Consuls," 213.

84. Johns, 120.

85. Bell Irvin Wiley, "The Confederate Letters of John W. Hagan, Part I," *Georgia Historical Quarterly* 38, no. 2 (June 1954): 196.

86. Brenda C. McKean, *Blood and War at My Doorstep: North Carolina Civilians in the War Between the States* (Bloomington, IN: Xlibris Corporation, 2011), 292.

87. Williams, *Rich Man's War*, 85. ORA, Series 4, Volume 3, 1170.
88. Crawford, 138. Stephen V. Ash, *When the Yankees Came: Conflict and Chaos in the Occupied South, 1861–1865* (Chapel Hill: University of North Carolina Press, 1995), 222.
89. Robert F. Durden, *The Gray and the Black: The Confederate Debate on Emancipation* (Baton Rouge: Louisiana State University Press, 2000), 187–203. Judith W. McGuire, *Diary of a Southern Refugee during the War* (Richmond, VA: J.W. Randolph & English, 1889), 341. Sarah Dorsey, *Recollections of Henry Watkins Allen* (New Orleans, LA: Doolady, 1866), 287. Jerry B. Lincecum, Edward H. Phillips, and Peggy A. Redshaw, *Gideon Lincecum's Sword: Civil War Letters from the Texas Home Front* (Denton: University of North Texas Press, 2001), 325. Emma LeConte, diary entry for April 20, 1865. LeConte and Furman Family Papers. University of North Carolina (Southern Historical Collection); Chapel Hill, North Carolina.
90. Galloway, 110–111.
91. Mills Lane, *Dear Mother: Don't Grieve about Me. If I Get Killed, I'll Only Be Dead: Letters from Georgia Soldiers in the Civil War* (Savannah: Library of Georgia, 1990), 344–345.
92. Richard A. Baumgartner, *Blood and Sacrifice: The Civil War Journal of a Confederate Soldier* (Huntington, WV: Blue Acorn Press, 1994), 194.
93. Richard Maury, diary entries for February 5, 19, and 20, 1865. Richard Maury Papers.
94. Thomas W. Cutrer, *Our Trust Is in the God of Battles: The Civil War Letters of Robert Franklin Bunting, Chaplain, Terry's Texas Rangers, C.S.A.* (Knoxville: University of Tennessee Press, 2006), 313.
95. Armstead L. Robinson, "In the Shadow of Old John Brown: Insurrection Anxiety and Confederate Mobilization, 1861–1863," Journal of Negro History 65, no. 4 (Autumn 1980): 281.
96. ORA, Volume 6, Part 2, 1295.
97. Douglas Cater, letter to cousin dated February 3, 1865. Cater Family Papers. Library of Congress (Manuscript Collection); Washington, DC.
98. Hague, 142–143 and 175. John E. Fisher, *They Rode with Forrest and Wheeler: A Chronicle of Five Tennessee Brothers' Service in the Confederate Western Cavalry* (Jefferson, NC: McFarland, 1995), 202–203.
99. James G. Martin, letter to wife dated January 22, 1865. Starke, Marchant, and Martin Family Papers. Southern Historical Collection, University of North Carolina; Chapel Hill, North Carolina. Winters, 422.
100. Burr, 252.
101. John Q. Anderson, *Brokenburn: The Journal of Kate Stone, 1861–1868* (Baton Rouge: Louisiana State University Press, 1995), 339–340.

102. ORA, Series 4, Volume 3, Part 1, 492. Scheiber, 232–233.

103. Reed, 39–40. Jayne E. Blair, *Tragedy at Montpelier: The Untold Story of Ten Confederate Deserters from North Carolina* (Berwyn Heights, MD: Heritage Books, 2003), 57.

104. McKean, 394. Crawford, 147.

105. Taylor, "Feed the Troops or Fight the Drought," in Howell, 287.

106. Richard M. McMurry, *Footprints of a Regiment: A Recollection of the 1ˢᵗ Georgia Regulars, 1861–1865* (Atlanta, GA: Longstreet Press, 1992), 151. The maypop (passiflora incarnate) is an indigenous plant in the South that produces an egg-sized fruit.

107. Benjamin Rountree, "Letters from a Confederate Soldier," *The Georgia Review* 19, no. 3 (Fall 1964): 293 and 295.

108. Cawthon, 544 and 545.

109. Frank Babin to Henrietta Babin, letter dated February 12, 1865. Gras-Lauzin Papers. Louisiana State University (Hill Memorial Library); Baton Rouge, Louisiana.

110. James L. Skinner, *The Death of a Confederate: Selections from the Letters of the Archibald Smith Family of Roswell, Georgia, 1864–1956* (Athens: University of Georgia Press, 1996), 167. Lucille Griffith, *Yours till Death: Civil War Letters of John W. Cotton* (Tuscaloosa: University of Alabama Press, 1951), 125–126. This passage had numerous spelling errors that were corrected by the author.

111. Paul D. Sporer, *End of an Era: The Last Days of Traditional Southern Culture as Seen Through the Eyes of a Young Confederate Soldier* (1899; repr., Chester, NY: Anza Publishing, 2005), 304. Joseph T. Durkin, *John Dooley, Confederate Soldier: His War Journal* (Washington, DC: Georgetown University Press, 1945), 182.

112. William W. Heartsill, *Fourteen hundred and 91 days in the Confederate Army* (Marshall, TX: Heartsill, 1876), 231.

113. Frank Babin, letter to Henrietta Lauzin dated February 12, 1865. Gras-Lauzin Papers.

114. Stephen Ambrose, "Yeoman Discontent in the Confederacy," *Civil War History* 8, no. 3 (Summer 1962): 259.

115. Victoria E. Bynum, *The Long Shadow of the Civil War* (Chapel Hill: University of North Carolina Press, 2010), 19 and 23. James Marten, *Texas Divided: Loyalty and Dissent in the Lone Star State, 1856–1874* (Lexington: University Press of Kentucky, 1990), 87–88.

116. Robinson, *Justice in Gray*, 385.

117. Escott, "Joseph E. Brown," 60.

118. Marten, 86.

119. Christian, 2.

120. Ramsdell, *Laws and Joint Resolutions*, 34–35 and 130–131.

121. Barton A. Myers also provides a spectrum of Confederate sympathies by viewing the white Southern population as unwavering Unionists, neutral citizens, and committed Confederates. Barton A. Myers, *Rebels Against the Confederacy: North Carolina's Unionists* (New York: Cambridge University Press, 2014), 18.

122. David Brown, "North Carolinian Ambivalence: Rethinking Loyalty and Disaffection in the Civil War Piedmont" in Paul D. Escott, *North Carolinians the Era of the Civil War and Reconstruction* (Chapel Hill: University of North Carolina Press, 2008), 14–15. Aaron Astor, *Rebels on the Border: Civil War, Emancipation, and the Reconstruction of Kentucky and Missouri* (Baton Rouge: Louisiana State University Press, 2012), 85–87. Tatum, 9 and 12–13. Smith, *Mississippi in the Civil War*, 128–130. Michael B. Dougan, *Confederate Arkansas: The People and Politics of a Frontier State in Wartime* (Tuscaloosa: University of Alabama Press, 1976), 105 and 109.

123. Thomas G. Dyer, "Vermont Yankees in King Cotton's Court," in John Inscoe and Robert Kenzer, *Enemies of the Country: New Perspectives on Unionists in the Civil War South* (Athens: University of Georgia Press, 2001), 132–133. Dougan, 105 and 109.

124. Escott, *Many Excellent People*, 34.

125. Bruce Levine, *The Fall of the House of Dixie: The Civil War and the Social Revolution that Transformed the South* (New York: Random House, 2013), 38–44 and 71–73. ORA, Series 1, Volume 4, Part 1, 249.

126. Danielson, 118. Tatum, 55. Storey, 59–60, 87–94, and 123.

127. Judkin Browning, *Shifting Loyalties: The Union Occupation of Eastern North Carolina* (Chapel Hill: University of North Carolina Press, 2011), 166–168. Astor, 96–97.

128. ORA, Series 4, Volume 3, Part 1, 67–70.

129. Brown, in Escott, *North* Carolinians, 22–23. Marten, 90–91.

130. McMillan, 116–117.

131. William W. Rogers, *Confederate Home Front: Montgomery during the Civil War* (Tuscaloosa: University of Alabama Press, 1999), 133.

132. Danielson, 152–154.

133. Richard M. McMurry, *An Uncompromising Secessionist: The Civil War of George Knox Miller, Eighth (Wade's) Confederate Cavalry* (Tuscaloosa: University of Alabama Press, 2007), 148–149.

134. James M. Silver, "The Breakdown in Morale in Central Mississippi in 1864: Letters of Judge Robert S. Hudson," *Journal of Mississippi History* 16, no. 2 (April 1954): 101–102.

135. James, "Mississippi Agriculture," 129.

136. H. Grady Howell, *Going to Meet the Yankees: A History of the "Bloody Sixth" Mississippi Infantry, C.S.A.* (Jackson, MS: Chickasaw Bayou Press, 1981), 209.

137. Danielson, 147–148.
138. Gary D. Joiner and Jimmy H. Sandefur, "Private Julius L. Knapp, U.S.A.: A Union Soldier's Point of View," in Gary D. Joiner, ed., *Little to Eat and Thin Mud to Drink: Letters, Diaries, and Memoirs from the Red River Campaigns, 1863–1864* (Knoxville: University of Tennessee Press, 2007), 104. Williams, in Fowler and Parker, 40–41.
139. McMillan, 105.
140. ORA, Series 1, Volume 47, Part 2, 31. Carlson, 613–614. Williams, in Fowler and Parker, 41–42. Tatum, 74–75.
141. Daniel E. Sutherland, *A Savage Conflict: The Decisive Role of Guerrillas in the American Civil War* (Chapel Hill: University of North Carolina Press, 2009), 248–250.
142. ORA, Series 4, Volume 2, Part 1, 680 and Series 1, Volume 32, Part 1, 671–672. Fleming, 118.
143. Fleming, 109–110.
144. Christopher L. McIlwain, *Civil War Alabama* (Tuscaloosa: University of Alabama Press, 2016), 130.
145. Silver, 106–107.
146. ORA, Series 4, Volume 3, Part 1, 1042–1043.
147. Silver, 104. Howell, 204–205. Sutherland, *A Savage Conflict*, 106–107.
148. Jones, *Rebel War Clerk*, 2:444.
149. Escott, *Many Excellent People*, 63–69. Auman, "Neighbor against Neighbor," *North Carolina Historical Review* 90, no. 1 (January 1984): 88. Tench Tilghman, diary entry for February 11, 1865. Tench Tilghman Diary (microfilm), University of North Carolina (Southern Historical Collection); Chapel Hill, North Carolina.
150. W.T. Block, "Some Notes on the Civil War Jayhawkers of Confederate Louisiana," http://www.wtblock.com/wtblockjr/jayhawke.htm. Bell I. Wiley, *This Infernal War: The Confederate Letters of Sgt. Edwin H. Fay* (Austin: University of Texas Press, 1958), 419. Arthur W. Bergeron, *A Thrilling Narrative: The Memoir of a Southern Unionist* (Fayetteville: University of Arkansas Press, 2006), 5–12. ORA, Series 1, Volume 34, Part 2, 358, 714, and 944. *Harper's Weekly*, May 7, 1864, 294. Reed, 45–46. Sutherland, *A Savage Conflict*, 212–213.
151. *Official Records of the Union and Confederate Navies in the War of the Rebellion*, 31 volumes (hereafter as ORN) (Washington, DC: Government Printing Office, 1894–1927), Series 1, Volume 27, 74.
152. Reiger, 292–293.
153. ORA, Series 1, Volume 35, Part 2, 12.
154. ORA, Series 1, Volume 35, Part 2, 606–608.
155. William T. Cash, "Taylor County History and Civil War Deserters," *Florida Historical Quarterly* 27, no. 1 (July 1948): 49–53.

156. Taylor, *Rebel Storehouse*, 112–113. George E. Buker, *Blockaders, Refugees, and Contrabands: Civil War on Florida's Gulf Coast, 1861–1865* (Tuscaloosa: University of Alabama Press, 1993), 150 and 156–159. ORA, Series 1, Volume 35, Part 1, 390. Buker, 153–154. Johns, 161–164.

157. David Pickering and Judy Falls, *Brush Men and Vigilantes: Civil War Dissent in Texas* (College Station: Texas A&M University Press, 2000), 24–27. See also Bertram Wyatt-Brown, *Southern Honor: Ethics and Behavior in the Old South* (New York: Oxford University Press, 1982) and Wilbur J. Cash, *The Mind of the South* (New York: Knopf, 1941).

158. Storey, 60–66. Reiger, 295–297. Danielson, 110. Marten, 91.

159. John Adams, *Warrior at Heart: Governor John Milton, King Cotton, and Rebel Florida 1860–1865* (Victoria, British Columbia: FriesenPres, 2015), 189. William L. Gammon, "Governor John Milton of Florida," (M.A. thesis, University of Florida, 1948), 243.

160. Fleming, 117.

161. Robert Mann, *Wartime Dissent in American: A History and Anthology* (New York: Palgrave, 2010), 43–44. *Arkansas True Democrat* [Little Rock, Arkansas] in H.L. Hanna, *The Press Covers the Invasion of Arkansas 1862: Vol. 1 January-June* (Widener, AK: Southern Heritage Press, 2011), 19.

162. Sutherland, *A Savage Conflict*, 257–260. Storey, 56.

163. Bynum, *Long Shadow of the Civil War*, 30–31. Scarboro, 146.

164. Williams, in Fowler and Parker, 35–37. Carlson 603–604. Storey, 69 and 81–84. Jack D.L. Holmes, "The Mississippi County that 'Seceded' from the Confederate States of America," *Civil War Times Illustrated* 3, no. 10 (February 1965): 49.

165. ORA, Series 4, Volume 2, Part 1, 783–785.

166. Crawford, 134 and 144.

167. Auman, "Neighbor against Neighbor," 83.

168. W. Buck Yearns and John G. Barrett, *North Carolina Civil War Documentary* (Chapel Hill: University of North Carolina Press, 1980), 103–105.

169. ORA, Series 1, Volume 45, Part 1, 1246–1248. McMillan, 93.

170. Williams, in Fowler and Parker, 35–37. Carlson 603–604.

171. ORA, Series 1, Volume 35, Part 2, 448–449. Buker, 153–154. Johns, 162–164.

172. Donald S. Frazier, "Out of Striking Distance: The Guerilla War in Louisiana," in Daniel E. Sutherland, *Guerillas, Unionists, and Violence on the Confederate Home Front* (Fayetteville: University of Arkansas Press, 1999), 163–165.

173. ORA, Series 1, Volume 32, Part 3, 662 and Series 1, Volume 52, Part 2, 658.

174. Holmes, 49. ORA, Series 1, Volume 52, Part 2, 657–658.

175. Howell, 217. Victoria E. Bynum, *The Free State of Jones: Mississippi's Longest Civil War* (Chapel Hill: University of North Carolina Press, 2001), 125.

176. ORA, Series 1, Volume 29, Part 2, 676 and 692 and Volume 27, Part 3, 1058–1068.

177. Daniel W. Barefoot, *General Robert F. Hoke: Lee's Modest Warrior* (Winston-Salem, NC: Blair, 1996), 99–100.

178. ORA, Series 1, Volume 43, Part 2, 889–800 and 906–908. Dotson, 425–429.

179. ORA, Series 1, Volume 35, Part 2, 64.

180. See Buker, Chapter 9, "William W. Strickland, Deserter," 98–114. ORA, Series 1, Volume 53, Part 1, 319–321.

181. Susan B. Eppes, *Through Some Eventful Years* (Macon, GA: J.W. Burke, 1926), 222–224.

182. Sutherland, *A Savage Conflict*, 256–257. Tracy J. Revels, *Grander in Her Daughters: Florida's Women during the Civil War* (Columbia: University of South Carolina Press, 2004), 88–89. Larry Rayburn, "'Wherever the Fight is Thickest': General James Patton Anderson of Florida," *Florida Historical Quarterly* 55, no. 3 (January 1982): 333. ORA, Series 1, Volume 53, Part 1, 351–352.

Notes for Chapter 2

1. ORA, Series 1, Volume 44, Part 1, 740–741.

2. Ibid. 820–821.

3. Frederick Marion, letter to sister dated March 29, 1865. Frederick Marion Papers. Abraham Lincoln Presidential Library; Springfield, Illinois.

4. Benjamin F. McGee, *History of the 72d Indiana Volunteer Infantry of the Mounted Lightning Brigade* (Lafayette, IN: Vater & Co., 1882), 258–259.

5. Frederick Marion, letter to sister dated March 29, 1865. Frederick Marion Papers. Frank Babin to Henrietta Babin, letter dated February 12, 1865. Gras-Lauzin Papers. William S. Hoole, *Alabama Tories: The First Alabama Cavalry, U.S.A., 1862–1865* (Tuscaloosa, AL: Confederate Publishing Co., 1960), 47.

6. Wade Sokolosky and Mark A. Smith, *To Prepare for Sherman's Coming: The Battle of Wise's Forks, March 1865* (El Dorado, CA: Savas Beatie, 2015), 10.

7. ORA, Series 1, Volume 47, Part 2, 1085.

8. Hudson, 179. ORA, Series 1, Volume 47, Part 2, 1202.

9. ORA, Series 1, Volume 49, Part 1, 616–777.
10. Francis F. McKinney, *Education in Violence: The Life of George H. Thomas and the History of the Army of the Cumberland* (Chicago, IL: Americana House, 1991), 435–436. Ben F. Fordney, *George Stoneman: A Biography of a Union General* (Jefferson, NC: McFarland, 2008), 107. ORA, Series 1, Volume 49, Part 1, 330.
11. Emma LeConte, diary entries for January 18, February 13, and February 18, 1865. Emma LeConte diary. (Southern Historical Collection). University of North Carolina; Chapel Hill, North Carolina.
12. Rachel S. Thorndike, *The Sherman Letters: Correspondence between General and Senator Sherman from 1837 to 1891* (London: Sampson, Low, Marston, & Co., 1894), 266. John G. Barrett, *Sherman's March through the Carolinas* (Chapel Hill: University of North Carolina Press, 2014), 91.
13. Edward G. Longacre, *Gentleman and Scholar: A Biography of Wade Hampton III* (Nashville, TN: Rutledge Hill, 2003), 226–227 and 304–305. Edward Longacre, *A Soldier to the Last: Maj. Gen. Joseph Wheeler in Blue and Gray* (Washington, DC: Potomac Books, 2007), 194. David Williamson, *The Third Battalion Mississippi Infantry and the 45th Mississippi Regiment* (Jefferson, NC: McFarland, 2004), 311. James F. Rhodes, "Who Burned Columbia?" *American Historical Review* 7, no. 3 (April 1902): 485–493.
14. ORA, Series 1, Volume 47, Part 2, 999–1000.
15. Hughes, *General William J. Hardee*, 273. ORA, Series 1, Volume 47, Part 2, 1181 and 1201–1204.
16. ORA, Series 1, Volume 47, Part 1, 1008.
17. John M. Otey, letter to Alfred Terry dated April 18, 1865. John M. Otey Papers. Museum of Mobile (Mobile Civil War Collection); Mobile, Alabama. Hughes, 278–279.
18. Richard M. McMurry, *John Bell Hood and the War for Southern Independence* (Lexington: University of Kentucky Press, 1982), 162–164.
19. Marshall Wingfield, *General A.P. Stewart: His Life and Letters* (Memphis: West Tennessee Historical Society, 1954), 96–97. Donald Stoker, *The Grand Design: Strategy and the U.S. Civil War* (New York: Oxford University Press, 2010), 379.
20. Wingfield, 98–99 and 101.
21. John Bell Hood, *Advance and Retreat: Personal Experiences in the United States and Confederate States Armies* (New Orleans: Hood Orphan Memorial Fund, 1880), 299–300.
22. Frey, 134. William R. Carter, *History of the First Regiment of Tennessee Volunteer Cavalry in the Great War of the Rebellion* (Knoxville, TN: Gaut-Odgen Co., 1902), 233. Derek Smith, *In the Lion's Mouth: Hood's*

Tragic Retreat from Nashville, 1864 (Mechanicsburg, PA: Stackpole, 2011), 118.

23. Stanley F. Horn, *The Army of Tennessee* (Wilmington, NC: Broadfoot Publishing, 1987), 419–420. Carter, 232–234. James H. Wilson, *Under the Old Flag: Recollections of Military Operations in the War for the Union, the Spanish War, the Boxer Rebellion, etc.* (New York: Appleton, 1912), 2:130. Wiley Sword, *The Confederates' Last Hurrah: Spring Hill, Franklin, and Nashville* (Lawrence: University Press of Kansas, 1993), 413. Richard R. Hancock, *Hancock's Diary: Or A History of the Second Tennessee Confederate Cavalry* (Nashville: Brandon Printing, 1887), 535. Stephen Lee, letter to Alexander Stewart dated December 16, 1864. Stephen D. Lee Papers (Southern Historical Collection), University of North Carolina; Chapel Hill, North Carolina. Horn, 419–420. Frey, 144.

24. Thomas Jordan and J.P. Pryor, *The Campaigns of Lieut. Gen. N.B. Forrest and Forrest's Cavalry* (Memphis: Blelock & Co., 1968), 655–656. Jeffrey N. Lash, "Major George Whitfield and Confederate Railroad Policy (1863–1865)," *Journal of Mississippi History* 42, no. 3 (August 1980): 192. Smith, *Into the Lion's Mouth*, 214. H. Grady Howell, *To Live and Die in Dixie: A Regimental History of the Third Mississippi Infantry, C. S. A.* (Jackson, MS: Chickasaw Bayou Press, 1991), 410–411. Sam R. Watkins, *Co. Aytch: Maury Grays, First Tennessee Regiment or, A Side Show of the Big Show* (Nashville: Cumberland Publishing, 1882), 229–230. Heartsill, 226.

25. Ridley, 439–440. Davis, "Richard Taylor," 107. Douglas J. Cater, *As It Was: Reminiscences of a Soldier of the Third Texas Cavalry and the Nineteenth Louisiana Infantry* (Austin, TX: State House Press, 1990), 204.

26. Robert P. Bender, *Worthy of the Cause for Which They Fight: The Civil War Diary of Brigadier General Daniel Harris Reynolds, 1861–1865* (Fayetteville: University of Arkansas Press, 2011), 170–171. Baumgartner, 194. Ridley, 439–440. Davis, "Richard Taylor," 107. Sword, 425.

27. Taylor, 250.

28. Baumgartner, *Blood and Sacrifice*, 194.

29. James L. McDonough, *Nashville: The Western Confederacy's Final Gamble* (Knoxville: University of Tennessee Press, 2004), 274. Alfred T. Roman, *The Military Operations of General Beauregard in the War Between the States*, Vol. 2 (New York: Harper & Bros., 1884), 331–32.

30. McMurry, *John Bell Hood*, 183.

31. Douglas Cater, letter to cousin dated February 3, 1865. Cater Family Papers.

32. John B. Hood, letters to Stephen D. Lee dated January 15, 1865, and November 29, 1866. Stephen D. Lee Papers.

33. Craig L. Symonds, *Joseph E. Johnston: A Civil War Biography* (New York: Norton, 1992), 352–353. Herman Hattaway, "The General Whom the President Elevated Too High: Davis and John Bell Hood," in Gabor S. Boritt, *Jefferson Davis' Generals* (New York: Oxford, 1999), 101. John B. Hood, *Advance and Retreat*, 311.
34. Charles L. DuFour, *Nine Men in Gray* (New York: Doubleday, 1963), 3–5.
35. Crist, *Papers of Jefferson Davis*, Volume 10, 512.
36. Taylor, 23–24.
37. T. Michael Parrish, *Richard Taylor: Soldier Prince of Dixie* (Chapel Hill: University of North Carolina Press, 1992), 136.
38. Davis, "Richard Taylor," 67–68.
39. Richard Taylor, *Destruction and Reconstruction: Personal Experiences of the Late War* (New York: Appleton, 1883), 102. ORA, Series 4, Part 2, 380.
40. Dabney H. Maury, "Sketch of General Richard Taylor," *Southern Historical Society Papers* 7 (1879): 343–345.
41. K. Jack Bauer, *Zachary Taylor, Soldier, Planter, Statesman of the Old Southwest* (Baton Rouge: Louisiana State University Press, 1993), 96. Holman Hamilton, *Zachary Taylor: Soldier in the White House* (Indianapolis: Bobbs-Merrill, 1951), 26–27. Jack Welsh, *Medical Histories of Confederate Generals* (Kent, OH: Kent State University Press, 1994), 210–211.
42. Napier Bartlett, *Military Record of Louisiana* (New Orleans: Graham and Co., 1875), 11. Wiley, *This Infernal War*, 427.
43. Hughes, 182–184 and 187.
44. Dabney H. Maury, *Recollections of a Virginian in the Mexican, Indian, and Civil Wars* (New York: Scribner's, 1894), 229.
45. To differentiate himself from other officers also named Smith, he always listed his last name as "Kirby Smith," without a dash in between. Consequently, his name will appear as such in this work.
46. Warner, *Generals in Gray: Lives of the Confederate Commanders* (Baton Rouge: Louisiana State University Press, 1959), 279–280.
47. William R. Boggs, *Military Reminiscences of Gen. Wm. R. Boggs, C.S.A.* (Durham, NC: Seeman, 1913), 54 and 57.
48. Forsythe, 35.
49. DuFour, 27. ORA, Series 1, Volume 26, Part 1, 212. Christopher G. Pena, *Scarred by War: Civil War in Southeast Louisiana* (Bloomington, IN: Authorhouse, 2004), 213–240. Edmund Kirby Smith, letter to Jefferson Davis dated June 6, 1864. Gilder Lehrman Collection. Gilder Lehrman Institute of American History, New York.
50. Ibid. Volume 26 Part 1, 394–395.

51. Parrish, 317–354. Robert L. Kerby, *Kirby Smith's Confederacy: The Trans-Mississippi South, 1863–1865* (New York: Columbia University Press, 1972), 320–321.

52. ORA, Series 1, Volume 41, Part 1, 90 and 117.

53. ORA, Volume 45, Part 22, 785 and 789.

54. Arthur W. Bergeron, *Confederate Mobile* (Jackson: University of Mississippi Press, 1991), 168. Davis, "Richard Taylor," 107. Stuart Salling, *Louisianans in the Western Confederacy: The Adams-Gibson Brigade in the Civil War* (Jefferson, NC: McFarland, 2010), 220. Homer L. Kerr, *Fighting with Ross' Texas Cavalry Brigade, C.S.A.* (Hillsboro, TX: Hill Jr. College Press, 1976), 203–205. Hale, 268–269. ORA, Volume 47, Part 2, 1078.

55. Joseph E. Johnston, *Narrative of Military Operations Directed during the Late War Between the States* (New York: Appleton, 1874), 373 and 394. ORA, Volume 47, Part 2, 1362. Horn, 423. Robert C. Black, *The Railroads of the Confederacy* (Chapel Hill: University of North Carolina Press, 1952), 271–272. Williamson, *Third Battalion Mississippi Infantry*, 300–301.

56. Harry V. Barnard, *Tattered Volunteers: The Twenty-Seventh Alabama Infantry Regiment, C.S.A.* (Northport, AL: Hermitage Press, 1965), 44. Bender, 172–176. John H. Curry, "A History of Company B, 40th Alabama Infantry," *Alabama Historical Quarterly* 17, no. 3 (Fall 1955): 217–218.

57. Williamson, *Third Battalion Mississippi Infantry*, 301.

58. Sokolosky and Smith, 47. Johnston, *Narrative*, 374. Sam D. Elliott, *Soldier of Tennessee: General Alexander P. Stewart and the Civil War in the West* (Baton Rouge: Louisiana State University Press, 1999), 269. Richard Taylor, letter to Joseph Johnston dated April 1, 1865. Louisiana Historical Collection (Department of Alabama, Mississippi, and Eastern Louisiana Collection); New Orleans, Louisiana.

59. Bevens, 231–233. Baumgartner, 201.

60. Bender, 173. Brown, *One of Cleburne's Command*, 162. R.M. Collins, *Chapters from the Unwritten History of the War Between the States* (St. Louis, MO: Nixon-Jones, 1893), 273–276. Williamson, *Third Battalion Mississippi Infantry*, 301. Rogers, 135. ORA, Volume 49, Part 1, 960–961.

61. Wiggins, 151. ORA, Series 1, Volume 47, Part 2, 1061.

62. Ridley, 441.

63. Richard M. McMurry, "Enemy at Richmond," 31. Jefferson Davis, "Autobiography of Jefferson Davis," *Confederate Veteran* 15, no. 5 (May 1907): 221.

64. ORA, Series 4, Volume 1, Part 1, 163–164.

65. Ibid. 605–608 and 611.
66. Ibid. Series 1, Volume 5, Part 1, 884–887.
67. Clement Eaton, *Jefferson Davis* (New York: Free Press, 1977), 158.
68. McMurry, "Enemy at Richmond," 8–10.
69. Symonds, 202–226.
70. Ibid. 245–248.
71. ORA, Series 1, Volume 33, Part 3, 801.
72. Rogers, 44–45.
73. McMurray, "Enemy in Richmond," 15–16. Symonds, 343. Joseph Johnston, letter to Edmund Kirby Smith dated January 30, 1865. Edmund Kirby Smith Papers. University of North Carolina (Southern Historical Collection); Chapel Hill, North Carolina (hereafter as Kirby Smith Papers (UNC)).
74. Gilbert Govan and James Livingood, *A Different Valor: The Story of General Joseph E. Johnston, C.S.A.* (Indianapolis, IN: Bobbs-Merrill, 1956), 340. Symonds, 340–342.
75. Bell I. Wiley, *Letters of Warren Akin: Confederate Congressman* (Athens: University of Georgia Press, 1959), 84.
76. ORA, Series 1, Volume 47, Part 2, 1078–1079.
77. Robert E. Lee, letter to Joseph Johnston dated February 22, 1865. Joseph Johnston Papers. College of William & Mary (Swem Library); Williamsburg, Virginia. ORA, Series 1, Volume 47, Part 2, 1248.
78. C. Vann Woodward, *Mary Chesnut's Civil War* (New Haven, CT: Yale University Press, 1981), 729. Herman Hattaway, *General Stephen D. Lee* (Jackson: University of Mississippi Press, 1976), 152–153. Joseph Johnston, *Narrative of Military Operations*, 372.
79. Nathaniel C. Hughes, *The Pride of the Confederate Artillery: The Washington Artillery in the Army of Tennessee* (Baton Rouge: Louisiana State University Press, 1997), 263–264.
80. Douglas Hale, *The Third Texas Cavalry in the Civil War* (Norman: University of Oklahoma Press, 1993), 268.
81. Richard Maury, diary entries for February 28 and March 18, 1865. Richard Maury Papers.
82. ORA, Series 1, Volume 47, Part 2, 1385, 1388, 1394, 1402, and 1408. Johnston, *Narrative of Military Operations*, 372 and 375. Hughes, *General William Hardee*, 273–274.
83. Govan and Livingood, 351.
84. Glenn Tucker, *Zeb Vance: Champion of Personal Freedom* (New York: Bobbs-Merrill, 1965), 371.
85. Sokolosky and Smith, 5–6.
86. Ibid. 11–12.
87. ORA, Series 1, Volume 47, Part 2, 1347.

88. Ibid. 1372–1373.
89. Ibid. 1372–1373.
90. Ibid. 1395–1396.
91. Davis and Swentor, 653.
92. Lash, 167–168. Joseph Johnston, letter to Zebulon Vance dated March 5, 1865. Joseph Johnston Papers.
93. Longacre, *Gentleman and Soldier*, 235.
94. Hughes, *Bentonville*, 28–29 and 37. David Williamson, *Third Battalion Mississippi Infantry*, 311. Longacre, *Gentleman and Soldier*, 235.
95. Johnston, *Narrative of Military Operations*, 582.
96. Hughes, *General William J. Hardee*, 281–286.
97. Daniel T. Davis and Phillip S. Greenwalt, *Calamity in Carolina: The Battles of Averasboro and Bentonville, March 1865* (El Dorado Hills, CA: Savas Beatie, 2015), 37–41.
98. George R. Farnum, "William B. Bate: Soldier of Dixie, Lawyer, and Statesman of the Union," *American Bar Association Journal* 30, no. 2 (February 1944): 105.
99. John Ott memoirs, 592. John Ott Papers. University of Michigan (Clements Library); Ann Arbor, Michigan. William G. Putney memoirs, 94. William G. Putney Papers. University of Michigan (Clements Library); Ann Arbor, Michigan.
100. Edward A. Pollard, *Lee and His Lieutenants: Comprising the Early Life, Public Services, and Campaigns of General Robert E. Lee* (New York: E.B. Treat & Co., 1867), 827.
101. David L. Anderson, "The Life of 'Wilhelm Yank': Letters from a German Soldier in the Civil War," *Michigan Historical Review* 16, no. 1 (Spring 1990): 89. John Ott memoirs, 595.
102. Barefoot, 298–299. Hughes, *Hardee*, 289. Bradley, *Bentonville*, 330–333.
103. Samuel W. Ravenel, "Ask the Survivors of Bentonville," *Confederate Veteran* 18, no. 3 (March 1910): 124. Hughes, *Hardee*, 290.
104. William G. Putney memoirs, 94.
105. R. Hugh Simmons, "The 12th Louisiana Infantry in North Carolina, January-April, 1865," *Louisiana History* 36, no. 1 (Winter 1995): 96.
106. Barefoot, 300–301.
107. Wilfred W. Black, "Marching with Sherman through Georgia and the Carolinas: The Civil War Diary of Jesse L. Dozer, Part II," *Georgia Historical Quarterly* 52, no. 4 (December 1968): 468.
108. Thomas W. Cutrer, "We are Stern and Resolved: The Civil War Letters of John Wesley Rabb, Terry's Texas Rangers," *Southwestern Historical Quarterly* 91, no. 2 (October 1987): 224–225.
109. Hughes, *Hardee*, 291 and 294.

110. Black, "Marching with Sherman," 469.

112. Bradley, *Bentonville*, 404–408. Symonds, 351. Ridley, *Battles and Sketches*, 466. Hughes, *Hardee*, 290.

113. Donald C. Seitz, *Braxton Bragg, General of the Confederacy* (Columbia, SC: State Company, 1924), 517–518.

114. Wade Hampton, "Battle of Bentonville," *Battles and Leaders of the Civil War*, Vol. 4 (New York: Century, 1884), 405. Rod Andrew, *Wade Hampton: Confederate Warrior to Southern Redeemer* (Chapel Hill: University of North Carolina Press, 2014), 287.

115. ORA, Series 1, Volume 47, Part 2, 1453–1454.

116. Ibid. Volume 53, Part 1, 415.

117. Richard Harwell and Philip N. Racine, *The Fiery Trail: A Union Officer's Account of Sherman's Last Campaign* (Knoxville: University of Tennessee Press, 1986), 200.

118. Waghelstein and Chisholm, 872.

119. David D. Porter, *Incidents and Anecdotes of the Civil War* (New York: Appleton, 1885), 285–287.

120. Ibid. 287.

121. James R. Solley, *Admiral Porter* (New York: Appleton, 1913), 442.

122. Sherman, *Memoirs*, Volume 2, 326–328.

123. Ibid. 328–331.

124. Grant, *Memoirs*, 739.

125. Seward, *Reminiscences of a War-Time*, 255–256.

126. *Collected Works of Abraham Lincoln*, 8:330–331. Jeffrey D. Wert, *General James Longstreet: The Confederacy's Most Controversial Soldier* (New York: Simon & Schuster, 1993), 397–398. Dowdey and Manarin, 911–912. Davis, *Breckinridge*, 494. ORA, Series 1, Volume 46, Part 2, 1275–1276.

Notes for Chapter 3

1. John Ott memoir, 600. John Ott Papers.

2. James L. McDonough, *William Tecumseh Sherman: In the Service of My Country* (New York: Norton, 2016), 618–623.

3. John Ott memoir, 601. John Ott Papers.

4. Zebulon Vance, letter to William T. Sherman dated April 12, 1865. Campbell Family Papers. Charles E. Slocum, *The Life and Service of Major-General Henry Warner Slocum* (Toledo, OH: Slocum Publishing, 1913), 306.

5. William T. Sherman, letter to Zebulon Vance dated April 12, 1865. Campbell Family Papers.

6. W.J. Sanders, "Governor Z.B. Vance: Story of the Last Days of the Confederacy in North Carolina," *Southern Historical Society Papers* 32 (1904): 166–167. Edward Warren, *A Doctor's Experiences in Three Continents* (Baltimore, MD: Cushings & Bailey, 1885), 337–338. Clement Dowd, *Life of Zebulon B. Vance* (Charlotte, NC: Observer Printing, 1897), 485–486.

7. Charles E. Slocum, 307. Zebulon Vance, letter to Cornelia Spencer dated February 17, 1866. Campbell Family Papers. Tucker, 399–401.

8. ORA, Series 1, Volume 47, Part 3, 815.

9. Ridley, 459.

10. Symonds, 355. Johnson Hagood, *Memoirs of the War of Secession* (Columbia, SC: State Company, 1910), 2:371. Mark L. Bradley, *This Astounding Close: The Road to Bennet Place* (Chapel Hill: University of North Carolina, 2000), 219–220. Ridley, 464.

11. Elliott, *Soldier of Tennessee*, 271.

12. Rodman L. Underwood, *Stephen Russell Mallory: A Biography of the Confederate Navy Secretary and United States Senator* (Jefferson, NC: McFarland, 2005), 174.

13. McFall, 73–74. ORA, Series 1, Volume 49, Part 2, 483–484 and 488. *Staunton* [Virginia] *Spectator*, October 31, 1865. Michael B. Ballard, *A Long Shadow: Jefferson Davis and the Final Days of the Confederacy* (Jackson: University of Mississippi Press, 1986), 133. Larry Gordon, *The Last Confederate General: John C. Vaughn and his East Tennessee Cavalry* (Minneapolis, MN: Zenith Press, 2009), 155–156.

14. McFall, 71. Brubaker, 5–6 and 14–15.

15. John S. Wise, *The End of an Era* (New York: Houghton, 1901), 415.

16. Chesson and Roberts, 367.

17. Brubaker, 25.

18. Davis, *Rise and Fall of the Confederate Government*, Volume 2, 677–678. James M. McPherson, *Embattled Rebel: Jefferson Davis and Commander in Chief* (New York: Penguin, 2014), 241. *Daily Progress* (Raleigh, NC), April 10, 1865. Richard W. Iobst, *Civil War Macon: The History of a Confederate City* (Macon, GA: Mercer University Press, 1999), 377.

19. James W. Raab, *J. Patton Anderson: Confederate General* (Jefferson, NC: McFarland, 2004), 159. Wise, 445–446.

20. Brubaker, 47 and 55.

21. Carl C. Rister, *Border Command: General Phil Sheridan in the West* (Westport, CT: Greenwood Press, 1974), 9.

22. McFall, 80. Durkin, 180–181.

23. Lawrence P. Jackson, *My Father's Name: A Black Virginia Family after the Civil War* (Chicago: University of Chicago Press, 2012), 159. *Evening Star* (Washington, DC), April 26, 1865.

24. Davis, *Long Surrender*, 62.

25. Robert M. Dunkerly, *The Confederate Surrender at Greensboro: The Final Days of the Army of Tennessee, April 1865* (Jefferson, NC: McFarland, 2013), 64.

26. Johnston, *Narrative of Military Operations*, 397–399. James J. Bowen, "The Strategy of Robert E. Lee," *Neale's Magazine* 2, no. 1 (July 1913): 64. Robert E. Lee, Jr., *Recollections and Letters of Robert E. Lee, C.S.A.* (New York: Cosimo, 2008), 121. Davis, *The Long Surrender*, 67.

27. John W. DuBose, *General Joseph Wheeler and the Army of Tennessee* (New York: Neale, 1912), 460.

28. Johnston, *Narrative of Military Operations*, 397–398. Davis, *Long Surrender*, 69.

29. Govan and Livingood, 362.

30. DuBose, 461.

31. Sherman, *Memoirs*, 703.

32. William E. Dodd, *Jefferson Davis* (Philadelphia, PA: Jacobs, 1907), 358. Horn, 427. Davis, *The Long Surrender*, 70–71. Govan and Livingood, 361.

33. William J. Cooper, *Jefferson Davis: His Essential Writings* (New York: Random House, 2004), 367.

34. Clark, 72.

35. Durkin, 192. John T. Wood, diary entry for April 17, 1865. John Taylor Woods Papers. University of North Carolina (Southern Historical Collection); Chapel Hill, North Carolina.

36. ORA, Series 1, Volume 47, Part 3, 221. Johnston, *Narrative of Military Operations*, 402–404.

37. Johnston, *Narrative of Military Operations*, 402. William T. Sherman, *Memoirs of General William T. Sherman* (Bloomington: Indiana University Press, 1957), 347–350.

38. Sherman, *Memoirs*, 349.

39. DuBose, 645.

40. Johnston, *Narrative of Military Operations*, 403.

41. Davis, *The Long Surrender*, 72.

42. Sherman, *Memoirs*, 832.

43. Jacqueline G. Campbell, *When Sherman Marched North from the Sea: Resistance on the Confederate Home Front* (Chapel Hill: University of North Carolina Press, 2003), 93.

44. Waghelstein and Chisholm, 893.

45. Tucker, 408–409.

46. ORA, Series 1, Volume 49, Part 2, 488.

47. Black, *Railroads of the Confederacy*, 268–269. Lash, *Destroyer of the Iron Horse*, 173–174.

48. Mark Grimsby, "Learning to Say 'Enough': Southern Generals and the Final Weeks of the Confederacy," in Mark Grimsby and Brooks D. Simpson, eds., *The Collapse of the Confederacy* (Lincoln: University of Nebraska Press, 2001), 63 and 68–70.
49. Ridley, 458.
50. DuBose, 464.
51. William C. Davis, *Breckinridge: Statesman, Soldier, Symbol* (Baton Rouge: Louisiana State University Press, 1974), 511.
52. Wise, 451.
53. Charles E. Slocum, 309.
54. Barrett, 4–6.
55. ORA, Series 1, Volume 47, Part 3, 411–412.
56. William Sherman, letter to wife dated April 18, 1865. Sherman Family Papers. Library of Congress (Manuscript Division); Washington, DC. Sherman was not the only officer with such concerns. See Andrew F. Lang, "Challenging the Union Citizen-Soldier Ideal," in Brian D. Knight and Barton A. Myers, *The Guerrilla Hunters: Irregular Conflict during the Civil War* (Baton Rouge: Louisiana State University Press, 2017), 305–334.
57. Silkenat, 227. Steven J. Ramold, "We Should Have Killed Them All: The Violent Reaction of Union Soldiers to the Assassination of Abraham Lincoln," *Journal of Illinois History* 10, no. 1 (Spring 2007).
58. Sherman, *Memoirs*, 839. Waghelstein and Chisholm, 895.
59. Michael Fellman, *Citizen Sherman: A Life of William Tecumseh Sherman* (New York: Random House, 1995), 241. Gordon, 150.
60. Charles E. Slocum, 308–309.
61. Frederic Bancroft and William A. Dunning, *The Reminiscences of Carl Schurz* (New York: McClure, 1908), 3:113–117.
62. Col. Thomas W. Osborn, one of Howard's staff officers, mentioned in his diary that Logan did not approve of the terms. Harwell and Racine, 211.
63. George W. Nichols, "Sherman's Great March," *Harper's New Monthly Magazine* 31, no. 5 (October 1865): 587.
64. Johnston, *Narrative of Military Operations*, 401.
65. ORA, Series 1, Volume 47, Part 3, 243.
66. Gideon Welles, *Diary of Gideon Welles, Secretary of the Navy under Lincoln and Johnson* (Boston, MA: Houghton-Mifflin, 1911), 2:296–297.
67. ORA, Series 1, Volume 47, Part 3, 263.
68. ORA, Series 1, Volume 47, Part 3, 287.
69. Abner Foreman, diary entry for April 24, 1865. Abner Foreman Papers. Abraham Lincoln Presidential Library; Springfield, Illinois.

70. Sherman, *Memoirs*, 425.

71. ORA, Series 1, Volume 47, Part 3, 293–294.

72. Ibid. 302.

73. Benjamin P. Thomas and Harold M. Hyman, *Stanton: The Life and Times of Lincoln's Secretary of War* (New York: Knopf, 1962), 410–411.

74. ORA, Series 1, Volume, 47, Part 3, 302–303.

75. Ibid. 835.

76. Gary R. Matthews, *Basil Wilson Duke, CSA: The Right Man in the Right Place* (Lexington: University of Kentucky Press, 2005), 200. ORA, Series 1, Volume 47, Part 3, 836. Johnston, *Narrative of Military Operations*, 411.

77. James L. McDonough, *Schofield: Union General of the Civil War and Reconstruction* (Tallahassee: Florida State University Press, 1972), 158–159. ORA, Series 1, Volume 47, Part 3, 313. Stanley P. Hirshson, *The White Tecumseh: A Biography of William T. Sherman* (New York: Wiley & Sons, 1997), 308.

78. ORA, Series 1, Volume 47, Part 3, 403.

79. *The Reports of Committees of the House of Representatives for the First Session of the Fortieth Congress, 1867* (Washington, DC: Government Printing Office, 1868), 717.

80. ORA, Series 1, Volume 47, Part 3, 840.

81. Ibid. 330–331.

82. Ibid. Volume 49, Part 2, 498.

83. Ibid. Volume 47, Part 3, 301–302.

Notes for Chapter 4

1. Henry Hitchcock, *Marching with Sherman: Passages from the Letters and Campaign Diaries of Henry Hitchcock, Major and Assistant Adjutant General of Volunteers, November 1864-May 1865* (New Haven, CT: Yale University Press, 1927), 319–320. Grant, *Memoirs*, 580.

2. *New York Herald,* April 24 and 25, 1865 (cited in the *Detroit Free Press*, April 30, 1865).

3. *Philadelphia Enquirer*, April 24, 1865.

4. *Detroit Free Press*, May 2, 1865.

5. *Cincinnati Enquirer*, April 26 and 29, 1865.

6. *Cincinnati Gazette*, April 25, 1865.

7. *Cincinnati Daily Commercial*, April 26, 1865.

8. *Brooklyn Daily Eagle*, April 27, 1865.

9. *New York Tribune*, April 28, 1865.

10. *Pittsburgh Daily Commercial*, May 31, 1865.
11. Frederick Marion, letter to sister dated May 27, 1865. Frederick Marion Papers.
12. Henry W. Slocum, "Final Operations of Sherman's Army," *Battles and Leaders of the Civil War* (New York: Yoseloff, 1887), 4:757.
13. Oscar O. Winther, *With Sherman to the Sea: The Civil War Letters, Diaries and Reminiscences of Theodore F. Upson* (Bloomington: Indiana University Press, 1958), 167.
14. John Ott memoir, 614. John Ott Papers.
15. Bancroft and Dunning, *The Reminiscences of Carl Schurz* (New York: McClure, 1908), 3:116–117.
16. ORA, Series 1, Volume 47, Part 3, 334–335. *Pittsburgh Daily Commercial*, May 31, 1865.
17. ORA, Series 1, Volume 47, Part 3, 311–312 and Volume 49, Part 2, 483–484.
18. Madeline V. Dahlgren, *Memoir of John A. Dahlgren, Rear Admiral, United States Navy* (Boston, MA: Osgood, 1882), 510–511.
19. ORA, Series 1, Volume 47, Part 3, 410.
20. Ibid. 3, 345–346.
21. Ibid. 454–455.
22. Martin Trowbridge, letter to wife dated May 23, 1865. Martin Trowbridge Papers. University of Michigan (Clements Library); Ann Arbor, Michigan.
23. Durkin, 197–198. Ridley, 458.
24. Johnston, *Narrative of Military Operations*, 410.
25. Crabtree and Patton, 701.
26. Ridley, 459.
27. Wise, 454.
28. Brown, *One of Cleburne's Command*, 168, 169, and 173.
29. George Childress, diary entries for April 15 and 17, 1865. George L. Childress Papers. Abraham Lincoln Presidential Library; Springfield, Illinois.
30. Charles Tanner, letter to father dated April 28, 1865. Charles A. Tanner Papers. University of North Carolina (Southern Historical Collection); Chapel Hill, North Carolina.
31. George W. Pepper, *Personal Recollections of Sherman's Campaigns in Georgia and the Carolinas* (Zanesville, OH: Dunne, 1866), 403.
32. ORA, Series 1, Volume 46, Part 1, 1304. "Gen. Thomas T. Munford," *Confederate Veteran* 26, no. 5 (May 1918): 227. Mary E. Dickison, *Dickison and His Men: Reminiscences of the War in Florida* (Gainesville: University of Florida Press, 1962), 230 and 239–240. Wise, 448–449. Durkin, 181.

33. John S. Mosby, *Memoirs of John S. Mosby* (Princeton, NJ: Collector's Reprints, 1998), 360. Kevin H. Siepel, *Rebel: The Life and Times of John Singleton Mosby* (New York: St. Martin's Press, 1983), 147–154. Jeffrey D. Wert, *Mosby's Rangers* (New York: Simon and Schuster, 1990), 289–290. Gordon B. Bonan, *The Edge of Mosby's Sword: The Life of Confederate Colonel William Henry Chapman* (Carbondale, IL: Southern Illinois University Press, 2009), 149–154.
34. Johnston, *Narrative of Military Operations*, 410.
35. James W. Raab, *W.W. Loring: Florida's Forgotten General* (Manhattan, KS: Sunflower University Press, 1996), 206–207.
36. Johnston, *Narrative of Military Operations*, 410. Ridley, 464.
37. "Henderson Deans Reminiscences," 8–12. (Southern Historical Collection). University of North Carolina; Chapel Hill, North Carolina.
38. ORA, Series 1, Volume 47, Part 3, 349 and 392.
39. Longacre, *A Soldier to the Last*, 203–204. DuBose, 469–470.
40. Manly W. Wellman, *Giant in Gray: A Biography of Wade Hampton of South Carolina* (New York: Scribner's, 1949), 185–189. Longacre, *Gentleman and Scholar*, 243–246.
41. *Cincinnati Daily Commercial*, April 27, 1865.
42. Johnston, *Narrative of Military Operations*, 414.
43. *Cincinnati Daily Commercial*, May 2, 1865.
44. William T. Sherman, letter to Joseph Johnston dated April 27, 1865. Joseph Johnston Papers.
45. ORA, Series 1, Volume 49, part 2, 683–683
46. David Urquhart, letter to William Perryman dated April 21, 1865. Starke, Marchant, and Martin Family Papers. ORA, Series 1, Volume 47, Part 3, 855.
47. Bender, 181–182.
48. Brown, *One of Cleburne's Command*, 173. Williamson, *Third Battalion Mississippi Infantry*, 322.
49. Curry, 221.
50. ORA, Series 1, Volume 47, Part 3, 392. Raab, *W.W. Loring*, 207.
51. *Cincinnati Daily Commercial*, April 27, 1865.
52. Michael B. Ballard, *Pemberton: The General Who Lost Vicksburg* (Jackson: University of Mississippi Press, 1991), 186.
53. Durkin, 177–178.
54. Kevin Levin, "When Johnny Comes Marching Home: The Demobilization of Lee's Army," in Davis and Robertson, 91. Brubaker, 38. Raphael Semmes, *Memoirs of Service Afloat during the War Between the States* (Baltimore, MD: Kelly, 1869), 819.
55. *Chattanooga Gazette*, May 8, 1865. Cumming, 232–233.
56. Eliza F. Andrews, *The War-time Journal of a Georgia Girl, 1864–1865* (New York: Appleton, 1908), 199.

57. Dorsey, 295.

58. Jewett, 213.

59. ORA, Series 1, Volume 46, Part 3, 826, 865, and 1063.

60. Richard B. Harwell, *A Confederate Diary of the Retreat from Petersburg, April 3–20, 1865* (Atlanta, GA: Emory University Press, 1953), 20–22.

61. Hairston Watkins, letter to sister dated April 16, 1865. Elizabeth Seawell Hairston Papers.

62. Ridley, 467.

63. Durkin, 197.

64. Davis, *Long Surrender*, 115.

65. James M. Morgan, *Recollections of a Rebel Reefer* (New York: Houghton-Mifflin, 1917), 237.

66. Govan and Livingood, 374. William J. McMurray, *History of the Twentieth Tennessee Regiment Volunteer Infantry, C.S.A.* (Nashville, TN: Publication Committee, 1904), 359.

67. Govan and Livingood, 372–374.

68. Tucker, 407. Johnston, *Narrative of Military Operations*, 417–418.

69. Joseph Johnston, General Order #23 issued May 2, 1865. Stephen D. Lee Papers. University of North Carolina (Southern Historical Collection); Chapel Hill, North Carolina.

70. Elliott, *Soldier of Tennessee*, 272.

71. Ridley, 466.

72. ORA, Series 1, Volume 47, Part 3, 873.

73. Govan and Livingood, 367.

74. *Pittsburgh Daily Commercial*, May 9, 1865. Govan and Livingood, 367.

75. Abner Foreman, diary entry for April 17, 1865. Abner Foreman Papers.

76. Brown, *One of Cleburne's Command*, 180.

77. Brown, *One of Cleburne's Command*, 181.

78. Hughes, *General William J. Hardee*, 298.

79. William Palmer, letter to James Martin dated April 28, 1865. Starke, Marchant, and Martin Family Papers.

80. Craig, 163. Milo W. Scott, diary entry for April 9, 1865.

81. *Cincinnati Daily Commercial*, May 12, 1865.

82. Grant, *Memoirs*, 652.

83. Thomas and Hyman, 406.

84. John F. Marszalek, *Sherman: A Soldier's Passion for Order* (New York: Free Press, 1993), 347. Mark Coburn, *Terrible Innocence: General Sherman at War* (New York: Hippocrene, 1993), 219.

85. See Wallace L. Ohrt, *Defiant Peacemaker: Nicholas Trist in the Mexican War* (College Station: Texas A&M University Press, 1998) and Jack Nortrup, "Nicholas Trist's Mission to Mexico: A Reinterpretation," *Southwestern Historical Quarterly* 71, no. 3 (January 1968): 321–346.

86. *New York Times*, April 23, 1865.

87. Matthew A. DeWolfe Howe, *Home Letters of General Sherman* (New York: Scribner's, 1909), 291. Fred H. Harrington, *Fighting Politician: Major General N.P. Banks* (Westport, CT. Greenwood, 1948), 164–174. James G. Hollandsworth, *Pretense of Glory: The Life of General Nathanial P. Banks* (Baton Rouge: Louisiana State University Press, 1998), 207–222.
88. McKinney, 449–451.
89. Peter Cozzens, *General John Pope: A Life for the Nation* (Urbana: University of Illinois Press, 2000), 247–249. ORA, Series 1, Volume 48, Part 1, 1202–1203.
90. Thomas and Hyman, 408.
91. Ibid. 343–345.
92. ORA, Series 1, Volume 47, Part 2, 36.
93. Roy P. Basler et al., eds., *The Collected Works of Abraham Lincoln* (New Brunswick, NJ: Rutgers University Press, 1953–1955), 6:429–429. John C. Rodrigue, *Lincoln and Reconstruction* (Carbondale: Southern Illinois University Press, 2013), 83–90. Burlingame, 2:594–596.
94. William B. Holberton, *Homeward Bound: The Demobilization of the Union and Confederate Armies, 1865–1866* (Mechanicsburg, PA: Stackpole, 2001), 7–16.
95. William Marvel, *Lincoln's Autocrat: The Life of Edwin Stanton* (Chapel Hill: University of North Carolina Press, 2015), 372–374.
96. Lew Wallace, *Lew Wallace: An Autobiography* (New York: Harpers, 1906), 2:670–671.
97. David M. DeWitt, *The Assassination of Abraham Lincoln and Its Expiation* (New York: Macmillan, 1909), 56.
98. Bradley, 209.
99. Sherman, *Memoirs*, 876. August Kautz, letter to Isabelle Savage dated May 16, 1865. August V. Kautz Papers. Abraham Lincoln Presidential Library; Springfield, Illinois.
100. Thomas and Hyman, 414–416.
101. John Ott memoirs, 630. John Ott Papers.
102. Herman Hattaway and Richard E. Beringer, *Jefferson Davis, Confederate President* (Lawrence: University Press of Kansas, 2002), 412–413.
103. Matthews, *Bail Wilson Duke*, 194. Longacre, *Gentleman and Soldier*, 242–243. Davis, *Long Surrender*, 90. DuBose, 464. Davis, *Jefferson Davis*, 614.
104. ORA, Series 1, Volume 47, Part 3, 821–828.
105. Davis, *Rise and Fall of the Confederate Government*, 2:689.
106. John T. Wood, diary entry for April 24, 1865. John Taylor Wood Papers.
107. Robert G. Kean, *Inside the Confederate Government: The Diary of Robert Garlick Kean* (New York: Oxford, 1957), 206–207.

108. Basil W. Duke, "Last Days of the Confederacy," *Battles and Leaders of the Civil War* (New York: Century Co., 1884), 4:764–765. Eli N. Evans, *Judah P. Benjamin: The Jewish Confederate* (New York: Free Press, 1988), 311. Underwood, *Stephen Russell Mallory*, 176.

109. Davis, *Rise and Fall of the Confederate Government*, 2:696. ORA, Series 1, Volume 47, Part 3, 826–828. Rembert W. Patrick, *Opinions of the Confederate Attorneys-General* (Buffalo, NY: Dennis & Co., 1950), 580–584. Davis, *Breckinridge*, 519.

110. Davis, *Long Surrender*, 127. Ballard, *A Long Shadow*, 133–134.

111. Lucien Wulsin, *The Story of the Fourth Regiment Ohio Veteran Volunteer Cavalry* (Cincinnati, OH: Fourth Ohio Cavalry Association, 1912), 103.

112. ORA, Series 1, Volume 49, Part 1, 390.

113. Marvel, 462.

114. Robert G. Athearn, *William Tecumseh Sherman and the Settlement of the West* (Norman: University of Oklahoma Press, 1956), 268–269. Charles B. Flood, *Grant and Sherman: The Friendship that Won the Civil War* (New York: Farrar, Straus, and Giroux, 2005), 394–395.

Notes for Chapter 5

1. Robert E. Lee, letter to Richard Taylor dated March 15, 1865. Richard Taylor Papers. Jackson Barracks; New Orleans, Louisiana.

2. Campbell Gibson, *Population of the 100 Largest Cities and Other Urban Places in the United States: 1790 to 1990* (Washington, DC: Bureau of the Census, 1998), 36. Harriet E. Amos, *Cotton City: Urban Development in Antebellum Mobile* (Tuscaloosa: University of Alabama Press, 1985), 212–216. B.L. Roberson, "Valor on the Eastern Shore: The Mobile Campaign of 1865," Confederate Historical Association of Belgium: http://chab-belgium.com/pdf/english/Mobile%20Bay.pdf, 3.

3. Hirshson, 87. ORA, Series 1, Volume 24, Part 3, 584.

4. Jeffrey N. Lash, "A Yankee in Gray: Danville Leadbetter and the Defense of Mobile Bay, 1861–1863," *Civil War History* 37, no. 3 (September 1991): 198–203.

5. Arsène L. Latour: *Historical Memoir of the War in West Florida and Louisiana in 1814–1815* (Philadelphia, PA: Conrad and Co., 1816), 30–45 and 208–225.

6. John M. Hammond, *Quaint and Historic Forts of North America* (Philadelphia, PA: Lippincott, 1915), 257–259. *Hand-book for the War* (Boston, MA: Wholesale Office, 1861), 23. Viktor von Scheliha, *A Treatise on Coast-defense* (London: E. & F.N. Spon, 1868), 17–18.

7. Lash, "A Yankee in Gray," 204.

8. James P. Duffy, *Lincoln's Admiral: The Civil War Campaigns of David Farragut* (Edison, NJ: Castle Books, 1997), 239–253.
9. Bruce S. Allardice, *More Generals in Grey* (Baton Rouge: Louisiana State University Press, 1995), 21. ORA, Series 1, Volume 39, Part 1, 426 and 436. ORN, Series 1, Volume 21, 539 and 615. Robert C. Conner, *General Gordon Granger: The Savior of Chickamauga and the Man Behind "Juneteenth"* (Havertown, PA: Casement Publishers, 2013), 153–157.
10. Lash, "A Yankee in Gray," 203.
11. James L. Nichols, "Confederate Engineers and the Defense of Mobile," *Alabama Review* 12, no. 3 (July 1959): 190–191. Disillusioned by lack of progress, von Sheliha had tried to resign earlier in the summer, but was denied the privilege of resigning his commission.
12. Also sometimes spelled as "Blakeley."
13. Nathaniel C. Hughes, *Liddell's Record: St. John Richardson Liddell, Brigadier General, CSA: Staff Officer and Brigade Commander, Army of Tennessee* (Dayton, OH: Morningside Press, 1985), 195. Nichols, 195.
14. Bergeron, *Confederate Mobile*, 157. Mumford diary, entry for August 27, 1864. ORA, Series 1, Volume 49, Part 1, 1055. ORN, Series 1, Volume 22, 269. Bergeron, *Confederate Mobile*, 154 and 170.
15. Bergeron, *Confederate Mobile*, 171. "History of MAWSS," http://www.mawss.com/history.htm.
16. Baumgartner, 209. Black, 287.
17. Nichols, 186 and 192–194. ORA, Series 1, Volume 49, Part 1, 864–865 and 876–877.
18. Bergeron, *Confederate Mobile*, 158 and 167–168. ORA, Series 1, Volume 39, Part 3, 910–911. Folmar, *From That Terrible Field*, 129–130. Arthur W. Bergeron, "The Twenty-second Louisiana Consolidated Infantry in the Defense of Mobile, 1864–1865," *Alabama Historical Quarterly* 38 (Fall 1976): 208. Clement A. Evans, *Confederate Military History: A Library of Confederate States History, in Twelve Volumes* (Atlanta: Confederate Publishing, 1899), 7: 225–226. Warner, *Generals in Gray*, 57–58.
19. Bergeron, *Confederate Mobile*, 158.
20. McMillan, 100–103. Bergeron, *Confederate Mobile*, 161–162. Bergeron used the term "galvanized Yankees" to describe the Union POWs, but this is incorrect terminology. "Galvanized Yankees" were Confederates who switched sides and fought for the Union, mostly on the western frontier. See Dee Brown, *The Galvanized Yankees* (Champaign: University of Illinois, 1963).
21. ORA, Series 1, Volume 49, Part 1, 1046–1048. Bergeron, *Confederate Mobile*, 168–169. Dabney Maury, letter to Richard Taylor

dated February 3, 1865. Louisiana Historical Center (Department of Alabama, Mississippi, and Eastern Louisiana Collection); New Orleans, Louisiana.

22. Hughes, *Liddell's Record*, 189.
23. ORA, Series 1, Volume 34, Part 3, 331–332.
24. Ibid. Volume 36, Part 2, 328–329.
25. George S. Denison, "Diary and Correspondence of Salmon P. Chase," *Annual Report of the American Historical Association* (Washington, DC: Government Printing Office, 1903), 2:438–440.
26. ORA, Series 1, Volume 34, Part 4, 451.
27. Ibid. Volume 41, Part 2, 465–466. Denison, 440.
28. Ibid. Volume 37, Part 2, 133.
29. Max L. Heyman, *Prudent Soldier: A Biography of Major General E.R.S. Canby* (Glendale, CA: Arthur H. Clark Co., 1959), 219–223.
30. ORA, Series 1, Volume 49, Part 1, 593 and 856–857.
31. Ibid. 875.
32. Heyman, 223–227.
33. ORA, Series 1, Volume 14, Part 1, 1338.
34. Ibid. Volume 48, Part 1, 1337. Kerby, 405.
35. Sean M. O'Brien, *Mobile, 1865: Last Stand of the Confederacy* (Westport, CT: Praeger, 2001), 23–24.
36. Charles C. Hughes, *The Civil War Memoir of Philip Daingerfield Stephenson, D.D.* (Conway, AR: UCA Press, 1995), 356–357. Hughes, *Pride of the Confederate Artillery*, 264. Douglas Cater, letter to cousin dated February 19, 1865. Cater Family Papers.
37. The soldiers were Privates Thomas Elam and Edward Wynn. *Mobile Register and Advertiser*, April 2, 1865. Arthur E. Green, *Mobile Confederates from Shiloh to Spanish Fort: The Story of the 21st Alabama Infantry Volunteers* (Westminster, MD: Heritage Books, 2012), 120 and 374.
38. ORA, Series 1, Volume 39, Part 2, 780.
39. *Richmond Dispatch*, March 29, 1865.
40. *Mobile Advertiser and Register*, March 14, 1865. Bergeron, *Confederate Mobile*, 172.
41. Folmar, *From that Terrible Field*, 157. Hughes, *Civil War Memoir*, 359.
42. Folmar, *From that Terrible Field*, 158.
43. Charles W. Treadway, "The Letters of Charles Wesley Treadway," *Foot Prints: Past and Present* (Richland County [Illinois] Genealogical and Historical Society) 9 (1986): 148.
44. Phillip E. Faller, *The Indiana Jackass Regiment in the Civil War: A History of the 21st Infantry/1st Heavy Artillery Regiment, with a Roster* (Jefferson, NC: McFarland, 2013), 235.
45. Bergeron, *Confederate Mobile*, 173.

46. Mumford diary, entry for March 11, 1865.

47. ORA, Series 1, Volume 49, Part 1, 92–93.

48. David Williamson, *The 47ᵗʰ Indiana Volunteer Infantry: A Civil War History* (Jefferson, NC: McFarland, 2012), 265.

49. ORA, Series 1, Volume 39, Part 2, 772. Bergeron, *Confederate Mobile*, 164.

50. Dabney H. Maury, "Defence of Mobile in 1865," *Southern Historical Society Papers* 3, no. 1 (January 1877): 7.

51. Dabney H. Maury, "Defense of Spanish Fort," *Southern Historical Society Papers* 39, no. 1 (April 1914): 133.

52. Christopher C. Andrews, *History of the Campaign of Mobile* (New York: Van Norstrand, 1889), 48.

53. Mark Lyons, letter to wife dated April 1, 1865. Mark Lyons Papers. McCall Rare Book and Manuscript Library, University of South Alabama; Mobile, Alabama.

54. Maury, "Defence of Mobile," 12. Andrews, *History of the Campaign of Mobile*, 146. ORA, Series 1, Volume 49, Part 2, 1162 and 1179. Hughes, *Liddell's Record*, 194.

55. Bergeron, *Confederate Mobile*, 175. Salling, 222 and 225. Williamson, *47ᵗʰ Indiana*, 270–271.

56. ORA, Series 1, Volume 49, Part 1, 314. Williamson, *47ᵗʰ Indiana*, 270.

57. P.D. Stephenson, "Defence of Spanish Fort," *Southern Historical Society Papers* 39, no. 1 (September 1914): 120.

58. ORA, Series 1, Volume 49, Part 2, 314. Terrence J. Winschel, *The Civil War Diary of a Common Soldier: William Wiley of the 77ᵗʰ Illinois Infantry* (Baton Rouge: Louisiana State University Press, 2001), 145.

59. Hughes, *Civil War Memoir*, 357.

60. Ibid. 359.

61. Stephenson, 122.

62. Henry W. Hart, letter to wife dated April 18, 1865. Henry W. Hart Papers. Mobile Public Library; Mobile, Alabama.

63. Maury, "Defence of Mobile," 7.

64. Winschel, 143–144.

65. Harry Carter, diary entries for March 25 and 29, 1865. Daniel Carter Beard Papers. Library of Congress (Manuscript Division); Washington, D.C.

66. Donald C. Elder, *A Damned Iowa Greyhound: The Civil War Letters of William Henry Harrison Clayton* (Iowa City: University of Iowa Press, 1998), 158–159.

67. Faller, 236–237.

68. Elder, 161 and 164.

69. James Drish, letter to wife dated April 4, 1865. James F. Drish Papers. Abraham Lincoln Presidential Library; Springfield, Illinois.

70. Walter J. Lemke, *Captain Edward Gee Miller of the 20th Wisconsin: His War, 1862–1865* (Washington, AR: Washington County Historical Society, 1960), 30.
71. ORA, Series 1, Volume 49, Part 2, 5–6.
72. Mildred Throne, "Civil War Letters of Abner Dunham, 12th Iowa Infantry," *Iowa Journal of History* 53, no. 4 (October 1955): 333–334.
73. Hughes, *Liddell's Record*, 193–194. Folmar, *From that Terrible Field*, 158.
74. Winschel, 145.
75. Throne, 335.
76. James Newton, letter to parents dated April 5, 1865. James K. Newton Papers, Wisconsin Historical Society; Madison, Wisconsin.
77. Throne, 336.
78. ORA, Series 1, Volume 49, Part 2, 1162. Salling, 224–225.
79. Throne, 336.
80. Winschel, 145–146.
81. William C. Holbrook, *A Narrative of the Services of the Officers and Enlisted Men of the 7th Regiment of Vermont Volunteers (Veterans) from 1862 to 1866* (New York: American Bank Note Company, 1882), 184–185.
82. Stephenson, 121. ORA, Series 1, Volume 49, Part 1, 239–240.
83. Throne, 336–337.
84. ORA, Series 1, Volume 49, Part 1, 239–240.
85. Dennis W. Belcher, *The 11th Missouri Volunteer Infantry in the Civil War: A History and Roster* (Jefferson, NC: McFarland, 2011), 212.
86. Hughes, *Civil War Memoir*," 362.
87. Winschel, 146.
88. Throne, 338.
89. James Newton, letter to mother dated April 2, 1865. James K. Newton Papers.
90. ORA, Series 1, Volume 49, Part 1, 225–226. ORA, Series 1, Volume 49, Part 2, 1176–1177.
91. Bergeron, *Confederate Mobile*, 174–176. George M. Blackburn, *Dear Carrie: The Civil War Letters of Thomas N. Stevens* (Mount Pleasant, MI: Central Michigan University Press, 1984), 308.
92. ORA, Series 1, Volume 49, Part 2, 1180–1181.
93. Faller, 240–242.
94. James Drish, letter to father dated April 1, 1865. James F. Drish Papers.
95. *McKinney [TX] Democrat*. November 21, 1901. ORA, Series 1, Volume 49, Part 2, 1184–1187.
96. Faller, 243.
97. James Newton, letter to mother dated April 2, 1865. James K. Newton Papers.

98. Mumford diary, entry for April 3, 1865.
99. Throne, 338–339. One of the tree mortars produced by the Seventh Minnesota during the siege of Spanish Fort is in the collection of the Minnesota Historical Society (http://www.mnopedia.org/multimedia/gum-tree-mortar-barrel).
100. ORA, Series 1, Volume 49, Part 2, 1191–1194.
101. Ibid. Part 1, 239–240 and Part 2, 16.
102. Stephenson, 122–124.
103. ORA, Series 1, Volume 49, Part 2, 153.
104. Lemke, 31.
105. Mark Lyons, letter to wife dated April 2, 1865. Mark Lyons Papers.
106. Maury, "The Defence of Mobile," 10–11.
107. Hughes, *Civil War Memoir*, 361.
108. ORA, Series 1, Volume 49, Part 1, 316 and Part 2, 1200–1201 and 1211. Salling, 226.
109. Cater, 208.
110. Hughes, *Civil War Memoir*, 364.
111. Stephenson, 122–124.
112. ORA, Series 1, Volume 49, Part 2, 1215.
113. Charles B. Johnson, *Muskets and Medicine: Or Army Life in the Sixties* (Philadelphia, PA: F.A. Davis, 1917), 225–226.
114. James Drish, letter to wife dated April 7, 1865. James F. Drish Papers.
115. ORA, Series 1, Volume 49, Part 1, 316 and Part 2, 1191 and 1204.
116. ORA, Series 1, Volume 49, Part 1, 96.
117. Stephenson, 124, Cortland, 63.
118. ORA, Series 1, Volume 49, Part 1, 316.
119. ORN, Series 1, Volume 49, Part 1, 279
120. The Fourteenth Texas Cavalry was dismounted after the Battle of Murfreesboro in 1862. When pledges to remount them came to nothing, the Fourteenth staged a minor mutiny, with the cry of "Hell or Horses," but their commanding officer persuaded them to return to duty.
121. William Bailey, "The Star Company of Ector's Texas Brigade," *Confederate Veteran* 22, no. 1 (January 1914): 404–405. Hughes, *Liddell's Record*, 195. Bergeron, *Confederate Mobile*, 181.
122. ORA, Series 1, Volume 49, Part 1, 278.
123. Faller, 250.
124. James Newton, letter to parents dated April 9, 1865. James K. Newton Papers.
125. Stephenson, 125–126.
126. Mary G. McBride and Ann M. McLaurin, *Randall Lee Gibson of Louisiana: Confederate General and New South Reformer* (Baton Route: Louisiana University Press, 2007), 112.

127. Faller, 250. Bergeron, *Confederate Mobile*, 181.

128. Lemke, 31.

129. Hughes, *Liddell's Record*, 195. ORA, Series 1, Volume 49, Part 1, 317. Blackburn, 309.

130. Cater, 209. Maury, "Spanish Fort," 131.

131. ORA, Series 1, Volume 49, Part 1, 102.

132. Maury, "Defence of Spanish Fort," 130–131. Hughes, *Liddell's Record*, 190–191.

133. Blackburn, 308.

134. James Newton, letter to parents dated April 9, 1865. James K. Newton Papers.

135. Throne, 339–340.

136. Williamson, *47ᵗʰ Indiana*, 277.

137. Milo Scott, diary entry for April 8, 1865. Milo W. Scott Papers. Chattanooga Public Library; Chattanooga, Tennessee.

138. Blackburn, 310.

139. James Newton, letter to parents dated April 9, 1865. James K. Newton Papers.

140. ORA, Series 1, Volume 49, Part 1, 313–318. Bergeron, *Confederate Mobile*, 182.

141. Hughes, *Liddell's Record*, 195. ORA, Series 1, Volume 49, Part 1, 317. Blackburn, 309.

142. Mumford diary, entry for April 9, 1865.

143. Maury, "Defence of Mobile," 1–3. Maury, "Defence of Spanish Fort," 130–134.

144. Lash, "A Yankee in Gray," 205–206. Robertson, "Valor on the Eastern Shore," 5. Hughes, *Liddell's Record*, 189. Nichols, 191. Elder, 171.

145. Buchanan, 244–245.

146. Vincent Cortright, "Last-Ditch Defenders at Mobile," *America's Civil War* 19, no. 6 (January 1997): 61.

147. Buchanan, 245.

Notes for Chapter 6

1. Taylor, *Destruction and Reconstruction*, 224.

2. ORA, Series 1, Volume 49, Part 1, 92.

3. Isaac Jackson, letters to brother dated February 28 and March 19, 1865. Isaac Jackson Papers, University of Michigan (Clements Library); Ann Arbor, Michigan.

4. Henry W. Hart, letter to wife dated March 6, 1865. Henry W. Hart Papers.

5. ORA, Series 1, Volume 49, Part 1, 309–310. "General Andrew Barclay Spurling"; http://www.cranberryisles.com/photos/andrew_spurling.html.

6. Isaac Jackson, letter to brother dated April 13, 1865. Isaac Jackson Papers.

7. ORA, Series 1, Volume 49, Part 1, 95. 159, and 280–281.

8. Roberson, "Valor on the Eastern Shore," 12.

9. Bergeron, *Confederate Mobile*, 183. Baumgartner, 210–212.

10. Henry W. Hart, letter to wife dated April 10, 1865. Henry W. Hart Papers.

11. Winschel, 150.

12. ORA, Series 1, Volume 49, Part 1, 282–283. Williamson, *47th Indiana*, 266–267.

13. Mumford diary, entry for April 9, 1865.

14. Edward W. Tarrant, "Siege and Capture of Fort Blakely," *Confederate Veteran* 23 (1915): 457–458. Maury, "Defense of Spanish Fort," 135. Bergeron, *Confederate Mobile*, 182–183. Hughes, *Liddell's Record*, 194. The exact number of defenders varies by source, as other sources set the number at 2,500 and another at 2,600.

15. Henry W. Hart, letter to wife dated April 10, 1865. Henry W. Hart Papers.

16. ORA, Series 1, Volume 49, Part 1, 248–250.

17. Andrews, *History of the Campaign of Mobile*, 123–127.

18. Isaac Jackson, letter to brother dated April 13, 1865. Isaac Jackson Papers.

19. Dabney Maury, letter to Maurice H. Garland dated April 2, 1865. Maurice H. Garland Papers. Alabama Department of Archives and History; Montgomery, Alabama.

20. Williamson, *47th Indiana*, 275.

21. Bergeron, *Confederate Mobile*, 186.

22. Henry W. Hart, letter to wife dated April 10, 1865. Henry W. Hart Papers.

23. Jerry Flint, letter to brother dated April 8, 1865. Jerry Flint Papers, University of Wisconsin-River Falls; River Falls, WI.

24. Russell W. Blount, *Besieged: Mobile 1865* (Gretna, LA: Pelican Publishing, 2015), 102.

25. Jerry Flint, letter to brother dated April 8, 1865. Jerry Flint Papers.

26. Hughes, *Liddell's Record*, 194–195.

27. Elihu Justice, diary entry for April 9, 1865. Elihu Justice Papers. Abraham Lincoln Presidential Library; Springfield, Illinois.

28. Faller, 251–253.

29. O'Brien, 187–189.

30. Don Russell, "Letters of a Drummer-Boy," *Indiana Magazine of History* 34, no. 3 (September 1938): 336.

31. *Prescott* [Wisconsin] *Journal*, May 6, 1865.

32. Isaac Jackson, letter to brothers dated April 13, 1865. Isaac Jackson Papers.
33. William Eddington, unpublished memoir, 20. William R. Eddington Papers. Abraham Lincoln Presidential Library; Springfield, Illinois.
34. Abner J. Wilkes, *A Short History of My Life in the Late War between the North and South* (Bethesda, MD: University Publications of America, 1990), 17. Winschel, 150.
35. ORA, Series 1, Volume 49, Part 2, 1198.
36. Mamie Yeary, *Reminiscences of the Boys in Gray, 1861–1865* (Dallas, TX: Wilkinson Printing, 1912), 555.
37. Hearn, *Mobile Bay*, 196.
38. Andrews, *History of the Campaign of Mobile*, 215.
39. Phillip T. Tucker, "The First Missouri Confederate Brigade's Last Stand at Fort Blakeley on Mobile Bay," *Alabama Review* 42, no. 4 (October 1989): 284.
40. Phil Gottschalk, *In Deadly Earnest: The History of the First Missouri Brigade, CSA* (New York: Macmillan, 1990), 521. *Chicago Tribune*, July 14, 1887.
41. Tarrant, 457.
42. Richard Fuchs, *An Unerring Fire: The Massacre at Fort Pillow* (Mechanicsburg, PA: Stackpole, 2017), 63–68. Thurman Sensing, *Champ Ferguson: Confederate Guerilla* (Nashville, TN: Vanderbilt University Press, 1994), 177–185.
43. ORA, Series 1, Volume 49, Part 1, 289–290.
44. Henry Crydenwise, letter to parents dated April 10, 1865. Henry Crydenwise Papers. Emory University; Atlanta, Georgia.
45. Andrews, *History of the Campaign of Mobile*, 210.
46. Charles C. Hughes, *Civil War Memoir of Philip Daingerfield Stephenson*, 368. Henry Chapman, letter to parents dated April 11, 1865. Walter A. Chapman Papers. Yale University; New Haven, Connecticut.
47. George S. Burkhardt, *Confederate Rage, Yankee Wrath: No Quarter in the Civil War* (Carbondale: Southern Illinois University Press, 2007), 239.
48. Walter Chapman, letter dated April 11, 1865. Walter A. Chapman Papers.
49. Hughes, *Liddell's Record*, 196. ORN, Series 1, Volume 22, 101–102.
50. ORA, Series 1, Volume 49, Part 1, 207–208.
51. Hughes, *Liddell's Record*, 196.
52. Blackburn, 311.
53. Mumford diary, entry for April 9, 1865.
54. Isaac Jackson, letter to brothers dated April 13, 1865. Isaac Jackson Papers.

55. Eddington memoir, 21. William R. Eddington Papers.
56. Isaac Jackson, letter to brothers dated April 13, 1865. Isaac Jackson Papers.
57. Winschel, 151.
58. Henry W. Hart, letter to wife dated April 10, 1865. Henry W. Hart Papers.
59. Buttolph, 4. Isaac Jackson, letter to brothers dated April 13, 1865. Isaac Jackson Papers.
60. Williamson, *47ᵗʰ Indiana*, 268.
61. ORN, Series, 1, Volume 21, 568–569. Edwin D. Lindgren, "The Impact of Mine Warfare upon U.S. Naval Operations during the Civil War" (M.A. thesis, Army Command and General Staff College, 1976), 55–69.
62. Faller, 246 and 249.
63. Winschel, 151.
64. Mumford diary, entry for April 9, 1865.
65. Bergeron, *Confederate Mobile*, 187–188. Maury, "The Defence of Mobile," 9–10. ORA, Series 1, Volume 49, Part 2, 1222. Robert P. Buchanan, "The Military Campaign for Mobile, 1864–1865" (M.A. thesis, Auburn University, 1963), 240–241, 240.
66. Mark Lyons, letter to wife dated April 10, 1865. Mark Lyons Papers. Andrews, *History of the Campaign of Mobile,* 231.
67. ORN, Series 1, Volume 22, 95, 102, and 139.
68. Mumford diary, entry for April 11, 1865.
69. *New York Times*, April 26, 1865.
70. Dabney Maury, letters to Richard Taylor dated April 11 and April 13, 1865. Louisiana Historical Collection (Department of Alabama, Mississippi, and Eastern Louisiana Collection); New Orleans, Louisiana.
71. Maury, "Defence of Mobile," 8. ORA, Series 1, Volume 49, Part 1, 151.
72. Mumford diary, entry for April 11, 1865. Daniel Geary, diary entry for April 11, 1865. Daniel Geary Papers. McCall Rare Book and Manuscript Library, University of South Alabama; Mobile, Alabama.
73. Mary D. Waring, "They Marched into Mobile to the Tune of 'Yankee Doodle,'" in Katherine M. Jones, *Heroines of Dixie: Confederate Women Tell Their Story of the War* (Indianapolis, IN: Bobbs-Merrill, 1955), 388–389. Buchanan, 240–241. J. Thomas Scharf, *History of the Confederate States Navy from its Organization to the Surrender of Its Last Vessel* (New York: Rogers & Sherwood, 1887), 595. Bergeron, *Confederate Mobile*, 188–191 and 595. *New York Times*, April 26, 1865.
74. William Rix, *Incidents in the Life of a Southern City during the War* (Rutland, VT: n.p., 1880), 21.

75. Scharf, 595. *New York Times*, April 26, 1865.
76. Conner, 168–169. Waring, 389. Bergeron, *Confederate Mobile*, 190–191.
77. William Fulton, letter to sister dated April 12, 1865. Mobile Public Library (Civil War Diaries and Letters (Mobile)); Mobile, Alabama.
78. Waring, 389. Cumming, 257–258.
79. *Mobile Daily News*, April 14, 1865. Elder, 171.
80. Henry W. Hart, letter to wife dated April 18, 1865. Henry W. Hart Papers.
81. *Cincinnati Daily Commercial*, May 10, 1865.
82. Blackburn, 318–319. Cumming, 260–262. John S. Morgan, "Diary of John S. Morgan, Company G, Thirty-Third Iowa Infantry," *Annals of Iowa* 8, no. 3 (April 1923): 604.
83. Winschel, 164–165.
84. Elder, 170 and 172.
85. Faller, 257.
86. Cater, 210. Buchanan, 241.
87. Hughes, *Pride of the Confederate Artillery*, 275.
88. Maury, *Recollections of a Virginian*, 225.
89. Mumford diary, entry for April 14, 1865.
90. Black, 289.
91. Milton Brown, letter to Richard Taylor dated April 17, 1865. Richard Taylor Papers. Jackson Barracks; New Orleans, Louisiana.
92. ORA, Series, 1, Volume 49, Part 2, 1255.
93. Baumgartner, 221–222.
94. Mumford diary, entries for April 18, 24, and 26, 1865.
95. Hughes, *Pride of the Confederate Artillery*, 275.
96. Ibid. Part 1, 99. *New York Times*, April 26, 1865.
97. Henry W. Hart, letters to wife dated May 2 and May 9, 1865. Henry W. Hart Papers.
98. Isaac Jackson, undated letter to brothers. Isaac Jackson Papers.
99. ORA, Series 1, Volume 49, Part 2, 468.
100. Ibid. 483.
101. Taylor Beatty, diary entry for May 26, 1865. Taylor Beatty Papers.
102. James Newton, letter to parents dated May 17, 1865. Newton K. Papers.
103. Edward Canby, letter to Richard Taylor dated April 19, 1865. Richard Taylor Papers. Louisiana State Museum; New Orleans, Louisiana.
104. Taylor, *Destruction and Reconstruction*, 204–206. Dufour, 36.
105. Robert S. Henry, *The Story of the Confederacy* (New York: DaCapo Press, 1989), 418.
106. ORA, Series 1, Volume 49, Part 1, 1035. John K. Folmar, "The War Comes to Central Alabama: Ebenezer Church, April 1, 1865," *Alabama Historical Quarterly* 26, no. 4 (Fall 1964): 190.

107. Robert M. Dunkerly, *To the Bitter End: Appomattox, Bennett Place, and the Surrenders of the Confederacy* (El Dorado Hills, CA: Savas Beatie, 2015), 79. ORA, Series 1, Volume 49, Part 2, 1255.

108. Richard Taylor, letter to Edward Canby dated April 22, 1865. Richard Taylor Papers. Louisiana State Museum; New Orleans, Louisiana.

109. Maury, *Recollections of a Virginian*, 204.

110. See John Cimprich, *Fort Pillow, a Civil War Massacre, and Public Memory: Civil War Battlefields and Historic Sites Recaptured* (Baton Rouge: Louisiana State University Press, 2011). Daniel E. Sutherland, *Reminiscences of a Private: William E. Bevins of the First Arkansas Infantry, C.S.A.* (Fayetteville: University of Arkansas Press, 1992), 219.

111. Taylor, *Destruction and Reconstruction*, 204.

112. ORA, Series 1, Volume 49, Part 2, 440. Heyman, 232. Parrish, *Richard Taylor*, 438.

113. Isaac Jackson, undated letter to brothers. Isaac Jackson Papers.

114. ORA, Series 1, Volume 49, Part 2, 1263–1264.

115. Parrish, *Richard Taylor*, 440.

116. Dunkerly, 83.

117. Taylor, *Destruction and Reconstruction*, 224.

118. Fisher, 204–205. Taylor, *Destruction and Reconstruction*, 224–225.

119. ORA, Series 1, Volume 49, Part 2, 575.

120. Ibid. 576–577.

121. Ibid. 577–578.

122. Edward Canby, letter to Richard Taylor dated April 30, 1865. Richard Taylor Papers. Louisiana State Museum; New Orleans, Louisiana.

123. Richard Taylor, "The Last Confederate Surrender," *Southern Historical Society Papers* 3, no. 3 (March 1877): 157.

124. ORA, Series 1, Volume 49, Part 2, 1275.

125. Ibid. 609. Yoseloff, 228.

126. *New York Times*, May 16, 1865.

127. ORA, Series 1, Volume 49, Part 2, 1283–1284.

128. David Silkenat, *Raising the White Flag: How Surrender Defined the American Civil War* (Chapel Hill: University of North Carolina Press, 2019), 247.

129. Baumgartner, 223.

130. Mumford diary, entry for May 2, 1865.

131. William T. Alderson, "The Civil War Reminiscences of John Johnston, 1861–1865, Part 2," *Tennessee Historical Quarterly* 14, no. 2 (June 1955): 173.

132. Winschel, 159.

133. Mumford diary, entry for May 4, 1865.

134. Winschel, 159.

135. Taylor, *Destruction and Reconstruction*, 277–279. Heyman, 235.

136. Baumgartner, 224.

137. McCaffrey, 89.

138. Mumford diary, entry for May 10, 1865.

139. Stephenson, 371.

140. Cater, 212.

141. Douglas Cater, letter to cousin dated February 19, 1865. Cater Family Papers.

142. B.P. Gallaway, *The Ragged Rebel: A Common Soldier in W.H. Parsons' Texas Cavalry, 1861–1865* (Austin: University of Texas Press, 1988), 130–131. Cater, *As It Was*, 213–218.

143. Arthur E. Green, *Southerners at War: The 38th Alabama Infantry Volunteers* (Shippensburg, PA: Burd Street Press, 1999), 338. Theresa Arnold-Scriber and Terry G. Scriber, *Ship Island, Mississippi: Rosters and History of the Civil War Prison* (Jefferson, NC: McFarland, 2012), 376–379,

144. ORA, Series 1, Volume 49, Part 2, 552 and 569. Jack Hurst, *Nathan Bedford Forrest: A Biography* (New York: Knopf, 1994), 255–257.

145. James Dinkins, *1861 to 1865 by an Old Johnnie: Personal Recollections and Experiences in the Confederate Army* (Dayton, OH: Morningside Bookshop, 1974), 256–257.

146. ORA, Series 1, Volume 49, Part 2, 609.

147. Cumming, 245.

148. Milo Scott, diary entries for May 4, 11, and 23, 1865.

149. John D. Cater, 213 and 215. Maury, *Recollections of a Virginian*, 226.

150. Craig, 163. Milo W. Scott, diary entry for April 9, 1865. Milo W. Scott Papers.

151. Heyman, 271. Stephenson, 371.

152. Brown, 171.

153. Buttolph, 20.

154. Iobst, 400. Thomas F Dornblaser, *Sabre Strokes of the Pennsylvania Dragoons in the War of 1861–1865* (Philadelphia: Lutheran Publication Society, 1884), 226–227.

155. Treadway, 156.

156. Hughes, *Civil War Memoirs*, 372.

157. Heyman, 271–272.

158. Douglas Cater, letter to cousin dated February 19, 1865. Cater Family Papers.

Notes for Chapter 7

1. McKinney, 453.

2. Wilson, *Under the Old Flag*, 2:105.

3. Frey, 133.
4. Jacob D. Cox, *Military Reminiscences of the Civil War* (New York: Scribner, 1900), 2:353–353. Steven Z. Starr, *The Union Cavalry in the Civil War* (Baton Rouge: Louisiana State University Press, 1979), 2:544–545.
5. ORA, Series 1, Volume 45, Part 2, 15–17, 55, 70–71, 84, 96–97, 114–116, 143, 155, 171, 180, and 195.
6. McKinney, 430–431.
7. Wilson, *Under the Old Flag*, 2:65–65 and 106. McKinney, 431–432. Jones, "Your Left Arm," 234.
8. ORA, Series 1, Volume 45, Part 2, 195.
9. McKinney, 430–432.
10. ORA, Series 1, Volume 45, Part 2, 610–611 and 614.
11. Ibid. 620–621.
12. McKinney, 430 and 441. Chris E. Fonvielle, *The Wilmington Campaign: Last Departing Rays of Hope* (Mechanicsburg, PA: Stackpole, 2001), 332. ORA, Volume 47, Part 2, 131.
13. ORA, Series 1, Volume 39, Part 3, 64. Adna R. Chaffee, "James Harrison Wilson, Cavalryman," *Cavalry Journal* 34, no. 140 (July 1925): 278–282. Ezra J. Warner, *Generals in Blue: Lives of the Union Commanders* (Baton Rouge: Louisiana State University Press, 1964), 566–567.
14. ORA, Series 1, Volume 39, Part 3, 64.
15. Chaffee, 283–284. ORA, Series 1, Volume 45, Part 1, 343.
16. Horn, 420. David V. Stroud, *Ector's Texas Brigade and the Army of Tennessee, 1862–1865* (Longview, TX: Ranger Publishing, 2004), 209–210.
17. ORA, Series 1, Volume 45, Part 2, 429–432.
18. McGee, 480–481. Glenn W. Sunderland, *Lightning at Hoover's Gap: The Story of Wilder's Brigade* (New York: Yoselof, 1969), 193 and 196.
19. Christopher D. McManus, Thomas H. Inglis, and Otho J. Hicks, *Morning to Midnight in the Saddle: Civil War Letters of a Soldier in Wilder's Lightning Brigade* (Bloomington, IN: Xlibris, 2012), 231.
20. Robert S. Merrill, *Civil War Diaries of Robert S. Merrill* (Cedarburg, WI: MGS Press, 1995), 194.
21. Charles Goodrich, letters to wife dated January 23, 25 and 31, 1865. Charles Perry Goodrich Papers. Wisconsin Historical Society; Madison, Wisconsin.
22. Sunderland, 196.
23. Charles B. Seidel, et al., *History of the Service of the Third Ohio Veteran Volunteer Cavalry in the War for the Preservation of the Union from 1861–1865* (Toledo, OH: Stoneman, 1910), 186–187.

24. Thomas Crofts, *History of the Service of the Third Ohio Veteran Volunteer Cavalry* (Columbus, OH: Stoneman Press, 1910), 187.
25. Charles Goodrich, letter to wife dated January 31, 1865. Charles Perry Goodrich Papers.
26. McManus, Inglis, and Hicks, 233 and 239.
27. ORA, Series 1, Volume 49, Part 1, 354.
28. William F. Scott, *The Story of a Cavalry Regiment: The Career of the Fourth Iowa Veteran Volunteers from Kansas to Georgia, 1861–1865* (New York: Putnam's, 1893), 426–428.
29. ORA, Series 1, Volume 45, Part 2, 18.
30. William L. Curry, *Four Years in the Saddle: The History of the First Regiment Ohio Volunteer Cavalry* (Columbus, OH: Champion Printing, 1898), 210.
31. Edward G. Longacre, *From Union Stars to Top Hat: A Biography of the Extraordinary General James Harrison Wilson* (Harrisburg, PA: Stackpole, 1972), 195.
32. Elbridge Colby, "Wilson's Cavalry Campaign of 1865," *Journal of the American Military Foundation* 2, no. 4 (Winter 1938): 207.
33. ORA, Series 1, Volume 45, Part 2, 609 and 616.
34. Taylor, *Destruction and Reconstruction*, 242–243.
35. Paul Ashdown and Edward Caudill, *The Myth of Nathan Bedford Forrest* (New York: Rowman & Littlefield, 2005), 49. ORA, Series 1, Volume 49, Part 1, 930–931.
36. Evans, *Confederate Military History*, 7:223–225. ORA, Series 1, Volume 49, Part 1, 1041–1042.
37. ORA, Series 1, Volume 45, Part 2, 756–757. Fisher, 181–183.
38. David Goodrich, letter to Charles Goodrich dated March 19, 1865. Charles Goodrich Papers.
39. ORA, Series 1, Volume 49, Part 1, 972.
40. Evans, 7:225. Wilson, *Under the Old Flag*, 2:196–197.
41. ORA, Series 1, Volume 49, Part 1, 961–962 and 1034–1035.
42. ORA, Series 1, Volume 49, Part 1, 708–709 and Volume 59, Part 1, 342. McKinney, 435.
43. James P. Jones, *Yankee Blitzkrieg: Wilson's Raid through Alabama and Georgia* (Athens: University of Georgia Press, 1976), 12. Jones, "Your Left Arm," 236.
44. ORA, Series 1, Volume 45, Part 2, 622–623.
45. McKinney, 435.
46. ORA, Series 1, Volume 49, Part 1, 908–909.
47. Starr, 2:542.
48. John W. Rowell, *Yankee Artillerymen: Through the Civil War with Eli Lilly's Indiana Battery* (Knoxville: University of Tennessee Press, 1975), 248. ORA, Series 1, Volume 49, Part 1, 355.

49. Starr, 2:566–567. Colby, 213.

50. Longacre, *From Union Stars to Top Hat*, 197–198.

51. ORA, Series 1, Volume 49, Part 1, 402–404. Colby, 207–208.

52. Ibid. Volume 45, Part 1, 954–955 and Part 2, 61.

53. Warner, *Generals in Blue*, 283–284, 296, and 519–520. David J. Fitzpatrick, *Emory Upton: Misunderstood Reformer* (Norman: University of Oklahoma Press, 2017), 28–53. Stephen E. Ambrose, *Upton and the Army* (Baton Rouge: Louisiana State University Press, 1964), 16–53.

54. Jones, "Your Left Arm," 244–245.

55. Merrill, 200.

56. McManus, Inglis, and Hicks, 244 and 247. Rex Miller, *Croxton's Raid* (Ft. Collins, CO: Old Army Press, 1979), 17.

57. Jones, "Your Left Arm," 237. Cumming, 109. Rogers, 131.

58. ORA, Series 1, Volume 49, Part 1, 1030–1031.

59. Benjamin Nourse, diary entries for March 10 and March 22, 1865. Benjamin Nourse Papers, Duke University (Perkins Library), Durham, NC.

60. *Sketches of War History, 1861–1865: Papers Read Before the Ohio Commandery of the Military Order of the Loyal Legion of the United States*, Volume 1 (Cincinnati, OH: Blake & Co., 1888), 86. Joseph G. Vale, *Minty and the Cavalry: A History of Cavalry Campaigns in the Western Armies* (Harrisburg, PA: Meyers, 1886), 424.

61. ORA, Series 1, Volume 49, Part 1, 908–909.

62. Wilson, *Under the Old Flag*, 2:190. Scott, 426–428. ORA, Series 1, Volume 49, Part 1, 356.

63. Miller, *Croxton's Raid*, 12–13. Fleming, 71.

64. ORA, Series 1, Volume 49, Part 1, 356.

65. ORA, Series 1, Volume 49, Part 1, 472.

66. Charles F. Hinricks, diary entry for March 25, 1865. Charles F. Hinricks Papers, University of Missouri (Western Historical Collections Manuscripts); Columbus, Missouri.

67. McGee, 529.

68. Merrill, 204–205.

69. Miller, *Croxton's Raid*, 23.

70. Danielson, 152–153.

71. Nancy Pape-Findley, *The Invincibles: The Story of the Fourth Ohio Veteran Volunteer Cavalry, 1861–1865* (Tecumseh, MI: Blood Road Publishing, 2002), 242. McGee, 531.

72. ORA, Series 1, Volume 49, Part 1, 411.

73. McGee, 527.

74. William O. Jones, *Journal of W.O. Crouse: August 4th, 1862 to July 1st, 1865* (Lafayette, IN: Tippecanoe County Historical Association), 24–25. McKinney, 434.

75. ORA, Series 1, Volume 49, Part 1, 908–909.
76. Ibid. 1023. James Dinkins, *Furl that Banner: Personal Recollections and Experiences in the Confederate Army* (Dayton, OH: Morningside Bookshop, 1975), 255.
77. Hale, *Third Texas Cavalry*, 270–271.
78. ORA, Series 1, Volume 49, Part 1, 1030. Robert S. Henry, *First with the Most: Forrest* (Indianapolis, IN: Bobbs-Merrill, 1944), 428. ORA, Series 1, Volume 49, Part 2, 1156.
79. "Telegrams Received by Lieut. Gen. Taylor at Selma, Dated from March 27 to April 2, 1865," Louisiana Historical Collection; New Orleans, Louisiana.
80. Howell Cobb, letter to P.G.T. Beauregard dated April 7, 1865. Louisiana Historical Association Collection (Army of Tennessee Papers). Tulane University; New Orleans, Louisiana.
81. Rowell, 251.
82. McGee, 531.
83. Samuel Newton, letter to parents dated May 12, 1865. James K. Newton Papers.
84. ORA, Series 1, Volume 49, Part 1, 350 and 405 and Part 2, 154. Crouse journal, 25. ORA, Series 1, Volume 49, Part 2, 154.
85. ORA, Series 1, Volume 49, Part 2, 154.
86. Rowell, 251.
87. Folmar, 193.
88. Merrill, 207.
89. Merrill, 206–207.
90. Miller, *Croxton's Raid*, 28.
91. Brian S. Wills, "The Confederate Sun Sets on Selma: Nathan Bedford Forrest and the Defense of Alabama in 1865," in Kenneth W. Noe, *The Yellowhammer War: The Civil War and Reconstruction in Alabama* (Tuscaloosa: University of Alabama Press, 2013), 77.
92. Jones, *Yankee Blitzkrieg*, 54–55. Thomas P. Clinton, "The Military Operations of General John T. Croxton in West Alabama, 1865," *Transactions of the Alabama Historical Society* 4 (Montgomery, AL: Alabama Historical Society, 1904), 451–453.
93. ORA, Series 1, Volume 49, Part 1, 421–422. Miller, *Croxton's Raid*, 36–53.
94. Clinton, 449–463.
95. Crouse journal, 25.
96. ORA, Series 1, Volume 49, Part 1, 358.
97. Ibid. 173.
98. James Chalmers, letter to Richard Taylor dated March 21, 1865. Louisiana Historical Collection (Department of Alabama, Mississippi, and Eastern Louisiana Collection); New Orleans, Louisiana.

99. Rowell, 253. James R. Chalmers, "Nathan Bedford Forrest and his Campaigns," *Southern Historical Society Papers* 7, no. 10 (October 1879): 485.

100. ORA, Series 1, Volume 45, Part 1, 642–644. John S. Fisher, *A Builder of the West: The Life of General William Jackson Palmer* (Caldwell, ID: Caxton Printers, 1939), 115–117.

101. Alderson, 169–170.

102. Folmar, "War Comes to Central Alabama," 187–202.

Notes for Chapter 8

1. Goff, 128 and 138. Richard J. Stockham, "Alabama Iron for the Confederacy: The Selma Works," *Alabama Review* 21, no. 3 (July 1968): 164–166.

2. Taylor, *Destruction and Reconstruction*, 219. Hurst, 251.

3. John A. Wyeth, *Life of Lieutenant-General Nathan Bedford Forrest* (New York: Harper, 1908), 603.

4. Crouse journal, 27.

5. Dornblaser, 209–210.

6. Sunderland, 202–203.

7. Longacre, *From Union Stars to Top Hat*, 207. Sunderland, 203–205. Colby, 210–211.

8. Longacre, *From Union Stars to Top Hat*, 207.

9. Frank A. Montgomery, *Reminiscences of a Mississippian in Peace and War* (Cincinnati, OH: Clarke, 1901), 241–245.

10. McManus, Inglis, and Hicks, 254.

11. Crouse journal, 27.

12. Edward A. Straub, *Life and Civil War Services of Edward A. Straub* (Milwaukee, WI: Yewdale & Sons, 1909), 38–39.

13. Hancock, 558–559.

14. Straub, 38–39.

15. Hancock, 558–559.

16. Sunderland, 205. ORA, Series 1, Volume 49, Part 1, 467.

17. Jones, *Yankee Blitzkrieg*, 88.

18. Longacre, *From Union Stars to Top Hat*, 209. Jones, "Your Left Arm," 239.

19. Crouse journal, 28.

20. Rowell 256.

21. Ebenezer N. Gilpin, *The Last Campaign: A Cavalryman's Journal* (Leavenworth, KS: Ketcheson Printing, 1908), 640–641.

22. Wulsin, 74.

23. Gilpin, 640–641.

24. Gilpin, 641–642.

25. Rowell 256.

26. Merrill, 209.

27. McManus, Inglis, and Hicks, 244. McIlwain, 258.

28. Samuel Newton, letter to parents dated May 12, 1865. James K. Newton Papers.

29. McManus, Inglis, and Hicks, 244. McIlwain, 258.

30. Henry T. Malone, "Atlanta Journalism during the Confederacy," *Georgia Historical Quarterly* 37, no. 3 (September 1953): 215. James W. Livingood, "The Chattanooga *Rebel*," *East Tennessee Historical Society's Publications* 39 (1967): 51–54.

31. Wilson, *Under the Old Flag*, 2:241–244.

32. Taylor Beatty, diary entry for April 4, 1865. Taylor Beatty Papers.

33. Chalmers, 485.

34. Rowell, 257. Colby, 211.

35. ORA, Series 1, Volume 48, Part 2, 818–819 and 919–920 and Volume 49, Part 1, 362. Jones, "Your Left Arm," 241. John Hardy, *Selma: Her Institutions and Her Men* (Selma, AL: Times Books, 1869), 52–53.

36. Isaac Jackson Papers, undated letter to brothers.

37. ORA, Series 1, Volume 49, Part 2, 218.

38. Crouse journal, 28.

39. Merrill, 211.

40. ORA, Series 1, Volume, 49, Part 1, 483.

41. Wulsin, 64. Crofts, 197.

42. Rogers, 127–128.

43. ORA, Series 1, Volume 49, Part 2, 1212 and 1239.

44. McMillan, 119.

45. Rogers, 142–144.

46. Rowell 257.

47. Cutrer, 312.

48. Rowell 257–258.

49. Crouse journal, 29. Rogers, 147.

50. ORA, Series 1, Volume 49, Part 1, 362–363 and 407.

51. Ibid. 407.

52. Crouse journal, 29.

53. ORA, Series 1, Volume 49, Part 1, 433–434.

54. Crouse journal, 30.

55. ORA, Series 1, Volume 49, Part 1, 428–429. William E. Brickell, "The Battle of Fort Tyler," *The Southern Practitioner* 22 (1900): lxi. Eleanor D. Scott and Carl Summers, Jr., *The Battle of West Point: April 16, 1865* (Valley, AL: Chattahoochee Valley Historical Society, 1997), 46, 58, and 66.

56. Brickell, lxi–lxii.

57. ORA, Series 1, Volume 49, Part 1, 428–429.

58. Crouse journal, 30–31.

59. James M. Madurner, letter to Charles Goodrich dated May 28, 1865. Charles Perry Goodrich Papers.

60. Brickell, lxii. ORA, Series 1, Volume 49, Part 1, 428–429. Scott and Summers, 37 and 60–61.

61. S.F. Power, "Personal Reminiscences of the Last Battle of the War, at West Point, Geo., April 15, 1865," *Confederate Veteran* 18, no. 1 (January 1910): 27–29. Brickell, lxi–lxii.

62. Crouse journal, 30–31.

63. Merrill, 215. Scott and Summers, 70.

64. Pollard, *The Lost Cause*, 725.

65. Crouse journal, 31. Brickell, lxii. ORA, Series 1, Volume 49, Part 1, 429–430.

66. Merrill, 215. Scott and Carl Summers, 38–39.

67. Stewart C. Edwards, "To Do the Manufacturing for the South: Private Industry in Confederate Columbus," *Georgia Historical Quarterly* 85, no. 4 (Winter 2001): 538–549.

68. Gordon L. Jones, *Confederate Odyssey: The George W. Wray, Jr. Civil War Collection at the Atlanta Historical Center* (Athens: University of Georgia Press, 2014), 197. Edwards, "Manufacturing," 543–546.

69. Amanda Rees, *Columbus History from the River: Historical Narratives from the White Water Express River Guides* https://history.columbusstate.edu/cc_projects/2014_History_from_the_River.pdf, 27–28. Edwards, "Manufacturing," 540–544.

70. Nancy Telfair, *A History of Columbus, Georgia, 1828–1928* (Columbus, GA: Historical Publishing Co, 1929), 134.

71. *Columbus Daily Sun*, April 15, 1865.

72. Iobst, 377–378.

73. Telfair, 134.

74. Colby, 213.

75. Bragg, *Joe Brown's Army*, 107.

76. ORA, Series 1, Volume 49, Part 1, 501.

77. Wilson, *Under the Old Flag*, 2:260. ORA, Series 1, Volume 49, Part 1, 442 and 498–503.

78. ORA, Series 1, Volume 49, Part 1, 344 and 408. In his postwar memoirs, Wilson listed Union casualties as a total of 28 dead and wounded. Wilson, *Under the Old Flag*, 2:265–266.

79. Charles A. Misulia, *Columbus, Georgia, 1865: The Last True Battle of the Civil War* (Tuscaloosa: University of Alabama Press, 2010), 161.

80. In his postwar memoirs, Wilson listed Union casualties as twenty-eight dead and wounded. Wilson, *Under the Old Flag*, 2:265–266. Misulia, 167–170 and 178–179.
81. Bragg, *Joe Brown's Army*, 107. Cumming, 221.
82. Wilson, *Under the Old Flag*, 2:266.
83. ORA, Series 1, Volume 49, Part 1, 344, 48, and 487. Williams, *Rich Man's War*, 181.
84. ORA, Series 1, Volume 49, Part 1, 487.
85. Charles D. Mitchell, "Field Notes of the Selma Campaign," *Sketches of War History, 1861–1865*, vol. 6 (Cincinnati, OH: Monfort & Company, 1908), 192.
86. ORA, Series 1, Volume 49, Part 1, 487. Charles J. Swift, *The Last Battle of the Civil War* (Columbus, GA: Gilbert Printing, 1915), 31. ORA, Series 1, Volume 49, Part 1, 344.
87. ORA, Series 1, Volume 49, Part 1, 102.
88. Iobst, 379–380, 387–388, and 391.
89. Sunderland, 209.
90. Crofts, 200–201. ORA, Series 1, Volume 49, Part 1, 457–459. Wilson, *Under the Old Flag*, 2:282.
91. Iobst, 394. Jones, "Your Left Arm," 238. Wilson, *Under the Old Flag*, 2:278–281. ORA, Series 1, Volume 49, Part 1, 102.
92. Felton, 91.
93. ORA, Series 1, Volume 49, Part 1, 368.
94. McManus, Inglis, and Hicks, 256.
95. Felton, 91.
96. Crofts, 203–204. ORA, Series 1, Volume 49, Part 2, 486.
97. Rogers, 100–101. ORA, Series 1, Volume 49, Part 2, 746–747. Ellen C. Long, *Florida Breezes: Or Florida, New and Old* (Jacksonville, FL: Ashmead, 1882), 380–381. Bertram H. Groene, "A Letter from Occupied Tallahassee," *Florida Historical Quarterly* 48, no. 1 (July 1969): 70. Rogers, 100. ORA, Series 1, Volume 49, Part 2, 524.
98. ORA, Series 1, Volume 49, Part 2, 746–747. James P. Jones and William W. Rogers, "The Surrender of Tallahassee," *Apalachee* 6, no. 1 (1967): 106. *Tallahassee Florida and Journal*, May 20, 1865.
99. Merrill, 222–223.
100. James M. Dancy, "Reminiscences of the Civil War," *Florida Historical Quarterly* 37, no. 1 (July 1958): 86.
101. William W. Davis, *Civil War and Reconstruction in Florida* (New York: Columbia University Press, 1913), 329.
102. ORA, Series 1, Volume 47, Part 3, 409, 444, and 485.
103. Ibid. 494.
104. Ibid. Volume 49, Part 2, 932.

105. ORA, Series 1, Volume 47, Part 3, 538 and 580–581.
106. Dickison, 212.
107. ORA, Series 1, Volume 49, Part 2, 396–397.
108. Ibid. 456 and 487. Gerald J. Smith, *One of the Most Daring of Men: The Life of Confederate General William Tatum Wofford* (Murfrees-boro, TN: Southern Heritage Press, 1997), 142–144.
109. ORA, Series 1, Volume 49, Part 2, 488 and 569 and 590–591.
110. Smith, *One of the Most Daring of Men*, 145–146.
111. ORA, Series 1, Volume 49, Part 2, 605–607, 736, and 748–749.
112. ORA, Series 1, Volume 49, Part 2, 890, 950, and 1053. Obituary of William T. Wofford, *The Courant American* (Catersville, Georgia), September 8, 1887. Avery, 338.
113. ORA, Series 1, Volume 49, Part 2, 768.
114. Avery, *State of Georgia*, 338–339.
115. ORA, Series 1, Volume 49, Part 2, 550 and 648–649.
116. Ibid. 671. 814–815, and 872. McKinney, 440.
117. Ibid. Volume 46, Part 3, 1298–1299 and Volume 49, Part 2, 960 and 1035–1036 and Series 1.
118. Colby, 213–214.
119. Fleming, 77.
120. ORA, Series 1, Volume 49, Part 1, 429–430.
121. Jerry Keenan "Wilson's Selma Raid," *Civil War Times Illustrated* 1, no. 9 (January 1963): 44.
122. Grant, *Memoirs*, 2:518.

Notes for Chapter 9

1. *Cincinnati Daily Commercial*, May 29, 1865.
2. Florence E. Holladay, "The Powers of the Commander of the Confed-erate Trans-Mississippi Department, 1863–1865, Part 1," *Southwestern Historical Quarterly* 21, no. 3 (January 1918): 279–282.
3. Woodworth, 54–55. ORA, Series 1, Volume 6, 788–789 and 787–798.
4. ORA, Series 1, Volume 17, Part 2, 788–792.
5. Ibid. Volume, 8, 826.
6. Ibid. Volume 53, Part 1, 804–805.
7. Robert R. Mackey, "Bushwhackers, Provosts and Tories: The Guerilla War in Arkansas" in Daniel E. Sutherland, ed., *Guerillas, Unionists, and Violence on the Confederate Home Front* (Fayetteville: University of Arkansas Press, 1999), 172. Diane Neal and Thomas W. Kremm, *The Lion of the South: General Thomas C. Hindman* (Macon, GA: Mercer University Press, 1993), 114–115. ORA, Series 1, Volume 13, 829.
8. Woodworth, 60–61.

9. ORA, Series 1, Volume 13, 848–849 and Volume 39, Part 1, 28–33. Robert G. Hartje, *Van Dorn: The Life and Times of a Confederate General* (Nashville, TN: Vanderbilt University Press, 1967), 163–165. ORA, Series 1, Volume 13, 856–858 and 936–943.

10. Walter C. Hilderman, *Theophilus Hunter Holmes: A North Carolina General in the Civil War* (Jefferson, NC: McFarland, 2013), 96. ORA, Series 1, Volume 15, 775.

11. Joseph H. Parks, *General Edmund Kirby Smith, C.S.A.* (Baton Rouge: Louisiana State University Press, 1954), 130–137, 197–199, and 220–239. Anderson P. Quisenberry, "The Confederate Campaign in Kentucky, 1862: The Battle of Perryville," *Register of Kentucky State Historical Society* 17, no. 49 (January 1919): 29–38. ORA, Series 1, Volume 22, Part 2, 798.

12. ORA, Series 1, Volume 22, Part 2, 802–803.

13. Ibid. Part 1, 925–927.

14. Holladay, Part 1, 290 and Part 2, 359.

15. Florence E. Holladay, "The Powers of the Commander of the Confederate Trans-Mississippi Department, 1863–1865, Part II," *Southwestern Historical Quarterly* 21, no. 4 (April 1918): 340.

16. Edmund Kirby Smith, letter to Robert W. Johnson dated March 16, 1865. Edmund Kirby Smith Papers (UNC).

17. ORA, Series 1, Volume 22, Part 2, 935–936.

18. Holladay, Part 1, 284–288. William T. Windham, "The Problem of Supply in the Trans-Mississippi Confederacy," *Journal of Southern History* 27, no. 2 (May 1961): 155. Jewett, 234. ORA, Series 1, Volume 22, Part 2, 2005–2009.

19. Sarah Wadley, diary entry for September 23, 1863. Sarah Lois Wadley Papers. University of North Carolina (Southern Historical Collection); Chapel Hill, North Carolina.

20. Ibid. 948.

21. Holladay, Part 1, 294–295. Ramsdell, *Confederate Laws*, 119–121.

22. Windham, 156–157.

23. Neal and Kremm, 120.

24. Ralph A. Wooster and Robert Wooster, "A People at War: East Texans during the Civil War," *East Texas Historical Journal* 28, no. 1 (1990): 8–10. Ralph A. Wooster, "Life in Civil War East Texas," *East Texas Historical Journal* 3 (October 1965): 96. Vera L. Dugas, "A Social and Economic History of Texas in the Civil War and Reconstruction Periods" (Ph.D. dissertation, University of Texas, 1963), 305. Holladay, Part 2, 335. ORA, Series 1, Volume 22, 1135. Day, 15. Charles M. Ramsdell, "The Texas State Military Board, 1862–1865," *Southwestern Historical Quarterly* 27, no. 4 (April 1924): 266.

25. Allen C. Ashcraft, "Texas, 1860–1866: The Lone Star State in the Civil War" (Ph.D. dissertation, Columbia University, 1960), 162–163. Charles W. Ramsdell, *Behind the Lines in the Southern Confederacy* (Baton Rouge: Louisiana State University Press, 1944), 73.

26. Thomas L. Connelly, "Vicksburg: Strategic Point or Propaganda Device?" *Military Affairs* 34, no. 2 (April 1970): 49. William A. Albaugh, *Tyler, Texas: The Story of the Confederate States Ordnance Works at Tyler, Texas, 1861–1865* (Mechanicsburg, PA: Stackpole, 1958), 135. Kerby, 381.

27. ORA, Series 1, Volume 13, 877–878 and 882–883. Hindman Report, 6.

28. Sheiber, 358. Ball, 121.

29. Sheiber, 357–360.

30. Cutrer and Parrish, 253–254.

31. ORA, Series 1, Volume 48, Part 1, 1381–1382.

32. Edmund Kirby Smith, letter to Robert W. Johnson dated March 16, 1865. Edmund Kirby Smith Papers (UNC).

33. Frank L. Owsley, *King Cotton Diplomacy: Foreign Relations of the Confederate States of America* (Chicago: University of Chicago Press, 1931), 31.

34. Fredericka Meiners, "The Texas Border Cotton Trade, 1862–1863," *Civil War History* 23, no. 4 (December 1977): 297 and 299. Henry, 342. Daddysman, 120–121. Surdam, 177–179.

35. Kenneth R. Jacobs, "The Confederate Diplomatic Missions to Mexico of John T. Pickett and Juan A. Quintero" (M.A. thesis, Hardin-Simmons University, 1970), 80.

36. ORA, Series 1, Volume 15, 900–901.

37. Ibid. Volume 53, Part 1, 845–846.

38. Meiners, 298–299. ORA, Series 1, Volume 53, Part 1, 867–868.

39. Tyler, 462–463.

40. Oates, 403. Alfred J. Hanna and Kathryn A. Hanna, "The Immigration Movement of the Intervention and Empire as Seen Through the Mexican Press," *Hispanic American Historical Review* 27, no. 2 (May 1947): 233. Robert W. Delaney, "Matamoros, Port for Texas during the Civil War," *Southwestern Historical Quarterly* 58, no. 4 (April 1955): 474.

41. James Freeman, letters to daughter dated February 15 and March 10, 1865, and letters to wife dated February 17, March 6, and March 10, 1865. James W. Freeman Papers, Dolph Briscoe Center for American History, University of Texas (Austin, Texas).

42. Stickles, 251. Windham, 162.

43. *Chattanooga Gazette*, May 8, 1865.

44. *Weekly State Gazette* (Austin, TX), March 29, 1865.

45. Strom, 93. Ellis, "Maritime Commerce," 189.

46. Dean B. Mahin, *One War at a Time: The International Dimensions of the American Civil War* (Washington, DC: Brassey's, 1999), 109–110.

47. Philip L. Russell, *The History of Mexico: From Pre-Conquest to Present* (New York: Taylor & Francis, 2010), 225. Brian Hamnett, *Juarez* (New York: Longman, 1994), 171. David Baguley, *Napoleon III and His Regime: An Extravaganza* (Baton Rouge: Louisiana State University Press, 2000), 177.

48. Rodman L. Underwood, *Waters of Discord: The Union Blockade of Texas during the Civil War* (Jefferson, NC: McFarland, 2003), 122–123.

49. ORA, Series 1, Volume 22, Part 2, 953 and Volume 24, Part 2, 437–438. John N. Edwards, *Biography, Memoirs, Reminiscences and Recollections: His Brilliant Career as Soldier, Author, and Journalist* (Kansas City: Jennie Edwards, 1889), 511–512. Hutchins bio on Texas Historical Association website (http://www.tshaonline.org/handbook/online/articles/fhu51).

50. Stanley Lebergott, "Through the Blockade: The Profitability and Extent of Cotton Smuggling, 1861–1865," *Journal of Economic History* 41, no. 4 (December 1981): 868. ORA, Series 1, Volume 34, Part 4, 639. Megee, 49–52. Holladay, Part 2, 344 and 352.

51. Holladay, Part 2, 349–350. ORA, Series 1, Volume 34, 638–639.

52. Daddysman, 132. Holladay, Part 2, 349–350.

53. Kerby, 385–386. Winters, 322.

54. Judith F. Gentry, "White Gold: The Confederate Government and Cotton in Louisiana," *Louisiana History* 33, no. 3 (Summer 1992): 233–235.

55. Stickles, 261–262. ORA, Volume 48, Part 1, 1343–1344.

56. Hans P. Gammel, *The Laws of Texas, 1822*–1897, vol. 5 (Austin, TX: Gammel Book Company, 1898), 499 and 680.

57. Holladay, Part 2, 356. Hendrickson, 241.

58. Day, 23–26.

59. Ibid. 27.

60. Edward T. Miller, "State Finances of Texas during the Civil War," *Quarterly of the Texas State Historical Society* 14, no. 1 (July 1910): 3–4. Daddysman, 130.

61. ORA, Series 1, Volume 34, Part 3, 730–732.

62. ORA, Series 1, Volume 53, Part 1, 986.

63. Ibid. Volume 34, Part 3, 821–822 and Volume 41, Part 4, 1133.

64. ORA, Series 1, Volume 41, Part 4, 1106. *Journal of the Senate of the United States of America* (39th Congress, 1st Session) (Washington, DC: Government Printing Office 1866), 147 and 191. Ramsdell, *Laws and Joint Resolutions*, 107, 110, and 144–145.

65. Samuel B. Thompson, *Confederate Purchasing Operations Abroad* (Chapel Hill: University of North Carolina Press, 1935), 117. Daddysman, 143.

66. Ronnie C. Tyler, "Cotton on the Border, 1861–1865," *Southwestern Historical Quarterly* 73, no. 4 (April 1970): 456. Jewett, 222 and 238. L. Tuffly Ellis, "Maritime Commerce on the Far Western Gulf, 1861–1865," *Southwestern Historical Quarterly* 77, no. 2 (October 1973): 224n. More than 300,000 bales went through Matamoros, about 20 percent of the 1.25 million bales shipped by the Confederacy during the war. Of the bales shipped out of Matamoros, about two-thirds went to Great Britain while most of the remainder wound up in American textile mills. Another 70,000 bales left through other ports, such as Galveston or Corpus Christi.

67. Marten, 87–88. Smith, in Sutherland, *Reminiscences of a Private,* 134 and 136. Tatum, 11, and 44–45.

68. Stephen B. Oates, *Rip Ford's Texas* (Austin: University of Texas Press, 1963), 338 n. 2. Lois C. Ellsworth, "San Antonio during the Civil War," (M.A. thesis, University of Texas, 1938), 47–48.

69. Anne J. Bailey, "Defiant Unionists: Militant Germans in Confederate Texas," in Inscoe and Kenzer, 215. Robert W. Shook, "The Battle of the Nueces, August 10, 1862," *Southwest Historical Quarterly* 66, no. 1 (July 1962): 31–42. Stanley S. McCowen, "Battle or Massacre?: The Incident on the Nueces, August 10, 1862," *Southwestern Historical Quarterly* 104, no. 1 (July 2000): 64–86.

70. Smith, "Limits of Dissent," 136–137. Samuel Acheson and Julie Ann O'Connell, "George Washington Diamond's Account of the Great Hanging at Gainesville, 1862," *Southwest Historical Quarterly* 65, no. 3 (January 1863): 374–376. John C. Roane, letter to Thomas C. Hindman dated November 2, 1862. John C. Roane Papers; Missouri State Archives (Jefferson City, Missouri).

71. Smith, "Limits of Dissent," 138–139. L. W. Kemp, "Young, William Cocke," Handbook of Texas Online (http://www.tshaonline.org/handbook/online/articles/fyo14).

72. Oates, *Rip Ford*, 338.

73. Marten, 87–91.

74. ORA, Series 1, Volume 15, Part 1, 926–927.

75. Ibid. Volume 34, Part 2, 911.

76. Smith, in Sutherland, 139.

77. Ibid. Volume 26, Part 2, 119.

78. Bob Alexander, *Six-Shooters and Shifting Sands: The Wild West Life of Texas Ranger Captain Frank Jones* (Denton: University of North Texas Press, 2015), 17.

79. Marten, 96.
80. Frances E. Abernethy, *Tales from the Big Thicket* (Denton: University of North Texas Press, 2002), 75–78.
81. Ibid. Volume 26, Part 2, 285.
82. Henry McCullough, letter to James A. Bourland dated October 29, 1863 (microfilm). James A. Bourland Papers. Library of Congress (Manuscript Division); Washington, DC. Sutherland, *A Savage Conflict*, 218–219. ORA, Series 1, Volume 26, Part 2, 394.
83. Frazier, in Sutherland, 163–165.
84. ORA, Series 1, Volume 26, Part 2, 455–456.
85. Welsh, 198–199.
86. ORA, Series 1, Volume 22, Part 2, 989.
87. Edmund Kirby Smith, letter to Jefferson Davis dated March 9, 1865. Edmund Kirby Smith Papers (UNC).
88. ORA, Series 1, Volume 52, Part 2, 763–764.
89. Jewett, 227 and 231.
90. Colin J. McRae, letter to Edmund Kirby Smith dated April 1, 1865; King & Co., letter to Edmund Kirby Smith dated May 27, 1865; and Edmund Kirby Smith, letter Edward R. Hood dated May 29, 1865. Edmund Kirby Smith Papers (UNC).
91. Jewett, 246.
92. Steven E. Woodworth, *No Band of Brothers: Problems in the Rebel High Command* (Columbia: University of Missouri Press, 1999), 53. Dorsey, 290. Kerby, 431–433.
93. Jewett, 245.

Notes for Chapter 10

1. William Hale, letter to wife dated February 11, 1865. William Job Hale Letters. Dolph Briscoe Center for American History, University of Texas; Austin, Texas.
2. Ramsdell, "Texas State Military Board," 255–256.
3. ORA, Series 1, Volume 48, Part 2, 1262–1263, 1276, and 1281–1282.
4. Jewett, 239.
5. ORN, Series 1, Volume 19, Part 1, 213, 254–255. ORA, Series 1, Volume 15, Part 1, 147–148. Edward T. Cotham, *Battle on the Bay: The Civil War Struggle of Galveston* (Austin: University of Texas Press, 1998), 73–86. James M. Schmidt, *Galveston and the Civil War: An Island City in the Maelstrom* (Charleston, SC: History Press, 2012), 54–64. Cotham, *Battle on the Bay*, 124–134.
6. Hollandsworth, 44–90.

7. ORA, Series 1, Volume 26, Part 1, 290–292. Edward T. Cotham, *Sabine Pass: The Confederacy's Thermopylae* (Austin: University of Texas Press, 2004), 92–102.

8. ORA, Series 1, Volume 26, Part 1, 294–297 and 311–312. Edward T. Cotham, "Nothing but Disaster: The Failure of Union Plans to Capture Texas," in Howell, 136–145. Barr, 23–27.

9. John W. Hunter, *The Fall of Brownsville on the Rio Grande, November 1863*. Jeffrey W. Hunt, *The Last Battle of the Civil War: Palmetto Ranch* (Austin: University of Texas Press, 2002), 16–24. Norman Rozeff, "The Story of Union Forces in South Texas During the Civil War," Harlingen Historical Preservation Society, 2011. (http://www.cchc.us/Articles/StoryOfUnionForces.pdf). Hollandsworth, 141–143. Oates, *Rip Ford*, 368.

10. Porter, 212.

11. Ludwell H. Johnson, *Red River Campaign: Politics and Cotton in the Civil War* (Baltimore, MD: Johns Hopkins University Press, 1958), 47. ORA, Series 1, Volume 43, Part 3, 534–535, 103–104, and 515, and Volume 14, Part 1, 412–5413. *Report of the Joint Committee on the Conduct of the War: Red River Expedition* (Washington, DC: Government Printing Office, 1865), 274.

12. Johnson, *Red River Campaign*, 48. ORA, Series 1, Volume 24, Part 3, 584.

13. ORA, Series I, Volume 34, Part 1, 167–176. Porter, 213. Forsyth, 71–72 and 192–193. Joiner and Sandefur, in Joiner, 102–103.

14. Joiner and Sandefur, in Joiner, 105–107 and 109. ORA, Series 1, Volume 34, Part 1, 183.

15. Gregory Urwin and Cathy Urwin, *History of the 33rd Iowa Infantry Volunteer Regiment* (Fayetteville: University of Arkansas Press, 1999), 71.

16. Boggs, 77. ORA, Series 1, 34, Part 1, 571–572.

17. James K. Ewer, *The Third Massachusetts Cavalry in the War for the Union* (Boston: Historical Committee of the Regimental Association, 1903), 169. Johnson, *Red River Campaign*, 268–272.

18. Ralph R. Rea, "Diary of Private John P. Wright, U.S.A., 1864–1865," *Arkansas Historical Quarterly* 15, no. 3 (Fall 1957): 316. ORA, Series 1, Volume 34, Part 3, 802, 810–811.

19. Johnson, *Red River Campaign*, 277–278.

20. Bruce Tap, *Over Lincoln's Shoulder: The Committee on the Conduct of the War* (Lawrence: University Press of Kansas, 1998), 224–226.

21. *Report of the Joint Committee on the Conduct of the War*, 28–29 and 270–271. Richard B. Irwin, "The Red River Campaign," *Battles and Leaders of the Civil War*, vol. 4 (New York: Century Co., 1887), 362–364.

22. Forsythe, 18.

23. ORA, Series 1, Volume 41, Part 1, 113–117.

24. Ibid. Volume 34, Part 1, 549 and 583–584.

25. Ibid. 540–548.

26. ORA, Series 1, Volume 34, Part 1, 540–541 and 598.

27. Ibid. Part 2, 1034, Part 4, 664, and Volume 41, Part 2, 1039.

28. Gary D. Joiner, "Lieutenant Edward Cunningham: A Kirby Smith Loyalist Complains About Richard Taylor," in Gary D. Joiner, ed., *Little to Eat and Thin Mud to Drink: Letters, Diaries, and Memoirs from the Red River Campaigns, 1863–1864* (Knoxville: University of Tennessee Press, 2007), 80.

29. Edmund Kirby Smith, letter to mother dated December 24, 1864. Edmund Kirby Smith Papers. University of North Carolina (Southern Historical Collection); Chapel Hill, North Carolina.

30. See William R. Brooksher, *Bloody Hill: The Civil War Battle of Wilson's Creek* (Washington, DC: Potomac Books, 1999).

31. Daniel O'Flaherty, *General Jo Shelby: Undefeated Rebel* (Chapel Hill: University of North Carolina Press, 1954), 214–215. Kerby, 333.

32. O'Flaherty, 214–216. Thomas M. Settles, *John Bankhead Magruder: A Military Reappraisal* (Baton Rouge: Louisiana State University Press, 2009), 276. Starr, 2:504–505.

33. Antony Arthur, *General Jo Shelby's March* (New York: Random House, 2010), 53. Starr, 2:503.

34. ORA, Series 1, Volume 41, Part 1, 728–729.

35. Albert Castel, *General Sterling Price and the Civil War in the West* (Baton Rouge: Louisiana State University Press, 1968), 213–219. Kyle S. Sinisi, *The Last Hurrah: Sterling Price's Missouri Expedition of 1864* (New York: Rowman & Littlefield, 2015), 77–87. George S. Grover, "The Price Campaign of 1864," *Missouri Historical Review* 6, no. 4 (July 1912): 167–181.

36. Samuel S. Curtis, *A Cruise on the Benton: A Narrative of Combat on the Missouri River in the Civil War* (Waynesboro, VA: M & R Books, 1967), 1–17.

37. John N. Edwards, *Shelby and His Men: Or the War in the West* (Cincinnati, OH: Miami Printing, 1867), 471.

38. Stephen B. Oates, *Confederate Cavalry West of the River* (Austin: University of Texas Press, 1961), 152. O'Flaherty, 226.

39. ORA, Series 1, Volume 41, Part 1, 625–640. Robert E. Shalhope, *Sterling Price: Portrait of a Southerner* (Columbia: University of Missouri Press, 1971), 246–247, 274.

40. Edwards, *Biography*, 232. ORA, Series 1, Volume 41, Part 1, 652–662.

41. ORA, Series 1, Volume 41, Part 4, 1068–1069.

42. Ibid. Volume 48, Part 1, 1418–1419.

43. Andrew F. Rolle, *The Lost Cause: The Confederate Exodus to Mexico* (Norman: University of Oklahoma Press, 1965), 15.

44. ORA, Series 1, Volume 41, Part 4, 1075–1076.

45. Starr, 3:170.

46. ORA, Series 1, Volume 41, Part 4, 1121–1122. Holladay, Part 2, 338.

47. Oates, *Confederate Cavalry West of the River*, 155. ORA, Series 4, Volume 44, Part 4, 1105–1106.

48. ORA, Series 1, Volume 41, Part 4, 1056–1057.

49. James Fremantle, *The Fremantle Diary: A Journal of the Confederacy* (Boston: Little & Brown, 1954), 58.

50. Francis R. Lubbock, *Six Decades in Texas: Or Memoirs of Francis Richard Lubbock, Governor of Texas in War Time, 1861–1863* (Austin, TX: Ben C. Jones and Co., 1900), 331.

51. ORA, Series 1, Volume 13, Part 1, 38.

52. Bill Stein, "Distress, Discontent, and Dissent: Colorado County, Texas, during the Civil War," in Howell, 309–310.

53. ORA, Series 1, Volume 48, Part 1, 1351–1352.

54. Oates, *Confederate Cavalry West of the River*, 155. ORA, Series 4, Volume 44, Part 4, 1105–1106.

55. Jon Harrison, "The Confederate Letters of John Simmons," *Chronicles of Smith County (Texas)* 14, no. 1 (Summer 1975): 49.

56. Frank Babin, letter to Henrietta Lauzin dated March 1, 1865. Gras-Lauzin Papers.

57. Joe M. Scott, *Four Years' Service in the Southern Army* (Fayetteville, AR: Washington County Historical Society, 1959), 46.

58. ORA, Series 1, Volume 41, Part 4, 716

59. Ibid. Volume 49, Part 1, 1228–1229.

60. Ibid. Volume 48, Part 2, 50–53.

61. Thomas D. Schoonover, *Mexican Lobby: Matías Romero in Washington 1861–1867* (Lexington: University of Kentucky Press, 2014), 58.

62. ORA, Series 1, Volume 49, Part 2, 283.

63. Pecquet, "Louisiana," 288. Harrison, 41–42. Albaugh, 169. ORA, Series 1, Volume 22, Part 2, 1137–1139 and Volume 48, Part 1, 1382–1383 and 1422.

64. ORN, Volume 22, 30, 61 and 123–124. Cotham, *Battle on the Bay*, 177–178.

65. Winters 415. Michael E. Banasik, *Serving with Honor: The Diary of Captain Eathan Allen Pinnell of the Eighth Missouri Infantry (Confederate)* (Iowa City, IA: Camp Pope Bookshop, 1999), 210 and 222.

66. ORA, Series 1, Volume 48, Part 1, 1409–1410.

67. John S.C. Abbott, *The History of the Civil War in America* (New York: Henry Bill, 1866), 2:605.
68. Edmund Kirby Smith, letter to mother dated January 17, 1865. Edmund Kirby Smith Papers (UNC).
69. Winters, 418.
70. William Heartsill, diary entry for April 19, 1865. Heartsill Papers.
71. ORA, Series 1, Volume 48, Part 2, 1284–1285.
72. Banasik, 217. Wiley, *This Infernal War*, 446.
73. William W. Heartsill, diary entry for May 9, 1865. Heartsill Papers.
74. For a full account of Charles Read's wartime exploits, including the attempted escape of the *Webb*, see R. Thomas Campbell, *Sea Hawk of the Confederacy: Lt. Charles W. Read and the Confederate Navy* (Shippensburg, PA: Burd Street Press, 1999). Wiley, *This Infernal War*, 446.

Notes for Chapter 11

1. ORA, Series 1, Volume 48, Part 1, 186–188.
2. Ibid. 186–189.
3. Ibid. 188–189.
4. Neal and Kremm, 203.
5. Arthur H. Noll, *General Kirby Smith* (Sewanee: TN: University of the South Press, 1907), 259.
6. Cutrer and Parrish, 259–260.
7. Davis, *The Long Surrender*, 110. Crist, *Papers of Jefferson Davis*, 2:514.
8. *Cincinnati Daily Commercial*, May 15, 1865. ORA, Series 1, Volume 48, Part 2, 591.
9. Dorsey, 287.
10. Rolle, 48.
11. Kerby, 417.
12. Henrickson, in Howell, 243.
13. Edmund Kirby Smith, letter to Henry Allen, Harris Flanagin, Pendleton Murrah, and Thomas Reynolds dated May 9, 1865. Edmund Kirby Smith Papers (UNC).
14. Hendrickson, in Howell, 421–422. Kerby, 393.
15. Dorsey, 288. ORA, Series 1, Volume 48, Part 1, 189 and 191.
16. Day, 29.
17. "Memorandum for the Marshall Conference." Edmund Kirby Smith Papers (UNC). John K. Damico, "Confederate Soldiers Take Matters into Their Own Hands: The End of the Civil War in North Louisiana," *Louisiana History* 39, no. 2 (Spring 1998): 199–200.

18. ORA, Series 1, Volume 48, Part 1, 188–189.

19. Edmund Kirby Smith, letter to John Sprague dated May 15, 1865. Edmund Kirby Smith Papers (UNC).

20. ORA, Series 1, Volume 49, Part 2, 608.

21. Vincent H. Cassidy and Amos E. Simpson, *Henry Watkins Allen of Louisiana* (Baton Rouge: Louisiana State University Press, 1964), 111.

22. Dorsey, 294.

23. ORA, Series I, Volume 48, Part 2, 240–250 and 1284–1285.

24. Perry Snyder, "Shreveport, Louisiana in the Civil War and Reconstruction" (Ph.D. dissertation, Florida State University, 1979), 125.

25. Edwards, *Shelby and His Men*, 445–446.

26. Jewett, 215.

27. William H. Tunnard, *A Southern Record: The History of the Third Regiment Louisiana Infantry* (Baton Rouge: printed for the author, 1866), 335–337.

28. Reed, 53.

29. ORA, Series 1, Volume 48, Part 2, 1294–1295.

30. Letter from William Purves to Joseph Brent dated March 23, 1865. Joseph Brent Papers. Jefferson Barracks; New Orleans, Louisiana.

31. ORA, Series 1, Volume 48, Part 2, 1310.

32. Ibid. 1313–1315.

33. Donald J. Stanton, Goodwin F. Berquist, and Paul C. Bowers, *The Civil War Reminiscences of General M. Jeff Thompson* (Dayton, OH: Morningside Press, 1988), 274 and 277.

34. ORA, Series 1, Volume 48, Part 1, 578, 658, and 1402. Stanton, Berquist, and Bowers, 278 and 281.

35. ORA, Series 1, Volume 48, Part 2, 117.

36. Stanton, Berquist, and Bowers, 285. ORA, Series 1, Volume 48, Part 2, 249.

37. ORA, Series 1, Volume 48, Part 1, 229.

38. ORA, Series 1, Volume 48, Part 1, 230–232 and 235 and Series 1, Volume 48, Part 2, 386–387.

39. ORA, Series 1, Volume 48, Part 1, 235–237.

40. Ibid. Part 2, 700.

41. Stanton, Berquist, and Bowers, 290.

42. ORA, Series 1, Volume 48, Part 1, 237.

43. Boggs, 84.

44. Winters, 425. Kerby, 422.

45. ORA, Series 1, Volume 48, Part 2, 1315.

46. Reed, 53–54.

47. Winters, 423–424. Tunnard, 337. Kerby, 426.

48. ORA, Series 1, Volume 48, Part 2, 1300 and 1312. Noll, 260–261.

49. Noll, 260–261.

50. ORA, Series 1, Volume 48, Part 2, 1308–1309 and 1316–1317. Silkenat, 260.
51. Cotham, *Battle of the Bay*, 179.
52. ORA, Series 1, Volume 48, Part 2, 1313–1314.
53. Ibid. 564–565.
54. William Heartsill, diary entry for May 20, 1865. William W. Heartsill Papers.
55. Stephen A. Townsend, *The Yankee Invasion of Texas* (College Station: Texas A&M University Press, 2006), 137–138.
56. ORA, Series 1, Volume 49, Part 2, 581, 603 and 1313.
57. Edmund Kirby Smith, letter to John Magruder dated May 26, 1865. Edmund Kirby Smith Papers (UNC). Kerby, 424.
58. ORA, Series 1, Volume 48, Part 2, 591 and 1319–1320. William P. Ballinger, diary entries for May 27, 28, 30, and 31, 1865. William Pitt Ballinger Diary. University of Alabama (W. Stanley Hoole Special Collections Library); Tuscaloosa, Alabama.
59. ORA, Series 1, Volume 48, Part 2, 700–701.
60. Noll, 261. Parks, 476.
61. Jewett, 212.
62. ORA, Series 1, Volume 48, 2: 515.
63. Williamson, *47ᵗʰ Indiana*, 283.
64. ORA, Series 1, Volume 49, Part 2, 591.
65. Parrish, 442–443. Taylor, *Destruction and Reconstruction*, 227–229. Heyman, 235.
66. ORA, Series 1, Volume 48, Part 2, 600–603 and 605–606.
67. Dunkerly, 117. *New York Times*, June 4, 1865. *Daily True Delta* [New Orleans], May 25 and 25, 1865.
68. Mary B. Townsend, *Yankee Warhorse: A Biography of Major General Peter Osterhaus* (Columbia: University of Missouri Press, 2010), 189.
69. Winters, 270. Stickles, 271–273.
70. ORA, Series 1, Volume 48, Part 2, 700–701.
71. Banasik, 227. ORA, Series 1, Volume 48, Part 2, 1320.
72. Stickles, 270. Townsend, 137. Watie's Cherokees were the last Confederate Army unit to surrender, receiving their paroles three weeks after Kirby Smith surrendered. For further information, see Bradley R. Clampitt, *The Civil War and Reconstruction in Indian Territory* (Lincoln: University of Nebraska Press, 2015), Clarissa W. Confer, *The Cherokee Nation in the Civil War* (Norman: University of Oklahoma Press, 2012), and W. Craig Gaines's *The Confederate Cherokees: John Drew's Regiment of Mounted Rifles* (Baton Rouge: Louisiana State University Press, 1992).
73. Edward Canby, letter to Edwin Kirby Smith dated May 27, 1865. Edwin Kirby Smith Papers (UNC).

74. Edmund Kirby Smith, letter to John Sprague dated May 15, 1865. Edmund Kirby Smith Papers (UNC).

75. Parks, 175.

76. ORA, Series 1, Volume 48, Part 1, 604–606.

77. Edmund Kirby Smith, letters to John Magruder dated June 2, 1865 and Benjamin Huger dated June 10, 1865, and Edward Canby, letter to Edwin Kirby Smith dated May 27, 1865. Edmund Kirby Smith Papers (UNC). ORA, Series 1, Volume 48, Part 2, 601–602.

78. Paul D. Casdorph, *Prince John Magruder: His Life and Campaigns* (New York: Wiley, 1996), 298.

79. Albert Castel, *General Sterling Price and the Civil War in the West* (Baton Rouge: Louisiana State University Press, 1968), 272.

80. Gary D. Joiner, *Little to Eat and Thin Mud to Drink: Letters, Diaries, and Memoirs from the Red River Campaigns, 1863–1864* (Knoxville: University of Tennessee Press, 2007), 28–29.

81. Ginny M. Raska and Mary Lynne G. Hill, *The Uncompromising Diary of Sallie McNeill, 1858–1867* (College Station: Texas A&M University Press, 2009), 125.

82. ORA, Series 1, Volume 48, Part 2, 816–817.

83. Oates, *Rip Ford*, 402–403.

84. Smith, in Sutherland, 148. "Last Order in Trans-Mississippi Department," *Confederate Veteran* 23, no. 10 (October 1915): 458.

85. Henry Richardson, letter to parents dated March 15, 1865. Richardson-Farrar Papers (Southern Historical Collection), University of North Carolina; Chapel Hill, North Carolina.

86. Kerby, 423.

87. John A. Johnson, diary entry for May 22, 1865. John Augustine Johnson Papers. Library of Congress (Manuscript Division); Washington, D.C.

88. Faller, 258.

89. Winschel, 160–161.

90. Jerry Flint Papers, letter to brother dated June 14, 1865. Jerry Flint Papers.

91. Alan S. Brown, *A Soldier's Life: The Civil War Experiences of Ben C. Johnson* (Kalamazoo: Western Michigan University Press, 1962), 120.

92. William J. Gould, diary entry for June 16, 1865. William J. Gould Papers. Library of Congress (Manuscript Division); Washington, D.C.

93. ORA, Series 1, Volume 47, Part 3, 866–867.

94. *Galveston Daily News*, June 20, 1865.

95. Blackburn, 328–329.

96. William T. Richter, "It Is Best to Go in Strong-Handed: Army Occupation of Texas, 1865–1866," *Arizona and the West* 27, no. 2 (Summer 1985): 123–126 and 130–131.

97. *Galveston Daily News*, December 30, 1865.

98. Cater, 219.

99. Washington Carson, letters to Kate dated August 10 and October 23, 1865. Washington Irving Carson Papers. Abraham Lincoln Presidential Library; Springfield, Illinois. Washington and Kate married on February 16, 1866.

100. Edward M. Coffman, "Memoirs of Hylan B. Lyon, Brigadier General, C.S.A." *Tennessee Historical Quarterly* 18, no. 1 (March 1959): 52–53. Sam D. Elliott, *Isham G. Harris of Tennessee: Confederate Governor and United States Senator* (Baton Rouge: Louisiana State University Press, 2010), 182–185 and 187.

101. Deryl P. Sellmeyer, *Jo Shelby's Iron Brigade* (Gretna, LA: Pelican Publishing, 2007), 281. Edwards, *Biography*, 251. O'Flaherty, 234–236 and 243. Rolle, 17–18.

102. Edmund Kirby Smith, letters to wife dated July 4 and August 21, 1865, and letter from Ulysses S. Grant dated October 16, 1865. Edmund Kirby Smith Papers (UNC).

103. John N. Edwards, "Shelby's Expedition to Mexico," *Missouri Historical Review* 18, no. 2 (January 1924): 252. ORA, Series 1, Volume 48, Part 2, 1292–1293. Settles, 283.

104. Stevenson, 612.

105. Hanna, 113, 115, and 121. Grady, 251. Rolle, 92–95 and 120. Davis, *The Long Surrender*, 277.

106. For examples, see Gabor S. Boritt, ed., *Why the Confederacy Lost* (New York: Oxford, 1992). Richard E. Beringer, Herman Hattaway, Archer Jones, and William N. Still, Jr., *Why the South Lost the Civil War* (Athens: University of Georgia, 1986). Herman Hattaway and Archer Jones, *How the North Won* (Urbana: University of Illinois Press, 1983), and Mark Grimsley and Brooks D. Simpson, eds., *The Collapse of the Confederacy* (Lincoln: University of Nebraska Press, 2001).

Notes for Conclusion

1. Banasik, 225.

2. ORA, Series 2, Volume 8, Part 1, 929.

3. Jonathan T. Dorris, *Pardon and Amnesty under Lincoln and Johnson: The Restoration of the Confederates to Their Rights and Privileges, 1861–1868* (Chapel Hill: University of North Carolina Press, 1953), 154. ORA, Series 2, Volume 8, Part 1, 585.

4. University of California. The American Presidency Project: http://www.presidency.ucsb.edu/ws/?pid=72212.

5. ORA, Series 2, Volume 8, Part 1, 709–710.

6. Ibid. 578–580. *New York Times*, May 30, 1865.

7. Maury, *Recollections of a Virginian*, 235–236 and 240.

8. Nathan Forrest to Stephen Lee, letter dated July 1, 1865. Stephen D. Lee Papers (Southern Historical Collection), University of North Carolina; Chapel Hill, North Carolina. Hurst, 267.

9. McKinney, 454.

10. Zuber, 190–191. Tucker, 407. ORA, Series 1, Volume 49, Part 2, 681–682 and 810.

11. Neff, 209. ORA, Series 3, Volume 5, 13–15.

12. J. Hubley Ashton, *Official Opinions of the Attorney Generals* (Washington, DC: Morrison, 1869), 11:323–324.

13. Neff, 206.

14. ORA, Series 3, Volume 5, 13–15.

15. Ibid. Volume 4, Part 1, 106.

16. James D. Richardson, *A Compilation of the Messages and Papers of the Presidents, 1787–1897* (Washington, DC: Government Printing Office, 1899), 6:434–438.

17. Stahr, *Seward: Lincoln's Indispensable Man* (New York: Simon & Schuster, 2012), 442–443.

18. ORA, Series 1, Volume 48, Part 1, 300.

19. Rister, 7.

20. Townsend, 138. Richard O'Conner, *Sheridan the Inevitable* (New York: Bobbs-Merrill, 1953), 280. Rister, 9. ORA, Series 1, Volume 48, Part 2, 476 and 525–526.

21. Philip H. Sheridan, *Personal Memoirs of P.H. Sheridan, General, United States Army*, vol. 2 (New York: Webster & Co., 1888), 214. Wilfred H. Callcott, *Liberalism in Mexico* (Hamden, CT: Archon Books, 1965), 71–72. Rister, 17–19.

22. Sheridan, 2:215–217. O'Conner, 278–279. Rister, 17.

23. ORA, Series 1, Volume 48, Part 2, 922–924.

24. Samuel F. Bemis, *American Secretaries of State and the Their Diplomacy*, vol. 7 (New York: Cooper Square, 1928), 106–110. Rolle, 31.

25. Stahr, *Seward*, 441. Schoonover, 66–67.

26. Ibid. 84–90 and 184.

27. Ibid. 90.

28. John A. Schofield, *Forty-Six Years in the Army* (New York: Century, 1897), 388–391.

29. Settles, 291. *Executive Documents Printed by Order of The House of Representatives during the Second Session of the Thirty-ninth Congress, 1866–67*, Volume 1 (Washington, DC: Government Printing Office, 1867), 574–575.

30. Mary M. McAllen, *Maximilian and Carlota: Europe's Last Empire in Mexico* (San Antonio, TX: Trinity University Press, 2014), 381–386.

Works Cited

Manuscript Collections

Ballinger, William Pitt, Diary. University of Alabama (W. Stanley Hoole Special Collections Library); Tuscaloosa, Alabama.

Beard, Daniel Carter Papers. Library of Congress (Manuscript Division); Washington, D.C.

Bourland, James A., Papers. Library of Congress (Manuscript Division); Washington, DC.

Brent, Joseph, Papers. Jefferson Barracks; New Orleans, Louisiana.

Carson, Washington Irving, Papers. Abraham Lincoln Presidential Library; Springfield, Illinois.

Cater Family Papers. Library of Congress (Manuscript Collection); Washington, DC.

Childress, George L., Papers. Abraham Lincoln Presidential Library; Springfield Illinois.

Civil War Diaries and Letters (Mobile) Collection. Mobile Public Library; Mobile, Alabama.

Chapman, Walter A. Papers. Yale University; New Haven, Connecticut.

Journal of W.O. Crouse: August 4th, 1862 to July 1st, 1865. Tippecanoe County Historical Association; Lafayette, Indiana.

Crydenwise, Henry, Papers. Emory University; Atlanta, Georgia.

Deans, Henderson, Reminiscences, University of North Carolina, Southern Historical Collection; Chapel Hill, North Carolina.

Drish, James F., Papers. Abraham Lincoln Presidential Library; Springfield, Illinois.

Eddington, William R., Papers. Abraham Lincoln Presidential Library; Springfield, Illinois.

Flint, Jerry, Papers, University of Wisconsin-River Falls; River Falls, WI.

Freeman James W., Papers, Dolph Briscoe Center for American History, University of Texas (Austin, Texas).

Foreman, Abner, Papers. Abraham Lincoln Presidential Library; Springfield, Illinois.

Garland, Maurice H., Papers. Alabama Department of Archives and History; Montgomery, Alabama.

Geary, Daniel, Papers. McCall Rare Book and Manuscript Library, University of South Alabama; Mobile, Alabama.

Goodrich, Charles Perry, Papers. Wisconsin Historical Society; Madison, Wisconsin.

Gould, William J., Papers. Library of Congress Manuscript Division; Washington, D.C.

Gras-Lauzin Papers. Louisiana State University, Hill Memorial Library; Baton Rouge, Louisiana.

Hairston, Elizabeth Seawell, Papers. University of North Carolina, Southern Historical Collection; Chapel Hill, North Carolina.

Hale, William Job, Letters. Dolph Briscoe Center for American History, University of Texas; Austin, Texas.

Hart, Henry W., Papers. Mobile Public Library; Mobile, Alabama.

Hinricks, Charles F., Papers, University of Missouri, Western Historical Collections Manuscripts; Columbus, Missouri.

Jackson, Isaac, Papers, University of Michigan, Clements Library; Ann Arbor, Michigan.

Justice, Elihu, Papers. Abraham Lincoln Presidential Library; Springfield, Illinois.

Johnson, John Augustine, Papers. Library of Congress, Manuscript Division; Washington, D.C.

Johnston, Joseph, Papers. College of William & Mary, Swem Library; Williamsburg, Virginia.

Kautz, August V., Papers. Abraham Lincoln Presidential Library; Springfield, Illinois.

Kirby Smith, Edmund, Papers. Gilder Lehrman Collection. Gilder Lehrman Institute of American History, New York.

Kirby Smith, Edmund, Papers. University of North Carolina, Southern Historical Collection; Chapel Hill, North Carolina.

LeConte and Furman Family Papers. University of North Carolina, Southern Historical Collection; Chapel Hill, North Carolina.

Lee, Stephen D., Papers. University of North Carolina, Southern Historical Collection; Chapel Hill, North Carolina.

Louisiana Historical Association Collection, Army of Tennessee Papers. Tulane University; New Orleans, Louisiana

Louisiana Historical Association Collection, Trans-Mississippi Department Papers. Tulane University; New Orleans, Louisiana.

Lyons, Mark, Papers. McCall Rare Book and Manuscript Library, University of South Alabama; Mobile, Alabama.

Mahood, Fontaine W., Papers. Virginia Historical Society; Richmond, Virginia.

Marion, Frederick, Papers. Abraham Lincoln Presidential Library; Springfield, Illinois.

Maury, Richard, Papers. Virginia Historical Society; Richmond, Virginia.

Mumford, William T., Diary. History Museum of Mobile, Jack Friend Research Library; Mobile, Alabama.

Newton, James K., Papers, Wisconsin Historical Society; Madison, Wisconsin.

Nourse, Benjamin, Papers, Duke University, Perkins Library, Durham, NC.

Otey, John M. Papers. Museum of Mobile, Mobile Civil War Collection; Mobile, Alabama.

Ott, John, Papers. University of Michigan, Clements Library; Ann Arbor, Michigan.

Peacock, John R., Papers. University of North Carolina, Southern Historical Collection; Chapel Hill, North Carolina.

Putney, William G., Papers. University of Michigan, Clements Library; Ann Arbor, Michigan.

Records of the Department of Alabama, Mississippi, and East Louisiana. Louisiana State Museum; New Orleans, Louisiana.

Richardson-Farrar Papers. University of North Carolina, Southern Historical Collection; Chapel Hill, North Carolina.

Roane, John C., Papers. Missouri State Archives; Jefferson City, Missouri.

Scott, Milo W., Papers. Chattanooga Public Library; Chattanooga, Tennessee.

Sherman Family Papers. Library of Congress (Manuscript Division); Washington, DC.

Stanton, William E., Papers. University of Texas Archives; Austin, Texas.

Starke, Marchant, and Martin Family Papers. University of North Carolina, Southern Historical Collection; Chapel Hill, North Carolina.

Tanner, Charles A., Papers. University of North Carolina, Southern Historical Collection; Chapel Hill, North Carolina.

Taylor, Richard, Papers. Jackson Barracks; New Orleans, Louisiana.

Taylor, Richard, Papers. Louisiana State Museum; New Orleans, Louisiana.

"Telegrams Received by Lieut. Gen. Taylor at Selma, Dated from March 27 to April 2, 1865," Louisiana State Museum; New Orleans, Louisiana.

Tilghman, Tench, Diary. University of North Carolina, Southern Historical Collection; Chapel Hill, North Carolina.

Trans-Mississippi Department Papers, Louisiana Historical Society Collection, Tulane University (New Orleans, Louisiana).

Trowbridge, Martin, Papers. University of Michigan, Clements Library; Ann Arbor, Michigan.

Virginia Enrollment Office Records. Virginia Historical Society; Richmond, Virginia.

Wadley, Sarah Lois, Papers. University of North Carolina, Southern Historical Collection; Chapel Hill, North Carolina.

Woods, John Taylor, Papers. University of North Carolina, Southern Historical Collection; Chapel Hill, North Carolina.

Government Documents:

*Accounts and Papers of the House of Commons (North America, No. 11
(1863))*. London: Harrison & Sons, 1863.

Candler, Alan D. *Confederate Records of Georgia*. 5 Vols. Atlanta, GA: Byrd,
1909.

Day, James M. *Senate and House Journals of the Tenth Legislature (First
Called Session) of the State of Texas, May 9, 1864–May 28, 1864*. Austin:
Texas State Library, 1965.

Gammel, Hans P. *The Laws of Texas, 1822*–1897. Vol. 5. Austin, TX: Gammel
Book Company, 1898.

*Journal of the Proceedings of the Senate of the General Assembly of the
State of Florida at the Thirteenth Session*. Tallahassee, FL: Florida
Sentinel, 1864.

Journal of the Congress of the Confederate States of America, 1861–1865.
Vol. 4. Washington, DC: Government Printing Office, 1904.

*Journal of the Senate of the United States of America (39th Congress,
1st Session)*. Washington, DC: Government Printing Office 1866.

National Archives and Records Administration, Record Group 109: Collections
of Papers of Confederate General Officers.

*Official Records of the Union and Confederate Navies in the War of the Rebel-
lion*, 31 Vols. Washington, DC: Government Printing Office, 1894–1927.

*Report of the Joint Committee on the Conduct of the War: Red River
Expedition*. Washington, DC: Government Printing Office, 1865.

Richardson, James D. *A Compilation of the Messages and Papers of the Presidents, 1787–1897*. Washington, DC: Government Printing Office, 1899.

Thian, Raphael P. *Correspondence of the Treasury Department*. Washington,
DC: Government Printing Office, 1879.

*The War of the Rebellion: A Compilation of the Official Records of the Union
and Confederate Armies*, 130 Volumes. Washington, DC: Government
Printing Office, 1880–1901.

Primary Sources

Abbott, John S.C. *The History of the Civil War in America*. New York: Henry
Bill, 1866.

Appleton's American Annual Cyclopedia. New York: Appleton's, 1865.

Andrews, Christopher C. *History of the Campaign of Mobile*. New York: Van Norstrand, 1889.

Andrews, Eliza F. *The War-time Journal of a Georgia Girl, 1864–1865*. New York: Appleton, 1908.

Ashton, J. Hubley. *Official Opinions of the Attorney Generals*. Washington, DC: Morrison, 1869.

Avery, Isaac W. *The History of the State of Georgia from 1850 to 1881: Embracing the Three Important Epochs: The Decade Before the War of 1861–5; the War; the Period of Reconstruction*. New York: Brown and Derby, 1881.

Bancroft, Frederic, and William A. Dunning, *The Reminiscences of Carl Schurz*. New York: McClure, 1908.

Bartlett, Napier. *Military Record of Louisiana*. New Orleans: Graham and Co., 1875.

Battles and Leaders of the Civil War. 40 Vols. New York: Century Co., 1893–1932.

Brickell, William E. "The Battle of Fort Tyler." *The Southern Practitioner* 22 (1900).

Capers, Henry D. *The Life and Times of C.G. Memminger*. Richmond, VA: Everett Waddey Co., 1893.

Carter, William R. *History of the First Regiment of Tennessee Volunteer Cavalry in the Great War of the Rebellion*. Knoxville, TN: Gaut-Odgen Co., 1902.

Chalmers, James R. "Nathan Bedford Forrest and his Campaigns." *Southern Historical Society Papers* 7, no. 10 (October 1879).

Chesnut, Mary B. *A Diary from Dixie*. New York: Appleton, 1905.

Cleveland, Henry. *Alexander H. Stephens*. Philadelphia, PA: National Publishing, 1866.

Collins, R.M. *Chapters from the Unwritten History of the War Between the States*. St. Louis, MO: Nixon-Jones, 1893.

Cox, Jacob D. *Military Reminiscences of the Civil War*. New York: Scribner, 1900.

Crist, Lynda T. *The Papers of Jefferson Davis*. 14 Vols. Baton Rouge: Louisiana State University Press, 1992.

Crofts, Thomas. *History of the Service of the Third Ohio Veteran Volunteer Cavalry*. Columbus, OH: Stoneman Press, 1910.

Curry, William L. *Four Years in the Saddle: The History of the First Regiment Ohio Volunteer Cavalry*. Columbus, OH: Champion Printing, 1898.

Davis, Jefferson. *Rise and Fall of the Confederate Government*. New York: Appleton, 1881.

Denison, George S. "Diary and Correspondence of Salmon P. Chase." *Annual Report of the American Historical Association*. Washington, DC: Government Printing Office, 1903.

Dornblaser, Thomas F. *Sabre Strokes of the Pennsylvania Dragoons in the War of 1861–1865* Philadelphia: Lutheran Publication Society, 1884.

Dorsey, Sarah. *Recollections of Henry Watkins Allen*. New Orleans, LA: Doolady, 1866.

Dowd, Clement. *Life of Zebulon B. Vance*. Charlotte, NC: Observer Printing, 1897.

Duke, Basil W. "Last Days of the Confederacy." *Battles and Leaders of the Civil War*. New York: Century Co., 1884.

Edwards, John N. *Biography, Memoirs, Reminiscences and Recollections: His Brilliant Career as Soldier, Author, and Journalist*. Kansas City: Jennie Edwards, 1889.

————. *Shelby and His Men: Or the War in the West*. Cincinnati, OH: Miami Printing, 1867.

Evans, Clement A. *Confederate Military History: A Library of Confederate States History*. Atlanta: Confederate Publishing, 1899.

Ewer, James K. *The Third Massachusetts Cavalry in the War for the Union*. Boston: Historical Committee of the Regimental Association, 1903.

Gilpin, Ebenezer N. *The Last Campaign: A Cavalryman's Journal*. Leavenworth, KS: Ketcheson Printing, 1908.

Hagood, Johnson. *Memoirs of the War of Secession*. Columbia, SC: State Company, 1910.

Hague, Parthenia A. *A Blockaded Family: Life in Southern Alabama during the Civil War*. New York: Houghton, Mifflin, and Co., 1888.

Hampton, Wade. "Battle of Bentonville." *Battles and Leaders of the Civil War*. Vol. 4. New York: Century, 1884.

Hancock, Richard R. *Hancock's Diary: Or A History of the Second Tennessee Confederate Cavalry*. Nashville: Brandon Printing, 1887.

Hardy, John. *Selma: Her Institutions and Her Men*. Selma, AL: Times Books, 1869.

Heartsill, William W. *Fourteen Hundred and 91 Days in the Confederate Army*. Marshall, TX: Heartsill, 1876.

Hindman, Thomas C. *Report of Major General Hindman of His Operations in the Trans-Mississippi District*. Richmond, VA: R.M. Smith, 1864.

Holbrook, William C. *A Narrative of the Services of the Officers and Enlisted Men of the 7th Regiment of Vermont Volunteers (Veterans) from 1862 to 1866*. New York: American Bank Note Company, 1882.

Hood, John Bell. *Advance and Retreat: Personal Experiences in the United States and Confederate States Armies*. New Orleans: Hood Orphan Memorial Fund, 1880.

Howe, Matthew A. DeWolfe. *Home Letters of General Sherman*. New York: Scribner's, 1909.

Johnston, Joseph E. *Narrative of Military Operations Directed during the Late War Between the States*. New York: Appleton, 1874.

Jones, John B. *A Rebel War Clerk's Diary at the Confederate States Capital*. New York: Lippincott, 1866.

Hammond, John M. *Quaint and Historic Forts of North America*. Philadelphia, PA: Lippincott, 1915.

Hand-book for the War. Boston, MA: Wholesale Office, 1861.

Latour, Arsène L. *Historical Memoir of the War in West Florida and Louisiana in 1814–1815* Philadelphia, PA: Conrad and Co., 1816.

Long, Ellen C. *Florida Breezes: Or Florida, New and Old*. Jacksonville, FL: Ashmead, 1882.

Lubbock, Francis R. *Six Decades in Texas: Or Memoirs of Francis Richard Lubbock, Governor of Texas in War Time, 1861–1863*. Austin, TX: Ben C. Jones and Co., 1900.

Maury, Dabney H. "Defence of Mobile in 1865." *Southern Historical Society Papers* 3, no. 1 (January 1877).

————. "Defense of Spanish Fort." *Southern Historical Society Papers* 39 (1914).

————. *Recollections of a Virginian in the Mexican, Indian, and Civil Wars* (New York: Scribner's, 1894).

————. "Sketch of General Richard Taylor." *Southern Historical Society Papers* 7 (1879).

McGuire, Judith W. *Diary of a Southern Refugee during the War*. Richmond, VA: J.W. Randolph & English, 1889.

McGee, Benjamin F. *History of the 72d Indiana Volunteer Infantry of the Mounted Lightning Brigade*. Lafayette, IN: Vater & Co., 1882.

McMurray, William J. *History of the Twentieth Tennessee Regiment Volunteer Infantry, C.S.A.* Nashville, TN: Publication Committee, 1904.

Mitchell, Charles D. "Field Notes of the Selma Campaign." *Sketches of War History, 1861–1865* Cincinnati, OH: Monfort & Company, 1908.

Montgomery, Frank A. *Reminiscences of a Mississippian in Peace and War*. Cincinnati, OH: Clarke, 1901.

Morgan, James M. *Recollections of a Rebel Reefer*. New York: Houghton-Mifflin, 1917.

Mosby, John S. *Memoirs of John S. Mosby*. Princeton, NJ: Collector's Reprints, 1998.

Nichols, George W. "Sherman's Great March." *Harper's New Monthly Magazine* 31, no. 5 (October 1865).

Pepper, George W. *Personal Recollections of Sherman's Campaigns in Georgia and the Carolinas*. Zanesville, OH: Dunne, 1866.

Pollard, Edward A. *Lee and His Lieutenants: Comprising the Early Life, Public Services, and Campaigns of General Robert E. Lee*. New York: E.B. Treat & Co., 1867.

————. *The Lost Cause: A New Southern History of the War of the Confederates*. New York: E.B. Treat, 1867.

Porter, David D. *Incidents and Anecdotes of the Civil War*. New York: Appleton, 1885.

Ridley, Bromfield L. *Battles and Sketches of the Army of Tennessee*. Mexico, MO: Missouri Printing, 1906.

Rix, William. *Incidents in the Life of a Southern City during the War*. Rutland, VT: n.p., 1880.

Roman, Alfred T. *The Military Operations of General Beauregard in the War Between the States*. Vol. 2. New York: Harper & Bros., 1884.

Scharf, J. Thomas. *History of the Confederate States Navy from its Organization to the Surrender of Its Last Vessel*. New York: Rogers & Sherwood, 1887.

von Scheliha, Viktor. *A Treatise on Coast-defense*. London: E. & F.N. Spon, 1868.

Schofield, John A. *Forty-Six Years in the Army*. New York: Century, 1897.

Scott, William F. *The Story of a Cavalry Regiment: The Career of the Fourth Iowa Veteran Volunteers from Kansas to Georgia, 1861–1865*. New York: Putnam's, 1893.

Seidel, Charles B. *History of the Service of the Third Ohio Veteran Volunteer Cavalry in the War for the Preservation of the Union from 1861–1865*. Toledo, OH: Stoneman, 1910.

Semmes, Raphael. *Memoirs of Service Afloat during the War Between the States*. Baltimore, MD: Kelly, 1869.

Sheridan, Philip H. *Personal Memoirs of P.H. Sheridan, General, United States Army*. Vol. 2. New York: Webster & Co., 1888.

Sherman, William T. *Memoirs of General William T. Sherman*. Bloomington: Indiana University Press, 1957.

Sketches of War History, 1861–1865: Papers Read Before the Ohio Commandery of the Military Order of the Loyal Legion of the United States. Vol. 1. Cincinnati, OH: Blake & Co., 1888.

Slocum, Henry W. "Final Operations of Sherman's Army." *Battles and Leaders of the Civil War*. New York: Yoseloff, 1887.

Smith, Ernest A. *The History of the Confederate Treasury*. Harrisburg, PA: Harrisburg Publishing, 1901.

Solley, James R. *Admiral Porter*. New York: Appleton, 1913.

Sporer, Paul D. *End of an Era: The Last Days of Traditional Southern Culture as Seen Through the Eyes of a Young Confederate Soldier*. 1899, repr., Chester, NY: Anza Publishing, 2005.

Stephens, Alexander H. *Recollections of Alexander H. Stephens*. New York Doubleday, 1910.

Stephenson, P.D. "Defence of Spanish Fort," *Southern Historical Society Papers* 39, no. 1 (September 1914).

Straub, Edward A. *Life and Civil War Services of Edward A. Straub*. Milwaukee, WI: Yewdale & Sons, 1909.

Taylor, Richard. *Destruction and Reconstruction: Personal Experiences of the Late War*. New York: Appleton, 1883.

————. "The Last Confederate Surrender," *Southern Historical Society Papers* 3, no. 3 (March 1877).

Thorndike, Rachel S. *The Sherman Letters: Correspondence between General and Senator Sherman from 1837 to 1891*. London: Sampson, Low, Marston, & Co., 1894.

Tunnard, William H. *A Southern Record: The History of the Third Regiment Louisiana Infantry*. Baton Rouge: printed for the author, 1866.

Vale, Joseph G. *Minty and the Cavalry: A History of Cavalry Campaigns in the Western Armies*. Harrisburg, PA: Meyers, 1886.

Wallace, Lew. *Lew Wallace: An Autobiography*. New York: Harpers, 1906.

Warren, Edward. *A Doctor's Experiences in Three Continents*. Baltimore, MD: Cushings & Bailey, 1885.

Watkins, Sam R. *Co. Aytch: Maury Grays, First Tennessee Regiment or, A Side Show of the Big Show*. Nashville: Cumberland Publishing, 1882.

Welles, Gideon. *Diary of Gideon Welles, Secretary of the Navy under Lincoln and Johnson*. Boston, MA: Houghton-Mifflin, 1911.

Wilson, James H. *Under the Old Flag: Recollections of Military Operations in the War for the Union, the Spanish War, the Boxer Rebellion, etc.* New York: Appleton, 1912.

Wise, John S. *The End of an Era*. New York: Houghton, 1901.

Wright, Louise. *A Southern Girl in '61: The War-Time Memories of a Confederate Senator's Daughter*. New York: Doubleday, 1905.

Wulsin, Lucien. *The Story of the Fourth Regiment Ohio Veteran Volunteer Cavalry*. Cincinnati, OH: Fourth Ohio Cavalry Association, 1912.

Secondary Sources (Books)

Abernethy, Frances E. *Tales from the Big Thicket*. Denton: University of North Texas Press, 2002.

Adams, John. *Warrior at Heart: Governor John Milton, King Cotton, and Rebel Florida 1860–1865*. Victoria, British Columbia: FriesenPres, 2015.

Albaugh, William A. *Tyler, Texas: The Story of the Confederate States Ordnance Works at Tyler, Texas, 1861–1865*. Mechanicsburg, PA: Stackpole, 1958.

Alexander, Bob. *Six-Shooters and Shifting Sands: The Wild West Life of Texas Ranger Captain Frank Jones*. Denton: University of North Texas Press, 2015.

Bruce S. Allardice, *More Generals in Grey*. Baton Rouge: Louisiana State University Press, 1995.

Ambrose, Stephen E. *Upton and the Army*. Baton Rouge: Louisiana State University Press, 1964.

Amos, Harriet E. *Cotton City: Urban Development in Antebellum Mobile*. Tuscaloosa: University of Alabama Press, 1985.

Anderson, John Q. *Brokenburn: The Journal of Kate Stone, 1861–1868*. Baton Rouge: Louisiana State University Press, 1995.

Andrew, Rod. *Wade Hampton: Confederate Warrior to Southern Redeemer*. Chapel Hill: University of North Carolina Press, 2014.

Arthur, Anthony. *General Jo Shelby's March*. New York: Random House, 2010.

Ash, Stephen V. *When the Yankees Came: Conflict and Chaos in the Occupied South, 1861–1865*. Chapel Hill: University of North Carolina Press, 1995.

Ashdown, Paul, and Edward Caudill. *The Myth of Nathan Bedford Forrest*. New York: Rowman & Littlefield, 2005.

Astor, Aaron. *Rebels on the Border: Civil War, Emancipation, and the Reconstruction of Kentucky and Missouri*. Baton Rouge: Louisiana State University Press, 2012.

Athearn, Robert G. *William Tecumseh Sherman and the Settlement of the West*. Norman: University of Oklahoma Press, 1956.

Baguley, David. *Napoleon III and His Regime: An Extravaganza*. Baton Rouge: Louisiana State University Press, 2000.

Ball, Douglas B. *Financial Failure and Confederate Defeat*. Urbana: University of Illinois Press, 1991.

Ballard. Michael B. *A Long Shadow: Jefferson Davis and the Final Days of the Confederacy*. Jackson: University of Mississippi Press, 1986.

————. *Pemberton: The General Who Lost Vicksburg*. Jackson: University of Mississippi Press, 1991.

Banasik, Michael E. *Serving with Honor: The Diary of Captain Eathan Allen Pinnell of the Eighth Missouri Infantry. Confederate*. Iowa City, IA: Camp Pope Bookshop, 1999.

Barefoot, Daniel W. *General Robert F. Hoke: Lee's Modest Warrior*. Winston-Salem, NC: Blair, 1996.

Barnard, Harry B. *Tattered Volunteers: The Twenty-Seventh Alabama Infantry Regiment, C.S.A.*. Northport, AL: Hermitage Press, 1965.

Barrett, John G. *Sherman's March through the Carolinas*. Chapel Hill: University of North Carolina Press, 1956.

Barringer, Paul B. *The Natural Bent: The Memoirs of Dr. Paul B. Barringer*. Chapel Hill: University of North Carolina Pres, 1949.

Basler, Roy P. *The Collected Works of Abraham Lincoln*. New Brunswick, NJ: Rutgers University Press, 1953–1955.

Bauer, K. Jack. *Zachary Taylor, Soldier, Planter, Statesman of the Old Southwest*. Baton Rouge: Louisiana State University Press, 1993.

Baumgartner, Richard A. *Blood and Sacrifice: The Civil War Journal of a Confederate Soldier*. Huntington, WV: Blue Acorn Press, 1994.

Belcher, Dennis W. *The 11th Missouri Volunteer Infantry in the Civil War: A History and Roster*. Jefferson, NC: McFarland, 2011.

Bemis, Samuel F. *American Secretaries of State and the Their Diplomacy*, Volume VII. New York: Cooper Square, 1928.

Bender, Robert P. *Worthy of the Cause for Which They Fight: The Civil War Diary of Brigadier General Daniel Harris Reynolds, 1861–1865*. Fayetteville: University of Arkansas Press, 2011.

Bergeron, Arthur W. *A Thrilling Narrative: The Memoir of a Southern Unionist*. Fayetteville: University of Arkansas Press, 2006.

————. *The Civil War Reminiscences of Major Silas T. Grisamore, C.S.A.* Baton Rouge: Louisiana State University Press, 1993.

————. *Confederate Mobile*. Jackson: University of Mississippi Press, 1991.

Beringer, Richard E., Herman Hattaway, Archer Jones, and William N. Still, Jr., *Why the South Lost the Civil War*. Athens: University of Georgia, 1986.

Black, Robert C. *The Railroads of the Confederacy*. Chapel Hill: University of North Carolina Press, 1952.

Blackburn, George M. *Dear Carrie: The Civil War Letters of Thomas N. Stevens*. Mount Pleasant, MI: Central Michigan University Press, 1984.

Blair, Jayne E. *Tragedy at Montpelier: The Untold Story of Ten Confederate Deserters from North Carolina*. Berwyn Heights, MD: Heritage Books, 2003.

Blair, William. *Virginia's Private War: Feeding Body and Soul in the Confederacy, 1861–1865*. New York: Oxford, 1998.

Blakey, Arch F. *General John H. Winder, C.S.A.*. Gainesville: University of Florida Press, 1990.

Blount, Russell W. *Besieged: Mobile 1865*. Gretna, LA: Pelican Publishing, 2015.

Bonan, Gordon B. *The Edge of Mosby's Sword: The Life of Confederate Colonel William Henry Chapman*. Carbondale: Southern Illinois University Press, 2009.

Boritt, Gabor S. *Jefferson Davis' Generals*. New York: Oxford, 1999.

————. *Why the Confederacy Lost*. New York: Oxford, 1992.

Bradley, Mark L. *This Astounding Close: The Road to Bennet Place*. Chapel Hill: University of North Carolina, 2000.

Boggs, William R. *Military Reminiscences of Gen. Wm. R. Boggs, C.S.A.* Durham, NC: Seeman, 1913.

Brooksher, William R. *Bloody Hill: The Civil War Battle of Wilson's Creek*. Washington, DC: Potomac Books, 1999.

Brown, Dee. *The Galvanized Yankees*. Champaign: University of Illinois Press, 1963.

Brown, Alan S. *A Soldier's Life: The Civil War Experiences of Ben C. Johnson*. Kalamazoo: Western Michigan University Press, 1962.

Browning, Judkin. *Shifting Loyalties: The Union Occupation of Eastern North Carolina*. Chapel Hill: University of North Carolina Press, 2011.

Brubaker, John H. *The Last Capital: Danville, Virginia, and the Final Days of the Confederacy*. Danville, VA: Womack Press, 1979.

Buker, George E. *Blockaders, Refugees, and Contrabands: Civil War on Florida's Gulf Coast, 1861–1865*. Tuscaloosa: University of Alabama Press, 1993.

Burkhardt, George S. *Confederate Rage, Yankee Wrath: No Quarter in the Civil War*. Carbondale: Southern Illinois University Press, 2007.

Burlingame, Michael. *Abraham Lincoln: A Life*. Baltimore, MD: Johns Hopkins University Press, 2008.

Burr, Virginia I. *The Secret Eye: The Journal of Ella Gertrude Clanton Thomas, 1848–1889*. Chapel Hill: University of North Carolina Press, 1990.

Bynum, Victoria E. *The Free State of Jones: Mississippi's Longest Civil War.* Chapel Hill: University of North Carolina Press, 2001.

————. *The Long Shadow of the Civil War.* Chapel Hill: University of North Carolina Press, 2010.

Callcott, Wilfred H. *Liberalism in Mexico.* Hamden, CT: Archon Books, 1965.

Campbell, Jacqueline G. *When Sherman Marched North from the Sea: Resistance on the Confederate Home Front.* Chapel Hill: University of North Carolina Press, 2003.

Campbell, R. Thomas. *Sea Hawk of the Confederacy: Lt. Charles W. Read and the Confederate Navy.* Shippensburg, PA: Burd Street Press, 1999.

Casdorph, Paul D. *Prince John Magruder: His Life and Campaigns.* New York: Wiley, 1996.

Cash, Wilbur J. *The Mind of the South.* New York: Knopf, 1941.

Castel, Albert. *General Sterling Price and the Civil War in the West.* Baton Rouge: Louisiana State University Press, 1968.

Cassidy, Vincent H., and Amos E. Simpson, *Henry Watkins Allen of Louisiana.* Baton Rouge: Louisiana State University Press, 1964.

Cater, Douglas J. *As It Was: Reminiscences of a Soldier of the Third Texas Cavalry and the Nineteenth Louisiana Infantry.* Austin, TX: State House Press, 1990.

Cimprich, John. *Fort Pillow, a Civil War Massacre, and Public Memory: Civil War Battlefields and Historic Sites Recaptured.* Baton Rouge: Louisiana State University Press, 2011.

Chesson, Michael B. and Leslie J. Roberts, *Exile in Richmond: The Confederate Journal of Henri Garidel.* Charlottesville: University of Virginia Press, 2001.

Clark, James C. *Last Train South: The Flight of the Confederate Government from Richmond.* Jefferson, NC: McFarland, 1984.

Coburn, Mark. *Terrible Innocence: General Sherman at War.* New York: Hippocrene, 1993.

Connelly, Thomas L., and Archer Jones, *The Politics of Command: Factions and Ideas in Confederate Strategy.* Baton Rouge: Louisiana State University Press, 1973.

Conner, Robert C. *General Gordon Granger: The Savior of Chickamauga and the Man behind "Juneteenth."* Havertown, PA: Casement Publishers, 2013.

Cooper, Edward S. *Louis Trezevant Wigfall: The Disintegration of the Union and Collapse of the Confederacy.* Madison, NJ: Fairleigh-Dickinson University Press, 2012.

Cooper, Edward S. *Traitors: The Secession Period, November 1860–July 1861*. Madison, NJ: Fairleigh Dickinson University Press, 2008.

Cooper, William J. *Jefferson Davis: His Essential Writings*. New York: Random House, 2004.

Corley, Florence F. *Confederate City: Augusta, Georgia, 1860–1865*. Columbia: University of South Carolina Press, 1960.

Corsan, W.C. *Two Months in the Confederate States: An Englishman's Travels through the South*. Baton Rouge: Louisiana State University Press, 1998.

Cotham, Edward T. *Battle on the Bay: The Civil War Struggle of Galveston*. Austin: University of Texas Press, 1998.

————. *Sabine Pass: The Confederacy's Thermopylae*. Austin: University of Texas Press, 2004.

Coulter, E. Merton. *The Confederate States of America, 1861–1865*. Baton Rouge: Louisiana State University Press, 1950.

Cozzens, Peter. *General John Pope: A Life for the Nation*. Urbana: University of Illinois Press, 2000.

Crabtree, Beth G. and James W. Patton, *Journal of a Secesh Land: The Diary of Catherine Ann Devereaux Edmonston, 1860–1866*. Raleigh, NC: Department of Cultural Resources, 1979.

Crawford, Martin. *Ashe County's Civil War: Community and Society in the Appalachian South*. Charlottesville: University of Virginia Press, 2001.

Curtis, Samuel S. *A Cruise on the Benton: A Narrative of Combat on the Missouri River in the Civil War*. Waynesboro, VA: M & R Books, 1967.

Cutrer, Thomas W. *Our Trust Is in the God of Battles: The Civil War Letters of Robert Franklin Bunting, Chaplain, Terry's Texas Rangers, C.S.A.* Knoxville: University of Tennessee Press, 2006.

————. and T. Michael Parrish. *Brothers in Gray: The Civil War Letters of the Pierson Family*. Baton Rouge: Louisiana State University Press, 1997.

Daddysman, James W. *The Matamoros Trade: Confederate Commerce, Diplomacy, and Intrigue*. Newark: University of Delaware Press, 1984.

Dahlgren, Madeline V. *Memoir of John A. Dahlgren, Rear Admiral, United States Navy*. Boston, MA: Osgood, 1882.

Danielson, Joseph W. *War's Desolating Scourge: The Union's Occupation of North Alabama*. Lawrence: University of Kansas Press, 2012.

Davis, Daniel T., and Phillip S. Greenwalt. *Calamity in Carolina: The Battles of Averasboro and Bentonville, March 1865*. El Dorado Hills, CA: Savas Beatie, 2015.

Davis, William C. *Breckinridge: Statesman, Soldier, Symbol.* Baton Rouge: Louisiana State University Press, 1974.

————. and James I. Robertson, eds. *Virginia at War: 1865.* Lexington: University of Kentucky Press, 2012.

————. and Meredith L. Swentor. *Bluegrass Confederate: The Headquarters Diary of Edward O. Guerrant.* Baton Rouge: Louisiana State University Press, 2005.

Davis, William W. *The Civil War and Reconstruction in Florida.* New York: Columbia University, 1913.

DeWitt, David M. *The Assassination of Abraham Lincoln and Its Expiation.* New York: Macmillan, 1909.

Dickison, Mary E. *Dickison and His Men: Reminiscences of the War in Florida.* Gainesville: University of Florida Press, 1962.

Dinkins, James. *1861 to 1865 By An Old Johnnie: Personal Recollections and Experiences In The Confederate Army.* Dayton, OH: Morningside Bookshop, 1974.

————. *Furl that Banner: Personal Recollections and Experiences in the Confederate Army.* Dayton, OH: Morningside Bookshop, 1975.

Dodd, William E. *Jefferson Davis.* Philadelphia, PA: Jacobs, 1907.

Dorris, Jonathan T. *Pardon and Amnesty under Lincoln and Johnson: The Restoration of the Confederates to Their Rights and Privileges, 1861–1868.* Chapel Hill: University of North Carolina Press, 1953.

Dougan, Michael B. *Confederate Arkansas: The People and Politics of a Frontier State in Wartime.* Tuscaloosa: University of Alabama Press, 1976.

DuBose, John W. *General Joseph Wheeler and the Army of Tennessee.* New York: Neale, 1912.

Duffy, James P. *Lincoln's Admiral: The Civil War Campaigns of David Farragut.* Edison, NJ: Castle Books, 1997.

DuFour, Charles L. *Nine Men in Gray.* New York: Doubleday, 1963.

Dunkerly, Robert M. *The Confederate Surrender at Greensboro: The Final Days of the Army of Tennessee, April 1865.* Jefferson, NC: McFarland, 2013.

————. *To the Bitter End: Appomattox, Bennett Place, and the Surrenders of the Confederacy.* El Dorado Hills, CA: Savas Beatie, 2015.

Durden, Robert F. *The Gray and the Black: The Confederate Debate on Emancipation.* Baton Rouge: Louisiana State University Press, 2000.

Durkin, Joseph T. *John Dooley, Confederate Soldier: His War Journal.* Washington, DC: Georgetown University Press, 1945.

Eaton, Clement. *Jefferson Davis*. New York: Free Press, 1977.

Elder, Donald C. *A Damned Iowa Greyhound: The Civil War Letters of William Henry Harrison Clayton*. Iowa City: University of Iowa Press, 1998.

Elliott, Sam D. *Isham G. Harris of Tennessee: Confederate Governor and United States Senator*. Baton Rouge: Louisiana State University Press, 2010.

————. *Soldier of Tennessee: General Alexander P. Stewart and the Civil War in the West*. Baton Rouge: Louisiana State University Press, 1999.

Eppes, Susan B. *Through Some Eventful Years*. Macon, GA: J.W. Burke, 1926.

Escott, Paul D. *Many Excellent People: Power and Privilege in North Carolina, 1850–1900*. Chapel Hill: University of North Carolina Press, 1985.

————. *North Carolinians the Era of the Civil War and Reconstruction*. Chapel Hill: University of North Carolina Press, 2008.

Evans, Eli N. *Judah P. Benjamin: The Jewish Confederate*. New York: Free Press, 1988.

Faller, Philip E. *The Indiana Jackass Regiment in the Civil War: A History of the 21st Infantry/1st Heavy Artillery Regiment, with a Roster*. Jefferson, NC: McFarland, 2013.

Fellman, Michael. *Citizen Sherman: A Life of William Tecumseh Sherman*. New York: Random House, 1995.

Felton, Rebeca L. *Country Life in Georgia in the Days of My Youth*. New York: Arno Press, 1980.

Fonvielle, Chris. E. *The Wilmington Campaign: Last Departing Rays of Hope*. Mechanicsburg, PA: Stackpole, 2001.

Fisher, John S. *A Builder of the West: The Life of General William Jackson Palmer*. Caldwell, ID: Caxton Printers, 1939.

Fisher, John E. *They Rode with Forrest and Wheeler: A Chronicle of Five Tennessee Brothers' Service in the Confederate Western Cavalry*. Jefferson, NC: McFarland, 1995.

Fitzpatrick, David J. *Emory Upton: Misunderstood Reformer*. Norman: University of Oklahoma Press, 2017.

Flood, Charles B. *Grant and Sherman: The Friendship that Won the Civil War*. New York: Farrar, Straus, and Giroux, 2005.

Folmar, John K. *From that Terrible Field: Civil War Letters of James M. Williams, Twenty-first Alabama Infantry Volunteers*. Tuscaloosa: University of Alabama Press, 1981.

Fordney, Ben F. *George Stoneman: A Biography of a Union General*. Jefferson, NC: McFarland, 2008.

Fowler, John D., and David B. Parker, eds. *Breaking the Heartland: The Civil War in Georgia*. Macon, GA: Mercer University Press, 2011.

Fremantle, James. *The Fremantle Diary: A Journal of the Confederacy*. Boston: Little & Brown, 1954.

Fuchs, Richard. *An Unerring Fire: The Massacre at Fort Pillow*. Mechanics-burg, PA: Stackpole, 2017.

Gallagher, Gary W. *The Confederate War: How Popular Will, Nationalism, and Military Strategy could not Stave Off Defeat*. Cambridge, MA: Harvard University Press, 1997.

Gallaway, B.P. *The Ragged Rebel: A Common Soldier in W.H. Parsons' Texas Cavalry, 1861–1865*. Austin: University of Texas Press, 1988.

Galloway, T.H. *Dear Old Roswell: Civil War Letters of the King Family of Roswell, Georgia*. Macon, GA: Mercer University Press, 2003.

Gibson, Campbell. *Population of the 100 Largest Cities and Other Urban Places in the United States: 1790 to 1990*. Washington, DC: Bureau of the Census, 1998.

Godrey, John M. *Monetary Expansion in the Confederacy*. New York: Arno Press, 1978.

Goff, Richard D. *Confederate Supply*. Durham, NC: Duke University Press, 1969.

Gordon, Larry. *The Last Confederate General: John C. Vaughn and His East Tennessee Cavalry*. Minneapolis, MN: Zenith Press, 2009.

Gottschalk, Phil. *In Deadly Earnest: The History of the First Missouri Brigade, CSA*. New York: Macmillan, 1990.

Green, Arthur E. *Mobile Confederates from Shiloh to Spanish Fort: The Story of the 21st Alabama Infantry Volunteers*. Westminster, MD: Heritage Books, 2012.

Griffith, Lucille. *Yours till Death: Civil War Letters of John W. Cotton*. Tusca-loosa: University of Alabama Press, 1951.

Grimsley, Mark and Brooks D. Simpson, eds. *The Collapse of the Confeder-acy*. Lincoln: University of Nebraska Press, 2001.

Hale, Douglas. *The Third Texas Cavalry in the Civil War*. Norman: University of Oklahoma Press, 1993.

Hamilton, Holman. *Zachary Taylor: Soldier in the White House*. Indianapolis: Bobbs-Merrill, 1951.

Hamnett, Brian. *Juarez*. New York: Longman, 1994.

Hanna, Harvey L. *The Press Covers the Invasion of Arkansas*. Widener, AR: Southern Heritage Press, 2012.

Hardy, Michael C. *The Thirty-seventh North Carolina Troops: Tar Heels in the Army of Northern Virginia*. Jefferson City, NC: McFarland, 2003.

Harwell, Richard B. *A Confederate Diary of the Retreat from Petersburg, April 3–20, 1865*. Atlanta, GA: Emory University Press, 1953.

————. and Philip N. Racine. *The Fiery Trail: A Union Officer's Account of Sherman's Last Campaign*. Knoxville: University of Tennessee Press, 1986.

Harrington, Fred H. *Fighting Politician: Major General N.P. Banks*. Westport, CT: Greenwood, 1948.

Hartje, Robert G. *Van Dorn: The Life and Times of a Confederate General*. Nashville, TN: Vanderbilt University Press, 1967.

Hattaway, Herman. *General Stephen D. Lee*. Jackson: University of Mississippi Press, 1976.

————. and Archer Jones. *How the North Won*. Urbana: University of Illinois Press, 1983.

————. and Richard E. Beringer. *Jefferson Davis, Confederate President*. Lawrence: University of Kansas Press, 2002.

Henry, Robert S. *First with the Most: Forrest*. Indianapolis, IN: Bobbs-Merrill, 1944.

————. *The Story of the Confederacy*. New York: DaCapo Press, 1989.

Heyman, Max L. *Prudent Soldier: A Biography of Major General E.R.S. Canby*. Glendale, CA: Arthur H. Clark Co., 1959.

Hilderman, Walter C. *Theophilus Hunter Holmes: A North Carolina General in the Civil War*. Jefferson, NC: McFarland, 2013.

Hirshson, Stanley P. *The White Tecumseh: A Biography of William T. Sherman*. New York: Wiley & Sons, 1997.

Hitchcock, Henry. *Marching with Sherman: Passages from the Letters and Campaign Diaries of Henry Hitchcock, Major and Assistant Adjutant General of Volunteers, November 1864–May 1865*. New Haven, CT: Yale University Press, 1927.

Hobart-Hampden, C. Augustus. *Never Caught: Personal Adventures Connected with Twelve Successful Trips in Blockade-Running during the American Civil War*. Carolina Beach, NC: Blockade Runner Museum, 1967.

Holberton, William B. *Homeward Bound: The Demobilization of the Union and Confederate Armies, 1865–1866*. Mechanicsburg, PA: Stackpole, 2001.

Hollandsworth, James G. *Pretense of Glory: The Life of General Nathanial P. Banks*. Baton Rouge: Louisiana State University Press, 1998.

Hoole, William S. *Alabama Tories: The First Alabama Cavalry, U.S.A., 1862–1865*. Tuscaloosa, AL: Confederate Publishing Co., 1960.

Horn, Stanley F. *The Army of Tennessee*. Wilmington, NC: Broadfoot Publishing, 1987.

Howell, H. Grady. *Going to Meet the Yankees: A History of the "Bloody Sixth" Mississippi Infantry, C.S.A.* Jackson, MS: Chickasaw Bayou Press, 1981.

————. *To Live and Die in Dixie: A Regimental History of the Third Mississippi Infantry, C. S. A.* Jackson, MS: Chickasaw Bayou Press, 1991.

Howell, Kenneth W. *The Seventh Star of the Confederacy: Texas during the Civil War*. Denton: University of North Texas Press, 2009.

Hughes, Charles C. *The Civil War Memoir of Philip Daingerfield Stephenson, D.D.* Conway, AR: UCA Press, 1995.

Hughes, Nathaniel C. *Liddell's Record: St. John Richardson Liddell, Brigadier General, CSA: Staff Officer and Brigade Commander, Army of Tennessee*. Dayton, OH: Morningside Press, 1985.

————. *The Pride of the Confederate Artillery: The Washington Artillery in the Army of Tennessee*. Baton Rouge: Louisiana State University Press, 1997.

Hunt, Jeffrey W. *The Last Battle of the Civil War: Palmetto Ranch*. Austin: University of Texas Press, 2002.

Hurst, Jack. *Nathan Bedford Forrest: A Biography*. New York: Knopf, 1994.

Inscoe, John, and Robert Kenzer. *Enemies of the Country: New Perspectives on Unionists in the Civil War South*. Athens: University of Georgia Press, 2001.

Iobst, Richard W. *Civil War Macon: The History of a Confederate City*. Macon, GA: Mercer University Press, 1999.

Jackson, Lawrence P. *My Father's Name: A Black Virginia Family after the Civil War*. Chicago: University of Chicago Press, 2012.

Johns, John E. *Florida during the Civil War*. Gainesville: University of Florida Press, 1963.

Johnson, Ludwell H. *Red River Campaign: Politics and Cotton in the Civil War*. Baltimore, MD: Johns Hopkins University Press, 1958.

Joiner, Gary D. *Little to Eat and Thin Mud to Drink: Letters, Diaries, and Memoirs from the Red River Campaigns, 1863–1864*. Knoxville: University of Tennessee Press, 2007.

Jones, Archer. *Civil War Command and Strategy: The Process of Victory and Defeat*. New York: Simon & Schuster, 2010.

Jones, Gordon L. *Confederate Odyssey: The George W. Wray, Jr. Civil War Collection at the Atlanta Historical Center*. Athens: University of Georgia Press, 2014.

Jones, James P. *Yankee Blitzkrieg: Wilson's Raid through Alabama and Georgia*. Athens: University of Georgia Press, 1976.

Jones, Katherine M. *Heroines of Dixie: Confederate Women Tell Their Story of the War*. New York: Bobbs-Merrill, 1955.

Jordan, Thomas and J.P. Pryor. *The Campaigns of Lieut. Gen. N.B. Forrest and Forrest's Cavalry*. Memphis: Blelock & Co., 1968.

Kean, Robert G. *Inside the Confederate Government: The Diary of Robert Garlick Kean*. New York: Oxford, 1957.

Kerby, Robert L. *Kirby Smith's Confederacy: The Trans-Mississippi South, 1863–1865*. New York: Columbia University Press, 1972.

Kerr, Homer L. *Fighting With Ross' Texas Cavalry Brigade, C.S.A.* Hillsboro, TX: Hill Jr. College Press, 1976.

Knight, Brian D. and Barton A. Myers. *The Guerrilla Hunters: Irregular Conflict during the Civil War*. Baton Rouge: Louisiana State University Press, 2017.

Lane, Mills. *Dear Mother: Don't Grieve about Me. If I Get Killed, I'll Only Be Dead: Letters from Georgia Soldiers in the Civil War*. Savannah: Library of Georgia, 1990.

Lee, Jr., Robert E. *Recollections and Letters of Robert E. Lee, C.S.A.* New York: Cosimo, 2008.

Lemke, Walter J. *Captain Edward Gee Miller of the 20th Wisconsin: His War, 1862–1865*. Washington, AR: Washington County Historical Society, 1960.

Levine, Bruce. *The Fall of the House of Dixie: The Civil War and the Social Revolution that Transformed the South*. New York: Random House, 2013.

Lincecum, Jerry B., Edward H. Phillips, and Peggy A. Redshaw. *Gideon Lincecum's Sword: Civil War Letters from the Texas Home Front*. Denton: University of North Texas Press, 2001.

Longacre, Edward. *A Soldier to the Last: Maj. Gen. Joseph Wheeler in Blue and Gray*. Washington, DC: Potomac Books, 2007.

————. *From Union Stars to Top Hat: A Biography of the Extraordinary General James Harrison Wilson*. Harrisburg, PA: Stackpole, 1972.

————. *Gentleman and Scholar: A Biography of Wade Hampton III*. Nashville, TN: Rutledge Hill, 2003.

Mahin, Dean B. *One War at a Time: The International Dimensions of the American Civil War*. Washington, DC: Brassey's, 1999.

Mann, Robert. *Wartime Dissent in American: A History and Anthology*. New York: Palgrave, 2010.

Marszalek, John F. *The Diary of Miss Emma Holmes, 1861–1866*. Baton Rouge: Louisiana State University Press, 1994.

Marszalek, John F. *Sherman: A Soldier's Passion for Order*. New York: Free Press, 1993.

Marten, James. *Texas Divided: Loyalty and Dissent in the Lone Star State, 1856–1874*. Lexington: University Press of Kentucky, 1990.

Martis, Kenneth C. *Historical Atlas of the Congresses of the Confederate States*. New York: Simon & Schuster, 1994.

Marvel, William. *Lincoln's Autocrat: The Life of Edwin Stanton*. Chapel Hill: University of North Carolina Press, 2015.

Matthews, Gary R. *Basil Wilson Duke, CSA: The Right Man in the Right Place*. Lexington: University of Kentucky Press, 2005.

May, Robert E. *Manifest Destiny's Underworld: Filibustering in Antebellum America*. Chapel Hill: University of North Carolina Press, 2004.

McAllen, Mary M. *Maximilian and Carlota: Europe's Last Empire in Mexico*. San Antonio, TX: Trinity University Press, 2014.

McBride, Mary G., and Ann M. McLaurin. *Randall Lee Gibson of Louisiana: Confederate General and New South Reformer*. Baton Rouge: Louisiana State University Press, 2007.

McCurry, Stephanie. *Confederate Reckoning: Power and Politics in the Civil War South*. Cambridge, MA: Harvard University Press, 2010.

McDonough, James L. *Nashville: The Western Confederacy's Final Gamble*. Knoxville: University of Tennessee Press, 2004.

————. *Schofield: Union General of the Civil War and Reconstruction*. Tallahassee: Florida State University Press, 1972.

————. *William Tecumseh Sherman: In the Service of My Country*. New York: Norton, 2016.

McIlwain, Christopher L. *Civil War Alabama*. Tuscaloosa: University of Alabama Press, 2016.

McKean, Brenda C. *Blood and War at my Doorstep: North Carolina Civilians in the War Between the States*. Bloomington, IN: Xlibris Corporation, 2011.

McKinney, Francis F. *Education in Violence: The Life of George H. Thomas and the History of the Army of the Cumberland*. Chicago, IL: Americana House, 1991.

McManus, Christopher D., Thomas H. Inglis, and Otho J. Hicks. *Morning to Midnight in the Saddle: Civil War Letters of a Soldier in Wilder's Lightning Brigade*. Bloomington, IN: Xlibris, 2012.

McMillan, Malcolm C. *The Disintegration of a Confederate States: Three Governors and Alabama's Wartime Home Front, 1861–1865*. Macon, GA: Mercer University Press, 1986.

McMurry, Richard M. *An Uncompromising Secessionist: The Civil War of George Knox Miller, Eighth. Wade's Confederate Cavalry.* Tuscaloosa: University of Alabama Press, 2007.

————. *Footprints of a Regiment: A Recollection of the 1st Georgia Regulars, 1861–1865.* Atlanta, GA: Longstreet Press, 1992.

————. *John Bell Hood and the War for Southern Independence.* Lexington: University of Kentucky Press, 1982.

McPherson, James M. *Embattled Rebel: Jefferson Davis and Commander in Chief.* New York: Penguin, 2014.

Merrill, Robert S. *Civil War Diaries of Robert S. Merrill.* Cedarburg, WI: MGS Press, 1995.

Misulia, Charles A. *Columbus, Georgia, 1865: The Last True Battle of the Civil War.* Tuscaloosa: University of Alabama Press, 2010.

Moore, Albert B. *Conscription and Conflict in the Confederacy.* New York: McMillan, 1924.

Myers, Barton A. *Rebels Against the Confederacy: North Carolina's Unionists.* New York: Cambridge University Press, 2014.

Neal, Diane, and Thomas W. Kremm, *The Lion of the South: General Thomas C. Hindman.* Macon, GA: Mercer University Press, 1993.

Neff, Spencer C. *Justice in Blue and Gray: A Legal History of the Civil War.* Cambridge, MA: Harvard University Press, 2010.

Noe, Kenneth W. *The Yellowhammer War: The Civil War and Reconstruction in Alabama.* Tuscaloosa: University of Alabama Press, 2013.

Noll, Arthur H. *General Kirby Smith.* Sewanee, TN: University of the South Press, 1907.

Oates, Stephen B. *Confederate Cavalry West of the River.* Austin: University of Texas Press, 1961.

————. *Rip Ford's Texas.* Austin: University of Texas Press, 1963.

O'Flaherty, Daniel. *General Jo Shelby: Undefeated Rebel.* Chapel Hill: University of North Carolina Press, 1954.

O'Brien, Sean M. *Mobile, 1865: Last Stand of the Confederacy.* Westport, CT: Praeger, 2001.

O'Conner, Richard. *Sheridan the Inevitable.* New York: Bobbs-Merrill, 1953.

Ohrt, Wallace L. *Defiant Peacemaker: Nicholas Trist in the Mexican War.* College Station: Texas A&M University Press, 1998.

Owens, Harry P. and James J. Cooke. *The Old South in the Crucible of War.* Jackson: University of Mississippi Press, 1983.

Owsley, Frank L. *King Cotton Diplomacy: Foreign Relations of the Confederate States of America.* Chicago: University of Chicago Press, 1931.

Pape-Findley, Nancy. *The Invincibles: The Story of the Fourth Ohio Veteran Volunteer Cavalry, 1861–1865*. Tecumseh, MI: Blood Road Publishing, 2002.

Parks, Joseph H. *General Edmund Kirby Smith, C.S.A.*. Baton Rouge: Louisiana State University Press, 1954.

Parrish, T. Michael. *Richard Taylor: Soldier Prince of Dixie*. Chapel Hill: University of North Carolina Press, 1992.

Patrick, Rembert W. *Opinions of the Confederate Attorneys-General*. Buffalo, NY: Dennis & Co., 1950.

Pena, Christopher G. *Scarred by War: Civil War in Southeast Louisiana*. Bloomington, IN: Authorhouse, 2004.

Peterson, Paul R. *Quantrill in Texas: The Forgotten Campaign*. Nashville, TN: Cumberland House, 2007.

Pickering, David, and Judy Falls. *Brush Men and Vigilantes: Civil War Dissent in Texas*. College Station: Texas A&M University Press, 2000.

Raab, James W. *J. Patton Anderson: Confederate General*. Jefferson, NC: McFarland, 2004.

———. *W.W. Loring: Florida's Forgotten General*. Manhattan, KS: Sunflower University Press, 1996.

Rable, George C. *The Confederate Republic: A Revolution Against Politics*. Chapel Hill: University of North Carolina Press, 1994.

Ramsdell, Charles W. *Behind the Lines in the Southern Confederacy*. Baton Rouge: Louisiana State University Press, 1944.

———. *Laws and Joint Resolutions of the Last Session of the Confederate Congress*. Durham, NC: Duke University Press, 1941.

Revels, Tracy J. *Grander in Her Daughters: Florida's Women during the Civil War*. Columbia: University of South Carolina Press, 2004.

Rister, Carl C. *Border Command: General Phil Sheridan in the West*. Westport, CT: Greenwood Press, 1974.

Robinson, Jr., William M. *Justice in Gray: A History of the Judicial System of the Confederate States of America*. Cambridge, MA: Harvard University Press, 1941.

Rodrigue, John C. *Lincoln and Reconstruction*. Carbondale: Southern Illinois University Press, 2013.

Rogers, William W. *Confederate Home Front: Montgomery during the Civil War*. Tuscaloosa: University of Alabama Press, 1999.

Rolle, Andrew F. *The Lost Cause: The Confederate Exodus to Mexico*. Norman: University of Oklahoma Press, 1965.

Rowell, John W. *Yankee Artillerymen: Through the Civil War with Eli Lilly's Indiana Battery*. Knoxville: University of Tennessee Press, 1975.

Rubin, Anne Sarah. *A Shattered Nation: The Rise and Fall of the Confederacy, 1861–1865*. Chapel Hill: University of North Carolina Press, 2005.

Russell, Philip L. *The History of Mexico: From Pre-Conquest to Present*. New York: Taylor & Francis, 2010.

Salling, Stuart. *Louisianans in the Western Confederacy: The Adams-Gibson Brigade in the Civil War*. Jefferson, NC: McFarland, 2010.

Sandburg, Carl. *Abraham Lincoln: The Prairie Years and the War Years*. New York: Houghton, Mifflin & Harcourt, 2002.

Sartain, James A. *History of Walker County*. Dalton, GA: A.J. Showalter, 1932.

Schmidt, James M. *Galveston and the Civil War: An Island City in the Maelstrom*. Charleston, SC: History Press, 2012.

Schoonover, Thomas D. *Mexican Lobby: Matías Romero in Washington 1861–1867*. Lexington: University of Kentucky Press, 2014.

Scott, Eleanor D., and Carl Summers, Jr.. *The Battle of West Point: April 16, 1865*. Valley, AL: Chattahoochee Valley Historical Society, 1997.

Scott, Joe M. *Four Years' Service in the Southern Army*. Fayetteville, AK: Washington County Historical Society, 1959.

Seitz, Donald C. *Braxton Bragg, General of the Confederacy*. Columbia, SC: State Company, 1924.

Sellmeyer, Deryl P. *Jo Shelby's Iron Brigade*. Gretna, LA: Pelican Publishing, 2007.

Sensing, Thurman. *Champ Ferguson: Confederate Guerilla*. Nashville, TN: Vanderbilt University Press, 1994.

Settles, Thomas M. *John Bankhead Magruder: A Military Reappraisal*. Baton Rouge: Louisiana State University Press, 2009.

Shalhope, Robert E. *Sterling Price: Portrait of a Southerner*. Columbia: University of Missouri Press, 1971.

Siepel, Kevin H. *Rebel: The Life and Times of John Singleton Mosby*. New York: St. Martin's Press, 1983.

Silkenat, David. *Raising the White Flag: How Surrender Defined the American Civil War*. Chapel Hill: University of North Carolina Press, 2019.

Sinisi, Kyle S. *The Last Hurrah: Sterling Price's Missouri Expedition of 1864*. New York: Rowman & Littlefield, 2015.

Skinner, James L. *The Death of a Confederate: Selections from the Letters of the Archibald Smith Family of Roswell, Georgia, 1864–1956*. Athens: University of Georgia Press, 1996.

Slocum, Charles E. *The Life and Service of Major-General Henry Warner Slocum*. Toledo, OH: Slocum Publishing, 1913.

Smith, Derek. *In the Lion's Mouth: Hood's Tragic Retreat from Nashville, 1864*. Mechanicsburg, PA: Stackpole, 2011.

Smith, Gerald J. *One of the Most Daring of Men: The Life of Confederate General William Tatum Wofford*. Murfreesboro, TN: Southern Heritage Press, 1997.

Smith, Timothy B. *Mississippi in the Civil War: The Home Front*. Jackson: University Press of Mississippi, 2010.

Sokolosky, Wade, and Mark A. Smith. *To Prepare for Sherman's Coming: The Battle of Wise's Forks, March 1865*. El Dorado, CA: Savas Beatie, 2015.

Stahr, Walter. *Seward: Lincoln's Indispensable Man*. New York: Simon & Schuster, 2012.

Standard, Diffie W. *Columbus, Georgia, in the Confederacy: The Social and Industrial Life of the Chattahoochee River Port*. New York: William-Frederick, 1954.

Stanton, Donald J., Goodwin F. Berquist, and Paul C. Bowers. *The Civil War Reminiscences of General M. Jeff Thompson*. Dayton, OH: Morningside Press, 1988.

Starr, Steven Z. *The Union Cavalry in the Civil War*. Baton Rouge: Louisiana State University Press, 1979.

Stickles, Arndt M. *Simon Bolivar Buckner: Borderland Knight*. Chapel Hill: University of North Carolina Press, 1940.

Stoker, Donald. *The Grand Design: Strategy and the U.S. Civil War*. New York: Oxford University Press, 2010.

Storey, Margaret M. *Loyalty and Loss: Alabama's Unionists in the Civil War and Reconstruction*. Baton Rouge: Louisiana State University Press, 2004.

Stroud, David V. *Ector's Texas Brigade and the Army of Tennessee, 1862–1865*. Longview, TX: Ranger Publishing, 2004.

Sunderland, Glenn W. *Lightning at Hoover's Gap: The Story of Wilder's Brigade.* New York: Yoselof, 1969.

Surdam, David G. *Northern Naval Superiority and the Economics of the American Civil War*. Columbia: University of South Carolina Press, 2001.

Suri, Jeremi. *Liberty's Surest Guardian: Rebuilding Nations after War from the Founders to Obama*. New York: Simon & Schuster, 2012.

Sutherland, Daniel E. *A Savage Conflict: The Decisive Role of Guerrillas in the American Civil War*. Chapel Hill: University of North Carolina Press, 2009.

————. *Guerillas, Unionists, and Violence on the Confederate Home Front*. Fayetteville: University of Arkansas Press, 1999.

Sutherland, Daniel E. *Reminiscences of a Private: William E. Bevins of the First Arkansas Infantry, C.S.A.* Fayetteville: University of Arkansas Press, 1992.

Swift, Charles J. *The Last Battle of the Civil War.* Columbus, GA: Gilbert Printing, 1915.

Sword, Wiley. *The Confederates' Last Hurrah: Spring Hill, Franklin, and Nashville.* Lawrence: University Press of Kansas, 1993.

Symonds, Craig L. *Joseph E. Johnston: A Civil War Biography.* New York: Norton, 1992.

Tap, Bruce. *Over Lincoln's Shoulder: The Committee on the Conduct of the War.* Lawrence: University Press of Kansas, 1998.

Tatum, Georgia Lee. *Disloyalty in the Confederacy.* Chapel Hill: University of North Carolina Press, 1934.

Taylor, Robert A. *Rebel Storehouse: Florida in the Confederate Economy.* Tuscaloosa: University of Alabama Press, 1995.

Telfair, Nancy. *A History of Columbus, Georgia, 1828–1928.* Columbus, GA: Historical Publishing Co, 1929.

Thomas, Benjamin P. and Harold M. Hyman. *Stanton: The Life and Times of Lincoln's Secretary of War.* New York: Knopf, 1962.

Thompson, Samuel B. *Confederate Purchasing Operations Abroad.* Chapel Hill: University of North Carolina Press, 1935.

Townsend, Mary B. *Yankee Warhorse: A Biography of Major General Peter Osterhaus.* Columbia: University of Missouri Press, 2010.

Townsend, Stephen A. *The Yankee Invasion of Texas.* College Station: Texas A&M University Press, 2006.

Tucker, Glenn. *Zeb Vance: Champion of Personal Freedom.* New York: Bobbs-Merrill, 1965.

Underwood, Rodman L. *Stephen Russell Mallory: A Biography of the Confederate Navy Secretary and United States Senator.* Jefferson, NC: McFarland, 2005.

————. *Waters of Discord: The Union Blockade of Texas during the Civil War.* Jefferson, NC: McFarland, 2003.

Urwin, Gregory, and Cathy Urwin. *History of the 33rd Iowa Infantry Volunteer Regiment.* Fayetteville: University of Arkansas Press, 1999.

Vandiver, Frank E. *Rebel Brass: The Confederate Command System.* New York: Greenwood Press, 1956.

Varhola, Michael J. *Everyday Life during the Civil War.* Cincinnati: Writer's Digest Books, 1999.

Volmer, John K. *From That Terrible Field: Civil War Letters of James M. Williams, Twenty-First Alabama Infantry Volunteers.* Tuscaloosa: University of Alabama Press, 1981.

Wagner-Pacifici, Robin. *The Art of Surrender: Decomposing Sovereignty at Conflict's End.* Chicago, IL: University of Chicago Press, 2005.

Warner, Ezra J. *Generals in Blue: Lives of the Union Commanders.* Baton Rouge: Louisiana State University Press, 1964.

—————. *Confederates in Gray: Lives of the Confederate Commanders.* Baton Rouge: Louisiana State University Press, 1959.

Wellman, Manly W. *Giant in Gray: A Biography of Wade Hampton of South Carolina.* New York: Scribner's, 1949.

Welsh, Jack. *Medical Histories of Confederate Generals.* Kent, OH: Kent State University Press, 1994.

Wert, Jeffrey D. *General James Longstreet: The Confederacy's Most Controversial Soldier.* New York: Simon & Schuster, 1993.

—————. *Mosby's Rangers.* New York: Simon and Schuster, 1990.

Wesley, Charles H. *The Collapse of the Confederacy.* New York: Russell & Russell, 1937.

Wiley, Bell I. *Letters of Warren Akin: Confederate Congressman.* Athens: University of Georgia Press, 1959.

—————. *This Infernal War: The Confederate Letters of Sgt. Edwin H. Fay.* Austin: University of Texas Press, 1958.

Wilkes, Abner A. *A Short History of My Life in the Late War between the North and South.* Bethesda, MD: University Publications of America, 1990.

Williams, David. *Rich Man's War: Class, Caste, and Confederate Defeat in the Lower Chattahoochee Valley.* Athens: University of Georgia Press, 1999).

Williamson, David. *The 47th Indiana Volunteer Infantry: A Civil War History.* Jefferson, NC: McFarland, 2012.

—————. *The Third Battalion Mississippi Infantry and the 45th Mississippi Regiment.* Jefferson, NC: McFarland, 2004.

Wingfield, Marshall. *General A.P. Stewart: His Life and Letters.* Memphis: West Tennessee Historical Society, 1954.

Winschel, Terrence J. *The Civil War Diary of a Common Soldier: William Wiley of the 77th Illinois Infantry.* Baton Rouge: Louisiana State University Press, 2001.

Winters, John D. *The Civil War in Louisiana.* Baton Rouge: Louisiana State University Press, 1991.

Winther, Oscar O. *With Sherman to the Sea: The Civil War Letters Diaries & Reminiscences of Theodore F. Upson.* Bloomington: Indiana University Press, 1958.

Woodward, C. Vann. *Mary Chesnut's Civil War.* New Haven, CT: Yale University Press, 1981.

Woodworth, Steven E. *No Band of Brothers: Problems in the Rebel High Command.* Columbia: University of Missouri Press, 1999.

Wright, Mike. *City under Siege: Richmond in the Civil War.* New York: Madison Books, 1995.

Wyatt-Brown, Bertram. *Southern Honor: Ethics and Behavior in the Old South.* New York: Oxford University Press, 1982.

Wyeth, John A. *Life of Lieutenant-General Nathan Bedford Forrest.* New York: Harper, 1908.

Yearns, W. Buck and John G. Barrett. *North Carolina Civil War Documentary.* Chapel Hill: University of North Carolina Press, 1980.

Yeary, Mamie. *Reminiscences of the Boys in Gray, 1861–1865.* Dallas, TX: Wilkinson Printing, 1912.

Zuber, Richard L. *Jonathan Worth: A Biography of a Southern Unionist.* Chapel Hill: University of North Carolina Press, 2011.

Secondary Sources (Articles)

Acheson, Samuel, and Julie Ann O'Connell. "George Washington Diamond's Account of the Great Hanging at Gainesville, 1862." *Southwest Historical Quarterly* 65, no. 3 (January 1863): 331–414.

Alderson, William T. "The Civil War Reminiscences of John Johnston, 1861–1865." *Tennessee Historical Quarterly* 14, no. 2 (June 1955): 156–178.

Ambrose, Stephen. "Yeoman Discontent in the Confederacy." *Civil War History* 8, no. 3 (Summer 1962): 259–268.

Anderson, David L. "The Life of 'Wilhelm Yank:' Letters from a German Soldier in the Civil War." *Michigan Historical Review* 16, no. 1 (Spring 1990): 73–93.

Auman, Williaim T. "Neighbor against Neighbor: The Inner Civil War in the Randolph County Area of Confederate North Carolina." *North Carolina Historical Review* 90, no. 1 (January 1984): 59–92.

Bauer, Craig A. "The Last Effort: The Secret Mission of the Confederate Diplomat, Duncan F. Kenner." *Louisiana History* 22, no. 1 (Winter 1981): 67–95.

Bergeron, Arthur W. "The Twenty-second Louisiana Consolidated Infantry in the Defense of Mobile, 1864–1865." *Alabama Historical Quarterly* 38 (Fall 1976): 204–213.

Black, Wilfred W. "Marching with Sherman through Georgia and the Carolinas: The Civil War Diary of Jesse L. Dozer, Part II." *Georgia Historical Quarterly* 52, no. 4 (December 1968): 451–479.

Bowen, James J. "The Strategy of Robert E. Lee." *Neale's Magazine* 2, no. 1 (July 1913): 55–66.

Burdekin, Richard C.K. and Marc D. Weidenmier. "Inflation Is Always and Everywhere a Monetary Phenomenon: Richmond and Houston in 1864." *American Economic Review* 91, no. 5 (December 2001): 1621–1630.

Cash, William T. "Taylor County History and Civil War Deserters." *Florida Historical Quarterly* 27, no. 1 (July 1948): 28–58.

Cawthon, John. "Letters of a North Louisiana Private to his Wife, 1862–1865." *Mississippi Valley Historical Review* 30, no. 4 (March 1944): 533–550.

Chaffee, Adna R. "James Harrison Wilson, Cavalryman." *Cavalry Journal* 34, no. 140 (July 1925): 271–289.

Christian, Rebecca. "Georgia and the Confederate Policy of Impressing Supplies." *Georgia Historical Quarterly* 29, no. 1 (March 1944): 1–33.

Clayton, James D. "Mississippi Agriculture, 1861–1865." *Journal of Mississippi History* 24, no. 3 (July 1962): 129–141.

Clinton, Thomas P. "The Military Operations of General John T. Croxton in West Alabama, 1865." *Transactions of the Alabama Historical Society* 4, no. 4 (1904): 449–463.

Coffman, Edward M. "Memoirs of Hylan B. Lyon, Brigadier General, C.S.A." *Tennessee Historical Quarterly* 18, no. 1 (March 1959): 35–53.

Colby, Elbridge. "Wilson's Cavalry Campaign of 1865." *Journal of the American Military Foundation* 2, no. 4 (Winter 1938): 204–221.

Connelly, Thomas L. "Vicksburg: Strategic Point or Propaganda Device?" *Military Affairs* 34, no. 2 (April 1970): 49–53.

Cortright, Vincent. "Last-Ditch Defenders at Mobile." *America's Civil War* 19, no. 6 (January 1997): 58–64.

Curry, John H. "A History of Company B, 40th Alabama Infantry." *Alabama Historical Quarterly* 17, no. 3 (Fall 1955): 159–222.

Cutrer, Thomas W. "We are Stern and Resolved: The Civil War Letters of John Wesley Rabb, Terry's Texas Rangers." *Southwestern Historical Quarterly* 91, no. 2 (October 1987): 185–226.

Damico, John K. "Confederate Soldiers Take Matters into Their Own Hands: The End of the Civil War in North Louisiana." *Louisiana History* 39, no. 2 (Spring 1998): 189–205.

Dancy, James M. "Reminiscences of the Civil War." *Florida Historical Quarterly* 37, No. 1 (July 1958): 66–89.

Delaney, Robert W. "Matamoros, Port for Texas during the Civil War." *Southwestern Historical Quarterly* 58, no. 4 (April 1955): 473–487.

Diamond, William. "Imports of the Confederate Government from Europe and Mexico." *Journal of Southern History* 6, no. 4 (November 1940): 470–503.

Edwards, John N. "Shelby's Expedition to Mexico." *Missouri Historical Review* 18, no. 2 (January 1924): 250–277.

Edwards, Stewart C. "To Do the Manufacturing for the South: Private Industry in Confederate Columbus." *Georgia Historical Quarterly* 85, no. 4 (Winter 2001): 538–554.

Ekelund, Robert B. John D. Jackson, and Mark Thornton. "The 'Unintended Consequences' of Confederate Trade Legislation." *Eastern Economic Journal* 30, no. 2 (Spring 2004): 187–205.

Ellis, L. Tuffly. "Maritime Commerce on the Far Western Gulf, 1861–1865." *Southwestern Historical Quarterly* 77, no. 2 (October 1973): 167–226.

Escott, Paul D. "Joseph E. Brown, Jefferson Davis, and the Problem of Poverty in the Confederacy." *Georgia Historical Quarterly* 61, no. 1 (Spring 1977): 59–71.

———. "Poverty and Government Aid for the Poor in Confederate North Carolina." *North Carolina Historical Review* 66, no. 4 (October 1984): 462–480.

Farnum, George R. "William B. Bate: Soldier of Dixie, Lawyer, and Statesman of the Union." *American Bar Association Journal* 30, no. 2 (February 1944): 104–105.

Folmar, John K. "The War Comes to Central Alabama: Ebenezer Church, April 1, 1865." *Alabama Historical Quarterly* 26, no. 4 (Fall 1964): 190.

Gentry, Judith F. "White Gold: The Confederate Government and Cotton in Louisiana." *Louisiana History* 33, no. 3 (Summer 1992): 229–240.

Groene, Bertram H. "A Letter from Occupied Tallahassee." *Florida Historical Quarterly* 48, no. 1 (July 1969): 70–75.

Grover, George S. "The Price Campaign of 1864." *Missouri Historical Review* 6, no. 4 (July 1912): 167–181.

Hanna, Alfred J. and Kathryn A. Hanna. "The Immigration Movement of the Intervention and Empire as Seen Through the Mexican Press." *Hispanic American Historical Review* 27, no. 2 (May 1947): 220–246.

Hay, Thomas R. "Joseph Emerson Brown, Governor of Georgia, 1857–1865." *Georgia Historical Quarterly* 13, no. 2 (June 1929): 89–109.

———. "Lucius B. Northrop: Commissary General of the Confederacy." *Civil War History* 9, no. 1 (March 1963): 4–23.

Harrison, Jon. "The Confederate Letters of John Simmons." *Chronicles of Smith County (Texas)* 14, no. 1 (Summer 1975): 25–57.

Holmes, Jack D.L. "The Mississippi County that 'Seceded' from the Confederate States of America." *Civil War Times Illustrated* 3, no. 10 (February 1965): 45–50.

Holladay, Florence E. "The Powers of the Commander of the Confederate Trans-Mississippi Department, 1863–1865. Part I." *Southwestern Historical Quarterly* 21, no. 3 (January 1918): 279–298.

————. "The Powers of the Commander of the Confederate Trans-Mississippi Department, 1863–1865, Part II." *Southwestern Historical Quarterly* 21, no. 4 (April 1918): 333–359.

Huff, Leo E. "The Martial Law Controversy in Arkansas, 1861–1865: A Case Study of Internal Confederate Conflict." *Arkansas Historical Quarterly* 37, no. 2 (Summer 1978): 147–167.

Lash, Jeffrey N. "A Yankee in Gray: Danville Leadbetter and the Defense of Mobile Bay, 1861–1863." *Civil War History* 37, no. 3 (September 1991): 197–218.

————. "Major George Whitfield and Confederate Railway Policy (1863–1865)." *Journal of Mississippi History* 42, no. 3 (August 1980): 172–193.

Lebergott, Stanley. "Through the Blockade: The Profitability and Extent of Cotton Smuggling, 1861–1865." *Journal of Economic History* 41, no. 4 (December 1981): 867–888.

————. "Why the South Lost: Commercial Purpose in the Confederacy: 1861–1865." *Journal of American History* 70, no. 1 (June 1983): 58–74.

Lindstrom, Diane. "Southern Dependence upon Interregional Grain Supplies: A Review of the Trade Flows, 1840–1860." *Agricultural History* 44, no. 1 (January 1970): 101–113.

Livingood, James W. "The Chattanooga *Rebel*." *East Tennessee Historical Society's Publications* 39 (1967): 52–55.

Malone, Henry T. "Atlanta Journalism during the Confederacy." *Georgia Historical Quarterly* 37, no. 3 (September 1953): 210–219.

McCowen, Stanley S. "Battle or Massacre?: The Incident on the Nueces, August 10, 1862." *Southwestern Historical Quarterly* 104, no. 1 (July 2000): 64–86.

McMurry, Richard M. "The Enemy at Richmond: Joseph E. Johnston and the Confederate Government." *Civil War History* 27, no. 1 (March 1981): 5–31.

Meiners, Fredericka. "The Texas Border Cotton Trade, 1862–1863." *Civil War History* 23, no. 4 (December 1977): 293–306.

Miller, Edward T. "State Finances of Texas during the Civil War." *Quarterly of the Texas State Historical Society* 14, no. 1 (July 1910): 1–23.

Moore, John H. "The Rives Peace Resolution-March, 1865." *West Virginia History* 26, no. 2 (April 1965): 153–160.

Morgan, John S. "Diary of John S. Morgan, Company G, Thirty-Third Iowa Infantry." *Annals of Iowa* 8, no. 3 (April 1923): 570–610.

Nichols, James L. "Confederate Engineers and the Defense of Mobile." *Alabama Review* 12, no. 3 (July 1959): 181–195.

Nortrup, Jack. "Nicholas Trists' Mission to Mexico: A Reinterpretation." *Southwestern Historical Quarterly* 71, no. 3 (January 1968): 321–346.

Parker, Daisy. "John Milton, Governor of Florida: A Loyal Confederate." *Florida Historical Quarterly* 20, no. 2 (April 1942): 346–361.

Pecquet, Gary M. "Public Finance in Confederate Louisiana." *Louisiana History* 29, no. 3 (Summer 1988): 253–297.

———. "State Finances in Arkansas, 1860–1865." *Arkansas Historical Quarterly* 48, no. 1 (Spring 1989): 65–72.

Power, S.F. "Personal Reminiscences of the Last Battle of the War, at West Point, Geo., April 15, 1865." *Confederate Veteran* 18, no. 1 (January 1910): 38–41.

Quisenberry, Anderson P. "The Confederate Campaign in Kentucky, 1862: The Battle of Perryville." *Register of Kentucky State Historical Society* 17, no. 49 (January 1919): 29–38.

Ramold, Steven J. "We Should Have Killed Them All: The Violent Reaction of Union Soldiers to the Assassination of Abraham Lincoln." *Journal of Illinois History* 10, no. 1 (Spring 2007): 27–48.

Ramsdell, Charles M. "The Texas State Military Board, 1862–1865." *Southwestern Historical Quarterly* 27, no. 4 (April 1924): 253–275.

Ravenel, Samuel W. "Ask the Survivors of Bentonville." *Confederate Veteran* 18, no. 3 (March 1910): 124.

Rayburn, Larry. "'Wherever the Fight is Thickest': General James Patton Anderson of Florida." *Florida Historical Quarterly* 55, no. 3 (January 1982): 313–336.

Rea, Ralph R. "Diary of Private John P. Wright, U.S.A., 1864–1865." *Arkansas Historical Quarterly* 15, no. 3 (Fall 1957): 304–318.

Reid, Brian H., and John White. "A Mob of Stragglers and Cowards: Desertion from the Union and Confederate Armies, 1861–1865." *Journal of Strategic Studies* 8, no. 1 (January 1985): 64–77.

Reiger, John F. "Deprivation, Disaffection, and Desertion in Confederate Florida." *Florida Historical Quarterly* 48, no. 3 (January 1970): 279–298.

Rhodes, James F. "Who Burned Columbia?" *American Historical Review* 7, no. 3 (April 1902): 485–493.

Richter, William T. "It is Best to Go in Strong-Handed: Army Occupation of Texas, 1865–1866." *Arizona and the West* 27, no. 2 (Summer 1985): 113–142.

Robinson, Armstead L. "In the Shadow of Old John Brown: Insurrection Anxiety and Confederate Mobilization, 1861–1863." *Journal of Negro History* 65, no. 4 (Autumn 1980): 279–297.

Rountree, Benjamin. "Letters from a Confederate Soldier." *The Georgia Review* 19, no. 3 (Fall 1964): 267–297.

Russell, Don. "Letters of a Drummer-Boy." *Indiana Magazine of History* 34, no. 3 (September 1938): 324–339.

Sacher, John M. "Our Interests and Destiny are the Same: Gov. Thomas Overton Moore and Confederate Loyalty." *Louisiana History* 49, no. 3 (Summer 2008): 261–286.

Sanders, W.J. "Governor Z.B. Vance: Story of the Last Days of the Confederacy in North Carolina." *Southern Historical Society Papers* 32 (1904): 164–168.

Scarboro, David D. "North Carolina and the Confederacy: The Weakness of States' Rights during the Civil War." *North Carolina Historical Review* 56, no. 2 (April 1979): 133–149.

Scheiber, Harry N. "The Pay of Troops and Confederate Morale in the Trans-Mississippi West." *Arkansas Historical Quarterly* 18, no. 4 (Winter 1959): 350–365.

Shook, Robert W. "The Battle of the Nueces, August 10, 1862." *Southwest Historical Quarterly* 66, no. 1 (July 1962): 31–42.

Simmons, R. Hugh. "The 12th Louisiana Infantry in North Carolina, January-April, 1865." *Louisiana History* 36, no. 1 (Winter 1995): 77–108.

Stockham, Richard J. "Alabama Iron for the Confederacy: The Selma Works." *Alabama Review* 21, no. 3 (July 1968): 163–172.

Strom, Steven. "Cotton and Profits Across the Border: William Marsh Rice in Mexico, 1863–1865." *Houston Review* 8, no. 2 (Summer 1986): 89–96.

Tarrant, Edward W. "Siege and Capture of Fort Blakely." *Confederate Veteran* 23, no. 10 (October 1915): 457–458.

Throne, Mildred. "Civil War Letters of Abner Dunham, 12th Iowa Infantry." *Iowa Journal of History* 53, no. 4 (October 1955): 303–340.

Treadway, Charles W. "The Letters of Charles Wesley Treadway." *Foot Prints: Past and Present* (Richland County [Illinois] Genealogical and Historical Society) 9 (1986): 148–177.

Tucker, Philip T. "The First Missouri Confederate Brigade's Last Stand at Fort Blakeley on Mobile Bay." *Alabama Review* 42, no. 4 (October 1989): 270–291.

Tyler, Ronnie C. "Cotton on the Border, 1861–1865." *Southwestern Historical Quarterly* 73, no. 4 (April 1970): 456–477.

Vandiver, Frank E. "Makeshifts of Confederate Ordnance." *Journal of Southern History* 17, no. 2 (May 1951): 180–193.

Waghelstein, John D., and Donald Chisholm. "The Road Not Taken: Conflict Termination and Guerrillaism in the American Civil War." *Journal of Strategic Studies* 29, no. 5 (October 2006): 871–904.

White, P.J. "Gen. Thomas T. Munford." *Confederate Veteran* 26, no. 5 (May 1918): 221 and 229.

Wight, Willard E. "Some Letters of Lucius Bellinger Northrop, 1860–1865." *Virginia Magazine of History and Biography* 68, no. 4 (October 1960): 456–477.

Wiley, Bell I. "The Confederate Letters of John W. Hagan, Part I." *Georgia Historical Quarterly* 38 (June 1954): 170–200.

Windham, William T. "The Problem of Supply in the Trans-Mississippi Confederacy." *Journal of Southern History* 27, no. 2 (May 1961): 149–168.

Wright, Gordon. "Conditions in the Confederacy as Seen by the French Consuls." *Journal of Southern History* 7, no. 2 (May 1941): 195–214.

Wooster, Ralph A. "Life in Civil War East Texas." *East Texas Historical Journal* 3 (October 1965): 93–102.

—————. and Robert Wooster. "A People at War: East Texans during the Civil War." *East Texas Historical Journal* 28, no. 1 (1990): 3–16.

Dissertations and Theses

Allen C. Ashcraft, Allen C. "Texas, 1860–1866: The Lone Star State in the Civil War." (Ph.D. dissertation, Columbia University, 1960).

Buchanan, Robert P. "The Military Campaign for Mobile, 1864–1865" (M.A. thesis, Auburn University, 1963).

Dugas, Vera L. "A Social and Economic History of Texas in the Civil War and Reconstruction Periods" (Ph.D. dissertation, University of Texas, 1963).

Ellsworth, Lois C. "San Antonio during the Civil War" (M.A. thesis, University of Texas, 1938), 47–48. William L. Gammon, "Governor John Milton of Florida" (M.A. thesis, University of Florida, 1948).

Jacobs, Kenneth R. "The Confederate Diplomatic Missions to Mexico of John T. Pickett and Juan A. Quintero" (M.A. thesis, Hardin-Simmons University, 1970).

Lindgren, Edwin D. "The Impact of Mine Warfare upon U.S. Naval Operations during the Civil War" (M.A. thesis, Army Command and General Staff College, 1976).

Snyder, Perry. "Shreveport, Louisiana in the Civil War and Reconstruction" (Ph.D. dissertation, Florida State University, 1979).

Strasser, William A. "Our Women Played Well Their Parts: East Tennessee Women in the Civil War Era, 1860–1870" (M.A. thesis, University of Tennessee, 1999).

Newspapers

Arkansas True Democrat [Little Rock, Arkansas].
Brooklyn Daily Eagle.
Chattanooga Gazette.
Chicago Tribune.
Cincinnati Daily Commercial.
Cincinnati Enquirer.
Cincinnati Gazette.
Columbus [Georgia] *Daily Sun.*
The Courant American [Catersville, Georgia].
Daily Progress [Raleigh, North Carolina].
Detroit Free Press.
Eutaw [Alabama] *Whig and Observer.*
Evening Star [Washington, DC].
Galveston Daily News.
Jacksonville [Alabama] *Republican.*
London Morning Star.
McKinney [Texas] *Democrat.*
Mobile Daily News.
Mobile Register and Advertiser.
New Bern [North Carolina] *Times.*
New York Herald.
New York Times.
New York Tribune.
Philadelphia Enquirer.
Pittsburgh Daily Commercial.
Prescott [Wisconsin] *Journal.*
Raleigh Weekly Standard.
Richmond Dispatch.
Richmond Examiner.
Staunton [Virginia] *Spectator.*
Tallahassee Florida and Journal.

Washington [Arkansas] *Telegraph.*
Weekly State Gazette [Austin, Texas].

Online Resources

Block, W.T. "Some Notes on the Civil War Jayhawkers of Confederate Louisiana:" http://www.wtblock.com/wtblockjr/jayhawke.htm.

"Columbus History from the River: Historical Narratives from the White Water Express River Guides:"https://history.columbusstate.edu/cc_ projects/2014_History_from_the_River.pdf, 27–28

"General Andrew Barclay Spurling:" http://www.cranberryisles.com/photos/andrew_spurling.html

Kemp, L. W. "Young, William Cocke" (Handbook of Texas Online): (http://www.tshaonline.org/handbook/online/articles/fyo14)

Roberson, B. L. "Valor on the Eastern Shore: The Mobile Campaign of 1865:" http://chab-belgium.com/pdf/english/Mobile%20Bay.pdf, 3

Rozeff, Norman. http://www.cchc.us/Articles/StoryOfUnionForces.pdf

University of California. The American Presidency Project: http://www.presidency.ucsb.edu/ws/?pid=72212

Index

A

B

F

G